Tatiana Todorova was born in the Soviet Union and grew up in Odessa, the largest seaport on the Black Sea. She studied at the Odessa State Mechnikov University, Faculty of Romance and Germanic Philology, Department of English Language and Literature, second language – French. After graduating from Odessa University, she moved to St. Petersburg, where she continued to study the history of art, painting and architecture, the history of all the museums of St. Petersburg on courses for guides and interpreters, then worked as a guide and interpreter in all the museums of the city, conducted excursions in English in the Hermitage and other museums of St. Petersburg for English-speaking tourists and delegations. She spent four years studying for a master's degree at the Theological Academy (non-denominational), studying the history of world religions and all subjects of theology, having written numerous essays on the topic of theology and the work of *Martin Luther, Ulrich Zwingli and John Calvin.* Her novel *Prelude and Allegro* was published in Russian in St. Petersburg and sold in a print run of 3,000 copies. She dedicated her life to her daughter, from five years old, teaching her the violin at the music schools of St. Petersburg. Her daughter Violetta Todorova then studied in America and became a soloist, concertmaster of the Fort Wayne Philharmonic and guest concertmaster of the Las Vegas Symphony Orchestra. The author lives in Chicago.

The novel is dedicated to my grandfather, Todor Todorov Karagochev.

Tatiana Todorova

TODOR TODOROV KARAGOCHEV

AUSTIN MACAULEY PUBLISHERS®
LONDON * CAMBRIDGE * NEW YORK * SHARJAH

Copyright © Tatiana Todorova 2025

All rights reserved. No part of this publication may be reproduced, distributed, or transmitted in any form or by any means, including photocopying, recording, or other electronic or mechanical methods, without the prior written permission of the publisher, except in the case of brief quotations embodied in critical reviews and certain other non-commercial uses permitted by copyright law. For permission requests, write to the publisher.

Any person who commits any unauthorized act in relation to this publication may be liable to criminal prosecution and civil claims for damages.

All of the events in this memoir are true to the best of author's memory. The views expressed in this memoir are solely those of the author.

Ordering Information
Quantity sales: Special discounts are available on quantity purchases by corporations, associations, and others. For details, contact the publisher at the address below.

Publisher's Cataloging-in-Publication data
Todorova, Tatiana
Todor Todorov Karagochev

ISBN 9798895432686 (Paperback)
ISBN 9798895432693 (Hardback)
ISBN 9798895432709 (ePub e-book)

Library of Congress Control Number: 2025903003

www.austinmacauley.com/us

First Published 2025
Austin Macauley Publishers LLC
40 Wall Street, 33rd Floor, Suite 3302
New York, NY 10005
USA

mail-usa@austinmacauley.com
+1 (646) 5125767

I would like to express my gratitude first of all to my grandfather, Todor Todorov Karagochev, the father of my mother Nadezhda Todorova; he lived a romantic and heroic life full of adventures and gave me the material to write this book. Thanks to his younger brother, Gocho, who was involved in the events and witnessed them, imprinted in his memory to pass on to future generations. Thanks to the wonderful team of the Austin Macauley Publishers, who highly praised my novel and published it for readers. I thank everyone who will buy and read my book to know and remember the heroes and their heroic actions, because as the ancient Greeks said, exploits worthy of not being forgotten will not be forgotten.

Table of Contents

Chapter 1: First Balkan War. Adrianople — 14

Chapter 2: Sworn Bro — 28

Chapter 3: Bodrovo — 35

Chapter 4: Second Balkan War — 42

Chapter 5 Election of Kmet. Grandfather Todor Karagochev — 58

Chapter 6: Alexander Stamboliysky. Beginning of the Great War — 65

Chapter 7: The Great War — 74

Chapter 8: Letter from the Front. Love and War — 82

Chapter 9: VIDIN — 88

Chapter 10: Dobro Pole. The Second Meeting with Ferdinand — 91

Chapter 11: Radomir, Vladay — 106

Chapter 12: Chirpan — 120

Chapter 13: Spanish Flu — 130

Chapter 14: Vidyu, Petyu, Mityu — 132

Chapter 15: Neuilly-Sur-Seine — 136

Chapter 16 Easter 1920 — 144

Chapter 17: Aidanlar — 154

Chapter 18: Haskovo Prosecutor — 160

Chapter 19: Resurrection — 179

Chapter 20: St. Ilijah Day — 181

Chapter 21: Dagger	190
Chapter 22: Alexander Stamboliysky Speech in Sofia	196
Chapter 23: Hajduk Ivan Ignatov	203
Chapter 24: Haskovo Prison	208
Chapter 25: Guenov-Kamine Plan	212
Chapter 26: Vidyu Gochev Karagochev	218
Chapter 27: Stamboliysky's Speech in Haskovo	225
Chapter 28: At the Abyss	233
Chapter 29: June 9, 1923	242
Chapter 30: Forever Bulgarian Shame	251
Chapter 31: June 1923	262
Chapter 32: July 1923	275
Chapter 33: September 1923	284
Chapter 34: After September 1923	299
Chapter 35: Chirpan Fair	302
Chapter 36: Butchevs the Yatacks	309
Chapter 37: Vengeance in Ezerovo	314
Chapter 38: Legends	318
Chapter 39: Winter 1923–1924	326
Chapter 40: Bukovo	337
Chapter 41: Spring 1924	343
Chapter 42: Choice	350
Chapter 43: Wedding in Bodrovo and Internment	362
Chapter 44: Cheta Hristo Botev	369
Chapter 45: Fight on the Pinnacle of Chala	385
Chapter 46: Popovo	397
Chapter 47: Returning Home	407

Chapter 48: Second Internment	415
Chapter 49: Manastir	425
Chapter 50: Belitsa	434
Chapter 51: Navasen	448
Chapter 52: Photo, Plovdiv, Sofia	455
Chapter 53: Georgy Pilashev	467
Chapter 54: Parting	484
Chapter 55: Mezek	502
Chapter 56: Mezek 2	516
Chapter 57: Political Emigration	533
Chapter 58: Georgy Dimitrov Karagochev. Susam	545
Chapter 59: Epilogue	561

Annotation
Historical Novel: Balkans 1912–1925

The pages of the novel resurrect before the reader the events of a hundred years ago from 1912 to 1925 in the Balkans, in particular, in Bulgaria during the two Balkan Wars, the echo of which was the Great War, which drew all countries and continents into its orbit and gave birth to a lost generation. Three wars led to dramatic events in Bulgaria: a coup d'état and the establishment of despotism, against which the heroes of the country rose to fight. Brave, fearless, daring, elusive, they defy the executioner's power and prepare the people for the uprising to overthrow the junta. The noble at heart and free spirited, they wage a heroic battle for freedom, risking their lives to save the life of another. It is a hymn to the beauty of nature of the Balkans. It is a wide panorama of life of the era and society. It is based on real events. It is dedicated to the memory of Alexander Stamboliysky; it is dedicated to the memory of all the freedom fighters of all the times and countries, as the great Greeks said the exploits worthy of not being forgotten will not be forgotten.

Chapter 1
First Balkan War.
Adrianople

The bombs, thrown by the Internal Macedonian-Adrianople Revolutionary Organization militants under the direction of Todor Alexandrov in Kochani and Shtip cities, reached their goal: they caused the massacre of the Bulgarians by the Turks throughout the European territory, which the Turks had been occupying during 500 years by October 1912, and brought the Balkans to war. The mortal enemies to each other, Serbia, Greece and Bulgaria, joined by Montenegro, were united in the Balkan Union to kick out the Turks from the territory of Europe and share the territory between the Balkan countries. Lurking from behind the Danube corner, Romania was watching for a right moment to tear off a piece of the Bulgarian land, extorting territorial compensation for 'neutrality'.

The tsar of Bulgarians Ferdinand of Saxe-Coburg and Gotha announced the beginning of the war on September 29, 1912, in his General Headquarters in his manifesto "To Bulgarian people", commanding: "I command the brave Bulgarian army to invade the Turkish domain! Friendly Balkan powers: Serbia, Greece and Montenegro will fight together with us for the same goal. The sympathy of those who love the truth and progress will be with us in this struggle of the cross against the crescent and freedom against the tyranny! Forward! God is with us!"

Sun-drenched Bulgaria with joy and blessings saw off her soldiers to the front, marching with torches to the cries of "Hurrah!" flattering flags, sinking in the flowers and music. In three days the war rashly began with resounding victories of the Bulgarian army which took Lozengrad and put to rout the Turkish army to the Chataldja fortifications. The Bulgarians advanced in a rush of feeling, accumulated in the historical memory of people from the songs and legends, passing by word of mouth from childhood, which they heard from cradle about the motherland Great Bulgaria, prosperous in former times, extending across the territory of Thrace and Macedonia, which had given the world Slavic alphabet and great culture; about their native land which the Turks had captured, enslaved, erased from the map of Europe, robbed, raped, tortured and murdered during 500 years; about their native land which Alexander II liberated and returned San Stefano Bulgaria on the map of Europe, but the criminal Berlin Congress dismembered, tore off Macedonia and Thrace and returned to the mercy of Turkey again.

And now, in defiance of the "Great Powers" and Alexander III, as well as the Balkan neighbors, Serbia in particular, who stabbed a knife in the back and attacked Bulgaria at that time of challenges, Bulgaria united with Eastern Rumelia in 1885, declared independence from Turkey in 1908, and now it remained in defiance of the same "Great Powers" and Nickolas II Thrace and Macedonia to free from the Turks and drive them out from the territory of Europe, where they had invaded 500 year ago. And now, having gathered together all forces, courage and heroism, hatred for the oppressor, the Bulgarians drove them south, and Turks retreated in stampede, leaving to the Bulgarians storages with ammunition and food, cannons, shells, airplanes, ranges, fortresses and Mustafa Pasha, Kash Kala, Lozengrad, Tomrish Juman, Baba-Eski, Lule-Burgas cities, and surrendered, abandoning the wounded to their fate.

The officers ran to a train at the station, having forgotten a saber, watch and documents, and soldiers pushed away the officers and hurried to get on the train first, until Mahmud Muhtar Pasha began to shoot his army, trying to stop stampede, and the commander of the Eastern Army Abdullah Pasha entered barrage detachments as an officer with a revolver behind the soldiers in every company with the order to shoot at the retreating. But it did not stop the retreat and did not help to himself, as he was displaced. Nazi Pasha, who replaced him, continued execution of his army for fleeing the battlefield.

And now, on October 31, 1912, the Bulgarian Tsar Ferdinand, being in Yambol, received a Turkish offer for truce. Ancient Yambol, situated on the banks of the Tundzha River, lived with the memory of four thousand years history, like all the other cities of Bulgaria where ancient Thracians, Greeks and Romans lived long time ago. The great Thracians created great culture here, antique Greek polis was here, Fillip II of Macedonia and his son

Alexander made history here; they were replaced by the Roman Empire with Diocletian, the emperor who gave the name "City of Zeus".

Ancient Yambol, becoming a city of the First Bulgarian Empire, was the place where the Bulgarian Tsar Ferdinand created history now in his headquarters of the First Army. He was standing in front of the mirror in the Military House, where the headquarters of the First Army was located, dressed in the ceremonial attire of the First Bulgarian Empire heyday tsars, embroidered with pearls and stones, and admired himself. It was the same attire, worn by the Byzantine tsars, from which the Bulgarians borrowed so much. He was looking at his Roman nose, small clear penetrating blue eyes, well-defined mouth over a short wedge-shaped trimmed beard, wavy ash blond hair and his emperor's attire, and he was quite pleased with himself, considering that he fully looked like an emperor of Rome.

"Your Majesty, I consider that it would be in our interests not to rush to let the allies know about the Turkish offer of truce," Dimitry Risov said.

He was in the hall together with Ferdinand and admired the precious stones glowing on the tsar's attire. Risov was a diplomat, Bulgarian ambassador in Rome, together with the Bulgarian ambassador in Paris Dimitry Stanchev and the Prime Minister Ivan Gueshov, he was a co-author of the Serbian-Bulgarian Defensive alliance, hatched, composed and approved in the trains, taking the leaders of the two countries to different sides. Ferdinand confirmed the treaty in a train between Oderberg and Vienna, and the prime minister of Serbia Milovanovich did it in a train between Vienna and Belgrade. This treaty was joined by Greece later.

Originally from Macedonia, Risov, an extraordinary man with vibrant energy, found himself on the crest of the fateful events in Bulgaria, fallen on his lot, beginning from the activity in the Bulgarian Secret Central Committee, resulting in the Uniting of the Principality of Bulgaria and Eastern Rumelia in 1885, fought in the chetas against the Turks on their territory and even was sentenced for two years in prison for criticizing the unconstitutional actions of the tsar. But now they are together, and Dmitry Risov, Ferdinand's adviser and confident, gifted, restless and rebellious fighter, determines foreign policy together with Ferdinand.

"Without a doubt, it would be a major fatal error if the Balkan states agree for truce before they defeat Turkey ultimately and finally!" Risov said.

"Can we believe Turkey at all!" Ferdinand exclaimed to agree with Dmitry Risov. "Do we have guarantee that pushing us to truce with false concessions now, they will not go on the offensive later again after they recover from defeat and gather strength! No, we'll not make such an error! I am giving the order to send a telegram to Gueshov: *I have to prohibit you to inform the allies about the Great Vizier's offer until I take into consideration the opinion of all my advisers, commanders of the three armies, politicians and responsible persons. Now I am leaving for Lozengrad and then by train to Chataldja to do it. Until then I ask you to undertake nothing in relation with the Great Vizier's telegram.*"

The telegram flew to Sofia to Prime Minister Gueshov, and Ferdinand was admiring a precious Venetian saddle for a white horse, on which he planned solemnly to enter Tsargrad like a Roman emperor, and the shining jewels on his attire.

"We shall enter Constantinople like victors," he declared solemnly, "and change the course of history. We shall improve a tragic error of the Great Schism of 1054 and join again on the Latin ground the split parts of the Christian Church. And it is on the Latin ground that Bulgaria will become great under the auspices of Pope of Rome!"

"Exactly so, Your Majesty!" Dimitry Risov supported Ferdinand, and his eyes were glowing. "Unitism for Bulgaria is her great future! It's high time to put an end to the Orthodoxy!"

"Orthodoxy will be crashed!"

"It can remain only in the form of rites, but in substance it'll be Uniate."

"And then Holy Pope Leo 13 will take back our excommunication from the Catholic Church for the Orthodox chrism of Prince Boris, as he will understand that we do great favor to Vatican by conducting this! We shall enter Constantinople at the head of the Bulgarian army and before the entire world we shall celebrate a solemn liturgy in St. Sofia cathedral in honor of liberation of the city from the infidels, and by this we shall announce to the entire world that the Schism of 1054 is put an end to."

"And the Holy See unites again under his wing both Eastern and Western churches in one, the same name of which 'Catholic' namely 'Universal' is imparted a new meaning and tone. And we not only return to bosom of the church, but we are worthy to be canonized like Louis the Saint or Philip II of Spain. His Eminence Metropolitan of Stara Zagora Methodius supports us,

Bulgarian exarchate will become apostolic!" Ferdinand was speaking pathetically, as he already saw himself on the Roman emperors' throne in Constantinople.

"There are all the necessary premises," Dimitry Risov supported Ferdinand enthusiastically. "Bulgaria has never been pure Orthodox, she was a motherland of different currents, such as Bogomils, Cathars, Paulicians and leaned to fall under the influence of Rome."

"And now, Bulgaria will return to Rome and the Holy See the Eastern Church and Constantinople, which thanks to us will become a stronghold of Catholicism and the straits."

"But what will Russia say, Your Majesty?" General Savov, who was present in the hall, inquired to be on the safe side.

"It's high time to be liberated from the liberator!" Ferdinand exclaimed. "It is Alexander II who liberated Bulgaria, but Alexander III and Nickolas II considered Bulgaria as a transdanubia province, hindered the Union in 1885 and Independence in 1908 and dethroned Prince Alexander Battenberg!" Ferdinand answered and thought to himself: *Luckily for me!*

"Russia hindered expansion and strengthening of Bulgaria, plotted and intrigued; it is hostile to all the vital forces of Europe!"

"Russia organized an attempt on you, Your Majesty!" Risov reminded.

"It is Holy See in Rome which is our only ally! Vatican will become a center of consolidation of anti-Russian coalition!" Ferdinand was speaking confidently.

"Then it's time for us to give the order to assault Chataldja!" Savov concluded logically.

"Do it!" Ferdinand confirmed.

And Savov rushed to Chataldja with the Ferdinand's order to assault. General Savov, "an evil fate of Chataldja", seemed to anticipate trouble and did not give the order to assault Chataldja. But nevertheless, he advised General Radko Dimitrov to assault the impregnable fortifications, all of a sudden appearing at the front on November 4.

"With the onset of darkness, I advise you to assault the redoubts south of the lake Derkos."

And the latter gave up, though he knew this could not be done. Tired of continuous fighting, having lost part of the army from cholera outbreak, not having enough cavalry and without heavy artillery, which was late to come from under Adrianople, the Bulgarians went on the offensive on the impregnable defense of Chataldja, which stretched from the Sea of Marmara to the Black Sea, where in addition to the fresh Turkish forces, having come from the Asia Minor, Turkish battleships entered near the coast of Derkos and opened fire on the Bulgarian troops. Nevertheless, the Turks retreated again, and the Bulgarians took the positions, but could not hold them and retreated in their turn and huddled in the trenches. Savov's advice of assault cost the Bulgarians 10 thousand killed and 2 thousand wounded, and he himself hurried away.

At that time, the Bulgarians took Nevrokop and Drama at the Western front and moved along the Struma River valley to Demir Hisar and Serres and from there to Thessaloniki, took Dedeagach, all the railway roads, captured Mehmet Yammer Pasha together with all his headquarters, 265 offices, 12000 soldiers, captured cannons, machine-guns, horses and provisions. Ivan Todorov Karagochev and his friend, Ivan Guenov, fought in the 10th Rhodopean regiment, and fortune still saved them on the battlefields for future events.

***

On March 23, 1913, at 1 pm, a deafening roar of guns around the entire circumference of the besieging ring of allied forces shook the age-old walls of Adrianople, heralding the approach of possible denouement.

"Is it the beginning of assault of the city-fortress and its inevitable fall, or it's a usual Serbian and Bulgarian cannonade?" flashed through the mind of the emaciated citizens of the city and its defenders, resigned to the fate and at heart seeking a speedy resolution of the issue.

5 months of the fortress siege were left behind since the beginning of the I Balkan War of the allies against Turkey. There were victories and defeat from the both sides, change of mood of the street crowd in the cities and villages of Bulgaria from overall euphoria, choking delight, singing of hymns, intoxication with patriotism, torchlight processions, dancing in the streets in national costumes, seeing off with the flowers like to the feast the warriors to the front to fight against the age-old enemy and enslaver, overall jubilation of the nation that "Lozengrad is ours!" till inevitable from the reverse side of victory severe hangover bitterness from snowballing messages about dead, wounded, maimed.

During those 5 months, the I Balkan War began, seemed to finish and continued again from the brilliant victories of the Bulgarian army at the very beginning under Mustafa Pasha, Vize, Suloglu, Lozengrad, stampeding the Turkish army, which abandoned troops and fortresses with provision, ammunition and artillery with everything else and stampeded in horror every which way from the chasing them Bulgarians to south to Tsargrad to stop here, gather strength and block the way to the impregnable bastions of Chataldja, where the ceremonial entrance on a white horse of the tsar Ferdinand never happened.

During that time, they concluded truce, and the members of the Balkan Union, staying comfortably in the St. James palace disposed by the king on December 13, 1912, sat down at the negotiating table in London, where the minister of Foreign Affairs Sir Edward Gray, who cherished hope for the early peace, made an ornate speech that "the relations between the governments are friendly and the diplomatic situation is favorable". And the peace was nearly made with Turkey, which had to cede the allies all her former European lands, including Adrianople or even its western part, but at that moment Young Turks committed another coup in Constantinople, murdered military minister Nofis Bay, dethroned the ministry of Kamil Pasha and declared: "You are cast down as you are for a shameful peace to cede Adrianople and almost all the European lands, but the nation which is ready for death demands the war!"

And the war resumed on January 21, 1913. And Adrianople, considering that he was still a key to Tsargrad, held on all that time, stood, besieged by the Bulgarian troops, which now decisively began the assault. Situated upon the confluence of 3 rivers on the undulated plain, to which gentle slope leads from menacingly towering mountains in the distance, Adrianople was impregnable, surrounded by the hills which were turned into the gigantic reinforced concrete forts by the German engineers. On them howitzers and heavy artillery did not admit to themselves on a gun-shot any enemy who dared to attack. The line of defense surrounded Adrianople with a triple circle: the rear one was in the city, the main one was in 03–3 km on the hills in front of the city, and the front one was 9–11 kms from the city, along which the wolf pits lurked as insurmountable barrier together with minefields, trenches and half miter columns, staggered in a checkerboard pattern, which were entangled with the barbed wire like an ominous lace, able to tear to shreds a human body. Hidden in the hills, the underground city-fortress, the streets of which securely concealed the armed standing to die its defenders, stretched along the circumference of Adrianople and blocked the path to the enemy. Interlacement of 3 flowing across the city rivers: Maritsa, Arda and Tundja naturally divides Adrianople on 4 parts, turned by the besiegers into 4 offensive sectors.

The artillery fire from all the cannons fell on the Turkish defense, setting fire and destroying their forts, and finished in 10 hours. The fire fell silent and the Turks went to bed, breathing freely.

"If they start assault, they will do it only at the north-west sector," Shukri Pasha, commander-in-chief of the fortress, said to his subordinates, pointing with a pencil on a map lying on the table at his headquarters in the Hadarlik fort.

Nobody dared to object. How many times, analyzing the situation, peering intently at the map of the area, Turkish command, trying to anticipate the++ enemy action, came to the conclusion that if the adversary go on assault, he can do it only at the north-west sector, where the railway line passes, and it is only here where the adversary could concentrate the number of weapons necessary for assault. Couldn't they drag the weapons in the bullock-cart along the field to the eastern sector where there is no railway rode! And it was the north-west sector who expected the assault, therefore it was fortified super-reliably. Situated in the checkerboard pattern, forts, furthest from the city, interchanged each other, and in case one falls, another one blocks the way to adversary.

The clock showed 2 am. The Turks, who were not in time to rest, jumped from their places, awakened by thunder and fire, unseen and unheard for all the time of siege. The fire of assault illuminated the night over Adrianople, but clouds of smoke from shells, crashing into the ground, again darkened and blinded everything around.

The Second Army commander Nickolas Ivanov's Order No. 60 was transmitted along the positions of the besiegers' troops: "Start assault at the eastern sector! The north-west, west and south sectors are to attack from all sides equally in order to demonstrative impact on the adversary to keep them on his places, to disable him to maneuver on a real sector of assault and deprive him of possibility to guess a real direction of the attack!"

Turks failed to guess. They had never seen how the Bulgarian and Serbian troops: second Serbian division, Timosh and Danube divisions were maneuvered from the Macedonian front to Adrianople through Sofia to help the Bulgarians. Now they assaulted the city at the north-west and western sectors, approached the Turkish trenches and rushed to attack. Unable to withstand the pressure, the Turks fled and hid behind the fort line, having abandoned their cannons and machine-guns, and the latter shot at their back. Bombarded with a hail of shrapnel, dumbfounded and blinded by the cannon roar and fire, the Turks did not perceive that the eastern sector was assaulted, denying its possibility.

Nevertheless, the impossible happened. Valor and talent of General Vazov, the commander of the eastern sector, made the impossible possible. Skillfully organized by him an endless caravan of buffaloes, harnessed to carts, each of which fit 3–4 shells, walking in a single file one after another along the paved road out of sight of the Turks, delivered arms to the eastern sector during months. Georgy Vazov, appointed commander of the eastern sector on January 22, 1913, since termination of negotiation with the Turks in London and the disruption of the peace treaty signed by them, prepared the offensive at the eastern sector, creating infantry fighting columns, strengthening tracking batteries, establishing a telephone connection between the infantry and artillery command and the batteries commanders, duplicating with a signal link.

A well-prepared operation suddenly began, rapidly unfolded, heralding victory. The Turkish forts at the eastern sector were closest to the city and lay along one line. The Bulgarian artillery swept them away one after another with enfilade fire. The Bulgarian commanders had accurate information about the location and structure of the Adrianople forts from the reports of the major Dyanko Nedelchev, who was sent as a diplomat to the city and during 2 years collected and transmitted a secret information, mapping the defense structures, and now he participated in the assault of Adrianople, aiming the Bulgarian cannons at the Turkish forts.

The Bulgarian officers led the soldiers into battle, and all of them, having mustering all their strength, merging into one gust, hurricane that knows no barriers and fell upon the eternal enemy, which having invaded Europe half of millennium ago, tormented their country, erasing it from the map of the world. And now it was a payback time. Rage gave them strength. They threw themselves on the barbed wire, which tore off pieces of their clothes and flesh, and without feeling pain rushed on, chasing the enemy. The Turks fiercely resisted, fell dead and wounded and retreated, unable to withstand the onslaught.

"All the cannons have been destroyed, the artillerists are dead, the Bulgarians enter the fort," the fort's commander of Aivazbaba telegraphed Shukri Pasha and shot himself.

Unable to withstand the Bulgarian fire and bayonet, the Turks admitted defeat and one by one ceded the forts Aidjioly, Kestenlink, Kurucheshme, Tolyoly, Kavkaz. From the Yildiz fort 4 dare-devils from the 29th Yambol regiment out of sight of 3 Turkish block posts, crawling, sneaked unnoticed, got to the quarter Kaen, crept to the high fence of the Selimiye II Mosque, of 3 human heights, deftly like acrobats limbed onto each shoulders, and the fourth one, Miho Stoyanov Gorgiev, from the Yambol city climbed by them on the very top of the fence, descended in the yard, opened the door to the 3, pushed off those who decided to block his way, penetrated into the minaret, climbed by a staircase on the very top and hoisted a Bulgarian banner. Fluttering over the high sultan Selimiye II Mosque minaret at the height of 52 meters, the Bulgarian banner served a signal for the Turks that the resistance is futile, and on March 26, at 8.30 am the commandant of the fortress Shukri Pasha announced the surrender of the Turkish garrison through his parliamentarians, who appeared before the commanders of the Bulgarian units. The Bulgarian warriors entered Adrianople.

***

Having joined his forces at the approaches of the fortress, General Vazov brought military in Adrianople from the side of Kauk. He was going along the main street of the city on his car and greeted a crowd, which met him with the joyful cry "Hurrah!" The general's gold epaulets, lined with galloons, sparkled on his blue overcoat with a red collar. His saber swayed at his left side. Famously twisted moustache and a small beard set off the tired face of 53-year-old general, with the generosity of the winner gazing at the defeated enemy. It was apotheosis of his glory, and pictures of the past flashed before his eyes in the memory.

He was born in Sopot city in a family with 10 children, who would grow up and become a part of the Bulgarian history, like his brother Ivan Vazov, the classic of the Bulgarian literature, whose novel "Under the Yoke" was a banner and manifest of the Bulgarian fighters against the Turkish enslavers; like his brother Vladimir, who would become a general, a participant and a winner of the battles and coups; like his other brothers: doctors and politicians. When he was 17, he lost his father, murdered by the Turks for the April uprising in 1876. It followed by the escape of his family to Adrianople, joining the Russian army of Alexander II, study at the Odessa infantry school and at the Saint-Petersburg Nickolas Engineering academy, participation in the war against the age-old Bulgarian enemy, the same like Turkey-Serbia, which treacherously stabbed in the back on November 2, 1885, when all the Bulgarian forces were concentrated at the south, guarding their reunification with the Eastern Rumelia under the banner of Alexander Battenberg; the organization of Alexander Battenberg to overthrow and escape to Russia, where he built everything he could in Turkestan, where a street was named in his honor Vazovskaya in the fortress Kushka in the very south point of the Russian Empire.

Then it was the amnesty and return to Bulgarian army and promotion in rank on April 24, 1897, the trumped-up prosecution for abuse in the engineering troops, but in fact for criticizing the tsar Ferdinand, who did not come up with anything new and did the same, as all the other tsars always and everywhere did: to prosecute the offender and throw him to jail. Then he was acquitted and continued to construct everything he could: from the first Bulgarian bus station Sofia-Samokov-Chamkoriya to all the military connections of the Balkan War.

The scenes from his past life with vital pictures floated before his eyes, and now he was reviewing the conquered Adrianople. The offices and adjutants followed him astride, and after them the soldiers, emaciated and tired from the battles not less than the defenders of the fortress, entered the city. The population of the city: Turks, Greeks, Jews, rejoicing that the siege was over, shouted: "Hurrah!" to the Bulgarian troops and met them with applause.

"Yesterday and today you've written a new glorious page in our history! Thank you! I am proud to be your commander!" Vazov addressed the eastern sector troops who entered the city, filling its streets.

Georgy Vazov was accompanied on the car by Ivan Vylkov, chief of staff, and Colonel Simeon Dobrevsky, chief of the engineering detachment. They solemnly passed along the main street of the city, crossed the Tundja River over the northern bridge, behind which the Turkish cavalry commandant's office was situated. They were accommodated there, and the captured Turkish generals and staff officers were waiting for their fate there. Vazov was looking through the commandant's office window and saw, how the streets were filled with the soldiers, he realized that there were too many of them and telegraphed the army commander: "The southern, western and north-west sectors troops do not enter the city, but remain at the captured forts!"

Soon, the guardsmen convoyed Shukri Pasha to the commandant's office, and he appeared before Vazov and the officers. He looked modest according to the situation, without a ceremonial gloss: he was dressed in a military frockcoat with general's epaulets, wide trousers, tucked into high officer's boots, and invariable Turkish fur hat. He had black moustaches, and a snow-white beard in a crescent form framed the oval of the face from one ear to another. He looked much older than his 56. He looked infinitely tired from the trials he had endured, but held himself with dignity. Admitting defeat, he greeted Vazov and handed him a saber.

"Thank you, Mr. General," Vazov responded and received the saber from the enemy.

A defeated enemy was standing before Vazov, a representative of the country which used to be a mighty empire, which had captured and enslaved the entire Balkan Peninsula, robbed and violated people, turned them into slaves who imbibed hatred to the enslavers with mother's milk and dream of revenge. Shukri Pasha had received education in France, became a general at 36 and ensanguined Thracian Strandja, where the uprising against Turks took place on August 2, 1903. Shukri Pasha held the defense of Adrianople during 5 months and now surrendered his saber and the city. And by this, Turkey surrendered ultimately, having been thrown away from the territory of Europe, from the Balkan Peninsula, which she had captured 500 year ago. Thereon the Balkan War ended.

"Mr. General," Shukri Pasha addressed General Vazov, "I ask you to allow me to keep my house in Hadarlik and your guarantee the general staff officers and me to keep our property. I also ask you to allow me to stay for this night in Hadarlik fortress, where my general staff was."

"Your request will be fulfilled, and now, please, get in your car, I have to hand you over to the army commander General Nikola Ivanov."

When in the evening the car with Georgy Vazov, Shukri Pasha and 2 staff officers drove up to the fort Hadarlik between the Maritsa and Tundja Rivers, 2 companies of the Serbian regiment were already there.

"They have violated the order to stay in the captured forts and not to enter the city," the officer told Vazov.

The second officer looked inquiringly at the general.

"Let them stay if they are already here," Vazov responded graciously.

"Gentlemen," he addressed the Serbs, "since you are here, in 3 km away from the fort line, where you were ordered to stay, guard Mr. Shukri Pasha and Hadarlik!"

When the car with the Bulgarian command disappeared behind an earthen rampart through the gates, built from red and white bricks, the Serbian soldiers winked at each other.

"We shall tell everybody that it is us who captured Shukri Pasha and that it is us to whom he surrendered."

Meanwhile, Vazov began to restore order in the city. Ragged and hungry, frustrated by defeat and rejoicing by the end of the siege, captured by the Bulgarians in the eastern sector, military crossed the bridge to the island Sarai on the Tundja River, where it would not be easy for them many days and nights. As it was not enough tents even for the Bulgarian soldiers, the captured Turks remained on the island Sarai under an open sky on the half frozen puddles to peel off bark from trees to gnaw, drowning out hunger, to kindle fires to keep warm, shake in a fever, writhing in convulsions of a cholera epidemic which attacked like a traitor in a difficult moment, defeating both Turkish and Bulgarians soldiers. The Bulgarians had captured about 55 thousand Turkish soldiers and officers all together. 35 thousand released Turkish officers returned to Turkey to their families, and Shukri Pasha went to Sofia. While parting, General Vazov told him: "Mr. General, do you realize that, having ordered to blow up the bridge across the Arda River, along which it is supplying of the city with food, and also having ordered to burn the warehouses with food, you also doomed the Turkish prisoners for starvation?"

"Yes, we did blow up the bridge, but I never ordered to burn the warehouses with food; it was bandits who did it," Pasha answered.

"In any case, in spite of the fact that our soldiers, due to the circumstances, until the food shipments arrive from Baba-Eski and Mustafa Pasha, do not receive enough quantity of food, I've ordered to cut a quarter of their ration and give it to the Turkish soldiers."

"Thank you, Mr. General!"

Shukri Pasha sat in a carriage, harnessed to 1 horse, driven by a Turk with downcast eyes. A long caravan of similar carriages were trailing behind them, the Turkish officers of lower rank were following their former commander to Sofia.

Chapter 2
Sworn Bro

The captive Shukri Pasha Turkish army tailed away on the Sarai Island on the Tundja River and also at the south-western forts of defense, as well as partly went to Bulgaria, and the General Vazov's troops entered the city. They had captured the city, ancient as history itself. Adrianople was founded by the emperor Hadrian in 124 on the place of the city capital of the Adrysian Kingdom Uskudana city of the Thracians who were in fact the first Europeans, having given the world Spartacus and buried countless treasures of gold and works of art in caves and mysteriously disappeared forever, and ceded their land to the Greeks, Romans, Byzantines, Bulgarians and Turks.

The fate of mankind was decided here many times from the outcome of the battle under Adrianople. On July 3, 324, Constantine defeated Licinius here. The emperor Valens was killed in the battle by the Goths here in 378. Here Trevel, Asparuh's son, "a holy savior of Europe" from the Muslims, defeated Arabian army to help Constantinople, having prolonged its existence for some more 700 years. And 100 years later, Khan Krum, a year before his death in 813, on June 22, defeated the Byzantine army of Michael I, putting it to flight, and reached the walls of Constantinople.

Here in 100 years, in summer 914, Simeon I captured Adrianople to force Byzantine Constantine VII to fulfill his promise and marry his daughter. Here, in 970 the Byzantines of Vardas Skliras defeated the allied army of the Bulgarians, Hungarians, Pechenegs and Russian Sviatoslav, who had robbed and plundered Bulgaria himself. Here, in April 14, 1205, Baldwin IX, the emperor of the freshly-minted Latin Empire, was defeated by Kaloyan, lost his army of crusaders, was taken captive and vanished into the Bulgarian dungeons.

Sprawling with all-merging black mass along the body of Byzantine and Balkans, the Turks went on capturing their cities one by one and took over Adrianople in spring 1361 and made it their capital, having moved it from captured Bursa, and from here they began threatening the entire Europe. They ceded Adrianople to Russian general Ivan Dibin without a fight in 1829, as the result of which Greece, Serbia, Moldavia and Walachia got autonomy from Osman Empire. In half a century, on January 20, 1878, the Turks ceded Adrianople to Russian General Skobelev, and Bulgaria who was absent from the world map for 500 years returned as a state again at the result of the war of Alexander II in 1878.

6 years before the Liberation, the governor of Adrianople Mustafa Effendi Susam capitulated before the Bulgarian Voevoda-hajduk Captain Petko in a letter, preserved for the descendants memory, where he admits the victory of Petko Voevoda, fulfills his requirements and releases from the Adrianople dungeons the Bulgarian captives, and in addition pays him 6 thousand gold Turkish liras. But never took place San-Stefano Bulgaria, robbed and fragmented at the Berlin Congress by the "Great Powers", who like a pack of hungry jackals surrounded the Turkish "patient" in agony in order to grab a piece of it for themselves and prevent any "great Bulgaria", neither "great Greece" nor "great Serbia" she (Bulgaria) lost Macedonia and Thrace which were returned under the Turkish rule. And now, with a thirst for revenge and determination to win, Bulgaria with the allies entered the Balkan War, cleaned Europe from the Turkish invasion, threw the enemy behind the Midia-Enez line and took legendary Adrianople by storm.

It was getting dark. 2 Bulgarian soldiers and sub-lieutenant of the 10th Rhodope Regiment Philu Borisov were going along the undulated street at the north-eastern outskirts of the city. Their military uniform, akin to the Russian model—cap, soldier's overcoat with a folded blanket over the shoulder—was enlivened with opanki and onuchi from coarse cloth, white before, but now gray with dirt, tied with leather straps, which immediately betrayed them to be Bulgarian soldiers. The sub-lieutenant wore a green color uniform, which did not differ from Russian form, and high officer's boots.

"Look, another one again is dragging something on his back, maybe stolen from somebody!" Ivan Todorov Karagochev said, pointing his companions at the other side of the rode.

The emaciated Greek, barely dragging his feet, carried on himself a chair of skillful work, ornate with carvings and velvet upholstery.

"Unfortunately, we can't take anything with us," Ivan Todorov Guenov responded discontentedly, "otherwise, we have to carry it on ourselves, but we can't carry many things on ourselves!"

"While we fought, shed blood, took by storm Adrianople, these rascals Greeks with Jews have plundered the city! But what if we take this chair away from him? It rightfully belongs to us!" sub-lieutenant Borisov exclaimed.

"Where will you get it? You will not carry it with yourself, will you?" Ivan objected, "Be happy that you remained alive! We went through the whole war and we aren't even wounded! The war is over, we'll return home soon!"

"We really did win over the cursed Turks!" Sub-Lieutenant Borisov exclaimed with his shining eyes. "They oppressed us for 500 years, and now we've vanquished them! Look, over there, it is their mosque of Selimiye II, it is ours now!"

He pointed with his hand at the Selim II mosque minarets, as high as the Babylon towers, which one could see from anywhere in the city.

"And now we have to give them our bread, haven't we!" Ivan Guenov said without hiding his anger. "General Vazov ordered to take away from us a quarter of our bread and give it to Turks! We are lack of food lately!"

"How far is it to go yet? Better to get some sleep! Where are we supposed to stay?" Ivan Karagochev inquired, who was dreaming only to undress, take off himself all the equipment, hanging on a soldier: a shovel, fire-cooking pot, flask with water, bag with bread, folded blanket, cartridge belt and a rifle with bayonet, and go to sleep, forgetting about everything.

"Our quarters are between Tundja and Maritsa; we'll pass by the mosque and get to our place."

They were approaching the center of the city, and the Greeks, who could drag on themselves everything from the Turkish houses, became more and more. Anticipating the fall of the city, they attacked Adrianople from inside before the Bulgarian troops entered it. The aged-old foe, the Turks, now received vengeance from all sides. The neighbors from the southern quarters, Greeks with the help of Jews penetrated into all the cracks, grabbed and dragged on themselves everything they could. They emerged from the lanes and disappeared around the corner, crossed 3 fellows' path and went to another side of the rode, went in front of them and behind, and like the oxen dragged on themselves the Turkish carpets, chairs, pillows, utensils and sacks with everything they could only cram. It was impossible to stop them, the same as it is impossible to stop a raging stream and rushing river during a flash-flood, capturing and carrying away with itself on its way. The more lucky and wealthy Greeks, possessing carts, carried on them mountains of loot along the streets, already filled with the Bulgarian military. And the emaciated, hungry and ragged Turkish soldiers were sitting on the ground along the fences or trudged to the gathering places, staring sadly on what was going on.

3 companions approached the Selimiye II Mosque. Sky-high towers-minarets surrounded from 4 sides for ages a fairy creation of Mimar Sinan. Born 29 years before Leonardo da Vinci death and challenged him with genius of his creations, Greek by birth and Joseph by name, who not by his choice of fate changed the Orthodox faith to the Muslim, he embodied it in stone forever, having presented the admiring gaze of the descendants 130 mosques, 50 madrasahs, 35 palaces and all the other things that could only be built: from the caravanserais and mausoleums to the shelters for the poor, kitchens, baths, hospitals, aqueducts, bridges and warehouses. For 20 years the epoch of Leonardo da Vinci was the epoch of the architect Sinan in the east who, at 80 years old, created the Selim II Mosque in Adrianople.

A son of Suleiman I "the Magnificent", Selim II, overweight and clumsy ugly pygmy with an inferiority complex, having dealt with all his brothers, as usual, villainously together with his father killed his brother Bayazit with all his sons, including a 2-year-old child, became a sultan of Ottoman Empire in 1566 and ruled without any merit, plunging in boozing, music and poetry, having captured only Cyprus for the sake of the Cyprus wine only and drunk more wine than he prayed. But he sent the architect Sinan to Adrianople to create a mosque of his name to make prayers there.

The companions approached the mosque fence and entered the inner court. There were many people there: Bulgarian military, Greek citizens, Turks, seeking for a shelter. All were staring around to steal something. But you can't steal beauty! Having crossed the threshold, the travelers froze with delight, stunned by unprecedented beauty. The grandiose creation of Sinan appeared before their eyes, complicated and unclear from outside, simple like all genius inside: light and delicate with lace carving, like lace interwoven multiple windows, priceless carpets and chandeliers, painting and mosaic, magic mihrab, pointing on Mecca and like a tsar's throne minbar, fountain in the center and a sultan's lodge for muezzin. A dome towered over your head, supported by 8 columns, which rivaled with the dome of St. Sofia in Constantinople. A hole from the Bulgarian shell gaped in the dome, but the damage was not irreparable. Overwhelmed and captive by the splendor of the view before him, Ivan Karagochev pronounced:

"What a beauty! I've never seen such a beauty; we don't have it in Bulgaria!"

"But all this is ours now!" Ivan Guenov answered.

"Both Lozengrad and Adrianople are ours together with this mosque!" Borisov supported his friend.

Squeezing through the crowd, they came out to the yard and, staring around at the arcades, multiple structures, contiguous to the mosque, they went around and saw a door. Exchanged glances, they came in. It was a library of the mosque. A Turk was sitting on the floor and tore Koran out of the heavy book cover, a Greek was cramming books into a sack, a Jew was rummaging through the shelves for the most valuable to steal. Having forgotten disagreements, they were robbing the mosque library all together. There were torn books on the floor and the traces of robbery.

"Get out of here, rascals!" Ivan Karagochev exclaimed, and Guenov with Borisov with a butt blow on their back pushed the robbers out of the library.

"All the doors must be closed and the sentries must be put," Ivan said who was feeling so sorry for the destroyed books.

"It'll be done, they were not in time yet, have just entered today," Borisov said.

They came out into the street and continued their way. They were approaching the bridge over the Tundja River, passing the nooks of the old city, along which old houses with sheds, fences with wickets were piled up. They heard groan round the one shed's corner and stopped. Ivan stopped and came to the place, where the sound came from. A wounded Turk was sitting on the ground; he leaned with his back against the shed's wall. His right arm was hanging like a whip, with a left arm he tried to squeeze a bleeding wound; apparently he was wounded in the shoulder. He looked alive yet like a skeleton, gray-colored; dirt and blood covered his tattered uniform of a common soldier and his suffering face, and his gaze begged for mercy. Ivan Todorov immediately unfastened his flask with water, leaned over the unfortunate Turk and gave him to drink. The latter sipped and looked gratefully at Ivan. His eyes filled with anxiety, when the other 2 came near.

"Don't be afraid," Ivan said, "the war is over; it is peace now."

Ivan opened his sack for food, took a piece of survived bread, broke off a piece, put it in the soldier's left hand. The latter groaned with pain, despair, joy and gratitude and greedily began to chew saving bread.

"Somebody of yours will pick you up," Ivan invigorated him.

They went on, came to the Tundja and crossed the bridge. Guenov stopped, exchanged glances with Borisov and said:

"You go, Ivan. I need to return. I also need to repay. General Vazov ordered to give away a quarter of our bread to Turks."

"I go with you," Borisov winked Guenov.

Ivan slowly went on, and the fellow countrymen hurried up to the place, where they had just been. On seeing how they approached, the Turk became agitated, anticipating evil. Borisov dealt a blow with a butt on his head and threw him down into dirt, then squeezed his throat with the butt and viciously said:

"To give you some bread, cursed Turk? During 500 years you violated my native Bulgaria, robbed and killed, turned my people into slaves! And now I must give you my bread? Rummage him!"

Guenov instantly rummaged the pockets of the Turk, lying on the ground, pulled out of his pockets some liras and a small black and white photo of his family, tattered it and threw in his face, then stuck a bayonet into his stomach. A stream of blood flowed out from the Turk's mouth. He trembled in convulsions and soon calmed down with wide open eyes.

Ivan slowly trudged on to the overnight place, and his companions soon overtook him. In several minutes they were at the wicket of the house, where they were quartered. A small shed by a Turkish house was a place, where they were supposed to stay overnight.

"Is the war over indeed, and we'll go home soon?" Ivan Karagochev exclaimed, taking off the entire load, hanging on him, and the soldier's overcoat.

His companions did the same and lay down on the long couch, standing along the walls.

"To go home soon, and I'll return to Borisovgrad to my people."

"And we'll go back to Bodrovo, next to you," Guenov said.

"We are the fellow countrymen and must stick together," Ivan pronounced, "we have gone through the entire war, fought shoulder to shoulder, god saved us, we aren't even wounded! Or are you wounded?"

He pointed on a cuff of Guenov, dirt with blood.

"No, I am not, just scratched on the wire during the assault."

"It's over now, we've won, the Turks are defeated, we must go on living and not remember the past."

"You are so fair always, aren't you!"

"I think about the old tradition of Bulgarian fraternization to become sworn brothers to support each other, to come to each other for aid, to save each other and their close people. Then, let's fraternize! We'll not let blood, how it used to be in old days, we have had enough blood, we'll fraternize spiritually."

"I agree," Guenov answered, "we are friends with you, countrymen, live in one village Bodrovo, our sons are of the same age."

"How I miss my home!" Ivan exclaimed. "How are there my family: Atanasa, my wife, my older sun Todor, he is 12 now, and all the housekeeping is on him. The young Gocho is 3 years old now."

"My son is also 12, they are of the same age," Guenov said

"Let's fraternize, I'll be a sorcerer and perform the rite," Borisov said, "we need some wine for that. I'll try to get it from the hosts."

He hurried out the door and soon returned with a small jug with wine.

"Ready, take an oath!"

Ivan Todorov Karagochev and Ivan Todorov Guenov were standing in front of each other, clasped with left hands and solemnly pronounced:

"We pledge allegiance to each other for internal friendship to stand for each other, never to betray, always come to the rescue and if something happens with us, to take care of the children of the other as ours."

"Shake hands and hug!" the sub-lieutenant said.

Both sworn brothers embraced brotherly, now bound spiritually. Borisov, as a sorcerer, witnessed the fraternization, and all drank some vine from the jug.

Chapter 3
Bodrovo

Having hidden behind the hills away from the universal roads, Bodrovo village managed to avoid the vicissitudes of universal history, hardships of war, enemy captures, burning and occupation. Only in 3 km to the north along the Tsargrad road across Philippopolis, destroying everything on their way, frantic hordes of crusaders marched past in former times, intoxicated with fantasy to free the tomb of the lord. The village, which like in a cradle the Rhodopes kept at its foothills, avoided meeting with the warriors of Christ, away from the dangerous ways.

During the Turkish slavery, there were no Turks here, who preferred flat places, lazy to climb the hills at the Rhodope foothills to rummage a hidden village, which therefore never had a Turkish name like almost all the other cities and villages, captured by the Turks. From time immemorial it was a settlement of the Thracians here first, whose famous Horseman slaying a dragon, found near by the archaeologists, once served as a model for the Christians, who copied it and created on its ground their tale character St. George the Victorious slaying the dragon; however, they had stolen the entire antique culture, copied and remade in their own way and then destroyed it with curses.

After the Thracians, the Romans lived here, who left after themselves only stones and bricks from once magnificent buildings. There was a settlement of the Bulgarians here of the time of the two Bulgarians Empires, when the Bulgarian tsars controlled the entire Balkan Peninsula and then stopped to exist on the map of Europe after the Turkish invasion.

And so, fleeing from the Turks, who preferred the lowlands, at the beginning of the 18th century freedom-loving Bulgarians began to flock here, who found a peaceful nook by the foothills of the Rhodope Mountains. A certain master Boduro, having firmly settled here by 1750, gave his name to the village, which was partly changed a bit into Bodrovo by 1887. He was followed by the singles and with families villagers who fled from the Turks; they built houses, plowed the fields, pastured flocks. Running from the mountains peaks and inflowing into Maritsa, Kayaliyka River gave them water; countless underground waters, here and there bursting to the surface, helped them to build cheshmas, tap-water fountains, for people and cattle to drink. Each yard had its own well; and by the beginning of the Balkan War there were strong farms in Bodrovo, created by the hard work of each of the generation of the families, each member of which knew and was proud of the genus, knew its founder, wrote down the lineage, which everyone cherishes in Bulgaria.

Karagochev's family house was situated not far from the entrance to the village from the northern side from the Kayaliyka River on the left side of the road. A high stone fence with wooden gates enclosed from the street side a territory of their spacious house and flowering garden. At the end of May the garden sparkled with all the colors of rainbow, which the fertile nature of the Balkans could only create. Fruit trees: apple, pear, apricot, cherry, peach trees blossomed with pink-white flowers, heralding a rich harvest. Unripe yet anise bushes, sesame and caraway greened in their beds, preparing their seeds to be used in almost subsistence farming. The bushes with cucumbers and tomatoes already filled the air with fragrance. A pergola, built specifically for grapes, supported its heavy vines, which wrapped around a metal frame with a continuous cover, through which from above lush clusters descended right on your head. Beds with onion, dill, parsley, celery, radish, eggplant, pepper greened, surrounded with the bushes of fragrant roses. There were household buildings and sheds for agricultural implements and cattle and fodder barn behind the house; and behind the village vast fields stretched with harvest and pasture-lands for livestock far away on the slopes of the hills. The entire household was on the shoulders of Atanasa and her older son Todor, as her husband Ivan Todorov Karagochev went to the Balkan War; and the war seemed to be finished, but he did not return, leaving in alarming expectations his family.

Ivan's father, the owner of the possessions, Todor Karagochev, was a strong and mighty man in his youth with strong body and spirit, having inherited from his father, grandfather and great-grandfather rebellious spirit of protest against evil and violence and noble desire for freedom during Turkish slavery, as all his ancestors were the hajduks, whom the Rhodope Mountains nursed with such generosity. The father of Todor Kara-Gocho-Todorov possessed vast pasture-lands to the west from the village between the lands Volchovsky Kairak and Pardjenaka, where in 1834 he built a conduit from a natural spring directly on his field with a tap, made from old rifle, through it water filled the containers for drinking for numerous flock, both his and the neighbors, who came later.

In 1884, he paid the masons who constructed a stone cheshma for drinking, having immortalized his name, carved in stone: "This cheshma is built with funds of Gocho Todorov Gochev, summer 1884." There was sheepfold household building and a county cottage nearby. Harvest ripened in the vast fields, numerous herds pastured on meadows of fabulous beauty, filling with wealth the Karagochev's house. Having inherited the property from his father, Todor ran successfully his farm, multiplying it, and together with his wife Mariyka brought up 7 children: 3 daughters, Kolia, Delia, Mina, and 4 sons: Angel, Gocho, Ivan and Dimitar. Children grew up, daughters got married and moved to their husbands; the sons got married, got their own families; a new house was built for each of them, where their children grew up, the grandchildren of old Todor.

Possessing 300 decares of land and numerous herds, Todor Karagochev was considered to be one of the rich families in the village. He raised his sons in the same way of hajduk's spirit of his ancestors: to be brave and courageous, noble and honest, to love the truth and appose evil. He equally gave his love to all his 4 sons. But something inexplicable happened to prove the proverb: "It is a small flock that has not a black sheep". Sis son Angel, fallen Angel, in the full sense of the word, appeared to be such a "black sheep" for woe to the entire family. His fall couldn't be explained either with his genes or upbringing, but only with some unknown to man a hostile force, which is stronger than him, bordering with double predestination, not giving answer to the eternal question, why is one person born noble in non-noble family and another one from nature is born and grows up a scoundrel in spite of all the attempts to bring him up in a noble spirit.

So, Angel repaid him with evil treachery and stab in the back for all the father's love and care and came to hate him as much as a filthy child can only hate his parent for all the good he received from him. Todor Karagochev invested a huge amount of money on the mill without any loans and credits, which he built by the river, purchased equipment in Germany, steam engine, and the mill successfully started functioning, bringing profit; all the inhabitants of Bodrovo and vicinity villages became the clients. Ivan, Todor's son, became the first machinist and the manager. But Angel, another son of Todor, had conspired with a notary in Haskovo and fabricated a false title to the mill for himself and declared himself a boss and his father and brother wage-earners.

In winter 1912 Todor Karagochev complained to the authorities that all 4 sons were sent to front and he remained alone with his daughters-in-law in a huge household, and he asks the authorities to return home one of his sons. By the evil of fate it was Angel who was returned from the war to help his father. Todor trusted him herds and granary with the fodder-food for the animals. Angel stole and sold all the fodder, starved the animals, did not give them food and water, just threw them dry hay and straw, and half of the sheep died from starvation. After that Angel moved to a new house with a garden and household buildings, built for him by his father, and stopped communicating with his father. He walked past his father in a hat, pulled down on one side, turning away to show contempt for his father and did not greet him. He crippled the health of his father, who began losing interest in life and slowly leaving it.

It was getting dark. In different corners of the room the kerosene lamps with tongues of fire lightened the interior of the country house, in which the grandfather Todor Karagochev lived together with the family of his son Ivan, who went to the war. A wooden floor was covered by the woolen carpets; the carpets also covered the walls of the room, creating warmth, comfort and beauty. The family photos hang right over the carpets. There was a clock with the candlesticks on the chest of drawers. There were copper and ceramic dishes on the shelves and a pyramid of carpets and blankets from the sheep's wool was neatly folded on a big sofa by the stove. The warmth in the stove came from a contiguous stove in a spacious kitchen behind a wall. They stoked the stove with firewood, prepared food on it; it heated several rooms, filling the house with warmth and comfort.

Todor Karagochev, his wife Mariyka, daughter-in-law Atanasa with her children were sitting at the table in a living room. Atanasa was young and pretty, but the colossal burden of housekeeping that fell on her fragile shoulders left an imprint on her face. Dressed in her woven and hand-sewn home cloths: long skirt, a shirt with embroidered sleeves and colored belt with a sleeveless cape on it, she was holding 3-year-old son Gocho in her arms; 7-year-old daughter Maria was sitting nearby, and her older son, Todor, named in honor of his grandfather, was sitting in front of her. A tasty village supper of sheep meat and vegetable stew, brinza-cheese, pies and freshly baked bread allowed them to eat as much as they wanted and kept them at the table. The mother Atanasa looked at her children with infinite tenderness, and she never ceased to amaze by the eldest of them. He was so much unlike his coevals that it surprised her, and she especially prayed god for his future, thought of which always filled her heart with inexplicable anxiety.

12-year-old Todor was so unusually handsome that those who looked at him were at a loss, thinking that they had never seen such a handsome boy. Fluffy black hair, glowing dark eyes, in which not childlike developed mind shone, gentle, slightly womanly oval of the face with chiseled features differed him from the other teenagers in the village, and all knew that Todor was not like all the others.

"I wish my father returns from the war!" Todor said.

"So do I! You are my only household assistant, my son! God willing, he'll be back soon, they say the war is over, we have won! There are no more Turks at the Balkans! Our father is a hero, he fought against the Turks and Bulgaria won!"

"Our father is a hero!" Todor said proudly. "And there were heroes in our village before who fought against the Turks: Petko Chakara and Ivan Chakalov were the chetniks in the Petko Voevoda squad."

"Yes, people told," the mother answered.

"Yes, they were!" the grandfather proved.

"How bravely they fought!" Todor exclaimed with admiration, rejoicing with the occasion to speak about his favorite heroes. "Petko was 17, when he courageously fought against the Turks at the head of his cheta-squad! First, there were 7 people in his squad, and Petko with his squad took vengeance upon the Turks, who had murdered his older brother, and killed them all. He was brave and smart, made an onslaught on Turks, who were several times more. And the Turks ran, they always ran in fear from Petko. Once he with his hajduks were fighting a battle against 130 Turks, was wounded, captured with his friends and thrown to jail. The hajduks made a plan to escape, undermined a wall of the prison with a simple scraper, but one Greek, who was in the same prison, betrayed and denounced them to the Turks; they could not escape, but they killed a warden. Petko was always lucky, when he and his cheta-squad were convoyed to Thessaloniki to be imprisoned in the Bloody Tower of the fortress, a warden lost a document on them. They came to Thessaloniki Pasha, and the latter asked them: "Who are they?" The warden reached into his pocket to get a document, but the pocket was empty, and he himself did not know anything. Here Petko says: 'We are the employees from Drama, we are supposed to be delivered there.' 'Then, go!' Pasha says. So, they came to one village near Drama, the wardens ate his fill, got drunk and fell asleep, and one teacher unshackled them, and they escaped. The Turks overtook them, a battle was at the cemetery, the cheta was captured, but Petko fell into a grave and was saved. He remained alone, forced his way through several Turkish patrols, assembled a new cheta-squad, and yataks-liaison-agents always helped him. Once Petko at the head of a new cheta fought in an unequal battle with Turks, commanded by Binbashi Osman, the one who cut off a head of Angel Voevoda, stuck it on a stake and was awarded for that. So, Petko defeated him in a battle, shaved Osman's left mustache and a right eyebrow and forced him to kiss under a horse tail, after that let him go together with the other Turks. And Angel Voevoda also was in Bodrovo, after he was wounded near Haskovo; his friends took him to Hadji Georgiev house, and he lived there during the whole winter."

"Yes, he did," the grandfather Todor confirmed.

And the grandson continued:

"After that Petko studied at the military academy in Athens, together with Garibaldi fought in Italy, fought against the Turks in Crete. And all the time there were traitors who betrayed him, like another Greek, who lured him into a trap in the Turkish embassy, but Petko managed to escape again. Once Petko with a new squad boarded a ship in Athens to arrive to Thrace to continue to fight. A storm blew up, and their ship was washed up upon the island, where the Turkish fortress was, and Petko with the chetniks changed into a Turkish military uniform and cheated a fortress commandant. He took them for 'inspection', gave them away boxes with food and with the fireworks escorted to the ship, because Petko fluently spoke Bulgarian, Turkish, Greek, Italian and French! Another time one Greek lured Petko to his house in a trap, the Turks surrounded the house, but Petko managed to get away again. Petko fought against bashi-buzuks who robbed and killed peasants, he protected the poor, acquitted them the stolen. He protected not only the Bulgarian peasants, but all the poor: Greek and even Turkish peasants, he released from prisons the innocent. He fought till the Liberation in 1878, when the Russians came and liberated Bulgaria, he also helped them. Petko was wounded 33 times and always emerged victorious from an unequal battle. Petko is a national hero, and it was Bulgarians who betrayed him. Prime Minister Stambolov ordered to take Petko captive and hand him over to the Turks or kill. The Bulgarians in Varna captured Petko, imprisoned him in the Roman fortress, tortured, tormented and mistreated, beat him, flayed him and spread rumors that he was not a folk hero, but a bandit. And it was a Mayer of Varna Spas Turchev who did it by the order of Stambolov because of envy and hatred for the folk hero. Therefore, it emerges that the Bulgarians are worse than the Turks! The tsar Ferdinand did a good thing to kill Stambolov!"

"Be quiet, son!" the mother was scared and looked around. "God forbid somebody will hear!"

"Let them hear!" Todor exclaimed. "The Bulgarian authorities dealt with the hero, they emerged to be worse than the Turks! It was a Turk who was the only one who stood up for Petko!"

The mother was anxiously gazing at her son, and her heart was pounding with disquiet. The sister Maria was listening to her brother with interest, she was fond of his stories about the brave heroes and their adventures.

"Well done, grandson!" his grandfather praised him. "Grow bold and fair! Don't betray your relatives and friends! You are our hope and support!"

"Be careful, grandson!" his grandmother Mariyka said and crossed herself.

Chapter 4
Second Balkan War

The spring of 1913, fragrant with greenery and flowers, warmed the land of the Balkans and its inhabitants with a bright sun in a cloudless sky, put an end to their suffering from cold in tents and trenches of defense, the siege and assault of Adrianople, on the fields of winter battles on both sides of the front. The spring 1913 came to an end. On May 30, having finished the Balkan War with a Peace Treaty in London, the allies kicked out the Turkish enslavers, who had occupied the Balkans 500 years ago, from the territory of Europe behind the line Midia-Enez. Macedonia and Thrace, liberated from the Turks, remained at the mercy of the winners. Clouds were gathering in the political sky, a tragic inevitability was approaching in gloomy darkness. On May 30, 1913, an issue of life and death was decided in the Vrana Palace of Ferdinand. He had named his palace Vrana in honor of vrana-crow, crows whom he adored together with all the other feathered, which flocks dwelled in a magnificent park, surrounding a magnificent palace. There were ponds and a lake, trees and bushes from the whole world, flowers, filling with fragrance the Garden of Eden, zoo with the reindeer, yaks, camels, llamas and two elephants—everything as it should be: tsar's luxury for the Bulgarian tsar who by the will of fate unexpectedly for himself became a former lieutenant of the Austrian army.

Situated on the first floor of the Vrana Palace a hall for the reception of ministers met all the canons of the Viennese palace style. A war party gathered there.

"Gentlemen, we must make a decision immediately!" Ferdinand addressed the senior officers. "Our allies behind our back are preparing a blow on our back. According to the information we received, the Serbian ambassador in Bucharest conveyed the proposal of the Serbian government to conclude a treaty against Bulgaria, and on May 2 the Greek ambassador made the same proposal; and yesterday, on May 29, the Greeks and Serbs concluded an agreement among themselves on a joint attack on Bulgaria."

"We must attack them first, it is necessary to launch a pre-emptive strike and not wait until our former allies attack us!" General Vladimir Vazov supported Ferdinand.

"Gentlemen, our army is emaciated by battles, illness and the hardships of the past war, but the spirit of the army was supported by a holy faith in our just cause of liberation!" Radko Dimitriev said. "But the war with allies will not inspire enthusiasm. However, it must be taken into account that if we demobilize the army, our enemies will attack us anyway, and it will not be easy for us to reassemble the army for a new war. The fact that their troops are concentrated for the attack in the area of Ovche Pole to the east of Uskub and northeast of Thessaloniki is the evidence of them to attack us."

"Gentlemen, we must attack," Dimitry Risov said, "there is no peaceful solution of the issue. While our army was fighting in Eastern Thrace, bearing the brunt of the war with Turks, our allies occupied the entire Macedonia and Thrace and subjected to genocide the entire Bulgarian population on these territories. They have seized those lands that belonged to us under the agreement, where the Bulgarian population lived, and expelled them from their lands from the very first days of the war. They have robbed and killed the others. We must return the lands, the rightfully ours!"

"What would you say, General Savov?" Ferdinand asked.

"Give me a written order, and I shall carry it out, Your Majesty!" General Savov, the deputy commander-in-chief answered.

"War," a common decision was made between the mutually hating each other top generals, who made up a war party under the leadership of the infringed and thirsty for vengeance tsar of Bulgarians Ferdinand I.

Meanwhile, desperate attempts were being made on the diplomatic field to prevent a new war, stop the impending catastrophe at any cost and preserve the Balkan alliance. On June 2, 1913, in the city of Tsarebrod near the Serbian-Bulgarian border there was a meeting between the Serbian Prime Minister Pashich and Bulgarian Prime Minister Gueshov, who were the initiators of the creation of the Balkan Union a year ago and were striving to preserve the Union.

"Mr. Pashich," Gueshov, a rich and old man, advocating peace and quiet, fighting against the "war party" in Bulgaria at the head with the tsar Ferdinand, addressed the Serbian, "the agreement was concluded between our countries, and with the joint efforts we have liberated the Balkans from the Turkish oppressors. According to this treaty, Macedonia should be guaranteed autonomy, and if the autonomy can't be achieved, then its territory is to be divided between our countries in such a way that the lands lying to the northwest of Shar-Planina go to Serbia, and the lands go to Bulgaria from the line Ohrid-Kriva Palanka, and these are undisputed zones. The territory between these lines is a disputable area and in a case of conflict, it is a subject to division with the help of Russian arbitration. While Bulgaria wore the brunt of the war in Eastern Thrace, Serbia, in violation of the treaty, occupied the whole Macedonia and subjected the entire Bulgarian population to unprecedented violence."

"Mr. Gueshov," Pashich, bound hand and foot by the Serbian war party led by the king Peter Karageorgievich, addressed the Bulgarian, "external circumstances significantly changed the content of the agreement concluded between our countries. The leading military circles of Serbia believe that Bulgaria was the first to violate the terms of the agreement by not providing Serbia with military assistance on the Western front, while Serbia has provided Bulgaria assistance with 2 divisions for the assault on Adrianople. Besides, the agreement did not imply Bulgarian occupation of Adrianople and Eastern Thrace. Bulgaria has received access to the Aegean Sea, which gives Serbia right to territorial compensation in Macedonia, since Serbia failed to gain foothold on the Adriatic coast due to the formation of the state of Albania."

Both ministers who tried to avoid war at the meeting on Tsarebrod on June 2, 1913, left for each other hope for peace and expressed their readiness to leave for Saint-Petersburg immediately for the arbitration court of Russia. Pashich did not know that he had just talked to the ex-Prime Minister of Bulgaria, since Gueshov 2 days ago, on May 30, having learned that the decision on the war had been made by Ferdinand with the military, resigned in protest.

Pushed around on all sides by the war supporters not to take any concessions at the Russian arbitration, Pashich was going to leave for Saint-Petersburg. In a few minutes before the departure he received a telegram, announcing starting of hostilities. He also resigned in protest. From the moment Pashich met with Gueshov in Tsarebrod, the events developed rapidly, and it seemed that the entire Balkan world as if on an inclined plane was rolling into abyss of a new war. On June 21, 1913, General Savov, who flatly refused to attack the former allies only on the basis of the verbal order from Ferdinand, what forced the tsar to sign a written order to attack, sent a telegram to the commander of the 4th army:

1) There is agreement between the Serbs and Greeks which purpose is to retain and divide the entire territory of Macedonia: the right bank of the Vardar, as well as Uskub, Kumanovo, Kratovo and Kriva Palanka for Serbia; Thessaloniki and regions of Pravishta and Nigrita for Greece.
2) Serbs do not recognize any treaty and do not allow arbitration within the treaty.
3) We insist the arbitrators to proceed from the foundations, laid down in the agreement, and consider exclusively the disputed zone. Since the undisputed zone belongs to us by treaty, we want the Serbs to evacuate from it, or at least this zone to be occupied by joint troops until negotiations are underway. We make the same offer to the Greeks.
4) These issues must be resolved within 10 days, or, in our opinion, the war is inevitable. Thus, within 10 days we'll have either demobilization or the war, depending on whether our proposals are accepted or rejected.
5) If we carry out the demobilization now, the above-mentioned territories will remain in the hands of the Greeks and Serbs, and it is difficult to assume that there is a serious agitation against the war.
6) The intelligent soldiers' attention should be directed to the fact that if the army is disorganized and incapable of action, the result will be as described in paragraph 5. Answer immediately whether the state of the army is such that it can be counted on for successful operations.

The next day, June 22, 1913, Danev, who had taken place of Gueshov, convened a Council of Ministers, informing them that at sleepless night he came to the conclusion that Serbia would still attack Bulgaria even after the arbitration; therefore it was impossible to demobilize the army. He was objected by the Minister of Finance that the war between the Christians would be a shame after the war for freedom. The other ministers supported him.

Danev, Savov, Theodorov rushed off to Ferdinand in Vrana to persuade him to go to Saint-Petersburg for arbitration. They were supported by the Bulgarian ambassador in Russia, warning of imminent troubles in case of war. General Georgy Vazov is appointed the Minister of War and together with the other ministers, supporters of peace, tries to stop the impending catastrophe. The public opinion was divided on pros and cons the war. The war party pushed the war. They are echoed by the Macedonian patriots, threatening to send the army to Sofia and kill Danev at the railway station if he dares to go to Saint-Petersburg. Danev is still preparing for departure, and the gunboat is already waiting for him in Varna port to transport him to Odessa. At this moment he learns that the enemy troops came into contact along the border line, that the Bulgarian troops had attacked the Serbs and Greeks, having received the Savov's telegram to the 4th army:

"In order that our silence during the Serbs' attack does not have a negative impact on the state of mind of our army and does not encourage the enemy, I order you to attack the enemy along the entire line of border as vigorously as possible without deploying all your forces or a prolonged battle. Try to gain a foothold in the Krivolak area at the right bank of Bregalnitsa. It is advisable that you make bombardment in the evening, continue an unrestrained attack during the night and at dawn. Begin the operation tomorrow evening, June 29."

The Second Army was ordered to attack Thessaloniki. The Balkan world had rolled to abyss and fell into it. In desperation, the cabinet of ministers, opponents of the war, makes the last attempt to stop the catastrophe, threatening to resign; Savov, rushing around to different sides, withdraws the order to attack, but it's too late. The former allies were just waiting an excuse to attack, though they were ready to attack without any excuse yet before the Bulgarian offensive. From the first days of the Balkan War, while Bulgaria was bearing the brunt of the war with Turks at the eastern front, Serbia had occupied the entire Macedonia, the disputed and undisputed zones, the zone that belonged to Bulgaria under the agreement from the line Ohrid-Kriva Palanka, the entire Macedonia where mainly Bulgarian population lived and committed genocide of the Bulgarians.

Serbian barbarians and savages, who surpassed the Turks in brutality, robbed and killed Bulgarians, burned Bulgarian villages to the ground, tortured and tormented defenseless people, cut out their tongues because they spoke Bulgarian, smashed Bulgarians schools and churches, killed teachers and priests, gouged out their eyes, cut off their fingers and ears, burned alive and rapped women and children, often calling yesterday's enemies, the Turks, into allies, arming them again to kill the Bulgarians. The Serbs had prepared the proclamation about the war against Bulgaria even before the Bulgarian onslaught.

In terms of brutality and barbarism, the Serbs were surpassed only by the Greeks, led by their King Constantine, who imagined themselves to be descendants of the great Hellenes. Constantine Glucksburg, having inherited from his father George I, who was killed in Thessaloniki on March 18, 1913, personally produced the visual pictures for the soldiers how to gouge out the eyes of the living Bulgarians, how to cut them into pieces with a knife and burn them alive. The founder of Nazism, King Constantine, imitating Mark Cato, was obsessed with the idea of fix: Bulgaria must be destroyed!

In the swirling whirlwind of insane chaos of insane ideas of "great Serbia", "great Greece" and "great Bulgaria" the corpse of the Ottoman Empire suddenly showed signs of life and moved beyond the Media-Enez line, burning with fire and a curved saber, massacring all alive which was not Turkish, resuming Lule-Burgas, Lozengrad, Adrianople; and from behind the northern Bulgarian border, like a robber, lurking around a corner to stab in the back, the Romanian hordes jumped out, crossed the Danube and moved on Sofia without meeting any resistance, as the entire Bulgarian army in a desperate attempt to recapture the lands inhabited with Bulgarians, fought with their yesterday's allies: the Serbs and Greeks in the southwest, suffering defeats and retreating. Another "robber-ally", impoverished and impudent Montenegro, did not fail to attack Bulgaria, hoping to tear off some piece for herself.

Danev, the Prime Minister of Bulgaria, also escaped, having resigned. After several days of the offensive, the Bulgarians failed to gain a foothold in the Krivolak area and hold their positions behind the Zletovska, Bregalnitsa, Kriva Lakavitsa rivers; they retreated with fierce battles with Serbs, responding them with the same coin of cruelty, with the only difference: the Bulgarian army was the only one from all the belligerent, who had received the order to follow the Geneva Convention and whose military tribunals tried for the war crimes up to execution. And at this time all the other armies committed the war crimes, following the orders from above. Soon the Serbs captured Kriva Palanka, pushed the Bulgarians back to their border, entered the Bulgarian territory and laid siege to Vidin, bombing houses, schools and the Red Cross hospital. And in the south on July 1, the Greeks attacked the Bulgarian garrison in Thessaloniki, who were killed, and the rest were captured, crammed into the holds of cargo ships and taken to the fortresses in the islands, where they vanished without a trace in casemates. Even before the Bulgarian attack, the King Constantine had arrived to Thessaloniki himself and personally led the army of the Greeks so that "Bulgaria is to be destroyed!"

The Bulgarians were late for 1 hour to enter Thessaloniki like the winners. The Bulgarian army approached the northern border of the city in an hour after the commander of the Ottoman army Hassan Tahsin Pasha, incited by the "great powers" through their consuls, had surrendered Thessaloniki without fight to the Greek army on October 26, 1912, and flatly refused to cede the city again to the Bulgarian army. Since that moment, 2 sentries had been standing on guard alongside one another, until they received the order to attack each other.

The second Bulgarian army under the command of Nikola Ivanov was maneuvered from Adrianople to South Macedonia and stood guard over the cities, recaptured from the Turks, stretching from the Lake Doiran, through Ku-Kush, Serres to Kavala near the Aegean Sea and, having received the order of General Savov, entered the Second Balkan War. General Savov had revoked the offensive, but it was too late. The Second Balkan War began by itself. Yesterday's allies, ready for attack long ago, went over to the offensive along the entire frontline. The Second Army, suffering defeats and losses, retreated to the north, abandoning the cities Kavala, Doxato, Drama, Ku-Kush, Serres. The commander of the army General Ivanov proceeded to Demir-Hissar by train through Serres. On July 5, 1913, General Volkov, the governor of Macedonia, the entire general staff and the Bulgarian garrison abandoned Serres, having left there the warehouses with weapons, ammunition and the archives.

Early morning, July 11, a regular army column, consisting of 1,5 battalions of infantrymen, a cavalry squadron and 1 artillery battery under the commands of Ivan Kirnikov approached Serres with the order to return to the city, restore order and evacuate the abandoned warehouses with weapons and ammunition. From the surrounding the city hills the Bulgarians quickly pushed back the army of Greek gangs, who met them with a fierce fire, and took up the positions on the hills themselves. Chaos reigned in the city: robbers, arson of different objects, gunfire from the windows and doors of various houses and mass exodus of the population from the city. Kirnikov aimed the cannon at a white house, from all the windows of which they fired, and stopped it with one blow. Dismounted cavalry troops and foot soldiers entered the main street of Serres to pass along, calling the population to order; the cavalry went on to the railway station and the infantry detachments went to the abandoned Bulgarian ammunition depots. The Bulgarians were hit by a hail of bullets from the Greek gangs who were sitting in the houses and hiding around the corners. The detachment that had entered the main street had to disperse and return the fire back.

Ivan Todorov and Ivan Guenov, shooting at the enemy and covering each other, approached the school building for girls. A bloody trace led outside and inside to the yard. They came in. Having gone through the Balkan War, two soldiers were dumbfounded by the spectacle that appeared before them. Everything was covered with human blood: the floor, the stairs to the upper floor, the railing of the stairs, the doors and door jambs, the door handles and the walls. They opened the door of the room and looked inside: the dead bodies of the Bulgarians filled the whole room; the bodies were heaped on top of each other in several rows with open eyes, in which the horror of death was frozen forever, with broken skulls and scattered brains, with stab wounds on their necks from the butcher's tools, used to slaughter sheep.

The heat from the midday July sun was saturated with poison of decaying flesh. The 2 soldiers recoiled back, but covering their nose and mouth with a handkerchief, began to open the doors of the other rooms with hope to find living. The pattern was repeated in every room: there were no living there. Overcoming the horror, they climbed the bloody stairs to the upper floor and kicked open a bloody door. The corpses of the unfortunate Bulgarians were piled one on another one, and somewhere from the bottom of this hill came a muffled groan of a half-dead. Ivan Todorov and Guenov began to disassemble the bodies of the dead and saw a man who was showing signs of life.

"Are you alive, brother?" Todorov asked and together with Guenov helped him get out to freedom.

"Help," the unfortunate moaned in semi-conscious state.

2 soldiers dragged the lucky unfortunate out from under a pile of corpses, grabbed him by the arms, hurried down the stairs and ran out into the street.

The survivor was a Bulgarian soldier, covered with his own and the others' blood with stab wounds on his shoulder, face and neck. Under the scorching July sun the bullets whistled in a crossfire, and the fire that had flared up from the ammunition depot, torched by the Greeks in the east of the city, moved from east to the west with the help of the strong eastern wind, with the tongues of flame passing through the wooden houses that stood closely next to each other along the narrow undulated eastern streets. Crouching from the bullets and running from cover to cover the 3 soldiers soon reached the hill, where the Bulgarian battalion was standing, which was never able to enter the city due to the heavy fire of the Greek gangs. Having gathered the soldiers, the battalion hastened to retreat, as the columns of the regular Greek forces were approaching Serres from 2 sides, ahead of which, pursued, the Bulgarian refuges were streaming. Turning back, the 3 soldiers saw a city, embroiled with flame, in which a school building with 250 bodies of Bulgarian martyrs, brutally tortured by the Greek savages, was burning with an ominous funeral pyre. Greek shells from the Greek cannons of the approaching units, sent after the retreating Bulgarians, fell on Serres, turning it into ruins.

Having moved on a considerable distance from Serres in the direction of the Rupel passage, Kirnikov's battalion called a halt for a night. The fighters, tired of incessant battles, retreats and transitions, sat down around the fire and listened to the story of Dimitar Lazarov, pulled out from under the mountain of corpses at Serres school before it burned down.

"So, what happened there?" Ivan Todorov asked the saved soldiers.

Dimitar Lazarov, whose wounds were bandaged by the Bulgarian soldiers, began his story.

"I was seized in the street by the armed Andarte-Greeks, hit on the head with a butt of a rifle and dragged to the bishop's palace. The bishop was a ringleader of the Greek gangs, and they had staged a show-trial in his palace. The bishop himself, armed from head to toe, was sitting in his chair like on the throne. There was a table and a chest of drawers near him. Andarte-Greeks and just Greek townspeople, all armed, were standing around. The bishop had called all the Greek inhabitants of the city to come to his palace, where there was a warehouse of weapons, and arm themselves to kill Bulgarians."

"They brought another group of Bulgarian captives. The trial began. They asked only one question: 'Are you Bulgarian?' After a captive answered: 'Yes', they hit him on the head, rummaged his pockets and took away everything he had: watch or money, and lay on the table before the bishop." The bishop took away everything and put in his drawer, then pronounced a sentence: "Do you know that our great King Constantine of Great Greece has ordered to exterminate all the Bulgarians till the last, until this filthy barbarian race is utterly destroyed never to be born again? Our King Constantine has ordered to destroy your Bulgaria, burn it to the ground because it has no right to exist among the civilized mankind, especially in the neighborhood with us, the descendants of the great Helens!"

"What a bastard!" the soldiers exclaimed. "He himself and his barbarians have nothing to do with the descendants of the Helens: they are just a mixture of Albanians and Slavs! The descendants of the Helens had sunk into oblivion a long time ago!"

Lazarov continued his story:

"Well, after his speech, the Greek bishop gave a sign to the Andartes, and they began to beat the captive and then sent him to the same school for girls, dragged him into the room where there were the other captives and threw him on the floor. Then it was my turn. I was found guilty because I am Bulgarian. I was robbed, beaten and sent to school, pushed into the room on the first floor. There were a lot of people; we were neither fed nor watered. Groups of Bulgarians were constantly brought in from the city and nearby villages. They were robbed, beaten and dragged to school, thrown into our room or the other rooms.

"Then they began to tie up 2–3 people and drag them to the rooms on the upper floor. We heard a cry, akin to the one that sheep make when they are slaughtered. The butchers kept on coming for a new group of Bulgarians, all their hands were covered with blood, they themselves were stained with blood, and their weapons were stained with blood. It was my turn. I was tied to another captive and dragged along with him to the upper floor, pushed into the room, where the dead were lying on the floor with their throats cut. Everything around was stained with blood there.

"The Andartes seized my comrade, pulled his head up by the hair, and another Andarte stabbed him in the neck, the butcher's eyes were shining with enthusiasm, and he exclaimed: 'Long live our Great King Constantine I of the Great Greece!' Then they grabbed me and with the same exclamation they stabbed me in the shoulder, face and neck. I sank into faint. The other dead bodies piled on me, I was feeling that I was alive, but I could not get out from under the bodies. And on Friday, July 11, I heard the roar of guns and shooting outside the window, I realized that the Bulgarian army had returned here to save us, and then I heard footsteps in school. I began to moan, and 2 Bulgarian soldiers have saved me. Thank them! They have pulled me out from under the pile of bodies and helped me to get out, and we got to our soldiers."

Dimitar Lazarov was speaking was difficulty, his wounds hurt, but his eyes shone with joy from the miracle that happened to him, which brought him back to life, in which he himself could hardly believe. His story made a horrible impression on the soldiers who listened to him, each of them was deeply anxious to survive and return home alive, and if to die, then to die heroically in a battle, but not to be slaughtered like a sheep by the Greek savages at Serres school.

The endless hills around the Struma Valley, covered with dense forests, plunged into darkness, night fell, and the soldiers of the Kurnikov's battalion fell into dead asleep, gaining strength for tomorrow battle.

***

4 days before, on July 8, 1913, the Bulgarian troops retreated from south to north through Demir-Hissar to the Rupel Passage to the Bulgarian border. An ambulance train with wounded and a cargo train with ammunition came from Serres. Another leader of the Christian church, Greek bishop of Demir-Hissar, the leader of a Greek gang, led 20 armed bandits out into the street. He gave them the order to make an onslaught on the Bulgarian wounded, and he himself showed an example, firing first in the forehead of a wounded soldier. The episcopal band held up the ambulance train at the station, burst into the cars and began shooting at the unarmed wounded. Then they attack the first cars and looted them, after that they opened fire on the streams of refugees from nearby villages, which flocked to Demir-Hissar. And it was only the Bulgarian battalion, returned to Demir-Hissar the next day, who managed to restore order for a day. The bishop had received a well-deserved bullet in the forehead in a shooting and plopped his physiognomy into a puddle, firing his last bullets from his revolver at the hated enemy.

The Greek army was advancing and the Bulgarian battalion left the city. Kavala, Doksato, Ku-Kush, burned by the Turks after the departure of Bulgarians, Akamdgeli, bombed by the Greek artillery, were left behind. The

Greek advanced, burning Bulgarian villages and fields to the ground together with the villagers, who decided not to escape, but stay and harvest from the fields, and with shells bombarded the streams of refugees, who decided to flee, raping women and children, stealing cattle and robbing everyone and everything on their way. Both warring armies, one advancing and another one retreating, entered the Rupel passage into the territory of Bulgaria between the Angistro and Belasitsa mountain ranges, where nearby at the foot of the mountains, as an ominous symbol of defeat, the village of Klyutch-Kleidion lay in the valley, where the Samuil's Bulgarian army was defeated 900 years ago by Byzantine emperor Basil II, the "Bulgarian slayer" who blinded all the Bulgarian soldiers, "broke the heart" of Samuil and in 4 years destroyed the First Bulgarian Kingdom in 1018. The Bulgarians retreated from the Greeks along the same pass, along which they attacked the Turks in October 1912, freeing from them Nevrokop, the Struma Valley, Demir-Hissar, Drama and Kavala.

Both armies entered the Kresna Gorge and advanced in grueling battles with each other up to the north along the valley and channel of the Struma, sandwiched between the Pirin Mountains. The Bulgarians were fighting with the desperation of those who had lost everything, and the Greeks, led by the maniac Constantine, were rushing to Sofia so that Bulgarian would be destroyed. The 1st and 4th armies, maneuvered from the Serbian front to help the Second Army, stopped the Greeks at Gorna Dzhumaya, in 100 km from Sofia. In the area of Razlog, the Bulgarians, having defeated the Greeks, had captured their luggage, where there were 100 letters from the Greek soldiers of the 19th regiment of the 7th division to their relatives, and the entire world saw those letters.

To Mr. Sotir Panayot, Vitziano village, parish Itiku
Trikala, Thessaloniki, river Nestor, July 12, 1913.

"Here in Brodi I've captured 5 Bulgarians and a girl from Serres. We have locked them in a jail and kept them there. We have killed the girl, and 5 Bulgarians suffered greatly: we have gouged out their eyes while they were alive, as the King Constantine taught us. With love from Kosti."

July 13, 1913, Nestos, village Bantsa.

"If you want to know the places where we pass: all the Bulgarian villagers and everyone fled. The rifle Mannlicher 'has eaten' all those who remained. We also burned all the villages, as the King Constantine taught us. The Bulgarians suffer the same fate from the Serbs. S. Nakis."

Rhodopes, the Bulgarian border, 11/7, 1913.

"Brother Meitso, we have burned all the Bulgarian villages from Serres to the border, as the King Constantine taught us. My address remains the same: 7th division, 19th regiment, 12th battalion, in Rhodopes."

S. Nakis in a desert. July 12, 1913.

"…on the Bulgarian territory we beat the Bulgarians who are retreating constantly, and we definitely go to Sofia. We enrage them by burning their villages, and wherever we find 1 or 2, we kill them like sparrows. Your brother Georg."

Zissis Kutumas Nikolau K.

"I hereby give you some news about the war we are waging against the Bulgarians. We have defeated them and reached the Bulgarian-Turkish border. They have fled to Bulgaria, and we have slaughtered all who remained. Only god knows how all this will end. I have nothing more to write to you. I remain your son Zissis Kutumas. Lots of compliments from Timus. He is fine, and all the other young men here are fine."

M. Zaharias Kalivanis Yerfos. Milipotamus Retimo, Crete, Rhodopes. July 13, 1913.

"We go on burning all the Bulgarian villages we occupy and kill all the Bulgarians, who fall into our hands, as King Constantine taught us. We have captured Nevrokop, and we have been well received by the Turks, who entered our ranks to fight against the Bulgarians. Our army has joint with the Serbian and Romanian armies, and we are in 32 km from Sofia. S. Z. Kalivanis."

To my brother Sotir. July 15, 1913.

"The Greek army burns all the Bulgarian villages, where there are Bulgarians, and we kill everyone we meet, as the King Constantine taught us. It is impossible to describe what is going on here. Only god knows how it will end. The time has come when we began to devour each other. With love from your brother Bekligis Panagis."

July 12, 1913. Bulgarian border.

"Everywhere we pass, even cats are not survived. We have bunt all the Bulgarians villages through which we passed. I can't describe it to you better. Your loving brother Georgy. My address is following: to Corporal Sterge Georg, 13 squadron, 3 battalion, 19 regiment, 7 division."

Dimitrius Talgarida in Mexista, Hunati-Ftiotis, July 11, 1913.

"I was given 16 soldiers to deliver to the division. I have brought only 2. I have killed them all."

Niko Theotilatus.

To George D. Karka (soldier), I section, Sanitarian Corps. 9 division, Argikosatro, Epirus.

"Nestor River, July 12, 1913. Dear brother Georg! Thank god, I am all right. Let me tell you that our division has reached the Nestor River that is the Bulgarian border, and the King's army has crossed that border. Fulfilling the order of the king, we set on fire all the Bulgarian villages. We turned out to be much crueler, than the Bulgarians. We rape every girl we meet."
"It's impossible to describe how the Bulgarians are destroyed and flee. All is fine with us. Say hello to our villagers and friends. After everything we have

been through, thanks god, I am not afraid of the Bulgarians. With regards, N. Zervas."

Aristiti Tapassia, Kamniati, Atanamov
Commune, Trikala, Thessaloniki. July 14, 1913.

"Dear cousin! We burn the villages and kill all the Bulgarians, women and children here. I heartily embrace you, your brother."

M. Georg P. Sumbili Mesali Atanasova, Kalamas.

"Rhodopes, July 12. Dear parents! We have captured several captives, whom we have killed, as we were ordered to do so. Wherever there is a Bulgarian village, we set it on fire and burn so that this filthy race of Bulgarians can't appear anywhere else. We are going on Sofia. I embrace you, your son Perilli Sumblis, 7th division, 19th regiment, 12th company Thessaloniki."

And so on there were 100 letters, captured in the luggage. So, allegedly, the heirs of the great Helens wrote, in fact having nothing to do with them, a vile tribe of savages with their King Constantine, for whose freedom the great Lord Byron vainly gave his life, ironically cast to the land of once great Hellens. Ancient Greece, which of course, having borrowed a lot from the great culture of Akkad and Sumer, laid the foundation of European civilization, formulated the main questions of philosophy, defined the criteria for beauty and created perfect works of art, so that all the subsequent generations could only imitate them from century to century.

King of Greece Constantine I, always arguing with his Prime Minister Venizelos, having lost half of his army, was rushing to Sofia, so that "Bulgaria would be destroyed," but having met standing to death Bulgarians, he failed to achieve his "great goal" and turned to the opposite direction and led his savages tribe back to the south, leaving behind scorched earth, killed Bulgarians, women and children burned alive, warriors, crucified on the trees, buried up to their throats in the ground with burned heads, gutted with a knife, stabbed with a bayonet, so that "this filthy Bulgarian race could never arise anywhere else".

The battle in the Kresna Gorge remained with the Bulgarian victory, and Greece was rebuffed back further to south. But, having lost a significant part of the land, conquered in the First Balkan War, Bulgaria signed peace in

Bucharest on August 10, 1913, still having access to the Aegean Sea from the mouth of the Mesta River to Enez. Having born on her shoulders the brunt of the struggle against the Turks, tattered, robbed and destroyed, Bulgaria lost the fertile Dobrudja, stolen from it by Rumania with the instigations of Russia who had revoked the treaty of 1902, and needed a break. She bitterly realized the vainness of the heroic siege and assault of Adrianople, the vainness of the shed blood in the battles for Lozengrad, Chataldja and could not deal with it. Bulgaria longed for vengeance, but it was the tsar Ferdinand who longed for vengeance most of all. "My vengeance will be terrible!" he exclaimed after they signed the Bucharest Treaty. And the "robbers-allies": Greece, Serbia and Rumania gnawed their elbows from frustration that they had failed to carry out their secret plan of 1868 of destruction of Bulgaria and division its territory among themselves, but only managed to gnaw off by piece from all sides like the jackals. Thus the Second Balkan War ended, and Bulgaria healed her wounds with resentment for the entire world.

Chapter 5
Election of Kmet.
Grandfather Todor Karagochev

The II Balkan War ended with disgrace and defeat of Bulgaria, its complete ruin, having filled houses with widows' and orphans' lamentation for the dead, of lamentation of parents, who lost their children. Those who survived gloomily rejoiced. All 3 sons of Todor Karagochev: Ivan, Dimitar and Gocho returned home safe and sound together with the other fellow villagers and Ivan's "sworn-brother" and namesake Ivan Todorov Guenov. Having received back its working hands, Bodrovo restored its farms and returned to peaceful life.

The premises of the village administration, Kmetstvo, was located on the territory of the courtyard, belonging to the St. Georgy church. This church was built in 1808 by a wealthy peasant Hadji Georgy, who had a lot of land of 1000 decares and numerous herds, a beautiful house and a lot of money. The legend said that he got rich very simply: he inherited from his father Ivan who had found a treasure with gold. 2 tax collectors, having collected taxes in Sofia and Philippopolis, were carrying a chest with gold to Istanbul. On the way one guard killed another one, turned off the Tsargrad rode toward Bodrovo, hiding behind the hills, and buried the chest in the ground, having marked the place with a huge stone, and disappeared somewhere, waiting for a right moment to return for the buried treasure.

Ivan, who owned this land, pulled the stone to another place, plowing the land. One day the Turk returned and began to inquire, where the stone was, allegedly, there was a grave of his father under it; having found nothing, dumbfounded he left. Ivan immediately realized that something valuable should be buried under the stone and, remembering where the stone had been before, dug up the ground there and found a chest with gold, which he passed on to his son Hadji George. George built the church in Bodrovo with joy in honor of the namesake St. Georgy. The church did not have gilded domes, it was in a form of a house with a sloping roof, but beautifully decorated inside with wooden carvings, mosaics and marble. A building for school was built in the church yard, later a new 3-story building was built for school in the center of the village, and next to the old school in the church yard there was a building for kmet.

The office of the head of the village opened its doors to Ivan Todorov Karagochev, who had been elected a kmet and defeated the other candidates, including his "sworn-brother" and friend Ivan Guenov. To the delight of his family and the other supporters in the village, Ivan Todorov settled into his new office and successfully began his work. The door of his office opened, and his frontline friend Ivan Guenov appeared on the threshold. Guenov's cheek bones twitched nervously, and his eyes glowed furiously with anger. By an effort of will, suppressing his overwhelming emotions, he began to speak with Ivan Todorov.

"Friend, you can't do this to me! You have won the elections and became a kmet, but it was me who wanted it! All my life I wanted to become a head of the village! Resign your position and give it up to me!"

Ivan Todorov became embarrassed and began to explain to his friend:

"I was not eager for the office, putting life at stake, as we went on the attack at the war. The vast majority of the villagers, or rather almost all of them have voted for me, and you know that. How can I resign my office now and hand it over to another person, for whom people did not vote! This is impossible! Get over it, Kamine!"

"That's right, Kamine! Since childhood they have been calling me so, because I managed to wade through the flooded Kayaliyka River. Kamine, Camine means 'I'll come through,' I'll wade through. I've waded always and everywhere. I can't admit defeat at the elections!"

"But how can I betray the villagers, who voted for me? People will say that I am not worthy of the kmet's office, that I am afraid, that I could not cope with the work and therefore refused and deceived them!"

"Remember how you and I fought, how we attacked the enemy, how we stormed Adrianople! After all, we are the sworn-brothers!" Kamine insisted.

"No!" Ivan Todorov snapped.

Nearly choking with rage and clenching his fists, Kamine turned toward the door.

"You will regret it," he gritted through his teeth, going out to the street.

Envy and malice, hatred and thirst for revenge were tearing him from inside.

At the end of spring of 1913, when the Balkan Wars were still going on, 12-year-old Todor went with his cousin Vidyu, 16-year-old, the son of uncle Gocho, to graze their flocks of sheep on the meadows, belonging to the family near Volchovsky Kairak, and so they remained there for the whole summer, coming to the village from time to time for food. They drove the flock into a sheepfold for a night, and in the morning they took them out to the meadows, where the poor sheep, which had endured hungry winter with uncle Angel, grazed and gained strength and health. Having mastered all the skills of the craft from early childhood, 2 shepherd boys took cake of the sheep with joy and love, helping their families, which remained without adult men. One evening, having corralled the sheep into the sheepfold, Todor and Vidyu ate hearty bread with butter and feta-cheese, ate a piece of salted bacon with vegetables, drank it with milk and fell on the hay in the corner to rest.

"Todor, you and I we have become the shepherd boys," Vidyu said.

"We have become shepherd boys like the famous voevodas, they became shepherds very early and helped their parents, remember, like Angel Voevoda and Captain Petko Voevoda!"

"Angel Voevoda, when he was little, grazed sheep somewhere in our area."

"He tended the other people sheep, but we do our own," Vidyu said thoughtfully.

"And how he beat the Turks!" Todor exclaimed with youthful enthusiasm, remembering by heart the songs and legends, heard from the cradle. "Angel with his cheta once went to Odrin to protect the Bulgarians who were robbed and killed by the Turks and Arnauts, then they realized that it was Jew Mushon, the Odrin Bey, who was the main enemy, as he himself sent his Arnauts to deal with the Bulgarians and steal their last. They understood that it was him who had to be punished. And at that moment the Odrin Bey lived in Tsargrad. So, they arrived at the port Chanakkale, suddenly some Turk from Haskovo recognized them. They hid from him and board some kind a ship, the ship sets sail and sailed to Burgas, and it was too late to get off the ship. Then they grab the captain and force him to turn the ship around and sail back to Tsargrad.

The captain complies, they sail back to Tsargrad, get off the ship, find the Jewish Bey Mushon, penetrate into his house, take all the gold and kill the Bey."

"At first, they did not want to kill the Bey, they only tied and gagged him, but he still started yelling, and they had to kill him," Vidyu specified, "gold was dearer for him than life."

"Yes, they had to kill him," Todor agreed, "and then Angel Voevoda with his squad excited fear on the Turks, always defeated them with their courage and cunning, and the Turks always retreated and never could catch Angel with his people."

"And why there is only one Angel Voevoda and another Angel is our uncle?" Vidyu grinned bitterly.

"He stole our mill and starved half the sheep!" Todor exclaimed indignantly. "Because of him our grandfather fell ill!"

"Hush!" Vidyu whispered, stopping Todor. "Somebody is walking there!"

Both boys fell silent and listened. There was sound of footsteps and the creak of the opening door. Against the evening twilight a male figure appeared in the doorway. The boys stood still and froze in place. The uninvited guest lingered for a moment at the door, peering into a dark space of the room, then resolutely stepped inside, grabbed the first sheep that came across and pushed her out into the outer pen, enclosed with the wooden fence around the sheepfold. He turned around, repeated the same thing with another sheep and pushed her out, stepped over the threshold of the sheepfold and vanished from view. In an instant the boys grabbed 2 sticks, standing next to the wall, and noiselessly jumped to the door, freezing from both sides of it. The door opened, and the night thief returned for the next sheep. He stepped over the threshold, cautiously holding the revolver in his outstretched hand, on which immediately received a blow from Todor, and having dropped the revolver, the sheep thief fell on the floor from a deafening blow with a stick on his head, which Vidyu inflicted on him. Agile like a cat, 12-year-old Todor jumped on the uninvited guest, lying on the floor helping Vidyu to tie his hands behind his back with a rope. Todor picked up the revolver expertly and pointed it at the sheep thief.

"Get up, let's go!" Vidyu told him, holding his hands tied behind his back on an outstretched rope, like a dog on a leash.

Having waked up, the sheep thief looked around with vexation and, on seeing 2 boys, grew bolder for a moment, but when he saw his revolver in the hands of one of them, became humbled, got to his feet and stepped over the threshold. Holding him at gunpoint with one hand, Todor corralled 2 sheep into the sheepfold, and the boys led the captive to the kmet's building in the Bodrovo village. They were walking along the trodden rural path under the light of the Moon, and the sheep thief walked in front on a leash on an outstretched rope, which Vidyu, walking behind, was holding firmly, and Todor was walking beside him with a revolver in his hands. Then the boys spotted that the prisoner was dressed in a military uniform, dirty, tattered and warn.

"A deserter?" they inquired.

"None of your business!" the prisoner snarled and walked gloomily in silence.

The distance from the sheepfold on their land to the village was considerable, but finally, having overcome it, they entered Bodrovo from the north side, where there was a building of the kmet not far from the right side of the main road. The building of the community with the office of the head of the village was located in the courtyard of St. Georgy church, and 2 guards were on duty there at night. They had accepted the bound prisoner and in the morning handed him over to the kmet Tosho Bonev, who with obvious displeasure at the fact that his nephew turned out to be a deserter, escaping from the front of the Balkan War, sent him to Haskovo community in the morning. And Todor with Vidyu, who after this case gained fame as brave boys, were pleased with themselves and rejoiced that they had managed to defend their property without fear of armed robber, and from the corner of their eye with pleasure noticed the admiring glances of the girls of the village, passing by them.

The hot summer of 1913 replaced spring and with its scorching sun greened up the hillsides with blooming herbs, flowers and plentiful harvest, which finally the men, who had survived after the 2 Balkan Wars and returned to the village, would be able to harvest. 3 sons of Todor Karagochev: Ivan, Gocho and Dimitar also had survived in the battles of the 2 wars and returned home. Ivan was elected kmet, head of the village, to the pride of the whole family, and it seemed that the grandfather Todor could only enjoy life. But shocked with the betrayal of his son Angel, he failed to recover, became gloomy, unsociable, talked to himself, losing his health and strength every day.

Vidyu and Todor continued to graze sheep on the meadows near Volchovsky Kairak, and one day they saw a rider, approaching them. It was their cousin Georgy, their uncle Dimitar's son.

"Let's go home, grandpa Todor is really bad, he wants to see you!" Georgy blurted out breathless.

Todor and Vidyu herded the sheep into the sheepfold, mounted their horses and galloped to the village. Soon Bodrovo, located on the hill, appeared. They hastily entered the house. There were all relatives there, except Angel: 3 sons, daughter-in-law, grandchildren and grandma Mariyka. Grandfather Todor was lying in bed and dropping off. He was akin of a ghost. His once mighty body was exhausted and lay helplessly in bed, with which the snow-white head and mustache merged in color. His dimmed eyes reflected the endless longing with which science of his life flashed through his memory: childhood, caring hands and smile of his mother, her songs and legends about the hajduks. His father Kara-Gochev, the son of hajduk and hajduk himself, the endless struggle with the hated Turks, peace and refuge in Bodrovo, their big house, herds of sheep, fields with crops, green fields on the hursts at the foothills of the Rhodopes, children, grandchildren, the betrayal of his own son Angel… The heart of the grandfather sank for the last time and stopped forever. The strong and brave heart of Todor was broken by the monster, into which his son Angel turned, betraying him, robbing him and ceasing to communicating with him, passing by with contempt in a hat, pulled down on his side, not saying hello, turning away from his own father.

They buried the grandfather Todor in the rural cemetery south from Bodrovo on a hillside next to his father and grandfather. Thus, Todor Karagochev, the last hajduk, passed away and found peace at his beloved Rhodopes, the father of 3 daughters and 4 sons and grandchildren, one of whom was 12-year-old Todor Ivanov Todorov Karagochev, named after him.

Alexander Stamboliysky

Chapter 6
Alexander Stamboliysky
Beginning of the Great War

On September 17, 1915, in the Red Salon, located on the second floor of the palace of the tsar Ferdinand in Sofia there were following politicians, waiting for an audience: Alexander Stamboliysky, the head of the Bulgarian Agrarian Union, and the leaders of the parties opposing tsar Ferdinand's foreign policy: Ivan Gueshov, head of the People's Party, Stoyan Danev, the leader of the Progressive Liberal Party, Alexander Malinov, head of the Democratic Party and Naicho Tsanev, leader of the Radical Democratic Party. In the center of Sofia on the Prince Alexander I Square the palace of the tsar Ferdinand stood as an ominous symbol of absolutism, long outdated in Europe, but fitting right in belated Bulgaria at the dawn of the XX century.

Once upon a time, there was a Turkish palace and a mosque on this place, and under the palace there were torture chambers and prison, where the fighters for freedom of Bulgaria against the Turks died, where Vasil Levsky was a prisoner, and opposite the Konak the head of Georgy Benkovsky stood, impaled on a stake like a gloomy sign of triumph of barbarism over progress and tyranny over freedom. After the Liberation, the mosque and the Turkish Konak were demolished, and on its foundation over the prison torture chamber they built a palace for the Bulgarian Prince Alexander Battenberg, whose reign from 1879 to 1886 promised to bring Bulgaria only benefit, progress and prosperity, which after the assassination of the tsar Liberator Alexander II was contrary to the interests of Russia, seeing a "Transdanubia province" in Bulgaria.

Overthrown by the machinations of Alexander III, Alexander Battenberg, having united Bulgaria, split by the Berlin Congress, and rebuffed the Serbs, attacking it, was forced to leave his beloved Bulgaria, his palace and die untimely in the prime of 36 years old with longing for the abandoned Bulgaria. As if evil fate played a cruel joke with Bulgaria, it slipped Ferdinand of Saxe-Coburg and Gotha into her in order to lead to the disaster. The first catastrophe fell on Bulgaria on July 1, 1913, with the Second Balkan Warm the second one was gleaming on horizon.

"Was it really necessary to win liberation from Turkey with blood in order personally to hand over your freedom into the hands of a self-proclaimed tyrant?" Alexander Stamboliysky was thinking gloomily, measuring with a contemptuous glance tsar Ferdinand who entered the Red Hall.

Next to the tsar his son Boris and the head of his office Dobrovich were going. Having greeted the delegation of the opposition, Ferdinand listened with vacant indifference to the opinion of each of them and, passing by his royal ears their appeals for an alliance with the Entente or neutrality, resolutely approached Alexander Stamboliysky. With hatred he extended his hand for a handshake, measuring with defiantly cowardly look the mighty figure of the peasants' leader. With his little grey cunning eyes Ferdinand peered into the large brown eyes of Stamboliysky with a fiery look and wondered, why he did not tremble before him. Ferdinand, who was not accustomed to the objection of his courtiers, established the regime of personal power in Bulgaria and, having turned the ideals of parliamentarism and democracy inside out, had crushed the Tarnovo Constitution with all its problems, having left only candy wrapper from it. The Constitutional monarchy turned out to be absolutism in fact. Elections of parliament by people on the basis of universal suffrage, ministry responsible to parliament, which the Tarnovo Constitution, allegedly, guaranteed in theory, turned out to be just a smokescreen, hiding Ferdinand's scams. Like a cardsharper he shuffled his marked deck of cards, transferring the politicians, ministers, parties from one place to another for his own benefits, dissolved the People's Assembly, rescinded the ministers, involved them into corruption schemes, fabricated accusations, accused in crimes, threw them to jail, then pardoned, kept on a hook, demanding personal loyalty out of fear of reprisals. He had hung the whole country on a hook, despising its people, and corrupted the politicians. He had killed Stambolov and destroyed Radev, he had planted corruption, betrayal, slander, lies and denunciations. He hated noble people, he hated Alexander Stamboliysky just as he hated those who couldn't be corrupted and intimidated and deprived of their opinion. He looked at him with hatred and fear, recalling how he himself appeared at the

People's Assembly, sat down in the armchair with a hat on his head and began to rant, and when all the parliamentarians were standing, the Stamboliysky's party sat down at his command, demonstrating disrespect for the tsar. And in 1913 Stamboliysky publicly challenged him for the repressions against the Ministry of Justice Radev, and in 1914 he publicly pointed on him as the culprit of the national catastrophe.

The mighty figure of Alexander Stamboliysky: tall, broad shoulders, a lush mop of black hair, dashingly curled moustaches, a clean-shaved chin, large brown eyes, beautiful regular features, a proud look, independent spirit, nobility, courage and dignity of the peasants' leader contrasted with the personality of the tsar Ferdinand with his grey cunning eyes, a washcloth hanging gray mustaches and a disgusting goatee, with a long hooked nose, inherited from his mother Clementine, with deceit, meanness and megalomania of the Byzantine emperor, who never took place, but still pursued his goal: to enter Constantinople as a winner on a white horse in the attire of the Bulgarian Empire kings. A supporter of people's power Stamboliysky hated Ferdinand, as he hated all tyranny and tyrants and, overcoming a feeling of hostility, he began his speech.

"Your Majesty, contrary to the decision taken by the Agrarian Union not to communicate with you, with the consent of the Agrarian Parliamentary Group, I decided together with the representatives of the opposition groups to come to the meeting with you. Deep feelings for my country and imminence of our motherland made me do it. I've come to you not seeking power, but in order to express, to the best of my ability, the opinion of the vast majority of Agrarian people of Bulgaria on the burning questions that all of us concern.

Before proceeding to the essence of topical issues, I consider it necessary to state that I am absolutely free from the well-known feelings of the Bulgarian people, fighting with each other in the socio-political field, so-called 'Russophile' and 'Germanophile'. I have always been overwhelmed with only one feeling and one understanding of the vitally important question of the destiny of the motherland: will Bulgaria be whole and unharmed, protected in this monstrous size world storm and, if possible, with minimal sacrifices gain maximum benefit before the altar of the national ideals. Your Majesty, I do not operate with fabrications, but with facts. I live among these people and I know their sick soul and gloomy mood.

My task was always to revive the fighting national spirit of the people, but one feeling remained in their soul regarding the big fateful issue which remains close to our heart.

1) Feeling for Russia has not disappeared. It's unfortunate, but it's true. It's unfortunate because it fetters a free scope of large statehood.
2) The terrible impression of the undergone pogrom has not disappeared.
3) His faith in governors is killed.
4) Fear of war and especially unpopular war, and war on several fronts is a terrible nightmare in his mind that gnaws him.
5) And the most important, his faith in you, Your Majesty, is completely shaken and killed. In his eyes, in the eyes of people after the pogrom in July 29, 1913, your reputation of a subtle diplomat was ultimately debunked.

Is it possible, in the presence of all this, to start an unpopular military action! And with whom? With your current government which has no support on this issue even in its own circles! No! Definitely not! Assessing the situation, I sincerely declare to you, reject the intention of your government to take this destined for it dangerous and destructive path! Remain neutral until the position of this world storm is fully cleared up! Use all your efforts to get closer to the people and direct your and your government's intentions for the common good! Look over this storm and over the impressions from it, over everything that surrounds us and remember that all this is a temporary phenomenon which will fly away, and human and legal international relations will be established throughout the world and especially on the Balkan Peninsula!

Your Majesty, before I finish, I consider it necessary to remind you one page from our recent history, which you can take note for your actions and intentions. In 1913, shortly after the demobilizations of the troops we began to receive letters, the delegations from the kmets of Bulgaria came to us through which the embittered and unfortunate Bulgarian people wanted us to lead the struggle to identify and punish quickly and decisively the perpetrators of the defeat, among which you take the first place. It is true that the gentlemen, who are near you, are trying in every possible way to evade responsibility, but we have never separated them from you. At that time we believed that the defeat was a malicious act of you and your ministers and feared for the fate of Bulgaria from the Romanian invasion, therefore we resolutely opposed this cruel popular intention and successfully rejected it.

Remember, however, if you commit another criminal act in the morning, we, the members of the Agrarian Union, shall not only interfere with people's indignation against you, but we ourselves shall become it's spokesmen and announce you a cruel, but just verdict. In conclusion, let me read you and give you a written summary of all that you have heard from me."

And Stamboliysky began to read the official appeal to Ferdinand.

"You Majesty, when the representative of the Agrarian Union for the first time has come to you, he must bravely convey the truth to you, especially at such a fateful moment, when Bulgaria is going through the most difficult days for her. This truth is that every action that you take with your government is previously condemned before the conscience of the Bulgarian people, because they lost faith in you personally and in your reputation as a subtle diplomat after the catastrophe of July 29, 1913 has been debunked in their soul, because they lost faith in each of the parties that rule Bulgaria, as the wounds and horrors of the Balkan Wars are still fresh and haunt the people's consciousness like a nightmare. Therefore, we warn you:

1) Keep your government of any venture.
2) Stay neutral.
3) Do not undertake any serious act without convening the parliament and without nation-wide cabinet, which will consider everything, which represents different currents in society, in order to calm the country and revive faith among people, without which people can't create their own destiny, but can only prematurely convert their land to the grave.
4) Do not forget that the soul of people is split, and today's government is least of all able to rally it and direct it to exploits and fateful deeds. This split soul can very soon turn the country into an arena of revolts and riots.

Thank you for having the patience to listen to me!"

Alexander Stamboliysky finished reading and handed over a folder with the appeal to the tsar to Strashimir Dobrovich, the head of Ferdinand's cabinet.

The chiefs of the opposition parties, who were present in the Red Hall, with bated breath anxiously looked alternately at Stamboliysky and then at Ferdinand. Gasping with anger, Ferdinand thought to himself: "If you only knew how much I despise you! You are backward, downtrodden, slavish people, to whom I descended to rule you, and I am your master!"

So Ferdinand thought, who 11 days ago, on September 6, 1915, concluded an alliance treaty between Bulgaria and Germany and signed a military convention of 2 states with Austria-Hungary without the knowledge of the majority of the Bulgarian ministers and without the consent of the People's Assembly. None of those present in the hall knew about it. And in order to make things as clear as mud, the tsar began to argue with Stamboliysky.

"Do you know what a painful impression made on me the resolution of the Agrarian Congress, which forbade you to communicate with me!"

"This resolution was one temporary measure that met the needs of the moment," Stamboliysky replied calmly.

"But you advise me to get closer to people, and you yourself avoid me!"

"We fled from you, when everybody, even the closest ones, fled from you."

"You were too audacious with me in your speeches!"

"I was only completely frank with you and only used my right to freedom of speech, which does not really exist, and I told you what you are obliged to know."

"Why do you consider only, me alone responsible for everything? There were the other factors too."

"This is not only my belief, but the whole nation think so. There is a huge gap in the Constitution: it gives you wide scope to be everything."

"What did Mr. Radoslavov tell you during your meeting with him?" Ferdinand inquired.

"We concluded from his words that the government is already ultimately in the orbit of the Central Powers," Stamboliysky replied.

"But what did he tell you?" Ferdinand anxiously tried to find out, not wanting his agreement with the Austro-German block to become known before the mobilization announcement.

"It concerns us and our friends," Stamboliysky answered.

"I insist: what exactly did Mr. Radoslavov say?"

"I don't remember, and I am not obliged to report you!" Stamboliysky rebuffed sharply.

"You, Mr. Stamboliysky, threaten me with riots and rebellions, you inform me that no one has faith in me and my ability and that you yourself are ready to announce a people's verdict to me?"

"Yes, I do."

"Know that I have my own path, a clearly defined policy, and I'll boldly follow this path, ignoring your threats. And when I follow this path, I believe that I serve the people much better than you do!"

"It's questionable. If you want to go your own way, go! And I shall go my own way which is not connected with pogrom like your way. I warn you once again: remain neutral, otherwise you will lose both the throne and your head!"

"Don't pity my head, I am old, think of your young head!" Ferdinand exclaimed, ending the conversation and ordered to himself: "Take, seize, destroy, throw him to jail and kill him!"

Alexander Stamboliysky with the leaders of the opposition parties left the royal palace with a painful premonition of an impending new catastrophe, which he could not prevent, but a tireless campaigner for people's cause, he did not retreat.

"Only people is the source of power, only the people himself must determine their own destiny and repel the tyrant, again pushing the country into the abyss, and only people can overthrow the tyrant!"

He went to the Union House on 1 Vrabcha Street, where the printing house of the Agrarian Union was located, and printed out his appeal to the tsar as a separate brochure, as well as the dialogue with the tsar that followed, loaded a cart drawn by 2 oxen with the boxes of brochures and set off with his assistants from village to village to speak with the people, so that the people could rebuff to the war that brings death. They reached the village Bodrovo. The kmet of the village Ivan Todorov Karagochev met the leader of the Agrarian Union and called everyone to meet him in a large hall of school, which was immediately filled with the villagers. In the front row of the hall 14-year-old Todor Todorov, anxious for the political struggle knowledge, was sitting, next to him his faithful friend Ivan Ignatov was and the cousins Vidyu and Georgy. All people were listening attentively to every word of Stamboliysky, who had attached a geographical map of the world to the blackboard and, showing at the countries with a pointer, told about their population, economic potential and intention to join one of two blocks that had been fighting with each other for a year.

"A simple arithmetic calculations show that in this insane war the Entente will win, and the Austro-Germanic block will be defeated. If the tsar Ferdinand and the Radoslavov government drag Bulgaria into the war on the side of Austria and Germany, then they'll doom the country to death, and the fate of Bulgaria will be hard!" Alexander Stamboliysky exclaimed, "All of us must not allow this! Bulgaria suffered 2 Balkan Wars and must remain neutral!"

"Down with the war on the side of Austria and Germany!" Todor exclaimed, whom Alexander Stamboliysky immediately noticed against the background of the rest, sitting in the hall.

"Well done, young man!" Stamboliysky praised him. "What is your name?"

"My name is Todor Todorov."

"This is my son," Ivan Todorov, the kmet of Bodrovo, said.

Stamboliysky with the assistances returned to his native village Slavovitsa, where Ferdinand's patrol was waiting near his house, who arrested him, took to Sofia and sent him to Sofia Central prison. The verdict was not long in coming. "For the speech to His Majesty the tsar, in which he expressed the most daring insults, accusations and threats of riots and rebellions, Alexander Stamboliysky is sentenced to death!" The tsarist prosecutor Markov read it out with pleasure, peering maliciously into Stamboliysky's eyes.

"Well, are you satisfied?" Markov wondered.

"I boldly believe that I've fulfilled my duty worthy and valiantly at this historical and fateful moment for my country. And if what my friends and I have done had an impact to prevent the catastrophe of the country, I'll readily accept full responsibility before the law!" Stamboliysky answered proudly, openly looking into the eyes of the Ferdinand's retinue servants.

"And I am satisfied! Let's continue your iniquity! Condemn 2–3 more honest and selfless persons, but you will need all these saints at the end of the war to save Bulgaria!" Tsanko Tsarkovsky Bakalov exclaimed, Stamboliysky's like-minded supporter, who was sitting next to him in the dock.

The death sentence of Alexander Stamboliysky was commuted to life imprisonment, and the door of a prison was slammed behind him. The tsar Ferdinand had destroyed almost the entire Agrarian Union and threw them to prison at the head of the prominent figures: Tsanko Tsarkovsky Bakalov,

Marko Turlakov, Raiko Daskalov, Nedelcho Georgiev, Grigor Boyadjinov, and Georgy Alexandrov; and in a few days, on September 23, 1915, he dragged Bulgaria into the Great War in one bound with the Austro-German block.

Chapter 7
The Great War

It was already 2 years that the world had been blazing in the Great War, drawing more and more new countries and continents into its funnel, each of which fought for its freedom and independence, without thinking about what exactly it consisted of. Europe burned, pitted with tranches, in which soldiers of the war lived and fought, rotted alive next to the rats and drowned in the mud from water that filled the tranches, so that only feet in boots stuck out on the surface, as if offering: "Need boots? Take it, I don't need them anymore!" Sponsored by Andrew Carnegie the Inquiry International Commission of the Circumstances of the Balkan Wars, whose members, noble and eminent personalities, had accomplished an amazing feat—they were in hot pursuit of the 2 Balkan Wars, interviewing witnesses, recording their stories, establishing the truth of the events and conveying to posterity—suddenly stopped and retreated, dumbfounded by the horrors of the new war that engulfed the whole world. The horrors of the 2 Balkan Wars faded by the scale of the horrors of the new war, which flared up less than a year later and was their direct continuation.

It all started with a quarrel between the relatives, the representatives of the royal families, almost all the offspring of Queen Victoria who held in their tenacious claws the countries and peoples inhabiting them: cousins, uncles and nephews, second brothers and sisters—they hated each other as much as only relatives are capable to hate. With jealousy they followed each other: who had more power, land, wealth and colonies. Preparing for the war, they sent each other telegrams with appeal: "Dear Willy!" "Dear Nicky!" and assurances of love and peace. Having unleashed the war, they sent millions of people to slaughter, to exterminate each other, to destroy cities, to sink ships, to destroy material and cultural values, to change the course of history. The drug addict

Gavrilo Princip helped them to start the war under a plausible excuse. Having received, together with a gang of patriots, weapons from the hands of the Serbian government at the instigation and of Russia and Hungary, Princip pulled the trigger, unleashing the monarchial relatives to attack each other.

All participated in the vile conspiracy, and its ends led to Vienna, where everyone hated Franz Ferdinand for his intellect, dignity and nobility, for his morganatic marriage with his beloved woman, for pacifism, peacefulness, Catholicism, for plans to reform the Austro-Hungarian Empire. All were the Princip's accomplices: from Vienna to Oskar Potiorek, The governor of Bosnia and Herzegovina, and the driver Leopold Loik. Potiorek had invited Franz Ferdinand to Sarajevo at the direction of Franz Joseph, previously divulged in detail the route of the cortege, deprived him of his guard and threw under the terrorists' bombs; after the explosion of bomb by a wrong car and accidental rescue of Franz Ferdinand, already at the Town Hall he insisted to continue the trip around the city instead of urgently to leave the city, persuading everyone that there were no terrorists in Sarajevo, did not strengthen the security and together with the driver Leopold Loik drove the car straight to the place where Gavrilo Princip was located, where Appel Embankment along the Miljacka River at the Latin Bridge at the corner of the lane, leading to the Franz Joseph Street. There Princip shot in the stomach of pregnant Sophie and in the neck of Franz Ferdinand, having fired 7 bullets into them, which had started the Great War, in which Oskar Potiorek became the commander-in-chief of the armed forces in the Balkans, successfully failed all the operations and before that had organized Serbian pogroms in Bosnia and Herzegovina.

Potiorek had lied that there were no terrorists in Sarajevo, pushing the unfortunate Franz Ferdinand and Sophie to continue their journey through the city. There were terrorists, and Potiorek knew very well about it, they were thoroughly trained, supplied with weapons, taught to shoot, delivered to the place of rout of the cortege by those who weaved on order a web of conspiracy, into which all were engulfed: the Austrian military and the court, consumptive fanatics-murderers from Mlada Bosna, the military junta of Serbia from the "Black Hand", headed by Dragutin Dimitrievich, behind which the figures from the government gleamed at the head of the regent Alexander, and the secret agents of the Russian court, who finally financed the entire operation. The interests of the opposing sides miraculously intertwined and, having killed the peacemaker and the reformer, they let the aggressors off the chain and unleashed the war.

However, during the July crisis there were moments of hesitation. Morocco, rending asunder, all the contradictions of the powers, disputes over the Baghdad railway, mutual hatred of the royal relatives, their squabble over the division of colonies around the world—everything froze on the verge of disaster, waiting for Russia to respond the demand to stop mobilization. But Russia did not stop the mobilization, accusing Germany and Austria of secret mobilization, and having mobilized her troops, moved them to the German and Austrian borders even before the final deadline for responding to the Austrian ultimatum to Serbia, which accepted all its points except the last one and did not allow Austrian detectives to search organizers of the assassination of Franz Ferdinand, as they would immediately go on the regent Alexander.

Austria shelled Belgrade on August 28, 1914. In response to the general mobilization in Russia and the advance of her troops to the Austrian and German borders, Germany declared war on Russia on August 1, and countries and continents fell like dominoes, declaring war on each other and involving their colonies around the world into it. Barefooted Africans from the French colonies went to war as if on a pleasure trip, dancing to the sounds of tambourine. From the distant Canada, Australia and New Zealand subjects of the British crown landed on the hostile shores of the upcoming battles. They were followed by the inhabitants of all other English colonies from India to the tiny islands in the oceans. Almost everyone hurried to the Middle East to the final division of the "sick" Ottoman Empire in order to snatch a piece for themselves, and the tsarist Russia led the race, raving about Constantinople and the straits, drawing England into the war. And in the Far East Japan and China also took side of the Entente. They walked as if at a review, countries and continents, fluttering banners, as at the opening of the Olympic Games they passed before the mankind eyes, dragging unfortunate animals behind them: horses and oxen, even donkeys and camels—ready to fight, but hardly realizing what awaited them in the war.

And as Alexander Stamboliysky correctly calculated, the numerous superiority was on the side the Entente, but the Austro-Germanic block was not going to yield, and the entire world blazed in the fire of the Great War, in the flame that flared up from a sparkle, striking in Balkans, where the flame of allegedly finished 2 Balkan Wars still smoldered, and where the war for the influence of 2 obsolete empires never ended: the patchwork Austro-Hungarian and the tsarist Russian Empire. The geographic names of the globe became the names of the great battles, land soaked in blood and strewn with human bones, evidence of crimes against humanity of those who drove millions of people to exterminate each other. Tiny Luxemburg, Belgian cities—Namur, Liege, Brussels, Antwerp, Langemark, Charleroi, Mons, Ypres, Ostend, all the land of Alsace and Lorraine, the land of Arden, Picardy, the river Marne River, cities of France: Verdun, Amiens, Calais, Lille, Noyon, Laon, Soissons, Nancy, Reims, Cambrai, Arras—became a symbol of carnage, of bloodshed in vain, heroism and crimes, the criminal madness of crowned relatives at the head of European countries.

There were moments when everything was calm on the Western front: the guns fell silent and it was quiet, as if waking up from a nightmare, the belligerents on both sides of the front crawled out of the trenches, gathered on a neutral territory to smoke together, treat each other with cigarettes, exchange souvenirs for Christmas and play football together, until a blank shot was heard from behind, calling to return to the tranches to continue to kill each other. Especially at such moments the soldiers thought about why they kill, suffer and die for the sake of some "offended" Serbia, which itself was a source of terrorism and turmoil.

Bulgarian Tsar Ferdinand swayed as if on a swing, approaching one or another warring party, trying to bargain for more, and finally made a wrong choice: he had stuck to the wrong side and made his belated and senseless entry into the war on a wrong side. Having responded on Stamboliysky's warning with a death sentence, commuted to life imprisonment, ignoring the warning of 40 scientists, public figures and writers at the head of Ivan Vazov and 109 political figures, tsar Ferdinand entered the war on the side of the Austro-Germanic block, previously having gotten rid of the heroes of the First Balkan War—General Georgy Vazov, Radko Dimitriev and Nikola Ivanov—the heroes of Adrianople. Ferdinand did not give a damn for the public committee, created by Georgy Vazov, which issued an appeal to him and the government to maintain neutrality in the World War; Ferdinand did not give a damn for this appeal, signed by the entire outstanding Vazov family: General Georgy Vazov, writer Ivan Vazov, deputy of the National Assembly and future minister Boris Vazov.

Knowing his worth as the tsar of the country with unique geographical position, important for the both warring parties at the approaches of Turkey and the straits, Ferdinand waited and bargained for the whole year, closely following the course of the battles. He had been watching how the 2 blocks exterminated each other on the Western front, gloated over the "great Russian retreat" in summer 1915 on the Easter front, remembering how the Russians tried to kill him 8 times, was amazed at the Gallipoli operation, in which the Great Britain fleet was defeated, and the British, French, Australians and New Zealanders taken together could not defeat the retarded Turks, the same Turks who were defeated 3 year ago during the First Balkan War, the Turks who were put into stampede by the Bulgarian warriors, the Turks who at the mere sight of the advancing Bulgarians fled in panic, abandoning Lozengrad, Babeeski, Lule-Burgas. Ferdinand and Prime Minister Radoslavov, seduced by the success by the Austro-Germanic block, decided to join it and now together with the Turks to exact vengeance upon their defeat in the Second Balkan War and return the territories, seized by Serbia, Greece and Rumania. And if the Entente asked for neutrality, promising help to return the territories, then Germany and Austro-Hungary demanded to fight for them. And Ferdinand drove Bulgaria to fight.

***

Under the jingle of pro-Germanic propaganda the Bulgarian regiments were sent again for the same Macedonia, Thrace and Dobrudja now only under the command of the German Field Marshal August von Mackensen. October 14, 1915 Bulgaria declared war on Serbia and the next day attacked the Serbian troops, having crossed the border, in response of which they received an ultimatum of declaring war from the Entente. The Entente had declared war on Bulgaria, landed an expeditionary force in Thessaloniki and opened the Thessaloniki Front. The Entente hurried up to the aid of Serbia, but it was too late, since Serbian Serbia no longer existed, and having dug the trenches from the Adriatic Sea to the Aegean Sea, blocked the path of Bulgaria to Thessaloniki and bridled Greece like a wild horse that kicked, reared up and strove to drop the rider and rush into battle along with Germany, for which King Constantine had tender feelings, the author of a manual for the Greeks how to gouge the eyes of living Bulgarians, until finally, on June 12, 1917, the allies abdicated him from throne and expelled with a kick in his ass out of the country and enthroned as a puppet under Venizelos his son Alexander who became the King of Greece, but not for a long time, as soon he would be bitten by a rabid monkey and go to the world to come.

Serbian Serbia ceased to exist after 2 months: by December 11, 1915. Hardened in the battles of the 2 Balkan Wars that had just died down and equipped with the German weapons, the Bulgarian army took one city after another of Serbia itself and Macedonia, occupied by Serbia, the territory from Ohrid to Kriva Palanka, which was supposed to be ceded to Bulgaria under the treaty of the Balkan Union, but occupied by Serbia: Zajechar, Knjazhevats, Pirot, Leskovats, Kumanovo, Skopje, Tsarevo Selo, Kochani, Vranje, Monastir and above all Nis, the city of 3 emperors, where Constantine the Great, Constantine III and Justinian were born, and where the Bulgarian Tsar Ferdinand and the German emperor Wilhelm II met to celebrate the victory over the defeated Serbia. The Serbian army fiercely resisted, suffered heavy losses, dragging along itself their government, which had left Prizren, the streams of refugees and Austro-German captives, as well as the entire Montenegrin army who fought, was defeated and retreated along with the Serbs on their own territory. Ragged, dirty, emaciated and hungry, the Serbian soldiers trudged along the impassibility of Montenegro and Albania, dragging carts and unfortunate animals, falling into the snowdrifts on mountain paths, slid along the icy rocks and shivered from cold, died by the thousands and covered with their corpses all the way to the ports of Albania.

The Bulgarians drove them to Valona and Durazzo, from where the allied fleet transported them to Tunisia and the island of Corfu, where remaining under the open air, they continued to die from hunger and cold due to the lack of proper supply organization, and their corpses were lowered into the waters of Adriatic, where Serbia had been striving so actively all the time. The survived Serbian warriors would recover and get stronger, will unite with the allies at the Thessaloniki Front to strike back at the hated enemies: Austria, Germany and Bulgaria. And those Serbs who remained on the territory of Serbia at the end of February 191 7 raised an apprising, captured a number of villages, invaded into the Bulgarian Bosilengrad and immediately proceeded to the favorite deed: they destroyed all who were not Serbs, burned the city and the Bulgarian border villages, wherever they could only reach, burned women and children alive.

As always, Rumania, lurking around the corner how to grab a piece of foreign territory amid the general madness that swept the word and finding the right moment for herself, in August 1916 entered the war on the side of the Entente, thereby aggravating the already difficult position of the Allies who were immediately forced to provide assistance for her, which all the same turned out to be futile for her, as Rumania was still defeated by the forces of Germany, Austria-Hungary and Bulgaria, which returned her historical lands of the First Bulgarian Kingdom—Dobrujia, or rather, Southern Dobrujia, as in the Northern Dobrujia—a condominium of all 4 powers of the central block was established. The mirage of San-Stefano Bulgaria became the reality, and only the far-sighted saw in it a soup bubble that swelled to the limit and threatened to burst, because it was a void inside: a German colony into which Ferdinand turned Bulgaria.

***

In general, everything was calm at Thessaloniki Front in 1917. Only in the spring the bloody fights in two battles at Lake Doiran, which ended in a draw, had died down, since the Entente army, lacking artillery, could not expel the Bulgarians from the occupied heights, and the Bulgarians who had settled on those peaks in bunkers, named "Devil's eye sockets", rained the adversary with the steel fire from German flamethrowers and cannons, for which the commander of the 9th Pleven Division Colonel Vladimir Vazov, the brother of Georgy Vazov, received the rank of general as a reward. And the battle of Bitola on the Baba Mountains claimed countless lives.

The Entente soldiers had dug out trenches from the Adriatic to Orfano on the Aegean Sea, actually having carried out archaeological excavations, in which they found artifacts of several thousand years old, vestments of ancient warriors, jewelry, ceramics, gold, which replenished the Louvre and British Museum collections. Taking advantage of the quiet at the Thessaloniki Front, the soldiers of the Entente had fun playing football and with the amateur theater. And only damn insects-vampires attacked the soldiers, who found themselves in the Struma Valley; gigantic mosquitoes, almost the size of sparrows, penetrated into a tiny slit under the clothes, dug into a human body with a ruthless sting, like a spear, sucked out blood, littering in poison in return, infected with malaria and took to the grave thousands of lives of unfortunate soldiers, who had survived from the enemy bullets, who in horrendous agony, burning in fever, covered with blisters of bites, on the verge of insanity, tattered their body from unbearable itching and died in meaningless death.

The survived continued to live, waiting for the breakthrough of the Bulgarian front, but for now they patrolled the Struma Valley by bicycles and horses and in the middle of the ruins of the Thracian-Macedonian villages, destroyed to the ground by 2 Balkan Wars 4 years ago, built new roads with the help of the same faithful assistances: mules and oxen, carrying countless loads.

On July 2, 1917, Greece entered the war on the side of the Entente, having gotten rid of the King Constantine. Bulgaria had occupied Kavala, Serres and Drama, which she freed from the Turks in the First Balkan War, and the entire right bank of the river at the mouth of Maritsa. Under the roar of the Bulgarian army victories the opponents of the war fell silent and anxiously expected of what would happen next.

Chapter 8
Letter from the Front
Love and War

The Bodrovo village became empty again, having lost the men gone to the front of the Great War. 3 brothers of Ivan Todorov also went to fight: Dimitar, Angel and Gocho together with his eldest son Todor. But Ivan Todorov himself did not go to the war, as he had been elected the kmet and remained at the head of Bodrovo to solve all the problems of his native village that were aggravated by the new war. The country had great problems in the Great War. Having bound the country with German ties, Ferdinand handed it over as a colony to Germany to plunder. The Germans scoured along the country, as if in their patrimony, and captured everything in their path: from the last loaf of bread from a Bulgarian peasant in a village to the plants and factories, coal mines and springs. They traveled throughout the villages of Bulgaria on the carts, drawn by oven, broke into the peasants houses, rummaged them, turned everything upside down, robbed people, dooming them to starvation, took away all the food to the last kg of bread. Special teams of Bulgarian soldiers diligently helped the Germans to make requisitions. All the products, taken from the Bulgarian peasants, were thrown onto the carts, which were pulled by oxen along the impassibility of Bulgaria right into the throat of Germany and for the military needs. They were followed by the endless herds of oxen, buffaloes and cows, as well as the horses, taken away from the same peasants, who went to fight. The Germans pumped out raw materials for devalued rag-money, having captured the Pernik and Bobov-Dol coal mines and "Plakalnitsa" copper mines. Ferdinand's printing press filled the country with a mass of paper money with the shortage of goods under the roar of pro-German propaganda of the evening newspaper "Deutsche Balkan Zeitung," and only in Bodrovo Ivan Todorov on his own tried to protect the villagers from robbery.

He loaded 1200 kg of wheat on the cart, harnessed to oxen, and handed it over from his home to the military; a couple of oxen and a small amount of wheat were requisitioned from several well-to-do families; from the rest it was one ox, and he did not allow anything to be taken from the poor, to break into the houses, to rummage, though he knew that many people simply hid their property from robbery. It was a kmet who was charged with the duty to provide requisitions.

Once again, all the men from Bodrovo as well as from all over the country left to fight and put overwork in the fields on the shoulders of the adolescents and women. And the soldiers of the war died one after another, struck down by a bullet, a fragment of shell and malaria with cholera. And the mournful cry of the family was heard from one house in village, then from another one, where, having received a death notice, those who remained, sobbed, suffering.

Once, the mail was delivered to the kmet's office, where Ivan Todorov worked. There was one letter from the front for him. With excitement he opened the letter and began to read.

"To Ivan Todorov Karagochev, the kmet of the Bodrovo village, from Ivan Todorov Guenov. Dear friend, we were with you on the fronts of the Balkan Wars, you know what it's like. It whistles in the ears from the explosions of shells, and it rains with bullets and shrapnel. Now I am in the rear for a short time, but I found out that our unit is to be thrown to the line of defense. My friend, I do not believe that I shall survive and stay alive, if I get to the frontline. So, I beg you to help me! Take advantage of your power as the kmet and apply to some authorities with a request that I'd be discharged from the army. I know, it's not easy to do, but I also know that you can do it. Do this as a token of our brotherhood and our friendship! Goodbye. Your devoted friend, Ivan T. Guenov-Kamine."

After reading the letter, Ivan Todorov became agitated, complex feelings overwhelmed him, they replaced each other instantly and caused complete confusion. Having received a letter from the front a few moments ago, Ivan took it in his hands with excitement and fear, fearing to read the funeral, because his 3 brothers, nephew Todor and other relatives fought at the front. On seeing that the letter was not a notice of death, but from the old friend who is safe and sound, he was delighted, but after reading the letter, he became agitated. His relatives were fighting and did not ask to go home, and he did not try to call them back with his authority of the kmet, but the friend asks for help… Ivan Todorov was thinking about what to do, he recalled the past years. The scenes of the Balkan Wars flashed in his memory, the assault of Adrianople, when they risked their lives together and miraculously remained alive. And then there were the elections of kmet, his friend lost, and if the black cat ran between them; he saw how hatred and envy sparkled in the eyes of Ivan Kamine. Ivan Todorov did not want to recall his friend from the front, because all his relatives were fighting, but he began to solicit. He applied to various authorities and acquaintances, and soon Ivan Guenov, Kamine by nickname, returned to Bodrovo and took up his farm.

Meanwhile, life went on as usual, the hot sun still shone in the clear sky of Bulgaria, orchards with fruit trees bloomed; nobody canceled youth and love, and the roar of cannons at the front line could not stifle the heart beats of young beings at the age of 17, for the first time embraced by a feeling of love. The house where Kristina Nalbantova lived was located on the north-eastern outskirts of Bodrovo, behind it some houses with gardens were situated, and behind them yellow-green hills with crops and forests undulated up to the foot of the mountains. And in the distance the Rhodopes rose, sung by Homer, Virgil and Ovid, where Orpheus once sang his songs, challenging Apollo and Hades, where on the pinnacle of the rocks of Perpericon and Tatul there is a sanctuary of Dionysus and megaliths of the 12th century BC, where a man asked for love and happiness, invoking the deity. Christina's house, as it should be, was surrounded by a flowering garden, where fruit trees, berries, fruits and flowers grew, and all the magical gifts of nature that fertile land of Bulgaria can only give birth to. The midday August sun warmed every blade of grass on the ground and the quivering hearts of two young people in love with each other, who were 17 years old. Being in rapture from love and intoxicated with the smell of flowering roses, they were sitting next to each other on a bench in the garden under an apple tree, huddled against each other, brunches descended above them under the weight of ripe fruits, and the other world did not exist for them at that moment.

Todor grew up and matured and his rare beauty blinded all the girls and embittered his peers, ill-wishers and adults. Long, thick black hair undulated on his mature shoulders, the chiseled features of the amazingly beautiful face took on finished forms. A sensual mouth, slightly sunken cheekbones, a well-lined nose on a perfectly shaped oval of the face and a piercing gaze of deep dark eyes imparted him the appearance of a young prince, placed by fate in the wrong place at the wrong time. Nature endowed him with noble features, a free rebellious spirit and a desire for beauty. He was sitting next to his beloved girl in new clothes: a red shirt made of German silk descended over the dark linen trousers, covering the upper part of the hips and was girt with a belt that embraced his slender tall figure. And his slender long legs were tied with leather straps of new cervulis from pig skin, which he made with his own hands. For Kristina he was the most handsome young man in the world, which probably really was, and for Todor Christina was the most beautiful girl not only in Bodrovo, Philippopolis and Sofia, but in the whole world. And for both the world was concentrated here and now: in a cozy nook of the orchard under the canopy of the branches of a blooming apple tree among berries, flowers and intoxicating aroma of blossoming roses. Roses embroidered with colored cord, adorned Kristina's long skirt, her light blouse and apron on the thin waist of her slender figure. Her thin graceful fingers, bright dark eyes under a fan of lush eyelashes on a beautiful face enchanted Todor, who was passionately in love. He was holding her hand in his hands, and both of them seemed to be pierced by a heart as if with the electric current.

"Todore, I am so glad that you broke away from work in the field and came to the village and we could meet," Christina said in a half-whisper, lowering her eyes.

"I missed you so much, I really missed you. I thought about us all the time."

Todor whispered, pressing her hand to his cheek and lightly touching it with his lips.

"Is it difficult for you to work in the field alone?"

"Yes, it is, but I manage somehow. My father is kmet, he is busy at work in the village, uncle Dimitar is at the front, cousins Vidyu and Georgy take care of the animals, so I have to work in the fields alone with the oxen. Harvest is soon, tobacco ripened as well as coriander, anise and bread."

"Todor, you are the best in the world," Christina whispered embarrassedly.

"And for me, you are the most beautiful in the world, Christina," Todor answered, kissing her fingers.

They were silent, thinking about each other, enjoying every moment spent together. They were silent and were talking, talking about trifles, about what have been, but they did not dare to think or speak about what would be, since the future was foggy, anxious, incomprehensible.

"So, our school has been ended," Christina said sadly.

"Our studies are over, but we still need to study further, while nothing is known yet."

"We don't know what's in store for us."

They did not notice how time flew by, the sun had declined to sunset, with its huge red ball touched the horizon, and in the south in the distance, like a giant black fence at dusk, the Rhodopes blackened, behind which the flame of the Great War was still raging.

"Christina!" they heard her mother's voice, calling her daughter home.

"I have to go," Christina whispered, moving even closer to him.

They touched with their cheeks and, unable to resist the feeling surging over both, sank their lips in a passionate kiss in a gentle embrace. He accompanied her to the house and slipped quietly out of the garden.

"Are you here?" Todor was delighted to run into a tall figure of his friend, who was waiting for him around the corner of the garden in the street.

"I've been waiting for you the whole evening!" Ivan Ignatov answered with delight to meet Todor. "At last!"

Ivan Ignatov was a distant relative of Todor and his best friend, who could be trusted with the secrets of the heart. He was tall, with broad shoulders and strong arms, akin a hero-warrior, with lush hair and handsome face.

"Mityu Kitev Dinkovsky has gathered his gang, and they are waiting for you," Ivan warned his friend, "don't go along this road, let's go around the gardens! You know how he hates you!"

"No, I'll not hide," Todor flared up with excitement and headed along the road.

Ivan Ignatov, like a true friend, followed him. They barely walked along, when Mityu Kitev and his friends appeared before them, having jumped out from round the corner, all 6 of them were holding sticks in their hands. Todor and Ivan stopped, assessing the situation with a quick glance. Todor was clutching a small revolver in his pocket, deciding whether he would use it or not. The ugly Mityu Kitev, stifling with anger and hatred, said menacingly:

"Why did you, the kmet's son, show up here to Christine?"

He swung his stick and lowered it, aiming at Todor's head. Agile and fast, Todor dodged a blow and in an instant with all his might hit the bandit on the head with a butt of a revolver. The freak fell on the ground, having dropped his stick, which Todor picked up at the same second and, holding it firmly in his hands, describing an arc, walked with it over the heads of the entire gang, which in indecision tried to surround them. Ivan Ignatov, brave and strong, mighty as a hero, just as deftly dodged a blow of a stick and hit somebody's jaw, from which a tooth immediately popped out. Deftly turning on one leg, Todor with another leg kicked the other jaw with all his might and blood spurted from it. The entire gang took to their heels, having dropped the sticks. In a fit of anger, Todor rushed after them, but Ivan grabbed his hand and stopped him.

"Let them run!"

The boys burst into laughing and, merrily chatting, went home.

"Tomorrow at dawn I need to go to the field to work, it's a lot of work," Todor said.

"And tomorrow I'll graze my flocks," Ivan answered.

Chapter 9
VIDIN

High on a hill, with a steep descent constituting a high right bank of the Danube at the site of the river bend, there was the Vidin fortress, where Alexander Stamboliysky was imprisoned after the Central Sofia prison by the evil will of the Bulgarian Tsar Ferdinand. Built during the Great Rome in the I century AD, the fortress-city Bononia stood menacingly as a symbol of the conquest of the new provinces by Rome, where the civilization of the ancient Thracians had previously flourished. Following the fall of the Great Rome, Bononia fell under the blow of the barbarian hordes of the Avars, moving into Europe from the Central Asia, and was reborn again under a new name, serving new masters: Byzantines, Bulgarians.

Vidin became a castle-fortress of the Bulgarians, who invaded the banks of the Danube from the banks of the Volga under the leadership Khan Asparuh, who subduing the Slavs, defeated the Byzantines and founded the I Bulgarian kingdom in 679. Vidin stood on guard of the Bulgarian kingdom until its fall, having withstood 8 months of the siege of the Byzantine Basil II "Bulgar Slayer", was captured by the Byzantians, then again captured by the Bulgarians: the brothers Peter, Asen and Kalayan in 1185. The troops of the III Crusade and the next Crusade of Sigismund I passed through Vidin, whose defeat near Nikopol in 1396 put an end to the existence of the II Bulgarian Kingdom. And even after that, he continued to hold on.

Standing high on the banks of the Danube on the Roman foundation, the Vidin castle-fortress, encircled with unapproachable moat, with mighty walls, bastions and towers, had strength and audacity to challenge the Bulgarian kingdom, declared its independence and separate from it. For this he was a stronghold for the rebellions kings, like Ivan Stratsimir. Vidin held out to the last also under the last Bulgarian tsar, the son of Stratsimir, Constantine II until his death in 1422 was the last stronghold of the Bulgarian kingdom.

Captured by the Turks, Vidin did not stop fighting from century to century, every now and then surrendered to the German emperors, who repulsed it from the Turks and strengthened its walls and bastions. Strengthening and reviving even more, Vidin founded strength to challenge the Ottoman Empire at the turn of the 18th and 19th centuries, when the rebellious Pasha Osman Pazvantoglu revolted against the progressive reformer Sultan Selim III and declared himself the ruler of the castle-fortress and the entire territory around it.

In 1850 the peasants of Vidin revolted against the Turks and finally, in early 1878 Vidin and Bulgaria were liberated from the Turks thanks to the Russian army of Alexander II the Liberator.

The centuries-old stones of the castle-fortress bore the traces of all the eras and peoples that succeeded each other: from Romans to the Turks, when looking at them, the pictures of the past centuries flashed before the eyes of Alexander Stamboliysky. He was imprisoned behind the bars of the famous dungeons of the Vidin castle-fortress on the villainous order of the tsar Ferdinand, transferred there from the Central Sofia prison. The gloomy centuries-old stones of the fortress, which had seen everything in their lifetime for 2 thousand years of existence, blocked his path to freedom into the outside world, where the Great War had been blazing for 4 years, against which he premonished the tsar Ferdinand, putting his freedom and life at stake. Having commuted the death penalty for life imprisonment, the bigot Ferdinand commuted his quick death with slow dying in the Vidin dungeon and enjoyed his torment. Emaciated from suffering, tormented by chronic illness, obsessed with thoughts of the vicissitudes of fate, Alexander Stamboliysky, using a ray from a narrow hole high above his head, wrote down on the paper his main desire, expressed the feeling that overwhelmed his heart:

"If only Bulgaria would remain safe and sound in this universal storm, gruesome in its scope!"

Nearby the diary of Alexander Stamboliysky was laying, written out by day and hour during these 3 years of imprisonment—a chronicle of his suffering, illness and continuous hard work. Nearby, the manuscript of the program of the Agrarian Union of Bulgaria was lying. Stamboliysky sat down to write a letter.

"Dear friend Tsanko! You've become a minister, use your position inside this palace group and the military-castle-fortress of power in order to destroy censorship and the military state of siege of Bulgaria. Work to stop the bloody military-political terror and the persecution of the soldiers and politicians for the front breakthrough with 10 times the enemy's superior forces and for the revolution that shook the Ferdinand's throne. You have entered the government not in order to save my head, which I myself have saved from the hands of the executioners, but in order to save the life of our dearest fine friend Raiko Daskalov, who is our invaluable, irreplaceable and great fighter for our Agrarian cause!"

Stamboliysky fell into thinking, remembering his friends, his party comrades-in-arms. Suddenly the door of the dungeon opened, and a guard entered.

"Mr. Stamboliysky, the government of Radoslavov has been dismissed, and a new cabinet has come to power, headed by Alexander Malinov. By the order of a new Prime Minister Alexander Malinov you are being transferred back to the Central Sofia prison. Come out with your things, Mr. Stamboliysky!"

"Thanks god, at least I'll be next to my party comrades. I'll be in the capital," Stamboliysky answered.

It was the end of July 1918.

Chapter 10
Dobro Pole
The Second Meeting with Ferdinand

It was the way Alexander Stamboliysky premonished the tsar Ferdinand, who for the true prophecy threw Stamboliysky to die behind bars. A whirlwind of events, rapidly occurring, every moment changed the fate of the country and the people. After a long preparation, having thoroughly developed the operation, having gathered their forces into a fist, the allies went on the offensive along the entire line of the Thessaloniki Front, having a significant numerical superiority over the Bulgarian army in manpower and artillery. Having inflicted the main blow in the area of the heights Dobro Pole, they broke through the Bulgarian defense line, made a breach in it, which grew and expanded to 160 km before the eyes. The Bulgarians retreated. They descended from the hills, leaving the carts and wounded, abandoned the trenches, where they fed the insects for 3 years and, pursued by the allies troops, retreated back. One by one they abandoned the cities and villages of Macedonia, where long time ago the Bulgarian kingdom flourished, subsequently erased from the map of the world for 500 years by the Ottoman conquers, against the remnants of which together with the Serbs, Greeks and Montenegrins the Bulgarians entered the I Balkan War in 1912, and while the Bulgarians besieged and stormed Adrianople and drove the Turks from Thrace, the Serbs stabbed them in the back and occupied Macedonia, where exterminated the Bulgarian population, which they tortured and killed and burned alive and burned their homes, thereby forcing Bulgaria to enter the II Balkan War in July 1913, which ended with an ultimate defeat of Bulgaria. For this reason the Bulgarian Tsar Ferdinand, craving the revenge to resume Macedonia, entered the World War on the wrong side.

Now the Bulgarians were retreating, abandoning the Macedonian cities, which they triumphantly took with light speed, passing through all Macedonia 3 years ago, and threw the Serbs into the waters of the Adriatic, to which Serbia was maniacally striving. Then, 3 years ago, during the rapid victorious offensive of the Bulgarians, they could've taken Thessaloniki on the move, if they had not been stopped then in front of its walls by their boss Germany, to which the tsar Ferdinand had subordinated the Bulgarian army, as well as the entire Bulgaria. And now, 3 years later, the Serbs were taken revenge and together with the Greeks, Italians, Englishmen and African rangers expelled the Bulgarians from the land of Macedonia. The Bulgarians were retreating. The German command from the headquarters in Skopje ordered the Bulgarians to retreat to Tetovo – Skopje – old border line in order to align the frontline and promised reinforcements. The Bulgarians were retreating, turning the retreat into a stampede. Pursued by the Entente, they were fleeing as far as they could run, hungry, exhausted, sick, for 3 years having fed the insects in the trenches and for 7 years continuously fighting since the beginning of the Balkan War, dirty and skinned, often half-dressed and barefooted, with wounds on their legs and gaping shreds of their naked bodies through the holes in the tatters, rotted in the war. Driven by the righteous anger, they were fleeing, drawing into their mighty stream all those indignant at the war, crossed the line of retreat, set by the Germans, reached Borovo and Pechevo and rushed to Kyustendil, where there was a command headquarters, and from there to Radomir with the slogan: "To Sofia! The perpetrators of the national catastrophe—to justice! Down with the tsar Ferdinand and the monarchy! Long live republic!"

In Sofia the door of Alexander Stamboliysky's cell in the central prison opened, and the guard announced:

"Mr. Stamboliysky, by order of the Minister-Chairman Alexander Malinov, you have been released. Come out with your things."

On September 25, 1918, at 10 am Alexander Stamboliysky left the prison building, holding a bag with his things and precious manuscripts, over which he had been working indefatigably while sitting in the dungeons. He breathed with the fresh air of freedom and rushed along the Sofia streets in car that was sent for him. Sofia was teeming with the German and Austrian agents, who spied on each other of treason, as Austria and Germany were turning before the eyes from the allies into opponents, each of which frantically tried to bypass the other for himself to find a way out of the impending catastrophe. The catastrophe had already become a reality for Ferdinand.

The car stopped at the building of the Agrarian Bank, where the Ministerial Council met. Alexander Stamboliysky entered the conference hall.

"Mr. Stamboliysky, the fatherland is in danger, and we have high expectations for you. You must help us, because you opposed the entry of Bulgaria into the war in alliance with the Central Powers, you advocated neutrality!" Alexander Malinov, the prime minister, addressed him, barely able to stand from sleepless nights and overexertion.

"And that's why you threw me to jail for life as alms to commute the death penalty?" Stamboliysky exclaimed indignantly.

"After all, you know that it was the will of His Majesty, we have nothing to do with it!" General Savov, the Minister of the War, tried to save the situation.

"His Majesty," how mockingly and ridiculously it sounds! And what is the "majesty" in "His Majesty"? "That he brought the country to the second national catastrophe?" Stamboliysky exclaimed.

"Mr. Stamboliysky, calm down, I beg you!" Minister Lyapchev intervened. "let's leave the past and unite our efforts in order to save our fatherland. You know what's going on at the front, don't you?"

"Yes, I do know everything," Stamboliysky answered, "all the news reaches the prison."

"Our plan is as follows: you go to the rebel soldiers and appeal to them to remain calm, to refrain from rebellion, not ruin the front and wait for the further instructions from the command. We know that you are trusted and respected by the soldiers and your authority is great among people! They will listen to you."

Alexander Stamboliysky bitterly grinned, recalling his torment in jail during 3 years.

"My condition is: immediately release all the political prisoners, all the leaders of the Agrarian Union, who have been languishing in a dungeon, first of all, Raiko Daskalov, my friend and comrade-in-arms, an outstanding politician and statesman, who was villainously imprisoned, like all the others. It is Raiko Daskalov only, whom I'll go to the front with!"

"We have prepared a decree to release all the political prisoners, so far, His Majesty, Tsar Ferdinand, has signed a decree on your release only," Malinov said.

"Release everyone immediately!" Stamboliysky exclaimed.

"I am sure that the issue will be solved today." Malinov replied. "But about the truce and Bulgaria's withdrawn from the war, we have been working hard on this for a long time, overcoming the resistance of the tsar Ferdinand, who intends to wage the war to a victorious end. We are sending a delegation to Thessaloniki to begin negotiations for peace. Minister Lyapchev, diplomat Radev and General Lukov will go, they will leave tomorrow. Wouldn't you agree to accompany them to Sveti Vrach? The path is dangerous, and they may be attacked by the rioting soldiers, and then the negotiations will be disrupted."

"I can go either to the front with Raiko Daskalov or to accompany the delegation," Stamboliysky replied, being in the strong excitement from the assignments that had piled on him, on which the fate of the country dependent, "perhaps, I'll go to the front."

"You leave tomorrow, September 26, and now the tsar Ferdinand is calling you to him."

Alexander Stamboliysky left the ministry and went to the palace to meet with the tsar Ferdinand. Meanwhile, Ferdinand, having no moment of peace, rushed between Skopje, Sofia and his train "Hope," checking its readiness for departure. He still cherished the hope of winning the Great War in alliance with Germany and Austria-Hungary in the third great war for the Great Bulgaria after the first war of the tsar Simeon II and the second one of the tsar Samuil. He hurried by train to Skopje to the General Headquarters of the German command to assure the allies of their intention to wage the war till victorious end, summoned Minister of War Savov and Minister Lyapchev there and was indignant, when they failed to arrive on the order of Prime Minister Malinov, who forbade them to go and urged Ferdinand himself to stay in Sofia. Ferdinand saw that the ministers were preparing an armistice plan behind his back and expressed his protest to them, as they "violate his rights as the commander-in-chief." And in the meantime, he fortified Sofia with Germans and strengthened the guard of his train, ready to flee at any minute. Now he was counting on the support of Alexander Stamboliysky. It was Alexander Stamboliysky only who could calm the rebellious soldiers and bring them back to the front to continue the war to a victorious end. At 5.30 pm, on

September 15, 1918, Alexander Stamboliysky entered Ferdinand's reception room in the Sofia palace.

"Good afternoon, Your Majesty! Mr. Minister of War told me that you had a wish to see me. I am at your disposal."

"Good afternoon, Mr. Stamboliysky, so we are seeing each other again," Ferdinand grinned slyly, shook Stamboliysky's hand and seated him opposite himself.

"After 3 whole years, Your Majesty!"

"Yes, after 3 stormy years."

"And in such a tragic hour!"

"Very tragic!"

"This tragedy has emerged exclusively as a result of that disastrous policy that I prevented you yet on September 4, 1915."

"These tragic events have emerged as a result solely of your desires and you subversive activities! These are all your fruits!"

"Mine?"

"Yes, yours! You tirelessly and systematically acted to disrupt the front and have already managed to reap the benefits!"

"Your Majesty, do you remember that after my meeting with you on September 4, 1915, I was sentenced to death, commuted to life imprisonment, and I was thrown to prison, where I've spent 3 years, and I have been released only today at 10 am? Do you remember that I was tortured behind the bars as the most dangerous robber and I was thrown into the most terrible dungeons under special police and warden supervision? Both your liberal government and today's radical democratic one mocked at me with a special regime: they did not allow me to see anyone."

"But you wrote," Ferdinand retorted cowardly.

"Yes, I wrote, but several censorships hung over everything I wrote with the tip of the sword: prison, police, postural and military one. And above all this there was the most brutal main censorship; it threw into fire what I wrote: in military-police department there were the whole bags with my letters and the letters for me. My rare and accidental meetings with the visitors were immediately reported to the district office and further on to the prime minister immediately. I'm sure, you can't even imagine clearly how terrible my prison regime was! And how is it possible that I, a detainee of an aggravated rigorous imprisonment, to be accused of disrupting the front! Apparently, I possess some kind of supernatural power that can overcome all obstacles to achieve my hellish intentions! Your Majesty, I indignantly reject all accusations against me of disrupting the front! I had neither desire nor the ability to do it."

"But your friends did it!"

"What friends, aren't they from the Agrarian Parliament Group?"

"That's it."

"It has nothing to do with reality. They did nothing at all and therefore couldn't do any evil. It's a sin to blame them for this. Do you know that all the groups have merged into one formless, lifeless mass, which is called 'the liberal majority' in the Bulgarian parliament; they are only waiting for both time and events themselves to deliver for them funeral chariot."

"But who has disrupted the front?" stupid Ferdinand wondered.

"That was done by time, events, circumstances and the strength of the enemy."

"How come? What do you want to say?"

"The patience of the Bulgarian soldier reached the extreme limit, his strength ended, and the explosion was inevitable."

"No, he had to endure more!" the tsar insisted.

"How long? I, like a Bulgarian soldier, want to know how long you have to endure! The offensive strength of Germany is broken, presumably, and the defensive too. After the USA has entered the war, the Bulgarian soldier already believed that he would be beaten. And at the appeal as 'hold the front!' he wondered: 'Until when?' The situation is irresistible any more, and your ministers, who visited the front, faced this question with their own eyes, and they have no answer to it, they only contributed to disrupt the front."

"The front was disrupted by the criminal agitation."

"A more destructive force than agitation was complete failure of your diplomacy: this is the II Bucharest Treaty, the issue of Northern Dobrujia, the issue of the border along the Maritsa and other claims of Turkey against us, but above all it is theft of the government, the cause of why the troops turned out to be naked and hungry."

"But the government of the liberals has gone, today we have a new government."

"The villainous government of Radoslavov, Tonchev, Petkov left too late and was replaced by another government of impotence, hesitation, sleep, fear, campaigning and inaction. Collapse is imminent and now I pass to another topic. Your Majesty, I want to know why the other political prisoners have not yet been released. I feel very embarrassed that I am free, while the other politicians, who were thrown into dungeons a year after me, are still there! It is my duty as a man and friend now, while I am standing before you, to insist for their immediate release."

"What kind of political prisoners are you talking about?" the tsar pretended to be ignorant.

"About all, You Majesty!" Stamboliysky answered sharply.

"Who exactly?"

"Those, and above all, Nikola Genadiev, who were thrown into jail for the so-called Fernan de Closier scam for so-called espionage."

"I have released them all," the tsar lied.

"Wrong, Your Majesty. Today I've met with the Minister of War and learned that only I have been released."

"I am telling you that I've signed a decree today, and they have been released."

"I repeat that you are mistaken, the decrees on their release were handed to you, but you have not signed them."

"Believe me, Mr. Stamboliysky," Ferdinand continued to lie, "today, recently I have signed a decree on their release, including Mr. Genadiev and his friends. But why do you care so much about Mr. Genadiev? Do you know him well?"

"I met and got acquainted with Mr. Genadiev in prison. And I stand for all the political prisoners, among which there are my good ideological friends: Raiko Daskalov, Nedelcho Georgiev, Turlakov and others."

"Among them there is one very bad person: Prudkin."

"You are very ill-informed, Your Majesty," Stamboliysky objected, "Anton Prudkin is not a bad person. It is his personal enemies who spread lies and slanderous gossips against him. And what happened with Kosta Todorov? He is a worthy Bulgarian, an officer of the French army. And what's about the socialists who are condemned for nothing?"

"We'll release all of them gradually," Ferdinand changed the subject, "Now a great drought has come, even Vardar has become shallow. Have you been to Vardar in Macedonia?"

"No, I haven't, Your Majesty. When I was going to go there, they threw me behind the bars."

"What beautiful lands are there!" Ferdinand said dreamily. "And I managed to bring all these beauties and riches to Bulgaria as if on a platter, and she ruined everything in an instant."

"Yes, it is a great misfortune, Your Majesty, the Bulgarian weapon conquered these lands, but then we lost them. But we need to remain calm."

"What a disgrace!" the tsar exclaimed. "Shame on a Bulgarian soldier, shame on me, shame before the history."

"First of all, this is a shame for Bulgarian diplomacy and only then for the soldier," Stamboliysky objected.

"Why?" Ferdinand did not understand.

"Because this diplomacy for the entire duration of the war for 3 years showed unimaginable deafness and blindness to the gruesome need that the Bulgarian soldier endured, it tormented him and impoverished."

"Actually, within 7 years," the tsar let slip.

"Quite right, 7 years with the previous wars. The Bulgarian warrior showed amazing heroism in the most gruesome conditions with the horrendous equipment. 300–400 thousand naked, barefooted, hungry soldiers and sick warriors had to hold a 500-km front, which was almost equal to the German one and exceeded the Austrian one, defended by millions of soldiers. This warrior was surrounded by enemies and nearby, and in the rear, like the vile insects they ate away his material, moral and vital combat capability. A warrior was even deprived of vocation. It was as a medieval force that came to life and descended from the pages of a historical book tormented him like a disenfranchised slave. And with all this, this warrior endured with the last strength and held on. However, when the situation at the front became irrepressible due to many reasons, he did like an honest boss does with his hired workers: he had warned them in 3 months before that peace must be concluded at any cost."

"I know nothing about it." Like a fool, the tsar continued to deny everything.

"Your Majesty, if I, a Bulgarian prisoner, who was kept under a strict regime, became aware of this, then I can't imagine, how it didn't become known to you!"

"I repeat, I don't know anything about this," the tsar did not give up.

"Perhaps so, but in this case, it is an even a bigger scandal, related to the behavior of the High Command and the government. They did know about it.

Not only the soldiers' fighting spirit, but also the officers' moral was broken. Both of them had one common desire: immediate peace. Both senior offices and the entire leadership of the army were convinced of this! The military set September 23 as the deadline for their patience. I am sure that your son Prince Boris, the heir to the throne, who often communicated with the army, is aware of this. And also the ministers often heard about this from the soldiers and officers. In a word, this fact was known to all the authority political circles in Bulgaria, and it couldn't be ignored."

"And why only some units with their bad equipment have disrupted the front, while the others held on?"

"Your Majesty, this should not surprise you at all. Our entire front was a single severely emaciated organism, which a day earlier or a day later was inclined toward an incurable disease. When a human body is exhausted and incurably ill, the disease does not manifest itself immediately in the whole body, but separate organs fail one after another, but the cause is a general incurable disease of a body. The same thing happened with the Bulgarian front and with the Bulgarian army. The units fell ill at Dobro Pole, because the enemy's blow was concentrated there. If the enemy had struck elsewhere, the result would've been the same. The fate of our front has been predestined, and the reason for this is the complete exhaustion of the army. And the Entente has decided to put an end to us, our allies were far away, and our defeat was inevitable sooner or later."

"What do we do?" Ferdinand said contritely. "I thought and thought and couldn't think of anything."

"Your Majesty, the time has come not to think, but to act immediately, actually, the answer has already been given by you. The Minister of War told me that you are ready to agree to a proposal for an armistice and peace. I fully approve this idea, it is reasonable and the only one possible. I beg you: in the interests of the country immediately move this proposal for a truce and wait for the response from the enemy. Any other course of action is absolutely impossible. The continuation of the war means the death of Bulgaria."

"What respond will be from our enemies?" Ferdinand exclaimed in horror.

"We'll see it immediately. I assume that they'll want us to return to the borders before October 1915, lay down our arm and abandon our allies."

"How do you know about it?"

"From common sense, logic and some other sources."

"But this is capitulation!" Ferdinand was horrified.

"Complete capitulation!"

"Shameful capitulation!"

"Inevitable capitulation!"

"And it does not bother you?"

"As a Bulgarian, this hurts me deeply, as a politician, I don't care, because I predicted this, I was convinced of this and expected this sad end. This could've been prevented if there were smart and courage people in the country, who would conclude a separate peace in time."

"It was unthinkable and impossible."

"But it became possible."

"That would be a gruesome betrayal which I could not allow in any case."

"I appreciate your honesty. You played for broke in this alliance with Germany, and only exceptional external and internal events could change course of foreign policy."

"In the name of this policy, I was called to wear the crown of Bulgaria! And despite all the misfortunes on my path, I continue to follow it. I was and remain a great friend and ally of the Central Powers. Noble blood flows in my veins!" Ferdinand declared proudly.

"I have no doubt about it, since I have tasted a lot from your nobility!" Stamboliysky answered.

"You are as rude as a redneck."

"But I have no 'noble' vice."

"You are unimaginably audacious."

"But extremely truthful."

"Your language is intolerant."

"But my heart and soul are captivating, as the Russians say, the tong is sharp, but the heart is gold, while you have the opposite."

"You allow gross threats against me."

"But with all this, not a single hair fell from your head through any fault."

"You have not quite recovered yet," Ferdinand suddenly said solicitously.

"It is too late, Your Majesty, to show regret and solicitude for my health. Yes, I have just come out of jail, but I feel like I am in my prime. In the fire of the most gruesome suffering, I forged my will. And the events of 1912 eloquently demonstrated my intellectual abilities and political insight. In those stormy fateful days, everything that I predicted came true. Practice has shown that the advantage is on my side in comparison with your statesmen and advisers, who are characterized only with their hesitation, uncertainty and instability. You do know it yourself, if in these fateful days for Bulgaria you sent for me to entrust power to me. I am glad that despite everything that has happened between us, you find me capable of governing, while all your henchmen with their incompetence have doomed our fatherland to gruesome upheavals and trials. I myself firmly believed in my strength and ability to solve the most difficult tasks in governing. But let's get back to the burning and touching topic: what needs to be done at the moment. I repeat, immediately and unconditionally agree of a truce and peace at any cost. Any other decision would be stupid and disastrous. Your Majesty, give your consent as soon as possible, otherwise and the present day will be lost for Bulgaria."

"Oh, how hard is my situation! All my life I've been loyal to the Central Powers! I'm determined never to evade them!"

"Your Majesty, we have not a slightest doubt about your loyalty to the Central Powers. I was convinced of this even at our first meeting, even before mobilization, from where a sharp conflict arose between us. But today the situation has changed. After all, you have the ability to deftly maneuver through a change of cabinet and influence on public opinion at such moments in order to conclude a truce so that neither morality nor feelings with relations get hurt."

"But the war is not over yet, Mr. Stamboliysky!"

"But it'll be finished soon. By her entry into the war, Bulgaria contributed to its continuation today by her surrender, she'll contribute to its completion."

"It's questionable."

"There is a question, but there is a clear answer to it."

"The military strength of the Central Powers is not yet broken."

"But one way or another, it'll be broken soon."

"This is a common misconception."

"Germany's first victorious performance and how long she held on gave you some reasons to think so."

"But even now neither Germany, nor Austro-Hungary has been defeated."

"I was and remain an inevitable opponent of Bulgarian entry into the war not because I underestimated the German strength, but because I underestimated the strength of England. I was a student in Germany, and I have an idea about its strength and capabilities, and I also know about the possibilities of both Austria and Hungary."

"What a magnificent people these Hungarians are!" Ferdinand exclaimed.

"But my belief that the Central Powers will be defeated is based on the historical facts. If England had entered the war, I never allowed her to lay down her sword before she wins." No, I believed and I affirm that she will draw the entire world into the war and win. If America breaks off the relations with Germany, I publicly and loudly declared: "Tell me when the first American steamship enters Europe, will you sign with both hands the imminent and final defeat of the Central Powers?" I never succumbed to the stupid versions of various Bulgarian politicians that America was preparing to intervene not against Germany, but against Japan.

Moreover, I believed that France would fight up to the last ditch, protecting her national interests. And indeed, we see that the Frenchmen as in the past and today have brilliant military qualities. My deepest conviction was and remains: the Entente will smash the Central forces; Bulgaria remains the last to be overthrown. Her fate today was predestined even at the moment for her entry into this Great War. It is necessary to give a proposal for a truce immediately and sincerely support it, no matter how bitter and hard it may be. Oh, how much work and effort was spent and now everything is lost!"

"Such is fate!"

"What are you going to do, Your Majesty?"

"What do you think?"

"Rumors are circulating about the plans to replace the cabinet, but the decision should not be delayed!"

"The people want you, Mr. Stamboliysky, but the current government has influence from abroad."

"I don't lust for power. At least you know about it. But I see that the events are developing in such a way that I have to accept it."

"You are against the dynasty, aren't you?"

"What evidence do you have for this?"

"I know it."

"I am for popular sovereignty."

"You are looking for favorable conditions to expel the whole dynasty."

"Your Majesty, the question of your and other dynasties will be discussed in a new world, which is just emerging. If the new time announces to the whole world, and especially in the Balkans, we'll put an end to the dynasties. You will find your new path without waiting for us or anyone else to point it out. I have no doubt that after this new catastrophe, indignation against you will be spontaneous, but whether it'll affect the entire dynasty, I don't know. As for me, I think that democracy can be established in the presence of a dynasty and vice versa: oligarchy, corporatism, personal regime and monarchism can flourish in a republican country also. The South and Central African satrap republics are clear proof of it. I believe that the principle of periodic re-election of the head of a state is useful and good, but our state institutions are not yet sufficiently developed for this principle. The electoral system has not been advanced. This process is still being developed and improved. I repeat, I feel no resentments against the dynasty and especially against the heir to the throne. He has great sympathy among the Bulgarian politicians."

"Mr. Stamboliysky, you are a very ungrateful person! We have been talking already an hour and a half, and you still haven't found any time to thank me for letting you out of prison!"

"Yes, Your Majesty, I don't find that I am obliged to thank you for anything. On the contrary, I expected an apology from you for throwing me in a jail for nothing. You've let me go today because you expect the destruction of our fatherland. After I crossed the threshold of the dungeon and went out, I felt an acute pain and heavy burden from all I saw. Since then, I have been responsible for what is happening as a Bulgarian and as a politician. It's too late. You let me go in these tragic moments, which brought me not joy, but sorrow. Why did you keep me in jail for so long?"

"Why haven't you written me even 2 lines?"

"I am always armed with patience and calmness, and I am not used to asking for help."

"If you knew my attitude towards you, you would not send your reproach to me. It was not me who let you go, the others were fussing about your release. You are a good person but you are too bold, brave and sharp in your speech, direct and honest, unselfish selfless, you are an unbridled and exuberant fanatic of your ideas. You've done great damage to Bulgaria by avoiding me for long times! How much evil could've been avoided! You are a very dangerous person! And what are you going to do now?"

"Now I'm going to render a service to the fatherland with everything I can."

"How?"

"By all possible means, it is necessary to restore the front and resist until our proposal for a truce is accepted. It is necessary to stop the fleeing units of the front, which are approaching Sofia. We discussed this issue with the Minister of War and came to the conclusion that I with my friends and with other delegates from other groups, and from the ministry should come to the most vulnerable sectors of the front in order to calm and reason the insurgent military. I am ready for this mission."

"Great idea, Mr. Stamboliysky! Let me shake your hand and congratulate you! Hurry up!"

"I shall go to do this huge and useful work."

"Go. Mr. Stamboliysky, carry out this mission! You are rendering a great service to me and the country. But you need to hurry!"

"I am going, Your Majesty, and if my mission is successful, I'll render great benefits to the fatherland."

"I am sure, you can do it. I am also convinced that we shall continue to work with you and together shall heal the wounds of Bulgaria. Our people are hardworking, sober and honest."

"But her rulers are not like that."

"We'll change them."

"There are humpbacked, which only grave will improve."

"Everything can be achieved with efforts."

"Habits are the second nature of human."

"We shall forget everything old and improve everything."

"I don't know. It's too much to deal with, but I hope."

"I believe in your patriotism."

"And I believe in myself, I hope for my strength."

"You are still young and full of energy, the brightest and purest idealism both are in you."

"And irresistible desire for the most serious creative work."

"Your ideas and my ideals will meet."

"I doubt it."

"Believe me, Mr. Stamboliysky, Bulgarian people should be given ideal management."

"This is what I've fought for and shall continue to fight for."

"How did you do in prison?"

"I survived in hard prison conditions and used the time in a way that no other Bulgarian prisoner: sullenly and continuously worked on myself and my ideas. I did not hold a grudge against anyone for the misfortunes that befell me. I said about this to the former minister Popov, who on behalf of the entire cabinet came to me in prison to ask for help. I've always been flattered by thought that I am suffering for just cause and as a result of the fulfillment of my governmental and political duty."

"What do you plan to do after?"

"First of all, after the conclusion of peace I need to revive, heal and recreate the Bulgarian Agrarian Union. After that I'll direct al my efforts to the renewal and revival of the ill-fated Bulgaria, which has survived so many long unfortunate wars."

"Vaya con Dios, Mr. Stamboliysky! Good luck!"

Alexander Stamboliysky was impatient to leave, but he had to exchange bare formalities with Prince Boris, the son of Ferdinand, who came in the office. Finally, he went out of the royal palace into the fresh air, he could feel his heart pounding with excitement, as he considered the conversation that had just taken place.

"I shall remember this second meeting with the tsar Ferdinand, however like that first one 3 years ago, and I'll write it down for posterity," he thought.

He hurried home. On the same day he hugged his faithful friend and associate Raiko Daskalov, who was released from prison on the same day along with the other political prisoners. They did not sleep all night, discussing events at the front, and drew up a plan of action.

On the same evening a delegation from Bulgaria of 3 people: Minister Lyapchev, General Lukov and Minister Plenipotentiary Radev left by car to Sveti Vrach and from there to Thessaloniki to offer peace, overcoming bridges, barricaded by the rebels along the way, escaping the chases and hiding where it was possible.

Chapter 11
Radomir, Vladay

The train was moving along the path through the undulated Struma River bed, which flowed down from the slopes of the Vitosha Mountains, and meandering, pierced its channel through the mountains ranges, pushed them apart, forming a valley, along which Thracian cities arose in antiquity, which became Bulgarian, having outlived Greece, Rome, Byzantine and Ottoman Empire. The river, which had changed many names, kept for itself the name of the king of the Thracian Edons-Strumon, the son of Ares and the muse Helika, who found death in its waters, according the ancient tragedy Strumon threw himself into the river, having heard the news of the death of his son Res and thus gave the river his name.

The train was leaving Sofia to the south-west along the Struma Valley, crossing its bends, in the distance, as always, the hills and mountains rose, covered with reserved forests and groves, still green, but already with a touch of the yellow-red color of September autumn, and the cranes from the banks of Struma were preparing to fly to south, drawing the Bulgarian letters in the sky with their wedges. The travelers were talking, ready to fulfill the mission, entrusted to them.

"Mr. Stamboliysky, we rely on you," General Savov said, "the soldiers got mad, the army got out of control. They only repeat your name, they whisper to each other and ready to carry out only your orders."

"After all, everyone knew that Alexander Stamboliysky opposed this war and premonished the tsar Ferdinand that he would destroy both Bulgaria and his throne, if he gets involved in this war in alliance with the Central Powers," said Nikola Sakarov, a 37-year-old member of the National Assembly from the Bulgarian Workers' Social-Democratic Party of the Broad Socialists, a graduate of the Berlin University, Ph. D., specialist in political economy, finance and statistics; he was traveling with the Alexander Stamboliysky delegation to the insurgent soldiers.

"And for this he was sentenced to life imprisonment," Alexander Girginov stated the fact; he was also on the train as part of the delegation.

He was 39 years old. A graduate of Leipzig University, a lawyer, historian and publicist, a talented writer and a noble man, he represented the Democratic Party. Alexander Stamboliysky, who was in the center of the attention all the time, replied:

"I was not the only one who was thrown into prison by monarchy for the truth. All my associates from the Agrarian Union were repressed. And look at Raiko Daskalov, this noble and heroic young man. All the reactionary pro-German monarchist forces, all the criminals responsible for the catastrophe had fabricated a false accusation against him on the so-called 'de Closier Scam!' Precisely because Raiko, like me, like all the honest people of Bulgaria, called for neutrality and predicted the Entente victory!"

"Thank you, Alexander! During the prison hardships we had happy moments of joy to communicate with you!"

32-year-old Raiko Daskalov was the youngest of the delegates. A graduate of the Berlin University Faculty of Finance, a brilliant mind, a noble and courageous hero, a "golden pen" and a fiery speaker, he was the most faithful friend of Alexander Stamboliysky, whom he considered an idol, and both put the fate of the country above their own lives.

"Gentlemen, you must agree: it's a shame for the country to have such political regime under which the best sons of Bulgaria are thrown into prison for their very best qualities!" Stamboliysky said.

"Thrown to prison by the monarchy!" Daskalov clarified.

"Even 100 years ago, Thomas Jefferson wrote that the European monarchs are fools and mad, that the order in which marriage bounds connected kings only with their royal families existed in Europe for centuries. Take animals of any kind, imprison them whether in a stable, rich apartments or in a palace hall in a state of inactivity and idleness, feed them to the full, satisfy all their sexual appetites, immerse them in sensual pleasures, encourage all their passions, make so that everyone bows before them and shield them from everything that made them think—and in a few generations, these animals will become only a body, a flesh only without a gleam of mind. This is the regime in which kings are raised and educated, and this had been going on for centuries. I am sure that the time will come and the issue of the existence of monarchy will be raised with all certainty."

"This moment will come very soon!" Raiko Daskalov said.

The train approached the railway station of the city Radomir and stopped. The travelers headed to the exit. Raiko Daskalov leaned over Alexander Stamboliysky and said quietly:

"We shall act according to our plan."

"And according to the circumstances," Stamboliysky nodded.

The travelers got out of the car and set foot on the land of Radomir. Armed soldiers were standing along the entire platform, and at the exit of the car the delegation from Sofia was met by the delegation from the insurgent military:

"Allow me to introduce myself: sub-officer, chairman of the revolutionary committee Vasil Draganov."

"On behalf of the government, we have arrived here to find out the situation and calm the troops," Alexander Stamboliysky said.

"The city is completely taken by the rebellious soldiers. Revolutionary committees have been formed. This is a revolution, gentlemen! We are ready to march on Sofia in order to bring to justice the perpetrators of the catastrophe. I beg you, follow us, you can take a break after the road in the hotel and then appeal to the soldiers."

They got into the cars and drove to the central boulevard, which crossed the whole city parallel to the Struma from south to north, deviating slightly to the east, and drove to the central square next to the building of the City Community, where the leaders of the newly created revolutionary committees were. The air of Radomir was permeated with the spirit of the revolution: it blew everywhere, having flown from the pinnacles of the Dobro Pole Hills, bringing with it a storm of the people's anger. It could not be stopped, as it was impossible to stop the streams of fiery lava, flowing from the peaks of a volcanic eruption. Like a volcano, the anger of the people exploded on the peaks of Dobro Pole and other breaches of the broken front and poured out like an avalanche, sweeping away all barriers. This anger absorbed all the 3 wars hardships of 7 years and now led the soldiers to Sofia. They were abandoning the occupied territories and returned within the borders of Bulgaria, which was never destined to become San-Stefano. Barefooted and tattered, hungry and sick, they bravely fought for the mythical image of San-Stefano Bulgaria, expanded to the limits by Ferdinand's ego, and without reaching it, now they were returning back. They were surmounting the ridges along the passes, crossing the Struma River, captured Gorna Dzhumaya, where they had stopped to gather the forces to go to Sofia for the culprits of everything that had happened. Their revolution could not be stopped, it could be only shot or led.

This was suspected by the members of the delegation from Sofia, headed by Alexander Stamboliysky, who after a shot respite from the trip in the hotel were already standing in front of the soldiers on the balcony of the City Hall. The entire central square of Radomir was filled with the soldiers, who were unshakable in their revolution.

"Soldiers of Bulgaria! I greet you; I am Alexander Stamboliysky, who was sentenced to death, commuted to life imprisonment, because I was against this war, in which the country was dragged by its rulers. And just yesterday I was released from the prison together with my fellow comrades-in-arms from the Agrarian Union, and Raiko Daskalov is among them, he is also present here with us."

"Stamboliysky! Stamboliysky! Stamboliysky! Daskalov! Daskalov! Daskalov!" the soldiers were chanting the names of their idols, and the square was buzzing throughout the city.

"We were released from the prison only, because the news had reached Sofia that the revolutionary soldiers from the front were coming to Sofia to punish the guilty and free the innocent."

"Stamboliysky! Stamboliysky! Stamboliysky! Daskalov! Daskalov! Daskalov!" the soldiers continued to greet them.

"Thank you, dear friends, for your support!" Stamboliysky continued. "We have also arrived here from Sofia to support you. You fought bravely in the battles of the unjust war, into which the tsar Ferdinand had dragged our country, and won victories, but the outcome of the war had been predestined, and the fate of the country had been predetermined on the day when Ferdinand entered the war on the side of the Central Powers, since the forces of the Entente were superior. And now, when the Thessaloniki Front has been disrupted and the Entente is advancing, you, exhausted by the war, have turned your weapons against your tormentors!"

"Stamboliysky! Stamboliysky! Stamboliysky! Daskalov! Daskalov! Daskalov!" the soldiers were scanning in response to their idols.

"But we are urging you: let no more Bulgarian blood be shed from any weapons."

The central square of Radomir, crammed with thousands of soldiers, continued to buzz. Alexander Stamboliysky continued:

"Yesterday, September 25 at our request and on the long-overdue decision of Prime Minister Alexander Malinov a delegation from Sofia was sent to Thessaloniki with a request of truce. The criminal war is over! Let nobody's blood be shed! Don't take any actions on your own anymore! Await further orders! Keep calm! We are with you!"

"Down with the tsar! Down with the monarchy! Long live republic! Stamboliysky! Daskalov!" the square scanned.

Alexander Stamboliysky gave floor to Raiko Daskalov.

"Brave soldiers! You have been fought bravely and selflessly against superior enemy's forces! You were weaker, and the hour has struck, when the weak must fall. It was impossible to win, and Dobro Pole emerged to be the result of the entire domestic and foreign policies of the Bulgarian rulers! The blood of the Bulgarian soldiers was shed in vain, and billions were wasted! Bulgaria was betrayed by her rulers, who ruled the country for 3 years and could not conclude a separate peace! You, valiant soldiers, under the superior enemy's pressure lost faith in your superiors and rulers, who abandoned the country to crumble into hell, you exploded with irresistible anger like a whirlwind and ignited the flame of revolution!"

"Revolution! Down with the tsar! Down with the monarchy! Long live republic! Stamboliysky! Daskalov!" the soldiers chanted.

"We are on your side!" Raiko Daskalov continued. "Our task is immediately to put an end to this senseless and objectionable for people war, to stop the invading enemy at least on our border and punish those responsible for the war and catastrophe and guilty of those shameful deeds that were carried out on the occupied lands, punish those who have tarnished the bright brow of the suffering Bulgarian people-martyr! We are all disgusted by their deeds, and the hour of reckoning is near! For now, we urge you to remain calm and await further instructions!"

The square was buzzing, the soldiers chanted the names of their idols, and their determination to march on Sofia was unshakable. Nikola Sakarov and Alexander Girginov made an appeal to remain calm. Several persons responded to General Savov proposal to go home on a specially provided train. Around the corner of the house on the square lieutenant Borisov was hiding, who was automatically brought into Radomir by a stream of retreating soldiers, he mentally pointed the muzzle of his pistol at the head of Alexander Stamboliysky and then hurried to the station to slip away from Radomir at the first opportunity.

The members of the delegation left from the balcony to the hall in the community building and began to discuss further actions. All were confused.

"What do you advise, Mr. Stamboliysky?" Girginov asked.

"I suggest to go to Kyustendil and learn the situation in the army there and the state of the General Staff," Stamboliysky answered.

"You go, gentlemen, I am staying here to control the army," Raiko Daskalov answered, "we'll be in touch."

"Let's hurry, gentlemen," Sakarov and Savov supported.

In the morning of September 27 the train took them to Kyustendil; it was moving southwest along the Struma Valley on both sides of which there were the same mountains, and soon crossed the river and approached the city, ancient as Europe itself, since had been founded in the 5th century BC by the Thracians and the first Europeans. Located in a valley, surrounded by the hills and mountains, the city abounded with the mineral springs, over which the Romans built there baths, preserved to amazement of their descendants, who unearthed them. The Romans replaced the Thracians and Greeks and turned the city into resort, in which hot healing waters flowed from underground, enclosed in pipes and stone fountains. Roman Ulma Pantalia, the most important fortified city, was at the intersections of all the Roman roads from Serdica and Philippopolis, from the Danube, Thrace and Macedonia. The ruins of a fortress, built by one of the mighty emperors of Rome Marcus Aurelius and by his worst son Commodus, towered majestically on the pinnacle of the Hisarlyk Hill. The city of 25 thousand years was a living witness of history, having seen in its lifetime the rise, twilight and collapse of the empire, the brilliance of ancient culture, the barbarians invasion, the legendary Byzantium, the Bulgarian Kingdom, the Ottomans, the struggle against them, Liberation and now had become the center of the revolution of the people against the tyranny of the Bulgarian Tsar Ferdinand.

The train stopped at the station in Kyustendil, and the delegation from Sofia set foot on its land. Like Radomir, Kyustendil was filled with the rebellious soldiers, led by the revolutionary committees, determined to march on Sofia.

"Lieutenant Boev," the commander of the armed soldiers, who met the delegation at the platform at the exit from the car, introduced himself, "we are in charge of the military-revolutionary committee in Kyustendil."

"We have arrived, as you know, from Sofia and Radomir," Alexander Stamboliysky said, "we need to go the general staff of the army."

"You are too late, gentlemen, the leaders of the general staff have left for the Thessaloniki to join the Bulgarian delegation to conclude a truce, and the rest left the city. You can see for yourself! Let's go!"

The cars brought everyone to the City Hall building, where yet recently the General Staff of the Bulgarian army had been located. They came inside to a foyer: the rooms and halls were filled with the revolutionary soldiers, who recognized the guest and began to greet them as in Radomir. The hands of the clock were approaching noon.

"Mr. Stamboliysky, the telephone call is for you," lieutenant Boev turned to the guest.

Stamboliysky went to another room, where there was a telephone.

"Alexander, Raiko is speaking," Stamboliysky heard his friend's voice, "Ferdinand has sent a telegram to General Zhekov in Vienna that there would be no truce. Prime Minister Malinov has been declared a traitor for sending the delegation to Thessaloniki to conclude a separate peace. Ferdinand is strengthening Sofia and awaits the approach of the German units. The army can't be stopped; the soldiers are unshakable with or without us they will go on Sofia. I've decided to lead the rebellious army and lead it to Sofia. Alexander, are you with us?"

Stamboliysky, like Daskalov who got out of life imprisonment in dungeons right into the thick of revolutionary events, was contemplating for a moment and immediately answered:

"Of course, I am with you, I am with people! What we were discussing with you the night before last should happen now, not sometime in future. Ferdinand and the monarchy must be overthrown immediately!"

"The plan of actions is as follows: I announce the manifesto, signed by Stamboliysky and Daskalov, on the overthrow of Ferdinand and the monarchy and proclaim the republic. Let's give her a name of our city Radomir. I am sending the telegrams and manifests all over the country. We connect the soldiers from Kyustendil and Radomir. We organize the transfer of all the rebel forces to Radomir. From Radomir we move to Sofia, I shall lead the army, and you go to Sofia and try to win Sofia over to our side. Our task is to ensure that no blood is shed."

"I gather all who are in Kyustendil, and we go to Radomir," Stamboliysky answered.

The events developed rapidly, and the trains immediately carried all the rebels from Kyustendil to Radomir, where the leaders of the uprising addressed them with an appeal:

"Soldiers of Bulgaria! Tsar Ferdinand has betrayed all of us. He is not going to conclude a truce, but intends to establish a dictatorship and shoot all the rebels and re-harness the rest in a yoke and continue the war. Ferdinand declared: 'We are not defeated!' and ordered to fight the Entente to the end. In case of a continuation of the retreat, he is intended to pull the Bulgarian army to the Arabokonaksky pass in the Stara Planina Mountains and from there to give a general battle to the Entente. And if we are defeated there too, we shall go to the Danube to Shumen to join the army of Mackensen there and give a general battle to the Entente. And if we are defeated there too, we shall do what the Serbs did in 1915: through the territory of Albania they united with the Entente. We shall link with the Germans through Rumania and Austria. Ferdinand must be overthrown, the revolutionary soldiers must march on Sofia. When the tsar perishes, he'll entail the entire Bulgarian people. Ferdinand wants to strangle Bulgarian people with his bloody hands. We won't let him do it!"

"Down with Ferdinand! Down with the monarchy! Stamboliysky! Daskalov!" the soldiers chanted again, ready to start marching immediately.

"Listen, everyone!" Daskalov proclaimed. "Today, September 27, 1918, the former tsar Ferdinand, his dynasty and the former government have been overthrown. Bulgaria is proclaimed to be a People's Republic. All the heads of the district administration, district chiefs, commandants, elders, military commanders must comply with the orders and instructions of the Provisional Government; it is responsible for the order in the country. This circular is to be announced to all the military units and to the entire Bulgarian people. Chairman of the Provisional Government is Alexander Stamboliysky. Commander-in-chief is Raiko Daskalov."

"Hurrah!" the soldiers cheered and chanted the names of their leaders.

And Stamboliysky with Daskalov formed infantry battalions and machine-gun-companies out of 30 thousand rebellions and sent by telegraph the

Radomir Republic appeal to Sofia and all the other settlements in Bulgaria, and in response to disorderly conduct Daskalov sent a telegram to Sofia to the Bulgarian government:

"From the information that I have, I found out that you have not yet resigned. I order you to do it immediately. I am coming tomorrow."

Tomorrow, September 28, 1918, a 30-thousand rebels' army, led by Raiko Daskalov, moved from Radomir to Sofia to bring her to the side of the revolution peacefully.

***

He fearlessly entered the cabinet of ministers in the government building alone, unarmed, into the camp of the enemies, whom he tried to win over to the side of the people. All the ministers were sitting stone-faced at the table, looking around cowardly, hostile, concerned only to save their own person and the privileges. Like the corrupt judges before to condemn an innocent, they heard his last word:

"Gentlemen, it is impossible to stop the revolution. The suffering of the soldiers in the war was great, the crime of the rulers who had dragged Bulgaria into this war was great, the desire of the soldiers to punish the guilty and restore justice was great. They would go to with or without us. We considered our duty to be together with people. To prevent blood shed we propose that the government will resign, accept the Radomir Republic, proclaimed by people, and overthrow the monarchy."

"How dare you, Mr. Stamboliysky, to come here and offer us such a thing?"

"You are a rebel!"

"You have no excuse!"

"There is nothing to talk about!"

On seeing senseless to continue the conversation, Alexander Stamboliysky left the government house, and an order flew after him:

"To arrest, to detain, to send him back to prison!"

Stamboliysky hurried to the club of the Narrow Socialists still with hope to find the allies there, but the Narrow Socialists had betrayed the people's revolution, and all the deputies of the People's Assembly cowardly shunned Stamboliysky. He was wandering alone through the Sofia streets in despair, realizing that there were no allies. Like a gruesome nightmare the meeting with Dimitar Blagoev 3 days ago rose before his eyes, and a dialogue sounded in his ears. He recalled how he had come for support to Dimitar Blagoev in his house on Debar Street in the center of Sofia on the same day of his release from the prison immediately after meeting with Ferdinand. 62-year-old Blagoev was constantly ill lately, he met him lying in bed. After the words of greeting and enquiring about his health, Alexander Stamboliysky got down to the main thing.

"Tomorrow I'm going with Daskalov, Savov, Sakarov, Girginov and some others to meet the insurgent soldiers in order to assess the situation, the balance of power and calm them down. If it turns out to be impossible to stop them, then this is a real revolution, which there is a reason to lead, to take power, overthrow the monarchy and proclaim a republic. Can we count on you? Because the Narrow Socialists, BSDP, have significant forces inside the country, will you come out with us?"

"I reject your proposal categorically. We shall not be able to take power together with you, as we are fundamentally different from you."

"Actually, we don't differ much. In general, we accept your program except one thing: we do not bother small owners. We shall not be able to take power without you: you have strong positions in the cities, and we are strong in the village. But if we manage to take power, will you share the government of the country with us? We could divide ministerial seats equally between our parties and carry out reforms, give land to the peasants who cultivate it."

"I reject your proposal categorically. We are not ready to participate in power and are not going to participate in the government of the country together with you, Bulgarian Agrarian National Union Party, which is not for socialism, as you are not a true party. Only us, the Narrow Socialists of BSDP, are the true party, only we have the truth. If you renounce your Agrarian Union and join our party, accept our program, only then, perhaps, cooperation is possible."

"If we manage to take power and form our own government of the country and begin to govern, then do you agree to give us, at least, 50 people from your party of socialists in the telegraph and railway business? Our party members are mostly peasants, specialists in agriculture."

"We can't do this, we'll not give."

"Will you report on my proposal to the leadership of your party, and will you put it up for discussion?"

"No, I shall not, because I reject your proposal categorically."

Alexander Stamboliysky said goodbye and went out into the street, discouraged, shocked and dumbfounded by Blagoev disgusting demagogy and complete betrayal.

"Here the practice has proved, what party is with the people: Agrarian Union or BSDP socialists. It turns out that the true people party is the Agrarian Union of Bulgaria. Unthinkable! Unbelievable! Incredible! Blagoev has written mountains of books about the revolution, and when the revolution has taken place, he betrayed it, he rejected it!"

Alexander Stamboliysky was wondering alone through the indifferent city, remembering his visit to Blagoev, and realized that there were no allies and he could not help Raiko Daskalov in any way. Pursued by a new order of arrest, he disappeared in the darkness of the Sofia streets and went into illegality.

***

Meanwhile, Raiko Daskalov was leading the rebel army to Sofia, having sent her a notification telegram:

"From the information I possess I found out you failed to resign, I order you to do it immediately. I am coming tomorrow."

By September 28, 1918, the trains brought the military units, retreating from the Southern Front, joined republican army of Daskalov, who had approached through Pernik the village Vladay, located in 15 km from Sofia. The village Vladay, or Vladaya, named after someone's name, either female or male in the early Middle Ages, opened a direct path to the capital. Ahead there was a passage between the Lyulin and Vitosha Mountains, along which the Vladay River rushed straight into the center of Sofia. The river, not wide, but narrow, swiftly carried its crystal clear waters, paving the way for a valley between mountains ranges, along which there was a road for the rebels and the railway lines. Having received no answer to his ultimatum to surrender the city, Raiko Daskalov led the rebellious soldiers to the capital. Not giving a damn about the doctrinarism and betrayal of the leader of the party, the BSDP ordinary members next to Daskalov led the detachments into the battle to overthrow the monarchy. The rebel army moved from Vladay and split into 3 streams like a trident to stab into the heart of the monarchy. 3 streams like lava of soldiers, boiling with anger, were advancing with a fight, flowing around the hills through the hollows and approached the city of Sofia. The left column from the side of the hills Lyulin Mountains range with a fight entered the city borders in the Gorna Banya area. The left column captured possessions at Boyan. And the central one, under the command of Raiko Daskalov, moved straight along the road and railway lines and took the village of Knyazhevo with fight.

In the twilight of September 29, shells burst along the entire south-western border of Sofia, machine-guns scribbled and the fragments scattered in all directions. One of them pierced the body of Raiko Daskalov, who was in front, fighting bravely. Raiko, wounded by shrapnel, fell down. His comrades-in-arms carried him away from the battlefield.

"We are winning, Mr. Daskalov," the chief of the staff of the rebels, sergeant major Damyanov reported, "lieutenant Dimitrov and lieutenant Boev took Gorna Banya; Stefanov and Sharankov took Boyana."

"We have taken Knyazhevo," Daskalov said, "I believe it is possible to postpone the encirclement of Sofia until dawn. According to my information, the cadets of the military school are mainly at the disposal of the enemy."

"Mr. Daskalov, maybe that's why, when the advantage is on our side and we are standing on the threshold of Sofia, we must not delay moving forward and take the city right now?" Damyanov objected.

"Let's give the soldiers to rest until dawn, and at dawn we shall resume the assault," wounded Daskalov ordered, who was barely on his feet, exhausted by sleepless nights and stress of the last days.

The rebels, according Daskalov's order stopped the assault and, deadly tired, fell asleep until dawn in the darkness of the coming night. In front of them there was Sofia, which was within easy reach. The roar of German guns woke them up at dawn. The fatal mistake of the assault on the capital, postponed until dawn, cost them victory and many lives. At the fatal night of September 29–30, 1918, when they fell asleep, having postponed the assault on Sofia until dawn, the 217th German division was rushing at breakneck speed to rescue Ferdinand. It had come up during the night before dawn just in time, took all the positions, where the rebels were and delivered the main blow at the Sugar Factory railway station near the village Knyazhevo.

Wounded Daskalov raised the army into battle, but now the forces were not equal. Ferdinand shot the soldiers with the German cannons, the Germans, shining with helmets, shot at the Bulgarians, yesterday's allies, and stabbed them with bayonets. Machine-guns were scribbling, as if with death, by a scythe scythed the soldiers' lives, a spatter of blood and shreds of the tattered bodies with fountain scattered through dust and smoke, and the glare of fire. Next to the Germans, a detachment of Macedonian punitive forces was commanded by the chief of IMARO (Internal Macedonian-Adrianopolitan Revolutionary Organization) Alexander Protogerov. A maniac-killer and a henchman, he abetted his Macedonian bandits to tatter Bulgarian soldiers, taking revenge that they failed to keep his Macedonia.

Hiding around the corner, Lieutenant Filyu Borisov was aiming at the head of the soldiers and shot; he had reached Knyazhevo, hid here and waited for his own people to shoot at the rebellious soldiers. And behind another corner of the Sugar Factory building another man was standing: a 20-year-old youth, handsome like god, with a soul of poet, a genius by nature, a military school cadet, by evil irony of fate, thrown to suppress the revolution, which he sang in his poems. He was watching with horror the massacre, at which Ferdinand shot like a butcher the people's revolution, periodically shooting into the air for the sake of appearance, trying not to hit anyone, and mentally took off himself his military uniform in order to become a writer and convey to posterity the truth of the events, to which he was a witness. The young man's name was Hristo Dimitrov Izmirliev.

The revolution was suppressed, the reaction came, the rebels who survived retreated, shedding blood and losing ground. The Protogerov's Macedonians were dragging the wounded chief of the rebellions staff Damyanov along the ground, kicking him, having captured. Wounded Raiko Daskalov took refuge and escaped to Thessaloniki, having survived. The Radomir Republic like lightning flashed as a beautiful dream, having existed 4 days.

At the same night, September 29–30, leaflets were dropped from the plane over the ongoing massacre of the Great War on the Thessaloniki Front about the truce, concluded in Thessaloniki between the Entente and Bulgaria, which was refuted by the Germans and Ferdinand. And in 3 days later, on October 3, 1918, the former Bulgarian Tsar Ferdinand was sitting with his things in the train car, departing from the "Nadezhda" railway station in Sofia. He was looking out of the car's window and was ready to jump out to continue his fight for the "Great Bulgaria". He was recalling 30 years of his reign in Bulgaria and thought about the vicissitudes of fate. The maternal grandson of the French king Louis-Philippe and paternal grandson of Ferdinand of Saxe-Coburg-Saalfield, Ferdinand himself simply served as a lieutenant in the Austrian hussar regiment and met the Bulgarians at the Vienna operetta theater, to whom he offered himself to become their king. First he became their prince, as the Turks continued to boss Bulgaria; and only finally, having gotten rid of them in 1908, on September 22, he became their tsar, having survived several attempts on his life from the assassins from Saint-Petersburg. An admirer of birds, beasts, plants, gardens and forests, all living things, except the Bulgarians, whom he called "canaille," he fell in love with their country, which became his kingdom, where he had ruled with sovereignty. The Tarnovo Constitution turned out to be just a fig leaf, with which he covered up his personal power regime. He juggled the ministers and shuffled the cabinet of ministers like a deck of cards, dismissing the objectionable, and provoked a crisis, and conducted the parliamentary elections so that obedient pawns were elected, and the elections themselves were of a sham character, as Ferdinand controlled them with the police violence, administrator pressure and machinations before and after voting, bribes, demagogy and lies. Ferdinand provoked 2 national catastrophes and the ultimate destruction of the country in the Second Balkan and Great War, having gotten involved in the Great War on the wrong side, he dreamed of the Great San-Stefano Bulgaria, he dreamed to enter Constantinople on a white horse in robes of the Bulgarian emperors and put an end with the barbarian Orthodoxy under the auspices of the Pope of Rome. His great dreams were not destined to be realized although. He had reined his fill in the country of Bulgaria, where he had brought luxury of the courtyard, etiquette, intrigues, balls and necessary concomitant of the monarchy slavery and servility of the flunkeydom, who always want to be slaves, flunkies of the tsar.

The train started, and Ferdinand was looking out of the window on the land of Bulgaria, to set foot on which he was never destined any more. Tears were glittering in his eyes. The former Prime Minister Radoslavov also fled together with the tsar. The Entente, who had defeated Bulgaria, overthrew Ferdinand together with the rebellious soldiers, but taking vengeance on her for the vainly spilled blood of her soldiers at the Thessaloniki Front and the entire war delay for more than a year due to the fault of Bulgaria, did not allow the republic establishment and, as a punishment and break of development, enthroned Ferdinand's son Boris III. This break turned out to be fatal.

Chapter 12
Chirpan

Bodrovo, like entire Bulgaria, healed the wounds, inflicted with another war, mourned the dead and gathered with forces to live on, overcoming hunger, poverty and diseases. The Karagochev family continued to be wealthy in comparison with the poor families, who had nothing. 300 decares of land, remained after division it between 4 brothers, the grandfather Todor's sons, provided them with a wealthy position. From century to century the land transmitted by inheritance, and herd, grazing on it, gave them life, and their life was on that land. They lived with work and love for their land.

The house of Ivan Todorov Karagochev was filled with the aroma of baked bread and vertuta-apple pie. The finest puff pastry was rolled out, pieces of chopped apple were placed in it, the dough with apples was rolled into a tube, twisted in rings and baked in the furnace. The aroma from the baked pie got you drunk, and the taste could not be conveyed in words. On the table in Ivan's house a huge loaf of hot bread, just removed from the fire, was smoking, the golden crisp of which excited your appetite; brinza-cheese, cottage cheese, milk, roast lamb with potatoes and all kinds of vegetables with fresh greens for salads, which grew in abundance on their land, were on the table. The entire family gathered at the table to see off Todor: Ivan, his father, Atanasa, his mother, 13-year-old sister Mariyka, 9-year-old brother Gocho and his grandmother Mariyka.

"We are going right after lunch," Ivan said, "I am thinking about a small production of footwear to open in Haskovo. For this, I am sending Todor to Chirpan city to learn this craft. I've made inquiries, there is one master there, the owner of his shoe workshop, he recruits the apprentices for fee; they learn how to make shoes. I have already agreed with him about you, Todor. You'll live there with him, learn to make shoes, we'll open our workshop if it goes successfully, we'll expand the business and hire employers. Todor will manage the whole business."

"My grandson likes this job," the grandma Mariyka said, "what beautiful cervulis he had made himself!"

"Be careful there, son," Atanasa, the mother, said, "if you don't like it, go back home!"

"I like this idea to open the production in Haskovo," Todor answered, in whose soul contradicting feelings rivaled: love for his land, his house, which he never left, parting with his beloved girl and interest in his father's idea to open shoe production in Haskovo.

Although deep in mind he felt that the fate had intended him path different from heading production of shoes. 9-year-old brother Gocho was upset by his brother's departure, as he loved him endlessly and admired him.

"Thanks god that the war is over and all our people have returned home alive," Ivan said.

"If I were at the war," Todor exclaimed, "I would be along with the rebellious soldiers together with Raiko Daskalov and Alexander Stamboliysky. Do you remember, father, how Stamboliysky came to our school and proved that the Central Powers would be defeated and the Entente would win, and if Ferdinand draws Bulgaria into the war in alliance with Germany and Austro-Hungary, then Bulgaria would be defeated? Everything happened exactly as he premonished! It's so pity that the rebels failed to dethrone the tsar!"

"Save you god, son!" the mother and grandma exclaimed in chorus.

"Yes, Alexander Stamboliysky was right, sorry for him and Raiko Daskalov, they are the only people's intercessors," Ivan said bitterly.

Ivan with his son got on a cart and set off. Their path lay north; they descended from the Bodrovo hills, crossed the Maritsa River in Borisovograd, and soon the houses and gardens of Chirpan appeared in the distance, which like the rest Bulgarian cities had in its ancestors the Thracians, Greek and Romans, who founded their settlements there in the old days of antiquity. Once at the times of Turks, Chirpan was famous for its craftsmen, artisans and workshops, who produced everything in the world and sold their goods to the Turks. During the latter 7 years of 3 wars the whole country was impoverished, the artisans, who lost the customers, went bankrupt and the workshops closed. In some places they remained, among them was the production of shoes of Hristo Kundurdjiyata.

Ivan and his son drove into the city completely covered with vineyards and gardens, the city of the poet Peyo Yavorov, who had so tragically passed away 4 years ago. They drove up to the gates of the house of Hristo Kundurdjiyata, who was waiting for them in a company of his apprentices. About 50 years old, untidy, thick in body, with bristles of an unshaved beard and mustache, in hanging wide trousers, on top of which a homespun shirt belted with a sash and a vest, the master-owner of the workshop grinned pretty wide on seeing a cart, loaded with bags to the top with flower, on top of which there were woolen blankets and baskets with food. Immediately he ordered the apprentices to unload the cart and transfer all the goods to the house.

"This is my son Todor. This is Hristo Kundurdjiyata, your teacher, obey him in everything, he'll teach you all the secrets of shoe production!" Ivan said, introducing his son to Hristo and turning to his son.

Todor greeted everyone, feeling a riveted glance of a young girl on him. She was standing nearby, slack-jawed, staring at him in a stupor and gloating him with her gaze.

"My wife Helen," Hristo introduced the girl, "go, Elena, show Todor his room."

"Goodbye, son," Ivan parted with Todor, gave him some money, turned the oxen and slowly set off on his way back home to Bodrovo, where a heap of things was waiting for him in his kmet's office, his own fields and heard of cattle on his own meadows.

He was worried about his son, who had aroused hatred of envious people in his own village, and was glad that he had removed him from them, imagining how Todor would learn the shoe business and head their own production in Haskovo. He was glad that the damned war, the third in a row, had ended, the first 2 of which he himself was a participant, and thought how happily they would live further in prosperity and peace.

Meanwhile, Hristo was gently stroking with his hand 20 sacks of flower, having been carried by the apprentices in his 2-story house, and was admiring the woolen blankets and baskets with food.

"Let's go, Todor, I'll show you your duties," he turned to the new apprentice, scanning him from head to feet, "look at him! What a handsome young man!" he said with annoyance. "And why do you only need to study footwear production! You could've married a prince!" he said half in jest, half seriously.

"Soon there will be no princesses, the republic will be!" "Todor found something to answer, also, half-jokingly, half seriously."

"Shush! Shush!" the master shushed at him cowardly, fearfully looking around, "otherwise somebody hears!"

They entered the yard, and Hristo brought him up to date.

"Here is the stable, come in."

Todor and Hristo went inside, where 4 horses were resting in stalls.

"I love horses," Todor said, "we have 6 horses in our farm."

"That's good, you'll feed them, water them, comb them and take them out to pasture, in one word, take care of them."

"Good," Todor shrugged.

"Further, there is a shed for firewood, this is where firewood is chopped, collected and taken to the shed."

"Ok, it's not hard for me."

"And also, you have to sweep the yard, clean the barn and the stable."

"How about learning to make footwear?" Todor asked.

"Wow, what a speedy one! Not all at once! When the time comes, I'll let you know," master Hristo slyly screwed up his eyes, blurring in a disgusting smile, "well, for now that's, probably, all."

"Let's go back to the workshop!" he commanded 5 apprentices, "who having unloaded the flour, were waiting in the yard."

The whole company left behind the gate and went to the Hristo's footwear shop.

"What the hell is this?" Todor swore and looked around. "Ok, it's not hard for me!"

Accustomed to work from childhood, Todor, on whose shoulders the entire household was from the age of 11 years old, from the moment his father left for the Balkan War, set to work and soon completed it. A small, clean, cozy room with an iron bed, on which a mattress lay with a colorful bed linen, a table, a chair and a chest of drawers—everything you need for a temporary stay, and Todor liked it. He laid out his things and put several books on the table, which he brought with him.

"Ok, I'll survive the stable and the barn, I am used to it," he was thinking, lying down on the bed to rest, "maybe I'll have to work as a servant for this Hristo-shoemaker for a couple of days and then I'll start studying in his workshop."

There was a knock at the door.

"Yes, who is there?"

"It's me, Elena. Todor, let's go, I'll feed you, you are, probably, hungry."

"Ok, I'll be right there," he replied and left his room.

"Let's go to the kitchen, sit down at the table," Elena said, serving him a bowl of chicken soup, a piece of chicken with fried potatoes and mushrooms and a piece of puff pastry.

"And you?" Todor asked, scanning her.

"I'll have a cake too," Elena said, sitting down at the table.

He immediately evaluated her appearance. She was about 25, half the age of her loathsome husband, quite pretty, all sparkling with all the colors of the embroidery that adorned her shirt and vest, and apron, and a fluffy long skirt made of soft wool. She did not take her eyes off the 17-year-old Todor, as if some unknown force shackled her gaze to him. Not at all embarrassed, Todor, accustomed to female attention, said:

"Well, bon appetite!"

Elena turned out to be a pleasant interlocutor, they chatted at ease, as 2 strangers sometimes easily enter into a conversation, when they see each other for the first time. She looked at him as if spellbound, unable to take her eyes off the young man, whose beauty had turned her whole idea of the world upside down. And this handsome man was in her house, sitting at the same table with her, talking with her.

Meanwhile, time flew by unnoticed. Todor thanked her for dinner, helped to clean the table and disappeared into his room. He woke up early next morning, freshened up, washed himself at the well and went to the stable to the horses and to the barn to feed, water, clean, sweep the whole yard and chop wood, putting it in the shed. Hristo, the shoe-man was nowhere, and his wife Elena was nearby, as if shackled, and the more she looked at him, the more the feeling to him that struck her heart, paralyzing her will. She was drawn to him against her will, and she followed him on his heels. He understood that she was in love with him and tried to avoid her company, but closed in the same space with her, fenced around the yard and the walls of her house, he did not always cope with the task. He missed his home, yearned for Christina, who was waiting for him in Bodrovo, and cursed his position of a servant and slave, which he unexpectedly fell into. Thus, a week of his "footwear production study" had passed, and early on Saturday morning, having received Elena's permission, he took a horse and went home for a weekend. The horse galloped south across the river, passing fields, orchards and wine yards, and soon he saw the hills, in the depth of which, hiding from the outside world, Bodrovo hid away from the cross roads.

2 days at home flew by quickly. Todor's joyful meeting with family and close friends, Ivan Ignatov and Christina, lifted his spirits; they laughed at the situation that Todor got into, having turned everything into a joke. And in the good mood he returned to Chirpan on Monday early in the morning. He got into the stable right from the road, and everything repeated again.

"That's it, this is the end of the job!" Todor decided and next day on Tuesday he went in search of the Hristo's workshop.

He walked on several blocks, crossing from one road to another, asking along the way where the workshop was. Soon he saw a 2-story building. On the first floor, all kinds of shoes for sale were displayed in the window: from cervulis with cords to boots, and there was a store.

Todor went inside and climbed up to the second floor. Hristo's workshop was in front of him. 10 apprentices were sitting at the machines, cut out parts, connected them, pieces of leather and patterns were hanging on the walls; there was a fragrant smell of the solution for processing leather. 10 slaves made shoes here, which Hristo sold downstairs in the store. On seeing Todor here, he was very surprised.

"What are you doing here?"

"My father planned to open a shoe factory in Haskovo like yours, that's why he brought me to you to study footwear-making, but not for me to work for you as a slave!"

"What? How many else of you here want my business? Why should I create competition for myself!"

"What?"

"Oh, no, what kind of competition will it be: you are in Haskovo, I am in Chirpan!" Hristo came to his senses with annoyance that he let it slip. "No competition will be! It's just I have such an order: for the first, an apprentice works at home with the housework, for the second month, he goes to the workshop to clean here and only then…"

"Oh, you fat freak!" Todor thought, looking at his pig's snout, covered with dirty bristles, fleshy filthy nose and dirty smacking lips, in the corners of which dried saliva glowed. "It is not without a reason that your wife is head over heels in love with me! Then it is you who should pay me for work, but not me to pay you!" he said, looking into Hristo's eyes.

"Oh, you a bully! How dare you to contradict me! Get out of here immediately!"

"I won't leave!"

"Get out or I'll drive you out with a hammer!" Hristo growled furiously, ultimately throwing off his mask.

"I can rebuff!" Todor answered calmly, "I shall not leave!"

"All right, all right," Hristo backed off, having received a rebuff, "why should we quarrel! Let's go this way: at home you will continue to do the same work that you did, this is before lunch, and in the afternoon you'll come here to sweep the workshop. So, this until the end of the month, so take a broom a sweep."

"Ok, I am doing it only for you, father! It was your idea to open a footwear factory," Todor thought and set about cleaning the workshop.

The month of October came to the end. Every day Todor cleaned the yard and took care of the animals until lunch, and after lunch he went to the workshop to clean it up. Elena, being in love with him, followed on the heels of him, but of course, did not go outside the gates of their courtyard and yearned alone, when Todor went for the workshop.

He fed and watered the horses and sat on a bench under a tree to rest. She came over and sat next to him. Living in abundance without any need to take care of daily bread, but in a confined space, surrounded by a fence around her yard and the wall of her house in a provincial town, she yearned for true love for a handsome young man. Suddenly he appeared like a miracle in responds to her dreams. She fell in love with him at the first sight, when she saw him. She gave herself up to her feelings without looking back. She hoped for reciprocity. The primal feelings swept over her whole, like the element raged in her heart, which she did not control. She gazed at his handsome face, deep black eyes, regular nose, sensual lips, slender figure, muscular shoulders and arms and felt an insane desire to throw herself into his arms and snuggle him to her. Her breast surged to the beat of the string feeling. She said:

"Todor, do you love anybody?"

He took her hand to comfort her.

"Elena, get distracted, do something else, read a book. I've been to the book store, there are a lot of books there, adventure novels…"

"From the adventure novels you want only adventures and romance," she answered wittily, squeezing his hand, from the touch of which a current seemed to run through her body.

Don't love me, girl,
Don't ruin your youth,
I came from afar,
The evil fate is gross.
To grieve at home
Mother left alone.
At the window she awaits
All the time days and nights.
Since, she has him one,
Her hope and joy, her beloved son
To support her later in her old age.

"Do you know who the author is?"
"I don't remember…"
"Peiko Yavorov. He glorified Chirpan. He lived here nearby. Like Hristo Botev, he wrote many poems about love, about hajduks, about their courageous struggle for freedom. He perished 4 years ago because of love and jealous woman. His wife got mad from love to him, was jealous of every woman so much that she committed suicide, after which he shot himself of scandal. It turns out, only sufferings are because of this love, love brings only suffering. Don't love me, Elena…"

The more he talked to her and dissuaded her from loving him, the more she loved him. He is handsome, smart, has read many books…
"Todor!"
"I have to go, sorry. Today is the last day I work as a slave for your husband."
"He bullies everyone like this, he takes money for training and uses students like servants. Only the work you do, has always been done by 2 persons."
"It ends today. Tomorrow, as he promised, I shall begin to study the production of footwear. My father wants to open a workshop in Haskovo."

Todor stood up from the bench, freed his hand from her hand and went to the workshop to sweep the floor there. He looked forward for tomorrow. He woke up early in the morning and out of habit hurried up to the stable to feed and water the horses. He was standing with his face to the horse, striking her muzzle and combing her mane. He felt that someone had entered the stable and out of the corner of his eye he saw a shadow flicker. He froze without turning around.

"This is a hello to you from Hristo!" Sabi blurted out quickly and raised a dagger over him.

In a blink of an eye, Todor dodged the blow, grabbed his hand, knocked the dagger out of it and hit him in a jaw. Dumbed by the blow, Sabi collapsed on the floor next to the dagger. Todor picked up the dagger, parted with the horses, he was used to, and left the stable. He went into his room, gathered his things and headed to the gates. Poor Elena was standing by the gate, anticipating something gruesome.

"Farewell, Elena, I'm leaving now, your Hristo sent a murderer to kill me."

"This is Sabi, his lackey. Did you kill him?"

"No, I didn't, he is alive, he'll come to his senses soon."

"Kiss me!"

Todor learned over to her and kissed in the cheek.

"I'll remember this all my life."

"Thank you, Elena, for your kindness! Tell you hubby, we'll meet one day."

Todor went out the gates and went home. His heart was filled with anger and desire for revenge. He felt sorry for his father and half ton of flour that Hristo had stolen. They were worth their weight in gold in the country impoverished by war.

"Oh, father, naive, kindhearted, unfortunate father," he repeated to himself, "you don't know how to choose friends; you chose a wrong workshop and a wrong master for me, but now it's too late. Apparently, I was not destined to boss the footwear business. And with you, Hristo, we shall meet again one day!"

Todor left the city, endless meadows and forests of yellow-red color, painted with the colors of autumn, opened before him. It was the end of October. He was walking by foot, crossing the Maritsa River valley and the river itself. Behind him, far to the north, the peaks of the Balkans barely loomed in a haze of fog, and in front of him, ahead to the south, the pinnacles of the Rhodopes loomed, their foothills with hills, in the depth of which his house was in the village of Bodrovo.

Chapter 13
Spanish Flu

He crossed over the threshold of his house, barely on his feet, with difficulty reached the bed in his room and collapsed on the bed, as if knocked down. The heat threw him into cold, he was burning from the high temperature, feeling as if he was lying naked on the snow and freezing. Fever shook his body, which he no longer controlled, unable to move an arm or leg, feeling freezing needles piercing all his flesh. He plugged into unconsciousness, and his family treated him with anise oil, which they produced themselves from anise, growing in their fields; suspecting possible contagiousness of the disease, they guessed to cover their nose and mouth with a handkerchief.

The disease, brought from the fronts of the Great War, was ironically named after the country that did not participate in the war—Spain. Spain which did not participate in the war, was free from the military censorship and was the first to premonished the world about the threat of a pandemic, while the censorship of war in the warring countries by criminal silence continued to spread of the disease. The Spanish disease, generated by the Great War, sounded like the final chord of the war and claimed more lives than the war itself. It struck countries in all 4 cardinal points and in October 1918 reached Bulgaria, Bodrovo, hiding in the hills at the foot of the Rhodopes. Here and there the dead were buried, although, not on the same scale, as in the other counties, where the disease mowed down entire villages.

Todor was ill for 2 weeks and went on the mend; the youth and health defeated the disease. His grandma Mariyka and mother Atanasa prayed for him like crazy without ceasing; his father worried, secretly wiping away a tear. 9-year-old Gocho nearly cried, helped with household, trying to replace his older brother. Finally, Todor came to his senses. He was very weak and exhausted by illness, but he was alive, and all the household members wept for joy. He began to get up from bed, the fever subsided, he was already on his feet.

"I'll go to Christina," he said to his mother and began to dress.

"Todor, wait, don't go," Atanasa said with fear, sitting him back on the bed.

"I shall go, I can already walk," Todor answered in a weak voice, "I'll go to visit her, I worry about her."

Mom continued to hold her son's hand and finally decided to speak.

"So, she's gone... Christina died..."

As if struck by thunder, Todor grabbed the iron headboard and ground with pain. He did not want to believe what he had heard and did not quite understand what was happening. He felt acute pain in his heart, as if was stabbed with a dagger. Struck by the illness of love, which had paralyzed his will, he had neither desire nor strength to live on without his beloved. Against his will, his hand automatically reached for revolver, which lay in a chest of drawers near the bed. He opened a drawer, the revolver was not there; his relatives had hidden it in advance. Grandma and mom burst into tears, pitting Todor, in the depth of their soul rejoicing that he was alive.

"Poor girl...poor her mother...husband died in the war, and now her daughter died too from this strange disease..."

The death of his beloved girl struck, dumbfounded and broke Todor's heart, changed his character and left an imprint on his soul. He became withdrawn, silent and gloomy. His mental anguish was echoed by the passing autumn, tearing the last yellow leaves from the branches, and his soul, like a bare skeleton of trees ached with pain, exposing its nerves.

On November 28, 1918, the government of Alexander Malinov resigned, the government of Theodor Theodorov came to power. An amnesty for all the political emigrants was declared. Alexander Stamboliysky and Raiko Daskalov came out of illegality and returned to political life, heading the Bulgarian Agrarian Union.

Thus, the year 1918 ended. Bulgaria froze in anticipation of the allies' verdict.

Chapter 14
Vidyu, Petyu, Mityu

Todor turned 18 on the fifth day of the New Year. His beauty became even brighter, more mature, more masculine: a tall, slender figure, muscular shoulders, a beautiful oval of face, slightly sunken cheeks, a sensual mouth, bottomless black eyes, piercing look, which embarrassed all the girls in the neighborhood. He gradually returned to life after the shock he had endure, as spring brings back to life all the living things after hibernation, dressing the yesterday's yet completely bare skeletons of trees in green foliage. He tried not to recall the past, which could not be changed, and the future was completely vague.

Spring filled their garden with all the scents of life, white and pink flowers covered the branches of fruit trees, the crescent and stars were glowing in the black sky. Todor was lying on the couch, covered with a thick woolen blanket and listened to the night sounds. Midnight was approaching. He heard the clatter of the hooves of oxen, harnessed to the cart, which drove up to their gates. Todor got up, went to the gate and let Vidyu in.

"Is everything all right?" Vidyu asked.

"Yes, everyone sleeps, let's go."

They walked quietly past the outbuildings at the back of the yard; there was another barn behind the threshing floor. They went inside, opened the cellar door and went down the steps underground. The cellar was long, at the end of it there was another exit to a waste-land behind the yard. This underground passage was dug back in the days of Turkish domination to escape in case of the Turks attack. They lit a kerosene lamp. The light from the lamp illuminated the dungeon. In the cellar there were boxes with weapons, hidden by the kmet Ivan Todorov from the military inspectorate of the Entente.

At the sight of the boxes with guns, carbines, revolvers and bandoliers Vidyu was completely delighted, and his eyes glowed.

"Let's take 6 rifles," Todor said.

"Fine, let's take 2 more carbines."

"Take them out faster."

They took the rifles, carbines and carried them out from the cellar to the cart. They returned a couple more times to take 10 boxes with cartridges, doused the lamp, closed the cellar and loaded the boxes into the cart, looking around to check that nobody was watching them. There was no one around, everyone was sleeping late at night. They set off. They went east to the village of Aidanlar, where Vidyu's father Gocho, Ivan's brother, the second son of grandfather Todor, had recently moved. Having sold his hose and land in Bodrovo, Gocho bought vast pastures near Aidanlar, built a 2-story house, barns, threshing floor, sheds, cellars and another 2-story house for his eldest son Todor and increased livestock. The oxen were slowly pulling the cart with weapons toward Aidanlar. The bright moon lit their way.

"Let's revive the romance of hajduks!" Vidyu said cheerfully.

Vidyu retained a cheerful disposition from childhood, when he and Todor were boys, pasturing their herds in the fields during the Balkan Wars, where their fathers-brothers fought. The free rebellious spirit, inherited in the genes from the hajduks ancestors, inspired him with a dream of reviving the traditions of the hajduks, the legends about which they lived with from their childhood. A healthy, red-cheeked, black-eyed Vidyu with a shock of black hair looked like a hajduk himself, the only missing thing was a gun, and now he had one.

"Yes, it would be interesting," Todor answered thoughtfully, "but there are no more Turkish conquerors, and the former Turkish conquerors became the allies in the Great War."

"There are no Turks, but there are enough of our own ones," Vidyu answered, "many of our own ones are worse than the Turks."

"That's for sure," Todor agreed, thinking about Hristo, the shoemaker, "how many rebel soldiers they shot at Vladay!"

"And after that they caught them in their homes in all the villages and cities of Bulgaria and tortured them to death!"

"Think about Petko Voevoda! He fought against the Turks from childhood, and his own people betrayed him, as soon as they were liberated from the

Turks. It was the Bulgarians who, on the orders of Stefan Stambolov, seized the hero Petko, threw him into the dungeon in the Varna fortress and tortured him. And Hristo Botev and Vasil Levsky were also betrayed by their own people: the Bulgarians! These scoundrels are worse than the Turks!"

These stories worried Todor from childhood and indignation burned in his soul. He was silent for a while, then changed the subject.

"How are your friends, the Armanovs?" Todor asked. "Do you still feed them?"

"Yes, I do," Vidyu answered happily, "I share food with them, the eldest Petyu, as he hid from the army last year and did not go to the war, turned out to be outlaw, since then he has been coming to us for food. And the younger Mityu was hired as a farmhand to one or the other, slept at night where he could and then joined his brother, and they began to rob the rich on the roads. They are not like us: you and I have land, herds of cattle, houses, but they have nothing. Both their father Ganyu Armanov and their grandfather were beggars, so the Armanovs are orphans: they live only on what they rob."

"I don't like this shorty, the younger one, he is very insolent," Todor said disgustingly.

"Insolent, because he's hungry," Vidyu pronounced philosophically, "but you don't know him well, come, when he is there, get to know each other better."

Vidyu laughed.

"Once I was swimming in the river, stripped, left my things on the shore. He crept up and stole my dagger, this one, a gift from my grandpa," Todor pulled out from his belt and showed Vidyu an ancient dagger, the handle of which was decorated with precious stones and carving, "I jumped out of the water, overtook him in an instant, knocked him down on the ground and took away my dagger and kicked his ass."

"Well, that's why he is a thief to steal!" Vidyu burst into laughing. "What are your plans for the future?"

"I don't know yet," Todor replied thoughtfully, "my father wants to buy me a 2-story house in Plovdiv and open there some workshop. He wanted to make footwear, but you know how it all ended. Then he suggested a saddlery workshop, but I think that soon it'll not be needed, neither blinders nor horse harness will be needed any more, since horses will be replaced by cars."

"Oh, no!" Vidyu exclaimed. "How could it be without horses! Horses will be needed always!"

"While, I'll stay at home. I love my house, I love my land, my herds, they belonged to our family for centuries."

They drove through the Aidanlar forest and approached Vidyu's house. The vast meadows around belonged to Vidyu, his father Gocho and elder brother Todor. They unloaded the weapons and hid it in the cellar. Todor stayed overnight at Vidyu's place, they recalled the stories about hajduks, which they liked, for a long time.

Chapter 15
Neuilly-Sur-Seine

The "Madrid Castle" hotel vaguely resembled the Madrid Castle, which stood here nearby, built for Francis I by Girolamo Della Robbia, who decorated all the facades with his invention—terracotta tiles. The castle was barbarously demolished for bricks by Louis XVI on the eve of the revolution, and in memory of it in the 19th century, a hotel with the same name was built, outwardly resembling the former castle, but smaller in size, without faience lining, luxurious inside.

In this hotel, which stood on the outskirts of the Bois de Boulogne, at the outskirts of Paris, Neuilly-Sur-Seine, all the members of the Bulgarian delegation, who came to Paris to sum up the results of the Great War, were imprisoned as honorary prisoners. The delegation consisted of the entire political elite of the country, its prominent political and public figures: Minister of Justice Venelin Ganev, Minister of Trade, Industry and Labor Yanko Sakazov, former Minister of Education Mikhail Sarafov, former Prime Minister Ivan Gueshov, Chief of Staff of the army Ivan Lukov, Envoy Extraordinary and Minister Plenipotentiary in the USA Stefan Panaretov, founder of BWSDP (Bulgarian Workers' Social Democratic Party), a member of parliament, Nikola Sakarov. Head of the Union of Thracian Societies Dimitar Mikhalchev, translator and diplomat Nadezhda Stancheva—a total of 5 plenipotentiary delegates, 6 advisers, 11 experts, 5 private secretaries of plenipotentiary delegators; the delegation was headed by the Minister-Chairman Theodor Theodorov and Alexander Stamboliysky, the head of the BANU (Bulgarian Agrarian National Union) and Minister of Public Construction, Communications and Improvement.

The entire delegation, which arrived by the Orient Express from Sofia through Ruse, Danube and whole Europe, was met on July 26 at the Lyon

Station in Paris by Colonel Henri with his people, who after greeting the guests, kindly escorted them by cars to the Madrid Castle hotel and placed under arrest.

"It's prohibited for you to go out, to talk to anyone, to receive any information and share it with the others; the visitors can't come in, you must wait for a draft agreement in silence!" Colonel Henri ordered and kindly offered the Bulgarians his service as an intermediary between the delegation and the conference, to participate in which they had no right.

The prisoners of the "Madrid Castle" could admire the beauty of the Bois de Boulogne from the windows of the hotel.

Seized with ominous premonitions of impending disaster, Alexander Stamboliysky wrote to his friend Raiko Daskalov, who remained in Sofia:

"I am back in jail. Our delegation is in custody here. Nobody can go out and come in. They take us out by cars under custody. Its evidently, they will brutally hack us off".

The agonizing expectation of the verdict and painful approach to the scaffolds began. The victors charged the vanquished. The eternal enemy of Bulgaria Serbia, which had grown like a cancerous tumor in the Kingdom of Serbs, Croats and Slovenes, KSCS, had created an International Commission to investigate the Bulgarian atrocities in Serbia, and the permanent Nikola Pashich, representing KSCS, appealed to Supreme Council of the Conference to condemn Bulgaria for the atrocities, and with a wave of his conductor's baton "Le Temp" welcomed the arrival of the Bulgarian delegation to Paris with an article:

"The Prime Minister of Bulgaria Mr. Theodorov was an absolute follower of the policy of Radoslavov, and the systematic extermination of the civilian population in Serbia was carried out on his and Radoclavov's orders. The investigation proved the guilt of Bulgaria in the destruction of the civilian population in Serres, Drama and Kavala, who died from starvation, committed by the orders of Theodorov and Radoslavov".

It was useless for the delegation to protest and explain to the public that ignorant and illiterate journalists had confused everything and lied, that at the instigation of the Serbs they did not distinguish who was who, that the former Prime Minister Radoslavov fled from the country together with Ferdinand and the current Prime Minister Theodorov was against the war of Bulgaria against the Entente, and Alexander Stamboliysky advocated neutrality for which was sentenced to death, commuted for life imprisonment.

The protest letters, written by the delegates, were transmitted through Colonel Henri to the conference and vanished into the black hole, unanswered. Although the facts of the Bulgarian atrocities took place, and the delegates could not either refute or change them, they could only oppose them to the Serbian and Greek atrocities, which differed from the Bulgarian ones in a much greater degree of atrocity and were committed by the orders of the leaders of their countries, the same like during the recent Balkan Wars. And in Bulgaria the military were punished for this and were read out in advance the rules of warfare in accordance with the Geneva Convention. Under the pretext of protection from the Bulgarian atrocities the Serbs swung at the Bulgarian territory and demanded the Bulgarian cities: Vidin, Kula, Belogradchik, Tsaribrod, Breznik, Pernik, Bosilegrad, Radomir and Kyustendil, inhabited by the Bulgarians correspondingly.

The permanent Greek Prime Minister Venizelos at first never mentioned anything about the Western Thrace, but decided to concentrate all his attention on Asia Minor and carefully probed the soil in this direction. But seeing the futility of the dreams of Greek rule in Asia Minor, he returned to the Thrace and began to demand it to tear away from Bulgaria and join to Greece.

"The transfer of Western Thrace to the Greeks will deprive Bulgaria of access to the Aegean Sea and is fraught with negative economic consequences for her!" the only defenders of Bulgaria USA and Italy stood up for her.

"Cut off Bulgaria from the coast of Aegean Sea, since Bulgaria can arrange a submarine base in Porto Lago and again attack the Entente alone!" Venizelos intimidated the conference.

"The Principal Allied Associated Powers undertake to ensure that Bulgaria's free economic access to the Aegean Sea is guaranteed. The terms of this guarantee will be established later," the Supreme Council of the Conference decided and proceeded to the accusation of the Western Thrace by the Entente forces even before the end of the conference.

Like the Bulgarian Tsar Ferdinand, Rumania waited for a long time on which side to enter the World War, barging for foreign territories with both sides, and finally, on August 27, 1916, entered the war on the side of the Entente, with which harmed it. Rumania was immediately defeated in the battles with the enemy, and the Entente had to withdraw troops from their fronts and rush to rescue Romania. The allies failed to save her, and having lost all her territory and the troops, Romania, in the end, on May 7, 1918, withdrew from the war and concluded a separate peace treaty with the Central Powers, but in one day before the end of the war she managed to reenter the war against the Central Powers on the side of the Entente in order to be in time for the division of the pie. Where Rumania had succeeded was to defeat Bela Kun's Hungarian revolution with her troops and now demanded a reward for this from the conference. Now Rumania has swung at the Southern Dobrudja—the main granary of Bulgaria. Now she again, as in the days of the Balkan Wars, as a robber peeked out from the behind the Danube corner to attack Bulgaria. On seeing Bulgaria defeated and prostrated, she went on the offensive.

The Bulgarian delegates learned all this from the newspapers publications, they were allowed to read, from the snatches of rumors that penetrated through the walls of the "Madrid Castle", through the guards, through the notes, secretly handed over to them by those who sympathized with them. Under the guard they were taken in turn by car on excursions, were accompanied for a walk to the Bois de Boulogne and the Russian church, where they managed to exchange notes secretly with their supporters. So, painfully dragged on the days and hours of waiting for the verdict. Going broke, they themselves paid for the luxurious apartments of the Madrid Castle and collected money for food and cigarettes for the Bulgarian prisoners of war, jailed in the citadel of the city of Corte on the island Corsica.

Incited by Serbia and Greece, the French press raged with inventions against Bulgaria, making her the only culprit of all the troubles of the Great War in order to set public opinion against her. In response, the Bulgarians prepared the documents about the events of the Balkan Wars, about the Greek soldiers' letters with a report on the fulfillment of the order of their King Constantine to gouge out eyes of the Bulgarians, of their dismember them and burn alive, which the Serbs did the same.

At the meantime, Sakarov, Ganev and Stamboliysky were amazed, when they got acquainted with the secret archive of the Ministry of Foreign Affairs, which Mikhail Sarafov provided them about how the former Prime Minister Radoslavov refused all the proposals of the Entente from July 1914 to September 1915 to remain neutral or fight against Turkey. The Entente offered Bulgaria a border with Turkey along Media-Enos, Kavala with the inland territories and the undisputed zone of Macedonia. Radoslavov and Ferdinand refused all this and dragged Bulgaria into the war against Entente. Everybody came to the conclusion that these documents were the basis to judge Radoslavov for betrayal and treason and immediately made an appeal to the conference about the decision of the new leaders of Bulgaria to bring to justice the members of Radoslavov government including him himself.

At that moment a telegram arrived from Sofia about the results of the elections to the People's Assembly of Bulgaria: Alexander Stamboliysky and the Agrarian Union, headed by him, won. As the leader of the winning party, Alexander Stamboliysky received the Premier's power and began forming the cabinet.

Meanwhile, the Serbs set fire to the bridge over the railway station in Vranje and blamed the Bulgarians, demanding the speedy transfer of the Bulgarian lands to them. Meanwhile, Gueshov left for London, but Lloyd George refused to accept him. Kosta Todorov, a French captain, wrote articles for the French newspapers in defense of Bulgaria. The delegates asked at least to hold a plebiscite in the lands that their neighbors-enemies had swung at, but Serbia, Greece and Rumania prevented this, stating that even without a plebiscite it was clear that there were no Bulgarians in these lands, but only solid Serbs, Greeks and Romanians. And Rumania put up armed guards in Northern and Southern Dobrujia, already considering it their own. Darkness was looming over Bulgaria, bringing denouement closer.

14 points of the idealist Wilson, in which he had formulated the principles of a just world: the right of nations to self-determination, the division of lands on the ethnic principle—the conference did not take into action and formulated its draft treaty, which it handed over to the Bulgarian delegation on Friday, September 19, 1919 at 10.30 am at the Ministry of Foreign Affairs. France, which most of all hated Bulgaria for the Thessaloniki Front, brought down her guillotine on her and cut off 1/10 of her territory of 11 thousand square km and handed it over to Serbia, Greece and Romania. The Bulgarian lands, inhabited by the Bulgarians, were transferred to the neighbor-enemies—Strumnitsa, Bosilegrad, Tsaribrod and the Kula region—to KSHS; Western Thrace was torn away from Bulgaria under the jurisdiction of the Entente, and the entire Dobrujia, the granary of Bulgaria, was transferred to Romania. Bulgaria had no longer the access to the Aegean Sea: the White Sea Thrace, as the Bulgarians called it, was no longer their land.

Having learned about the decision of the conference, in order not to be tortured and exterminated by the new owners, the streams of refugees abandoned their homes and lands and began to flow to Bulgaria, as during the Balkan Wars. Bulgaria had to pay the winners 2,250 million gold francs over 37 years, that is a quarter of her pre-war national income, and supply Greece, Romania and KSHS with thousands of cattle, tons of coal and everything else that was possible. Bulgaria was forbidden to have aviation, conscript army, and she had to hand over her weapons to the military commission of Entente.

The delegation received a draft treaty in which they had not right to change anything, and in a desperate attempt to improve the situation Theodor Theodorov made his last speech, calling for plebiscite.

"The legal borders of Bulgaria have been established in the most solid way by history, ethnography and international acts. But as soon as they are disputed, let the relevant sections of the population be called upon to speak out for themselves about their future. We'll bow before their vote without reproach and without a grief…"

Having received deathly silence in response, next day, September 20, the delegation left for Sofia to bring to the attention of the People's Assembly the contents of the agreement, which they were given 25 days to familiarize themselves with. On October 6, Theodorov resigned from the post of prime minister, and Alexander Stamboliysky became a leader of the country. There were 2 people who remained in the "Madrid Castle": Ganev and Sarafov.

In Sofia the People's Assembly found it necessary to sign the treaty, as not signing meant the continuation of the war and ultimate occupation of Bulgaria. On October 13, Sarafov in a letter to Clemenceau announced that the delegation would sign the agreement.

On November 19, Alexander Stamboliysky returned back to Neuilly with a new composition of the delegation. He had brought with him 2 letters of appeal with plea of prudence: 1 letter was to the Chairman of the Conference, and the other one was to the neighbors: KSHS, Greece and Romania. He urged them to come to their senses and retreat, not to seize the Bulgarian lands, but to establish a lasting peace at the Balkans. He explained to them that the old government of Bulgaria had been condemned, and the new one, which he headed, would continue to lead the country along the path of peace and friendship with the Entente. He offered them Bulgaria as a friendly partner.

The letters, handed over to Colonel Henri to the neighbors, the latter returned back and ordered to send by post, since the conference could not be an intermediary.

It was November 27, 1919. On November 27, 1919, at 10.30 am Alexander Stamboliysky together with the plenipotentiary delegates got into the cars and, accompanied by Colonel Henri and French officers, went to the City Hall of Neuilly-sur-Seine. They were escorted to the Great Hall of the Municipality, where plenipotentiary delegates from the Entente countries gathered. Clemenceau made a speech about the coming peace and solemnly said:

"I ask the head of the delegation of the Kingdom of Bulgaria to the table to sign a peace treaty."

Full of dignity, Stamboliysky approached the table, sat down in the armchair and put his signature. Those present gloatingly were peering over his shoulder and closely followed the movement of his hand. The military gave him military honors. By signing the treaty, he drew a line under the old: a new stage in the history of Bulgaria began. He wrote to Raiko Daskalov:

"Some kind of painful jet passed through my soul, because I put my signature under the result of the other people policy, which I fought against and because of which I suffered. I said to myself at that moment: 'What vicissitudes fate can bring to a person! Did I ever think that I would stay alive, that I would get out of prison and with my own hands I, the most implacable opponent of Ferdinand and Radoslavov, would reap its fruits?' But at that moment some kind of bright ray illumined my soul and made it so that I with complete calmness and firmness put my signature under the terrible peace treaty. This light ray arose from my deep faith in the triumph of truth and justice!"

The delegates left the City Hall as free people, now they were allowed to receive journalists, give interviews and freely walk around the city. In an interview with journalists Alexander Stamboliysky said that he would dismantle the old regime in Bulgaria within 3 years. On November 29, in the evening the Bulgarian delegation, headed by Alexander Stamboliysky, left for Sofia. At the station of Lyon Colonel Henri, Commandant Gozman, Mr. Jackoli, Lord Hay, Mr. Poiset from the Prefecture, who had become accustomed and made friends with them, came to say goodbye to them, and Captain Lanresh accompanied them all the way on the train. Thus, the Great War ended. The Treaty of Versailles and its integral part the Treaty of Neuilly-sur-Seine summed up the results of the war. It laid a mine under a fragile peace and filled many souls with anger and the thirst of vengeance. The Great War engendered a lost generation.

Chapter 16
Easter 1920

It was the end of April of 1920. The yet cold night air was filled with all the aroma of awaking nature. Bright stars and the moon in the sky pierced the blackness of the southern night, illuminating the path for the walkers. Todor and Ivan Ignatov were returning from another party, which young people often arranged at home. They were walking home and chattered merrily along the way. Ivan Ignatov was Todor's closest friend and was his distant relative. He looked like a hajduk, a hero of ancient legends: tall, broad-shouldered and mighty young man with a lush mop of dark hair, beautifully framing his high forehead. Big clear eyes betrayed in him a simple-hearted, kind person, and he was infinitely devoted to his friend Todor Todorov. 2 handsome young men were walking along the vicinity road from the south-western side of the village and chattered merrily, recalling the party.

"Stop, Todor, look, somebody is coming," Ivan Ignatov said, pointing to his friend with his hand on 2 male figures, coming towards them in the direction from the village.

Those 2 also stopped, peering into the darkness, then resolutely continued their way and stopped again, having approached Todor and Ivan at a close distance. One was about 25 years old, very thin, unkempt, unattractive with blond hair. Another one was of very small stature with long blond hair, from a distance he could be taken for a girl if he puts on a woman's dress. Todor and Ivan immediately recognized them: they were the Armanov-Ganev brothers, armed with rifles and daggers. Next to the brothers 2 donkeys dutifully trudged along, each of them was loaded with 2 sacks, crammed to the top. Mityu, small in stature, raised a rifle and aimed it at unarmed Todor. Ivan Ignatov became numb. Todor recognized the rifles: they were some of those that he and Vidyu had stolen from his cellar and taken to the Vidyu's cellar.

"Immediately, put your gun down!" the older brother Petyu commanded. But Mityu continued to aim.

"Yes, put down the gun, Mityu, your brother rightly says," Todor said calmly, looking into his eyes, "put your gun down and come close to me. Let's see who wins."

Mityu grunted discontentedly and lowered his gun, but he did not dare to approach Todor, knowing that the latter didn't have equal in fight.

"Get out of the way!" he commanded angrily.

"What, are we hindering you, won't you get here with your donkeys with balls?" Todor asked mockingly. "And what are you dragging in the bags from our village?"

"Let's go, Todor, it's too late already, I want to sleep," Ivan Ignatov pulled him by the hand.

"Stay away from our village!" Todor told the Armanov brothers.

"Exactly in your village there are wealthy people, by the way, all your relatives are, Todor."

"It is my relatives who support both of you," Todor reminded them, "if not my relatives, your brother and you would no longer exist, you would die from hunger. My brother Vidyu constantly feeds you both."

"It's true, Mityu," Petyu said, "we must be grateful, because Todor is Vidyu's cousin and he would not like that we quarrel."

At the thought of Vidyu's food, which they systematically received in his house, Mityu and Petyu felt their mouths watering, and the Armanov brothers wished to be in Vidyu's house immediately.

"Ok, let's go."

Todor and Ivan continued their way home, and the travelers parted ways.

"No doubt, they've robbed somebody!" Ivan Ignatov burst into laughing.

They went home and fell asleep soundly after a fun night.

The main road to Bodrovo opened the entrance to the village from the north-west, it went parallel to the Kayaliyka River, turned into the village and crossed its entire territory to the east. Along the main road there was St, Georgy church with the building of kmet's office in the courtyard and a school; Todor's house also overlooked the main road. The villagers liked to come out here to gossip, spread rumors, discuss current affairs, especially when something extraordinary happened.

In the evening of the holy Monday of the Holy Week before Easter, the villagers were flocking on the main road of the main street and vividly discussed the night incident in the village.

"Last night they have robbed the shop of the Ignatov brothers. Have you heard?"

"No way, we got the hajduks-robbers here."

"It looks like they are new comers."

"Or, maybe one of ours?"

"No, ours can't."

"Here, Ivan Todorov is coming, our former kmet; he was a good kmet, human, fair, did not give us to be plundered by the Germans during the war! How did it happen that we have another kmet?"

"We don't know."

Ivan Todorov approached the neighbors to inquire what had happened. On hearing the news of the night robbery of the shop, he exchanged a few words with the people and returned home. Todor got up, had breakfast and prepared to go to the field. The house was getting ready for the Easter.

"Son, at night they've robbed the shop of the Ignatov brothers, the father and uncle of your friend Ivan. Don't you know anything about it?"

"I don't know, father," Todor answered, remembering the night party and the meeting.

"After all, you returned from the party late at night, maybe you saw someone or heard anything?"

"I don't know, father, we were at our gatherings at uncle Kolyu Kolev, then we returned home with Ivan late, we did not hear anything."

At that moment there was a loud knock on the gates of the house, and the assistant of the new kmet entered; he demanded Todor.

"Get ready, Todor, kmet calls you."

Ivan Todorov got excited.

"Why do you want my son?"

"Kmet calls all the boys, a robbery was committed last night. He wants to talk to everyone."

"Don't worry, father, I'll be back soon," Todor said, putting on new shoes and cervulis.

They came out of the gates, turned left, crossed the road and approached St. George Church, in the courtyard of which there was a 2-story building of the kmet's office. Young people from all over the village gathered there. Kmet called them one by one to his office and inquired about the night robbery. Nobody knew anything. The turn came to Ivan Ignatov, Todor and their friend Panyu Kiryakov. The telephone rang in the kmet's office.

"Send these three to the Borisovograd police."

Todor, Ivan Ignatov and Panyu were put in a cart drawn by oxen and sent to Borisovograd, accompanied by the kmet's assistant. The city was named after Boris III, the son of the escaped tsar Ferdinand, who was born on January 20, 1894. The former Ottoman name of the city was Hadji Yeles with several variations later; a small settlement that stood on the Thracian land at the crossroad on the right bank of the Maritsa River. The cart with the detainees entered Borisovograd from the south-east along the road from Bodrovo and headed to the city center. The 2-story police building was situated at the central square, which had a shape of a rectangle with a park in the center and the buildings of the Community and the Cyril and Methodius library on its sides.

The detainees were pushed into the police building. The gloomy tattered inside building and the vicious mugs of the policemen did not bode well. Ivan Ignatov and Panyu were locked in a cell, and Todor was pushed into the interrogation room. 2 policemen grinned evilly. 2 more entered: the head of the police Enyu Gogov and Ivan Todorov Guenov, nicknamed Kamine, a bailiff. Gogov was short, stout, unkempt, with a round, greasy physiognomy, on which a nasty moustache hang below the chin; he was from the neighboring Debar. So, unable to become a kmet of Bodrovo, Ivan Todorov's best friend became a bailiff in Borisovograd. He was the first to strike Todor in the face with his fist with all the strength of the best friend.

"Confess, the bitch bastard, was it you who robbed the shop of the Ignatov brothers last night?"

Kamine nodded to 2 policemen, standing nearby. They threw Todor with his hands tied to the floor and started kicking him. Enyu Gogov, the chief of the police station, bared his teeth of satisfaction. Todor was looking at Kamine's face with contempt, remembering how many times he came to their house for birthday party, name day, Christmas, etc., how many times Todor's father Ivan received him in their house as a dear friend and the best guest, treated him to food and drink and showed him cordial hospitality. And Kamine, remembering his friendship with Todor's father, joined the 2 policemen and kicked Todor, lying out on the floor in blood.

"Speak, confess, your bastard, was it you who robbed the Ignatov's shop? We'll beat you until you confess!"

He and the policemen struck blows all over Todor's body and his swollen bloodied face, reveling in pleasure.

"Look at you, what a handsome boy turned up! So, the most handsome, like they say, has come into being?" Kamine snarled angrily through his teeth, striking, remembering how ugly and insignificant his own son was. "I'll rot you in prison if you don't die!"

"You are a thief and a robber! It is you who robbed the shop! Confess! You will be in jail for life!"

Blows and pain drowned out Todor's consciousness, filling him with anger and a thirst for revenge. He lost the sense of time, which seemed to stretch on forever. He did not remember how the day ended and it began to get dark, he could hardly hear the words of the policemen through the noise.

"Ok, we are tired, we need to rest, there are two more his friends."

They dragged Todor along the floor downstairs, leaving a bloody trace, and threw him into a cage.

"Hey, you the villain, is it you who robbed the Ignatovs' shop?" the policemen, tired from beating Todor, turned to Ivan Ignatov.

"But it is me myself who is Ignatov!" Ivan was naively surprised at such an absurd accusation. "This is my shop! It belongs to my father and his brother!"

"So you've robbed yourself!" not at all embarrassed by the Ivan's logic, Ivan Kamine declared and the first stroke at the mighty body of Todor's friend.

The Holy Week of the torture of 3 young men had crossed the middle. It was Thursday. They were bitten 4 days in a row. The villagers were preparing for the Easter feast of 1920. All the houses, clean and decorated, emitted the aroma of baked kalachi-cakes, solemnly standing on plates with the rainbow-colored eggs around the edges. Sadness and depression reigned in Todor's house, despite the expectation of replenishment in the family: Ivan Todorov's wife, Todor's mother Atanasa was in the ninth month of her pregnancy and was about to give birth. Kolyu Kolev, Ivan Todorov's second cousin, entered the house, and Ivan pleadingly addressed him:

"Kolyu, help! After all, the Borisovograd police chief is your friend. Go there and ask what happened to Todor! 4 days have passed, and there is no news from him. They took 3 of them with Ivan Ignatov and Panyu Kiryakov yet on Monday, and it is Thursday today already. Tell the police that the boys were at your house at gatherings almost the whole night, they could not rob the shop! And what about Ivan Ignatov? Has he robbed himself, robbed his father's shop, which is his by inheritance?"

"Don't worry, Ivan, I'll go right away, I'll tell them everything," Kolyu answered and hurried on a cart drawn by oxen to Borisovograd.

At the end of the same day Todor returned home, beaten, dirty, tattered, humiliated; everything turned upside down in his mind. With tears his family rushed to hug him, horrified by his appearance.

"Son, how could it happen?"

"This is all your 'best friend' Kamine, father!" Todor replied bitterly.

"How so! Were all 3 of you released?"

"No, just me."

The next day, Friday morning, Todor went to work in the fields, inhaling the aroma of green fields and admiring the beauty, which he loved more than anything in the world, and nature could heal his wounds. On Good Friday people remembered the Passion of Christ, and in the torture chamber of Borisovograd police the unfortunate Ivan Ignatov began to be beaten even harder than in the past 4 days.

"Confess, robber, confess that it is you and your friend Todor, robbers and hajduks, who committed a robbery! Confess that Todor robbed the shop together with you!" gloating Kamine inquired, peering into Ivan's bloody face. "Just say 'yes', and we'll stop beating you!"

"Yes," Ivan Ignatov, half-dead wheezed.

"Yes! We'll put it down on the record!" the executioners triumphed. "So, let's write it down exactly so! And now confess, where did you hide the loot: in Bodrovo, in Debar, in Ezerovo?" Kamine gave a sign to the policemen, and they struck with their feet on Ivan's swollen body, helplessly lying on the floor.

Through the bloody veil that covered his eyes he could barely distinguish their physiognomies.

"No, you hajduks-robbers, hid the loot in Aidanlar in the house of Todor's relatives! This place is secluded and next to the dense forest is the most convenient place to hide the good! Speak, robber, is it in Aidanlar you hid the loot?"

"Yes," Ivan Ignatov wheezed, who no longer cared.

"Let's record it in the protocol!" the executioners, led by Kamine, rejoiced and telegraphed to the kmet in Bodrovo:

"Detain Todor Todorov. Ivan Ignatov confessed the robbery."

Next morning Ivan Ignatov, tied up, was mounted on a horse and another policeman on another horse escorted him to the house of Vidyu and his father in Aidanlar. Vidyu was not in. Together with his older brother Todor and their father Gocho he went to work in the fields. The mother and Vidyu's wife were in the house. They greeted the unexpected guests with outward calm. Bloody, swollen, barely standing Ivan Ignatov and armed policeman entered the house.

"I have an order to search your house," the policeman said.

"Search," the women replied coolly.

The policeman, inhaling the aroma of the baked kalachi-cakes, staring with envy at the furnishing of the 2-story house, slowly went around room after room, finding nothing.

"Where did you hide the loot?" he turned back to Ivan Ignatov, but the later had gone.

In horror, the policeman started to run to the exit, sending threats to the hostess of the house.

"I'll show you! You will answer me for the abetting the robbery!"

Angry policeman ran out into the yard: neither Ivan nor the horse were there. He jumped on his horse and rode into the dense forest, which was contiguous to the Karagochev's house. After having driven a couple of meters, he slowed down and, looking around in fear, slowly drove along the path, leading the forest. The Aidanlar forest ended, and he set off a gallop across an open countryside, bypassing the hills, towards Bodrovo. On the top of the Sirka rock, above the cave of Angel Voevoda the Armanov brothers were vigilantly watching him. Mityu Ganev pointed a rifle at the policeman and took aim.

"Leave it, let him go, today is Easter," his more peaceful older brother Petyu Ganev-Armanov said and pushed the rifle away.

Mityu lowered the rifle and grinned. The policeman safely galloped past Sirka and drove into Bodrovo at noon. Gasping, he came into the office of the kmet Niko Enchev.

"Mr. Kmet, Ivan Ignatov confessed that Todor Todorov together with him robbed the shop of the Ignatov brothers. The order of the Borisovograd police station chief is Todor Todorov to be arrested and convoyed to Borisovograd."

"It's Easter now, fear god, postpone the arrest for 3 days!" the kmet answered irritably.

"There is no way I can, I have the order to arrest and deliver, and shoot while trying to escape!"

"I am the boss here! I am the kmet of Bodrovo and won't let you arrest him on Easter! He is from a wealthy, respectable family; his father was the kmet here before me, and he is a hero of the Balkan Wars! Have a Christian conscience and humanity! And if Ivan Ignatov confessed from your beating, this does not mean that they are actually guilty!"

"Then I place responsibility on you!" the policeman answered and hurried away.

"That's the story!" discouraged kmet said, his festive mood was spoiled. "All the same it is necessary to detain Todor and place him to my office," he decided and sent field watchmen to bring Todor.

"He is out, he has gone to the field, he'll be back soon," Todor's father Ivan answered.

The watchmen sat down on a bench near the kmet's building to wait for Todor. After some time they saw him on a cart drawn by 2 oxen entered the village along the main road. Todor had chopped a full cart of firewood and drove it home. Having approached the kmet's building, he stopped, looking with contempt at the 2 watchmen.

"Get off the cart, the order from Borisovograd is to arrest you," they said.

"They let me go on Thursday," Todor said angrily.

"Todor, come to me, we'll talk," Niko Enchev said, coming out of the building onto the road.

Todor, hating his sad fate, got down from the cart and came to the kmet.

"Take the oxen to his yard, it's close, across the street, and tell his relatives to hand over a bag with food and a blanket," kmet ordered 2 watchmen and led Todor to his office.

He told Todor in detail about the policeman visit, about the new order to arrest him, about the confession of Ivan Ignatov and his escape. Todor, frowning, listened to the kmet, not understanding what was happening to him. He was born and raised in a wealthy family of ancient lineage, graduated from school, from childhood worked in the vast fields, belonging to the family, almost himself carried the entire household on his shoulders since his father left to fight in the Balkan Wars, went to study to the shoemaker in Chirpan at his father's will, where he was robbed and was tried to be killed; he fell in love with a girl, who died from the disease brought by the war, and now misfortune had fallen on him without his fault: lawlessness was being committed in the name of the law! "What is it: damn fate, and what the hell does she want, or a matter of chance, but still, why?"

"Tell me, Todor, are you guilty?" Niko Enchev asked.

"Of course not! I did not steal anything, I don't need anything from Ivan's shop, we are not poor, and Ivan Ignatov did not steal anything from his own shop! This is all Ivan Todorov Guenov, nickname Kamine, my father's 'friend', who hates him because it was my father, not him, who was elected the kmet after the Balkan Wars, and he decided to take revenge on him by destroying his son, that is me."

"I've heard about it, there are rumors, people talk. Let us do it this way, I have to detain you, but I'll not give you to them during 3 days of feast, you will stay here in the same room with a Russian white emigrant, and then, maybe, justice will be restored during these 3 days."

Todor agreed, thinking it over a further plan of action. Kmet took him to the next room, where there were 2 beds, a table and 2 bedside tables, and a white emigrant from Russia Maxim temporary lived, who was thrown from Russia to a Bulgarian village on the hills at the Rhodopes by the storm of the revolution and vicissitudes of fate. Maxim friendly met Todor and told him his story, lamenting the hard lot of a stranger in a foreign country, where he was forced to work in the other people fields for a piece of bread, and tired, fell asleep soundly by midnight. Todor was thinking what to do next. He saw that "the triumph of justice" was not expected, that the big power was far away in Sofia, and here the scoundrels did lunching, and if he falls into their hands again, they would kill him.

Todor made a decision to run away. He looked at the unfortunate Russian emigrant, soundly sleeping, and came to the window. The 2-story building of the Bodrovo Municipality was located on the territory of the St. George courtyard on the main road of the village, coming from north-west. There were no bars on the window. Todor looked out of the window. A solemn service was going on in the church, crammed with people, people huddled in the courtyard to meet "resurrection of Christ", to whom they prayed, hoping that he would, allegedly, resurrect them too for eternal life and at the same time deliver them from all their troubles.

Todor patiently was waiting for the service to end and the people to disperse. Finally, everything was quit. He easily opened the window, jumped out into the courtyard of the church and quickly vanished in the darkness of the May night. He made his way through the gardens and orchards, passing his house, in the direction of the south-east, leading to Aidanlar. He cursed his fate, which made him run away past his native house, where the comfort and prosperity awaited him, and go towards the unknown. He was making his way at night, passing the fields and hills along the paths, familiar from childhood, where he walked, admiring nature, where in the field he pastured his herds in freedom. Now he felt that his freedom was threatened and they were trying to take it away from him. But, born with a free spirit, he will not give up his freedom! He made his way through the dense Aidanlar forest and approached the court of his uncle Gocho and his son Vidyu, Todor's cousin. It was already dawned.

Todor knocked on the gates and went inside. Vidyu led him into the house to the kitchen, where preparations for the feast were in full swing. Cauldrons with sheep and mutton meat were boiling on the fire, and cauldrons with cooked food that emitted intoxicating odors that could not be resisted, were standing on the floor. Ivan Ignatov was sitting on a bench in the corner, peeling potatoes.

"There he is! Todor has come!" he said cheerfully, trying to smile at his bruised and swollen face from beatings.

Todor looked at his friend and took pity on him. They hugged tightly and told each other what had happened.

"I escaped."

"So did I."

"Well, what are we going to do now?" Ivan asked.

"I don't know, but we'll not give up the Armanovs."

"Maybe we'll go to Sofia and complain about the butchers?"

"I don't know, maybe."

Sunday has come. The villagers had fun and celebrated the "resurrection of Christ." Two families in Bodrovo—Ignat Mitev and Ivan Todorov—were heart broken. They were tormented by uncertainty and suffered from emotional pain, worrying about their sons. This was how Easter 1920 passed.

Chapter 17
Aidanlar

In a week after Easter 1920, Ivan Todorov's fourth child was born: the youngest daughter, who was named Mitra. And 3 days after her birth, 15 mounted policemen, armed to the teeth, from Borisovograd, led by Ivan Guenov-Kamine, raided Bodrovo. They dismounted by at the gates of Ivan Todorov's yard and began to clatter on the gates loudly, so that all the neighbors of the village could hear. There appeared to be many, who wanted to stare at the persecution of their former kmet, and they immediately came in flocks by Ivan's gates, whose house was located on the main road of the village, peering with curiosity into the yard. Ivan Todorov opened the gate, he had not experienced such emotions since the time of the Balkan Wars. The adversary was standing on the threshold of his house.

"You have been detained, Mr. Todorov, by order of the Borisovograd police department chief!" caustically grinning, Guenov-Kamine gave full value to each word.

"Where is a written confirmation of this?" Ivan asked anxiously.

"Escort the detainee to the kmet's building!" Guenov-Kamine turned the policemen. "There is a written confirmation there."

Ivan's oldest daughter, 15-year-old Maria, and 11-year-old Gocho, who were standing nearby, clutched at the hands of their father, not allowing him to go anywhere, and his wife Atanasa, who had not recovered yet after giving birth, was lying in bed next to the cradle, in which her 3-day-old baby was peacefully sleeping.

"I'll be back soon, don't be afraid, children, protect your mother!" Ivan addressed his son and daughter, freeing his hands from them. "We have laws, the Constitution and the new government in Sofia."

Guenov-Kamine grinned derisively, meaning that neither laws nor Constitution had ever worked before, why then they would start working now under the new government! The policemen pushed Ivan forward and convoyed him to the kmet's building, which was located nearby across the road. The rest of the policemen rushed into the yard and into the house, peering in all corners, repeating one question:

"Where is Todor?"

The frighten children and their mother Atanasa, distraught from stun, answered:

"We don't know. He is not in the house."

Here Ivan came into the house and rushed to calm his wife. The baby woke up from the noise and cried.

"What are you doing?" Ivan turned to the policemen with anger. "The kmet let me go and confirmed that there is no written order to arrest me!"

"No problem, if there is no, then it will be!" Guenov-Kamine said brazenly, with hatred looking into the eyes of his best friend.

He walked like the owner from one room to another of the 2-storied house, "looking for Todor, the robber," recalling how Ivan cordially accepted him and treated him with delicious food. He hated this table, where he ate and drank for many years at all the feasts, birthdays, name days, christening, New Year parties and Easter in addition. Only at the past Easter he had not been here. He hated this house, where there was comfort and prosperity, as he lived differently. He hated Todor, because his son was ugly and negligible; he hated his friend Ivan for kindness and generosity, as he himself was evil and base; he hated Ivan for that piece of bread that he gave to the wounded Turk in Adrianople, to whom he returned to kill. He hated Ivan, because he was elected kmet during the Great War and he saved him front the front, and returned him home, because if he himself had been kmet, he would not had gone to the war at all, as kmet Ivan had been dismissed from the war. He hated Ivan for so long time he had to pretend to be his friend and lie, and only now the time has come to remove the mask and take revenge. What kind of the "sworn-brother" are you for me? You are my sworn foe, and I'll destroy you!

The policemen, having failed to find Todor, pulled out food supplies from the cellar—cheese, milk, meat, eggs, feta-cheese, kulichi-cakes—and sat down at the table to feast. Having stuffed his belly, Guenov-Kamine announced: "You, Ivan Todorov, and all of you, are given 3 days to give up Todor. If you fail to find him during 3 days, you'll be interned from Bodrovo, your house will be sealed, and your fields will go to state ownership."

"There is no such a law!" Ivan exclaimed angrily.

"It does not matter! I am the law here!" Kamine answered brazenly.

3 days passed. For 3 days the policemen, led by the bailiff Kamine, robbed Ivan's house, raking out food supplies from his cellar, and 15 people guzzled for breakfast, lunch and dinner and also fed their 15 horses. After 3 days 15 policemen with Kamine at the head surrounded the house of Ivan Todorov, around which all the villagers of Bodrovo flocked, and poking with their rifles butts, forced Ivan to harness the cart with 2 oxen and load there only most necessary things for the road. Not believing what was happening, Ivan put some things in the cart, thinking about how to bring the scoundrels to justice for lynching.

"That's it, that's enough for you!" Kamine commanded and ordered everyone to get into the cart.

Nobody moved.

"Do you want us to force you to get in the cart?" Guenov-Kamine said menacingly through his teeth and moved toward Gocho with Maria.

They roared with all their might.

"Get in! Is it you who generated the hajduk-robber? Get into the cart!" the policemen hissed and moved toward Atanasa, who was holding a 6-day-old baby in her arms.

She screamed with all her might and rushed to run with the baby back into the house, but the policemen blocked her path. Ivan regretted that he had shown weakness, succumbed to threats and harnessed the cart.

"We are not going anywhere!" he said decisively.

The children roared, the wife screamed, the new-born baby cried, and the villagers, who had gathered around, stared. At that moment the kmet ran up to the Ivan's house, out of breath whizzing with difficulty catching his breath from running, and shouted:

"Stop the outrage! This is my village, and I am the power here, and I shall not allow you to committee the lawlessness! There is no such a law! This is called arbitrariness, and you will answer for this lawlessness! I shall immediately inform Sofia about the violation of the law by the Borisovograd police! I shall complain to the head of the government Stamboliysky!"

On hearing the words of the kmet, Guenov-Kamine immediately retreated and lowered his tone, cowardly backing away.

"Ok, ok, we are just doing our job, doing our duty, why to go straight to Sofia to Stamboliysky!"

"The lawlessness that you committee, hiding behind the law, has nothing to do with the law and duty!" the kmet said menacingly and turned to Ivan. "Unharness the cart, Ivan!"

Kmet came close to sobbing Atanasa, who was holding the child in her arms, surrounded by the policemen, and began to calm her down and shame the policemen. At that moment annoyed Kamine said through his teeth to Ivan, who was unloading the cart:

"I give you a week. Find your son and hand him over to the police, otherwise no one will save you next time! Yes, give me 1000 leva to compensate for the theft from the Ignatov brothers."

"You won't get anything: neither my son, nor a lev, you swindler!" Ivan answered, unharnessing the oxen.

He remembered the Balkan Wars, in which he participated. If here in peaceful time, during the ruling of the Agrarian Union of Stamboliysky, a peasant leader, who recently came to power, doing everything possible for the good of the peasantry, local villains, spitting on the law, committee lawlessness, then what the adversary did to each other on the occupied territory then, during the time of the wars! Thousands of refugees, deprived of their homes and land, exhausted, flew in an endless stream in search of a new shelter. And now, after the Great War, there were again refugees from the territory, cut off by the Entente. He was happy with one thing: a complete break with his best sworn-friend, namesake Ivan Todorov Guenov-Kamine. Ivan thanked the kmet Niko Enchev for his support and waiting after the mounted policemen, led by the bailiff, disappeared from the sight on the main road, headed in the opposite direction to the south-east to Aidanlar. He walked on foot, looking back to see if no one was watching him, and furtively hiding from one bush to another, secretly making his way to his older brother Gocho, in whose house, he knew for sure, he would find support. Ivan left Bodrovo, behind which green expanses, meadows, stretched, where the neighbors grazed their cattle and sowed fields. In the distance his own land was visible, waiting for care. The spring air intoxicated with aroma of awakened nature, the sun was shining brightly, the leaves on the trees and bushes were green, and his head turned white, covered with grey hair from the hardships fallen on him.

Aidanlar was in 6 km from Bodrovo, which took him an hour and a half. He passed to the Aidanlar forest and approached the house of Gocho, his older brother. Kind and generous, brave and freedom-loving Gocho, like him, a descendant of their hajduks ancestors, who bravely fought against the Turks, he always gave shelter to the persecuted. And Ivan knew for sure that his son Todor, persecuted by the executioners, would definitely be here. He knocked, and Gocho's wife opened the gate. All the men were at work in the field. Ivan came inside the house, he was hospitably fed, and time slowly dragged on in anticipation. Ivan's heart was rent asunder, he did not know what to do, where to find justice against the executioners, he felt sorry for his son, thought about his new-born daughter, he worried about the abandoned farm. The day came to an end, it began to get dark, soon the gates opened, and Gocho with Vidyu came in. At the same moment Todor and Ivan Ignatov slipped into the house with lightning speed and noiselessly.

"Son," Ivan shed tears and pressed Todor to his chest, "hello to you too, Ivan."

"Hello, Bay Ivan."

"Thank you too, brother Gocho, that you did not leave our fugitives, but sheltered and fed them."

"How not to shelter, how not to feed, brother Ivan!" Gocho answered and hugged Ivan, whom he had not seen for a long time. "So, we have met, otherwise it was work, affairs, there was no time to see each other, and it is trouble that brought us together."

"A terrible trouble, this is a question of the young men life. Today they tried to expel us from our own house together with the new-born child, so to say, to intern us, but kmet Niko Enchev interceded. Guenov-Kamine said that if you don't give up in a week, he would certainly intern us."

"Why do you listen to him, brother! There is no war now, and you are not to blame for anything! Now the Agrarian Union and Stamboliysky are at power! Can't we find protection for arbitrariness!"

"Oh, how would we find protection! Stamboliysky is far away in Sofia, and we are here," Ivan Todorov sighed.

"So, what shall we do?"

"I'll not surrender to executioners and murderers, I want to live, my life just begins!" Todor said angrily.

"I'll not surrender, if I surrender, they'll kill us," Ivan Ignatov confirmed.

"Do not give up!" Gocho and Vidyu supported them.

"Tell me, son, are you really not guilty?" Ivan Todorov asked. "And you, Ivan?"

"I am not guilty, father, I did not rob my friend Ivan Ignatov shop, I am not a beggar, and Ivan Ignatov did not steal from himself."

"Yes, I did not rob my own shop, my father's shop!" Ivan Ignatov laughed.

"And don't you know who robbed?"

"No, we don't know," Todor hastily answered.

"All of you, come to the table!" Vidyu's wife called the men, and everyone with appetite pounced on the abundance of food in Gocho's house.

They discussed after midnight whether or not to surrender, but they did not come to any decision.

"We need to apply to the higher authority, up to Stamboliysky," Todor said, "we'll not surrender to the Borisovograd murderers and to your friend Guenov-Kamine. Maybe we'll appear at the higher instance, let them investigate and find out who robbed this shop. We must start from Haskovo."

So they decided. It was a deep night. Everyone exhausted fell asleep. When Ivan Todorov woke up in the morning, there were no fugitives in the house, they had already disappeared into the thick of Aidanlar forest. Ivan took a donkey from his brother Gocho, sat on him and slowly went to Haskovo to seek the justice.

Chapter 18
Haskovo Prosecutor

The faithful donkey dutifully stamped his legs, carrying Ivan Todorov on his back, moving south-west from Aidanlar to Haskovo. Peasants worked everywhere, they sowed the fields and the shepherds grazed their cattle in the meadows. The bright sun illuminated the rural idyll, which he wanted to return to his house. In the middle of the way they passed the ancient Klokotnitsa, where in 1230 Ivan Asen II defeated Theodor Komnenos Duk, having turned the II Bulgarian Kingdom into the ruler of the Balkans, subjugated the entire territory from Ohrid to Adrianople and Thessaloniki, all Thrace and Macedonia. The donkey walked another half way and approached Haskovo. Ivan remembered capture of Adrianople, the Balkan Wars, which never returned the II Bulgarian Kingdom. It seemed to him that the war was never over, the war continued, but now the enemy was secret, hidden under the guise of legality, but he knew that the truth was on his side. He rode on a donkey into the ancient land of Haskovo of 7 thousand years old. Thracian culture flourished here in antiquity, older than the Greek one, which now was buried under the hills of Haskovo and waited for its discoverers. The donkey covered the distance of 17, 5 km in a little over an hour and drove into the central part of the city right to the building of the prosecutor of the district court.

Ivan tied the donkey and came into the office. Prosecutor Vasil Nikolov received Ivan Todorov with the exceptional courtesy. He was a middle-aged man of middle income, who dreamed of more. His small sly eyes darted slyly on his round, double-chinned face, and his figure suffered a little bit from overweight. He saw a lot in his lifetime, he knew better than others how changeable life is, capable to turn everything upside down in an instant. He saw that everything in life is relative. Yesterday's prisoner of the dungeon in the Vidin fortress Alexander Stamboliysky is the Minister-Chairman and the leader of the country today. Yesterday's tsar Ferdinand with unlimited power is a fugitive and criminal today along with yesterday's Prime Minister Radoslavov. And listening to the story of Ivan Todorov from capture of Adrianople and fraternizing with Ivan Guenov, nicknamed Kamine, and misfortunes that fell upon them because of the revenge of a false friend, the prosecutor thought only of one thing: how wealthy was the client before him.

"Can we save the innocent young men?" Ivan asked in pleading voice with his eyes wet with tears.

"Can we save them?" the prosecutor asked thoughtfully in a philosophical way, continuing to think about his own business, and if in a friendly way switching to "you is", reassuringly answered. "Of course we can. We can save them and release, conduct an investigation, confirm their innocence, as they claim. But it all depends upon whether you are able to pay for the whole procedure. This matter is not simple, but difficult, complex and confusing. I shall have to negotiate with higher people, they also do their job. Now I don't know whether you, Ivan, can cover all the legal costs? And, by the way, if you don't have money, then you can sell some fields, as far as I know, you have enough land, haven't you? And there will be buyers."

The prosecutor was talking and played for time without deciding how much to request, fearing not to miscalculate. This made him nervous, and his eyes were darting even faster. And to Ivan's direct question "how much?" he named a random amount: "50 thousand leva". He froze, twitching nervously, waiting for an answer.

"Ok, I'll pay," Ivan answered without haggling.

Not believing his ears and luck, the prosecutor twitched so much that could not sit in his chair, stood up, almost dancing, and began to talk about the complexity of the intricacies of the Ivan's case, but he absolutely assured:

"Not a single hair will fall from their head. Bring both of them and the money. I'll solve the problem."

The prosecutor was so kind that he opened the door for Ivan and escorted him out into the street.

"Don't worry, justice will prevail."

Ivan thanked the prosecutor, sat on his donkey and set off on his way back.

2 weeks have passed. The nature of mid-May blossomed magnificently with every moment, brightly coloring the slopes of the hills and valleys, pleasing the eyes. Ivan Todorov longed for the joy of life, but a heavy burden

crushed his heart. He was sitting on the bank of the pond under a willow next to the youngest son Gocho and, looking at the still water, tried to restore peace of mind. Nearby his horse was grazing in the pasture, and sheep with goats and oxen nibbled grass, drinking cold water. A fast stream flowed down from the foothills of the Rhodopes, forming a flowing pond, and continued its run to the Maritsa valley. There was a small forest next to the pasture. On completing the school year in Bodrovo, Gocho, who was almost 12 years old, tended his cattle as a shepherd, replacing his older brother, to help his parents. Often in a cheerful company with his cousin Georgy, the son of uncle Dimitar, and other children from the village, he had fun in nature, while their animals grazed, and he knew by heart all the lands in the area. While the animals were peacefully grazing on the green meadow, Gocho was sitting on the bank of the pond next to his father, empathizing with him and thought about the fate of his brother.

"It's been 2 weeks since we haven't seen Todor. I am looking for him everywhere and can't find him," the father said.

"They definitely come to visit Vidyu in Aidanlar," Gocho assured, trying to calm his father.

"Probably I missed them, I came to Aidanlar, but they were no longer there. Until they come to the prosecutor and he testifies that the charges against them are dropped, they are in an illegal position," Ivan said bitterly, "Guenov-Kamine can easily shoot them somewhere."

Here Gocho turned back to see how the animals were grazing and saw 2 horsemen, riding out of the forest.

"Father, look!" he took Ivan by the hand and pointed toward the forest.

2 young men were driving astride horses, which were approaching them with a calm step. Ivan's son Todor and his best friend Ivan Ignatov were dressed as hajduks. On the legs they had new leather cervulis and leather straps, wrapping snow-white onuchis to the knees, into which dark linen trousers were tucked, and a dark shirt, intercepted by a wide belt, on which a revolver in a holster and a dagger in a sheath hung. Bothe had lush black curls, fluttering in the wind and touching their shoulders. A light tan covered their skin. Todor, darker and refined, with delightful features, was definitely handsome; he became matured and had a thoughtful look after the recent events. Ivan Ignatov was larger with broad shoulders, tall as a hero, with bigger features, less swarthy skin, with scarlet blush on his cheeks. He always smiled and joked, and quickly forgot hardships, but he could not stand physical pain only and

easily admitted what he never did, if only not to endure pain in order to escape from the clutches of the executioners to freedom and take revenge on the offenders.

"You are crazy!" Ivan Todorov attacked them. "They are looking for you everywhere to grab and even kill, and I am looking for you everywhere to save. And you are playing the hajduks here. I have made a deal with the prosecutor in Haskovo, I must bring you to him and pay 50 thousand leva, and he will protect you."

Ivan Todorov nearly cried with excitement and joy that he found his son with his friend.

"All right, father, if so, then we shall go with you," Todor answered seriously.

"And I am with you," Ivan Ignatov agreed.

12-year-old Gocho hugged his brother, whom he loved very much and was proud of him and did not want to part with him.

"Stay here, son, look after the animals," Ivan Todorov said, and the 3 riders went to Aidanlar, where they left weapons in the shelter, took 50 thousand leva, hidden by Ivan, and went to Haskovo prosecutor.

The prosecutor, who already lost hope, was incredibly happy, when 3 men entered his office. He was full of pleasantries and assured Ivan that he would settle this difficult matter. Ivan Todorov gave him a bag with 50thousand leva, which he immediately hid in his safe, and escorted Ivan out into the street. Ivan mounted his horse, took 2 horses of Todor and Ivan Ignatov by the bridle and headed to Bodrovo. The prosecutor questioned 2 young men and took them to a special room for detainees and ordered them to wait.

2 weeks have passed. The prosecutor Vasil Nikolov was indecisive and himself waited how the "case" would end, until he saw that in fact there was no "case," because there was no statement of robbery against the accused from the Ignatov brothers. There is only a personal revenge of the bailiff of the Borisovograd police Guenov in a criminal abetting with the police chief Gogov and his policemen. But most of all, the prosecutor Nikolov did not want to share Ivan Todorov's money with anyone else "to settle the case", which did not exist, and without saying anything to anyone, he hid the money away and ordered to leave the door of the detainees open, where Todor with Ivan Ignatov were under his custody, whom someone somehow sometimes fed and watered. On seeing that the door was open and no one held them, Todor with Ivan went

out into the street, got into a cart, drawn by the horses, and coachman took them home to Bodrovo.

On June 3 the inhabitants for the Bodrovo village celebrated the Day of Constantine and Helena. In the south-eastern part of the village in the large meadow under the canopy the villagers set up the tables, on which they arranged on the dishes food, cooked at home, and brought with them to the party. From the very morning people began to gather for the feast. Inhabitants from neighboring villages arrived for the feast in Bodrovo on the carts, pulled by oxen, and brought with them various goods for sale, as well as food for a joint meal. Food was laid out on the tables, and goods for sale were on stalls. Rakia and wine complemented the tables. 6 policemen from Borisovograd, headed by Guenov-Kamine, "guarded order," vigilantly watching everyone who came to the party. One policeman elbowed Guenov-Kamine:

"Look, who's there."

All the policemen and Guenov-Kamine stared at the new guests. A cheta of 6 people, dressed as hajduks, came to the feast: Todor, Ivan Ignatov, Vidyu with his friend Todor Trendofilov, who were joined by the brothers Valko and Peter Buchev. All were armed like hajduks and each had 2 revolvers, hung on a belt with a dagger in a sheaths, and bandoliers full of cartridges across the chest. They boldly entered the glade full of people and joined the feast under the greetings of the present. On seeing them, Guenov-Kamine turned green with anger and went into a furious rage. The second policeman nodded to the third one, and nearly headed toward the young men. Guenov-Kamine stopped them and said:

"Let's go, we'll take them one by one."

Guenov-Kamine and 3 policemen, who beat Todor and Ivan Ignatov at the police station of Borisovograd, retreated and quietly vanished from the feast. The other 2 remaining policemen filled their stomachs with free food and got drunk so that apart food and rakia did not notice anything and no one. Disappearance of 4 policemen relieved tension, and after seeing that they had escaped, the young men relaxed and immersed in the general joy. They ate to their fill of delicious food, displayed on the dishes under the canopy, where a giant catfish, caught from Maritsa River and expertly cooked by Ivan Todorov, flaunted. They ate fried lamb meat, lush lies, drank wine, and it seemed, having forgotten about all the hardships, they started dancing. With graceful body movements handsome Todor took a girl by the hand and led her into a round-dance, which was joined by a hero-bogatir Ivan Ignatov and the others. Holding hands, all the dancing men and women in drunken merriment joyfully performed their favorite dance, familiar from childhood, moved in a circle in a round-dance on the spacious meadow to the sounds of music and the smells of blossoming nature. Local musicians vividly played the bagpipes, moved the bow on the fiddle, struck the doira to delight of the dancers.

"Sing, Todor!" was heard from all sides.

Everyone knew that Todor had a unique voice, and they stopped to rest from dancing, sitting on the grass. A fire was lit nearby. Todor sang a hajduk song, and his voice with beauty and strength echoed over the hills, reaching the Rhodopes, competing with Orpheus. It penetrated the hearts and souls of the audience, filling them with joy and peace, some of women had tears in their eyes. Young and handsome young men, born for love and happiness, having forgotten about hardships, completely surrendered to joy and merged with nature. They still ate and drank, and danced roundelay, until the fire began to die out and the sun leaned toward the hills in the west, ready to hide. The hawkers were putting things into the carts, counting profits, preparing to leave for home. The villagers from Bodrovo cleared the tables and went home. Vidyu with Todor Trendofilov mounted horses and galloped off to Aidanlar, making sure that their friends safely went home. General merriment on the St. Konstantin and Helena Day ended.

Todor soundly fell asleep at his home. Next morning he was already in the field to plow the land with his cousin Georgy, the son of the uncle Dimitar. 2 large plows on wheels, each of which is attached to a harness of 2 oxen, diverged in different directions, harrowing the ground, leaving even furrows for sowing tobacco. George and Todor led the oxen. Wheat was undulation in the neighboring field, almost ripe to harvest. A little further on there was a gentle hill, on top of which anise ripened on their land. The entire family of Todor was there: his father Ivan, mother Atanasa with a baby, sleeping peacefully in a cradle, their older daughter Maria and their youngest son Gocho. They carefully pulled out weeds, clearing the ground for anise. It was time to rest. They broke away from work, had lunch in nature, and Ivan with his son Gocho were standing on the top of the hill and admired the wonderful view. Nearby, on the green velvety bushes of anise snow-white lace of flowers sparkled and emanated a delicate aroma, and below the endless fields and meadows, belonging to the family, stretched, where ripe ears of wheat shimmered with gold; his son Todor and nephew Georgy worked nearby on the field, preparing the land for sewing tobacco. In the distance on the meadow, contiguous to the forest, their herds grazed. The summer sun warmed this fertile land, yielding a generous harvest, created by their peaceful labor. Ivan Todorov enjoyed the beauty of nature, among which he grew up and loved it from childhood. He was glad that he managed to keep the land, received from his father, and increase wealth by buying additional plots to the east and south from Bodrovo. So, the ideal of peaceful labor on their land, returned to their home, giving them everything they needed. He thought bitterly of 50 thousand leva, a huge amount of money, given to a cunning prosecutor, but he was glad, everything was all over and his son was free.

Suddenly he saw in the distance armed policemen, who were racing on horseback along the highway from Borisovograd, approaching the field, where his son Todor was working, and fired from their rifles. On hearing the shooting and seeing the mounted policemen, Todor left the plow, harnessed to the oxen, and rushed to save himself with lightning speed. The magical picture of nature of the fields with meadows, belonging to him, which just admired Ivan Todorov and filled his soul with peace and tranquility, faded before his eyes and, seeing how armed enemies were shooting at his son Todor who fleeing, instantly disappeared from his eyes, Ivan felt acute bitterness in his mouth, lost strength and sank down on the grass. The eldest daughter Maria and his wife Atanasa, on seeing what was happening, burst into tears, and the youngest son Gocho also wept, bringing a jug of water to the lips of his exhausted father, sitting on the grass. Baby Mitra woke up in her cradle and also burst into tears.

Todor carefully made his way through the hiding him ears of wheat and, crouching down, reached the end of the field, where the path several meters wide separated it from the forest, and looked out through behind the ripe ears: the policemen were at the other end of the field. With the speed of lightning he ran across the path and disappeared into the forest, which in fact was not a dense forest, but coppice, dividing the land of different owners, who at that time were working at their fields. Todor saw that 3 policemen drove into the coppice from the other end and realized that he had nowhere to run. Hiding from tree to tree, he crept back to the path in front of the field. Prickly bushes grew along the edge of the path and, as far as he knew, there was an old fox hole nearby. He knew these lands from childhood. The hole, dug in the ground, was quite spacious; he crept up to this hole and managed to squeeze into, bending his knees and tucking under him.

He froze, listening to every sound outside. The policemen continued to ride the horses around and fire from their rifles just like that at random, hoping to shoot Todor somewhere. He heard the footsteps of a horse next to the hole. The horse stopped, the policeman looked around, the horse took a step back and with her back leg stepped with her horseshoe spike right on the thigh of Todor, who was lying in the hole under the ground huddled up. His legs pressed into the loose earth, otherwise Todor would lose them, but he felt the full weight of the spikes on his thigh. He nearly lost consciousness from the pain, but having gathered all the strength of his spirit into a fist, he did not move and did not make a sound. Having missed Todor, the policemen, full of anger, galloped back to Borisovograd.

Like a beast driven into the hole, Todor lay underground, suffering from pain, until the sun rolled behind the hills and black darkness of night came. He made a slight movement, trying to get out of the hole, and the pain became even worse. The leg did not obey, and he had to drag it. Overcoming the pain, he finally crawled out of the hole. Convinced that the bone was not broken, he sat down with his back against the trunk of a tree. He was very cold. The night was chilly. The bright stars in the black sky illuminated the path home. Leaning his hands on the tree, he found the strength to rise to his feet and, hobbling, went to Bodrovo. He entered the village from the south-east side, where on the outskirts the house of his grandfather Tekha, his mother's father, was situated. Todor found a shelter at his place. The entire thigh was swollen and blue from the strongest hematoma, all soft tissue were damaged and crushed. The grandfather Tekha put Todor to bed, made rakia compress and treated him with anise oil and herbal infusions, hiding him from everyone in his home for 10 days. Anger and striving for vengeance flared up in Todor's soul, more and more often now he thought about the former hajduks and their exploits of the past, when they fought for freedom during the time of Turkish slavery, but now these Bulgarians were worse than the Turks.

After recovering and getting to his feet, Todor hugged his grandpa Tekha, who shed tears from excitement, thanked him and left his home.

"Take care of yourself, grandson," grandpa Tekha told him with his eyes wet with tears.

Todor went through the whole village to his house, where all the household members greeted him with tears. Dumbly, Todor took 2 revolvers, bandoliers, hidden in the barn, mounted a horse and galloped to Aidanlar to Vidyu, a friend of all the hajduks. Ivan Ignatov was also there, waiting for Todor in the Vidyu's house, and they all hugged tightly after parting. Todor told them about his misfortune adventures, and Ivan Ignatov told about how he was captured on the same day, when the policemen made an onslaught on Todor, and how he fooled them and escaped.

"They seized me in our field, where I plowed the land," Ivan said, "they tied my hands and instructed our policeman from Bodrovo Peter Slavov to convoy me through our Bodrovo and the White River. The policeman was on a horse, and I was walking next to him. We approached Bodrovo, and I told him: 'That's it, I won't go any further. Even if you kill me, I won't go through our village with my hands tied! Let's do it this way: or untie my hands, or I won't go! Or let's turn right and go around Bodrovo. Why should we go through Bodrovo?' And he answered me: 'You know, we don't feed detainees in Borisovograd police, there is nothing to feed them with, we don't have any bread, we ourselves don't have anything to eat, we are not like you, the land lords. And there is nothing to sleep on, nothing to lie on, nothing to cover yourself with, that's why a detainee is obliged to appear with his bread crumbs and with his blanket. That's why we are going through the Bodrovo community, they must contact your relatives, and they must deliver a bag with bread crumbs and a blanket to the community for you."

And I say to him: "Come on, you go for bread crumbs and a blanket yourself, and I'll wait for you here." You know our Peter, he is a god-natured person, there are some like him, but he is an exception, so he agreed. I also tell him: "Come on, go, where I can go? My hands are tied!" So, he went, and I untied my hands, mounted his horse and ran astride to Aidanlar. "Where else! Thanks to our Vidyu, he accepts and feeds all the fugitives, gives them food and drink! What should we do without him!"

Vidyu smiled with pleasure from praise in his address. It was his clement: pursuit, chasing, escape, secret meetings and fight for freedom against evil.

"Yes, our Vidyu also fed The Ganev-Armanovs and gave them shelter," Todor said, "by the way, how are they? Where are they, Mityu and Petyu?"

"They haven't been around for a long time," Vidyu answered, "they say they went to Turkey together with some Turks, who joined them."

"Maybe we'll look for them, find them and join them, create our own cheta?" Ivan Ignatov suggested. "And we shall fight the villains who pursue us, we'll become hajduks?"

"While we only dress up like hajduks, playing hajduks," Todor said thoughtfully, "but if they force us, we'll fight for ourselves."

"That's right," Vidyu caught up, "the enemies made an onslaught on us and declared war, we must give them a fight."

"But if we start fighting with them, we shall finally place ourselves outside the law, we'll have to go to illegality, we won't be able to return home," Todor said, rent with doubts, "and now it's not the Turkish yoke, not war, but peaceful time, and we are not poor vagabonds like Ganev-Armanovs, but wealthy peasants, we own houses, the land that our ancestors owned! We need to solve the problem legally. Tsar Ferdinand fled with Radoslavov long time ago, and it is Alexander Stamboliysky, a peasant leader, who is at power. Can't we find law and justice against the Borisovograd murderers in police uniform!"

"Eh," Ivan Ignatov sighed, "Ferdinand fled, but his son Boris, the rascal, remained! God is high, and Alexander Stamboliysky is far away in Sofia, and here in Bodrovo and Borisovograd murderers-bastards run the show. Your father has already tried to resolve the issue, 'according to the law,' he paid the Haskovo prosecutor 50 thousand leva, and after that the murderers-policemen shoot at you! It means that we should go to Sofia," Todor answered. "Let's go first to look for Mityu Ganev with his brother Petyu," Ivan said.

"Yes, go, find Mityu Ganev and his cheta, come to our house for food and lodging for the night," Vidyu offered to help, and his father Gocho supported him along with his older brother Todor.

They talked yet for a long time, argued, trying to decide what to do, ate their fill of Vidyu's food: fried lamb, roast, delicious soup with meat and vegetables, feta-cheese, milk, which cheered them up. They feasted heartily, drank some rakia and fell asleep soundly in the morning. Next day they saddled their horses and left to look for the brothers Mityu and Petyu Ganev-Armanov, just in case, to talk, chat, see how they were, what they were doing, although it was known what they did. They walked along the familiar paths through valleys and hills, along the forest paths, along the bed of streams, went into neighboring villages, asked the peasants—Ganev-Armanovs were nowhere, nobody had seen them for a long time; apparently, they had gone to Turkey.

However, drawn to their native lands, homesick, they approached the area, which was located south-east of Bodrovo. The locals called it Sulman Dere. An extensive meadow lay in lowland, and on the south side a dense forest was contiguous to it, it slowly ascended a gentle slope of a hill, beyond which there was a small mountain, which was told legends about. An undulated path ascended to the pinnacle of the hill from the meadow, passing centuries-old oaks, ash-trees, hornbeams and maples. There was a green terrace at the top, decorated with flowering shrubs, and the entrance to a cave, hiding from frying eyes. In this cave at one time Angel Voevoda used to stay, who was fed by a source of pure water, springing out of the ground next to the cave.

A herd of cows, sheep, oxen and horses were grazing in the sun-drenched green meadow, in which Todor recognized his animals.

"Gocho must be around here somewhere. Maybe he is near the fountain on the hill?" Ivan Ignatov said.

They dismounted, tethered their horses to the trees and climbed the undulated path to the green terrace. A trunk of a tree felled by storm and cleared from brunches served as a bench for travelers. Gocho was sitting on this log under a lilac shrub and read a book. On seeing Todor with Ivan, he jumped to his feet and threw himself at his brother's neck. They embraced.

"What are you reading?" Todor asked.

"Duma's 'Three Musketeers', where did you go? How are you, Todor?"

"We bypassed all the Rhodopes, home draws."

"At home we have no peace, everyone is worried about you. When will you be back?"

"We must think it over," Todor answered.

They sat down on the log next to Gocho and lit cigarettes.

"This is a legendary place," Todor said, "in this cave all the hajduks hid at all times and they drank water from this spring."

The purest transparent icy water spouted like a fountain from vertical slope of the mountain next to the cave and flowed by stream down into the valley.

"Tell us, Todor."

"This cave and this spring are located in the very center of the intersection of all the paths, along which our heroes-voevodas used to go from south to north, from Rhodopes to the Balkans and from east to west: from Straudzha to Pirin and Rila. They all hid in this cave and drank water from this spring. One of the legends that grandpa Todor told about Volchan Voevoda says that this fearless warrior, who was at the head of cheta of 100 people, collected countless treasures. In addition that they attacked rich caravans, going to Tsargrad, Volchan found the treasures of the Thracians and Romans, and he hid the treasures somewhere here, where we are now, somewhere in the depth of the cave."

True, the whole cave has been rummaged, but nothing has been found. Volchan hid the treasures exactly in such a way that no one would find it, and only he alone knew where exactly this place was. They say that here at this source Volchan met with Indje Voevoda; Indje commanded an entire army of 500 people. Brave and fearless, he suddenly swooped down on the Janissaries and smashed them. He managed to organize a whole republic. And Indje also possessed countless treasures after he had robbed a fair in Sliven. These treasures are also hidden somewhere, maybe here, maybe somewhere else. Stoyan Voevoda has also been here, when he returned from the island of Thasos; he and his friends passed through these lands, gathered a cheta, smashed the Turks and went to Macedonia to fight.

They fought the Turks already after the liberation in 1878, when Bulgaria was divided at the Berlin Congress and Macedonia was given back to the Turks. Stoyan was betrayed and killed by his own people: the Russians. There has always been betrayal, intrigues, enmity between their own. So, Petko Voevoda was betrayed by his own people: the Bulgarians. Petko fought with the Turks in our area and, of course, hid in this cave and drank water from this source. And immediately after the Liberation the Bulgarians betrayed him, this is the most shameful betrayal done by Bulgaria: the betrayal of Petko Voevoda. Stefan Stambolov's government tried to seize Petko and hand him over to the Turks, because he, Stambolov envied Petko, his popularity, his valor, bravery and heroism. True, they did not hand him over to the Turks, but they seized him, threw him into the dungeon in the Varna fortress, where he was tortured, maimed and starved on the order of Stambolov.

So, our own Bulgarians turned out to be meaner and more disgusting than the Turks. Well, this cave itself bears the name of Angel Voevoda, since it served as his shelter a long time. After all, he was from our lands and fought with the Turks in our lands: in Hadji Yeles, as Borisovgrad used to be called, as well as in Plovdiv and Haskovo, he also visited our Bodrovo. All these hajduks-heroes did not submit to tyranny, violence and slavery, but rose to fight for freedom."

"So, we have to do the same," Ivan Ignatov sighed sadly, "although there are no Turks long ago, but the Bulgarians rule, more than that, the country is headed by the peasant leader Alexander Stamboliysky, the defender of all peasants."

"Alexander Stamboliysky and his Agrarian Union have nothing to do with it. These Borisovograd bandits were the same before Stamboliysky and during the Agrarian Union, and will remain the same forever, no matter what power is. We must fight against them with weapons in our hands only and settle scores."

Todor was sitting on the log near Gocho and looked at his younger brother, whom he also missed. Suddenly he saw that Gocho was frozen in horror and staring straight ahead. Out of the corner of his eye Todor saw a giant snake right in front of them, it raised its head to attack. Ivan Ignatov felt silent and froze in mid-sentence, looking straight ahead in horror. The Rhodopes are teeming with snakes of various varieties, but none of them has ever seen such a gigantic monster. Todor also froze and then in a blink of an eye grabbed the snake by the head and cut it off with his dagger. Both Gocho and Ivan shuddered in disgust, feeling that the danger was very close. They saw Todor as their protector. They discussed the incident for a long time, and then changed the subject and returned to the previous topic.

"That's how to destroy all our enemies!"

"I've decided to return home, to see my parents, to help them, I'm tired from wandering," Ivan Ignatov said.

"So do I," Todor decided, "I need to visit home, how long can this last!"

The decision was suddenly made by both of them. They went down from the hill to the valley, where Todor's animals were grazing, Ivan Ignatov went home, and Todor stayed with Gocho to help him to huddle the herd into the paddock for a night.

Ivan mounted the horse and galloped to Bodrovo, where his yearning relatives were waiting, and before they had time to rejoice at their son return, cry with joy and hug Ivan, the Borisovgrad policemen broke into his home, overpowered him, tied his hands, threw him on a saddle of a horse and took him to Borisovgrad police station.

"Is it you who committed 15 robberies of banks of the large bankers and tobacconists?" Guenov-Kamine began interrogation of Ivan Ignatov in the chamber of torture, hitting him with all his might with the whip. "Is it you with Todor in the same gang with Mityu Ganev who robbed everyone around?"

Blows with whip, boots and sticks rained one after another down on Ivan Ignatov, distraught with pain, and soon he mumbled through a bloody mouth:

"Yes, it's me who robbed everyone with Mityu Ganev, it's me myself who is Mityu Ganev."

190 cm tall hero-bogatir Ivan Ignatov took on the appearance of Mityu Ganev, whose height barely reached 160 cm, in a mockery of the executioners, whom he swore to himself, if he survives, to kill everyone.

When Todor with Gocho entered their house in the evening, at that time Ivan Ignatov, all in blood, had been lying long on the floor in the Borisovograd police torture chamber, but they did not know about it.

"Son, you must surrender to the prosecutor!" the father began to beg Todor after joyful tears of meeting with his son. "You must return to the prosecutor, to whom I've paid 50 thousand leva and who promised to release you and drop all false charges from you, he must give us a written document, confirming that you have been released so that the police would no longer persecute you!"

"Ok, father, I'll return to the prosecutor and surrender so that he gives us a document, stating that I am free, but if they kill me, know, that it is you who will be guilty of this!" Todor answered and left his house at nightfall, saddled the horse and galloped to Haskovo, where he waited until the morning for the prosecutor Vasil Nikolov, and went into his office, when he came to work.

"Oh, Todor, hello," Nikolov greeted him kindly, whose eyes slyly ran in different directions at the thought of the money, received from Todor's father, "how are you doing?"

"Mr. prosecutor, my father Ivan Todorov Karagochev sent me to you. The policemen from Borisovograd shot at me, I miraculously survived. My father said that you must give us a document, confirming that all charges against me were dropped, so that the police would not pursue me."

"Yes, yes, Todor, I am going to go to Plovdiv to the district court on your case. We shall go together with you."

***

They went down the stairs and got into the prosecutor's car.

"I have my horse here," Todor said.

"Ok, don't worry, you'll pick it up on the way back."

The prosecutor Nikolov instructed the driver, and the car drove from Haskovo. On the way Nikolov talked nonstop about the fact that there was no reason to worry, that there was no case in fact, since there was no written statement from Ignat Mitev and his brother about the robbery of their shop, and he stressfully thought about the fate of 50 thousand leva, which he had received from Todor's father, which he safely hid in his safe without any intention of sharing them with anybody else. Would it be necessary to share it in Plovdiv, giving "the case" an official turn or let things drift and not tell anyone anything, as there is no "case", he was thinking about frantically, not knowing what to fix on. But in connection with the recent events, the latter hardly seemed to be possible.

Having already passed half way and approaching Debar, which was on the direct road to Plovdiv, the car suddenly turned sharply to the right in the direction of Borisovograd. Todor's heart went cold, and he looked inquiringly at the prosecutor Nikolov.

"Don't worry, Todor," the prosecutor Nikolov comforted Todor with a false smile, "I've decided not to take you with me to Plovdiv, but to leave you in Borisovograd. I'll pick you up on the way back after I receive a document from the District Court in Plovdiv that all charges against you are dropped."

Todor's heart began to pound even faster, as the car approached the central square of Borisovograd, where the building of the city police was situated. He was so young and so handsome, he wanted to be alive and healthy, he so wanted to live!

Meanwhile, the car stopped near the police building. The prosecutor took Todor out of the car and led inside.

"Sergeant Nesterov, the duty officer of the police department," the policeman introduced himself in a string in front of the prosecutor.

"I hand you over Todor Ivanov Todorov Karagochev from Bodrovo until I return from Plovdiv. On the way back I'll pick him up, and so that not a single hair is harmed on his head, otherwise you'll respond before the law! There are laws and justice in Bulgaria!" the prosecutor Vasil Nesterov harangued pathetically and disappeared behind the door.

"Well, well, well! We shall guard you so that you don't get anywhere," sergeant Nesterov muttered maliciously through his teeth, handcuffing Todor and locking him in an iron cage.

Todor was trembling, and his heart was pounding strongly. If he had gone one-on-one with each of them in a fair fight, he would have defended himself and defeated them all. But the fight with the Borisovograd sadistic murderers was not fair, and he did not want to be slaughtered by them with the handcuffs on his hands, like a sheep to be slaughtered.

"Here it is your law to you, father! Damned be your law and damned be me myself for listening to you!" Todor thought in despair.

Soon the iron latch was open, and Nesterov on duty dragged Todor into the interrogation room. Police chief Enyu Gogov and his best friend Guenov-Kamine were already waiting for them there.

"Ah, a bitch bastard got caught?" Guenov grumbled ominously through his teeth and approached Todor with a whip.

The other 2 were already waiting with the sticks. They tore off Todor's clothes, and Guenov-Kamine swung and hit Todor with whip with all his might. The whip dissected Todor flesh, and the blood spurted from the wounds. Guenov-Kamine was delighted. Nesterov and Gogov threw Todor to the floor. Without making a sound, Todor tried to cover his face with his bound hands so that the executioners would not mutilate it. Guenov-Kamine beat with his whip, tearing off his living skin, with sadistic pleasure he admired how the perfect beauty of the young man body was covered with bloody harrows. The whip in Guenov's hands, whistling and wriggling, dug into the youth's body with devilish zigzags, tattering his flesh and flaying it. The chief Gogov and sergeant Nesterov alternately rained blows of sticks on Todor after Guenov's blow with a whip, grinning with pleasure.

"Take it, damned hajduk!" they said, taking turns inflecting blows.

The whistle of the whip, the blows, showering his body, the abuse of the sadists, inhuman pain drowned out Todor's consciousness, he sank into darkness and non-existence, and time stopped for him. The day came to an end, and it began to get dark. The executioners finally lost their strength, and their striking hands fell like whips, and fetid sweat ran down from their faces.

"We need to take a break," Gogov, the chief, suggested, and finally Guenov-Kamine with all his might kicked Todor, who was lying motionless on the floor on his stomach with his face to the floor.

"Dead!" Guenov-Kamine announced, staring at the Todor's motionless body, tattered and turned into a dark red mass, lying lifelessly in a puddle of blood.

"Really, he is dead!" Gogov, the police chief, confirmed, inflicting another kick in the side of the lifeless body.

"Let's go to have drink, let celebrate!" Gogov called everyone into his office.

The sadistic killers threw away the whip and sticks and went to celebrate the victory. They poured a bottle of rakia into the glasses, made a toast "for victory!" and poured the contents of the glasses into their throats. Much cheered up, they began to share their impressions of the pleasure they had just experienced.

"Oh, I forgot to say that the prosecutor ordered to tell you that nothing bad would happen to the hajduk," stammering from alcohol, Nesterov on duty squeezed out of himself, washing down with another sip of rakia.

"We need to come up with something," Guenov-Kamine winked at the chief Gogov with a drunken eye, adding drunken swearing.

"Let's say this," the drunken Gogov rejoiced, "we'll say that we interrogated him in according with the law, and he confessed to robbery a shop and that he hid the loot in Aidanlar; we took him to Aidanlar to find what he hid, but the robber escaped on the way!"

"Yes, let's say this," 2 policemen agreed, "and now we'll tell our people to dig a hole somewhere on the bank of the Maritsa and bury him there."

"Let's drink to victory, friends!"

They filled their glasses with some more rakia and made a toast. They just raised the glasses to their mouths, when the telephone rang. The chief Gogov hurriedly put the glass on the table, spitting half of rakia, and with a trembling hands picked up the receiver.

"The head of the city police of Borisovograd, captain Gogov is here."

"Mr. Gogov, this is the prosecutor of the Plovdiv District Court. Can you hear me well?"

"Yes, sir! That's right, Mr. Prosecutor," drunken Gogov stretched himself into a string, trying to sober up.

"So, listen, right now at your department is Todor, Ivanov, by his father, Todorov Karagochev, by his surname. I am aware of what happened. I warn you, if you lay a finger on him, if something happens to him, you will respond to the fullest extent of the law before Sofia! My colleague, the Haskovo prosecutor, and I are heading there, we are going to Sofia on this case."

The chief Gogov tried to sober up and was thinking on his feet what to answer: whether Todor escaped on the way to Aidanlar and was shot while trying to escape, or whether he ran away directly from the Borisovograd police, but he did not come up with anything and only mumbled:

"Yes, Mr. Prosecutor!"

"Immediately send our men to dig a grave near Maritsa!" Guenov-Kamine said, and everybody began to fuss.

They returned to their torture chamber, Todor's lifeless body was lying on the floor in the puddle of blood. They took him by the arms and legs and dragged him out of the police building through the back door into the courtyard, in the depth of which there was a pile of horse manure. They swung Todor's body and threw him into this heap. They sent the assistances to Maritsa River to dig a grave. They themselves returned to the chief Gogov's office to drink some more rakia. Soon the grave was ready on the bank of the Maritsa River in a secluded nook under the willow. They returned back to the dung heap, dragged Todor out of it and threw him on the ground. It was necessary to throw him into a cart and take him to the dug hole on the river bank. Again they took him by the arms and legs, he stirred and began to breath.

"So, he is alive, bitch's hajduk!" the chief Gogov delighted.

"What are you happy about?" Guenov-Kamine barked angrily, lighting a cigarette.

"Now it's better him alive than dead," Gogov concluded logically, "get him back!"

They dragged half-alive, half-dead Todor back to the torture chamber, threw him on the floor and went out to Gogov's office to finish drinking rakia. Night came. Everything plunged in the darkness.

2 days passed. Todor's father, Ivan Todorov, knocked on the door of the Haskovo prosecutor Vasil Nikolov's office.

"Oh, Ivan, come in! How are you?" Nikolov greeted him kindly.

Exhausted of being anxious about his son, Ivan could hardly stand on his feet.

"Where is Todor?" he asked the prosecutor.

"Todor is all right, as I promised. After all, there is no 'case'. There is no statement from the Mitevs. All the suspicions and charges have been cleaned from Todor. Here is the decision of the district court of Plovdiv that he was released and any persecution of him is illegal."

Prosecutor Nikolov handed Ivan Todorov a paper.

"Where is my son?" Ivan repeated his question.

"Well, we shall find out now," Nikolov answered and called Gogov's office.

"Where is Todor Todorov?"

"He is here with us, sick little bit…"

"Bring him to Haskovo immediately! He was released, and all the suspicions and charges were acquitted of him."

"Yes, Mr. prosecutor!" Gogov answered.

"Go home, Ivan, Todor will be brought here, and then he will return home to Bodrovo on his horse."

The unfortunate father thanked the prosecutor and went home on his cart. The policemen harnessed the oxen to a cart, threw Todor into the cart and took him to Haskovo. The cart jumped and creaked, Todor fell into oblivion. The policemen brought him to the building of the District Court in Haskovo, threw his naked body on the pavement stones next to the court, threw his clothes on him and left him like that. Passers-by flocked about bloody, mutilated, covered in dung naked Todor, who seemed not to breath and to be dead, and wondered who was he. Finally, an ox-drawn cart drove past with a fellow villager from Bodrovo, who took Todor home in his cart.

Chapter 19
Resurrection

Ivan and his brother Dimitar carried him into the house in their arms. Nobody knew if he would survive. Todor's house was flood deluged with tears. Their grief and joy had no end, because Todor was mutilated and because he was alive. The tattered body of Todor was laid on the bed with his back up, as he could only lie on his stomach. Fortunately, his face had not been mutilated, because in the chamber of torture he lay on the floor on his stomach with his face to the floor and thus saved his face from damage. And on the rest of the body there was no living place. On seeing his wounds, the mother Atanasa and grandma Mariyka loudly burst into tears, while the father Ivan clutched at his heart and sank emaciated into a chair, fainting. His brother Dimitar, who was standing nearby, supported him and shared a tear himself.

"I've been to 2 Balkan Wars, I saw suffering and death, the wounded and killed in battle, but I could not imagine that the authority representatives could so mutilate an innocent person in peace time! Damn you, Bulgarian barbarians! You are worse than the Turks, who bossed the Balkans for 500 years! And you be trice cursed, false friend—'sworn-brother' Ivan Todorov Guenov-Kamine!"

Ivan suddenly recalled the wounded Turk, lying on the ground in Adrianople, to whom he gave a piece of bread and some water. Then the 3 men moved away from him, and Guenov-Kamine with the lieutenant Filyu Borisov returned back under some pretext. They came back to kill him! This Turk suddenly occurred to him. How could he be so blind and did not see that in fact he did not have any friends and he let into his life and into his house a sworn foe, who assumed the guise of a friend, and now this foe tried to torture to death his son. Ivan sobbed loudly, and his brother Dimitar tried to calm him down.

"Well, well, brother, calm down, Todor is alive, his wounds will heal and he will live!"

He hugged his brother by the shoulders, stroked his gray hair and wept softly himself. The women were the first to pull themselves together and began to treat Todor. His entire back, thighs, lower back were cut almost to the bones by the blows of Guenov's scourge and were nothing but swollen blue-red mess from the blows of sticks, smeared with dung, the infected wounds of which festered, threatening blood poisoning. The women began to cleanse his body from dung and dirt by millimeter, wash the wounds, apply compresses with medical herbs and give Todor strong broth and tea honey, since he had not eaten or drank anything for several days.

Todor again lost consciousness from unbearable pain. In delirium and fever, in unconsciousness and semi-consciousness, suffering from unbearable pain from wounds all over the body, Todor fought for his life, balancing on the verge of life and death. Then he fell into oblivion, then returned to reality and again and again saw before him the mugs and snouts of the monsters, the whistle of the whip, boots and clubs falling on his beautiful body. He drove away from himself the nightmare visions, but they overtook him again and again, and when he regained consciousness, he already knew that he would kill them all. He lay on his stomach, less affected from the torture, and his back with flayed skin, completely covered with festering wounds, and his mother and grandmother treated him, praying to god.

The father Ivan only cried and more and more came to the tavern to flood his grief with rakia. 12-year-old Gocho looked after the herd of animals, and 15-year-old Maria helped around the house. 2 weeks passed like this. Todor's life vanquished death. Gruesome wounds cleaned and closed up and began to be healed. The fever subsided, and the appetite appeared. Delicious dishes were prepared for Todor. Finally he got on his feet, leaning on a stick, and took a few steps. He began to move first around the room, then slowly went out into the courtyard and breathed with fresh air, and soon he got stronger enough to walk along the main street in Bodrovo. True, not long and not far, and soon, staggering, he returned to his house. He knew that he would kill them all.

Chapter 20
St. Ilijah Day

A month passed, July ended, the hot summer of 1920 was in full swing. Under the life-giving rays of the Bulgarian sun on the fertile fields, contiguous to Bodrovo, ripe crop of wheat, rye, anise, tobacco undulated, which was carefully looked after by the villagers, who worked in their fields and grazed their herd on the rich pastures of the valleys and hills.

Todor continued to stay at home, slowly healing his wounds. On August 1 in the morning Ivan Ignatov came to see his friend after the separation. He was holding in his hands a tightly tied small sack. On seeing Todor, yellow as a lemon, emaciated, resembling a skeleton, Ivan smiled as guilty, as if embarrassed by his heroic body, full of health: after all, he got much less from the sadistic executioners than Todor. The friends hugged and shed tears from the friendly feelings that overwhelmed them.

"How are you, Todor?" Ivan asked, deeply sympathizing with his friend.

"I am recovering slowly, but my spiritual wounds will never heal!"

"They won't get away with it!" Ivan replied angrily.

"I'll kill them all," Todor said slowly and clearly rapping out every word, and his eyes were sparkling.

"We'll kill them," Ivan Ignatov supported his friend, squeezing his hand, "don't worry, Todor, you'll recover finally. You were and will always be the most handsome young man of all! All the girls are crazy about you, you know!"

"Not all of them, but only half," Todor replied, smiling, "and half of the girls are crazy about you! You are a hero-bogatir and very handsome man!"

The friends laughed and cheered. Ivan handed Todor a small tightly tied bag, with which he had come.

"This is for you, Todor, from our mutual acquaintance."

Todor took the bag with interest, took out its contents and put it on the table. It was a package tightly wrapped in a piece of bright silk fabric and tied with a red silk ribbon as a valuable gift. Ivan was watching with interest. Todor untied the ribbon, unwound the bundle and put the present on the table: 2 boxes of expensive Greek cigars and big bundles of large banknotes, neatly folded in a box, there was also a letter. Todor opened the letter and began to read.

"Todor, you suffered a lot because of me and for me, and you did not betray me and my brother Petyu. We all admire your courage and nobility. Remember, I'll take vengeance on your enemies, when they fall into our hands. The weapons that we have—revolvers, rifles and cartridges—we received from Vidyu. It is he who gave us weapons. But we also have other weapons, and it will be enough for everyone, who decides to join us. If you decide to become a hajduk to revenge on all your enemies, come to us, and we'll welcome you with joy. Everything is wonderful with my brother Petyu and me. Thank you, Todor! Mityu Ganev."

"So, this is how it is, that means that Mityu Ganev is not any longer angry with me that I hit hard on his neck and beat him, because he stole my dagger from me, when I was swimming in the river, and then I took my dagger from him?"

"No, he is not angry at all," Ivan Ignatov, pleased, answered, "he is not angry, and he worries about you very much."

"Where did you see him?"

"Near the Aidanlar forest, we also have pastures there, next to the Vidyu's lands, you know. All this time I've been tending our flocks together with Vidyu's animals. We've teamed up with him and took turns tending our flocks. I pastured my animals and his, and then he pastured his animals and mine, and sometime we did together. The Armanov brothers used to come to him, as before, to the sheepfold or chalet. Mityu Ganev is anxious about you very much, and he is grateful to you for not betraying him under the torture of the Borisovograd policemen, he also swore that he would kill them all."

"You can kill them all, except for one: Guenov-Kamine!" Todor said seriously. "Leave this one to me."

"I don't mind," Ivan Ignatov agreed.

"The fame of Mityu Ganev spread all over Rhodopes," Todor said, smiling.

"Perhaps, all over Bulgaria," Ivan corrected, "there was no bank that he would not rob, there was no rich banker that he would not rob, while he always gives part of the loot to the destitute. He swoops with his people like a whirlwind, robs and instantly vanishes without a trace. Everyone knows that it was Mityu Ganev, but there are no proves."

"Well done!" Todor laughed. "So, it was not Mityu Ganev who stole my dagger after all, when you and I were resting in Khodzovi Bunar? Then I fell asleep, and it was your turn to be on guard and protect both of us, and you fell asleep treacherously, and someone pulled my dagger out of my pocket. So, it wasn't Mityu Ganev, was he?"

"No, it wasn't him," Ivan Ignatov answered guilty, "forgive me for falling asleep then!"

"I forgave you long ago," Todor answered.

"Somehow I found out about your dagger, there is information that it is in the hands of the Macedonian chetnik Argir. It was him who stole your dagger from your pocket. Several people of Argir live in Bodrovo."

"We'll meet one day," Todor replied.

"Ok, Todor, get ready, all our friends will be at the party, we'll get them there."

"Remember, Guenov-Kamine is mine!" Todor said. "We are leaving after lunch."

Ivan Ignatov hurried home to get ready for the trip to the party, and Todor, having hidden the parcel from Mityu Ganev in a safe place, began to harness the oxen to the cart and prepare for departure. After lunch, Maria, 15-year-old sister dressed up, Atanasa, the mother, in a new fancy dress, who left the child in her husband's care. Gocho, joyful, in a new shirt, cousin Mika, Uncle Dimitar's daughter, and Todor, dressed in all new clothes, were sitting in the cart, ready to go to the feast. The father Ivan, who had no reason yet for the feasts, stayed at home with his 3-month-old daughter Mitra and with tears in his eyes adjured Todor not to drink too much and not to get involved in any affairs and not to mess with the enemies. Having promised his father to take care of himself, Todor, who was still barely able to sit, found strength to sit on a sack with straw and drive a cart, headed the oxen along the main road of Bodrovo from the village to the north to the Tsaregrad highway, where in a place called Saladin, between the villages of Byala Reka and Varbitsa they were preparing for the main feast of the Thrace villagers: the Elijah Day.

Having left all the work in the fields and around the house on that day, August 1, people flocked to the Saladin glade to pay homage to Elijah the

Prophet, who inherited to the ancient Greek Zeus and ancient Roman Jupiter, and ancient Slavic Perun, and in the round dances of drunken joy to enlist his support in the abundance of harvest, since Saint Elijah, just like Zeus, Jupiter and Perun, the lord of thunder, heavenly fire and rain, was the patron of harvest and fertility. All the roads to Saladin from the nearby villages were filled with caravans of carts full with dressed-up merry people, who were dragged by the harnessed oxen, buffaloes, horses, mules and donkeys. Creak of carts, cheerful chatter and singing were in the air of the cloudless hot day, and like streams they were flowing to one direction: to a huge glade between the Byala Reka and Varbitsa villages.

Steadfastly overcoming the still unsolved pain in the whole body, Todor was driving the oxen, which dragged his relatives, to the gathering place for the feast. They drove through their fields in the lands of Koor Bunar, which were located not far from Tsaregrad highway and Saladin glade. Ripe corn stood in the fields, ready for harvest, and the sight of the fertile land that belonged to him, filled Todor's soul with a sense of peace, tranquility and joy, and a passionate desire for life and happiness, but continuing pain in the whole body from the slightest movement reminded him the inflicted offense and resurrected in his memory the torture chamber in the Borisovograd police. And the proud spirit of the hajduks, whose blood flowed in his veins, made his brave heart pound with an inevitable thirst of revenge. His was thinking about his ancestors and was proud of them. And the founder of the clan Todor Chaunov since 1782, and his father, and all the descendants in the male line up to the Todor's grandfather were the hajduks, fearless warriors, who fought for freedom against the Turkish enslavers, and he inherited from them freedom and hatred to slavery, rebellious spirit, fearlessness and willingness to fight.

They drove on an elevation, from which they could see a huge glade of Saladin, located in the valley, on which the inhabitants of the nearby villages, festively dressed in rainbow-colored and decorated with the flowers clothes, gathered to glorify the patron saint of the harvest and natural elements Elijah the Prophet, like their distant ancestors glorified Zeus, Jupiter and Perun in the festive mysteries, and above all not so much to glorify the mythical deities, but to have fun for themselves, to communicate with each other with a dream and hope, if possible, to meet friends and beloved. Torn apart by contradictions and need to choose between war and peace, Todor drove the oxen to the Saladin glade. On the edge of the glade, away from the festivities, there were many carts of arriving guests, and animals were grazing nearby. They stopped nearby. Todor and Gocho unharnessed the oxen, simply tying them to the cart and giving them the opportunity to graze, and they all disappeared in the crowd.

The overall feast was in full swing, and the noise of merriment shook the air over Saladin glade. Fancy-dressed villagers from all around, having postponed all their affairs and concerns, had fun with all their hearts. The adventurous dealers sold their goods on numerous stalls, placed everywhere, which were bursting with abundance of goods. There were also here all kinds of fruits and berries that only grew on the fertile land of Thrace, pastries and sweets and jewelry. A huge fair of all kinds of goods was at the service for the guests. The children were swinging, the musicians were playing, under a huge canopy there was a long table, on which everything was prepared for common mess. Circus artists gave a performance on a specially arranged stage in front of which there were benches for public. And several tents stood at a distance. In one of the tent there was a table for the Borisovograd police, at which the whole campaign of Todor's enemies feasted: Enyu Gogov, Guenov-Kamine, petty officer Nesterov and a couple of policemen, and a small detachment of policemen guarded them outside.

Burning with a thirst of thirst for revenge, Todor, gloomy as a cloud, quietly walked around the fun fair and assessed the situation. His keen eye saw a tent aside, in which the enemies were feasting, guarded by the police outside, and he realized that the place was not suitable for revenge, which should be postponed until later, until a more favorable moment. And now he can have fun himself. Having gone further toward the arena for circus performances, Todor met with a distant relative Slav Deligerchev and his daughter Kalina, who were accompanied by a campaign of dressed-up girls. On seeing Todor, they could not hide their joy, they grabbed him by the arms and engulf with themselves. At that moment Todor turned gloomy, noticing ahead of him Nadyu, the son of Guenov-Kamine, a daddy's boy, who hated Todor as fiercely as his father. Todor failed to go unnoticed and turn aside, because the cheerful girls were holding him tightly by the arms. Nadyu noticed the hated Todor, turned aside and hurried to the policemen's tent to report to his father. Gasping, he ran into the tent and whispered to his father:

"Todor is here."

"It's time to get out of here," Guenov-Kamine announced fearfully.

"So what, if he is here?" Enyu Gogov, the police chief, grinned indifferently, drunk from rakia, pouring himself another glass. "We have a whole detachment here, what can he do to us alone!"

Enyu Gogov giggled merrily.

"Surely, the entire gang is here, headed by Mityu Ganev," Guenov-Kamine worried, objected, "they are the best shooters, and if they make an onslaught on us, our guards will not save us. And Todor is from the hajduks' lineage, fearless hajduks, and you know who the hajduks are, so, we'll be crushed if they decide to take vengeance on us here and now. It's time to get out!"

The whole company with displeasure broke away from the table with food and drinks and left the tent. They left the merry fair astride on the horses to Borisovograd under the protection of the policemen detachment. And the cheerful company of fancy girls carried Todor further and further right under a huge tent, where there was a huge table with food and drinks and where the merry guests were already feasting. Having occupied the vacant seats, the company proceeded to the feast with appetite. Having eaten a little and drank a glass of rakia, Todor got up from the table and calmed the confused girls, assuring them that he would be back in a couple of minutes. He carefully made his way to the tent of the policemen and looked inside: there was nobody there; there was no external guard, only 3 policemen were walking aside. Todor realized that all the foes had fled and decided to forget about them on St. Elijah Day and indulge in fun, postponing the vengeance for later. He returned under the huge canopy to the table for common mess, where the girls, led by Kalina, were impatiently waiting for him and gave himself up into their hands. The girls, competing with each other, served Todor dishes with food and poured rakia. Avoiding get drunk, Todor mostly ate and had fun, looking at the fancy dressed girls, decorated with flowers, who went crazy over him.

Having eaten and drunk, the cheerful company got up from the table and, chanting "horo-round-dance," went through the already playing round dances in search for a free space for their own horo. Finally Todor saw a round-dance of young people, over whom the heroic head of Ivan Ignatov towered. A group of musicians was playing nearby for them, and Todor went with the girls straight to his friend to join him. Todor saw that next to Ivan Ignatov, tenaciously holding his hand, an unfamiliar girl of not a tall statue was dancing: her fair braid, descending bellow her shoulders, was covered with a bright silk scarf, tied back under the braid, over which a hat with brim, lowering to the eyelashes, was put on, so that beautifully made up eyes were shining from under the brim of the hat on a pretty face, well-groomed, powdered, with rouge on her cheekbones and brightly painted lips. The non-tall girl barely reached the mighty chest of Ivan Ignatov; she tenaciously held his hand in a whirlwind of horo-round-dance and did not take her eyes of Todor. Although the girl was unfamiliar, it seemed to Todor that he had already seen those eyes somewhere, although he could not remember where. She was wearing an ankle-length wide skirt that rose like a bell in a whirlwind of dance, a bright embroidered apron over the skirt and an embroidered blouse with long sleeves and a colorful sleeveless jacket over the blouse. Flowers decorated all the clothes. Five strangers, holding each other and Ivan Ignatov by the hands, were dancing on another side of him. All were wearing cowboy hats down to their eyes, and silk handkerchiefs covered their mouths. By the type of costumes Todor decided that they might be from the village of Susam. He did not know anybody of them, but he noticed that they were keeping their eyes on him. When the horo-round-dance went around the next circle and Ivan Ignatov caught up with Todor, he tried to join the horo-dance next to his friend and unknown girl who tenaciously held him. But he failed to open their hands, the horo-dance left, and Todor with his girls managed to enter the horo-dance in another place. Having joined the dance with the girls, Todor, masterfully dancing, immediately headed the horo and led it along. The sun had rolled to the sunset. Bright stars in the black sky illuminated the feast in the Saladin glade, kerosene lamps burned everywhere, and a huge bonfire, scattering sparks and glare around the illuminated faces of the dancers.

Deftly moving their feet, the dancers followed Todor under the beautiful music, in a swift whirlwind of horo they circled at the bosom of nature, leaving all their hardships outside the Saladin glade. Todor also rejoiced; he was held by the hands of the beautiful girls on both sides, and dancing masterfully, he carried them along in a whirlwind of a huge horo-round-dance. Here he happened to notice that Ivan Ignatov, his unknown girl and 5 strangers had disappeared from the round-dance, but he did not attach much importance to this.

At the distance another horo-round-dance was playing, led by a stately and handsome young man named Rayu. Both horo-dances were spinning in a dizzying whirlwind, dangerously approaching each other, and like meteors, avoiding collision, diverged in different directions. Nearby 3 policemen were standing and stared as if spellbound at both horo-dances.

Having disappeared from the round-dance, Ivan Ignatov, the girl and other 5 strangers-companions imperceptibly, quietly and swiftly approached the policemen's tent, which turned out to be empty.

"This time they are lucky, never mind, they won't go far, sooner or lately they will answer for everything they did!" said the "girl," under which Mityu Ganev-Armanov was disguised.

His faithful companion and his brother Petyu was together with him and 4 new friends.

"The bastards will not leave, we'll kill everyone!" Ivan Ignatov said.

He said goodbye to his friends, who mounted their horses, tethered up at the edge of the glade, and rode off to the top of Dragoina. Ivan Ignatov went under the shed for a little more refreshment. Both horo-round dances slowed down their rhythm well and soon stopped to rest. Taking advantage of the hitch, Todor freed his hands from the women hands and eluded them with a lightning speed. He went under the shed, where Ivan Ignatov was feasting, and sat down next to him.

"Tired," he said to his friend, wheezing hard, "my health hasn't mended yet, and who was it with you: a girl and 5 strangers?"

Ivan Ignatov smiled and paused to answer.

"No! Really? I got it now!" Todor exclaimed.

"Hush!" Ivan Ignatov pressed his index finger to his lips and looked around.

"And I thought that these eyes of this girl are familiar to me, I've already seen them somewhere," Todor whispered, "this is Mityu Ganev! He is so masterfully disguises that he can penetrate everywhere without being recognized."

"Exactly," Ivan Ignatov answered quietly, satisfied, "only the foes have fled."

"Remember what I asked you: you can kill them all except Guenov-Kamine! Leave that one for me!"

"Agreed."

Todor parted with his friend and went to his cart, where his mother and younger brother Gocho were already soundly sleeping. It was 4 o'clock in the morning. The rest of the relatives stayed at the feast until morning. Todor and

Gocho harnessed the oxen and went home to Bodrovo. The villagers of Thrace celebrated the Elijah Day 1920 until the next day noon and then left the Saladin glade to plunge into the world of their everyday affairs.

Chapter 21
Dagger

The summer of 1920 was coming to an end. The work in the household of Todorov-Karagochevs was in full swing. Todor and his father Ivan on the oxen-drawn cart carried sheaves of wheat home from the fields, where a threshing floor and a barn were situated in the backyard. With the oxen help the threshing machine separated the grain, and the straw was stored for future use to feed livestock. They harvest corn from the fields, cleaned and prepared for storage and use. When their own corn was harvested, they went to the aid of relatives, who had an estate even larger than they had. Ivan's sister Mika successfully married a rich man Chakalov, who together with their 2 brother Zapryan and Georgy inherited from his father thousands of decares of land and huge herds of cattle. Ivan Chakalov owned 5000 decares of land to the south of Aidanlar, where corn was not yet harvested on the field, as hired workers from nearby villages could not cope with the work. Ivan' brother Dimitar Todorov Karagochev with his son Georgy, Todor and 11-year-old Gocho responded to a request for help and in 2 carts, pulled by oxen, went to their field to collect corn. They were riding merrily with songs and stories, soon reached the field of Ivan Chakalov, where the hired villagers were working, and having joined them, finished the work by the end of the day.

The vast fertile land near Aidanlar gave a generous harvest to the villagers, and a few carts with corn remained to be taken to the village of Bodrovo. Children frolicked nearby, chasing a hare that flashed in the grass. The men satisfied with their work done sat down on the grass to rest and smoke a cigarette before going home.

"It's high time to go home," uncle Dimitar said, finishing his cigarette.

"Have a rest, we need to water the oxen," Todor answered, getting up from the grass.

"I am with you," Gocho immediately joined his brother, leaving the frolic with the children.

They led the oxen for a water to a stream, flowing nearby, knowing by heart all the paths and reservoirs in the area. Suddenly Todor stopped and pushed his brother Gocho:

"Step aside!" he told him sharply.

From the side of the stream a huge giant was walking toward them, followed by 2 oxen from a watering place. The stranger was dressed in a white shirt, black wide trousers and traditional cervulis; he had a revolver hanging on his belt, and from the pocket on the right thigh the handle of the ancient dagger peeped out, sparkling with precious stones, in which Todor immediately recognized his gift from the grandpa, the dagger stolen during his sleep, when they wandered with Ivan Ignatov through the forests and mountains, lay down to rest, Ivan Ignatov was supposed to be on guard while Todor was sleeping, but he treacherously fell asleep, and by this nearly lost his friendship with Todor. Having woken up, Todor discovered that the dagger had been stolen, Ivan was sleeping and nearly killed him for that. And now, sparkling with stones, the handle of the dagger strikes out of the pocket of a huge stranger, who is walking straight toward them. Gocho, frightened, jumped aside, and the stranger caught up with Todor. Furious, Todor said in authoritarian voice:

"Stop and show me this dagger, give it to me in my hands!"

"Who else are you to want my dagger?" the stranger said in response.

"Give me the dagger in my hands so that I can see it! If it's your dagger, I'll give it back to you, I want to see it. It looks like my dagger that was stolen from me."

"Get out of my way!" the stranger shouted angrily.

But even before he had time to flash his eyes menacingly, he immediately screwed his eyes shut in pain. With a lighting speed Todor jumped up to him and with bare hand, clenched into a fist, struck him in the nose, from which blood spurred. At that moment Todor snatched his dagger from his pocket and tucked it into his belt, grabbed the revolver, hanging on the stranger's belt, threw it into his left hand and with his right hand began to beat the giant on his back with a stick. The later, having closed his eyes in pain, grabbed his nose with both hands, allowed himself to be disarmed and turned to Todor with his wide back, on which Todor pounded with a stick with force and soon broke the stick. At the same moment the revolver moved to the Todor's right hand and aimed at the stranger's head. Being unarmed, the later quickly went forward, but after moving a few meters, he turned back.

"You will answer for that! I am the Macedonian Voevoda, I have my own people in Bodrovo, we'll deal with you! We'll cut you into pieces!"

"Oh, how brave you are! You and your people will cut me into pieces, several dozen for against one man! And what is if without your people, one-on-one right now? Look, I'll put down the revolver and dagger, come on, come, the Macedonian Voevoda!"

But the stranger, holding his nose with both hands, stepped back.

"And for your information: I am the Bulgarian Voevoda!" Todor told the giant. "Your people invited me to their squad, but it's not in my way with them. Why did you steal my dagger, when I was sleeping, why didn't you kill us with Ivan Ignatov? Tell me, did you steal my dagger yourself, or did Mityu Ganev give it to you?"

But the Macedonian did not answer anything and, leading his 2 oxen, hastened to leave. Gocho was standing aside and, frozen with excitement, watched with fear what was happening. He admired his older brother, whom he loved very much and most of all he wanted to be like him.

"Todor, how brave and strong you are! How cleverly you've defeated this giant!" he exclaimed, coming to his brother and snuggling up to him.

They continued their journey to the reservoir, watered the oxen and with corn harvest returned to Bodrovo.

The summer of 1920 was over. Todor's house was filled with harvest from the fields, but the work continued with the onset of autumn. The villagers continued to plow the land to sow winter crops to harvest it in spring. Todor, on whom the whole household continued to hold on, skillfully drove a pair of oxen harnessed to a plow, which laid even harrows behind it, and seeds of winter crops were sown in them. In the neighboring fields of the Chorbadzhiis, large owners of the land, hired season workers worked, with whom Todor met shortly at noon during a break for rest. They gathered near the stream, which flowed through the coppice that separated the fields of different owners, sat on the grass to smoke a cigarette. Todor joined them. He knew some of them, somebody lived in Bodrovo, others were not from these places, they came from the west, all were the Macedonian committees at the head of their Voevoda, named Strakhil. They went around the villages, recruited supporters and put together a detachment of the Macedonian chetniks, whose number, according to rumors, had already reached up to 80 people. Todor approached them, sat down on the grass and lit a cigarette.

"Well, Todor, have you thought over our proposal?" Strakhil Voevoda addressed him.

His telling name was consonant with his appearance—terrible, formidable, unkempt, large and muscular—he struck fear into those around him with his appearance and held his detachment in obedience.

"Come on, join our squad, we need fellows like you, we'll fight for the freedom of Macedonia!"

"Why should I join your detachment, if recently one Macedonian from your gang swore to kill me, and even with your help!" Todor answered Strakhil, smoking a cigarette and with another hand clutching a loaded pistol in his pocket.

"Who was he?"

"They call him Argir, a hefty stranger not from our area. We ran into each other near Aidanlar, I beat him up nicely," Todor answered, watching the people around him.

Everybody started, a little surprised, and listened carefully.

"Argir? And you beat him? Can't be! He is so hefty and fierce! He is a Voevoda-foreman, he has 10 chetniks under him! And you dared to beat our Voevoda?" the Macedonians were furious.

And Todor, vigilantly watching them, finished smoking his cigarette and clutched 2 loaded pistols with both hands in his both pockets.

"Maybe you'll tell us how it was?" the terrible Strakhil gritted through his teeth.

Todor began his story from the very beginning, from the persecutions, with which an evil fate overshadowed his youth, and the fierce and terrible, but devilishly sentimental Macedonians were listening to him with their mouths open, and some even shed a tear.

"So," Todor continued, "when, pursued by the foes and expelled from our home, Ivan Ignatov and I wandered through the forests and mountains in search of Mityu Ganev, but could not find him anywhere, we stopped to rest in one of our places, I fell asleep, and Ivan Ignatov had to be on guard and protect both of us, but tired, he also fell asleep, someone pulled a dagger out of my pocket. It was an ancient dagger, a gift from my grandfather, which he in his turn inherited from his grandfather. It was our family heirloom. I was very angry with Ivan, when I woke up and discovered the loss, we quarreled with him in the end and parted, but then after the well-known events, when the foes continued to pursue him and me, I made peace with my old friend and before we came to the Elijah Day party, he told me what he managed to find out: my dagger was stolen by the Macedonian Argir."

Todor ended his story with a skirmish with Argir at Aidanlar and the returned dagger.

"Also, I took his revolver from him," Todor said calmly and handed the revolver to Strakhil.

At that moment, everyone saw a man descending from the hill, large and gloomy, approaching them.

"Here he is, the bastard, hold him, we'll cut him to pieces now!" Argir growled menacingly, pointing at Todor. "It was he who stole my revolver and a dagger!"

Argir was about to move toward Todor, but Strakhil Voevoda blocked his path.

"Or maybe the other way round: it was you who stole his dagger, although you know that our charter forbids robbery and self-will, and you even allowed a civilian to disarm you!" Strakhil continued.

He unloaded the revolver, removing all the bullets from it, and handed it to Argir. The latter, embarrassed, stepped aside, taking his revolver.

"Todor," Strakhil Voevoda turned to him, "join our squadron! I'll appoint you an under-Voevoda-foreman commander and you'll have 10 people under you command. We shall return to Pirin region, from where we'll fight for the freedom of Macedonia!"

All the chetniks looked ta Todor with envy.

"Thank you for the invitation," Todor answered, "but I have my own way. Here I have a house, land and a farm. My path is a path of peace. After all, the war is over, besides, Alexander Stamboliysky banned Chetism, he signed a peace treaty with the Kingdom of Serbs, Croats and Slovenes."

At the mention of the name of Alexander Stamboliysky, all the Macedonians became furious and cursed him. Todor chose to say goodbye and leave to his field to continue work. And the Macedonians roared for a long time, seething with anger and savored the details how they would cut

Alexander Stamboliysky into pieces and throw them to dogs, while praising the Greek Prime Minister Venizelos.

Chapter 22
Alexander Stamboliysky Speech in Sofia

Rural life went on as usual. Having completed work in the fields, in late autumn and winter, the villagers locked themselves in their homes, where in turn, one or the other organized sit-round-gatherings parties. At those parties the schemes were machinated, intrigues were plotted of one against the others, gossips and rumors spread, the hearts were broken from unrequired love, engagements were announced and happy or unhappy marriages were contracted. The fun took place under the light of kerosene lamps and the pleasant sound of cracking fire in the furnace, drowned out by loud songs and mysterious stories and legends of the old times. The girls did not sit idly at the parties, but were engaged in needlework: they sewed and embroidered or wove rugs from wool and made various figures from corn leaves, collected a dowry for themselves mysteriously sighing for the beloved. And the young men watched the girls through songs and speeches, choosing a favorite for themselves, to whom they sent matchmakers.

Todor, whose beauty broke the hearts of all the girls in Bodrovo and in the nearby villages, which caused poisonous anger against him on the part of the young people, visited the sit-round-gatherings, killing time, pondered on his future life and scanned the young girls, hesitating to stop his choice on any of them. Christina constantly treacherously came to his mind, but he resolutely expelled away from himself the ominous ghost of death, preventing him from continue to live.

Not finding reciprocity, the girls, one after another, holding a grudge against Todor, in spite of the whole world, married anyone who sent matchmakers, and soon there was not a single unmarried woman left in Bodrovo and in surrounding lands, except for the cousin Kalina Petrova and a girl from the neighboring village Ezerovo large and rosy-cheeked, who was called "white" Rada Plunkova for her milky skin color. Both girls organized sit-round-gathering parties in their houses, where the fate of their future life was often decided. Kalina Petrova, a sweet and kind girl, secretly in the depth of her heart was in love with Todor and dreamed to marry him. He saw this and understood that all the same nothing would work out of it, and one day he came to their house finally to explain himself. She took him to separate room so that no one would overhear in hope of hearing the most important thing.

"You and I are relatives, cousins, marriage between us is impossible," Todor pronounced the sentence coldly, and discouraged, she escorted him out the door, where the matchmakers from Guenov-Kamine and his son Nadyu were standing on the threshold.

They bumped face to face. Todor left, and the matchmakers entered the house to convey a marriage proposal to Nadyu. Kalina pulled herself together after the endured stroke just suffered and answered indifferently:

"I shall never marry Nadyu, the son of Guenov, as I am already engaged to another one."

The matchmakers said goodbye and left. They conveyed the answer to those who sent them, mentioned that they encountered Todor Todorov in her house, what led Guenov-Kamine and his son Nadyu, who had secretly sighed for Kalina, into even greater anger and a thirst for revenge. And Kalina soon, in order to drown out the pain of a broken heart, married a resident of a neighboring village.

With Rada Plunkova there was a mutual love and a secret liaison with Todor's best friend Ivan Ignatov. Having considered their plans for their life together, burning with sincere love for Rada, he finally came to her house to ask her father for her hand.

"You, Ivan, are a robber and hajduk!" Plunkov became menacingly furious and pointed Ivan at the door, "Guenov-Kamine told us everything about you, so that your foot will never set in our house anymore! My daughter will never marry you!"

Round, rosy-cheeked and craven Rada, who sincerely loved Ivan, for everything depending upon her father in an almost patriarchal traditional society, did not find courage to spit on her obscurantist father and leave home together with Ivan Ignatov. Her courage was only enough to go out with him into the yard, where 3 bandits were waiting for Ivan with sticks and revolvers aimed at him, and vulgarly exclaim:

"Oh, if you kill Ivan Ignatov, then kill me too and put me in one and the same coffin with him!"

The bandits never fired, and Ivan Ignatov, morally destroyed and crushed, hurried to leave the village Ezerovo, knowing exactly what to do next.

"So, that's you talk, I am a robber-hajduk, then I shall become him!"

"Let's go, Ivan, let's take a walk round Sofia, let's get some fresh air, the New Year is coming soon," Todor invited his friend next morning, and boarding the train at the nearest station, they soon arrived and admired the pre-New Year capital.

Sofia, ancient as Europe itself, located on an elevated plain, surrounded on all sides by the mountains, visible in a distance, ancient Serdika, renamed Sofia in the Middle Ages, all stood on an ancient foundation. Excavated ancient amphitheaters, fortresses' walls and towers peeped out of the ground here and there and reminded the contemporaries of their heroic past. 30 thousand years BC a man found a comfortable place of residence here and founded a settlement that turned into a city for the Celtic-Thracian tribe Serdi, which immortalized his name in the name of the city in the 7th century BC. The Romans, who subjected everything in their path to their power and expelled the Thracians and Greeks, turned Serdika into a large and important city on the Roman route from Sigidunum to Byzantium under Trayan, and the emperors Aurelian and Galerius were born here at all. Constantine the Great called Serdika "my Rome" and dreamed to move the capital here. Serdika survived the invasion of the barbarians and revival under Byzantium, and entry into the Bulgarian Kingdom, and Ottoman rule, after the liberation of which she became known as Sofia, the capital of Bulgaria. Each of the epochs left its cultural monuments in the city, and the frescoes in the Bayan Church of the 12th century, pained according to all the laws of perspective and 3-dimensional space long before Simone Martine's timid hints at these laws in his painting in the era of the Proto-Renaissance testify to the fact that it was here, long before Italy, where the Renaissance began.

The Iskar River crosses the eastern part of the city from the south and carries its waters to the north, cutting a passage through the Balkan Mountains, and flows into the Danube, and the small rivers, flowing through the city, with bridges over them, embankments and gardens create a spectacular picture. One of them, Vladay, recalls the heroic events of the recent past: the Vladay uprising, named after the village of Vladaya, situated on the banks of this river near Sofia, where the heroic soldiers reached in a noble impulse to overthrow the odious monarchy and establish republic.

Todor and his friend Ivan walked along the streets of Sofia and admired the city: paved with stone pavements, beautiful stone houses, shops filled with goods, advertisements about thriving business were everywhere. Citizens streamed in one direction toward the city center. Todor and Ivan joined them.

In one of the central squares of the city, Alexander Stamboliysky spoke from the corner balcony of the building of the Ministry of Foreign Affairs, overlooking the square. Next to him on the balcony were the member of Stamboliysky's cabinet, the kmet of Sofia Krum Popov and his faithful companion and comrade-in-arms Raiko Daskalov. Daskalov acted as the head of the country during Stamboliysky's foreign trips, and now Stamboliysky was telling a large crowd of townspeople, which had gathered at the square, about his 100-day trip abroad.

Todor and Ivan Ignatov squeezed through the crowd, trying to get as close as possible to the balcony. Soon they were standing under the very wall of the ministry building and listened to Stamboliysky's speech. His mighty figure towered nobly from the balcony above all those gathered and his loud voice sounded majestically over the square, trying to penetrate into the depth of everyone's heart and thoughts:

"Bulgarian people! I can tell you that we've solved all the tasks that were assigned to us. We have achieved that the reparations of 2 billion 250 million francs imposed on Bulgaria by the victorious powers, were reduced to 550 million francs for 60 year of payment. Today Bulgaria is advancing, because she is governed by the Agrarian Union, the same Union that opposed Ferdinand and the war, and she is advancing, because it is new Bulgaria with completely new political organization and with new principles of diplomacy. Instead of a gun and ax we have a slogan that proclaims peacefulness, friendly relations with the neighbors and friendly relations with the states of the Entente.

Most recently, the Great War ended with complete defeat of Bulgaria, having left a deep imprint on the soul of every Bulgarian. Before the roar of cannons on the battlefields and the wailing of relatives, who lost their loved ones in the war, silenced, when the 'chauvinist patriots' started talking about 'revenge' and new adventures. The whole world is a witness how the entire Agrarian Union and its leaders, having put their life and freedom at stake, resolutely opposed Bulgarian entry into the world slaughter, were thrown to jail for this by the tsar Ferdinand and suffered a lot, having freedom and life of Bulgaria as the highest good and goal of their lives. We, the Agrarian Union, were against the war then and are against the war now. As long as we, the Agrarian Union with Alexander Stamboliysky, govern Bulgaria, there will be no war, no 'revenge' and no adventures! We resolutely stand for peace with all the countries and especially for peace with our neighbors.

For this purpose, we have made a trip throughout Europe, lasting 100 days, which resulted in the establishment of diplomatic relations with foreign countries. We were deprived of the Aegean Sea, and Greece occupied Eastern Thrace even before the signing of the Treaty of Neuilly, and we are trying to resolve this issue and resume access to the Aegean Sea, but only by peaceful means! It's true that the Serbian chauvinists threaten us with a new war and threaten our lands even more. And if they make an onslaught on us, we'll be able to defend our borders. But our task is not to succumb to the provocations of our neighbors and to prevent a new war, which Bulgaria will no longer survive! Therefore, we conclude a peace treaty with the Kingdom of Serbs, Croats and Slovenes! We also ban the action of the chetas from the Pirin region, who raid the neighboring kingdom and commit terroristic attacks there. Our goal is peace! For peace we traveled all over Europe, the countries, which have their own contradictions and their own interests in the Balkans. Our goal is to have peaceful relations with each of them.

We started our journey with a visit to London. Yet at the time of signing the Treaty of Neuilly he was more favorable toward us than Georges Clemenceau, and therefore we decided to visit England, where we were met with a friendly welcome and enthusiastic reviews of the British press, and Lloyd George invited us to another dinner after we left England for France, so that we had to interrupt our meeting with Georges Clemenceau for a while and return to London again to dine with the prime minister of the British empire once more. And we arrived to Paris again, the entire Ministry of Foreign Affairs met us there more favorably. The British press wrote enthusiastically about our visit. We also met with the Pope of Rome, we concluded diplomatic treaties with foreign countries. Our position on the Bosphorus and the Dardanelles coincides with the position of Russia: the straits should not belong to Turkey, but should have an international status and be free for the passage of the ships of all the states."

His noble speech sounded majestically, emotionally and loudly, captivating the crowd of citizens, gathered at the square, and everyone knew that this was true: as long as Alexander Stamboliysky is alive, and as long as he is the leader of Bulgaria, there would be no war. The inhabitants of Sofia were listening to him with admiration and somewhere in the corner the Macedonian autonomists clenched their fist. Todor and Ivan noticed that a young man, about their age, was standing next to them, tall, thin, of pleasant appearance, and he was listening as if spellbound, catching every word of the Minister-Chairman.

"His supporter?" Todor asked.

"His is my hero!" the young man answered. "I myself am a member of the Youth Organization of the Agrarian Union, and he is our leader."

"I can bet that I know Alexander Stamboliysky even earlier than you," Todor said.

"Really?"

"I met him 5 years ago, in autumn of 1915. He came to us in Bodrovo to agitate against the war and convinced that the Entente would win this war. We met in the hall of our school, I was sitting at the front desk and supported him."

"That's true, I was there too," Ivan Ignatov confirmed.

"Mikhail Guenovsky, a member of the Youth Organization of the Agrarian Union," the young man introduced himself and extended his hand.

"Todor Todorov, and this is my friend Ivan Ignatov, we are both from the village Bodrovo."

Young men shook hands and got acquainted, smiling. Ivan even cheered up, having forgotten for a while about the offense, inflicted on him in the village Ezerovo.

"Maybe we'll meet again!" Todor said. "The world is small."

"Especially the Bulgarian world!" Guenovsky answered and added. "Alexander Stamboliysky is the best of all! He is the best leader of Bulgaria that has ever been. He is the most talented and noble, the most intelligent and honest, the most courageous and kind! I am ready to give my life for him!"

"So it is," Todor agreed, "only the fate gave him a difficult time, and the task is difficult for him: to raise the country, destroyed by the war."

Alexander Stamboliysky finished his speech, which lasted several hours, an explosion of applause was heard in response to him, and the townspeople began to disperse. Todor and Ivan said goodbye to their new acquaintance and went to the station. They walked in high spirits, discussing what they had heard. They were strongly impressed by Alexander Stamboliysky's speech and the meeting with Mikhail Guenovsky.

"Mikhail Guenovsky is educated, he knows a lot," Todor said, "maybe you and I should move to Sofia and enter some university, for example, the Agrarian People's University, founded by Alexander Stamboliysky?"

"What about our farm?" Ivan was surprised. "The city life is not for me. I am a free bird, I am a resident of fields, forests and mountains. It's enough for me many books that I read, there are books in our home and in our Bodrovo library."

"Yes, fortunately, we have a wonderful library. I also take books there and read them one after another, and I want to know even more, to get a higher education, I dream about it."

They passed by the royal palace, where at that time the new tsar of Bulgaria Boris III was sitting, having shut himself alone. Deprived by the Stamboliysky government of the prerogative to form executive bodies, deprived of the right to represent the country in the international arena, deprived of the opportunities to exercise the functions of the supreme commander-in-chief, which was claimed by tsar Boris, the son of the former tsar Ferdinand, he sat locked in his palace, gnashing his teeth and clenching his fists. He hatched plans for "revenge" and prepared for vengeance.

Thus, 1920 ended for Bulgaria.

Chapter 23
Hajduk Ivan Ignatov

Alexander Stamboliysky on his mighty shoulders pulled Bulgaria out of the consequences of the war. Clamped in the grip of the Neuilly Treaty, Bulgaria did not have right to have a regular army, and she did not have funds for a contract army. There were not enough people to guard the borders, and the neighbors kept getting impudent. In order somehow to organize the youth, Stamboliysky adopts a law of compulsory labor service, socially equalizing the entire population. He declared socially useful work obligatory for all able-bodied men from the age of 20 for a period of one year and women from 16 years of age for a period of one year, regardless of their position in society and property status. With their work for the country young people had to help to overcome the post-war period devastation. Young people from all levels of life, equalized by position, gathered in detachments, built roads and bridges, restored the economy, and the neighbors of Bulgaria—Greece, Romania and Kingdom of SHS—immediately raised a howl and protested against the "laborists", enraged by too rapid pace of economic recovery in Bulgaria, calling it "militarization".

And the young people themselves all over the country gladly joined the labor detachments, where there were no military discipline, uniform and difficulties, but there was complete freedom and feasible work for the good of the motherland. Along the way they communicated, got acquainted with each other and made new friends. They worked 5 days a week and went home for a weekend.

Todor, who became 20 on the fifth day of the New Year 1921, also worked in one of these detachments on the construction of a road near Bodrovo. Ivan Ignatov did not get into a labor detachment, as he was one year younger than Todor, and continued to make plans how to become a hajduk.

Spring awakened nature from hibernation, having painted everything in bright colors, and bare black, seemingly dead skeletons of trees and bushes, retaining life-giving force as a secret, as if by a wave of a magician, they bloomed with green foliage. Meadows and gardens were painted with all the colors of rainbow, and white and pink flowers on the fruit trees filled the air with an intoxicating aroma and desire for life. The blooming spring and the bright sun, warming all living things around, filled the soul with hope and joyful expectation of the best. Farmers plowed and sowed the fields in anticipation of a rich harvest.

Todor worked in a labor camp near Bodrovo, building a road, and several hired workers worked in their fields. Todor's father Ivan, 12-year-old Gocho helped to pasture the herds. At the weekend Todor was at home. The feast of June 3, St. Constantine and Helena, marked the summer, which came into force and replaced spring. The feast was traditionally held in Bodrovo on the south-eastern outskirts on a huge flowering meadow, where the villagers and guests from nearby villages who arrived there, had fun, communicating, drank and ate with friends and settle accounts with foes. The young swirled in the whirlwind in horo-round-dance, intoxicated with youth, sips of rakia and the blossoming nature around. They argued among themselves who danced better, gathered in rival factions, arranged brawls and gave vent to the passions, emotions and bubbling power-energy of the inhabitants of the south.

Todor set the tone in the horo-round dances, and his mortal foe Guenov-Kamine did not even show up at the feats, even if he was surrounded by policemen, because he knew that a whole detachment of his faithful companions had gathered behind Todor's back: Mityu Ganev and his older brother Peter, several Turks and Greeks, Ivan Ignatov with his cousins Peter and Valko Buchevs and Todor's cousin Vidyu with his older brother Todor. Guenov-Kamine avoided direct collisions and cherished plans for revenge behind the back. The festive fun in Bodrovo on the "Helena's Day" was followed by everyday work in the fields, pastures and labor camps, and then again horo-round dances, rakia, food and showdowns at the "Holy Spirit" gatherings in the village of Skobelevo near Borisovograd and then again on "Elijah Day" on the glade of Saladin. The religious names of the feasts had nothing to do with their content and were only transmitted according to tradition from the ancient time, when the believers in Christ half-heartedly with pagan rites entreated the deities, drank, ate and rejoiced in their honor, so that they would send them prosperity, life and harvest in the fields.

Thus, the summer of 1991 flew by in the horo-round dances of fun and work, and by the beginning of autumn a new house of the Todorov-Karagochevs was built. The father Ivan with the hired workers built a new house nearby for the family, hoping that Todor would soon find a life partner, get married, and the new house would be mainly for him. Everything was ready for the move and the housewarming party. Todor took a week off in the labor detachment for the construction the road to work in his fields and at home, and now he was sleeping peacefully in a summer shed in his garden, resting from a day's work.

"Get up, Todor!" he heard through his dream and immediately woke from a push in the side.

Armed Ivan Ignatov and Blagon Ganev Zabanarov were standing in front of him.

"What happened?" Todor grumbled, displeased that his sleep was interrupted.

"We stole a herd of sheep, divided it into 2 parts, hid most of it in a safe nook of Petyu Mitev, and the smaller part, the sheep are standing here nearby, we need to drive to Ezerovo. I was requested sheep by Peter Hubinov Manikov and Rusi Panev, they will buy them for half price."

"What? What the heck? Are you out of mind?" Todor could not believe his ears.

"Don't you have your own sheep? You have a house, fields and herds of cattle and even the notorious shop to boot! Are you crazy?"

"I became a hajduk," Ivan Ignatov answered calmly, "I said that I would become a hajduk, so I became him; yes, I have a house and flocks, but I became a hajduk, I stole even more sheep, so that I could have them even more, and we'll sell some, we need money. We shall put together our detachment, and I'll take vengeance on those who tormented me and humiliated me. Help us to drive some of the sheep to Ezerovo and be a witness to the deal, so that they don't deceive us."

"You have already been deceived!" Todor became indignant. "Who requested you sheep in Ezerovo: Panev and Manikov? They are provocateurs, hired by Guenov-Kamine, don't you understand? They want to lure you into a trap, and you are dragging me there too? My father has just built a new house for me, we are moving tomorrow morning, I want finally to live in peace! I don't need your sheep! Leave these sheep, disband them! Hajduks fought for freedom, but they were not sheep thieves!"

"How is it to disband?" Ivan Ignatov, as if distraught, stood his ground. "We stole them from our enemies with such difficulties and drove some here, there is still a little left: to drive them to Ezerovo."

"Why do you need it?"

"I've decided so! I was beaten and tortured in the Borisovograd police, accused of what I never did; they attributed robberies to me that I did not commit; they did not allow me to marry my beloved girl, accusing me of being a robber, bandit and hajduk! So, I became him to take vengeance on them all."

"You are a blockhead," Todor was indignant, "with these sheep you will not vengeance in your enemies, but you will fall into the clutches of Guenov-Kamine into a trap and behind bars!"

"Are you my friend or not? Help me only to drag the sheep to Ezerovo, so that we get paid!"

Cursing his fate, his friend and everything in the world, Todor got up, took a revolver and against his will left the barn. A small herd of sheep, 4? in number, was grazing peacefully in a distance. Todor's heart began to beat, and blood throbbed in his temples. His feet marched against his will, a terrible premonition stabled like a dagger into his heart: this is the end of your peaceful life and this is a turning point on your path, the milestone. Rejoicing that his friend had not abandoned him, Ivan Ignatov cheerfully drove the sheep, and Blagon Zabanarov helped him. They descended from the hill, on which Bodrovo stood, passed through the valley and climbed the hilly area to the village Ezerovo. It was a black night, and only bright stars illuminated their path. They approached the nearby houses of Peter Hubinov and Rusi Panev. Todor was standing aside, holding a revolver in his pocket, when Ivan Ignatov and Blagon Zabanarov called them out of the house. Todor's heart continued to beat, he cursed himself for not resisting Ivan's request, for having yielded to him, and his legs have brought him here against his will. And now he is participating in this circus, in this madness. With a sharp eye through the darkness he saw that Peter ad Rusi refused to buy the sheep, they even refused to take them for free and soon disappeared behind the fence of their houses. The unfortunate sheep bleated, demanding lodging for the night, and the faint rays of the rising sun gleamed in the east. Ivan Ignatov and Blagon went back with empty pocket.

"Did I warn you that it was a trap?" Todor said in rage through his teeth. "And you have dragged me into this affair."

Deathly silence accompanied them all the way home, everyone was dumb, and only tired sheep bleated, asking to go home. Soon they reached Bodrovo. The darkness merged into light, and Todor rebuffed:

"I go home, take them wherever you want."

He hid behind the gates of his house, and Ivan Ignatov with Blagon Zabanarov went around the village from the south-east and hid the sheep in the empty house of Scheryu Elev at the end of the village. There they were seized at the same day, and on the same day they appeared in the torture chamber of the Borisovograd police. And a day later Todor joined them. His body, healed from wounds, was cracking at the seams again. Through the veil of oblivion the mugs of Guenov-Kamine and the policemen flashed before his eyes, pocking him in face with a written statement from Rusi Panev and Peter Manikov from Ezerovo that an armed gang of 3 people in led by Todor Todorov broke into their house at night, trying to rob, threatened with weapons, extorted money and forced to buy a stolen flock of sheep. His blood flooded his swollen eyes, he could barely distinguish their filthy mugs in semi-consciousness; whistle of the scourge cutting through his body to the bones echoed with a chorus of ridicule and abuse, and then the blackness of non-existence engulfed his being, and he was already more dead than alive.

For 27 days the sadistic butchers tortured him in their own pleasure in Borisovograd police and sent him unconscious on a cart to Haskovo with a mountain of documents about the unsolved crimes. All the statements about unsolved robberies in recent years now have been solved by the Borisovograd policemen. All these robberies were committed by Todor Todorov, and his half-dead body in a cart was presented as evidence in the case. The butchers-sadists in Haskovo beat his half-dead body for the other 20 days and signed "confessions" with his hand, hanging lifeless like a whip. On the basis of these "confessions" the court of Haskovo threw his half-dead body into the Haskovo prison, where Ivan Ignatov with Blagon Zabanarov had been jailed long ago.

Chapter 24
Haskovo Prison

December in the foothills of the Rhodopes was cold. The village Zhelti Bryag, located on their plain, which was a part of the Haskovo region, was knee-deep in snow. A dilapidated shed, warmed only with hay, could hardly warm Mityu and Petyu Ganev-Armanovs and their friend Georgy Staikov, who were hiding there, shivering from cold.

"We should put a sentry on guard," Mityu said, shivering from cold.

"Who will find us here and even in such a weather!" Petyu objected.

"Maybe we'll move to another place, where we light a bonfire?" Georgy Staikov asked.

And before he could finish his question, a formidable voice from outside answered him:

"Give up, you are surrounded!"

All 3 men jumped on their feet and snapped at the weapons. Mityu Ganev looked out through a crack in the wooden wall of the shed and saw that numerous policemen with the guns pointed at them surrounded the cabin. Mityu fired at the first person at random. In response there was a fire, and the bullets, ahead of each other, fell on the dilapidated shed, only shreds bounced off it in different directions. All the rebels fired back as best they could. The skirmish continued for some time, then the revolver fell out of the hands of Petyu, who was wounded in both hands, and Mityu bled, the bullet hit him in the shoulder. The policemen snapped into the shed and grabbed the 2 wounded, but the third one was not there.

Having taken advantage of the turmoil and the fact that all the policemen moved to the entrance of the shed, Georgy Staikov escaped through a hole in the back wall of the shed and disappeared. In the handcuffs put on their bloody hands, the Armanovs were dragged out of the shed, thrown into a cart and taken to the Haskovo prison.

"There are still patriotic heroes in Bulgaria!" the policemen said with a smug smile. "They denounced us about you and informed where you are hiding!"

The cart with the Armanov brothers, whose fame was ahead of their actions, since there was no bank in the country, which they would not rob, and there was no rich man in the country, whom they would not steal from, having shared with the destitute, drove to Haskovo and unloaded them in prison.

Built in 1885, when after the Liberation the failed San-Stefano Bulgaria was again divided into several parts and its southern part with its center in Philippopolis and the entire Haskovo region remained a Turkish province called South Rumelia, a prison in the north-western part of Haskovo still retained the traces of Turkish rule. These were one-story buildings, stretching along the perimeter of a rectangle of 100 x 60 meters with 3 courtyards, where cells for prisoners faced. In one part there were cell for those still awaiting trial.

In one of the cells of the prison there was Ivan Ignatov, imprisoned for 2,5 years and Blagon Zabanarov, sentenced for 3 years, since during the investigation it turned out that it was he who initiated the theft of the sheep and incited Ivan Ignatov to do this, and the later agreed "to become a hajduk". In the next cell Mityu Ganev-Armanov, underage, having escaped the death sentence, was sitting in proud solitude, having been sentenced for 101 years imprison, unlike his brother Petyu, who was sentenced to death by hanging. The condemned to death Petyu, Kolyu Panev from the village of Bodrovo and Todor, sentence for 2, 5 years, were sitting in a neighboring cell. In a small narrow chamber a coat peg hung on the wall, and there were 3 mattresses stuffed with straw in striped covers on the floor. The same striped prison uniform was on the prisoners. A barred window and a wooden door overlooked the courtyard of the prison, where the prisoners went for a walk.

After beating and torturing the half-dead body of Todor, who once again escaped death, lay like a palliasse on a straw mattress on the floor and by some miracle retained the breath of life in the depth of itself. Neither his mother Atanasa with the grandma Mariyka were there to treat his wounds, neither his father Ivan nor his younger brother Gocho were there to support his spirit, but there was an unbroken spirit in him and a feeling that it was not the end yet and the fate was preparing him for the greater struggle. His deep wounds heeled and skinned over, and his face became even more handsome. Soon his neighbors Petyu Ganev and Kolyu Panev made the company with him, and all of them met with Ivan Ignatov and Blagon Zabanarov, and Mityu Ganev in the inner courtyard for walks. Everyone was overshadowed only by the death sentence for Petyu Ganev. It darkened them, but not for long. Without waiting for the execution, Petyu Ganev and his friend Kolyu Panev decided to run away, and on one of the black nights of spring 1922, with help of the friends everything was ready for their jailbreak.

That night it was heavy rain, muffing any other sounds and thickening the impenetrable darkness even more. Todor handed Petyu and Kolyu the key to the lock in the cell door and tightly twisted long linen rope with a "cat" at the end. It was a device, resembling the cat's claws: 4 sharp hooks that could catch on any wall so that you could climb up the rope, as they did so in the ancient times.

"Blagon Zabanarov got the key, he is a picklock master," Todor said, "and Ivan Ignatov brought the rope with hooks after they were taken somewhere to work outside the prison. He wound a rope around his waist under the prison clothes and managed to bring it here."

"Let's run with us!" Petyu and Kolyu said.

"I thought about it and decided to stay," Todor answered, "I am afraid that if I run away, it will be worse for Ivan, Blagon with Mityu, and I'll never be able to get home legally. And I want to go back to my house. Well, run, there is not much time. Do you understand everything? Remember the route?"

The fugitives nodded their heads that they remembered. They hugged for parting, said goodbye and thanked Todor for his help. Petyu easily opened the lock in the wooden door, and both of them slipped out and closed the lock from outside. It was a heavy rain, and the sentry in the courtyard hid themselves in a wooden booth. Petyu and Kolyu slipped imperceptibly past the booth to the wall, dividing the yards. Swinging the hooks, they threw them up with all their might. The hooks flew up, dragging the rope with them, and firmly hooked on the top of the wall. Having pulled the rope slightly and making sure that the hooks were motionless, both took turns climbing the wall, got along it to the roof of the neighboring prison building and made their way for a long time along the wet and slippery roof to the back wall of the prison, and then went down the drainpipe to the outside and were free. A heavy downpour hid all traces. Wet and excited, they started to run as fast as they could outside of

Haskovo, bypassing the fields and meadows, toward Aidanlar, where they found home and shelter. Their faithful companions Vidyu and Todor Karagochev and their kindhearted father Gocho received them, gave cloths to change and fed them.

Next morning the wardens opened the door of the cell and found one person instead of 3 in it and raised the alarm, and began to beat Todor again, inquiring him how his cell matchers had escaped.

"I was sleeping and did not see anything," Todor answered only, enduring the beatings.

Suspecting the intervention of the higher powers in the matter, the wardens crossed themselves in horror, appealing to the help of these higher powers: there were no signs of the lock breaking, the door was locked, but the prisoners had gone. A search and interrogation of prisoners from the other cells began, and after somebody said that he saw Petyu and Kolyu exchanging words with some guard, they suspected those guards of complicity.

In Borisovograd police station the already drunk pot-bellied chief Gogov poured himself another glass of rakia, foreman Nesterov helpfully served him a piece of cheese for a snack. Guenov-Kamine was smoking a pipe and blew a puff of smoke.

"What are we going to do?" the chief Gogov asked.

"What if the rest run away?"

"There is a plan," Guenov-Kamine answered, thinking cunningly, emitting clouds of smoke from his mouth, "we are already working on it."

Chapter 25
Guenov-Kamine Plan

Having watered the earth abundantly, the rain stopped. The sun warmed the earth more and more every day, the spring of 1922 resurrected the dead skeletons of trees and black branches of bushes to life. Flowers flashed like bright lights through the lush greenery, and the meadows were covered with green grass like the velvet. A huge herd of sheep, goat and cows of the Karagochevs peacefully grazed in the meadows, devouring the grass. Ivan's brother and Todor's uncle Gocho tended his flock with joy in the heart. He gazed at the vast lands and rejoiced at life, often recalled his late father Todor, who managed to preserve these lands, inherited from his ancestors, increase them and pass on to his sons. He thought about his brothers, everyone was worthy—both Ivan and Dimitar—only the traitor Angel brought his father to grave. None of the relatives had any connections with him.

He thought about his brother Ivan and about misfortune that fell on him because of his son Todor, who like an evil fate was pursued by misfortune one after another, and now he is in prison. In the depth of his soul he rejoiced at his own sons: both Vidyu and older Todor grew up, matured, both got married, gave birth to his grandchildren, already have their own farm and houses, handsome, heroes, brave, courageous knights with the spirit of freedom inherited from their ancestors—hajduks. They are kind and fair, like the heroes of the ancient legends, which all of them heard from the cradle and passed on to their children. The known Mityu and Petyu Ganev-Armanov so many times found shelter and refuge, and home in their house! And the same nephew Todor with his friend Ivan Ignatov could always find support and help here in hard times.

"Poor boys are tormented now in Haskovo prison! Thanks god that my sons are all right!" aging Gocho thought to himself, and his heart was filled with joy and tranquility: in his old age there will be someone to look after him in a nice house.

His summer cabin stood at the edge of the field near the stream, and Gocho's sons Vidyu with Todor were working in the field. In the valley Kostadin Petrov Stanchev was resting from work; they called him Kosta, Gocho took him temporarily for a season work, since he really asked, and they all needed help. Kosta, a young fellow with small ugly features, small shifty eyes, filthy and stinky, fell on the hay in a summer cabin to rest. The door suddenly opened, and Petyu Ganev with Kolyu Panev appeared on the threshold. Kosta began to fuss and get nervous and wanted to go out, but the entered blocked the way.

"We need to talk," Petyu told him.

"Yes," Kosta bleated cowardly like a sheep, glancing at the door, "how are you?"

"Tell us: is it true that Vidyu with Todor began to cooperate with the police?"

"How come? Not at all! Can't be!" Kosta exclaimed falsely and rolled his small eyes to avoid meeting their eyes.

"Tell the truth!" Petyu said threateningly. "And who are you anyway? How long have you been working here? If you work here, you should know everything. Everyone says that Vidyu with Todor became the police informers."

"Well, I'll tell you everything," Kosta whispered, looking around, "yes, it's true: they work for police. I got hired here to work, spin around everywhere, I see and hear everything, and I know everything. The police hired them and gave them 2 guns to kill you."

Blood hit Petyu in the face, and he turned purple with anger. Kolyu could not believe it.

"You are lying, dog! Why would police give them rifles, when they have their own weapons?"

"This is so that they don't jeopardize with their guns. After all, you are being chased everywhere, all people look for you, so Vidyu with Todor decided to get rid of you, they are tired to feed you all the time for nothing."

"You are lying!" Petyu roared, though Kosta repeated them word for word what they had already heard in all the nearby villages.

"And here is another thing, you don't know who betrayed you in December," Kosta whispered even more quietly, looking around cowardly, "then, in winter, when you were hiding in Zhelti Bryag, you don't know who betrayed you, do you? It was them, Vidyu with Todor who found out where you were hiding and reported to police."

The blows rained down one after another, and poor Petyu no longer knew whether he should have heard it or not.

"Only don't tell them that it was me who told you," Kosta whispered pleadingly, "otherwise, they'll kill me and you won't know anything else."

"I'll kill you myself if you've lied!" Petyu threatened ruefully, and they with Kolyu disappeared from sight.

Several days passed. The happy father and wealthy owner Gocho continued to graze his heard in peace, contemplating his possessions, and enjoyed life. Vidyu with his older brother Todor were working in the field. Peace and happiness overflowed their hearts; they had everything one could dream about: fertile lands, herds and wealthy houses, happy families and already their own children. Suddenly Petyu with Kolyu appeared in front of them with aimed rifles.

"What is it, a joke?" Vidyu was dumbfounded.

"Tell the truth," Petyu said threateningly, "was it you who handed over Mityu with me to police last winter? Do you work for police now?"

The dumbfounded Gocho's sons wanted to snap at the weapons, but the guns lay in the cart aside.

"We are unarmed, put the guns down!" Todor replied.

"Are you crazy?" Vidyu could not believe what was happening. "What's going on?"

"Everyone says that it is you who betrayed us, you hired to the police to kill us and you betrayed us last winter."

"What we have lived to see!" Vidyu exclaimed. "You pointed your guns at us, unarmed, and this is after all that we've done for you! After all our entire family has done for you! We fed and watered you for free for many years, sheltered you, and slandered us and pointed your guns at us!"

Petyu with Kolyu retreated and lowered their rifles.

"But why do all people tell us about it in Bodrovo and in Ezerovo, and in other nearby villages, and somebody else told us about it?" Petyu pronounced, but did not name who exactly told. "If you regretted the food that you fed us with the brother, if you planned to get rid of us, then why you didn't just say: 'Don't come here anymore, there is no more food?' If you want to kill us, then take this rifle and kill us! Why did you go to the police?"

Petyu handed Vidyu the rifle. There was a pause.

"Wake up, fools, you've been deceived, don't you understand?" Vidyu exclaimed excitedly, not touching the rifle. "I can even guess whose plan is this, for sure this is the plan of our uncle Ivan's 'best friend' Guenov-Kamine, the plan is to set us against each other, so that you kill us, and there will be nobody to feed you, and then you'll disappear too. The only thing is not clear, if every one of our lineage, whom he hates, die, then what will this Guenov-Kamine live further with! What will he do next! Remember, how many times we saved you with Mityu and hid from the police! Aren't you for shame?"

Petyu with Kolyu put their rifles down and embarrassed.

"Excuse us, if we offended you, if all this is a lie, forgive us, just everybody says it. We are leaving this place, we'll go far away, and you won't see us again. We won't bother you anymore. Thank you for everything you've done for me and Mityu."

Everyone was standing in silence thoughtful. Then Petyu with Kolyu went round and disappeared from view.

Some time passed. In order not to upset his father, Vidyu with Todor did not say anything to him, and Gocho continued to graze his herds, enjoying life and nature.

"What a happy father I am!" Gocho thought happily, looking at his sons.

He was proud of them and sympathized with his brother Ivan, whose oldest son Todor was behind bars in jail. Gocho and his sons owned herds, fields, houses and small cabins throughout the territory of their possessions: barns and sheds, summer cabins, sheepfold, arbors and verandas. Vidyu, having finished working in his field, went to the house of his brother Todor, but the later was not at home.

"Uncle Vidyu, I'll go with you to look for dad," the 7-year-old son of Todor, Vidyu's nephew, addressed to him. Vidyu put his nephew in the cart drawn by oxen, and they drove to a remote place of their possessions, where there was a summer cabin next to the sheepfold. They rode to the stream next to the sheepfold, unharnessed the oxen and let them graze and drink water. Dobri Bursukov from Bodrovo was watering his oxen near the stream.

"Haven't you seen Todor?" Vidyu asked.

"No, I haven't, I've been here for a long time, but I've not seen him, my oxen are still drinking."

"Come with me to our cabin," Vidyu called him, and they approached a wooded summer lodge that belonged to their family, standing in the distance. There was silence, there was no sound.

"Probably, he is not here," Vidyu said, "if he was here, then his dog would recognize us and greet. He always walks with his dog."

They approached the house, 7-year-old Gocho trailed behind them.

"Where is dad?" the boy asked.

The door of the lodge was wide open, and they came in and saw Todor sitting in the corner of the room.

"Finally, we have found you!" Vidyu rejoiced.

"Dad, dad, look what a pipe uncle Vidyu gave me!"

Todor did not answer. Vidyu walked up to him. Todor was sitting with his head bowed and said nothing. Vidyu noticed that there was a hole from a bullet in his temple and a trickle of gore on his face. Todor Gochev was dead. Overcoming shock so that not to lose consciousness, Vidyu grabbed his little nephew in his arms and ran outside, only now noticing the corpse of the unfortunate dogs lying in the bushes. Shocked, Dobri Bursukov did not even try to console him.

"What's with dad?" little Gocho asked naively, in the depth of his childish soul suspecting bad had happened.

"Wait here, don't follow me," Vidyu ordered and, overcoming grief and shock, returned back to the lodge.

He searched his brother's clothes and found that the military parabellum, which the latter carried with him, was gone. Together with Dobri Bursukov they carried Todor's body to the cart, put him in the cart and, having taken Todor's 7-year-old son, Gocho, in their arms, went home to Aidanlar.

"It is Petyu Ganev and Kolyu Panev who did it!" the Haskovo police concluded and with this the investigation was finished.

The next day Gocho, the father, distraught with grief, buried his eldest son. All the relatives from Bodrovo came to the funeral: brother Ivan with his family, brother Dimitar with his family. The family of Todor Gochev—his widow with a child—plunged into despair. The employee Kosta was nowhere. Thus, in the prime of his life, a handsome young man, a hero and a knight, a kind soul, a fearless descendant of the hajduks, Todor Gochev Karagochev passed away.

Chapter 26
Vidyu Gochev Karagochev

A few days after the funeral of his brother, having lost his mind from grief, with rage and thirst of revenge, Vidyu Gochev went to Haskovo to the chief of the District Police Department with a request to help him to catch his brother's killers. He was provided with a rifle, cartridges, several grenades against receipt and a small detachment of 6 agents, armed civilians. All 7 went through the forests, mountains and fields to search for the killers of Todor Gochev: Petyu Ganev-Armanov with Kolyu Panev. Thus, Vidyu Gochev became a police agent.

Having got mad from grief of losing his older brother, whom he loved very much, Vidyu with a veil over his eyes, neither seeing nor hearing the voice of reason, without thinking clearly, stupidly went forward with the detachment of police agents, bypassing all the surrounding lands around. Before his eyes the pictures were from the past, how they grew up with his brother, how they were friends all the life, as they were spiritually close, had the same disposition, how the elder brother always helped him and supported in everything, how both lived in the neighborhood in abundance in their houses, in which Ganev-Armanov brothers were constantly given shelter, were constantly fed and watered boldly by the brothers, who did not fear of the police, since they were constantly wanted for robbery. He recalled how they gave shelter to the cousin Todor Todorov and his friend Ivan Ignatov, when they were persecuted. And then a gruesome picture in the summer lodge rose before his eyes: the dead body of Todor with a bullet in his head, a crying child and the widow, the father distraught from grief. Vidyu's hands were clutching the rifle, and one thought was pounding in his temples: revenge! He expelled all the other thoughts which occurred to him. He did not want to think why Petyu and Kolyu would kill Todor, and even secretly, if they could've killed both them publicly then in the field, if they had been told that Vidyu with Todor became the police agents and handed them over with Mityu. Or maybe even now the same enemies had lied to him that Petyu with Kolyu had killed Todor. He expelled from him thoughts of prudence, he did not want to think about why they killed the unfortunate dogs and, having killed Todor, stole his parabellum, while they had a lot of their own weapons. Why should Petyu with Kolyu kill Todor secretly, if Petyu with his brother Mityu made so many daring raids on banks and rich people, who got rich in war and speculations, and then shared the loot with the poor! After all, he knew both Mityu and Petyu Ganev very well for many years of communication; he knew that they were "noble robbers" like Robin Good, but not murderers to shoot from around the corner at those who helped them. Away with the thought of mind! Blinded by the thirst of vengeance, grief and rage, Vidyu stubbornly marched through the surrounding lands with his detachment of volunteers in search of Petyu and Kolyu, who were nowhere to be found. Petyu and Kolyu vanished, and nobody knew anything and said nothing about them.

The detachment of the "detectives" on a vicious impulse went around one village after another, but failed to find anybody. Vidyu fed the entire detachment at his own expense. Provision was over. The tension grew. He felt hostility.

"They gave us 7 days for search of the killers," one of the agents said, either joking or seriously, "if we don't find them in 7 days, we'll kill you."

Vidyu felt that he had fallen into a trap.

"Who will go with me to Bodrovo? I need only one person, we shall bring food, let the rest wait here."

Vidyu suddenly realized that he was surrounded by the enemies on all sides. But if at least someone agrees to go with him to Bodrovo, that one is not adversary and perhaps could be relied upon.

"I'll go with you," one volunteer answered, his name was Peter, he was from the village of Starozagora.

5 detectives lay down on the grass to rest, and the sixth, Peter, went together with Vidyu to Bodrovo. Uncle Ivan's house in Bodrovo was the same place of shelter and hospitality for Vidyu, as his house in Aidanlar was for Todor Todorov and all those who sought refuge. It was the house of true companions. Together with Peter they came into the uncle's spacious well-to-

do house, and Vidyu threw himself on Ivan's neck and burst into tears, Ivan also had some tears in his yes.

"Cry, nephew, cry, cry out grief! Gruesome grief fell upon all of us!" Ivan said, barely holding back tears, "But how is my brother Gocho, your father?"

"Completely got mad," Vidyu answered, sobbing, "I feel that I myself gradually losing my mind. I received the detachment of 6 men from the Haskovo police. Here is Peter, one of them. We walk all over the district to find the killers of our Todor: Petyu Ganev and Kolyu Panev, but we can't find them anywhere."

"We'll talk later," uncle Ivan interrupted him, "we'll have dinner first."

Peter introduced himself and greeted Ivan, who invited him to the table. Well-coming house of the Todorovs was distinguished by its hospitality, the same as the Karagochevs house in Aidanlar. They ate with appetite and drank some rakia. 13-year-old Gocho Todorov, Ivan's youngest son, rejoiced at the guests and looked at them with interest. His cousin Vidyu and his companion Peter were armed from head to toe, had rifles, revolvers, cartridge cases crisscrossed around their chests and grenades in the pockets of their wide trousers. He vigilantly scanned everything, eagerly absorbed the information and imprinted it in his memory in order to keep for life. He listened to what they were saying. It got dark. Ivan, avoiding a direct conversation on the case, waited until they went to bed. He put Peter to spend the night in another room, as he did not know whether the latter could be trusted, and only then fell into talking with Vidyu.

"Well, tell me," he said to Vidyu.

"We go on walking, uncle Ivan, but nowhere can find the killers of Todor: Petyu Ganev and Kolyu Panev," Vidyu said gloomily.

"But who told you that it was Petyu with Kolyu who killed Todor?" Ivan asked.

"How is it who? The policemen said right away," Vidyu answered in confusion, "the policemen said at once. Then, they, Petyu with Kolyu, came to us and pointed their rifles at us and accused us of being the police agents and that we had handed them over with Mityu then, last winter."

"And who told them about you?"

"The police."

"The same policemen did? It is the same policemen spread rumors that Todor and you were the police agents, and Petyu with Kolyu pointed their rifles at you, but they did not shoot. And if they wanted to kill you, they would've killed you at once when they pointed the guns at you. Could Petyu shoot you after all good you with Todor and your father had done for him and Mityu?"

Vidyu began to ponder on, recollecting all these past years, how they feasted together in his house, how they hunted together the common enemies, the Borisovograd policemen, in order to help Todor Todorov, uncle Ivan's son.

"And now I've abandoned the whole household, abandoned my poor father and hunt for them. And we are stamped with work at home. There are some hired employees, but they need an eye on. And Kosta is gone at all…"

"Which Kosta?" Ivan asked worriedly.

"Kosta, his name is Kostadin Petrov, Stanchev, our hired worker, my father hired him for work, he is kind of strange."

"You don't have to say anymore," Ivan answered, who felt like being stabbed in the heart with a dagger. "Do you know that this Kosta is Guenov-Kamine nephew? I've known him since his childhood…"

The gruesome truth flashed like lightning in Vidyu's consciousness and made him wake up.

"I remember him when he was little yet," uncle Ivan continued, "after all, we used to be friends with Guenov-Kamine, fought together in 2 Balkan Wars, took Adrianople together with general Georgy Vazov, we even fraternized. How many times he came to our house, ate and drank! Or, rather I thought that we were friends, and he came to us and was jealous. And I remember his nephew: such a wile creature! And why did you father hire him?"

Vidyu seemed completely came to his senses, woke up from the lethargic sleep, in which had been since the murder of his brother, and veil fell from his eyes. The true picture of what had happened suddenly emerged clearly in his mind. He realized what a trap he had fallen into.

"Thus, you became a police agent and an abettor of the real killers, our common adversaries, these mad dogs! They've killed your brother, then they will kill my Todor, then they will kill you and all of us one by one!"

There was silence. Dumbfound Vidyu understood and realized the full horror of what had happened.

"What to do now?" he asked helplessly.

"Can this Peter be trusted?" Ivan asked quietly, nodding his head to the next room, where the guest was sleeping.

"I don't know," Vidyu hesitated, "I don't trust anyone anymore, though, I think that yes, you can trust him."

"Then rely on him, and you have to part with the rest of the group, leave them. It would be nice if you go somewhere, to Plovdiv, for example. Stay there for a while and then come back. Just do not try to sell the estate. We inherited these lands from our grandfathers, from our ancestors, we are obliged to preserve them and pass to our children and grandchildren. And if you want to find Petyu with Kolyu, only, of course, not to kill them, but on contrary, to warn them, then you need to look for them near the water reservoirs: rivers, streams, fountains, familiar to all of you from childhood, where the hajduks quenched their thirst in old days."

Vidyu spent the rest of the night in a restless sleep and had nightmares as if they were real. In the morning they with Peter thanked Ivan for his hospitality, for diner and for the food that Ivan gave them for the squad of hungry detectives. They parted. Vidyu and Peter met their detachment of the "detectives" at the main road of Bodrovo, not far from Ivan's house, those came out of the Bodrovo kmet's building, where they were provided with an overnight stay, but were not given any food, and they pounced with appetite on the food, brought by Vidyu with Peter.

The summer of 1922, which replaced spring, was coming to an end, and the detachment of the "detectives" that had gone on 7 day campaign continued to wander around the nearby lands in a futile search for the fugitives. Vidyu fed them at his own expense and did not know how to put an end to this circus, because he felt surrounded by them at gun point and felt trust only to Peter. Finally they met with Petyu Ganev and Kolyu Panev by the ancient water source. The "detectives" sat in ambush at a considerable distance from the water, fearing to come closer, and waited. 2 armed men came out of the bushes and approached the source, drank water and began to fill their baklagas-canteens. Vidyu took aim with his rifle and was about to shoot into the air, so that the latter would see the ambush and hide.

"Do not shoot!" one of the "detectives" roughly snapped him by the elbow, and all 5 pointed their rifles at Vidyu.

At that moment Peter pointed his rifle at them in Vidyu's defense.

"Don't shoot, we'll take them alive," the "detectives" said, "otherwise, if you miss, they will shoot us all. Petyu Ganev has no equal in accuracy of shooting. And you want to kill him, so that he would not tell a lot, for example, how you, your late brother Todor and your father were his accomplices and hid him?"

"Put down the barrels," Vidyu answered, feeling gratitude to Peter, "if you decide to kill me, then before death I must finish off at least one of you."

5 ones put their rifles down and looked in the direction of the water source: there was nobody there anymore.

Some time passed, and Vidyu abandoned the detachment of the volunteers-detectives and went to Aidanlar home, allegedly for food for them. He never returned to them. He arrived to Haskovo policemen handed over the rifle and cartridges against receipt and reported that the fugitives had not been found. And after some time, Peter was found dead, thrown onto the rail road tracks. Again, in a state of insanity, Vidyu, without asking his father, sold all his property for nothing: the houses, herds, lands inherited from his ancestors, loaded the remaining belongings into the oxen-harnessed cart and went with the family to the village of Ezerovo, where he counted to build a new house on the acquired land. In Ezerovo Vidyu led the oxen to the forge to renew the shoes for the oxen, as the old ones were worn out, and in the forge he found Kosta, on whose belt a military parabellum hung that belonged to his murdered brother Todor. Hardly realizing what was happening, Vidyu cursed himself that he had sold the Aidanlar estate, but there was no turning back.

Vidyu did not follow the political life in the country and did not know what was really going on. He fought with the adversaries from Borisovograd and Haskovo and thought that this was the power and did not know that the criminals in police uniform committed lawlessness in defiance of the power of the Agrarian Union. He did not know that the government of Alexander Stamboliysky began radical reforms in agriculture to provide land for the destitute peasants and passed a law on the alienation of uncultivated land in favor of the state for further redistribution among the poor. The inalienable norm of cultivated land was 300 decares, and for the forests, fields and pastures—500 decares. The land areas abandoned, uncultivated, wasted, rotting in desolation, exceeding these norms, were alienated in favor of the state, if the owner did not assume the obligation to use rationally the surplus land holdings in the near future and build enterprises related to agriculture on them, so as not to rot the land, but turn it into vineyards, orchards and pastures for the prosperity of his own and entire Bulgaria. And in this regard, the transactions for the purchase and sale of land made after February 17, 1920 that is from the moment when the law was published were declared invalid. But Vidyu did not know this, as he "was not engaged in politics," and therefore, cursing himself for selling the estate, he fell into a state of even greater insanity.

In the same state of insanity he gave "on parole" the money from the sale of property to the freshly-minted "friends" from Ezerovo: Mityu Hadzhiev and Ilia Pyankov who entreated him for a loan for the construction of a new mill, the income from which Vidyu, allegedly, would receive too. New "friends" in collusion with another bandit Mikhail Mandaliata lured Vidyu into a trap and killed him with an ax blow at his head.

On the eve of his death, on February 20, 1923, Vidyu came for the last time to visit the house of his uncle Ivan Todorov in Bodrovo, where his name day was celebrated. They rejoiced, sang, ate and drank. Vidyu Gochev left and never returned. 3 bandits hit on the head with an ax not to return the money. Bleeding, he was crawling on his stomach along the land of Ezerovo, no one helped him, and when his distraught father Gocho found him lying on the ground in a puddle of blood, it was too late.

Thus the good-natured, handsome, hero, valiant Vidyu Gocho Karagochev passed away, thus in an instant the entire family vanished, a rich estate disappeared, becoming a legend, as the one they gave shelter to: Mityu Ganev-Armanov, the legend of Aidanlar forest.

Following him, those whom Vidyu, blinded by a thirst of "revenge," mistakenly chased after, whom he had given shelter before—Petyu Ganev-Armanov and his friend Kolyu Panev—also passed away. They were killed by the traitors when they were peacefully sleeping in a barn in the village Kirilovo of Svilengrad region. The freshly minted "sworn-brothers" acquired in the village of Kirilovo—the brothers Ilia, Dimitar and Ivan Karaboyuv—killed them in their sleep in order to receive the reward promised by the Haskovo police. But when they brought the bodies of the dead to Haskovo, the Haskovo police threw the killers in jail in order not to pay the promised reward, which they took for themselves, having declared that the bodies could not be identified. Gruesome news awaited the heroes who were imprisoned in the city of Haskovo.

Chapter 27
Stamboliysky's Speech in Haskovo

The gruesome news of the death of the brothers plunged Todor Todorov, Mityu Ganev and Ivan Ignatov into despair. A gruesome grief crushed them, and it also pushed them to take a decision step: to escape from the jail in order to take revenge. By mid-May of 2023 everything was ready for the escape of Mityu Ganev. The friends decided that Mityu Ganev, who had a life sentence, should run away first, and they would escape after him. It was not difficult for them to escape, but they did not want to run away and leave Mityu in jail. Mentally, Mityu Ganev was already parting with his cell in jail, ready to escape. Everything was going according to plan, until one of the freshly-minted friends whispered in the ear of the guards:

"Today Mityu Ganev is escaping from the prison. I hope I'll be rewarded."

At that moment the guard stormed into Mityu's cell and put him into a solitary confinement cell and then locked him in another cell. The rat-informer grinned wickedly. The next morning the chief of the Haskovo prison called Sofia by telephone:

"Robber Mityu Ganev planned to escape from my prison, which is not suitable for him, as it does not have proper security. Please, transfer him to another prison!"

Om May 12, 1923, Mityu Ganev-Armanov, chained and handcuffed, escorted by 15 policemen, went by train along the route from Haskovo to Sliven, located north-east of Haskovo. In Simeonovgrad there was a transfer to another train and a change of convoy. 2 policemen from Simeonovgrad, who met the arrivals at the station, mockingly asked:

"15 armed policemen escort 1 ironclad prisoner, who is shorter than all of you?"

"We hand him over to you, then you convoy him to Sliven. This is a famous robber Mityu Ganev, haven't you heard?"

"Yes, we have heard, but never seen him before," 2 policemen answered, sympathetically looking at the heavy fetters on the hands and feet of Mityu Ganev, "is it really he, the same one? But he looks like a teenager."

"Sign a receipt."

The Haskovo convoy handed over the escorted one to the Simeonovgrad convoy against receipt and went back to Haskovo. And the new guard of 2 people and Mityu Ganev in chains waited for a long time train to Sliven, which finally arrived, crammed so that to get into any car was impossible. Helping Mityu Ganev in chains to climb the steps of the car, the policemen stopped at its open place and sat down on both sides of Mityu, who became in middle of them and also sat down on the floor, sighing heavily. The train started moving.

"At least, take off the handcuffs," he asked them pitifully, "so that I could smoke quietly. Where shall I go in iron shackles on my legs!"

The policemen looked at each other and, apparently, there was something human in them, removed the handcuffs from Mityu Ganev and gave him a cigarette and lightened it. Mityu inhaled with pleasure and began to thank them almost with tears in his eyes. All 3 were gazing from the open space of the train car, which was heading from Simeonovgrad to Sliven to the north-east. Landscapes of the ancient city flashed before their eyes, where human being settled in pre-historic times, and in antiquity the baths and temples flaunted, and where the last Roman emperors found refuge for themselves and built the fortress of Constantine with underground labyrinths, where they hid their treasures of the emperors of Rome. Forests flashed. The policemen now and then shifted their gaze from the beautiful landscapes to Mityu, then again admired the nature. Finally they saw that Mityu, having finished smoking his cigarette, was peaceful dozing, tired. They also lay down on the floor. The train went along some more distance, and suddenly, unexpectedly, Mityu Ganev hopped up to his feet and, like a spring, jumped from the train car with ease. He rolled head over hills on the grass and vanished into the thickets of the forest. In the place, where he had just been, heavy iron chains were lying next to the policemen. How they fell off his feet, remains a mystery. The dumbfounded policemen, bulging their eyes, stared after Mityu Ganev, who had vanished in the distance, and only after a while they guessed to stop the train already at a considerable distance from the incident and start vain search.

The news that the famous robber of all the times and peoples Mityu Ganev escaped from custody spread all over Bulgaria with a lightning speed and, having penetrated the walls of the Haskovo prison, cheered up its inhabitants. In the morning of May 13, 1923, Todor Todorov and Ivan Ignatov were ready to escape. It was not difficult to escape from the Haskovo prison, you just had to make up your mind, realizing that if you were an owner of a house and land, you will never be able legally to return to your house and land.

In the morning of May 13, 1923, the prisoners of the Haskovo prison were sent to work to the city garden, which was created at the banks of the Haskovskaya River and landscaped by the hands of the prisoners, they also built a road, leading to the garden. The prisoners were dressed in the civilian clothes not to embarrass the townspeople, and they were without any chains. More than that, they freely moved back and forth. The dinner time was approaching. By 11 am Todor Todorov, Ivan Ignatov, Blagon Zabanarov, Ivan's mate in the case of the stolen sheep, and several other men received a responsible task to go back the prison for bread and soup in cans for the prisoners, working in the garden. Having moved away from the construction side at a required distance to hide, everyone at Todor's signal rushed in all directions. The lush green forest rustled in the distance, and everything around had already long blossomed and smelled with spring of 1923.

"Let's run to the forest!" Ivan Ignatov pulled Todor by the hand.

"Wait, we'll make it, do you see something is happening in the city."

From everywhere streams of people flocked to the central part of the city, stretching in a chain along the roads and paths.

"Crazy? Let's run, faster!" Ivan tried to stop Todor.

"Nobody will find us in the crowd," Todor answered to Ivan's horror and headed in the opposite direction straight to the center of the city.

Soon they merged with the crowd and completely lost among it. A crowd of people with the flowers in their hands greeted Stamboliysky, who was riding a white horse, accompanied by his party companions. The white horse was walking slowly, the Prime Minister of Bulgaria was sitting majestically in a saddle, apparently, this is how the tsar Ferdinand once dreamed to enter the conquered Tsargrad. Soon the procession reached the high tribune, Stamboliysky got on it and greeted the audience. The enthusiastic roar of the crowd subsided, and Stamboliysky began his speech.

"Bulgarian people! We won! We fought on all the lines, and we won. The last struggle that we are waging and in which victory will be ours is the struggle for the triumph of order and law! And it is not the anarchists that we are fighting with, let it pass, leave them alone, let them arrange themselves as they like, if they do not do anything illegal. I hope, everyone remembers how, after talking with some anarchists and learning from them that their friends were arrested and beaten by police in the 6th police station in Sofia, we immediately ordered that they all be released.

The Macedonian terrorists committed a terrorist act in the National Theater against us and our ministers: Bakalov, Yanev and Obov. The person who threw the bomb is an unimaginable villain, and only accidentally did not destroy the mass of people in the stalls of the theater. As for me, I declare that I forgive him, since he is a blind instrument of others, and as long as I live, I shall never allow blood to be shed and human life taken away because of me.

I am fulfilling my role of the head of the state as a role of a warrior, placed on the battle front in order to fulfill my duty before the fatherland. Our enemies are these who, hiding behind the law, beat and torture people, commit atrocities and lawlessness in their official positions, and if they are the members of the Agrarian Union at the same time, then they disgrace our party, and we shall inevitably purge the cadres. There is no place in the Agrarian Union for the executioners and sadists, and also there is no place for any exploiters: covetous men, knackers, parasites, speculators, moneybag-bankers, who profited from the war, innkeepers and rural and urban chorbajis.

We are opposite to the fact that any large landowner, who owns thousands of decares of land, would not use this land for the good of the country, would not cultivate it, would not grow agricultural crops on it, but would rot it and this land stands in desolation, not benefiting anyone. Therefore, back in February 1920, we adopted the land ownership law and left the inalienable norm of 300 decares for exploited plots and 500 decares of land with fields, forests and pastures, and everything that is above the norm will be taken away and give to the poor and landless peasants, if the owner of the land does not undertake not to rot his land in desolation, but to turn it into the flowering gardens, pastures and vineyards, or to build agricultural production enterprises.

The Agrarian Union today is the only political organization in the world with its own political ideology, and we have many enemies: they are attacking us from the right and from the left. From the left they call us bourgeois and rural bigwigs, and from the right they slander us that we are the 'Bolsheviks' who almost made an alliance with Moscow. The Communists enjoy our sympathy, because they represent the urban workers of Bulgaria, and we could be allies. But look what happens: taking advantage of our sympathy for them, they constantly lie and slander us, organize strikes and stoppages to undermine our power. They accuse us of terror against them. In the most difficult time for us, in winter 1919–1920, they staged a railway strike only in order to blackmail for themselves an equal number of portfolios in the government, and this strike could have political consequences.

We had just returned from Neuilly-Sur-Seine; the peace treaty had just been signed. We didn't know where we were and what we could do. The international position of Bulgaria was so difficult that a strike could lead to dangerous political consequences. Serbs, Greeks and Romanians only expected that we would give them a reason to occupy us.

But this storm has already passed. The then struggle for life and death is already in the past. And what is today? The Communists continue to slander that we organize terror against them! And where is this terror? Was at least one representative of their party or one leader arrested by our government and put on trial for political activities? The Communists freely participate in the life of the country, have seats in the People's Assembly, freely hold their meetings and publish their bulletin 'Rabotnichesko Delo'. And Vasil Kolarov, Georgy Dimitrov and Hristo Kabakchiev go the Congress of the Communists, where they play leading roles, make reports, are elected to the leadership of the Comintern, and after that they freely return to Bulgaria. Has anyone made a claim against them? How many times the Entente complained to me: "Why do you allow them to go to Moscow?" And because of this, I was suspected of having connections with Moscow. And I only answered them with a counter question, why do they tolerate their Communists and why do they let them go to the Comintern to Moscow. Where is the terror against them from us?

There is terror! But this terror is not against the Communists, but it is against us, the Agrarians! In the entire history of their activities in Bulgaria, especially during our rule, has the Communists party suffered such sacrifices like we, the Agrarians, have suffered with the terrorist murder of Alexander Dimitrov! Not a single hair fell from the head of the Communists through our fault. It is really so difficult for them to understand that every blow inflicted on us from the right, given under the current disposition of the political forces, is also a blow against them! The victors in the war demanded from us to outlaw the Communist Party, we did not obey their demand and did not ban the Communist Party, as they did it in Yugoslavia and Romania. But, god forbid, if the flayers from the Black Block and the Military League, and the terrorists from IMRO with the help of the neighbors overthrow our government, the next day there will be not a trace of the freedom that the power of the Agrarian Union provides Bulgaria, and will be no trace of them. And this threat is real. There is terror against us, the Agrarians, but we fight, because we are the organization of fighters and we are not afraid of death.

We started the war against illegal Macedonians. They seek out all means to bring the Black Block to power and anticipate their destructive work. For 5 years now they have bear claiming to be fighting against Bulgaria. Let them answer: has at least one Greek or Serbian minister received threatening letters? But namely Greece and Serbia own Macedonia. The Macedonian terrorists killed our dear companion Alexander Dimitrov. Our comrade-in-arms, our Minister of War and outstanding politician of the Agrarian Union Alexander Dimitrov was murdered by the Macedonian assassins on October 22, 1921, during our trip abroad.

The Macedonian assassins seized Kyustendil, dragged many people out of their homes and killed them, attempted on the lives of Raiko Daskalov, Tsanko Tsarkovsky and our other ministers. And just now, on May 3, 1923, having set up an ambush from around the corner, they shot down a whole truck with the Bulgarian soldiers in Sveti Vrach. Their aim is clear: to overthrow the Agrarian Union government. We do not covet to shed blood, but these Macedonian terrorists hung the Bulgarian citizens and killed the Bulgarian soldiers from an ambush. We'll wage war against them, arrest their abettors and harborers. And if they encroach on the life of one of us, we'll take the measures that the merciless struggle dictates to us, so that the sword falls from their hands, so that the barbarism does not come.

We have one new Christianity: these are the ideas of the Agrarian Movement. And just as in old days barbarism did not stop the victorious march of Christianity, so today our enemies will not be able to stop the solemn victorious march of the Agrarian Teaching. We have concluded an agreement in Nish, under which we undertake to guarantee peace on our border with Yugoslavia not allow the chetas to cross the borders. At the same time we proclaim the right of nations to self-determination. We attach international treaties as a guarantee of the rights of national minorities.

But every Balkan people should have a suitable outlet to the sea. We are for the Balkan Federation. And in order for the Balkan people to unite peacefully, first of all it is necessary to declare a republic in Bulgaria. The most important thing: the Agrarian Union is the power of the people and our highest goal is democracy. The time has come to liquidate the monarchy, without which it is impossible to realize a new higher stage of democracy. Our goal is to declare a republic in Bulgaria, a labor republic, in which power comes from the people and belongs to the people, and the People's Assembly will be the highest power in the Labor Republic of Bulgaria.

We with our lawyers are working on the text of the new Constitution, which will be one of the most democratic in the world. It'll strengthen the principles of self-government in the grassroots cells—communities and neighborhoods. The new Constitution will proclaim the principle of democracy, which will be created by the Agrarian administration: referendums, labor property, public education, public justice, etc. It is necessary to provide labor property, honest human labor, inviolability of a home, fundamental human rights and freedom. But we'll take away these guarantees of property, which was the fruit of robbery as the result of suffering of the people. The Constitution will be clear, precise and define, always and in everything patronize the working people, but not the exploiters, oppressors and robbers. I've see here the tobacco manufactures banks: huge new buildings of the private banks.

Believe me, Herskovits, it'll be all yours. The bankers will hand them over to cooperators and syndicates; if they do not do it voluntarily, we'll take them away. You will be the witnesses: next time, when I come to Haskovo, all these capitals and capitalist enterprises will be in the hands of the cooperative people. We do not support capitalism and the private capitalist system. We are against capitalism.

This autumn the monarchy will be abolished, and Bulgaria will be declared a republic. We are moving toward this goal we shall fight for it, as our dear friend and a poet Sergei Rumantsev wrote:

"Life is a continuous battle here
And in that battle is real life!

Fight for and be the first for mere
Love of our people's strife!"

Alexander Stamboliysky spoke for several hours, and his speech was constantly interrupted by the applause of the crowd. His speech was directed to the future, but there were some tragic notes of self-doom in it. He compared himself to a warrior and said:

"A true warrior and a true social fighter march proudly and confidently against any danger that life places in his path. And in this bold and steady movement forward, in this encounter with dangers along the path of struggle, the wrestler finds a truly reasonable meaning of life…"

2 friends, who escaped from the prison, were listening with their mouths open and then slipped unnoticed to the outskirts of the city and hid in the thickets of the forests outside Haskovo. On that day, May 13, 1923, the imprisoned builders of the city garden vainly waited for lunch, on that day they were left without it.

Chapter 28
At the Abyss

The air was filled with alarm of a storm, threatening to break out. Astute people sensed that something was happening or would soon happen. A philistine, going about his own things, as always, knew nothing and did not want to know anything, and the people, who participated in the events, knew perfectly well what was happening. A harbinger of a storm, a huge black cloud appeared on the horizon and, growing, was moving closer and closer.

April 25, 1923 was a warm evening, and the tsar of the Bulgarians Boris III, the son of Ferdinand, enjoyed the fragrance of nature in his Botanic Garden of the Vrana Palace.

"How wonderful my father arranged everything here," nostalgically recalling childhood, said Boris, smiling, whose already tiny eyes almost disappeared with a smile, turning into tiny slits, and most of his face was occupied by a long nose and disgusting square form black mustache under it.

Tsar Boris was in a sweet state of expectation of the pleasant.

"Yes, Your Majesty," Kostadin Muraviev servilely assented, smiling to the tsar in response, "soon everything will be decided, you must return to your proper place which belongs to you by right. Everything goes according to plan."

It was a young 30-year-old man of elegant appearance with a shock of black hair, flauntingly raised and licked back like a cock's comb, and rather rotund round cheeks, slightly hanging down, imparting him a frowning look. The freshly-minted Minister of War of the Stamboliysky government, who became him barely of 30 years old, was in the company of the tsar Boris in the garden.

"He has arrived," his adjutant reported to Boris, and a young military man approached them.

"Lieutenant Popov has arrived on behalf of the Plovdiv Garrison chief," the arrived reported, stretching out in a string.

"At ease," Boris answered him, "we have a private conversation."

"I have a confidential assignment from colonel Stoyanov to clarify the issue, regarding your approval of some upcoming events."

"I do approve all the upcoming events in advance, lieutenant, so speak directly and report in detail."

"Colonel Stoyanov instructed me to find out your attitude to the fact that a military upheaval is being prepared against the government of Alexander Stamboliysky."

"Go on," the tsar said smugly, exchanging glances with Muraviev.

"So, the conspiracy has been preparing for more than a year, and almost all the officers of the Plovdiv garrison are involved in it. And now emerges the question of which side the head of the garrison colonel Stoyanov will take. Colonel Stoyanov through the Major Porkov received a letter from Colonel Vylkov, in which Colonel Vylkov categorically demands an answer and consent to take side of the conspirators."

"And what's about colonel Stoyanov?"

"He is indecisive. He replied that his consent would depend on the Haskovo and Sliven garrisons. He received information that the head of the Haskovo garrison Colonel Zlatov had been on the side of conspiracy from the very beginning. Then Colonel Stoyanov sent his confidant Major Porkov to Sliven. Major Porkov returned and reported that the head of the Sliven garrison colonel Khumbadjiev was also among the conspirators, all of them are just waiting for the signal to move and waiting for the consent of the head of the Plovdiv garrison, who sent me to you to find out your position."

"Whose side are you on?" the tsar asked with a sly smile.

"I am like the others," Lieutenant Popov reported.

"Well done, you are a true patriot, be sure, you will be rewarded. Tell Colonel Stoyanov that I not only approve the upcoming events, but it is me who organized them. So, it's Colonel Stoyanov's duty to act as our fatherland and the Lord require."

"Can I be dismissed?"

"Dismissed."

The faithful adjutant of Colonel Stoyanov, Lieutenant Popov, hurried from the palace to report that the assignment entrusted to him had been fulfilled with honor. Having received the answer from the tsar, the head of the Plovdiv garrison Colonel Stoyanov some more for a long time did not agree to betray his motherland, doubted, tormented by remorse and cowardly looked around, fearing to be arrested from one side or another, and then, finally, he made up his mind and gave Vylkov his consent, with what he put a huge weight on the scales, hanging in favor of the conspirators, since the success of the entire operation in southern Bulgaria depended on the position of the Plovdiv garrison.

After the end of the visit of Lieutenant Popov, Boris III and Muraviev discussed the technical details of the upcoming operation and its political consequences for a long time, and then, satisfied with progress of the case and with themselves, they went home.

Despising the danger, Alexander Stamboliysky secluded himself at his villa in Slavovitsa, where he was working on the draft of the new Constitution, abolishing the monarchy and proclaiming the republic, and ordered no one to let in. The Orange Guard soldiers guarded the villa, and the guards reported on a guest's visit:

"Mr. Koev, the governor of the Plovdiv district, persistently asks to receive him."

"I said that I do not accept any visitors," Stamboliysky got angry, as he was interrupted from his work.

"He insists," the guard replied.

"Let him in."

Gasping and wheezing, an agitated Koev entered the prime minister's office. He was holding an envelope in his hands.

"Mr. Stamboliysky, the upheaval is being prepared against you! You are in danger!"

"Oh, it is this you are talking about! I do know it. I know that the Macedonian autonomists have sentenced me to death long ago."

"You are wrong!" Koev said hastily, afraid of not being in time. "The Macedonians have nothing to do with it. The conspiracy is prepared by the military, and they use the Macedonians simply for a screen."

"You did not say anything new," Stamboliysky said absently, completely immersed in the draft of the new Constitution, "these don't like me either, because their business is to fight, and I am against war, I am for peace."

"Look here!" Koev handed Stamboliysky the envelope with the documents. "Here are 18 names of the military and members of the Black Block, the leaders of the National Liberals of Plovdiv, their meetings and negotiations. At first, I learned about the conspiracy from 2 officers, honest officers. They told me in detail that for a year the conspiracy has been prepared to overthrow the government of the Agrarian Union. They even told me the technical details of the upcoming conspiracy. After that I managed to establish personal contacts with the conspirators, as I made it clear to them that I was on their side. Almost all the officers of the Plovdiv garrison are in the ranks of the conspirators. Under an oath that I gave them not to reveal the secrets, I received from them all the exact data and these documents."

Stamboliysky was holding the envelope in his hands without opening it.

"The Minister of War Muraviev convinces me that the danger comes only from the Macedonians."

"Lies!" Koev exclaimed irritably. "Macedonians will be used only as the distraction, and some ministers are involved in the conspiracy!"

"Immediately go to the Minister of Internal Affairs Hristo Stoyanov and the Minister of War Kostadin Muraviev and tell them what you've told me, let them take all measures."

Stamboliysky called by the government telephone and ordered Stoyanov and Muraviev to receive Koev. Koev left Stamboliysky's villa, got into his official vehicle and rushed back to Sofia. And Stamboliysky with a despair of the doomed returned to work on the draft of the new Constitution of the Republic of Bulgaria.

A few hours later, overcoming incredible difficulties, Koev reached the office of Hristo Stoyanov, the Minister of Internal Affairs, and reported to him about the impending upheaval. Dumbly, Hristo Stoyanov listened to Koev to the end, trying to find out what exactly he knows, and sent him to Kostadin Muraviev. With a sinking heart, understanding what was going on, Koev began to report to Muraviev.

"Shut up!" Muraviev interrupted him rudely. "I'll order to arrest you now for treason! Who gave you the right to interfere into the state affairs?"

"We need to alarm the villages," Koev continued stubbornly.

"Get out of here, and if you tell anyone else, you'll be shot for treason!" Muraviev threatened and sent the unexpected visitor out, cursing him.

Depressed Koev, clearly seeing the impending catastrophe before him, left and began to look for ways to get in touch with other ministers. And Kostadin Muraviev, joyfully anticipating the grandiose changes in his life, already saw himself in the role of the prince and son-in-law of the tsar Boris III, as he was a lover of his vile and ugly sister Evdokia.

The whole of Bulgaria was buzzing and resembled a huge beehive: couriers-conspirators scurried back and forth like bees under the auspices of their queen Boris. United in a conspiracy against people, all the scum of the Bulgarian society called themselves "People's Conspiracy" and from April 1922 began to operate actively. All the dissatisfied with life: all the bourgeois parties, military, active and retired, joined the People's Conspiracy. They hated Alexander Stamboliysky for 2 national catastrophes, for the defeat in the Great War, for the Peace in Neuilly, for the participating in the Vladay Apprising on the side of the soldiers, for erecting a monument to the heroic soldiers, who were shot near Sofia by the walls of the Sugar factory.

They hated Stamboliysky for 500 years of Turkish slavery, the blinding of the Bulgarian soldiers by the Byzantine emperor Vasil II the Bulgar Slayer. They seethed with anger, spitting, ready to take revenge. They were joined by the "Constitutional Block", created on June 6, 1922, nicknamed the "Black", which united all the bourgeois parties that had lost their positions with the defeat of Bulgaria in the Great War.

In all the cities of Bulgaria, the conspirators recruited supporters in military garrisons and police stations, established contacts, sent instructions. Between the center in Sofia and the provinces, the couriers scurried with secret reports, instructions and orders to clear the technical details of the upheaval, the announcement of the exact date that everyone was eagerly awaiting.

The tobacco producers of Bulgaria provided them with money. In Sofia, Plovdiv and the other cities of Bulgaria the palaces of nouveau-riche sprang up like the mushrooms after rain; the speculators-merchants, having come from nowhere, became millionaires as the result of the war. Against the post-war disasters, they erected luxuriant palaces, restaurants, shops and banks and teased the impoverished people with their luxury. Tobacco merchants prospered especially. The conspirators relied on their money. The press organ "Tobacco," created by them, became a platform for the enemies of the Agrarians, and the editor-in-chief of "Tobacco" was the first chairman of the "People's Conspiracy." Streams of lie, slander and street swearing at the address of the Agrarian Union spewed out of themselves "Tobacco" and the bulletin "Struggle," akin to it in spirit with a pharisaic name; only he waged a struggle against good in favor of evil. It was only the "Epoch" that competed with them in terms of lies, slander and abomination; it belonged to the broad socialists, headed by the editor-in-chief Grigor Cheshmedjiev, who took revenge on Stamboliysky for not taking him to the ministers. The bulletin "Slovo" was a propaganda organ of the "Conspiracy" itself, while the "Illinden" and "Nezavisimaya Macedonia" were the messengers of the IMRO, which sentenced Stamboliysky to death. There were no lies that their brains turned inside out would not invent, there was no slander that their bestial spirit would not concoct and, characterizing themselves in essence, they brought down streams of abuse on Stamboliysky.

From the left flank the Communists of Bulgaria muddied the water, slandered and yelped as they could in unison with "Tobacco" and "Struggle" in the "Rabotnichesky Vestnik" and did not want to go to any proposals from Stamboliysky about the alliance against the "Black Block." They were opposed by the Agrarian Banner, in which the bright articles of Alexander Stamboliysky and Raiko Daskalov smashed and ridiculed all the filth of the "People's Conspiracy," telling people about what really happened in the country.

Fighting on 2 fronts, both with the BCP (Bulgarian Communist Party) and with the "Conspiracy," Stamboliysky carried out agricultural reforms and brought the defeated country back to life. Crowds of refugees, who flowed into Bulgaria from the torn away Macedonia and Thrace, received shelter and roof over their heads. By labor service he raised all the people to rebuild the country, defended honest labor and gave free medicine for the poor. And in the elections on April 22, 1923, BANU won a crushing victory. In the lower levels, in the fighting nuclei of the Orange Guard, created to defend the Agrarian Union, they knew what was happening and, preparing to fight, they gathered their secret meetings, stocked upon weapons, hidden in the villages from the commission of the Entente, and took an oath:

"We swear in the name of god, the Holy Gospel, the cross of the Lord and in the name of the interests of the fatherland that at the cost of our lives we shall keep sacredly and indestructibly the ideas and principles of the Agrarian Union and all laws created by it, to keep in absolute secrecy all the orders of the Union and definitely fulfill them with readiness. If I break this solemn oath I've given, I shall answer with my head."

***

Contrary to the danger, confident of the rightness of the cause, Alexander Stamboliysky expelled from himself a tragic foreboding of trouble. He recalled the warning of General Savov from Paris, where he was a plenipotentiary minister of Bulgaria, about an upheaval, being prepared in the country. Savov learned about it from the French Freemasons, who were closely associated with the Bulgarian Freemasons, who were all traitors-conspirators. Savov asked to take measures. Stamboliysky was in a hurry to complete his work. Secluded in Slavovitsa, he worked hard on the draft of the new Constitution. Built a year ago for the Minister-Chairman a 2-story villa with an attic next to his native house was situated in 3 km from Slavovitsa and in 90 km from Sofia in a valley surrounded on all sides with high hills and mountains between the left bank of the Maritsa and its tributary.

A massive antique writing desk, leather sofa and armchairs in his study, where he worked on the Constitution, became a favorite place, where he sought for seclusion lately, where he had a sense of peace. His work was interrupted by the visit of the distinguished guests. On June 7, 1923, Tsar Boris III arrived to visit Stamboliysky with his sister Nadezhda and Evdokia. A luxurious welcome met the guests. Stamboliysky villa was a nook of a flowering paradise on earth. Built in 1922 a small 2-story house with an attic and a veranda, situated next to his native house, where he grew up and spent his childhood, was surrounded by a flowering garden and orchard in which watermelons and melons ripened against the background of fragrant roses, jasmine and lilacs.

In the distance, on the hills growers were green, behind which the fields with ripening wheat stretched, the villagers worked, and the high mountains on all sides seemed to guard the peaceful life of all the inhabitants. The blessed June sun, warming all living things on earth, illuminated the idyllic picture of the earthly paradise, which, it seemed, no forces of darkness would ever dare to encroach upon.

Squealing with delight, the "grand princesses," the sisters of Boris Nadezhda and Evdokia, accompanied by the retainers went for a ride astride horses around the neighborhood, while their brother remained in the villa and spoke with Stamboliysky. They were sitting in and arbor in the garden among the roses, jasmine and lilac and were engaged in a small talk about agriculture, necessity of its mechanization, about the harvest and export of grain and corn. The tsar was not at all interested in this topic and started talking about his own:

"My father would like to return to Bulgaria and end his days in this country, which became his second home."

"This is out of the question," Stamboliysky replied firmly, looking at the tsar, "the people will not accept this, will not understand this and will not allow it. No one has forgotten how much trouble Ferdinand brought to Bulgaria and how much grief for her people."

Boris gloomed, and the fake friendly smile disappeared from his long-nosed face, but restraining himself, he continued:

"Mr. Stamboliysky, do you intend to abandon your plans for state reforms of the liquidation of the monarchy, given by god, and establishment of a republic?"

"This is also out of the question," Stamboliysky answered calmly, "the monarchy has outlived its usefulness, it is a break for social development, its time has ended. Our goal is to establish rule of the people in the form of republic, and you can even put forward your candidacy for the post of president of the republic and participate in elections, and if the people elect you, if they vote for you by their majority, then you have the right to become its first president, but only for the period determined by the Constitution."

The tsar again squeezed out of himself a gracious smile. Here his sisters returned from a walk, and Stamboliysky invited them all to the table, laid on the veranda. The hungry pounced upon the delicious rustic home-made dinner of Stamboliysky, and when they devoured it with appetite, bringing joy to the owner, he was informed that the other visitors had arrived and wanted to see him urgently. Apologizing, Stamboliysky left the table, came out of the house and went to the gates of the yard. Party comrades-in-arms Petko Petkov, Stoyan Kalichev and Jordan Vishovgradsky were standing there. They were in the highest degree of anxiety. In an exited voice they began to speak.

"Mr. Stamboliysky, the tsar is preparing a military upheaval, the entire army is set in motion. Sofia is surrounded by troops, the Minister of War Muraviev is a traitor! Arrest the tsar right here and now, otherwise the irredeemable will happen!"

"You are crazy! Even if it's true, I can't do it. He is the guest in my house, he is sitting at my table. There will be a big scandal."

"Mr. Stamboliysky, this is the only chance to prevent the tragedy, there will be no other chance!"

"The people is with us, the police, the Orange Guard will protect us."

"There are traitors in the police, the Minister of the Interior Hristo Stoyanov is also under suspension, and the Orange Guard has disappeared!"

"It is impossible! The general elections have just passed on April 22, and we won a complete victory, you know, don't you!"

"We know that the tsar has been preparing an upheaval for a year now, they have everything ready, they will strike at any moment. Maybe, he came to you just to mock. Arrest him, he is the enemy of the state!"

"Go away! I can't do this!"

Stamboliysky resolutely asked them to go outside the gates and in a complete desperation they withdrew to face the catastrophe. The guests were very pleased with the reception and the dinner at Stamboliysky home; they did not skimp on pleasantries and, having eaten and drunk to their fill and having enjoyed, the host's hospitality, they hurried to leave. Having gone behind the gates, the tsar chuckled and pronounced venomously:

"Well, farewell the Minister-Chairman!"

"We won't see each other again!" the ugly Evdokia said with an evil smile and, exchanging glances with her brother and sister, she giggled; all 3 of them giggled.

Chapter 29
June 9, 1923

The next evening, June 8, 1923, the tsar Boris III had another meeting in the pergola of his garden in his Vrana Palace. General Ivan Rusev and the Minister of the War of the government of Alexander Stamboliysky Konstantin Muraviev reported on the progress of the upcoming operation.

"Have we everything ready?" the tsar asked, looking inquiringly at the colonel, general and minister.

"That's right, Your Majesty!" everyone reported, stretching along the string.

"Speak more quietly, gentlemen," Boris answered, cowardly looking around, where extraneous ears could be hiding behind thickets of bushes, "well?"

"The army is on alert," the Minister of the War reported confidently.

"The entire army?" the tsar specified.

"Almost all, and those who are against us are disarmed and destroyed," General Rusev informed, pleased with himself. "We carried out a number of operations to neutralize them. Thus, for example, Lieutenant Tuleshov, loyal to Stamboliysky, was summoned from Shumen a month and a half ago together with his regiment, and the day before yesterday we deftly removed him from the regiment and summoned him to Shumen district court in a case trumped up against him; thus the regiment was left without the commander and entered our disposal. And we'll deal with Tuleshov later."

"Wonderful!" the tsar approved.

"In this way we neutralized and eliminated officers loyal to the government through out of the country."

"What about the police?"

"The police is also neutralized. The police stations are surrounded by our military detachments under the pretext of strengthening the police. Each police station in Sofia has been guarded over by one military branch, and somewhere the whole platoon under the guise of helping police in the course of a possible planned attack of the Macedonian autonomists."

"As a result, we have 6500 military personnel in Sofia against 435 police officers. Thus, the police stations are taken over by the military and completely deprived of the possibility of resisting the upheaval. And in some other cities, to our knowledge, there are police stations, such as Borisovograd and Haskovo, where the policemen are our people. By order of Hristo Stoyanov, the weapons that were in the police station were transferred to the military barracks."

"Is the Minister of the Interior Hristo Stoyanov still with us?" the tsar asked.

"That's right, it would've been impossible to disarm the police."

The tsar grinned contentedly: 2 key ministers: the Minister of the Internal Affairs and the Minister of War are the traitors of Stamboliysky.

"Orange Guard?"

"It no longer exists," Muraviev and Rusev reported ahead of each other, who will be the first to report, "we deftly took away from them the weapons that Raiko Daskalov supplied them after the events in Kyustendil last December, and thereby we disarmed them. By order of the minister, the Orange Guard fighters, who arrived in Sofia after Kyustendil and received weapons from Raiko Daskalov, were ordered to hand over the weapons to the military by the next order. Glory to our Lord Jesus Christ that Raiko Daskalov is not in Bulgaria, as he was recently sent to Prague as the ambassador!"

At the mention of the name of Raiko Daskalov, the tsar twitched in the nervous convulsions of hatred for him and all the other leaders of the Agrarian Union.

"These two ones will answer for their Radomir Republic!" he said angrily, "I'll show them the 'Republic', I'll show them the Balkan Federation!"

"That's right, Your Majesty!" the speakers confirmed and continued:

"Almost all the weapons are in our hands. In some villages the Orange Guard fighters hid their weapons secluded from the Entente, so our people removed the bolts from their guns and hid them in safe place in accordance with the order of the minister." Also, the Minister Stoyanov issued the following order: 'Any initiative for self-defense during the upcoming actions is prohibited!' The governor of the district of Plovdiv, a well-known supporter of Stamboliysky, obviously knows something about the impending coup and began to take initiative against it, so Hristo Stoyanov personally answered him: "None of your business! I forbid you to take any actions on your own behalf, you cannot do anything except what I order you! So, get out of here and wait for the instructions from the ministry!"

"Excellent!" the tsar approved, "By the way, it's good that Georgy Vazov is not in the country: he is being treated in Germany. And what's about his brother Vladimir?"

"General Vladimir Vazov is one of our leaders."

"Two Vazov brothers: Vladimir and Georgy would go separate ways, I think," the tsar said thoughtfully. "Yes, it's good that Georgy Vazov is not in Bulgaria."

"And what's about our broad socialists?"

"All are bought in bulk together with their leader Krastyu Pastuhov and their bulletin 'Naroden Glas' and the journalist Dimo Kazasov. Not only broad socialists are with us, but also some figures from the BANU, such as Dimitar Dragiev. He-he-he!"

"Amazing! And how are there our comrades the Macedonian terrorists from IMRO? They will not let us down, will they? When I last met with the Colonel Vylkov, he assured me that he is in direct contact with them and that everything is all right."

"That's right, Your Majesty, the autonomists from IMRO are our true comrades and allies. Todor Alexandrov promised us 200 fighters for the most important thing."

"He-he-he," the tsar Boris chuckled mockingly, "but Stamboliysky saved them from prison along with the General Protogerov and others, when they were in prison in Sofia for atrocities in Serbia during the Great War, and Serbia demanded their extradition by decision of Neuilly Treaty. Stamboliysky staged their escape from prison and saved him on his own head."

"He is our well-known humanist," Muraviev pronounced mockingly, "but we'll not be such humanists and will not make such a mistake."

"By the way, don't you pity him?" the tsar asked as if checking the degree of loyalty of the young minister. "He is your uncle, and you are his nephew, he raised you, fed you."

"I am not his nephew, but I am his wife's nephew," Kostadin Muraviev was offended, seething with anger. "I hate him from childhood!"

"Yes, there is no greater hatred in the world than the hatred of a nephew to his uncle," the tsar uttered philosophically.

And Kostadin Muraviev turned purple with anger, recalling juicy details of his birth, when a passing Russian officer knocked up his mother and disappeared in an unknown direction, and Alexander Stamboliysky, married to his mother's sister, took him a child, raised him, fed him, educated him and made him Minister of War, when Muraviev was barely 30.

"Yes, by the way, you owe the post of the War Minister to me," the tsar reminded. "Let's finish, gentlemen, time does not wait."

"That's right, Your Majesty! We have to hurry, they are waiting for us!"

"Is everything clear, gentlemen?" the tsar concluded in parting, ending the meeting. "To behead, certainly to behead, and I want to have proof! Kill everyone: Krum Popov, Tsvatko Avramov, Tsanko Bakalov, Stoyan Kalichev and all the rest! And in Prague track down and kill Raiko Daskalov! And promise IMRO 5 million leva a year."

"That's right, Your Majesty!" the conspirators confirmed and hurried to leave the Palace of Vrana.

They got into the car and rushed to Sofia, where Muraviev vanished into unknown direction, and Rusev arrived home, where the visitors were already waiting for him. The last evening in peaceful Bulgaria was coming to an end.

In a dark nook of a dark courtyard, a dark house was situated. In this house of General Rusev, nicknamed by the people Dobropolsky for being first to run without looking back, abandoning the army, when the allies broke through the front on Dobro Pole, 9 abettors were waiting: Sofia University professor Alexander Tsankov, Colonel Vylkov, who together with General Vazov captured Shukri Pasha 10 year ago, Officer Nikola Rachev, Professor Yanaki Mollov, Colonel Hristo Halfov, the tsar's adjutant, Peter Todorov, the deputy of the People's Assembly from the Radical Democratic Party, lawyer Tsvatko Bobashevsky from the so-called "People's Party," Kimon Georgiev, the lieutenant-colonel, and Dimo Kazasov, the journalist from the broad socialists.

They were sitting in a dark room with no light on, shaking with fear. The clock hand was approaching the midnight and started to count the first moments of June 9, 1923. Those gathered in the room understood that they were doing something out of the ordinary, for which they had come here that night, but they did not truly realize the consequences, although they had been preparing for this step for a year. They were turning history back from light to darkness, eternal darkness, from which the dawn will never come again. They were not completely sure of the success of what they had started, and therefore they were sitting in the gloom of the dark room, where only one candle burned, throwing gleam on the mugs of the monsters, and nervously looked at the clock that was stopping time. The hands of the clock seemed never wanted to move toward the gaping abyss, slowing down and forever saying goodbye to peaceful life in Bulgaria. Extend it even for a moment!

The participants were freezing in horror, then, having taken courage, they walked round the room and hissed like the poisonous snakes at Vylkov, who, the bravest of all, dared to approach the window and pushed back the curtain to look out:

"Don't come to the window, you will destroy all of us!"

"Calm down, don't spread panic!" the brave Vylkov hissed back at them like a viper, prudently moving from the window.

It seemed the eternity passed before the clock struck 3 am, and when the telephone rang, everyone froze in their seats in horror, bit daring to breath General Ivan Rusev picked up the phone, listened to the message and announced gratitude on behalf of god and the entire Bulgaria, and the audience exhaled and burst out crying of happiness, weeping.

"Behold, gentlemen, it is happening! An hour and half ago the army proceeded to carry out the tasks, assigned to it! Everything is going according to the plan!"

Here clamor and howl began, and Tsankov squalled louder than the others, waving his fists:

"To suppress all the attempts of resistance! To shoot! To hang! To kill! To crush! And now we'll draw up the composition of the new government! As I was promised, according to the agreement, I am appointed the Minister-Chairman, I hope! There are no other suggestions, are they?"

"No!" the audience confirmed, and in the clamor and noise, interrupting each other, they distributed the ministerial portfolios, appointing themselves ministers of the government.

And only when the machine-gun fire outside the window muffled their hubbub, they froze again in a daze with their mouth open, without any wish to part with their newly acquired portfolios of power.

"Everything is going according to plan, it is the post office and telegraph are being captured," Rusev explained the situation, and the joyful uproar broke out even louder, which no machine-gun fire outside the window could muffle any longer.

Tsankov, screaming louder than the others, in addition to the post of the Minister-Chairman received 3 more ministerial portfolios: Foreign Affairs, Education, and Military. The clamor of bacchanalia suddenly was muffled by the noise of the grenade explosion outside the window and furious knock on the front door. Instantly everyone fell silent and dashed to hide in all directions: some crawled under a long rectangular table, covered with a white table cloth, some tried to squeeze into a fire-place chimney or to cover themselves behind any ledges of the furniture corners. The knocking continued, and there was a cry: "Open! Long live Bulgaria!" The owner of the house, General Rusev, boldly opened the door, and the jubilant officers burst into the room and, saluting the general, continued to yell:

"Hurrah!" and "Christ is risen!"

"Indeed he is risen!" the self-appointed ministers confirmed, crawling out from under the table and out of chimney.

Their joy knew no end. They sang "Many years" and "Shumi Maritsa," washing down with cognac, hugging and kissing each other.

"Gentlemen officers!" Rusev addressed them, "Let me introduced you to a new cabinet of ministers of Bulgaria at the head of the Minister-Chairman Alexander Tsankov! Due to the fact that the government of Alexander Stamboliysky voluntarily resigned," he added.

"Christ is risen!"

"Indeed he is risen!"

"God is with us!"

Yes, god is always with you and with such like you, who would doubt: the whole history of mankind is evidence to this!

They triumphed in the victory, and each scribbled in his notebook everything that happened that night, they wrote down for posterity every word and every minute of action on that fateful night that forever divided Bulgaria into 2 camps: executioners-murderers and folk heroes-fighters against them; they wrote down their bloody names in the history of Bulgaria.

Meanwhile, the putsch soldiers like pewter were marching through the streets of Bulgaria, obediently and stupidly carrying out the criminal order. The "non-political" dark instrument of evil went forward to attack their native country, to kill the fellow citizens. They were joined by the mobilized, called under a threat of reprisals for failure to appear, all from 24 to 40 years old for free food and 50 leva reward "voluntarily" went to the villages to suppress the spontaneous riots of peasants. On that night on June 9, 1923, the conspirators broke into the houses of the Agrarian Union leaders, dragged them out of bed unclothed, pushed them into the trucks and dumped them in the barracks' basements, in the central prison and police stations, among which there was only the second police station, headed by the chief Stefan Svetozarov, resisted. All the other stations surrendered to the military without fight or were captured, like the first disarmed police station, headed by Boris Hristov, was captured, as Muraviev forced him to give up the canister. The fighters of the Orange Guard, disarmed by Muraviev in advance, were seized and dragged to the cellars, where the Agrarian Union leaders were already languishing. The putschists suppressed by machine-gun fire individual pockets of resistance.

The cities were captured by the military, in Sofia they filled all the streets, central squares and approaches to the government buildings. The people hid in the morning, not understanding what was happening, and looked out from behind the curtains of the windows, and in the evening, emboldened and cheerful, they flocked out into the streets, read the "Manifestos" pasted on every corner and, shouting "Hosanna!" and "Glory to god!" joyfully greeted the fascist coup soldiers, who were saluted with a special pleasure in fascist salute by the Italian embassy from the balcony.

Plovdiv also triumphed, where by morning they captured the post office, the district administration, the mayor's office, the police department and all the other facilities, as well as the railway station, where the Minister of Justice Spas Dupariev had just been, but in front of the nose of the fascists managed to escape in a car together with the District Governor Koev. Their attempts to raise an uprising in Asenovograd region were suppressed by a machine-gun fire and roar of canons of the military units. At the same time in Plovdiv the people jubilated, having read the "Manifestos," in the same way as they jubilated on October 13, 1922, greeting Raiko Daskalov, Stamboliysky's faithful comrade-in-arms and his devoted friend, where he arrived at the Plovdiv railway station, where the townspeople enthusiastically met and escorted with orange banners, music, shouts of "Hurrah!" and tears in their eyes, when, having mounted the white horse, he rode it, accompanied by the

Orange Guard, and sobbed to tears, listening to his speech at the square. In the same way the same townspeople with banners, only now not orange, music, tears in their eyes and shouts of "Hurrah" welcomed his butchers and killers.

Music sounded, and priests served solemn prayers for the glory of the upheaval, and the bulletins of the rival factions explained to the people that "tyranny has fallen" and "Nero II has fallen." Universal merriment and triumph reigned. The leaders of the BCP also triumphed, having acted in alliance with the putschists. The universal fun became even greater, when it was solemnly publicly announced that the upheaval had been carried out on the order of the tsar.

The freshly-minted "ministers": Tsankov, Kazasov, Smilov, Karakulkov, the former chief of the palace guard, accompanied by a horse escort, solemnly arrived to the tsar at the Vrana Palace early in the morning, immediately after they left the conspirators' headquarters in General Rusev's house to report on the fulfillment of the task and sign new decrees. Having inspired, organized and carried out the fascist upheaval in the country, the tsar Boris III was suddenly frightened of what he had done, ordered the guard not to let anyone in and disappeared to an unknown direction, so that the arrived escort had to argue with the guards for a long time and then, having pushed them away, voluntarily enter the alley of the park, enter the palace and wait on the chairs for a long time under the glances of the frightened servants, ask them where the tsar was, go upstairs on the second floor to the bedroom, make sure that he was not there, then wait some more for a long time, go out into the park and look for him, peering under each bush. And already in the afternoon, when the enraged Tsankov clamored that he would proclaim a republic, since the tsar, having disappeared, in fact declared self-denial, the tsar suddenly appeared in front of them from no one knew where and, having taken courage, greeted them, congratulated on "fulfillment of duty to Bulgaria" and invited everyone in the Hunting lodge, where he warmly accepted them, listened to their report, checked the lists of the new cabinet of ministers, where they corresponded to the previous agreement with him, once again congratulated them and solemnly signed a decree on the appointment of the new government headed by the professor Alexander Tsankov in connection with the fact that the "government of Alexander Stamboliysky voluntarily resigned."

"Gentlemen, I hope you understand that the victory cannot be completed until the object is neutralized," the tsar said, "I wish I have the evidence and proof."

"That's right, Your Majesty! Will be done!" all the arrivals stretched out to string.

The townspeople had fun, washing themselves with tears of joy until the late evening under the order of the fascist junta to kill, shoot, hang and burn them alive. This is how ended the day of June 9, 1923 in Bulgaria.

Chapter 30
Forever Bulgarian Shame

Having survived several attempts upon his life, Alexander Stamboliysky still could not believe what happened even when it had happened. He could not realize the degree of moral bestiality and ethical decline of the people for whom he suffered, fought and worked all his conscious life. In the morning of June 9, 1923, he telephoned from his villa in Slavovitsa to Pazardzik to find out what was going on. He was responded that nothing was happening, that everything was calm, and everything was in order. And when suddenly in the morning of June 9 a negotiator came to his villa, guarded by the guardsmen, with a note that the government of the Agrarian Union was overthrown, and he was offered to surrender, so that the blood would not be shed, he did not take it seriously.

"Who sent you?" he asked the negotiator.

"Major Popov from Plovdiv, you have been ordered to arrest."

"Tell Major Popov the following: *Mr. major, I am the Prime Minister of Bulgaria, in whose name I order you. Pick up your shit and go back, where you have come from, and wait for forgiveness there! Wake up from the insanity that has come over you and understand that the days are gone long ago, when a bunch of unbridled crazy thugs like you could shake and overthrow the government. Get out and try to find for yourself another country, where you can find refuge. And the Bulgarian people will be able to defend their Minister-Chairman Alexander Stamboliysky*! June 9, 1923."

He wrote his message on a piece of paper and handed it to the negotiator, and the later returned to Major Popov with Stamboliysky's response. Major Popov with the cavalry detachment from Plovdiv scoured around Slavovitsa, but did not dare to attack, since both Slavovitsa and the villa were guarded by the armed Orange Guard fighters with a canister. He really wanted to be the first to capture Stamboliysky and receive a reward from the new government, but being afraid to attack the armed guards, he rode off to Pazardzik with his detachment.

And Alexander Stamboliysky still believed that the people would be able to protect him. Meanwhile, the people of Bulgaria fell, and it was the lowest degree of their fall. Of course, not the entire people, but half of them, but half of the fallen was enough for the whole country to fall. Bulgaria was divided into 2 camps, into 2 rebeldom, 2 warring camps, and the civil war began.

The last night of June 10, 1923, Stamboliysky spent in his house, and in the morning of June 10, accompanied by the loyal soldiers of the Orange Guard under the commander of Capitan Yonovsky and his faithful brother Vasil, went to Pazardzik to raise the uprising. 1500 villagers, armed with something, joined them from the vicinity of Slavovitsa. Stamboliysky with his brother and Yonovsky were riding in a car, the guardsmen rode astride, the peasants from the vicinal villages with guns and knives were walking or riding astride. They reached Pazardzik, on the approaches of which the commander of the military garrison Slaveyko Vasiliev met them with the artillery and canister fire. The battle was not equal, but the warriors of Stamboliysky fought bravely, defending the people's leader and their country. They held on to the very end. Artillery buckshot knocked out the heroes one by one from the ranks and, falling slain, they washed the ground with their blood, on which the legends and memory of them will grow for centuries.

On the night of June 11 Stamboliysky remained alone. He was in time to ride on the car away from Pazardzik toward the north-west. Realizing that he would rather be detained on the car, he left the car, having hidden it in the grove in the bushes, and set off on foot, not knowing where to go. He was walking through the meadows and fields familiar for him from his childhood and recalled his life. Here, nearby in Slavovitsa village he was born on March 1, 1879, in a simple rural house, surrounded by a low stone fence. His father Stoimen Stamboliysky, a simple peasant, already old, was still alive.

His brother Vasil was his faithful friend. Provably, he had just died near Pazardzik. In childhood they loved this land of fabulous beauty, and from childhood Stamboliysky dreamed to benefit it. He recalled his student years at the university in Munich, when he lost his health from violent political activity and unrest and then suffered greatly from illness. Having returned to Bulgaria with European education, he plunged headlong into political life and headed the Agrarian Union immediately after its foundation and soon became a member of the National Assembly, the most brilliant politician, whose talent the others viciously envied. A mass of written works, the program of the Union, works written in prison and not yet published, when he languished in the dungeons of the Central Sofia prison and in the Vidin fortress for protesting against the war. The heroic days during the Vladay uprising, when he took the side of the people against the obscurant monarchy. Again wandering outside the law after the defeat of the Radomir Republic, then the amnesty, entry into power and blows of insidious fate, which handed him the pen to sign the peace treaty in Neuilly after the defeat of Bulgaria in the war, against which he languished in the dungeons.

Then his work with party comrades at the head of the country, reforms for its benefit and the triumph of glory in the last parliamentary elections on April 22, 1923. Crowds of thousands of the supporters at his speeches to the people in all the Bulgarian cities, and now he, the Prime Minister of Bulgaria, legally elected by the people of the country, secretly, hiding, makes his way through the groves and fields, alone on the whole earth, and a pack of Bulgarian dregs is chasing him to kill. Where are you, the people, for whom I suffered so much, where are you, my friends and supporters, where are you, my comrades-in-arms of the Union!

Stamboliysky did not know what was happening in the country. He did not know that at that time in all the cities and villages of Bulgaria there was an unequal battle between the people and the fascist junta of the tsar, who shot them with machine-guns, buckshot and cannons, suppressed resistance with fire. The junta grabbed them and threw into the cellars, where the sadistic butchers and fascist barbarians, led by the tsar Boris, tortured them, cut into pieces and stuffed them alive into the furnaces. He did not know that all his associates in the Union were captured and thrown into the dungeons or killed. He recalled the Youth Organization of the Agrarian Union and the Agrarian University he had created.

He suddenly remembered a recent meeting in the house of Krum Popov with a wonderful young man Mikhail Guenovsky, who was then a fighter of the Orange Guard, but wanted to quit, and he, Stamboliysky, ordered to admit him to the Agrarian University. What a clever, educated and noble man he was, what a devoted my supporter he was, and how attentively he listened to everything I said! Where is this young man now, what is his fate!

Stamboliysky did not know that Mikhail Guenovsky at that time was bravely fighting the fascist junta at Grivitsa, where the warriors had fought for the liberation of Bulgaria from the Turks in 1878. Loyal to Stamboliysky, with a detachment of Orange Guard soldiers he wages an unequal battle against 33rd Svintsovsky infantry squad, which comes to their rear, capturing the Levsky station, defeats the Orange Guard with superior forces, grabs their entire surviving detachment of 30 people, sends them to the city of Svintsov and throws them into the dungeons, where they are torched.

The scenes from the past life flash before the eyes of Stamboliysky, he recalls epochal events, fleeting meetings, the little things that make the life. He suddenly remembered the 12-year-old Todor Todorov in the village of Bodrovo, sitting in the front row in the school where he Stamboliysky, agitated with visual aids for neutrality in the World War 10 years ago. He remembered his burning eyes, the delight with which he listened to his every word, and understanding. This boy remained in his memory, and now he remembered him. What is his fate? Whose side are you on now, an unusual boy from Bodrovo!

Emaciated by wanderings, hungry and tired, Stamboliysky exhausted and internally devastated, alone in the whole world, Alexander Stamboliysky, the people's leader of Bulgaria, continued his way, wading through bushes, streams and passing the fields. He approached one village, then another one, foreboding an ambush around the corner, remained outsides the settlements. In a distance to the south the tops of the Rhodope Mountains towered in blue color like fence, and he thought that he would have to cross them to Turkcy or Yugoslavia in order to survive and continue struggle. A gleam of hope flashed in his mind, having strengthened unbroken spirit. This idea seemed to him the only one correct, and, excited, again he sat down to rest, having found a shelter at the side of the road behind a bush. He saw a peasant riding along the road in cart drawn by oxen and came closer to the road to ask for a piece of bread. The peasant held the oxen for a minute, stopped them and, apparently not recognizing, handed him a piece of bread with some cheese, then withdrew. Stamboliysky thanked, took the food, returned to a secluded nook, sat down on the grass and greedily began to eat. He thought: "How much good I've done to the peasants and now a peasant is saving me from starvation!" With gratitude he ate a simple peasant meal, sitting on the grass, and recalled dinners at receptions at Lloyd George in London, with Clemenceau in Paris, in Geneva and Genoa, at the reception at the Pope of Rome, when he was solemnly received as the Prime Minister of Bulgaria, the envoy of peace. How could this happen! How did I let this happen! This is my fault, because I've been warned so many times that the tsar prepared the upheaval and Muraviev is a traitor. Why did I give him the post of the Minister of War! But it was the tsar who encouraged me to do this. Oh you, my wife's nephew, I raised you, fed you with food and drink, gave you education, and you stabbed me with a knife in my back! Without a complicity of the Minister of the War, a military conspiracy would not have been possible! Damn you, bastard!

The day came to an end, the sun, warming the earth, sank to sunset, a breeze blew, and chilled Alexander Stamboliysky lay down on the grass, having firmly decided to cross the mountains in the morning. But this requires a faithful person, a guide, a companion. At night he was shaking from cold, the fever rose, but lying huddled up, he fell asleep for a while. Early in the morning, waking up from a dream, he returned to reality. It was June 12, 1923. In the distance, hidden behind the hills in the thickets of the grove, was a village of Golak, and he went there to find a guide. Another village appeared on the way and, feeling nausea and pain in the stomach from hunger, he decided to come to that village, where there was a tavern on the edge. He came in there, sat down at the table and asked for some food. From the very morning there were several people in the tavern, they stared at him with curiosity. Stamboliysky failed to eat and gain strength. He rose from the table and courageously looked in the face of doom.

"Here, here, there he is, Stamboliysky himself!" a young freak yelled at the top of his voice, pointing the way to an armed gang, pouncing through the door.

"Don't yell, Bikov, we are seeing, now he'll not get anywhere from us!" the bandits said, grabbed Stamboliysky by the hands and dragged him to the exit.

Oh, Bulgaria, the country of heroes and their traitors! You gave birth to great freedom fighters and the scum-rats who betrayed them all: Petko Voevoda, Vasil Levsky, Hristo Botev, Alexander Stamboliysky! The traitor Bikov gloatingly smiled, demanding a reward.

"Wait, Bikov, we'll deal with you later," the killers answered and dragged Stamboliysky along with them.

They tied his hands and threw him into a cart, which was approached by the armed villagers from all sides.

"Back up, you dogs, I'll shoot you!" one of the bandits threatened and shot at the peasant who fell, and the other peasants opened fire at the bandits. A peasant who did not have a gun approached the bandits with a raised dagger and, struck by a bullet, fell on the ground. Several bandits killed by peasants also fell, while the others jumped on the horses, tethered near the tavern, and quickly drove the cart south-east toward Vetren. The peasants failed to recapture Stamboliysky.

In Vetren they telephoned from the kmet's office to Pazardzik and reported about the detention of the object. The cart was driving, creaking the wheels, through the ancient land of Vetren, and Stamboliysky was proudly sitting in it, despising the filth that had grabbed him. He proudly held his head and courageously saw ahead the impending tragedy, akin to the ancient one, like the great antiquity heroes, whom this land was connected with.

Here the military route of the Romans lay through the passage between the mountains, called Suki, and now the Bulgarian bitches-suki are taking along it Stamboliysky to slaughter; they are driving past the Roman fortress and the Trojan Gate through the land of Vetren, which was sung in his poems by Alphonse de Lamartine, who was here in 1835 and predicted a "great future" for Bulgaria after freedom from Turks. And now this great future in the face of Stamboliysky is taken to Golgotha in order to prevent its fulfillment.

They arrived in Pazardzik, and the bandits handed Stamboliysky over into the hands of Slaveyko Vasiliev, the commander of the Pazardzik garrison. The competitors scoured around and squabbled among themselves like dogs, snatching from the hands of each other the prey: the same cavalry squadron of Major Popov from Plovdiv, 2 more squadrons and a training team from the 9th squad with the head of Captain Sotirov, the artillerymen with 2 Polish cannons at the head of Captain Dimitrov under the overall command of Lieutenant-Colonel Hristov, the commander of the 3rd Cavalry Regiment. The whole pack of rabid dogs snatched Stamboliysky from the hands of the bandits, who boastfully declared:

"No, it is us who have gotten him!"

These bandits were the civilian volunteers from the same Plovdiv. Slaveyko Vasiliev called Sofia and after a minute of conversation he stretched himself along a string: "Yes sir!" and proceeded to carry out the order.

"Captain Harlakov, you've received the instructions from Sofia, you know what to do. Proceed to you duties!"

"Yes, sir!"

"All the others disperse! You are free, gentlemen, the object is passed to the special detachment of captain Harlakov."

Perplexed, when would be the reward, all the rest left for Plovdiv. The bound Stamboliysky was transferred to a truck, and a special detachment, consisting of lieutenants Harlakov, Savov, Pavlov and Dinchev, in the same truck rushed back to Slavovitsa, at the approaches of which a detachment of the Macedonian cutthroats with Velichko Skopsky at the head was already waiting for them. Bearded, stinking non-humans, overgrown with hair, in human form, hung from head to toe with the revolvers, bandoliers and knives, 30 in number, with a drunken cackle and squeal of triumph joined the Bulgarian officers and dragged the bound Stamboliysky from the truck to his home. Alexander for the last time saw his yard and garden, his native rural house nearby, where he was born 44 years ago, where his old father Stoimen was still alive. For the last time he saw his villa from outside, where his initials and the year of construction were carved in stone by monogram: 1922. He was dragged into his own house, and a pack of thugs barely squeezed in.

"Former Minister-Chairman of Bulgaria Alexander Stamboliysky, by the decision of the Council of Ministers of Bulgaria represented by Kazasov, Rusev, Vylkov, Halfov, Stanchev, Smilov and all the other members of the Ministerial Council, chaired by the Minister-Chairman Professor Alexander Tsankov, as well as by the Internal Macedonian Revolutionary Organization, you are sentences to death!" captain Harlakov solemnly announced the verdict and spat in the face of the bound Stamboliysky.

All the others followed his example, dragging their knives with a cackle.

"But don't worry," Harlakov continued, "you won't die right away, you will still live for some time. By the way, I myself am a member of IMRO, and we are all the fighters of Todor Alexandrov, whom you saved from prison."

The thugs cackled one louder than the other, closely surrounding the bound Prime Minister Stamboliysky, who dumbly looked into their eyes. One beastly mug of the Macedonians was more horrendous than another, among which Argir stood out for his large size.

"Have you seen how he is looking at us?" Harlakov asked, "Now we'll improve it. Hold him!"

The murderers seized Stamboliysky and tied him to a chair, which they were holding from all sides, and the Macedonian brought his knife to

Stamboliysky's eye: the gleam of the blade was the last thing that this eye saw, for which eternal darkness came. The bandit was about to cut the captive's second eye, but Harlakov hit him on the arm and pushed him away.

"Leave it for the last, he must see everything. Drag him!"

They dragged the bound brother Vasil Stamboliysky into the room, tied him to another chair and began to cut him with knives. All the circles of hell closed over the 2 Stamboliysky brothers, and their martyrdom began, once and forever having given the answer to the odious question whether there is god. The devil himself would intercede for 2 martyrs, if he was, and would punish their butchers, while god was sleeping, but there was neither devil nor god, and there was no one to stop the sadists. With each stroke of the knife, with which they slaughtered the unfortunate martyrs, the executioners got into frenzy and cackled even louder, so that Harlakov had to stop them and reminded:

"Don't cut deep, so that he doesn't die at once!"

"With what hand did the Minister-Chairman sign the Peace of Neuilly and then the agreement in Nis with the Kingdom of the SCS on the prohibition of chetas? Ah, this is one, with the right one? Hold him firmly, and you cut, no, not you, otherwise you will lie later that it was Macedonians who killed Stamboliysky! No, It is the Bulgarian offices who killed Stamboliysky, and you, Macedonians were called here for fun!"

A Bulgarian officer began to cut off the right hand of Alexander Stamboliysky above the wrist and was cutting it so slowly that the others lost patience. Then the butchers cut off his genitals and cackled even louder. The bleeding Stamboliysky brothers untied from the chairs and thrown on the floor were left lying in blood alone, and the sadists-butchers went to another room to feast and rest from hard work. They drank rakia and clamored from the rooftops, gathering strength to continue work.

Stamboliysky found the last strength in himself, crawled up to the wall and, rising himself, wrote on the wall with his blood: "1923 A. S." The strength left him, but in the depth of his mighty nature and heroic body the breath of life was still barely warm. His brother Vasil was already dead on the floor. This is how the day of June 12, 1923 ended for Bulgaria.

Slowly fading away, his courageous heart continued to pound the whole next day of June 13, 1923 and the night until morning of the 14th, when all this time a gang of non-humans in the guise of people stabbed his body with knifes, inflicting shallow wounds so that he would not die immediately, cut off him pieces, flayed, cut open his stomach and cackled with pleasure in a drunken rage. Slowly fading, the brave heart of Alexander Stamboliysky made the last beat and stopped, his noble spirit left the tormented body, Alexander Stamboliysky, the best of the sons of Bulgaria, ever born on that earth, and the noblest of her rulers passed away. He died in inhuman torment akin only to the suffering of the victims of the Christian Inquisition.

He became a legend and made the hearts of the noble descendants honoring his name beat in love and hatred for his butchers.

"He is dead!" the butchers were disappointed, when they saw that the naked, tattered body of Stamboliysky was lying in the blood motionlessly and no longer breathed.

"Damn it, he died so soon! Cut off their heads! The tsar wishes to have proofs."

They cut off the heads of the Stamboliysky brothers and threw them into 2 sacks, and they dragged the bodies out of the house and dug them in the vineyard in the garden.

"Thank you for your service! The tsar allocates 5 million leva per year to IMRO for your activity!" Harlakov said, and the Bulgarian officers said goodbye to the Macedonians.

And the later, inspired by the feat of arms they committed went to Macedonia to continue robbery there and raid the vicinal lands. Harlakov and his abettors took 2 sacks and went to Sofia. In Sofia the feast continued everywhere, and banners fluttered on the royal palace. In the Alexander Nevsky church they prayed services to the glory of the new power. A flock of people crammed in the center of the city, you could hardly squeeze through around the Lyavov bridge and along the Maria Louise street. The mounted police guarded the roadway from the "Macedonia" hotel. The stare of the idlers were turned toward the Central Station.

3 dames were sitting on a bench in the park aside and had a conversation.

"I know everything in the world, I've read everything, I am learned: Stamboliysky died on the prostitute, and only then they cut off his head," one dame said importantly, quickly blinking her eyes and rolling her pupils, so that only her eyes whites were gleaming, at the same time she gained much air into the mouth to release another portion of verbal diarrhea.

"How could you 'read everything' if you don't have a single book in your house!" the second dame remarked mockingly and objected to her, "No,

Stamboliysky did not die on a prostitute, but the patriots of Bulgaria killed him, and they did a right thing, because it is he to blame for all the troubles of the country! It is his fault for our defeat in 2 national catastrophes: both in the Second Balkan War and World War! It is because of him the Entente defeated Bulgaria! It is he to sign the Neuilly Treaty! Stamboliysky is a thief! He stole all the Bulgaria!"

"Why are you talking only about the politics? As for me, I am not involved in politics, I don't care if it Stamboliysky or Tsankov! But, perhaps, it's better under Tsankov, because Stamboliysky banned deep neckline! And now it is freedom! Here, look!" grimacing, the third dame exclaimed and unbuttoned her dress on the breast.

"They are coming, they are coming!" was heard from all sides, and the crowd of idlers rushed their eyes to the road along which Harlakov's military detachment was driving in cars, consisting of Krystev, Savov, Pavlov, Dinchev and the other officers, who joined them at the station.

They were carrying 2 heads of the Stamboliysky brothers in 2 sacks. In a stupor of horror, delight, curiosity and moronic indifference, the idlers stared at the bloody spectacle that brought them back to the days of the Turkish slavery. They followed with their eyes the escort, which solemnly drove through the center of Sofia and disappeared from sight, heading for Vrana.

The tsar received what he wanted: the faithful lackeys delivered proof of the death of the prime minister to his feet and laid 2 sacks with cut-off heads. With pleasure he gazed at the mutilated Stamboliysky's head with parts of his face cut off, in which both eyes were cut out, and the head of his brother Vasil and then uttered philosophically:

"Let's act mercifully, gentlemen, because we are the Orthodox Christians, let's act like the Christians: take these 2 heads back and bury them next to the bodies. Thank you for your service to our beloved Bulgaria! Our Lord Jesus Christ is with us!"

"It will be done, Your Majesty!" the butchers reported and took the sacks back to Slavovitsa.

Having seen the Stamboliysky's head and making sure that he was dead, the tsar Boris III signed a long-prepared yet on June 9, which was immediately published and hung on all the corners:

"Order № 107 of June 14, 1923. By the order of the Supreme Leader, His Majesty the tsar, the army chose to sacrifice itself, but save the fatherland from possible upheavals that would've taken place if the army not intervened so that to maintain order in the country. Dear officers, cadets, sub-officers and soldiers, I sincerely thank you for your dignity and selfless behavior on June 9 and after. I am personally put by fate at the head of the carriers of the idea of duty to motherland in difficult moments, and I am ready to sacrifice myself for the good of the fatherland."

Plovdiv did not lag behind the capital, rang all the bells, served prayers and on June 14, to the glory of what had happened, solemnly hosted the 52 person cooperative theater that arrived from Sofia, led by Mimi Balkanskaya, who parted with democracy in Bulgaria with Oskar Strauss "Last Waltz". Stupid musicians, who never involve in politics, always and everywhere ignorant in everything that does not concern music and ready to serve any satanic regime, with great enthusiasm, grimacing, performed the freshly-minted march "The 9th June," which was composed in one night by the band-master of the military school Atanasov.

The venal press raged, praising the upheaval, and vilified already dead Alexander Stamboliysky. The craven governments of the western countries swallowed the fascist coup in Bulgaria, but their press raised the alarm and went to Slavovitsa in search of the prime minister's body. Having preceded them on one hour, the kmet of Slavovitsa ordered to hide the traces of the crime. The bodies of 2 martyrs together with their heads were dug out of the vineyard in Slavovitsa and transferred away by truck. They were reburied on the sand bank of the Maritsa between Vetren and Saranovo, so that the foreign journalists, who saw the empty pits, never saw their mutilated bodies—proof of the crime against humanity.

Chapter 31
June 1923

The fascist coup on June 9, 1923, put an end to the democratic development of Bulgaria and forever split the country into 2 warring camps. The fallen part of it triumphed over itself, and the better half of the country rose to fight. While the fallen part of Bulgaria was feasting on a satanic Sabbath and in the devilish whirlwind of horo-round-dance all the bastards of the country hooved it on the bones of the beastly tortured Stamboliysky brothers, spreading vilification and lie against Alexander, its better part armed itself with anything to take vengeance.

Having killed Stamboliysky and almost all his ministerial council, the new ministerial council of Professor Tsankov together with Tsar Boris III, having usurped power, raged further, destroying the very memory of the national hero. They invaded his house in Sofia, which was located on the outskirts of the city behind the Sugar factory, a small 2-story house with one room on each floor, where there was complete order, with which books were placed on the shelves, documents and letters were folded, the works of Stamboliysky himself—the savages crashed everything. They dragged his works, books and documents into the yard and set them on fire. Grimacing and salivating with rabidity, the savages read by syllables the names of the senders: Chicherin, Kristyu Rakovsky, Vintsenti Vitos, Antonin Shvekhla, Elephteros Venizelos, Adolf Damashke, doctor Lupus, Voya Lazich, Francesco Nitti, doctor Milan Hodja. And what is that? Oh, the history of Bulgaria written by Alexander Stamboliysky himself? Is it the draft of the new Constitution? They threw into the fire the boxes with letters, his writings, his library.

They broke into the Union House of the Agrarians at 1 Vrabcha Street, dragged the boxes and bags with the documents of BANU into the yard, threw them into a huge pile of priceless papers and set it on fire. They broke into the

Stamboliysky's office in the Ministerial Council and the Ministry of Foreign Affairs, pulled the entire archive of documents and set it on fire. The entire archive of the Agrarian Union, all the publications of the Agrarian Bulletin, the manuscripts of Stamboliysky, letters and books were burning in a hellish flame, and the fascist scum of the Black Block in officer's straps hooved the satanic horo-round-dance by the fire, and the monsters: those who "don't engage in politics" danced nearby.

"Stamboliysky is a thief! He died on a prostitute! And before that he plundered all Bulgaria!" the dung worms spewed in the way, how the light is hated by the darkness, anger hates goodness, how the dawn is hated by the sunset, the cowardly traitor hates courage and bravery, stupidity hates talent, and zero hates nobility.

Ominous shadows danced around the fire, and the flame devoured the Agrarian Union. But it could not gobble it all. Love for the people's leader, hatred for his butchers, bright memory of Stamboliysky raised the people to struggle throughout the country. Armed with knives, hunting rifles and clubs, the peasants flocked to the cities, where the same peasants, dressed in soldier's uniform, stupidly fulfilling a criminal order met them with buckshot and shells of machine-guns.

The secretary for the Organizational Affairs of the central Comity of the Communist Party of Bulgaria communist Lukanov cursed up the hill and down dale everything that had happened and with longing eyes caressed the furnishings of his office in the Party House in the center of Sofia: elegant furniture, library, conference hall, spacious rooms and upholstered furniture. Most of all cherishing the comfort and peace of his office, Lukanov feared like plague of the practical application of the communist ideas in life and preferred a safe occupation of the theory of "armed struggle" for power to its implementation. He did not find peace for a long time, fidgeted in a chair, rolled from one side to another on a soft sofa, foreboding the catastrophe of losing everything he had, if the Communists enter the struggle and finally with the abetting of Georgy Dimitrov sent a telegram to the post office to Pleven and to the Pleven garrison, where the leader Asen Halachev led the rebel detachment to storm:

"Stop fighting, give up your weapons, surrender to the fascist invaders! Let the urban bourgeoisie, that is the fascist invaders, and the rural bourgeoisie, that is the peasants of the Agrarian Union, kill each other, and we, the Communists, will stand aside and watch and maintain neutrality."

The telegram did not stop Halachev, but lured him into a trap in the garrison "for negotiations," where he was immediately seized and tortured to death. Left without the commander, the rebel detachment was immediately defeated. The telegram of Lukanov, who concealed from his fellow party members another telegram from Comintern in Moscow to support Stamboliysky, was published in the "Rabotnichesky Vestnik," pasted on fences and distributed in the villages and cities, where part of the Communists was waiting up, and the decent people, spitting on the telegram, following their hearts, but not the party discipline, founded the rebellion detachments together with peasants. The uprising broke out spontaneously throughout the country.

In the Borisovograd city police station in the office of the chief Enyu Gogov, the police bailiff Guenov-Kamine, foreman Nesterov and another policeman celebrated the victory, and the rest tortured the rebel captives one by one in the torture chamber, with which the lockup was crammed.

"Gentlemen, our people have taken the power. Let's drink to our common victory!" proclaimed a toast and raised another glass fat man Enyu Gogov, barely holding on in his chair, drunk to the point of losing consciousness.

"Now we'll fulfill our duty and our work freely, without looking back at Haskovo, Plovdiv and Sofia," Guenov-Kamine shared his thoughts happily, rubbing his hands with pleasure.

"Yes, sir!" sergeant Nesterov dutifully reported, obligingly filling the bosses' glasses with rakia.

"Our people are everywhere: in Haskovo, and in Plovdiv, and in Sofia! We immediately swore allegiance to the new government, but some other districts, as I heard, resisted the legitimate authorities."

"So now they are also our adversaries, and now we'll wage struggle with them!"

"Now we'll catch and destroy our main enemies, you know, gentlemen, whom I am talking about."

"Yes, sir!" the foreman Nesterov reported.

"We'll show them!"

"They escaped from the Haskovo prison yet under Stamboliysky and still haven't been captured!"

"Now they'll get caught! How are there our people coping in the interrogation chamber?" Guenov-Kamine asked with irritation, slamming the door of the office more tightly, through which inhuman screams were heard, and 5 policemen were shoving into the furnace with the head an almost already dead the rebel, bound hands and feet.

In the evening a detachment of rebels from the vicinal villages was rebuffed from the Borisovograd borders, and 10 mounted policemen galloped along the boundary, dividing the corn fields, chasing the remnants of the fleeing villagers. One peasant, faithful to the end to his hero Stamboliysky, continued to drag behind him an orange banner of the Agrarian Union instead of the rifle, what hampered him to run, but he did not abandon the banner and escaped with all his strength from a horseman, approaching him. In a moment the mounted policeman overtook the fugitive and cackled at the top of his lungs:

"We'll annihilate this orange plague! Go-go-go-go! Ha-ha-ha-ha!"

The peasant stopped and continued to hold the orange banner. He was looking straight into the eyes of policeman. The policeman cackled, drew his saber, swung it over the peasant's head, and immediately a shot rang out, and the policeman staggered and fell down from his horse with a bullet in his forehead. The peasant crossed himself and began to look around. The remaining 9 policemen, chasing the peasants, scattered across the field, one after another fell from the horses. The peasants gathered at the boundary, not yet fully aware of what was happening. Here young men came out of the corn thickets, dressed like hajduks, armed from head to toe, with daggers and parabellums on their belts next to the grenades. Their black shirts were crisscrossed on their chests by bandoliers filled with cartridges. One was tall and large like a hero—Ivan Ignatov—and another one was slender, thin, handsome like god with a piercing gaze of the black eyes—Todor Todorov Karagochev.

"Who are you? Are you orange Agrarians or red Communists?" the peasants asked.

"We are neither Agrarians nor Communists, we are on our own, we have our own accounts with them," Todor answered, "we are the people's avengers."

"Understand," the peasants rejoiced, not yet believing in their miraculous salvation, "what a precise shooting! 10 shots and 10 flayers fell dead! If only we could shoot like that!"

Here a young man, the commander of a rebel detachment in the military uniform of an officer came up to them, emerging from the thickets of corn. Slender, tall, handsome, he introduced himself:

"George. This is all that remained from our detachment. We had 70 people. Thank you for helping us, we are almost out of ammo."

"Hurry up, we are leaving," Todor commanded, "they can send the military. Take their guns and horses and ride the hell out of here!"

"Lord bless you!" the standard-bearer crossed the young men, who disappeared in the thickets of corn, reached a hillock covered with grove, where the faithful horses were waiting for them.

The policemen were those who tortured Ivan and Todor in the police station, robbed his house and tormented his family. The major foes remained yet.

Todor and Ivan set their horses at a gallop and, having driven some distance from the cornfield, where the killed foes were lying, they took a calm step. They rode quietly toward the west, swaying in their saddles, to which sacks with food and baklagas-canteens with water were tied.

"Let's go far away from here, wait a while, then come back," Todor said.

"To our hides?" Ivan asked.

"Where else? We have no way home. We no longer have a home. They've deprived us of our home. Now our home is forest and mountains, and our secret caves in them."

"Not only home, they have taken away from us our country!" Ivan sighed.

"Damn Black blockers, tsankovites! They'll be called now '9 June conspirators.' And our policemen-flayers immediately swore allegiance to them!" Todor muttered through his teeth, clenching his fists.

"Yes, they are of the same kind."

"Now there is nowhere to complain: there is neither court of justice nor lawyers, neither prosecutor nor government with ministers. There is no Stamboliysky." Todor pondered.

"Yes, sorry for him," sentimental Ivan almost sobbed, "do you remember how we listened to him 2 times in Sofia and in Haskovo! I am sorry for him and for us, for Vidyu and Todor, for Petyu and Kolyu!"

"There will be never such a prime minister like Stamboliysky!" Todor exclaimed with all his heart, "I wonder how he died? They write that the villagers and Orange Guards attacked the truck, in which he was transported, and released him, and then there was a chase, and he was accidentally shot dead. But it is the sellout beasts from 'Slovo', 'Mir', 'Epoch', 'Fatherland' who write this, the same scum who vilify him. Can we believe them! Especially, at the end: 'The government is sorry!' There is no more any government! There is a gang of murderers and thieves who illegally seized power and killed the legitimate government. And we have only one thing left: to take vengeance on the butchers!"

"Yes, if earlier the Borisovograd policemen and Haskovo jailers acted with us illegally, then there was always a hope that you could complain to Plovdiv or Sofia and find justice there and punish the criminals, but now there is nowhere and no one to complain to: in the entire country the power has been captured by criminals and murderers," Ivan sighed hopelessly, "it is clear that the uprising of the peasants is suppressed everywhere. The forces are not equal."

"There is neither leadership nor plan for uprising, there is no leader. There is no Voevoda. And the Communists are traitors!" Todor was indignant with anger. "They lied that they are with people! Liars, traitors and scoundrels! They abandoned the peasants, betrayed Stamboliysky! Their sellout scumbags drove along with the Black blockers on the trucks and threatened the peasants with reprisals, demanding them to go home. Only a few decent Communists led the detachments into battle, violating the criminal order of their leaders to abandon the peasants."

"And how many bastards-traitors are among the soldiers, participating in the fascist coup against their people and against themselves! They are all peasants too, aren't they?" Ivan was silent for a while and then asked his friend, "What are we going to do?"

"Let's gather a squad and fight. We already have 3 men, I hope, they will wait for us in our hide. Then we'll meet with Mityu Ganev at our appointed place. The Borisovograd pack at the head of Guenov-Kamine are the first to answer for the murder of Vidyu and Todor."

Todor and Ivan pondered on the catastrophe and hopelessness of their position and the position of the entire country in general, and each of them was glad to have a faithful companion who could be relied upon. The horses were walking in measured step, the riders in the saddles swayed with them, keeping the surrounded area under control with a keen eye. They were walking westward, following the setting sun that was moving ahead of them. Soon a huge orange ball touched the ground in front of them, scattering orange gleams across the darkening abyss, and as if wounded, slowly fading, fell into the chasm. Darkness hung over their heads and the forest, all over Bulgaria. The era of Alexander Stamboliysky, the era of the reforms and hopes, the symbol of which and its guard was orange, has set like a rolling orange ball of the sun. Utter darkness, sorrow and grief have merged their country.

They drove out of the forest and saw in front of them a lonely koshara-lodge, near it there were no signs of life: neither man nor cattle. They dismounted and cautiously approached the fence of the paddock, looked inside the koshara, the creaking door gave away, and they came in, having left the horses in the paddock. They had a place to sleep. What a night they have spent away from their home and their bed!

Early in the morning, having eaten some food they had stored, they looked around, saddle their horses and set off. The fields with ripe wheat stood empty: the peasants, defeated in battles during a spontaneous rebellion, hid in all directions. The entire course of normal human life was stopped. They bypassed the villages, sinking in sorrow, where in each village the kmets were overthrown, put in jail or killed, and instead the Tsankov's triples were placed to create outrage. On the right in the distance Philippopolis-Plovdiv was barely noticeable, located, like Rome, on 7 hills, an ancient coeval of Europe, part of the legendary ancient history, a shameful traitor and abettor of the putschists, who did not stop the fascists with a step or word, feasting with them their satanic Sabbath of victory.

And on the left, on the banks of the Chaya River Stanimakha remained behind, the ancient city in the ravine, like at the bottom of a bowl, surrounded by the mountains and dotted with churches, and in them bas-reliefs with even before the Christian gods. The Asen's fortress towered in the Rhodopes to the south. Rebuilt by Ivan Asen II, the fortress stood there before since ancient times. Like a pinnacle of a spear, a unique castle stuck out on the top of a marble rock, and from it a view of the entire Thracian valley and the ancient Greek path through the mountains passes from Philippopolis to Xanti opened up. The marble steps, carved right into the rock, took you in a spiral to its top. Snow-white marble blinded the eyes, and it seemed that all this miracle of nature and man was chiseled from marble by sculptor and erected on the top of Rhodopes as a symbol of power over this land.

The riders moved forward and lower to the south, but higher in the Rhodopes the Bochkov Monastery remained, the fairy-puppet scenery of the ancient buildings of which among the fragrance of flowers always attracted people from everywhere, and along the wide road of the gentle slope of the hill leading to it, the bazar used to rustle before, where the hawkers offered all kinds of goods to the visitors, now was empty.

There were left behind Ustovo, Raykovo, Smolian, the lands once owned by Momchil Voevoda, who created a squad which defeated the enemies and smashed the Turks even before the Turkish yoke, about whom the legends were spoken and Bulgarian songs were sung from the childhood.

The horsemen rode westward along forest paths, passing hills and ravines, giving rest to the horses and stopping to eat. Nature was in full bloom in mid-June, filling the fields with the ripened wheat, barley, corn, and instead of to work in the fields, the peasants revolted spontaneously and were smashed, fled, hid or were captured and killed. They made their way along the boundaries of unharvested fields, or partially harvested, found an empty cabin on the bank of a stream and, having tethered the horses, remained in it for a night. On the right behind Pazardzik remained in the distance, the ancient city of bazaars, from which it got its name, where trade flourished for centuries, panairs-fairs, where merchants sold goods and byers bought them, where Kostadin Muraviev sold his conscience, as came from here originally, and officers sold out the honor, having captured Stamboliysky here.

The smell of hay in the hut reminded them of the stubbles left in Bodrovo, the abandoned farm and home filled their hearts with aching longing.

"Maybe we'll go back?" Ivan Ignatov asked.

"We'll decide it in the morning," Todor replied.

Dawn and the rising sun, a sound sleep in the hut enlivened them, and in the morning they decided to ride a little more through the unfamiliar area and scan it, just in case. Carefully they moved along the northern border of the town of Saranievo along the Maritsa River, where the horses drank to their fill, passing the Thracian hills, where the ruins of the ancient Greek fortress-city Pistiros, treasures and the works of art were hidden under ground. And to the left in the south the Stamboliysky government recently, 2 years ago, built a station and laid a railway, which was supposed to lead southwest to Necrop along the valley of the Mesta River, to be tunneled through the mountains and pass through them. They were in time to build a railway only to the village Lydzhene, and they were killed.

Todor with Ivan Ignatov crossed the bridge over the Maritsa, which went to the left to the south-west, from where it flowed from the Maritsa lakes far in the Rila Mountains, dismounted and went on foot along the tributary of the Maritsa Khazar Dere, leading the horses by the bridle. The tributary was not deep, weeping willows and thickest of shrubs grew close to the sand bank, and Vetren could be seen in the ravine between the hills ahead. Here no one could know them, but they made their way carefully, with a keen eye scanning the area and pondered on to return. It was unrealistic and dangerous to recruit a squad in a remote unfamiliar land.

They were walking along the sand bank, inhaling the aroma of the summer June and suddenly began to feel a nauseating sweetish smell of the frightening death. They stopped dead in their tracks and saw the infernal companions: disgusting buzzing flies, which swarmed, pushing each other, over a gruesome mound of sand. Suddenly Todor turned sharply and grabbed a man, hiding in the bushes, out to the sand, and he appeared before them. It was a young lad of their age or younger, dressed as a villager, he was looking at them with fear, and a tear gleamed in his eye.

"Who are you?" Todor asked.

"I am local, from Vetren."

"What are you doing her? Why are you watching us?" Todor interrogated him, and all 3 sensed that they could not breathe from the stench.

They covered their noses, and the young man replied:

"I am scared alone, afraid I won't cope, here," he pointed to the bushes, where they saw a handle from a spade, "I am scared to come up…"

"What is here?"

"There…" the boy pointed to a fetid mound on the sand, over which the damned flies were buzzing, "help me, I need help."

3 of them came closer to the ominous mound, covering their noses, and Todor with Ivan ducked aside, and the boy who knew what the matter was stayed in place, wiping a tear. The waters of Khazar Dere, rolling in soft waves, washed away the sand bit by bit from the gruesome hillock, exposing what was under it. In front of them lay a naked, only in the white socks, decapitated body of Alexander Stamboliysky, and next to him the hand of his brother Vasil was

sticking out of the sand. The drunken butchers dug up the bodies of 2 martyrs from the vineyard in Slavovitsa, so that the foreign journalists, approaching the Stamboliysky's villa, would not see them, and having preceded them by an hour, they transported the bodies by truck to the sand bank Khazar Dere and buried them in the sand by the river. In drunken merriment they did not bury them deep, only superficially having thrown sand on the bodies, which was washed away by the river.

The 3 boys covered their mouths and noses with handkerchiefs and came closer. The headless body of Stamboliysky was lying helplessly on the sand, submissively to a criminal fate. His genital organ was cut off, his right hand was cut off above the wrist, the nails on the left hand were torn off and the whole body was pierced with daggers like a sieve and cut with the shallow wounds, 80 in number. Only on the stomach there was a deep cut, 10 centimeters long. Dumbfounded from the hideous view, the boys were standing silently, unable to move. Todor was clenching his fists, Ivan eyelid was twitching, and the boy from Vetren was wiping away a tear.

"I need help, help me," the boy was the first to break the silence, "we must bury."

"I see that you are a good person," Todor said, "can you get 2 more spades? One is not enough, we'll wait."

"Yes, of course, I'll be back soon."

"Do you believe him?" Ivan asked.

"It does not look he would betray us, but just in case, follow him."

Ivan vanished in the bushes, and Todor with the horses was left next to the hellish nightmare. His heart was clenching with pain, and the desire for vengeance intensified even more. He did not wait for long. Soon the friend Ivan emerged from the bushes, holding 2 spades, and the boy nearby, in his hands there were 2 woolen elongated rugs, embroidered with a bright pattern, and a long rope.

"What's your name?" Todor asked.

"Nikola Vasilev from Vetren."

"I am Todor, and this is my friend Ivan."

Ivan nodded, as if saying that they had already met. Nikola took his spade out of the bushes and they began carefully to break up the mound of sand, from which the Vasil's hand was sticking out. They dug out his headless body, like his brother's body, it was cut and pricked with wounds, but fewer in number.

The boys pulled themselves together and, having stifled the horror, fear and disgust, set to work. They cut 2 holes in the rugs with a knife, threaded ropes through them like loops and tied them to the horses' saddles. 3 of them lifted the body of Stamboliysky and laid it on one rug, and the body of Vasil on the other.

"Wait, that's not all," Nikola said, "I am scared myself."

He pointed to a bush. There were 2 severed heads lying around. The head of Stamboliysky was gnawed by dogs on the right side, 2 hollows gaped instead of the eyes, his face was all cut with a knife, only his mustaches were preserved. The brother Vasil's head was also all cut with shallow wounds. Overcoming the surging feelings, Todor took 2 heads and put them on 2 rugs next to the bodies. They slowly led the horses away from the shore, going around the bushes, toward the small grove. Nikola was going behind and made sure everything was in order. They stopped at a small glade, where an old tree grew, and decided to bury the bodies here. With 3 spades they dug a deep hole in the ground, lowered there the body of Stamboliysky and his brother Vasil near him. They put 2 heads together with them. They untied 2 rugs from the horses and covered the bodies with them, filled with earth, having made a small hill.

"Let's remember this oak," Todor said and made a notch on the trunk of the oak with a knife, "the time will come, and somebody... Someday..."

3 boys were dumbly standing under the crown of the age-old oak, the foliage of which seemed to sing a hajduk's song, slightly undulating in the wind. The horses were grazing peacefully.

"You are not from this vicinity, are you? Have you come from afar?" Nikola asked, scanning the military ammunition of Todor and Ivan.

"Yes, we have walked for a couple of days."

"Come to my koshara, you can rest there, there is food and drink there," Nikola called them.

"Let's go, Todor, I've been there, it's ok," Ivan supported.

They passed through a grove and entered the koshara standing in a ravine, surrounded by jasmine bushes. They took their bread and cheese, and Nikola found a baklaga with rakia, some milk and boiled eggs. They drank a sip of rakia to relieve an acute stress of the experience and started to talk to alleviate anguish.

"Are you an Agrarian?" Todor asked Nikola.

"Yes, I was in the Orange Friendship. What about you? Are you the Communists?"

"Fuck them! Venal bastards! They betrayed Stamboliysky! They betrayed the people! Abettors of the Tsankov fascists!" Todor flared up. "They shitted Stamboliysky even when he was alive!"

The sounded name of Stamboliysky plunged everyone into horror and shook them from horrendous visions, of what they had just experienced, from the gruesome picture that stood before their eyes.

"No, we are neither Communists nor Agrarians," Todor explained, "we are on our own, we have our own accounts with them."

"Poor, poor Stamboliysky is!" Ivan exclaimed with all his heart, "A martyr, and his brother Vasil is too! Judging by the number of wounds, there were many butchers! One thing is when you perish with the weapons in your hands in battle with enemies, and another thing is when you are alone, captured by the foes, and there is no one to rescue!" Ivan remembered his suffering in the police station.

"These are not human beings, these are monsters who are to be destroyed only!"

"Our country is seized by the enemies, and these enemies are worse than the Turks. At the very least, there was peaceful coexistence with the Turks for 500 years, but with these ones no peaceful coexistence can be, and they are our own, the Bulgarians!"

"Our kmet, the Agrarian, was tortured to death, they mutilated his face so that he was impossible to be recognized," Nikola said, "and they put their triples everywhere."

"Come with us!" Todor said, "We are gathering a platoon-cheta to take vengeance on the butchers. The money-bags-tobacconists who financed the fascist upheaval must pay!"

Nikola pondered on a minute and answered:

"Probably, not. Now I can't. Where shall I go from my land away? I like here. I have a home and a household, no, not yet I can go with you."

"Well, look, if you decide, you'll find us somewhere near Bodrovo someday. How did they defeat you, the Agrarians, so quickly and seize power?"

"There were too many traitors."

"The uprising of people in June was suppressed, but, I am sure, there will be another uprising, there will be continuation of struggle."

They talked for a long time, pouring out their soul to each other. The day was over. They spent the night right there in the Nikola's koshara, and in the morning they parted and set off on their way back.

"We'll meet one day!"

"Find us near Bodrovo!"

Chapter 32
July 1923

Having reached the outskirts of Bodrovo safely, Todor with Ivan Ignatov confidently, but carefully stepped along their native land, familiar to them from childhood, knowing by heart every ravine and stream. They bypassed from the south-west Bodrovo, where their house, farm and nearby fields with crops remained, where they, driven on their own land, could not openly return in defiance of the accursed fate. The scorching sun heated the fertile earth, raising from it all the fruits of the harvest that it could only produce. Yellow-green ears and stems, sparkling, covered the fields and valleys and undulated in breeze. The boys seemed to float on these waves of the ocean, being outlaw due to the wiles of unfortunate fate, set sail, not knowing which shore they would land on and what awaits them, the unfortunate ones, on the other shore. The sight of the familiar fields filled their souls with aching anguish and increased their desire for revenge on the foes, sharpened their confidence in their rightness to go to the very end. Along the familiar path, they went around a high hill on the right, behind which an entrance to a shallow ravine opened, a small river once flowed through it, but dried up in the sun, it turned into a thin stream. It murmured merrily and ran along the bottom of the ravine, overgrown with dense vegetation, weeping willows and hornbeams from the both sides.

They dismounted and walked slowly, leading the horses by the bridle, then tethered them to a low hornbeam, which like with a canopy covered the entire circumference with lush foliage, creating a pleasant shade. They walked some more along the ravine, looked around and instantly vanished into the thickets of boxwood bushes. On the side of the ravine, a small river, that once flowed here, washed out a depression in the soil, turned into a half-cave, half-dugout. Thoroughly camouflaged, it was impossible to be seen from outside, unless you know it was here. Deepened, reinforced with wooden beams and obscured from prying eyes, the dugout served as one of the hides for the cheta of Todor Todorov. Todor with Ivan Ignatov came in, where 3 barrels of the revolvers were pointed at them.

"Calm down, it's us," Todor said.

The companions of Todor and Ivan, who escaped with them from the Haskovo prison: Mityu Panev from Gorsky Izvor, Kolyu Trendofilov from Yablokovo and Rusi Stoyanov from Harmanly region greeted them joyfully, putting their guns down.

"Why so long? We are too tired to wait, and food is running out," Kolyu Trendofilov asked, a large, black-eyed, curly-haired, merry fellow, who ended up in Haskovo prison for some trifle.

"We walked to Slavovitsa," Todor answered and together with Ivan told them about the story.

All 5 were shivering from the details of the story about the death of Alexander Stamboliysky. They were silent.

"We are leaving to get food and in a couple of days to the action. We stick to the plan. No independent steps, the life of everyone else depends on the reckless act of any of you. We have the cheta, and I am your Voevoda," Todor said.

Inside the dugout, cut off on both sides wooden stumps served them as seats, and straw mattresses were used a bed, on which they rested from the road. When the midday subsided and the sun rolled toward set, hiding in the shade of foliage and calculating every step, the Todor's cheta set off toward the Aidanlar forest, beyond which the Todorov's meadows stretched and their herd of animals grazed. The young brother Gocho, who replaced Todor in the household, grazed goats, sheep, cows and oxen with the horses, who gave them dairy products, wool and draft power in all kinds of work. All the animals pastured in the meadows, gaining strength, moving from one place to another, and in the evening Gocho corralled them next to koshara. Todor expected to meet with him.

It got utterly dark. It gets dark quickly in the south, and a dark veil hid the cheta's moving. Moving past the Aidanlar forest, behind which till recently the lands of his Uncle Gocho and his sons Vidyu and Todor stretched, Todor could not hold back his tears and felt like a dagger had been stabbed in his heart. Ivan Ignatov experienced the same feelings. With unbearable pain the bright image of the Karagochev family arose in their memory: kind father Gocho, their hospitable house full of prosperity, where the table was busting with abundance of food, which they always shared with guests and always gave shelter the driven ones. How they would help Todor's cheta now! It was impossible to believe that the young handsome heroes, who could've had life to live and benefit people, were lying in the grave, killed by the maniac Guenov-Kamine, their house was devastated, and their old father Gocho wretched on the verge of insanity, languishing in grief somewhere in the village Ezerovo, having lost his 2 sons! 3 new friends of Todor and Ivan: Mityu, Kolyu and Rusi, who had heard so many times stories about this family, could only guess what their friends were going through.

The Aidanlar forest remained aloof; the Todor's cheta was approaching his meadows, where they expected to meet with young Gocho. Soon they saw the koshara, around which a huge paddock was fenced, where the animals rested after a day walk. Here they began to move especially carefully and silently, hiding from bush to bush, slowly approaching the koshara, and Ivan Ignatov, who saw best in the darkness, piercing it with his acute sight, showed the travelers that everything was fine. Bending down, they silently approached the pen and koshara, Ivan remained a sentry outside, and Todor with 3 friends came in. There were books and food on the table, a kerosene lamp was lightening, and Gocho with George were resting on the palliasses. Scared, they jumped on their feet, overjoyed, rushed to hug Todor.

"How you have grown, Gocho!" Todor exclaimed, hugging his young brother.

"We haven't seen each other for 2 years!" Gocho burst into tears, all this time yearning for his elder brother. "How are you, Todor?"

"You are already 14 years old! And I am 22… I am alive…"

"Hello, Georgy!" Todor turned to his cousin, and Georgy, the son of uncle Dimitar, 2 years younger than Todor, with eyes wet from joy, dashed to hug Todor. "Meet our new friends: Mityu, Kolyu and Rusi."

The young people greeted each other, and Gocho with Georgy gazed with admiration at the guests, dressed as hajduks and armed from head to toe. Full of cartridges, bandoliers crossed on the chest of each other of them, 2 revolvers, daggers and a couple of bombs hung on their belt.

"Wow!" Gocho and Georgy exclaimed in unison with admiration.

"Where is Ivan?"

"He is a sentry outside."

"Good," the boys breathed a sigh of relief, "so, he is with you, isn't he?"

"Do you want to eat?"

"We wouldn't refuse."

"We have a lot of food left, sit down at the table."

The guests sat down on the wooden benches around the table and with appetite began to eat bread, feta-cheese, milk and a juicy watermelon for a snack.

"We have just come about food," Todor said, "we need help for the first time. Gocho and you Georgy, will you help us?"

"Of course, we'll help!"

"Do you remember the old koshara of grandpa Techa?"

"Certainly."

"You'll bring food and drink there. We'll not come here again, it's too dangerous for you and for us."

"We understand," the cousin responded sadly, returning to reality.

"You'll help us a lot if you do this, and don't tell anyone, ok?"

"Of course."

"Let us remember in silence our cousins Vidyu and Todor, who were villainously killed by our foes," Todor said, and everyone was silent for a minute.

"Do you remember, Todor, how you and Vidyu in this same koshara grabbed a robber who wanted to steal our sheep?" Gocho asked. "You were 12 then and Vidyu was 16, and I was only 4 years old, but then I heard this story from everyone many times. And our father was at the Balkan Wars then along with his 3 brothers."

They were silent again, and memories cut Todor's heart again with acute ache from losing Vidyu and Todor Gochev.

"It is impossible to forget, I'll always remember this, and the killers will answer yet for their atrocity! What are you reading, Gocho?" Todor asked, scanning the books lying on the table, "Yeah, *Ilya Voevoda*, *Hadji Dimitar* and *Stefan Karadzha*. Why is the Bible here? Gocho, don't even think to believe in god like your obscurant villagers! There is no god: if only there was god, everything would be different, and those innocently killed by the villains would've been alive! Religion is like poison, with which the dark peasants are poisoned!"

"I read the Bible out of curiosity and inquisitiveness just to know what is written there," Gocho replied. "I read everything in general. I've read foreign classical literature, Ivan Vasov's novel *Under the Yoke*; *Bay Ganue* by Aleko Konstandinov, and I've learned Hristo Botev's poems by heart. There are all these books in our library in Bodrovo, you read them all, you know. And especially, I like to read about the hajduks."

"Yes, our hajduks used to fight against the Turks, the Turks were enemies, and now our own Bulgarians are enemies worse than the Turks," Todor said angrily, seeing before his eyes the tattered body of Alexander Stamboliysky with his brother and his murdered cousins. "The murderers-butchers committed the fascist upheaval, they kill and torture people, and the Bulgarian 'Bay Ganues' serve them! We don't have any longer our country, law, home, we can no longer return to our home. Gocho, how is there our house? How is father, mother, grandma Mariyka? How is sister Mary and little Mitra?"

Gocho sobbed, unable to hold back his tears, and sobbingly pronounced:

"It's hard for us without you, Todor. The entire household is falling, we are barely holding on, we are trying our best. We miss you. The father became completely unsociable, he is gloomy all the time, as if a part of him has been cut off. Mom pities you, often cries. Maria is already 18 years old, she wants to get married, and Mitra is 3 years old, she has grown up, so funny."

They went silent.

"Rusi, go and change Ivan, let him come inside and eat, but just look at both, so that there is no one!"

"Can I smoke?"

"No, you know that you can't. You can't smoke at the post, you can be noticed, but it's your duty to notice somebody appears."

"Ok, I just asked," said Rusi, of medium height, dark haired, snub-nosed boy thanked for food and went out from koshara, and Ivan Ignatov came in instead of him and sat down at the table.

Mutual greeting sounded sincerely, and Ivan Ignatov began to eat with appetite the offered food. Gocho continued:

"Grandma Mariyka called me recently, the conversation turned about you: how everything will be there, when you'll return. Grandma Mariyka told me: Gocho, your great-great grandfather Todor Chauna, he was born in 1782, was a hajduk for 12 years and Voevoda of a big squad, he acted under different names: Stoyan and Bosil. He was not from these parts, but from afar, from the

Balkan Mountains in the North. He himself was a son of hajduk. His father Gocho Zelengoro was a hajduk for 20 years. They had a house and fields in the village Djeravna in the valley at the foot of the Balkan Mountains, where Stara Planina is. They called him Zelengoro, which means "green wood", because he was very fond of the forest, the green forest, where the hajduks could hide under the crowns of trees, behind the green foliage. In the Kardjali Times of troubles, Gocho Zelengoro was the associate of Indje Voevoda, he was his right hand, and late he was his most faithful yatak. He himself was from the village Kotel, which is higher north in the Balkan Mountains from the Zheravna village. His grandson, your great-great-grandfather, Todor Chauna, the hajduk and a descendant of the hajduks, when it became dangerous to stay in Zheravna, gathered the entire household, loaded it into carts with mules and with all his family and hired workers together with a huge herd crossed the path, left the Balkan Mountains and went south. His daughters were beautiful, and 4 sons were heroes, one of which was Gocho, the father of your grandfather Todor. They lived for some time in Karasarle, but the Turks did not give them to live in peace and began to pester his beautiful daughters, and he killed them.

Again he gathered the entire household, herds of cattle, loaded everything in carts and drove the cattle south into the forests to our lands. Bodrovo did not exist then. So, they had to start building in a new place again, now far from the Turks. But this is not the end of the story yet, then I'll tell you the continuation. So, all the men in our lineage were the hajduks: proud, recalcitrant rebels, who did not tolerate any slavery and oppression, who fought for freedom. So, our Todor inherited all the traits of their character."

"I heard these stories from our late grandfather Todor," Todor said, who really felt the rebellious, proud hajduk's blood in him.

They talked almost all night, then Todor signaled to everyone that they had to go, and the young people proceeded to part.

"Thank you, Georgy, for your help," Todor hugged his cousin emotionally. "Thanks to your father, uncle Dimitar, for helping our family."

"You can count on us," Georgy answered. "I'll bring food to the old koshara of grandpa Techa, as agreed."

"And I'll bring what I can," Gocho said.

They got up from the table, hugged and said goodbye.

"I don't know if we see each other again," Todor said thoughtfully.

"Take care!" Gocho and Georgy wished them.

Todor's cheta came out of the koshara, the sheep and goats stretched out like cats with pleasure, having folded their paws under the heads, and were dozing peacefully before to set off in the morning. In the corner of the paddock a donkey was dozing sweetly on the side. The Todor's cheta set out on the return journey to their underground hide in the ravine south of his fields. Like a precious treasure they carried in their sacks all the food that Georgy with Gocho gave them. The moon and the stars, burning with bright lights, illuminated their path, the dark cover of green foliage hid them from foes.

***

2 days had passed. The July sun rose from the east, flooding with rays the underneath world. The lash foliage of bushes and trees of a small forest, which was contiguous to the Haskovo-Kardzhali highway, reliably hid the Todor's cheta, who had taken their positions since early morning. They crouched, hidden behind the greenery of dense vegetation, sparkling in the sun, at a turn of the road near the village of Kozlets, where any movement in one direction or another had to slow down for turning around the bend and there, where form both sides you could not see the road, to check what's going on behind the turn. Todor with Kolyu were sitting in an ambush at the very turn. Ivan Ignatov was in ambush from an opposite side of the road, and Mityu Panev was sitting in the bushes up the road toward Haskovo. Rusi Stoyanov was at the same distance down the road toward Kardzhali. All were at such a distance from each other, where they could hear a whistling or see a signal.

On the road paved with stone movement began from the morning: horses clattered with horseshoes, carrying on their backs a lone rider or a cart harnessed to them, oxen carts rumbled; a donkey loaded with bales walked slowly, shaking its sides, next to the owner; lone travelers went to work in both directions. Todor let all of them go, estimating their level of prosperity by appearance. The time was approaching noon, the sun was at its zenith and unbearably scorched the glowing stones of the road. Todor's friends, sitting in ambush, covered with the shade of the green foliage, almost emptied their baklagas with water and impatiently watched the road. Traffic almost stopped in the afternoon. Suddenly they heard a whistle coming from the south from Kardzhali. Rusi gave a signal that a car of a tobacco company was coming, since only the tobacco-speculators, who bought all the tobacco from the villagers for a pittance, concentrated in their hands its processing and sale, fabulously becoming rich in this way and financed the fascist coup against their country, drove cars.

The chetniks were ready. The convertible was traveling at a low speed and braked before turning. Todor shot at the car's tire, which spun like spinning top, limping on one leg with a punctured tire, and due to the momentum drove off the road straight into the bushes. In an instant the car was surrounded by 5 from head to toe armed boys, who opened the doors and commanded:

"Get out of the car! Hands up!"

A driver and 2 armed guards with their hands up began to get out of the damaged car. In one instant Todor disarmed the guards and took away their revolvers. Mityu Panev and Rusi Stoyanov with Ivan Ignatov tied their hands, Kolyu Trendofilov rummaged the car and pulled out 2 large suitcases from under the seats; they were immediately opened: there were tightly packed banknotes of golden leva. The chetniks did not try to hide their joy. Keeping their revolver sights from the 3 travelers, the chetniks tied them to the steering wheel of the car, wished them a happy journey to Haskovo bank and instantly vanished into the thickets of the forest along with the bags full of money and gold watches on chains.

"Help," the driver of the car mumbled helplessly, tied along with the guards to the steering wheel of the car, sticking sideways out of the bushes thickets.

The hajduks disappeared from sight, with a quick step they made their way through the forest to the glade, where their horses were tethered to the trees, jumped in the saddles and galloped north-west toward the Aidanlar forest. With a dense ring of forest surrounded the hollow, where there was the village in which the Karagochev family lived recently: uncle Gocho with his sons Vidyu and Todor, the forest covered the lowland around the village of Aidanlar and gradually rose up the high slopes of the hills to the south from the village. Alternating, the hills, now higher, now lower, rose south to the Rhodopes, forming a labyrinth of ravines and hills. The hajduks galloped to the foot of the hill covered with dense forest, dismounted, tethered the horses and set off further on foot. They climbed a mountain along a hidden path, reached a small terrace, where bushes of jasmine and boxwood grew, and behind the bushes there was an entrance to a cave, going inside the mountain. No one knew about it, except Todor with Ivan Ignatov: there was their second shelter, where they arranged a temporary home for themselves. In the depth of the cave in a cache they hid money, there was a hell amount of money, and, tired, they fell to rest on the palliasses. Loud laughter, echoing from the walls of a deep cave, broke the silence of the hidden shelter. They started to have fun, congratulating each other with a successful action.

"Maybe we split the money and go to Turkey?" Mityu Panev asked.

Todor stopped laughing immediately and answered confidently:

"Not now, I and Ivan have another goal: to take vengeance and exterminate the foes."

Ivan Ignatov confirmed the words of his friend.

"Ok, I've just asked," Mityu said embarrassedly, and the hajduks continued to laugh.

Chapter 33
September 1923

On August 26, 1923, the criminal gang of Boris III, consisting of Tsankov, Rusev, Vylkov and all the other murderers, who usurped the power in Bulgaria, fired 3 bullets in the back of Raiko Daskalov, Alexander Stamboliysky's ally, with the hands of the filthy assassin from IMRO Jordan Tsitsonkov, hired by them. The plenipotentiary Minister of the Agrarian Union government fell in a street of Prague, the best friend and associate of Alexander Stamboliysky, Raiko Daskalov, passed away, the great hero of Bulgaria, a brave, courageous, noble fighter for freedom against darkness and obscurity, the leader of the Vladay revolution for democracy and republic, a handsome young man of 27 years old died, having left wife and 2 children, having left defeated and decapitated the Agrarian Party, its herald in Prague the "Agrarian Banner," having left defeated and decapitated by all forces of evil, gathered in one fist of the tsar Boris, unfortunate Bulgaria. Gloom and darkness hung over the country, exterminating her best sons, to leave only the Bulgarian Bay Ganevs to serve the fascist regime.

The sectarians and doctrinaires, as Alexander Stamboliysky aptly called them, as vainly tried to conclude an alliance with them, the leaders of BCP, who used to betray him always and everywhere, betrayed him during the Vladay uprising and on June 9, 1923, acting as abettors of the fascist coup in the country, having thrust a knife in the back of Bulgaria with their "railway strike," when the defeated country healed the wounds of the war, fighting with him, clearing the way to power for the fascist junta of the putschists, having given the hero of Pleven Halachev for the mercy of the fascists by order them to surrender—the BCP did not even think of being tormented by remorse.

Continuing to enjoy the comfort in the gorgeous Party House, built with the workers' money, Lukanov, the BCP secretary for Organization Affairs, rocked with pleasure in soft armchairs, stoked the smooth polishing of the table, contemplated with pleasure the books, beautifully arranged on the shelves, and winked at the portraits of Marx and Engels, hanging on the walls in his office, fearing more than anything else to lose office comfort in case to join the fight against the fascist junta and be defeated. Therefore, secretly from his colleagues, he telegraphed to the Comintern in Moscow that "everything is fine and the new Tsankov government guaranteed the Communists their complete loyalty and support in case of cooperation." He stubbornly convinced his colleagues in this.

He was indulged by Georgy Dimitrov. And only thanks to the fact that fearless Vasil Kolarov, the Secretary of the Executive Bureau of the Comintern, left Moscow, arrived in Sevastopol, accompanied by 2 officers, crossed the stormy Black Sea, arrived in Varna by a winding path, ended up behind bars and safely freed and finally under the cover of night reached the Party House in Sofia, gathered a council and called the fascist abettors and traitors to responsibility, only after that the members of the BCP Council adopted a resolution on an armed uprising against the fascists.

The council meeting continued during 2 days: 5–6 August 1923. On the first day, on 5 August, 2 helpers brought a chair into the meeting room with gravely ill Dimitar Blagoev, the leader of the BCP, who had nothing more to lose and, descending into a grave, he blessed the coming uprising and left in the chair the Conference Hall, where he was not destined to ever return. Under the sparkling speech of Vasil Kolarov, who morally destroyed his fellow traitors, they finally felt ashamed and in full force—Georgy Dimitrov, Hristo Kabakchiev, Nikola Penev, Todor Petrov, Anton Ivanov, Kosta Yankov—on the next day of the meeting, on August 6th, 1923, signed a resolution to set a course for an armed uprising against the fascist junta of Boris III, Tsankov, Vylkov, Rusev. Lukanov remained true to himself and continued to put sticks into the wheels, foreboding the loss of his office comfort.

On August 6th, Kolarov read the resolution, he had received from the local cells, from the village of Dylboky of the Starozagorsk region and the other places that the people was sending the traitor Lukanov and the entire Central Committee, who had betrayed them, to hell and was preparing to rise without the leadership together with the Agrarians to fight against the fascists. Under the onslaught of Kolarov, the Central Committee signed a resolution: "The military organization must begin to collect weapons secretly and instruct the combat groups. The uprising is to be raised in September."

The couriers set off throughout the country to spread the news of the resolution for the uprising. In every city and village, large and small, there were district committees of the BCP. Grassroots cells, Youth communist unions. The couriers from the center brought news about the United Front with the Agrarian Union and the Social Democrats. The decapitated Agrarian Union continued to breathe, the surviving members of BANU, the supporters of Stamboliysky, seething with anger toward his killers, the military specialists and ordinary villagers continued to live; now they have united with the Communists and together with them began to prepare the uprising. The couriers delivered the instructions in oral and written form, risking their lives, keeping secrecy: they walked day and night, making their way through the thickets of forests, through fields and meadows, surmounting the hills and gorges, wading shallow rivers, went by trains and passing phaetons. They carried the message of the United Front of all the decent people against the criminal gang of murderous scum, who had seized power in Bulgaria by banditry. Like by web, the whole Bulgaria was connected by the local headquarters of the rebels and the couriers bringing the news.

According to the military-technical plan of the uprising, the country was divided into 5 military-revolutionary regions. Plovdiv became the center of the uprising throughout southern Bulgaria. The result of the uprising throughout the Southern Bulgaria depended on the success of the uprising in Plovdiv. Collection of weapons began in all the cities and villages. They took out from the basements of the kmet communities, shepherds' kosharas and rural cabins Mailicher rifles, drum revolvers, double-barreled shotguns, bayonets, sabers and grenades, hidden from the Balkan Wars; they cleaned the barrels and filled the bandoliers with cartridges. They were waiting for the signal to start the uprising.

The leaders in each locality had plans for the uprising, carefully worked out by the military-revolutionary committees. A joint blow of all the forces and throughout the country guaranteed the success of the uprising and victory. And the railroad strike was also needed to block the ruling junta from sending troops to suppress it. The traitors scum spied, sniffed and eavesdropped and informed the fascist tsar Boris III and Tsankov with Rusev that the uprising against the bandits was being prepared. On September 12, the junta launched a pre-emptive strike throughout the country. 2, 5 thousand BCP and BANU leaders were arrested, the Party House of Communists in Sofia, their club and the "Liberation" Cooperative were destroyed. The surviving members of the BCP Central Committee went into hiding.

In response, the very next day, September 13, without waiting for a general signal for the uprising, the brave city of Migledzh of the Kazanluk Region rebelled. The rebels captured the kmet's office and hoisted 2 banners on it: red and orange. The village of Golyamo Dryanovo joined them. All the villages around Pazardzik rebelled the next day. The bells rang on the towers of the churches, signaling the attack, the armed villagers, Communists and Agrarians, as well as all the honest citizens disarmed the policemen with lighting speed, put them behind bars, seized police stations and communities and hoisted banners on them: red of the Communists and orange of the Agrarians. Seething with a thirst of vengeance for the death of Stamboliysky, for his martyrdom and heroic death, the rebels flocked to Pazardzik, where the national leader, the hero Alexander Stamboliysky was captured and sent to torment in the hands of the butchers, and Golgotha-Slavovitsa blackened nearby, covered in blood.

On September 19, 5 policemen from Borisovograd, having dismounted and tethered their horses to the trees near the north-eastern border of Borisovograd, hid themselves and peeped out toward the bridge over Maritsa, and waited for somebody to put a bullet in the back, who would cross the bridge with weapons. Shots rang out, and explosions rumbled from all sides, where the rebels were fighting with the forces of the junta. 5 shots were fired right under their noses, and all 5 wounded in the right hand dropped their guns from the hands. 5 young people, armed from head to toes, dressed as hajduks, immediately picked up the guns and pointed on them. A slender, black-eyed handsome man with shoulder-length black hair parted in the middle, Todor Todorov, and his friend-hero Ivan Ignatov introduced 5 policemen to their 3 friends, who were unaware:

"Meet them, friends, these are the same policemen!"

"Wow, how lucky we are to catch the whole gang!" pleased Mityu Panev exclaimed.

"Hey, you, policemen, do you remember how you tormented me and my friend Ivan in your Borisovograd police station?" Todor asked angrily, holding the revolvers, aimed at them.

"Yes, yes, do you remember how you were killing me, damned dogs?" Ivan Ignatov asked, also holding 2 revolvers.

"Do you remember how you beat me almost to death and threw me into a dunghill, how you dug a hole on the bank of the Maritsa, where you were going to bury me alive? I miraculously survived. How many more people have you beaten to death after June 9th? How many more people have you tortured and burned alive in the furnace of you police station? Answer me, police scum! Do you remember how you abused my family and robbed my house?"

The cowardly butchers-policemen stared with fright and grimaced from pain of the wounds, they only silently opened their mouths. They were brave only with a whole gang together in front of one man in chains.

"Yes, people like them beat people to death not only after June 9, but also before that," Ivan corrected.

"And now Tsankov Bulgaria is full of people like them," Rusi Stoyanov said, aiming at them from 2 revolvers, "others were simply removed from the police."

"You, butchers, sadists, murderers of people, fascist henchmen, are sentenced to death penalty!" Todor pronounced the verdict, and all 5 put a mortal bullet in the policemen, intending to save cartridges.

"Well, we have taken the vengeance, the main foes remained: their bosses," Todor said and commanded the cheta to set off.

They untethered 5 police horses, which they took with them, and rode north on their horses. They crossed the Maritsa River, on the left bank of which fighting raged around Chirpan.

***

In the village Krushevo the insurgent villagers gathered on the square near kmet's office building, and the fascist defenders fled from the village in the northerly direction toward Chirpan, firing back. A retired lieutenant, a member of the Agrarian Union, the commander of the rebel detachment Nikola Zorov appealed the audience with a speech:

"Comrades members of the Agrarian Union and BCP, non-partisans and sympathizers, dear friends who have gathered here on the square near the village, I congratulate you with our victory! Today you defeated the criminal fascist junta that overthrew the legitimate government of the Agrarian Union in Bulgaria on June 9, this year, killed our Minister-Chairman Alexander Stamboliysky and usurped power in the country, having deluging it in blood. Here and now you have defeated the bandits and murderers of the Bulgarian people, which are rising now to fight all over the country."

"Hooray!" the rebels triumphed, then fell silent and turned their gaze together with the speaker to the main road of the village, crossing it from west to east.

5 horsemen were approaching the place with leisurely step along it. They were dressed in the hajduk style and armed from head to toe, each led another horse by the bridle, and along the stretched out in a chain horsemen, 8 well-dressed civilians in fashionable pointy-toed shoes were going. All looked at them with interest.

"Who are you?" the commander asked.

"I am Todor Todorov, and this is my cheta."

"And who are they?" the commander asked, pointing at the bound captives.

"We have caught them on the road, disarmed and captured; they tried to shoot at the peasants in the back."

"Spitz team?"

"Exactly they are, they betray themselves by their shoes: they all have the same ones with pointed toes. Isn't it Hristo Kundurdjiyata from Chirpan, the shoemaker, who supplies all of you with pointy-toed shoes?" Todor asked mockingly, pointing at the shoes of the captives.

"His Majesty tsar Boris III and Prime Minister Tsankov entrusted us with a state mission: to kill all the enemies of the state," the bravest of the captives declared importantly, "we'll shoot you in the back always and everywhere from around the corner or openly, because you are the rebels against our fatherland, the tsar and the church!"

"Let us shoot them right away!" Ivan Ignatov suggested and raised the revolver.

"Leave it, not now!" Todor stopped him. "Your mission is over, gentlemen-killers," he returned to the captives and the commander, "lock them up somewhere."

"Come on, take them to the back room of the kmet's building, there is already seating there under lock and key the 'holy trinity' of Tsankov, who tortured to death our kmet and sat down to rule instead of him."

The captives were pushed into the kmet's building and placed under lock in a room, guarded by a sentry. Todor whispered something in the ear of the commander, who changed his face, frowned and turned to the public.

"Friends, comrades, fighters for a just cause, Todor Todorov will now tell you something."

With excitement and a sinking heart, barely controlling himself, Todor told the audience about his trip with Ivan Ignatov to Slavovitsa region and about what they had witnessed. Ivan Ignatov, who was standing near him, confirmed everything. Angry exclamation flew over the square; the audience shuddered with horror…

"Help," Zorov turned to Todor, and together with him they climbed on the roof of the kmet's building and hoisted 2 banners: red of the Communists and orange of the Agrarians.

"And who are you: Agrarians or Communists?" the commander asked Todor.

"We are neither Agrarians nor Communists," Todor said, "we are on our own, we have personal scores with the fascists."

The telephone rang in the kmet's office, the assistant commander received calls and reported to everyone: "Svoboda is occupied by the rebels, the workers and Agrarians power has been declared in Perigleri, Medovo has surrendered to the rebels." Loud "Hurray!" flew all over the square. The tired rebels sat down, where they found any place, to rest, eat and go to battle.

"We are going on Chirpan. Are you with us?" the commander asked Todor.

"Of course, we are with you," the later answered, "the more so I have debt there, that is I am owed. Take 5 horses and 5 guns that we've brought."

"Nova Zagora is occupied by the rebels, the Tsankov fascists are surrendering," the news that had just been received by the telephone was publicly announced. "Under Stara Zagora there are heavy battles."

After resting and refreshing themselves with food cooked right there in the boilers, the rebels got up and moved north to Chirpan. The Todor's cheta was together with them. Some on foot, some astride, armed with rifles and revolvers, and some were with a dagger and saber or club, the rebels flocked to Chirpan in streams to take the city. They went to fight not for the slogans of the Comintern and not for the triumph of communism throughout the world, they went to fight for the restoration of the trampled power of the Agrarian Union, for the people's leader Alexander Stamboliysky, tortured by the beasts, for their lives and the lives of their loved ones, for their home, village and country, occupied by a criminal gang of bloody fascist killers. Here and there, there was fighting, now and then all looked back to the west up the Maritsa River toward Plovdiv, where explosions rumbled, and machine-guns scribbled. It was heavy artillery, which fired on the rebels from 60 rebellious villages, who were trying to attack Plovdiv…

***

The uprising against the fascists had already been going on for 7 days, and finally, on September 20, 1923, the Central Committee of the BCP, having secretly from the police gathered in a safe house in Sofia, decided to start a general uprising throughout the country at night on September 23. On September 20, they finally determined the day of the uprising to start: 23rd of September, and they made a decision about the uprising on September 15. The members of the Central Committee, except Lukanov, in an atmosphere of house-to-house arrests and terror, secretly gathered in a safe house and made a final decision on the date of the uprising.

Lukanov himself was not present at the meeting, as he was hiding in a closet in the same apartment, where the meeting was held, and the day before, on September 14, he secretly from the party members ordered to stop the general strike of large enterprises that had begun. On September 12, secretly from the comrades-in-arms, he sent his couriers throughout the country with a directive immediately to stop the uprising for those who raised it and not to raise it for those who were just preparing to raise it. With a telegram and courier note, Lukanov tried to stop the course of history, to suppress the storm of people's anger, to drown out human conscience, to strangle the people's struggle against fascism, just acting as an abettor of this fascism, its accomplice and henchman.

Lukanov was sitting, having hidden himself, in a remote dark and dusty closet, trembling with fear and yearning with nostalgia for his personal office in the luxurious Party House, which had been destroyed by the fascists on September 12, and for his parliamentary tribune in the Public Assembly, where he would deliver pompous speeches about the interests of the working people.

But Lukanov failed to stop the uprising with a telegram and notes behind the backs of his party members, the uprising had already been blazing since

September 13. Major Nikola Todorov Aguinsky, a member of the Agrarian Union, was appointed chief of the staff of the uprising, he on the next day, September 21, early in the morning went by car with the leaders of the Central Committee Georgy Dimitrov and Vasil Kolarov and Panov from Sofia through the Petrokhansky Pass to Virshets, from where it was planned to raise the uprising throughout the north-west, to capture the cities Vratsa and Ferdinand and together with the joint forces of the rebels of the entire north-west to cross the Balkans to Sofia, where the rebels inside the city were to be supported by the artillery battery of the Slatin redoubt, which was on the side of the rebels. Having changed their appearance and disguised as engineers, Dimitrov and Kolarov with Panov and Aguinsky with the forged documents of civilian engineers, overcoming the cordons at the Petrokhansky Pass, approached Virshets in a car.

At the same time in Sofia at the last meeting of the revolutionary committee at the safe house of Dimitar Guichev in Veslets street, Anton Ivanov, Nikola Panev, Todor Atanasov and Ivan Pashov lamented over the fatal news they had just received about redeployment of the artillery men of the Slatin redoubt, loyal to the rebels, to another place: that jeopardized the entire operation in Sofia, as the Slatin redoubt occupied the hill dominating over Sofia, and there was the main hope for it. Terrified by the foreboding news, all the members of the Committee shuddered at the rumble of grenades, the crackle of machine-guns on the door of their room and menacing cry: "Surrender, you are surrounded!" Who fell dead, who jumped out of the window, vanished and miraculously survived, who was captured by the police, being wounded. The defeat of the members of the Military-Revolutionary Committee and the uprising that had never begun in Sofia occurred on the denunciation of the traitor Major Simeon Vankov. In one country there were 2 majors, 2 personalities, 2 destinies, 2 paths. One was Major Nikola Todorov Aguinsky, a member of the Agrarian Union, appointed by the Central Committee as the chief of the staff of the general uprising. Another was Major Simeon Vankov, a member of BCP, was an agent-provocateur of the tsarist secret police, sent to the Central Committee to destroy them all, who betrayed all the plans of the rebels to the fascists. He led armed policemen to a safe house, where the last meeting of the Revolutionary Committee was taking place, thereby thwarting the uprising in Sofia. One was Major Aguinsky, who allowed himself to be arrested and refused to escape already at the entrance to Virshets, in order to lead a gang of bloodhounds astray and save Dimitrov with Kolarov, a brave hero of revolution, a member of the Agrarian Union. Another major was a pseudo-communist, a bastard-traitor, a fascist henchman. Bulgaria, a country of heroes and traitors, who betrayed them all, followed her chosen path of valor and betrayal.

Thanks to Major Aguinsky, arrested by the police, who knocked the bloodhounds out of the way, Georgy Dimitrov and Vasil Kolarov with Gavril Guenov safely reached Virshets and headed the uprising of the United Front. 2 banners of victory of the revolution rose above the Virshets kmet's office building: red and orange. The rebels took the village, having disarmed the police, at night of September 23. And then there were fights, heroism and betrayal, courage and cowardice. The city of Vratsa, designated as the center of the uprising, rushing into battle, failed to come out, was sitting and waiting to be liberated from outside, chickened out at the last moment. Vratsa, who had condemned the treacherous neutrality of the Central Committee on June 9, burning with a thirst of revenge on the fascists, declared that she herself would rise to fight for freedom even if the signal of the Central Committee for the general uprising is not given, did not rise, when this signal was given and predestined the outcome of the uprising.

Ad after that there was the victory of the rebels near Ferdinand, the ancient Roman Montanesia, named after the former Bulgarian tsar, surrendered to the rebels and solemnly greeted them with orange and red banners. The rebels were led into battle by the officer Hristo Mikhailov. The rebels took almost all the settlements of the north-west, except Vratsa, who betrayed them. The rebels acted according to a well-developed plan, simultaneously inflicted massive strikes on the enemy, invaded settlements and seized post office, police stations banks, railway stations, municipalities and district offices, freed political prisoners, who joined the rebel detachments, and they raised red and orange banners over the main buildings of a city or a village. In the district police departments, the arrested political prisoners were replaced with the Black Bloc supporters. Under the beat of a drummer, the workers and peasants government was created. There was a feast of the people. There was a hero of revolution, pope Andrew from the village Medkovets. With shoulder-length black curls, flattering in the wind of the revolution like a hajduk, he tried to deliver a cannon to the gates of the city of Lom, under the roar of guns he lead the rebels detachments into a battle to take the city. There was a hero of the revolution, pope Mikhail, who hid the weapons for the rebels and blessed his 2 sons to fight the fascists: Hristo and Ivan, the commander of the detachment that took Ferdinand. Then there was a forced retreat of the rebels from Ferdinand to the hills, as the enemy forces from Vratsa sent a train with troops and artillery by rail to recapture Ferdinand.

Then there was the ultimate defeat of the enemy forces in Ferdinand and resuming the city by the rebels, to whose aid the revolutionary detachments of Georg Damyanov from Lopushin and Gavril Guenov came in time. Guenov, who tried in vain to raise the uprising in Vratsa, retreated alone, walked throughout ravines and mountains, gathered people along the way, joined up with Georgy Damyanov and now with common forces, shouting "Hurrah!" the fighters of the revolution descended from the hills and in battle with the enemy rebuffed the city. The soldiers of the junta surrendered to the rebels, threw down their weapons and who, finally, waked up from the sleep of the mind, went over to the side of the people who rebelled for freedom. The herald on the market square again beat the drum, informing everyone that the city was again taken by the insurgent people, red and orange banners again flew up on the bank building, and Georgy Dimitrov and Vasil Kolarov finally arrived in Ferdinand from Vlrshets. They trudged through forests and mountains, rode a draisine and train and entered the city, greeted by the jubilant public and comrades-in-arms. They took over the political leadership of the uprising.

From the District Military-Revolutionary Committee, the couriers carried throughout the north-western land of Bulgaria appeals, orders and calls for everyone to rise up to fight the fascists and go to Ferdinand. And Ferdinand received a joyful telegram that Berkovitsa had been taken by the detachment of Hristo Mikhailov. All units in the United Front were going to storm Vratsa, as she herself did not rebel, but was sitting and waiting for somebody to come to free her from outside.

Then there was a battle for Boychinovtsy, where they had to turn, changing their route from Vratsa, and go to save the strategic point, since the tsarist echelon from Shumen drove hundreds of fascists with guns there. It was a battle that went down in history, covering its heroes with glory. Those who captured the plateau and hills above, the station, had the advantage in position, but it did not save them, and after heavy fighting, surrounded by the rebels, who increasingly closed the ring around them, retreated, fleeing. Hundreds of the fascist soldiers and fascist volunteers, the White Guard bastards of Baron

Wrangel, whom Stamboliysky sheltered and let into Bulgaria, and provided asylum, were now killing the Bulgarian people, serving the fascist junta that tortured Stamboliysky to death. All of them fled, stumbling, and dropped down the weapons under the onslaught of heroic rebels near Boychinovtsy. They tore off their shirts and pulled them on their rifles, raising a white flag, and surrendered to the mercy of the winners. Someone managed to escape to the Danube. Boychinovtsy were taken by the rebels. Emaciated and tired from battles and crossings, the soldiers of the revolution triumphed. They rejoiced and congratulated each other: they won a great victory, defeated the enemy and seized his weapons. They reveled in victory, they were ready to go to the end. They were standing at the railway station Boychinovtsy and listened with joy to the speech of the commander Gavril Guenov, who congratulated them. They thought and hoped that in all other villages and cities the victorious insurgents celebrated the same victory. And if it had been so, then it would've been a general victory. But it was not so…

And then it was September 26. There was a betrayal of those who did not rebel. There was a betrayal of the railroad workers of the Minister of the Broad Socialists Dimo Kazasov, a participant of the putsch on June 9. During the governing of Stamboliysky, in a difficult year of the trials for the country after the defeat in the Great War, the railway workers staged a general strike, stabbing the government of the Agrarian Union in the back, and now, during the uprising of the people against the fascist junta, they were not on strike and servilely served the junta. Hey worked without interruption, supplying trains and sending them filled with gangster vermin from the far ends of the country to the places, where the battles were fought, to suppress people. Trains filled with murderers flew by, cannon barrels stuck out of the windows, they arrived to the Krivodol station, halfway from Boychinovtsi and Vratsa. Hordes of fascist vermin accumulated in Krivodol, cutting off the road to the non-rebellious Vratsa. They spread in black masses, surrounding the rebel detachments, crept into Belogradchik, cutting off the retreat route to Yugoslavia. In heavy battles with superior forces, the rebels suffered a defeat, fell to the ground dead, retreated in despair, realizing that this was the end, because those, who did not rebel, betrayed. Because of them, Vidin fortress sent black forces along the Danube to Lom, and the remote Shumen sent a black train to Krivodol.

The rebellion had a chance to win if all had risen up, and they did what they had to do, but now, when all had failed to revolt, their chance was lost. Now the task was to retreat, to leave and be saved. The committee ordered the rebels to retreat to Serbia. The fascist vermin poured in black streams, surrounding, breaking, dispersing the rebel detachments. The rebel heroes bravely at the last moment were fighting their way through these streams and retreated to the Yugoslavia borders.

Georgy Dimitrov, Vasil Kolarov and Georgy Rusinov left Ferdinand in the direction of Lopushna-Chiprovtsy border of Yugoslavia. Serbia, a long-standing enemy of Bulgaria, which fought with her in mortal battles yet recently during the Second Balkan and the Great War, now gave shelter to the driven Bulgarians, saved them on her land, where the Communist Party was officially banned.

The bravely fighting heroes of the rebels safely crossed the border, they flocked in streams to the rescue coast of Yugoslavia, while the passage for them was provided by the detachment of Captain Mikhail Kupchev, who fought with the enemy. All left, only Kupchev remained, did not have time to leave, was captured by the fascists and cut into pieces alive. Gavrila Guenov was the last to leave Ferdinand and took all the detachment to Yugoslavia.

The hours and days of the uprising in September 1923 flew like a whirlwind in a blink of an eye and dragged on like the eternity, creating the history. This was the history of entire generation. There was everything in those days: preparation, hopes and plans of revolt, its bold start and the first victories, jubilant joy, the height of the fight, the liberation of settlements from the fascist vermin and flying red and orange banners of victory; smashed fleeing foes, dropping down the weapons, a roar of cannons, whistling bullets, victorious shouting "Hurrah!" of the winners, anxiously listening to the silence of un-rebellious cities and villages, the betrayal of those who did not rebel; echelons crammed with the scoundrels, rushing to the places of battles, tightening rings of fascist vermin around the detachments that suffered defeat, their heroic last struggle with a superior enemy and safe withdrawal to Yugoslavia. Those who rebelled against the fascists were heroes, and they did what they had to do. They had a hope for victory, and it was not their fault that the others did not rise.

Sofia did not rise without the leadership, and almost the entire leadership was betrayed by Major Vankov. Plovdiv did not rise without leadership, but almost the entire leadership was seized on the traitors' denunciation. Jordan Bozhilov, Nikola Guinev, engineer Patarganov, the leadership of the Military-Revolutionary Committee, developed a clear plan of uprising in the city and vicinal villages, but the plan failed, as the junta launched a pre-emptive strike. Because Plovdiv was designated as the center of the uprising of the entire South of Bulgaria, the secretaries of the local city committees from all over the district, representatives of BCP from Northern Bulgaria, Varna and other cities gathered there. The junta seized and threw behind bars 113 leaders of the BCP and BANU, blocked the entire city on September 12 and imposed a curfew. All party organizations and Agrarian friendships were left without leadership, and their will to take decisive actions was paralyzed. According to the plan, the rebel battle group was to attack the headquarters of the divisions, militant organizations were to attack police stations throughout the city, as well as the barracks, they had to take a post office and other important objects. Detachments from the villages of Markovo, Belashitsa, Kuklen and Karaagach were supposed to attack the city.

On September 19–20, the battles for Stara Zagora and Chirpan were unfolded, from where the fighters for freedom directed their gaze from the battlefields toward Plovdiv with hope. But Plovdiv was silent, attacked by the rebels of 60 villages around, he did not enter the battle, smashed by the arrests, lost heart and chickened out. The soldiers in the barracks, ready to go over the side of the revolution, vainly waited for the signal to attack; the rebellious Stara Zagora and Chirpan and the entire South Bulgaria vainly waited support. And at that time the uprising in the North-West was just beginning. The entire North-East and South-East did not revolt. In the south-eastern lands of Bulgaria the activists of the BCP and the Youth Union were sitting quietly, hiding, not daring to take any action. There was a powerful and numerous organization of the party with brave and determined warriors in every village ready to fight.

Scheryu Atanasov, an activist from the Youth Union of the BCP and his friends raised an uprising on June 9 without waiting for directives from the Central Committee. They themselves organized revolutionary committee and raised the people to revolt throughout the vicinal area. They formed combat detachments, sent couriers to all villages and districts, and by the ringing of bells on the towers of the churches, they raised everyone to fight. They took all the villages on the left and right bank of the Maritsa and founded in

Lyubimets the headquarters of the uprising. They seized the communities in Belitsa, Lozen, Bizer, Malko Gradishche, Jerusalemovo, Momkovo, Kirilovo, Ivanovo and Leshnikovo; they held rallies and hoisted red banners on the kmet's buildings. They seized the post office and the railway station. The armed platoons and companies of the rebels, commanded by Atanas Gogov, took the fight with the detachments of the fascists, which arrived from Harmanly, north of Lyubimets, and won, when they were overtaken by the fatal telegram of Lukanov in the "Rabotnichesky Vestnik" immediately to disperse and give up to the invaders: "It is two types of bourgeoisie: Agrarian, BANU of Stamboliysky, and urban: Tsankov fascists, who are fighting between themselves. Let them kill each other! The Communist Party observes neutrality!" Discouraged, dumbfounded and dissentient, rebels of June all were forced to disperse into illegality, as the junta began to catch them one by one and brutally deal with. Scheryu Atanasov took refuge in a labor detachment and then in a secret cave on the island Ada on Maritsa River together with friends, which could never return home. This was in June, 2023. Now, in September, they recalled the events of the first uprising and were sitting quietly, waiting to see what would happen. The Communists of the Central Committee reaped the fruits of their betrayal of Stamboliysky.

The rebels failed to take Pazardzik and Chirpan, though they fought valiantly; the shells of the fascist cannons smashed them, and they retreated, dispersed.

"We withdraw!" Todor commanded his cheta, and they galloped south from Chirpan beyond Maritsa and hid in their secret cave on the hill in the Aidanlar forest.

"Never mind, we'll meet another time, Hristo Kundurdjiyata, a shoemaker!"

Chapter 34
After September 1923

Several thousand participants in the uprising safely crossed the border and took refuge in Yugoslavia, which gave the asylum. The other remnants of the defeated detachments sheltered in the caves of the Balkan Mountains, hid in the forests in order to survive and sought refuge with friends. Black hordes of the fascist volunteers, policemen and military caught them one by one and subjected them to inhuman torment. As soon as the roar of cannons, with which the junta defeated the insurgents, ceased, from the border outpost of Chiprovtsy near Yugoslavian border to a distant rebellious village in the east, as soon as the flame of the flame of the struggle of the fighters for freedom died out, the flames of the bonfires blazed all over the country: this is the fascist junta of the tsar Boris, Tsankov and company burned the houses of the participants in the uprising, their parents, relatives or friends, just acquaintance or sympathizers. The junta drove women, old people and children out of their houses into the street and burned their houses. Dogs howled, children yelled, women wailed around the ashes, trying to pull out of the black ashes a thing, dear to their heart and memory. Everything crumbled into black dust, their house, household and all property was swallowed up by the sinister flame. Old people cried, raising the hands to indifferent sky: "Why, god, have you left us?" They remained in the street without a house and yard on the threshold of winter.

Captain Harlakov, the butcher of Stamboliysky, who was raised to the rank of colonel for atrocities, personally arrived, where the uprising was flared up most of all: to the north-west, and now he was raging in Ferdinand and its environs. He cut off with a knife hands and feet of the captives, who had anything to do with the uprising or had nothing at all. A cry of despair and deathly torment resounded throughout the land of the ill-fated country. The cries of suffering and groans of the tortured rushed over the fields, in the cities and villages, even of those who did not rebel, from the walls of the police stations, barracks turned into prisons, from the jails, full of people. The sadists tortured everyone for their own pleasure, burned them alive, beat them to death, cut off pieces of flesh and flayed, pulled bags with lime over their heads and tightened them under a neck, so that the unfortunate person breathed with it, shot them without a trial and investigation, "when trying to escape," drowned in rivers and lakes. The corpses of unfortunate fighter for freedom floated along the Danube, Maritsa and Arda and their tributaries. And in Plovdiv they tortured, killed and under killed, and the dead and half-dead were buried alive in the ground along the coast of the Maritsa. The ground along the river was heaving from the screams of those buried alive.

Hordes of fascist volunteers, civilians without a specific type of occupation, gathered in flocks at the invitation of the junta, dressed in civilian clothes and pointed-toe shoes, all in a row were sadistic maniacs, received power from the tsar to hound down, fish out and grab everyone they wanted, to torture and kill on suspicion of disloyalty to the fascist junta, that usurped power, without trial and investigation and bearing responsibility. Like cockroaches, they crept across the country with a black cloud, fulfilling their mission.

"They killed the Bulgarian people, so that the Turks did not kill them!" the poet Strashimirov exclaimed, and these words became a characteristic of the era.

The foreign countries shuddered from the barbaric atrocities of the tsar Boris and his henchman Tsankov and published articles caricatures on them. And the Bulgarian venal press, except the bulletin "Agrarian Banner" and the communist "Rabotnichesky Vestnik," sold itself in bulk to the ruling junta and at the request of Tsankov did not publish a word about what was happening in the country, but published secular gossips, stupid stories and juicy jokes, so that the population "does not engage in politics" and turns into moronic slaves. But those who are born free will never become slaves.

The civil war unleashed by the tsar Boris III on June 9, 1923, continued and gained momentum. The thirst for vengeance of the people was seething, and it was impossible to stop it. Soon the secret letter of Georgy Dimitrov and Vasil Kolarov, printed in Belgrade, was forwarded to Bulgaria through secret channels and distributed throughout the country:

"Dear comrades! After major revolutionary battles, which so far ended unsuccessfully for popular masses, we together with many other fighters were forced to leave you in order to continue serving the great cause of our people. Although we are temporarily far away from you, the role that has fallen to our lot in this struggle, obliges us to appeal to you with open letter. And the first words, with which we address you, are 'Heads up!' The White Guard rabble, trembling for its power, will not be able to break the fighting spirit of the working Bulgaria with bloody revenge! Defeat will teach us to win!"

"Against all odds, workers and peasants government will be established in Bulgaria! Together with you we fought for great people's cause. Now we are defeated. But the fight is not over, and our final victory is closer than our enemies think. We'll learn from our defeat, and tomorrow we'll be stronger than we were yesterday, and our foes will increasingly lose ground under their feet. Filled with deep faith in our cause, which is the sacred cause of people, we, all the working people, shall courageously endure the pain and suffering of defeat and with even greater energy and enthusiasm sacrifice ourselves to the service of cause of people, and shall not rest until we win."

"We'll gather again and unite our thinned ranks. We shall quickly begin to heal the wounds inflicted on us. With common efforts and sacrifices we'll help the remained widows and orphans, needy families and comrades driven to a foreign land. In particular we shall preserve and strengthen the alliance of all the working people of city and village, which in September battles was sealed by the joined shed blood of thousands of fighters, who fell for the common cause of the people. No despondency, no despair, no cowardice! Keep your heads up, glorious fighters! Long live the workers and peasants' government! Long live Bulgaria of workers!"

"Vasil Kolarov, Georgy Dimitrov, October 2023."

The leadership of the Central Committee of the BCP fled abroad, having left in Bulgaria deeply conspiratorial battle squads, which proceeded to take vengeance on the fascist junta for thousands of killed and tortured, for burned houses, for terror and violence, for unleashing a civil war on June 9, 1923, when they had committed a fascist upheaval, exterminated the best people of the country, the Agrarian Union leadership and brutally tortured Alexander Stamboliysky. Therefore, the political cheta named after Hristo Botev was born.

Chapter 35
Chirpan Fair

The groans and cries of the tortured were muffled by the buffoonery noise at a fair on the city Chirpan and loud music. Carousels spun like a whirlwind, hawkers loudly advertised goods, hidden and just pulled out for sale. Bright signs lifted the spirits. Dressed-up ladies spread gossips, gleaned from newspapers. A philistine was having fun, as if nothing had happened. He knew nothing and did not want to know what was happening in the country. On the road from the south, leading to Chirpan, a few days before its opening, carts pulled by oxen, filled to the top with various goods, carts harnessed to an emaciated horse, cars of wealthy tobacco merchants were drawn in a string to the fair.

The fair had just made a noise, began to play, to sing, having opened, and started to work. Filled with people, wondering if anyone else was still alive, it hummed, offering merchandise. The sellers and buyers clamored, bargained to the last and made a deal. A couple of oxen, cattle and small lives stock, a donkey passed from hand to hand. 18 merchants at the fair were not in good mood, they with rage recalled the past day. A day before the opening of the fair, the traffic along the Bansko Highway was especially intensive. The merchants and buyers went to the fair in Chirpan from Ivaylovgrad, far away on the edge of the earth near Greece, from Momchilgrad in the Rhodopes, from Kardzhali. The road descended from the Rhodope Mountains through Miniralny Baths and then passed near the Aidanlar forest along Gorsky Izvor to the Maritsa valley and to its left bank to Chirpan. The average wealthy, the poor and rich went to the fair, the smugglers from Greece rode along the Bansko Highway along the hills, covered with forests.

5 young men, armed to the teeth, dressed like hajduks, in cervulis and onuchis on the legs with interlaced leather straps, in dark trousers and jackets,

with daggers and revolvers on the belts, were sitting in ambush near the highway and waited for prey. There was still yellow foliage on the branches of the bushes and trees, which reliably hid them. All their attention was directed to the south of the road, along which carts loaded with goods descended down to the north.

"Only the rich!" Todor reminded.

"Certainly," the subordinated replied.

Around the hill, here the road gently curved and was surrounded on both sides by lush yellow-green bushes. Rusi whistled, giving a signal, and it was not clear whether it was a cry of some bird or the moan of an animal. Those in the ambush got ready. An ox-drawn cart drew level with them. A well-dressed merchant was riding on a cart. All 5 jumped out of the ambush in a blink of an eye, blocking his path, and surrounded him from all side. They pointed the revolvers at the driver.

"Hold on! Get off the road!" Todor commanded, and Ivan grabbed a team of oxen and began to turn it left, where a vicinal road led to a small glade behind the bushes.

The driver in the cart did not resist and led the oxen to a place, where those who seized him pointed out. The cart turned off the road, went around the bushes, drove through the trampled grass through a small grove into a glade surrounded on all sides by trees.

"Customs inspection!" Todor announced cheerfully to the detainee and ordered him to get of the cart. "Hand over the weapons!"

The detainee, glancing with fear at the 5 barrels of revolvers pointed at him, dutifully handed over his revolver. Ivan Ignatov at that time was searching the cart. He shrugged his shoulders and told his friends:

"Nothing special."

"I propose voluntarily to hand over jewelry and money," Todor turned to the detainee.

The merchant calmly took out a briefcase from under the seat on the cart and gave it to Todor. Todor caught the briefcase and without taking the revolver off the detainee, threw the briefcase to Ivan. Mityu, Kolyu and Rusi were standing around, also holding the revolvers, and with a keen eye scanned both the detainee and the situation around. At that time Ivan poured the contents of the briefcase on a canvas bag spread on the grass and counted the money that spilled out.

"60 thousand," he reported to everyone.

"Count the necessary," Todor commanded.

Ivan counted out 40 thousand and handed them to Todor, who gave them to the detainee.

"We do not take amounts up to 40 thousand leva," he explained to the merchant, who was shaking with horror and did not know what awaited him: either it was time to part with the life, or the robbers would only rob him. On seeing 40 thousand leva that Todor handed him as change, he did not understand what was happening and did not dare to take the money, not knowing what would happen next.

"Take it, take it, don't be afraid," Todor laughed, "we rob only the rich and share with poor. We do not take away sums up to 40 thousand leva: let people buy a pair of oxen or a donkey at the fair. You are free!"

The man was completely at a loss, then grabbed 40 thousand leva returned to him, kindly thanked for this, wished the hajduks good luck, climbed into the cart and immediately returned to the highway, descending to Chirpan. The companions-hajduks merrily laughed.

"So, we have 20 thousand leva!" merrily laughing, Ivan Ignatov showed his friends the prey and hid them in another bag.

"Let's go back!" Todor commanded, and the friends returned to the highway and froze in ambush.

They missed the poor looking peasants, who were pulled by emaciated nags, and in the same way as they detained the first merchant, they detained the following one after another. Ivan Ignatov remained already at the glade, where he guarded the sack with the loot, 5 horses and a mule were grazing nearby, waiting for their owners. The hajduks-companions gave back sums that did not exceed 40 thousand leva without regret and let the people go and counted for themselves everything else over 40 thousand, and gave 40 thousand back to the owner. Those, not having time to come to their senses, hurriedly retreated on their carts, wishing good luck to the hajduks-robbers. Banknotes and gold and silver things fell on the canvas bag on the grass, as well as weapons that they took away from everyone: either poor or rich.

"Weapons will still come in handy," they foresaw.

They worked all day long. The carts of either rich or poor were drawn in string along the Bansko Highway to Chirpan, where the fair was opened the next day, where until recently there were battles with the fascist junta for the city, which the rebels never managed to take.

One by one the hajduks detained 17 people, rummaged and took away sums exceeding 40 thousand leva; their mood was cheerful, the sack with the prey was filling up, the day was coming to a set. They returned to the highway, planning to detain 1 or 2 and leave. A right client appeared. He looked wealthy. He was riding on a cart filled to the brim with saddles for horses. Todor with company escorted the saddler to the glade. He handed over his gun, but said that he had no money: he was going to the fair only to sell the saddles and on the proceeds to buy something for his house. Ivan began to rummage his cart. The most beautiful patterned and skillfully crafted saddles emitted a pleasant aroma and reminded Todor of the shoe-shop of Hristo Kundurdjiyata in Chirpan. He became angry.

"Seek better!" he commanded.

Each of these saddles cost a fortune, but he says no money! Ivan began to rummage again, but found nothing. Mule seats were interspersed with horse saddles. The owner of the saddles was standing neither alive nor dead, being afraid to raise his eyes, and looked at the muzzles of the revolvers pointed at him and at his goods. Suddenly at that moment, a short man with long dark blond hair emerged from behind the bushes with a revolver in his hands and shouted loudly:

"All hands up!"

"Mityu!" everyone was delighted and began to hug with a newcomer.

"Mityu Ganev in propria persona!" laughing, he reported to the present.

The saddler shook with fear even more, not daring to raise his eyes.

"All right, you may go!" Todor told him. "Here our friend has arrived, we need to talk, we let you go."

"He says he has no money," Ivan said disappointedly to Mityu.

"Wait a minute," Mityu said and went to the saddler, who was trembling with fear, and scanned him attentively, then he came up to the cart and began sorting out leather saddles and seats for mules. He took a seat, to which a pillow on the back to an animal was attached, cut it with a knife, and from there hundreds of Turkish liras and gold ancient jewelry fell like from the cornucopia.

"No money, you say?" Todor turned to him angrily, and the saddler trembled with fear even more. "Ok, go, we have a joy: we've met with a friend!"

"We cannot be compared with you in ability to requisition of valuables!" all 5 burst into laughing.

The saddler, grieving for what he had lost, got into his cart and instantly disappeared from sight.

"Let's go!" Todor commanded, and they put a bag with the props on the back of the mule, which just came in handy and was given to Mityu Ganev.

The other jumped into the saddles of their horses, and they rode to their secret shelter-dwelling cave. Nobody knew about this cave, only they did.

The autumn Aidanlar forest became repainted in bright red-yellow colors and gradually lost its foliage, but still it was enough of it to hide its inhabitants. 6 riders galloped to the foot of the hill, dismounted, tethered their horses and climbed up the winding path, leading up.

"Where are we going?" Mityu asked.

"Look," Todor answered and showed him the entrance to the cave, hidden so that even Mityu Ganev was amazed, when he came inside.

A large cave, disguised by nature itself, turned by the cheta of Todor into a dwelling, opened before him. There were palliasses, on which they slept on the floor, there were wooden benches and a table, hammered from wooden boards. Todor lit several kerosene lamps. In the depth of the cave there were several more rooms, hollowed out in the rock by nature itself, to shelter young fellows, driven by fate. Mattresses, benches and the floor of the cave were covered with woolen rugs. A hearth was made near the wall.

"Wow!" Mityu Ganev exclaimed in amazement. "I know almost all the caves in Rhodopes, but I did not suspect about this one!"

"Well, it is impossible to know all the caves," Todor answered contentedly, "there are too many of them! There are many more such caves that no one knows about until now, since the time of the Thracians, who hid their gold in them. And this cave is mine, I accidentally found it back, when I was a teenager and shepherded our herd during the Balkan Wars, where my father with his brothers fought. And now my cheta is in this cave."

Young men dumped from a canvas bag its contents on the rugs on the floor of the cave. Banknotes and gold jewelry spilled on the floor, forming a solid slide. All laughed together.

"We give some of this to the poor and those who have been especially affected by recent events," Todor said.

"Sure thing," Mityu Ganev agreed.

"We are the cheta, we are the hajduks, and I am the Voevoda!" Todor said. "We have been looking for you, we have long wanted to meet you and unite with you. And, finally, you are with us. We have to decide: are you with us?"

"I am with you. And are you with me?" Mityu Ganev asked in response.

"We are with you," all 5 answered.

"I propose, there will be 2 voevodas in our cheta: you, Mityu and I remain, as I was, and Ivan Ignatov will be the under-Voevoda, our deputy, the standard-bearer. Mityu Panev, Kolyu Trendofilov and Rusi Stoyanov are subordinate to us."

Mityu Ganev, used to be the boss always and everywhere, thought for a moment and agreed.

"All right, Todor, you and I are the voevodas. All agreed?"

"Agree!" everyone replied.

"Then, let's swear," Todor said and picked up his dagger, and put it on the table.

Mityu Ganev brought his revolver and put it on the table crosswise with Todor dagger. All the rest stood in a circle around the table and touched the crossed revolver and the dagger with their right hand. Each of them uttered his name, and in chores they swore:

"We are the hajduks, we form the cheta, we admit 2 voevodas above ourselves: Todor Todorov and Mityu Ganev. We swear to maintain discipline, comply with the instructions of the 2 voevodas, come to the aid for a comrade and never betray our friends. We swear to take vengeance on our foes, who put us outside the law, as well as the fascist junta of the tsar Boris III and his killers: Tsankov, Vylkov, Rusev and the others, all the policemen, serving them, and the fascist volunteers. All of them deprived us of our country and our home, where we can't return anymore! Freedom or Death!"

Excited and tired, the hajduks lit a fire in the hearth, prepared supper and sat down at the table.

"It was easier for the Bulgarian hajduks, who used to fight against the Turks: it was clear to everyone who were the enemies—the Turks. The Turks captured and enslaved Bulgaria. They were foreign invaders. The hajduks used to fight against them for liberation of Bulgaria. And now everything is mixed up. There are no Turks, they are not only absent, but they were yet the allies of the Bulgarians in the Great War. And our foes are our own ones: the Bulgarians."

"During the time of the Turkish slavery not only the Turks were the enemies, but also our own Bulgarians: traitors who betrayed the hajduks to the Turks and killed them," Mityu Ganev said bitterly, mourning his brother Petyu.

"And now our own Bulgarians turned to be worse than the Turks," Ivan Ignatov added, longing for his home.

"I miss home," Todor confessed sadly, "I have my own home, herds of cattle, fields, everything is abandoned, and I can't return home because of our foes."

"At least you and Ivan have your own houses and fields, but I don't have any house and fields and never had. I grew up in poverty, bent my back as a hired worker," Mityu Ganev said angrily.

"I have a house and parents in Gorsky Izvor," Mityu Panev said thoughtfully.

"And I have it in Yablokovo," Kolyu Trendofilov said.

"And I also have a small house and a garden under Harmanly," Rusi Stoyanov joined his friends, "what will be with us next?"

"I don't know what will happen to us next, but I do know that we can no longer return home, because our foes have taken from us this opportunity. They've taken from us our home and our country, and we must take vengeance on them for this," Todor said.

"Mityu, where have you been all this time? We were looking for you everywhere, we wanted to meet with you. So many events have happened since our escape from Haskovo jail!" Ivan exclaimed.

"Yes, tell us!" everyone exclaimed, supported Ivan and, having sat down at the straw mattresses covered with rugs, lit cigarettes and listened for a long time the story of Mityu Ganev.

Chapter 36
Butchevs the Yatacks

In the village of Aidanlar, surrounded by the Aidanlar forests, it was fun in the tavern of Bay Zhelyazko. The gramophone was playing merrily, folk music sounded, and the drunken voices of the tavern visitors were singing along with it the old hajduk song about youthful prowess and freemen. About 15 peasants filled with rakia their grief and joy: some grieved, mourning their relatives and friends killed after June 9, 1923, the other rejoiced at the rich harvest, the other simply got drunk, indifferent to everything. Several kerosene lamps were burning, the light from which barely penetrated through a thick veil of the smokers' tobacco smoke. In a contiguous room in the kitchen, a stout wife of the tavern owner and her daughter were bustling around the stove. The innkeeper Zhelyazko served the guests and scanned them vigilantly, so that they drunk would not break anything.

"Have you heard what all people talk about them?" through the tobacco smoke and gramophone music the voices of the visitors, sitting at the table, were heard.

"The cheta of Todor Todorov and Mityu Ganev is a threat to our current government in our area."

"They are real hajduks, like resurrected hajduks from our history, when there were Turks here."

"The current ones are definitely worse than the Turks."

"That's for sure."

"How many people's lives they have laid down!"

"Who would've thought that after the 'liberation from Turkish slavery' our own slavery would come: the Bulgarian one!"

"Their cheta suddenly appears, robs the rich, steals from the speculators and vanishes instantly. Nobody can find them. And then they give back to the poor and the victims of the authorities what was taken from the speculators!"

"They are like Robin Hood!"

"Just like him! They are our Bulgarian Robin Hoods!"

"The entire country police is thrown in search of them, but there is no trace of them!"

2 young men were sitting at the separate table in the corner of the tavern near the wall, whispering to each other. Suddenly, one interrupted the conversation and pointed at the interlocutor with his hand at the front door, which opened, and 4 hajduks were standing on the threshold. Everyone in the tavern fell silent and looked in the direction of the door with their jawed dropped. Young men entered the tavern, armed from head to toe: bandoliers full of cartridges hung crosswise on their chests, a revolver and a dagger, as well as a couple of bombs were on their belts. On the legs they had cervulis, tied up with the leather straps over the white onuchis; dark shirts and jackets warmed them from the coming autumn. One was a handsome man with amazing facial features that awe the entire female sex, with a piercing gaze of black eyes and black curls to the shoulders divided into a strait parting. The second one was a short man with regular pretty features, shoulder-length dark blond hair and intimidating black eyes. The third one was a broad-shouldered hero, tall with a ruddy face, a merry fellow. And the forth one looked like him: a tall, large brunette with a cheerful look and pretty face. Everyone present in the tavern instantly recognized in them Todor Todorov, Mityu Ganev, Ivan Ignatov and Kolyu Trendofilov. Mityu Panev and Rusi Stoyanov remained on guard outside.

"Calm down, gentlemen! This is not a robbery: we do not rob ordinary people!" Todor turned to everyone.

"But we forbid you to leave!" Mityu Ganev commanded menacingly. "Everyone stay where you are and do not approach the front door, until we allow it!"

"Come in, gentlemen, you are welcomed!" Bay Zhelyazko, the owner of the tavern, began to fuss and invited the newly arrived guests to a separate table, standing near the wall. The guests comfortably sat down at the table, offered to them, and looked around. The gramophone began to play again, which fell silent for a moment, when the hajduks entered. Several kerosene lamps illuminated the tavern, on the wooden wall of which pictures of a shepherds' idyll hung. The present couldn't take their eyes off the hajduks.

"Well, what are you staring at? Keep having fun!" Mityu Ganev shouted at them, and everyone instantly drank in one gulp another glass of rakia to the music of the gramophone and now peeped at the hajduks only stealthily and immediately looked away in fear.

"What would you like, gentlemen?" Bay Zhelyazko asked obsequiously.

"What do you have, Bay Zhelyazko?" Todor asked.

"We'd like to have something to eat and drink," Mityu Ganev said.

"Mr. Todor, we have beef yahnia. Would you like us to cook something else?"

"We don't need anything else, bring yahnia," Todor answered.

"Mr. Mityu, what would you like to drink? We have Greek cognac, old and new wines, rakia."

Mityu looked at his friends and answered: "Bring us some cognac."

"Just a moment!" Bay Zhelyazko obligingly answered and immediately rushed to serve the guests.

Soon the table was set. A hot dish of beef stew with vegetables and a short glass of cognac satisfied men's hunger and cheered them up. They had fun, but vigilantly scanned all the present in the tavern. 2 young men, sitting at the nearby table in the corner, got up and approached them. The hajduks were ready to draw their revolvers immediately.

"We are the brothers, I am Kolyu, and this is my brother Tanyu," they introduced themselves, "we lived in the vicinity in Gorsky Izvor, but then…then we moved to Aidanlar; we bought 2 houses and land from Vidyu Gochev Karagochev."

Todor turned pale and instantly put his hand on the revolver's handle.

"Oh, it's you!" he said through his teeth.

His companions scanned every gesture and sound with tension.

"Can we sit at your table? Need to talk."

Todor looked at his friends and nodded his head to allow. The Buchev brothers moved their chairs up to the hajduks' table and sat down next to them.

"Long ago we wanted to meet and talk," Kolyu began hesitantly, "we are very sorry about what has happened."

"Yes, we are sorry," Tanyu continued, "we did not know anything. Vidyu offered us to buy all their property…very inexpensively…he needed it very urgently… So, we bought… Who would refuse…?"

Todor became furious, so that even his friends became worried.

"Of course, who would refuse? You bought an estate from Vidyu for 250 thousand leva, which is worth several million! Generally, it is priceless, as this is an inherited property from our grandfather, and our grandfather inherited these lands from his father and grandfather, who moved here from the Balkan Mountains! Vidyu was out of his mind, grieving for his murdered brother, he almost went crazy and sold you all the family property for nothing: for 250 thousand leva. They managed to buy a small house in Ezerovo for 150 thousand leva, and 100 thousand were stolen from him, and he was killed by the assassins sent by Guenov-Kamine. If Vidyu had stayed here at home, he would've been alive!"

"We are very sorry," the Buchev brothers guiltily confirmed, "but it is not our fault of what happened."

"We grew up together, Vidyu was our greatest friend and helper, he was always assistance in trouble," Todor spoke, barely holding his tears, "we'll take vengeance on his killers!"

"Although we are not guilty, we feel guilty, we'll help you, you can count on us, we'll become your yataks. When you need food, or any other help, come, we'll help you. We are also on your side, because we hate the damned fascists, who seized power in Bulgaria and overthrew the power of Stamboliysky."

The companions looked with gratitude at the Buchev brothers and felt a friendly disposition toward them. Excited, Todor, grieving for his murdered cousins-friends, and Ivan Ignatov left the tavern for fresh air to replace Mityu Panev and Rusi Stoyanov, who were guarding them, so that they could have supper in the tavern. The night was quiet, bright stars in the black sky illuminated the village Aidanlar, surrounded by the Aidanlar forest. There were no foes nearby. The hajduks were sitting in the tavern until late, ate the delicious food of Bay Zhelyazko to their fill, drank cognac, paid in full and got up from the table.

"You are free, gentlemen, you can go, who wishes."

Nobody budged and left the place. The hajduks and the Buchev brothers went out into the street, where Todor with Ivan were waiting for them.

"If you want, let's go to our place, spend the night with us, rest, and tomorrow we'll see."

After a moment of hesitation, Todor agreed and called all the others. All 8 went to Kolyu Buchev's house, where Vidyu Gochev once lived. The view of the house, where once Vidyu hospitably received the driven Mityu Ganev and his brother Petyu and Todor with Ivan Ignatov again made everyone excited, and they could not hide their feelings. Even the furnishings in the house remained almost the same, as Vidyu hurriedly pushed his father Gocho out of the house in order to urgently move to a new place in Ezerovo in order to be saved. The Buchev brothers arranged all the hajduks in 2 rooms. And they, tired, fell asleep soundly, they had not slept in a human house for a long time...

Chapter 37
Vengeance in Ezerovo

The village Ezerovo, located in vicinity next to Bodrovo in 2 km away on the banks of the Kayaliyka River at the foot of Dragoyna, was sleeping soundly at a dark cold autumn night, in which even stars in the sky could not be seen, because of the thick dark haze, enveloping everything around. Only in one house they did not sleep. In the window of the house, which stood on the southern outskirts of the village in a ravine at the foot of the hill, a kerosene lamp was burning. The owner of the house Mityu Hadzhiev hosted 2 his friends: Ilya Pyankov and Mikhail Mandaliata. All 3 were sitting at the table in a small shabby room by the kerosene light and drank rakia.

"What are we going to do?" Mityu Hadzhiev, the owner of the house, cowardly asked. "He takes revenge on everyone together with his gang, and there also Mityu Ganev showed up."

"I am sorry, what?" Mityu Mandaliata asked indignantly. "Why should we be afraid of him? We have a cover: Guenov-Kamine himself, the police bailiff of Borisovograd!"

"Yes, but they will get and him soon!" Ilia Pyankov mockingly remarked.

"We must track them down and hand them over to the police for a big reward, which has been promised for them."

At that moment the door of the room opened wide, and Todor's hajduks rushed in.

"So we are already here, bastards!" Todor informed them angrily, aiming his revolver at them.

5 other friends of Todor immediately surrounded the murderers of Vidyu Gochev, sitting at the table.

"Sit, don't twitch!" Mityu Ganev commanded, aiming at them from 2 revolvers.

3 ugly scoundrels twisted their physiognomies in ugly grimaces from horror and shook even more with fear. Todor came closer to the owner of the house, Mityu Hadzhiev and pocked him in the chest with the muzzle of his revolver.

"Money! All the money that is in the house, which you together with your accomplices stole from my cousin Vidyu, give it to me!"

"But I don't have all the money that we took from him, that is he gave it to us himself. I only have half of it, and the rest is with him," he pointed his finger in the direction of Ilia Pyankov, who turned pale with fear.

"And as for me, I have nothing to do with it at all, I did not take any money," Mikhail Mandaliata mumbled with hope for salvation, remembering, how exactly he struck the last blow with an ax to Vidyu's head, "It is they who took the money!"

At gunpoint Mityu Hadzhiev backed into a contiguous room and took out a bag with the money from a chest of drawers, and handed it to Todor, then both returned to the others.

"He has the rest," again he pointed his finger at Pyankov.

"Where is the money?" Todor turned to him.

"I'll bring it now."

"We'll find it ourselves! Tell me, where did you hide the money, stolen from my cousin?"

The later told in detail, where he kept the money.

"The key from your house!" Todor ordered.

The later pulled out the key from his house out of his pocket and handed it to Todor.

"Where is your money?" Todor turned to the third one.

The later handed over the key from his house and told, where he kept the money.

"And now, will you let us go?" Hadzhiev asked plaintively.

"A couple of more questions. Was it Guenov-Kamine who hired you?"

"Yes, we were promised a cover."

"Did you kill Todor, Vidyu's older brother?"

"No!" all 3 answered in chorus. "We did not kill him! That one was killed by Costa, Guenov-Kamine's nephew."

"For the robbery and murder of my beloved cousin Vidyu Gochev Karagochev, I, Todor Todorov Karagochev, sentence you to death!" Todor said and shot at Hadzhiev.

Mityu Ganev got ahead of Todor and fired 2 bullets into the forehead of Pyankov and Mandaliata.

"This is to you, bastards, for the robbery and murder of my beloved friend and yatak Vidyu Karagochev!"

They quenched the kerosene lamp and instantly slipped out of the house, where the faithful Rusi Stoyanov was waiting on guard in the street. Silently and noiselessly under the cover of thick dark night, they vanished from the Hadzhiev's house and, moving imperceptibly like shadows, crept up to the Pyankov's house, which stood next door. They opened the door with the key, silently got inside, found the money in the place, indicated by Pyankov, and slipped out. They did the same in the house of Mandaliata, unnoticed by anyone, they safely reached the opposite end of the village and knocked on the window of a small unpretentious house, where the unfortunate old man Gocho, the father of Vidyu and Todor, lived.

"Who is there?" Gocho asked and looked out of the window.

After seeing Todor, he unlocked the door. Todor and Ivan came in the house, the others remained outside. A kerosene lamp illuminated Gocho, and Ivan with Todor gasped, when they saw him. In front of them an old man, looking like about 100 years old, was standing, gray with grief, in whom it was difficult to recognize the former happy and cheerful Gocho Karagochev. Todor hugged him by the shoulders, and both shed tears.

"What a woe!" the unfortunate old man uttered through the tears, wiping his red eyes, inflamed from tears with a handkerchief.

"Here it is, take it, Uncle Gocho," Todor said and handed him 100 thousand leva, "those who stole it, returned the money."

"Come in, boys, eat something."

"We can't, uncle, we must hurry, we must go back."

"Todor, son, and you, Ivan, my sons loved you. Count on me, come, when you need help, food, I'll help in any way, I can feed you, I have some more weapons, I hid them; I am your yatak. I know, it is not easy for you yourself either, but I am your faithful yatak, remember it! And let Mityu Ganev also come, and all yours."

"Thank you, Uncle Gocho, hold on! We have punished the killers, though, not all of them yet."

"Thank you, Bay Gocho!" Ivan Ignatov said, touched, and kissed the old man's hand.

Both slipped out of the house; true friends were waiting in the street. All 6 imperceptibly like shadows reached the grove, where the faithful horses were waiting, which carried them away from Ezerovo in the direction of the Aidanlar forest.

Chapter 38
Legends

Having defeated the insurgent people, the fascist junta of the tsar Boris III triumphed and feasted at the expense of the vanquished. The groans of the rebels, tortured by the butchers, and buried alive were muffled by the roar of music at the balls. Bare-shouldered ladies in European attires waltzed with the officers, who had betrayed their country. Those, shining with the awards for the defeat of their own people, boasted who killed and how many. Rewards for the butchery from the tsar Boris rained down like from a cornucopia. The entire business, the treasury, all the fascists were in their service. The capital Sofia danced at the balls, and Plovdiv tried to keep up with her in this matter. The military parade of officers and sub-officers of reserve, who had crushed the insurgent people, rumbled along the Plovdiv streets. And nearby in the rank a regular army was marching, thrown by the tsar to home front. The philistine enthusiastically greeted the winners over himself.

In the course of recent fighting in September a "civilian committee" was created by the "patriots" in Plovdiv. They formed the detachments of fascist volunteers from the civilians: Shpits-commands. Under it, the officers companies and "militia squads" were formed. All their dark masses were thrown to the defeat of the insurgent people and after the defeat they continued to punish the population. The "Civil Committee" created the "People Defense" fund, where the donations from large banks and firms flocked. Millions of leva gathered in the fund to reward all those who killed people.

The triumphant Plovdiv decided to share a part of the fund with its southern neighbor, who was less wealthy: Haskovo. In the strictest secrecy 2 million leva were sent by a car to Haskovo to reward particularly distinguished policemen, Shpits and military. A driver, a bank employer and 3 armed guards were going by car. The car was going carefully, and armed guards vigilantly watched around. They were going along the highway, along the Maritsa valley, passing different villages in their way. On both sides of the road the fields stretched, fenced off by a line of trees from the road, and very close to the south hills rose. They had already been driving for several hours, passed Debar, on the left of which Borisovograd laid closer to Maritsa, passed Byala River and Varbitsa. All in the car were already very tired and eagerly wanted to get to Haskovo as soon as possible, to which it was a small part of the way left. They drove up to Gorsky Izvor, to the south of which the Aidanlar forest stretched, the name of which itself terrified the punishers. A road splits appeared ahead, a vicinal road led south from the highway, and the bushes and trees grew thickly between the roads. The coming autumn had bared them considerably, but some foliage still remained. There was nothing suspicious and nobody on the way. The car caught up with the folk and immediately, as a whirligig began to whirl, having received a bullet in the tire. A well-aimed bullet of Mityu Ganev hit right on the target and stopped the car.

"Hands up!" those who were sitting in the car heard and saw 6 barrels of the revolvers, out of nowhere, aimed at them.

One of the guards moved his hand, trying to grab his revolver.

"Don't!" he heard the voice of Ivan Ignatov, who in the blink of an eye took away his revolver and the revolvers of the other guards.

"Get out of the car!" Todor commanded, and Rusi was holding a rope ready.

All 5 slowly got out of the car and by the order stood with their back to a thick oak, which grew behind the road. In one instant they were tied with a rope to this oak, and the hajduks pulled out of the car 2 suitcases, crammed with 100 leva banknotes of 1 million leva each, wished them good luck and went to the horses tethered nearby. Ivan Ignatov carried the confiscated weapons in his bag.

"One question," the bank employer dared to utter, "how did you know that we are transferring the money? After all, it was a secret operation."

"Intelligence service reported!" Mityu Ganev laughed in response, and all 6 burst into laughing merrily.

"It's ok, you won't get lost, somebody will drive by and untie you," Todor consoled them.

The hajduks mounted their trusty horses and rushed off to the south, where the hills covered with Aidanlar forest rose. In vain on that day they waited in Haskovo for the rewards for the butchery.

The telephone rang in the Haskovo police chief's office.

"Yes, sir, that's right!" the chief answered his boss in Sofia.

He hung up and called Detective Topora to his office.

"There is the order from Sofia to start an extensive search. Gather a squad of our policemen and volunteers. Comb everything from the south to the north to Maritsa and from the north to the south to Kardzhali. Deploy the squad in Chernoochene!"

"So, after all several detachments have already been sent: they exterminated them all," Topora recalled, who was distinguished by courage only before a handcuffed prisoner and also differed by sadism and ferocity among his equals.

"Start doing it!" the police chief ordered. "The volunteers from Kardzhali and Harmanly are ready to join you."

"Yes, sir," Topora replied.

In a couple of days a small detachment of policemen and volunteers from Haskovo, Kardzhali and Harmanly settled down in a spacious house of the tax collector in the village of Chernoochene. The village was located in a ravine between the hills at the foot of Rhodopes and gradually rose up the hills from the hollow along the gentle slopes of the hills. And below in the south there was Kardzhali, once Turkish free land. In the specious house on the edge of the village, turned into the police headquarters, the detachment, sent to capture the Todorov-Ganev's hajduks, worked out the details of the upcoming search.

"Remember, these robbers are very daring, brave and dexterous!" detective Topora edified his subordinates. "And they have no equal in accuracy of shooting, especially their ringleaders: Ganev and Todorov! We'll rummage for them under every bush, behind every tree and stone! You must have heard the songs that are sung about them! Simple people have already composed songs and all sort of legends about them! I'll show them, this simple people!" here Topora clenched his fist, grimaced his physiognomy in the threat of reprisal. "I'll show them…! And we catch them, I'll show them!"

"So, we are already here!" the voice of Mityu Ganev sounded through the door, kicked out with his feet, into which the hajduks rolled in.

Mityu Ganev fired a bullet into the butcher Topora forehead, whose atrocities were known about. The later fell dead on the floor with his clenched fists, without having time to unclench them. In an instant the hajduks seized the weapons of the detachment, which now begged for mercy, and beat their asses with the sticks for memory of them, and kicked them out of the hut with a knock in the ass, so that they would run back, where they came from. The policemen and the volunteers ran out of the hut and took to their heels.

"Our yataks work well!" Todor said contentedly.

"Yes, well done that they warned us, where the booth of these dogs would be!" Ivan Ignatov said, smiling with his wide smile.

The companions-hajduks collected the weapons, seized from the squad, and a bag with money of the tax collector, in which there were 400 thousand leva, and galloped off toward the Aidanlar forest. They did not have time to rest in their cave. Every hour of their hajduk's life was filled with stormy events. Nobody knew about the cave of Todor, where they hid themselves. Encounters with the yataks took place outside the cave. There were many yataks-helpers. From Bodrovo itself and Aidanlar, and all the vicinity villages their assistant agents plied, delivered information, brought food, delivered them everything necessary. They met in kosharas in the fields and forests at a designated place near the water sources and secretly in the houses of the yataks, when they entered their village under the cover of night. They received the necessary information from everywhere, and even from the police, where there was always someone, who survived from the Agrarian Union, who hated the fascist junta that had tortured Stamboliysky.

The intelligence network of the yataks covered the entire Bulgarian Thrace. The shepherds, grazing the flocks, brought the cattle to a watering place and, having heard the signal bird's squawk, met one from the cheta and handed over a note, which they carefully hid in a bosom and orally conveyed the message. The people composed and sang songs about them, and the legends about them circulated around.

Listen, hey, tsar and your Tsankov!
Heroes are in Rhodopes!
Todorov, Ganev, Ignatov,
Valiant, deprived of all fears,

Fast as the wind and elusive,
Peoples' avengers to butchers.
Vylkov and Tsankov, and Rusev,
Tsarist and fascist coup plotters

Shaking with fear when hear
Vengeance of daring threesome.
Fall of you, putschists, is near,
Freedom from evil will be soon.

The hajduks generously paid the yataks for their help, but not all the yataks took from them money for help: only those who were in need. The policemen sent one detachment after another to capture them. The fascist volunteers prowled around and rummaged behind every bush and then fled in all directions, beaten with a stick on their ass. The Macedonians, who always served the fascist junta, came to the aid of the authorities. Hired by the tsar Boris, the Thracian-Macedonian terrorist group of Ivan Maximov ran in race, competing with gang of smugglers of Kafal Handji, who were promised an amnesty, if they eliminate Ganev Todorov cheta. Both groups competed with each other to be the first to eliminate the hajduks and receive a reward.

Cunning, dexterous and fearless, the hajduks liquidated them themselves with their own hands. The fame of the hajduks spread all over Bulgaria, and the boys, who carried the newspapers, shouted at the top of their lungs at every corner, outshouting each other:

"The cheta of Todorov-Ganev-Ignatov again robbed the rich chorbadji!"

They were credited with robberies, committed by the others, because the hajduks physically could not rob a bank in Varna, Plovdiv and Sofia at the same time. The hajduks decided to use this technique to deal with the enemies.

At that time a local gang robbed a small shop nearby in the village of Ortakoisko. The hajduks spread the rumor that the robbery had been carried out by the Ivan Maximov's gang, sent to catch the hajduks. These rumors spread faster than the lighting with the help of the yataks and reached the ears of the bosses of the IMRO. Enraged that Ivan Maximov committed a robbery without their sanction, thereby violating discipline, and even did not share the loot with the superiors, the bosses ordered to liquidate Maximov. The sentence was carried out by Maximov's best companion, his first hand and sworn-brother Alexi, who stabbed a knife into his back. The Maximov's gang broke up and, having suspected Kafal Handji's competitors in the intrigue, dealt with them in their own way.

There was a moment of respite for the hajduks. They were sitting around the hearth in their cave and discussed a plan for further action. They had just received a message from their yatak Rejeb Akaliolu from the Kolyu Trendofilov's native village Yablokovo that large tobacco merchants had stopped in the village Inishche on the left side of Maritsa. The hajduks set out for hunting the same night. They made their way unnoticed under the cover of night to the north, and on the edge of Gorsky Izvor they were met by the yatak Dimo Kumov and handed over a letter from the yatak from Haskovo. Todor read the letter and gave it to Mityu Ganev.

"We turn back!" they commanded the rest at the same moment, and the cheta instantly vanished from site in the opposite direction from Gorsky Izvor to the south.

In a short time a vehicle full of people was driving along the Tsaregrad highway from Haskovo. The auto drove along the highway to the village of Gorsky Izvor and turned left on the vicinity road toward Aidanlar. The way ran along a winding path from both sides of which bushes and trees grew, still retaining albeit thinned autumn foliage. Only the headlights of the car illuminated the path in the darkness. They drove into the lands of Bostanlak, and the car broke sharply. A wild pear tree, sawn down by Ivan Ignatov in advance, fell with roar in front of them and blocked the way. 8 armed people jumped out of the car with the physiognomies grown by beards and mustaches like the monkeys, which unmistakably betrayed the Macedonians in them, and vainly tried to see anything at least around. The first who was shaggy more than the others was the boss, a man about 50, the others were of different age.

Like the hajduks, they were dressed in cervulis with onuchis, the bandoliers girded their light colored jackets. The revolvers with daggers hung on the belts of each.

"Drop your weapons! Hands up!" they heard a menacing shout, coming from nowhere, because they could not see anything in the darkness.

Looking around and peering into the darkness, they began to take off and put in a pile everything that hung on them.

"Only move, and I'm shooting!" the same voice was heard, and armed Ivan Ignatov came out from behind the bushes and appeared before them.

"Back off!" he commanded, and they took a few steps back from the heap of weapons on the ground.

Ivan Ignatov picked up everything that the arrivals took of them and carried it to the other side of the fallen tree. At that moment the hajduks, cleverly disguised under the brunches, jumped out and took up a convenient position around them with the revolvers aimed at them.

"Oh, Tanyu Nikolov himself!" mockingly, Mityu Ganev turned to the main one, continuing to aim at him. "And what did you forget here in our lands, so far from your lands?"

The 50-year-old ringleader of the gang, shaggy like a monkey, politely greeted the hajduks.

"We are searching for you, Mityu! The fame of you has reached our lands, so we've come here to find you and invite you to join our ranks, so that you become Komitadji and together with us, with the Internal Thracian Revolutionary Organization, lead the uprising against the Greeks, who occupied Thrace!"

"You are lying, you scoundrel!" Todor shouted at him. "And where is your car from? Is it the tsar with Tsankov who gave it to you? How much did they promise you for killing us, like you killed Yane Sandansky in an ambush, having shot at his back?"

"I am not lying, Todor! I never lie! After all, you see that we've surrendered to you without resistance. There are 6 of you, and we are 8. The tsar sent us with the proposal to you to come over to our side. Here I have a letter, signed by the tsar."

"We don't serve the villains!" Todor cut him off.

"I have my own accounts with you!" Mityu Ganev said. "Do you remember how you taunted at me, when the police grabbed me and my brother Petyu for the first time and took us around Haskovo for show? No one taunted at us, only you alone approached me and my brother and began to taunt!"

"Well, oh, come on, Mityu, you've recalled the event long time ago! You were a 14-year-old boy then, who could've known that you would grow up and become such a famous Voevoda, which entire Bulgaria is buzzing about?" Tanyu Nikolov kindly answered. "And you, Todor, do you remember, we invited you to become our comitia, when you were 18 years old, but your father did not let you then?"

"It is not only you alone who invited me," Todor answered. "Strakhil also invited me, only you and I are not on the way, you shoot each other in the back! And now you've been hired yourself to the fascists, the tsar and Tsankov to kill us!"

"Todor, shall we let them go or not?" Mityu Ganev asked.

"Decide yourself!" Todor replied.

"That's what I've decided: step back, Tanyu, on 50 steps along the road and stop, and I'll shoot at you in this darkness; if you stay alive, we'll let all of you go."

Trembling with fear, Tanyu Voevoda backed away along the path, and Mityu Ganev shot at him in the darkness. The bullet flew through the Voevoda's lash, shaggy, sticking out in all directions hair, causing Mityu Ganev's laugh.

"You know, I never miss, let it be: we let you go! And don't dare to catch our eyes again, otherwise you'll not leave alive!"

The hajduks burst into laughing and turned their backs to leave. At that moment the hefty one from the Nikolov's gang jumped toward Todor, pulled out a hidden on his bosom dagger and swung it with the words:

"I killed Stamboliysky himself, and I'll kill you!"

Todor dodged the dagger in a blink of an eye, jumped and slashed his dagger across Agir's throat. The giant fell on the ground.

"Die, Macedonian scum, this is to you for Stamboliysky!"

Everyone froze instantly, and the rest of the Macedonians, having left the car, dashed to run in the opposite direction along the road they had come from; they ran after fleeing Voevoda Tanyu Nikolov. The way on Inishche for the hajduks was open.

Chapter 39
Winter 1923–1924

That year winter came early, and in early December 1923 snow fell, which could betray the hajduks. The brunches of the bushes and trees, behind the lush foliage of which the hajduks were hiding until recently, now became bare. The fields and meadows, where the shepherds grazed their cattle and the villagers harvested their crops, were empty: the cattle hid under the roofs in warm sheds, lying comfortably on soft hay close to each other with the prepared food in advance. The villagers hid in their houses behind the latches near the hot stoves. The white silence and problems with food supply appeared. Before snow covers everything, on which they could be tracked, they had to find refuge. For the last time before leaving in the outgoing 1923 they were sitting around the hearth in their cave and discussed the details of the departure.

"Friends, let's do the same what all the hajduks used to do before us, in the past," Todor said. "They gathered in the detachments and took revenge on their enemies with the onset of spring, when the forest, hiding them, turned green. Let's do the same!"

"I agree with you, Todor!" Mityu Ganev supported his friend. "Only you and you, Ivan, have your own house, but I don't have a house, there is a dilapidated hut. Together with my brother Petyu I grew up with other people and broke my back for the bosses. Where shall I go?"

"We'll split into 2 groups: I, Kolyu and Ivan will try to sneak secretly into Bodrovo, and 3 of you with Mityu Panev and Rusi, try to hide with our new friends in our old place in Aidanlar, where once Vidyu and Todor with their father Gocho used to live. In my opinion, the brothers Kolyu and Tanyu Buchevs are to be trusted."

"Eh, winter has always been a hardship for all the hajduks," Ivan Ignatov said.

"We are with you, friends!" Kolyu, Mityu and Rusi supported.

"We'll liaise with our yataks throw our old channels."

"And the horses need food, and they need to be in the stables. We'll take 3 horses to or stable to uncle Dimitar, and you try to accommodate 3 horses with the Buchevs in Aidanlar."

"Friends, our cache remains in this cave, and not a single soul should know about this cave!"

"Sure!"

"Half of the weapons remains here, and another part will be in our Hajduk Angel cave on Sirka; in case, we meet there, and never set foot here anymore in this cave! Soon the snow will cover everything, and we'll be tracked by the foot prints in the snow."

"Before we part, we'll pay a visit to old Ivan Duban, at least we'll sit in a warm house, before we leave."

"We've got everything ready."

The hajduks said goodbye to their cave, which had become their home, and promised to return here with the onset of green spring. They mounted their horses and galloped to old Duban, their faithful yatak. To the south of Bodrovo the hills rose higher and higher toward Rhodopes, on the top of one of them there was an estate of old man Duban. On horseback they were climbing a winding path that led along the gentle slope of the hill and knocked on the massive wooden gates, connecting the stone walls of the almost medieval castle-fortress. Dogs began to bark, the latch rumbled back, and the gate swung open. The riders drove into the yard. On seeing them, the dogs stopped barking and with the speed of the wind, wagging their tails, they came up and began to caress their friends. Old Duban met his friends:

"I've been waiting for you, come in!" he said and ordered the assistant to take the horses to the stables, feed and water them.

In front of them a tall, strong built, gray-haired old man was standing, like a century-old oak, covered with snow. He was old, but no one knew how old, just like the old man himself did not know, as he had lost count of his years. Originally he was from the village of Bodrovo. Once upon a time, in his youth he lived there in a wealthy 2-story house with his wife and 2 daughters; he was happy, loved his family and had extensive household. The villainous fate, if there is any, took away from him his beloved wife, who died being pregnant with the third child, and after her 2 of his daughters died one after another. Old

Duban hated his fate, moved away from people from Bodrovo to his field and hill, which he owned, and built his hermit fortress here. Stone walls ran along the perimeter of the entire plateau at the top of the hill and surrounded a vast courtyard, where a new house was built, a stable, barn, cattle shed and a luxurious garden, where all fruit trees, berries and flowers grew. Duban's workers harvested the fields at the foot of the hill, and Duban himself grew a garden and traded the fruits of his land. He fenced himself off from the whole world with a stone wall and now made friends with the hajduks only.

The guests went into the house, where the stove was heated red-hot in the spacious living room, it was warm and cozy. Minder was lined with carpets and cushions along the carpeted walls, and in the center there was a long table ready for dinner with guests.

"Well, hello, grandpa Duban!" the hajduks said and handed him a big hag filled to the brim with gifts. "Take it from us!"

Mityu and Todor began to pull out of the bag cognac, wine and cigarettes.

"Take this money from us!" Mityu Ganev handed him a pack of banknotes.

"I'll accept the gifts, how not to accept! Thank you for the gifts, but I won't take any money," old man Duban answered, "I won't receive you for money, I have enough my own money, but I don't have any heirs. Hide your money, you yourself will need it. Well, sit down at the table, boys, everything is ready."

A Duban's worker brought lamb, baked in the oven, and all sat down to feast, except for Kolyu and Rusi, who went out into the courtyard and climbed the stairs to the top of the wall, began to scan the Bansko Highway in both directions.

"Try my own rakia, which I made myself! Eat and drink, my dear guests, my boys!"

"Grandpa Duban, we drink to your health and thank you that we have found a shelter in your house many times, and you have often accepted us and fed us! To grandpa Duban!" all the hajduks answered in unison.

The grandpa Duban almost shed a tear, and everyone drank the filled glasses to the bottom. The baked lam turned out to be not one, but paired with another one, with which the hajduks ate to their fill; rakia, wine, a hot stove, homely comfort filled their souls with peace and tranquility. But the reality could not be forgotten even for a minute, and Mityu Panev and Ivan Ignatov went out into the yard to replace Kolyu and Rusi. The latter hurried up to the table.

"How are you, Bay Duban?" Todor asked. "How are things?"

"How my things can be, comparatively with you, my desolate boys!" old man Duban sighed. "I am engaged in housekeeping, gardening, rakia, trade: the same like always."

"And how is your nephew? Does he still 'help' you?"

"He still helps: carried my money to the bank, he conducts my accounts."

"Are you aware that he has opened his shop in Haskovo as the result of 'helping you'?"

"What can I do!" old man Duban sighed. "After all, I have nobody, but him, you know."

"We know, and we also know that it's high time for us to visit your nephew," Mityu Ganev answered, "and then back to you to return something."

"Tell me better, where will you spend winter, my unfortunate boys, because winter is not for the hajduks; it has always been like that, and in the old days the hajduks used to be at home in winter."

"Well, of course, we'll not stay in the forest, we have some plans."

"Boys, stay in my house, there is enough space for everyone; there are some funds, we shall re-winter, we'll survive."

"We can't, Bay Duban," Todor answered, "thank you for your kindness and hospitality, but we can't abuse it, we can't endanger both you and your house!"

"You know, what it's going on in the country!" Mityu exclaimed.

"I know, boys, I know!" Duban exclaimed excitedly. "Evil foes have conquered the unfortunate Bulgaria! The satanic spawn has seized the power! Poor Stamboliysky was tortured to death! All the Agrarians were tortured to death, common people were killed, the Communists were hunted down. After September mostly Communists are being exterminated. Have you heard anything about the Communists?"

"We've heard something. In any case, we have one enemy with them and with all the good people of Bulgaria: it is the tsar Boris III and his Tsankov's gang, which seized the country."

"Yes, you are good at dealing with them! I've heard a lot. Although I live as a hermit, but the earth is full of rumors. Your fame spread all over Bulgaria! These scoundrels have the army, police, rats-provocateurs, and you are 6 boys, a bunch of brave dare-devils, who strike them in the heart and vanish without a trace. Nobody can find you."

"If it was in the heart!" Todor exclaimed. "Then the monster would've died long ago!"

"No, no, you attack them to the very heart! Because their heart is the tobacco money! If it is not this, our Stamboliysky would've been alive. It was the tobacconists' money, on which the bandits staged a coup! How many officers have sold their homeland, tarnished the honor of an officer! And you take away from them this money and share it with the poor! So, it turns out that you strike them in the very heart!"

The guests were satisfied with the meat of the baked lambs, drank wine with rakia, talked until late night in the cozy warm house of their faithful yatak old man Duban, and then mounted their horses and set off.

"Take care of yourself, Bulgaria still needs you!" grandpa Duban told them at parting.

The hajduks descended from the hill and galloped along valley toward the vicinity hills to the north, on which Bodrovo was situated. In the house of Bodjan Volkov, standing on the south-west edge of the village, another faithful yatak was waiting for them. A wealthy large merchant lived in a specious house in abundance and helped the hajduks as much as he could. He was waiting for them and let them in his house.

"Did you get the news?" he asked them.

"Yes, Bodjan, my cousin George said that you are waiting for us."

"Your Georgy is a real fighter, he is not afraid of anything, works as a liaison-agent flawlessly!" Bodjan praised him. "Yes, and a little Gocho also, only he is too small yet, he is only 14 years old."

"How long shall we fight yet? When will the peace come to our land?"

"It is not us who unleashed the war." Todor said.

"I know, I know, but I also want to know, when will be the end of this war?"

"Did you bring anything?" Mityu Ganev asked.

"It is this, I've called you here for. Look!"

Bodjan brought clothes for the young men from the contiguous room. He was laying out 6 sets of suits made of English wool, shirts and warm jackets on the minder-sofa standing along the wall. The hajduks' eyes lit up.

"Was it enough money?" Mityu Ganev asked.

"More than enough, there is some change even left."

"Keep change for yourself."

"I bought it in Sofia," Bodjan smiled.

"If the sellers knew for whom they sold these clothes!" Todor exclaimed, and all burst into laughing.

"Thank you, Bodjan, for your help!"

"Not at all! Thank you for not sitting idly and not hiding in the nooks, but fighting against our common foes!"

"But just for winter we need to hide."

"This is inevitable, it has always been like that: the hajduks dispersed for winter and always gathered in spring."

"This is what we are planning. Thank you again, Bodjan! The liaisons are the same! Let's hurry!"

"Happy to you and all of us to survive in this winter, and then we'll see what happens!" Bodjan wished, saying goodbye to the hajduks.

From the Bodjan's house on the edge of Bodrovo, they split into 2 groups and dispersed in different directions. Mityu Ganev, Mityu Panev and Rusi Stoyanov galloped to Aidanlar to the Buchev brothers, to the same place, when they used to find shelter with Vidyu and Todor Karagochevs, and Todor with Kolyu Trendofilov carefully made their way into the Todor's koshara and put 3 horses in his stables. Ivan Ignatov went to the house of his cousins Peter and Valko, who lived separately in a 2-story house with different entrances, located in the eastern part of the village Bodrovo, not far from the school.

Todor with his friend accommodated in his koshara, intently listening to every sound outside. Everything was calm, only the icy wind softly uttered a whine at uncomfortable frosty December night. Todor endured extraordinary excitement, being close to his home. Not far from him there was his native house, in which he was born and grew up, which he loved very much, and whose household he shouldered as a teenager, when his father went to fight in the Balkan Wars, a house full of prosperity, warmth and comfort, where he could not now openly return any longer. And nearby there was a new house, built by his father, where he was supposed to move on that ill-fated day, when he was arrested, tortured and thrown behind the bars without guilt.

He asked himself thousand times, why it all happened, why did his ill-fated destiny turn out this way, having made him a desolate and put him out law. And is there any kind of fate at all, which predestines a life of a person and by her whim spins it on her wheel of fortune, either lifting it on the pinnacle, or dropping it down to crush it with her own wheel, cruel, incomprehensible, bringing evil to every good person, a supernatural force that is called fate, before which a person is powerless, and if so, is a strong and proud person capable to challenge it and defeat it with his valor? Or it is not, there is no fate: there are only mistakes and miscalculations of a person? If all the misfortunes that happened to him were due to the fault of the devil "sworn-brother," his father's best friend Guenov-Kamine, who decided to hound his family because of the envy through the fault of his father himself, who was unable to choose friends? The questions tormented his vengeful heart and mind, and he knew only one thing: he was doing the right matter, and he would never bow before evil and never follow the slavish demagogy of turning the other cheek, when one was hit, and all his enemies would answer for their atrocities.

In the koshara-cabin they were met by the cousin George, who led them to his house, standing next door, where the family of the uncle Dimitar lived. They temporally accommodated in one of the rooms of his beautiful, specious 2-story house, in which his uncle Dimitar and his son George, risking his lives, provided shelter and hospitality to the rebellious hajduks. From time to time they were visited by the younger brother Gocho, who was proud of Todor and bowed to him. 14-year-old Gocho studied at the Bodrovo school in winter and in summer he grazed their herds of goats and sheep, which gave the family milk and wool, and when the animals peacefully pastured in the green meadows of the picturesque hills and valleys, Gocho next to them swallowed one book after another, which he always carried with him in a bag, kept in the koshara in a field far from home. He took books from the library: the teachers-enlighteners founded it in the village in the 19th century. Gocho saw in his elder brother Todor a romantic hero, a freedom fighter against evil, descended from the pages of his favorite novels. He felt himself involved in the struggle, and he was such, being faithful yatak of the hajduks, to whom he brought food and news from the outside world. He imprinted for life in his memory all the details of the events and dreamed, when he grows up, he remains alive, someday to tell about this great struggle to the future generations and descendants of their ancient lineage.

And long winter evenings and long night with short day stretched in anticipation of spring. Todor and Kolyu did not experience uncomforting in the George's house, but they felt uncomfortable in somebody's house, realizing that their presence endangered the owner of the house, and impatiently awaited the coming of spring and the moment, when they could leave the house. As in the house of Todor, in the house of George there was complete prosperity, beauty and comfort; the fire crackled hotly in the oven, glowed red-hot the metal rings of the stove on the top of the oven, on which delicious lunch and dinner was cooked, and outside the window was spinning snow whirlwinds, white silence reigned around, as all the inhabitants of Bodrovo hid themselves behind the latches in the houses, basking by the fire of the stoves, they were engaged in needlework, housework and gossip. And only the smoke from the chimneys of the stoves on the roofs of the houses, rising in a gray trickle to the winter sky, showed the continuous life inside the houses behind the heavy latches of the gates.

Sinking knee-deep in snow drifts, the policemen from time to time staged the cordon of the village and rummaged it, primarily in the house of Todor and Ivan Ignatov, as well as in the other suspicious places, but found nothing and nobody and returned back to their barracks in Borisovograd and Haskovo. And Todor with his friend Kolyu with a revolver in their hands were hiding during the rummage in the basement of George's house, which stood next to his own house.

On the fifth day of the New Year 1924, Todor turned 23 years old. His father was 23, when his son Todor was born. And now Ivan Todorov, who had gone through 2 Balkan Wars, the power of kmet in the harsh years of the Great War, the betrayal of his sworn-brother, the persecution of his son, hounding and misfortunes of Todor, as well as the celebrity of the son through the country in company with Mityu Ganev and Ivan Ignatov, about whom people created legends and sang songs, and after whom the entire police of Bulgaria and countless volunteers of shpits-commandos vainly chased…turned into untimely old man with gray hair, undermined health and shattered nerves and did not even know that his son was hiding next door in the house of his brother Dimitar.

And Todor, at the age of 23, was handsome like a god, handsome like in childhood and youth, and every year his beauty acquired the finished features of young man, for whom it seemed to live, love and enjoy life. But he, the master of his own house and land, where he can't openly return, a handsome young man, at the sight of whom all the females experienced awe, without a beloved one and love, without a family is hiding secretly in the other people house, having no idea, what his odyssey ends with.

2 months of the winter had passed, and February 1924 came, and the feeling that all the permissible periods to stay as the guests in a stranger house had been exceeded, filled them with the determination to leave this house. On one February night they left, having thanked uncle Dimitar and his son George for their hospitality, who flatly refused to take any reward from them. Under the cover of night, they made their way to the south-eastern end of the village to the house of uncle Angel; along the way they took with them their faithful friend Ivan Ignatov, whose departure was long dreamed by his cousins Peter and Valko Buchev, who had given him hospitality. All 3 knocked on the gates of uncle Angel, the elder brother of Todor's father Ivan. He opened.

"Hello, uncle!" Todor greeted him. "Will you let us in?"

"Hello, nephew! How have you grown up! How handsome you are, the same like in the childhood! Hello, guests!" Angel answered and let them inside the house, firmly locking the gates with a latch.

The spacious 2-story house of Angel was situated on the very edge of Bodrovo, in the south-east part in the middle of a large yard with household buildings. This piece of land and the house on it were allocated for him by his father, old grandpa Todor, when Angel betrayed and brought him to the grave. Having broken with his family, with all his brothers, Angel lived apart since then. And now the son of his brother Ivan with his comrades, armed from head to toe, whom all the newspapers of Bulgaria every day trumpeted about, were standing in front of him.

"Uncle, will you harbor us for a while?" Todor asked him. "We'll pay you as much as needed for a room and food."

"I don't even want to hear about the payment," Angel answered. "I am not poor, you know, I have my own mil…"

"Yes, I remember," Todor answered, feeling awkward: the old story with the mill was the shame for their family, but how much time has passed since then, and how many events had happened!

"I have enough money to feed all 3 of you, you'll have a room," Angel answered proudly, in whom, on seeing his nephew, suddenly the memory of the past, of youth, of brothers and father woke up.

Something human stirred in his heart and filled with nostalgia for the past and desire to do something good in order to somehow atone his guilt seized him.

"I've heard about you, you are famous all over the country. People already sing songs about you and create legends."

"Yes, it happens so," Todor answered. "These are my friends: Ivan and Kolyu."

"Well, I know Ivan, after all he from the same village. Well, come in, leave your things in your room and sit at the table."

The companions were happy to be together again in the beautiful, comfortable and spacious house of uncle Angel, who once betrayed his father Todor, but now, after many years, risking himself, did not betrayed them and sheltered them in his house, actually, to Todor's surprise. They chattered almost until midnight, telling about the time spent apart, and Ivan Ignatov told them, how he hid himself in their native school, situated next to the house of his cousins, when the police surrounded Bodrovo and rummaged, and how once nose to nose nearly collided with the school warden and son-in-law of the Guenov-Kamine's brother.

3 hajduks lived in the uncle Angel's house for 2 weeks, and not wanting to bother him anymore, left, having thanked him heartily, and he did not take any stotinka from them, in the depth of his heart feeling a pleasant sensation that at least something he returned the debt to the family, which he caused a gruesome moral and material damage.

It was the middle of February. There was still snow all over the place, driven by the blizzard, sweeping the snowdrifts, but the most part of the winter of 1924 was already behind, and the light of spring sun gleamed ahead. Homeless hajduks, who had his own house and land, where it was impossible to return, huddled in the houses of their yataks, spending 2–3 nights there, and having exhausted all the opportunities, at night went to their cave of Angel on Sirka, where their arsenal of weapons was hidden.

When they climbed the hill along the winding path and approached their second cave, where the Hajduk Angel once hid himself and his treasures, they heard familiar voices, and what a joyful surprise for them was to meet their friends: Mityu Ganev, Mityu Panev and Rusi Stoyanov. Their joy knew no bounds. In the Angel's cave there were palliasses and firewood, stored for the future, the weapons they had hidden here were in place. They built a fire and lay around it on the matrasses to rest, telling each other stories about their winter adventures.

"Friends, my cousin George told me that we were invited to Bukovo," Todor said.

"What for?" Mityu Ganev asked warily.

"I suspect why," Ivan Ignatov answered.

"And I even suspect who is calling us: the Communists! Will you say no, Todor?"

"Yes, it is them. The invitation was conveyed through George by Rudy Hristov; he himself is the Agrarian, and his son-in-law Georgy Pilashev is a communist. It is Pilashev who is calling us."

"Yes, he is the famous person," Mityu Ganev said, "but what do they want from us?"

"I propose to accept the invitation. We'll come to Bukovo, meet, talk, think," Todor suggested, "in any case we have common foes, and we fought against them together both in June and September 1923."

"Well, let's go," Mityu Ganev said, "just we'll take some extra grenades with us, just in case."

"I don't mind," each of the hajduks answered in turn.

"Maybe they will help us at least to find a place, where we can survive the rest of the winter, until spring comes."

"That's great, agreed. Tomorrow evening we'll go."

Chapter 40
Bukovo

From the cave of the Hajduk Angel on the hill of Sirka between Bodrovo and Aidanlar, their path lay to the south-west to the village of Bukovo higher and higher into the Rhodope Mountains. As soon as it began to get dark and twilight closed them from prying eyes, the hajduks descended from the hill, having captured an additional couple of grenades from the cave and set off. The treacherous snow imprinted their footprints in itself, and sweeping their traces on the approaches to the cave, they secretly, stealthily and imperceptibly, made their way further and further along the path, familiar to them from childhood, passing the hills, valleys and ravines. The bare skeletons of the bushes and trees, devoid of foliage, through which everything was visible, could not hide their hajduks in winter, and the risk of being noticed was very high. But luck was on their side, and silently, like dark shadows, not noticed by anyone, they moved in single file further and further to the south-west, where they had an appointment in the village of Bukovo, and finally reached their goal.

The Dragoyna ridge, covered with dense forest, rose in front of them, and right at its foot there was a picturesque village of Bukovo, standing on the ground, where the Thracians founded their settlement thousands of years ago. They built their fortress on the very top of Dragoyna, and the carved fantastic niche-eyes, through which they seemed to watch the course of the future history. The hajduks entered the Bukovo village.

The house of Rudy Hristov stood on the north-western outskirts of the village. They knocked on the gate, he opened it and let them in. Rudy Hristov was a member of the Agrarian Union, and his son-in-law Georgy Pilashev was a communist. They were waited for in the house. They took off their sheepskin coats in the entry, went into the living room and sat down at the table.

"Well, how do you do, hajduks! Welcome to my house!" the owner of the house Rudy Hristov greeted them.

"How do you do, Bay Rudy! We were called, so we've come." Todor answered. "These are my friends, you probably know them."

"Who does not know you!" Rudy answered with smile. "The entire country already knows about you."

"Well, tell us, why did you call us?"

"We need to talk."

At that moment the door opened, and a young man in a military uniform entered the room. He smiled, and it seemed that his kind, friendly smile illuminated the space, where they were, and glowed their rebellious souls with warmth. He was slender, tall and dazzlingly handsome. Dark hair and a thin line of mustache set off the regular, handsome features of his face; smartness and bearing betrayed a military man in him and noble postures and manners indicated his education. A retired military officer, a teacher in present, Georgy Pilashev greeted the guests.

"Meet my son-in-law Georgy Pilashev," Rudy Hristov introduced the man, entered the room.

"Yes, but we probably know each other!" Todor exclaimed. "After all, it was you then in the field with the peasants, retreating from Borisovograd, who were chased by the mounted policemen in June 1923! Ivan, it was he who was there!"

"Yes, Todor, yes, we met then in the field, when the remnants of our defeated detachments were pursued by the Borisovograd policemen, whom you and Ivan shot dead."

Ivan Ignatov amazingly confirmed, recalling the events of the last summer.

"You, Todor and Ivan, saved us then, we ran out of bullets, and if not you, they would've killed us!"

"Yes, the uprising of the peasants failed then, it was not organized, and not all came forward. And we have heard about you."

"And how we have heard about you! You are the celebrities! The government has never chased any of its enemies, like they chase you!"

"What government?" Todor exclaimed. "There is no government! The legitimate government of Alexander Stamboliysky was overthrown and killed, and power was seized by the fascist junta! These are criminals: butchers, murderers and thieves led by the tsar Boris III."

"That's right!" Georgy Pilashev exclaimed. "And the task of all good people is to fight against them!"

"So, we are all fighting against them and against our personal foes!" Todor exclaimed.

"All good people admire your fight. People create legends about you. 6 dare-devil boys challenged the entire Tsankov's gang. And you swoop in like a whirlwind, take from the rich Tsankov lackeys and then share with the poor and the destitute, and all the Tsankov's and tsar's policemen, all their spies, Macedonian henchmen and Wrangell's ones can't catch you! This is amazing!"

The hajduks smiled from the self-flattering praise.

"So," Georgy Pilashev continued, "we need you."

"Who? Who are you?" Mityu Ganev asked.

"Us, BCP."

"What for?"

"To unite our efforts in the fight against common foe."

"But you are traitors!" Todor objected.

Everyone was silent, Georgy Pilashev frowned, Todor continued.

"It all happened because of you! After all, it was you who betrayed Alexander Stamboliysky! You betrayed him during the uprising of the soldiers in 1918, when Raiko Daskalov and Alexander Stamboliysky proclaimed the Radomir Republic, and you refused to support him, and the rebels were crushed with the help of Germany. Yet then it was possible to throw off the tsar and everything would've turned out differently. All the time you put sticks in the wheels of Stamboliysky, when he became the leader of the state, by this you helped the fascists to seize power and kill Stamboliysky. He himself spoke about it in Haskovo a month before his death. We heard it, didn't we, Ivan?"

Ivan nodded his head to agree. Todor continued.

"You betrayed the people, when he rose to fight the fascists on June 9 last year. You betrayed Stamboliysky and the people and forced them to go home, and at the very beginning of the upheaval Stamboliysky was still alive, and you betrayed him and abandoned him to die in agonizing death in the hands of the butchers. It's all your fault!"

Everyone was silent, frowning, and Mityu Ganev intensively was listening to the words of Todor.

"You are very smart, Todor, and literate, you understand everything correctly," Georgy Pilashev interrupted the silence. "Unfortunately, everything you said is true, but only it is not true, as you said: 'All of you.' These fatal mistakes or it can be even said, crimes, were committed through the fault of some people in BCP leadership. And you know yourself that the rank and file Communists, the leaders of the district organizations came out on their own initiative to fight on June 9, 1923, including me. And in September 1923, the BCP ultimately redeemed its guilt and with the United Front came out to fight against the fascists. In alliance with the Agrarians we fought shoulder to shoulder together against our common foe. You know that, you yourself with your boys fought together with us near Chirpan, and we know about it."

"Yes, we helped them as much as we could."

"And you, Todor, know that after defeat of the uprising in September 1923, the fascists persecuted us, the Communists, not less than the Agrarians. Our brothers were seized, thrown to jail, tortured and killed. Our Central Committee was forced to emigrate abroad, the elite of our party was exterminated, all our district committees were crashed. They shot our people in the back in the street just like at the Agrarian Union leaders."

Todor wanted to say: "You yourself are to blame for that, as you shouldn't have betrayed Alexander Stamboliysky!" but he kept silent, and these words only sounded in his brain, haunting him. He was seeing himself that Georgy Pilashev was telling a bitter truth, and now they are allies, and they have a common foe. Pilashev continued.

"But, despite of the fact that BCP suffered irreparable losses, its ranks thinned out, but it is still alive and continues to act, continues to fight. So, on behalf of the BCP leadership, I propose you to conclude an alliance with us to fight a common foe. I invite you to join our ranks for the joint struggle against the fascist tsarism in our country. You are glowing heroes: fearless, bold, daring, well-aimed shooters and noble souls; you help the victims of government violence. You are unique, there are few like you, or rather there are no such like you, and if there were more people like you in our ranks, then we would win out fight! On the other hand, you are waging the struggle against your personal foes and struggle without any idea, and we offer you a joint struggle for lofty ideas."

"What are your ideas?" Mityu Ganev asked.

"Our ideas are a just world without violence and arbitrariness of power, without poverty and suffering of people, without such a structure, where a pack of rich people feast in palaces at the expense of the poor people who works for them and suffer hardships. Our ideas, first of all, are a republic without a tsar and his servants. Our ideas are freedom!"

Todor was thinking about the Radomir Republic, proclaimed by Stamboliysky and Daskalov during the soldiers uprising in 1918, which was betrayed by the Communists and bitterly regretted of what had happened. Meanwhile, Georgy Pilashev was speaking enthusiastically about the ideas of the Communists, about a just structure of the society, in whom he firmly believed. There was not a shadow of doubt in his beautiful eyes about the correctness of the wonderful ideas, for the implementation of which he was ready to sacrifice his life. The other hajduks were listening attentively with interest. And Mityu Ganev, who never trusted anyone, firmly decided not to give any of his consent to join the ranks of the BCP right away in any case.

"Well, what will you say, hajduks?" Georgy Pilashev asked them with a smile.

"I do not give my consent to join the BCP right away. I need to learn your program and your rules in more detail. Yes, and also I hope you offer us to join the Communists voluntarily, according to our will, and in case of our refusal, you'll not persecute us, as the Macedonians persecute and kill those who decide to leave their ranks? Keep in mind that Tsankov and the tsar have thrown all those forces against us: policemen, army, shpits and Macedonians, and we are rebuffing them, so we won't be afraid of you, if you decide to pursue us in case of our refusal to join your ranks!"

"What are you talking about, Mityu! First of all, we are not the Macedonians, but internationalists; secondly, of course, we offer you voluntarily to unite with us, as I have already said, for a voluntary struggle against our common enemy for an organized struggle. If you refuse, it's up to you, but we'll be very sorry that you are not with us."

"What do you say, Todor?" Mityu Ganev asked his friend.

"I agree with you. No answer: neither yes nor no I won't give now. I have to weight everything, I have to think it over."

Satisfied with the result of negotiations, Georgy Pilashev gave them several copies of the "Rabotnichesky Vestnik" for review and invited them to dinner. Rudy Hristov laid the table, and simple rustic dinner in a clean, warm house, where they were given a friendly welcome, melted the hearts of the rebellious hajduks.

"If you accept our offer, stay here with us, we'll find a place to accommodate you," Rudy Hristov and Pilashev suggested.

"Thank you, but we'll think it over first," Todor and Mityu answered.

After resting in the house of Rudy Hristov all day, they set off on their return journey at dusk. Exited and tired from the crossing, they were sitting around the fire in one of their caves of the Hajduk Angel and discussed the offer they were made, reading the "Vestnik." 6 boys, in whom the people saw the romantic heroes and about whom they created the legends and sang songs, were proud and freedom-loving rebels, but unfortunate and destitute wanderers, who could not return to their home and had to roam around the strangers' places in winter storms and hide in caves in summer, every moment risking being hunted down by Tsankov's bloodhounds. But they were as free as the wind, which blows where it wants, and in the end they could've surmount the ridges and go abroad. But if they join the BCP ranks, they we'll be forced to submit to the leadership; but on the other hand, they will not be alone in a chaotic war with windmills, but will have organization support and idea of struggle. They weighed all the pros and cons, and in 2 days, having quenched the fire in the Angel's cave, with the onset of twilight they went back to Bukovo to Rudy Hristov and Georgy Pilashev, where they remained until the end of that snowing, frosty Bulgarian winter of 1924. They sat by the hearth in a warm, comfortable house and listened to Georgy Pilashev communist lectures. They temporary cut off all liaisons with their yataks, and nobody knew, where they were. The most disturbing rumors about them spread throughout the region. They still did not give any consent to join the BCP, and Rudy Hristov with Georgy Pilashev were hospitable to them in advance, as a token of friendly disposition toward them and support.

Chapter 41
Spring 1924

March 1924 was still cold, but it symbolized the onset of spring, which means a new hope. The snow was melting, destroying the traces of the hajduks imprinted on it, and the vicinal roads became open for the passage of carts. On the road from the Bukovo village to the Bodrovo village a cart harnessed by 2 horses was rushing from the south-west to the north-east, in which the coachman was carrying an old woman Srebra Yurukova, who was jumping up and down with impatience to inform the people in Bodrovo about the news from Bukovo as soon as possible. The old woman Srebra was a sister of Rudy Hristov wife and unexpectedly appeared in their house. She saw the hajduks, who did not have time to hide from her, and dumbfound by the news, forgot what she had come for. It was too late to push her out of the door, as the hajduks had already caught her eye. After staying with her sister for a short time, Srebra got ready to go back.

"Don't dare to tell anybody what you saw here!" Rudy Hristov threatened her at parting. "Otherwise you won't come into my house anymore!"

"You will not be my sister, if you hint at least someone!" her sister confirmed to her, escorting her out of door.

"What are you talking about, sister, how can I! What are you talking about, son-in-law! How could you even think about me in such a way!" the old woman Srebra got offended and quickly jumped into the cart, which rushed her to the village Bodrovo.

"You must leave!" Rudy warned the hajduks. "It's dangerous to stay here."

The cart rushed through the fields and ravines, and the old woman Srebra was shaking in it with impatience to tell "in secret" the news to everyone. On the same day, she told the news to Atanasa, the Todor's mother, whom she met near the cheshma-fountain, that her son Todor was alive and hiding in Bukovo, where he is listening to the Georgy Pilashev communistic lectures. Atanasa brought the good news to her house, where she made everybody happy. And the old woman Srebra rushed to her son Hristoz, who on the occasion of such news arranged sit-round-gathering in his house the same evening, to which urgently they invited everyone, who "did not engage in politics" but was engaging in only one thing: denunciations and gossips.

In the cigar-smoked hut of Hristoz there was noise and hubbub from the discussion of the news that had just been heard, so that the old woman Vichka Pavlova, who was present at the sit-round-gathering and had a personal interest in the news under discussion, could hardly differ the words that reached her ears. She repeatedly re-asked about the gossip the villagers sitting next to her about the information, and they told each other the news, introducing their details to the story. Finally, she found it out: Todor Todorov is alive and together with his cheta is hiding in Bukovo with the communist Pilashev. The old woman Vichka, as if scalded, jumped up from her place at the sit-round-gathering and, stumbling, almost fell, but stood on her feet, which carried her out strait to her own house to her old husband.

"Old man, get ready, run, there is news: Todor is alive and hiding in Bodrovo!"

"Wait, old woman, tell me everything in order!"

"I am telling you: Todor is alive and hiding in Bukovo together with his gang! This is our chance, finally! Otherwise, wait for another chance, when the luck turns up!"

"Yes, yes, the reward is promised for him after all!"

"The reward is one thing, of course! And there is something else: our son is married to the second daughter of the grandfather Techa. The grandpa Techa is Todor's maternal grandfather, as he is the father of Atanasa, Todor's mother. So, if Todor dies, the inheritance of the grandpa Techa will not have to be divided between his 2 daughters, but will remain indivisible, and everything will go to one of his daughters: our daughter-in-law, that is, her husband, our son, and therefore to us!"

"That's what I understand, you and I have discussed this many times! But how will Todor die, if he is not caught, and only the policemen and agents, who are chasing him, die?"

"So, I am telling you: now Todor is in Bukovo, and if the policemen suddenly appear there, they will seize him and hang or shot him dead! Then the inheritance of grandpa Techa will be ours!"

"Yes, but by the time when the police gets to Bukovo, there will be no trace of them!"

"That's I am telling you, let's quickly run to the kmet's office and report it!"

"Are you crazy, old woman, it's night now, and the office is closed, there is no one there, everyone is sleeping, let's go early in the morning! And we also need to spread the rumors that it is Atanasa, Todor's mother, who told everyone that her son Todor is in Bukovo. When the police comes to Bukovo, they will kill not only Todor, but also Pilashev with all his family, then the Communists will decide to avenge Pilashev, then they will kill Atanasa with her entire family, and then the entire heritage will go to us."

"Let's hurry up!"

"I am telling you, let's go in the morning, there is nobody there now: it's night now!"

2 old persons hardly waited for the morning and early in the morning they knocked on the door of the Bodrovo kmet's office, where besides the kmet, there were some spies at that time. In a moment the telephones were ringing in Borisovograd and Haskovo, and a platoon of soldiers with mounted policemen rushed to Bukovo together with the truck with volunteers, Wranglers and Macedonians. They completely cordoned off Bukovo, blocked all the entrances and exits, rummaged the entire village and broke into the house of the Agrarian Rudy Hristov, who denied everything, pretending to be sick, and there were no traces of the hajduks: they disappeared along with Gregory Pilashev and were watching them from the secret Dragoyna Thracian cave on the top of the mountain.

***

A long-awaited spring has finally dressed the tree crowns and the brunches of bushes in green foliage that can hide its hajduks. And the hajduks of Todor Todorov and Mityu Ganev descended from the mountains and returned to their path of war. The liaisons with the yataks were restored. And the faithful horses, brought out from the winter stables, again carried their riders toward the fight with the foe. They hadn't yet given their consent to the Pilashev's proposal, and therefore they were as free as the wind and conceived their daring actions themselves. Having received information from the yataks that on that day a car of the owner of a rich tobacco company would pass along the highway from Sofia to Haskovo, the hajduks ambushed. Near the highway on the hillock there was a koliba-cabin of Panyu Petrov, an acquaintance, and they stayed there. Through binoculars from the koliba, the highway was visible in both direction, and they only had to wait. The risk was great, since it was daylight, but despising the danger, the hajduks, frozen, took up their positions inside the koliba, carefully watching the highway through their binoculars. Their faithful horses were grazing on the lines aside. They were waiting for a long time, but did not lose patience.

Finally, the car appeared on the highway. On the sign from Todor all the hajduks jumped out of the koliba and in a moment were at the edge of the highway, covered with bushes. Mityu Ganev shot and pierced the tire of the car, and it, falling on the damaged wheel, gnashed it along the road and stopped.

"Hands up!" Todor ordered.

The driver of the car and the wealthy merchant Azerl raised their hands, and the hajduks only had to grab from the merchant 3 huge bags with 7 million leva and instantly disapeared from view on their horses. The cave of Todor with their cache remained undisclosed by anyone and was waiting for its inhabitants. The boys, who had been quiet for the winter, selling the newspapers in the streets of Bulgaria, again yelled at the top of their lungs, shouting over each other: "The cheta of Todorov, Ganev, Ignatov robbed the Thracian Tobacco Company!" and so on every day, listing the objects of robbery. The fame of the cheta thundered throughout the country and outstripped their appearance, and they were ahead of any pursuit and, having successfully completed the "action of expropriation and fair redistribution," faster than lighting disappeared without a trace in the thickets of the forest, having left the pursuers to follow their nose. Meanwhile, their main foes continued to run free, and the thirst of revenge and hatred to them burned the soul of Todor and his companions and pushed them to action.

The police bailiff Ivan Todorov Guenov-Kamine at the weekend from the work at the Borisovograd police station, where he with the police chief Enyu Gogov, foreman Nesterov and some other new sadistic police officers tortured and killed the detainers, thrusting their heads into the firebox of the police station in the name of "Great Bulgaria," the "good of the state" and "law and order," relaxed in nature and sowed tobacco on his plot of land in the Metokha area, not far from Bodrovo. It was the end of May. The nature of Bulgaria completely revived from the winter non-existence, struck with its beauty both good and evil ones, and enemies, and friends. Yellow-green fields, sown fields, giving shoots, hills covered with green velvet, on which scarlet poppies dazzled like lights, flowering gardens seemed to be a nook of heavenly paradise. But there was no paradise on the land of Bulgaria, as there was hell, which the hajduks of Todor challenged. They hid behind the hillock in the bushes, overlooking the hill below, where the entire Guenov-Kamine family was planting tobacco. Behind the hill, covered with boxwood bushes, a stream flowed, carrying clear waters from the peaks of Rhodopes to the lower reaches of Maritsa.

Todor's heart beat with excitement, when he saw his butcher Guenov-Kamine, as if nothing had happened, enjoying life, surrounded by his family. His nephew Costa was by his uncle and helped him with his work in the field. Ivan Ignatov scanned the rural idyll below at the foot of the hill and tightly squeezed the handle of his revolver. Mityu Ganev carefully scanned the area around, and the other 3 hajduks were placed sentries on a higher hill, from where a view was opened in both directions on the Bansko Highway. Todor signaled to his friends not to make a sound or move. They were waiting. The sun rose in the zenith, flooding the yellow-green velvet of the hill and valleys with a dazzling light, and finally Guenov-Kamine separated from his family and headed toward the hill, behind which the stream flowed; his nephew Costa followed him. 2 foes came to the stream, drank some water and filled their baklaga-canteens with water to take with them, then undressed and climbed into the water to swim. They splashed like children, told something to each other, apparently remembering what they had done and laughed out loudly, enjoying swimming and nature. Then they got out of the water and began to dress. They froze in place, not having time to pull on their pants. 3 barrels of revolvers were aimed at them. Pale with horror, they froze, not uttering a sound. 3 shots from revolvers that hit them in the legs knocked them on the ground. Todor was ahead of his friends, first jumped to the fallen and fired another bullet into the Costa's stomach, instantly drew a dagger and staged it into Guenov-Kamine's belly.

"You are sentenced to death, butchers and murderers, for the murder of the brothers Vidyu and Todor Gochev Karagochev, for killing me and hounding my family, for killing and torturing the detained in Borisovograd police station and for the serving of the tsar-Tsankov junta!" Todor pronounced a sentence on them, who was immediately ahead of by Ivan Ignatov and Mityu Ganev, who jumped to the mortal foes stretched on the ground at their feet and staged their daggers in both. They pronounced them their sentences one after another. The riddled and blooded bodies of the exterminated foes were lying at the feet of the triumphant hajduks; the long-awaited revenge finally had come true. Todor, Ivan and Mityu bathed in the stream and washed their daggers, then instantly disappeared, hidden by the green foliage.

Several days had passed. Having received information of the yataks, the hajduks were sitting in ambush near the highway west of Gorsky Izvor. That day was clear and sunny, the nature of southern Bulgaria was blooming and fragrant, nothing foreboded danger to the Borisovograd police chief Enyu Gogov and his henchman Nesterov, who were driving in a car to Haskovo on official business. But frightened by the death of Guenov-Kamine, now they were afraid even of their shadow and cowardly looked around along the entire length of the road, especially when they were approaching Gorsky Izvor, to the south of which the Aidanlar forest stretched. Their fears were not in vain. Before they had time to think about the worst thing that could await them, the car screeched, gnashed, falling on a wheel with a punctured tire, spun like a whirligig and was forced to stop.

"Hands up!" they heard in their address and instantly raised their hands cowardly.

Out of nowhere the Todor's hajduks suddenly rose up in front of their noses and were standing around the car with revolvers aimed at them.

"You are sentenced to death, butchers and murderers, for torturing and killing me in Borisovograd police station, for the torturing and killing other prisoners, for burning them alive in furnace of your dungeons, for crimes against the people of Bulgaria!" Todor Todorov announced the verdict to them and set the trigger of the revolver.

"I, I, I did my duty, I did my job," the police chief Gogov bleated helplessly, whose pig-like snout turned white with horror.

Nesterov, the assistant, was shaking with fear.

"Die, butcher and sadist!" Todor shouted and shot 2 times at each.

Ivan Ignatov, Mityu Ganev and 3 others followed his example, and each shot at the hated policemen, who were already dead without it.

The spring of 1924 ended in Bulgaria.

Chapter 42
Choice

The gloomy prophesy of Alexander Stamboliysky, being martyred in the hands of the Bulgarian officers, who vainly tried to find an alliance with the Communists, came true: "But god forbid if the flayers from the Black Blok Military League and the terrorists from IMRO overthrow the government, the next day there will be no trace of them (the Communists)!"

All came true, as Alexander Stamboliysky predicted. The Communists of Bulgaria, who during the reign of the Stamboliysky's Agrarian Union freely carried out their activities and were only engaged in putting sticks in the wheels of the Agrarian Union, who had seats in the parliament, published their bulletin "Rabotnichesky Delo," openly held their meetings and rallies and were comfortable in their Union House; now, being declared to be outlaw, on April 4, 1924 they sneaked secretly to their conference in the Vitosha Mountains. They made their way in advance, to be in time by May 17. Driven and illegal, they stubbornly moved forward, trudging through 10 Vitosha pinnacles, with a huge dome hanging over Sofia. They surmounted gorges and ravines, climbed the pinnacles and finally reached a secluded place, surrounded by dense forest in the most remote nook on the glade of the top of Selimishki. A huge stone served as a table for them.

And at that time in their former Union (Party) House in the center of Sofia there was a headquarters of policemen, who sent all the decent people of the country to death. Yet in January 1924, the tsarist-Tsankov junta adopted the "Law of the Defense of the State," which forbade anyone, who was not an abettor of the fascists, to live and breathe. Each article of the "Law" ended with the words: "…punished with death." And if you provided shelter to a driven person, but did not know that he was persecuted, let it be: you will go to jail only for 16 years. Miraculously survived deputies of the National Assembly, still cherishing hope that parliamentary methods of combating the bloody junta of the tsar Boris III-Tsankov, which had overthrown the Agrarian Union power, beastly tortured to death its leader Alexander Stamboliysky on June 9, 1923, usurped the power and exterminated the people of Bulgaria, delivered fiery speeches from the rostrum of the parliament, which the junta had reassembled in Sofia for the sake of appearance in order to demonstrate to somebody that there was a parliament in Bulgaria. The deputies from the Agrarian Union and BCP made fiery speeches from the rostrum of the parliament about the atrocities of the junta, exposing it in murders of people, then went out to street and received a bullet in the back from the junta. The chairs of the murdered deputies became vacant in the National Assembly Congress Hall; they fell in the street, shot in the back, one after another. There is no parliamentary struggle against the fascist junta in a country, where democracy has been trampled!

18 representatives of the party districts of Bulgaria and 4 members of the Central Committee of the BCP, Bulgarian Communist Party, climbed to the pinnacle of Selimishki of the Eastern Range and opened their illegal conference on May 17, 1924. Once again they condemned the betrayal of Alexander Stamboliysky by their leadership on June 9, 1923 and confirmed the course for a new armed uprising in alliance together with the United Front, together with the Agrarian Union against the fascists. Shortly after the BCP leaders Georgy Dimitrov and Vasil Kolarov crossed the Yugoslavian border with the rebels after the uprising was crushed in September, they met with Alexander Obbov and Kosta Todorov in Serbia. The companions of Raiko Daskalov after his assassination by the tsar-Tsankov junta on August 1923, headed the foreign representation of the Agrarian Union. In the town Lanovo in the center of Serbia the leaders of the Agrarian Union and the BCP confirmed their further struggle against the fascists together by the United Front and preparation of the new uprising. Then, on October 7, 1923, there was a new meeting of Dimitrov and Todorov in Vienna, where the course for the new armed uprising by the United Front was confirmed. On February 20, 1924, already in Moscow, there was a meeting of the leaders of the Agrarian Union Kosta Todorov and Stefan Tsanov with the Communists' leaders Dimitrov and Kolarov, where the agreement was signed on the preparation of the new armed uprising. The date of the uprising had to be determined.

To prepare of the new uprising both sides began to found the united chetas to disturb the fascist authorities. On March 20, 1924, the political cheta of Haskovo region was founded, named after the legendary hajduk Hristo Botev. This cheta began to operate in the Haskovo region. It was far from the glory of the Todorov-Ganev-Ignatov cheta, but it also began to be spoken about its courage and audacity. Both chetas operated in on and the same place.

Meanwhile, the Todorov-Ganev-Ignatov's hajduks, satisfied with their bloody vengeance on the mortal foes, with a light heart continued their devil-devilish actions to "expropriate and re-distribute capital" and very easily escaped the chase. Their glory thundered throughout the country the same as before.

"They gave me money to buy oxen," the poor villager shared his secret with another in a whisper.

"And to me—for the purchase of agricultural inventory," the latter whispered to him in response.

"God bless them! Thank them!"

On a hot June day, there was heavy traffic on the highway, connecting Haskovo and Kardjali. Clopping with their hooves along the stone paved road, horses and oxen dutifully pulled their carts with goods, and rare cars transported the rich. In the gorge, where densely forested mountains were contiguous to the road on one side and a forested valley on another, a traffic jam occurred in the afternoon. The movement had stopped. A car and the carts were standing along the road one behind another.

"Customs control, gentlemen! No one move, stand still!" Todor commanded to all, and together with Ivan Ignatov and Mityu Ganev, and Rusi Stoyanov they took a blanket by the 4 ends and approached the first cart, on which a merchant was riding.

"Everyone, throw all the valuables and wallets on the blanket!" ordered Mityu Ganev, who was walking nearby and exercised control.

Kolyu Trendofilov was standing by the first cart and closed the traffic. The merchant threw his wallet on the blanket.

"You can go!" Mityu Ganev ordered and made the sign to Kolyu to let the merchant go.

The first cart left. The second on arrived up, followed by all the others in turn. After the merchants, sitting in the carts, threw their valuables and money on the blanket, they were allowed to go further, and Kolyu Trendofilov let them go. A car drove up. Poor and middle-level merchants did not go by car. Mityu Ganev looked inside the car. A tobacconist was sitting behind the wheel, shaking with fear, and white faced.

"What's in the bags?" Mityu Ganev asked, pointing with his hand at the several suitcases lying on the seat.

With trembling hands, already parting with life in his thoughts, the merchant held out the bags, crammed with paper-bills, which Rusi and Mityu threw on the blanket.

"There is a million and a half leva there, I am going to Kardjali to pay off the peasants. I've bought tobacco from them on credit," the tobacco dealer barely articulated from excitement and fear.

"Give it back!" Mityu Ganev ordered, and Rusi Stoyanov with Mityu Panev, handed the bags crammed with money back to the merchant.

With trembling hands, not believing his eyes, the merchant took back his bags with money and put them on the seat of the car.

"Do you have any valuables or wallet?" Mityu Ganev turned to him.

The merchant took a wallet out of his pocket and removed a silver watch on a chain from his belt and handed it to Mityu Ganev, who threw everything on the blanket.

"You can go! Allow!" Mityu Ganev said and gave a sign to Kolyu.

The merchant did not move from his place, dumbfounded from everything that was happening.

"Well, why are you standing? Go, don't stop traffic!" Mityu Ganev told him.

"How is it, is it all? I can go, can't I? Maybe you need anything else? Maybe I can help you somehow?"

"Someday you'll tell somebody about it?" Todor burst out laughing.

Not believing his eyes and ears, the merchant started the car and slowly drove forward, then gradually picking up speed, disappeared from view.

Thus, having collected tribute from all the passengers through the gorge, the hajduks tied 4 ends of the blanket, put it on the back of the mule and in a cheerful mood, galloped on their horses to the Todor's cave on the hills of the Aidanlar forest. They deliberately circled around, confusing their tracks, carefully approached the place of the cave, left the horses to graze at a certain distance, and on foot made their way to the hill, looking around. And only after making sure that there was no chase, they climbed the hill and got into the cave. The entrance to the cave was absolutely invisible from outside, as a ledge of a rock covered it. The hajduks dragged the tied blanket with the collected tribute inside, appreciated its contents with satisfaction, then hid it in their lurking-place, which was situated in the depth of the cave and actually was a separate room. They sat around the hearth and began to eat a roasted lamb.

"Maybe we split everything and go to Turkey or Greece?" Kolyu Trendofilov suggested. "The same thing like Petyu, Mityu Ganev's brother, has done?"

At the mention of Petyu Ganev all burst into laughing in unison, and Mityu Ganev frowned first and then also burst into laughing louder than the others.

"Petyu is great! He fooled everybody; everybody thought he was killed together with Kolyu Panev, but they turned out to be alive and fled to Turkey!"

"How I worried about my brother, grieved, but he, as it turned out, has already dodged everyone and appeared to be alive!"

"As it turned out, he is not only alive, but also lives in wealth. He bought an estate in Turkey, married his beloved girl, gave birth to a child and became a chorbadji!"

"It's all love! He fell in love with her even earlier, when we fled to Turkey, then he met her and fell in love. And so, he dodged all, returned to Turkey and married her."

"And how deftly they designed it together with Kolyu! They dug up 2 corpses of the villagers, killed by the Macedonians, wrapped them in blankets and put them in the koliba. They knew from the yataks that they had been betrayed, and an onslaught was being prepared. 2 traitors got in the koliba, shot 2 corpses and dragged them to the Haskovo police for ransom. And the police threw them to prison, not to give them reward and take it for themselves. At that time Petyu and Kolyu were already crossing the border, and Petyu hurried to his beloved. They bought fake documents and live in clover in Turkey."

"What a romantic story!"

At the words "love", "marriage", "estate", a soul-crushing melancholy seized the hearts of the hajduks, and each of them imagined himself in place in Petyu Ganev and Kolyu Panev with fake documents, which was not a problem somewhere in Turkey, in a cozy house, in a circle of his beloved family. And Todor and Ivan Ignatov, who had their estates here nearby in Bodrovo, recalled them with sad anguish and passionately desired to return home legally.

"Oh, I would give everything in the world to be in my house again!" Todor sighed.

"Is that true: everything in the world?" Mityu Ganev asked incredulously.

"And what prevents us from sharing what is there in our lurking-place and going abroad?" Rusi Stoyanov asked.

"Georgy Pilashev is waiting for a response from us," Todor answered seriously.

"And what shall we answer him?"

"Sooner or later we must give him a positive response," Todor replied.

A mirage of happiness, love, wealth and peace in their estate abroad, which was standing before their eyes, disappeared in front of the harsh reality, and the ghost of continuing the fight against the fascists again emerged.

"The opposite side also is seeking for meeting with us," Todor told his friends the news, and everyone became excited.

"And Hristo Botev cheta is great!" Mityu Ganev exclaimed. "They are already catching up with us in glory!"

All laughed.

"Our competitors!"

"Not competitors, but allies," Todor corrected, "we have a common foe."

Several days had passed. The hot summer of 1924 was in full swing. Blooming and fragrant nature amazed you with its beauty. The yellow-green seedlings of the harvest undulated in the breeze on the hills and dales, and the green foliage of bushes and trees hid their hajduks with their lush crowns. They were hiding in the Uncle Gocho old koshara, which hidden by the thickets of the bushes, stood at the very edge of the Bodrovo highway. When the busy movement began, they went out onto the road. They were acting according to their established scheme. They stopped the first cart with a merchant, by which they put Mityu Panev, and suggested him to give away the excess. The second cart drove up after the first one and was followed by the others. Shaking with fear and resigned to the inevitability, the merchants gave the hajduks what it was not pity to part with and what was by no means the last.

Suddenly the hajduks heard the cheerful neighing of the horses, which recognized Todor, remembering how he carefully fed them, watered them, combed their manes and kissed them on the muzzle in Chirpan. Todor patted them on the back of the neck and greeted Hristo Kundurdjiyata, who was sitting in the cart.

"Well, so, we've met," Todor informed him.

Neither alive nor dead from fear, Hristo raised his hands up, preparing for the worst. Mityu Ganev nodded his head to Todor; Todor took the horses by the bridle and turned the cart off the highway behind the koshara-shed, covered with the bushes.

"Get down!" Todor ordered.

Hristo obediently got down from his cart with his hands up.

"Well, have you recognized me?" Todor asked him mockingly.

"Hm…" Hristo mumbled.

"Do you remember how you robbed my family in the famine of 1918 and stole half a ton of grain from my father, brought you as payment for my teaching?"

"Hm…"

"Do you remember how you mocked me, humiliated me, forcing me to work for you as a servant for free instead of teaching me shoemaking?"

"Hm…"

"Do you remember how you sent a killer with a knife to kill me?"

"Hm…"

"You remain my last personal foe, whom I long to take vengeance on!"

"Have mercy, Todor! I am guilty before you, but it was so long ago, how long time has passed since then!" Hristo pleaded, thinking how to finish Todor off.

"The more time has passed, the more is my thirst for revenge! If it was not you, maybe my fate would have been different. My father dreamed to open a shoe factory and therefore he sent me to you to learn all the details of the craft. And you robbed us and sent an assassin to kill me. If it was not you, maybe we really would've had a shoe factory somewhere in Haskovo or in Plovdiv! I would've been in charge of it, as my father wanted. I have no mercy for you!" Todor exclaimed a stabbed the dagger into his heart.

The heavy, vile body of Hristo Kundurdjiyata, the Todor's last foe, fell to his feet.

"I think, your wife Elena will not grieve too much!" with these words Todor led him on his last journey.

He unharnessed the horses, leaving the cart next to its owner, and the hajduks took the horses with them, having hidden without a trace from prying eyes along with the tribute they had collected on the Bansko Highway.

Remembering the hard winter, when they wandered homeless, seeking for shelter at the yataks' houses, since they could not hide in their 2 caves with the cache and arsenal of weapons, now in summer, they arranged for themselves several additional luring places in Dragoina and Aida mountains, which were around Bukovo. They found several caves there, hidden on the mountain pinnacles, and turned them into their additional headquarters. In advance, in summer, they hid stocks weapons and clothing in them, brought crackers and canned food, which were a delicacy and could be obtained in the cities only.

***

And at this time near the city Sofia in the garden of the royal palace Vrana, the tsar had a meeting with the fascist junta ringleaders: Tsankov, Vylkov and Rusev. In the pavilion, where more than a year ago he discussed with them the details of the upcoming fascist upheaval in Bulgaria and assassination of Alexander Stamboliysky together with all the leaders of the Agrarian Union, now he was discussing with them the actions of the Todorov-Ganev-Ignatov cheta. In the arbor, fenced on all sides by bushes of boxwood, jasmine and fragrant roses, the tsar Boris III turned to the guests, called for the conversation, with a question:

"Have you prepared a decree for signature?"

"That's right, Your Majesty!" Rusev reported, and Tsankov pulled out from his briefcase a sheet of paper with a printed text.

"Everything is as we discussed with you at the previous meeting!" Vylkov reported ingratiatingly.

"What sum have you determined?" the tsar asked.

"I think, 300 thousand leva," Tsankov prompted.

"For all?" the tsar was surprised.

"No, what are you talking about, Your Majesty, for each of them," Rusev clarified, "but only…"

"What, only?" the tsar was surprised.

"Only, I don't really believe that they will accept our proposal."

"Why?"

"Because, they can't be bought. They take money from the rich tobacco dealers, our sponsors, by the way, and give part of it to the poor."

"Gentlemen, do everything to win them over to our side!" Promise them, in addition to "300 thousand leva for each, a house where they want: in Plovdiv or in Sofia! They won't be able to refuse this!" the tsar exclaimed. "Yes, and then an amnesty! They will not buy an amnesty for any money, and we give them a full amnesty for everything they've done!"

"That's right, Your Majesty!" General Rusev reported servilely, agreeing with everything that the tsar said.

"They must certainly take our side and help us to destroy the Hristo Botev cheta!" Tsankov squealed, twitching with excitement. "The Communists and Agrarians cheta Hristo Botev really causes us big trouble! They are the same bold, daring and elusive as our legendary hajduks, and I think, they can be exterminated only with the help of these hajduks, if they accept our offer!"

"Send reliable agent for negotiations, give them our decree and do not spoil the matter, do not threaten them! From now on, stop any persecution of them! Todor Todorov, Mityu Ganev and Ivan Ignatov with their friends must be ours!" the tsar ordered and signed the decree.

"That's right, Your Majesty!" Tsankov, Rusev and Vylkov confirmed the royal order, put the documents in their briefcase and respectfully retired.

The tsar Boris twirled the mustache gladly, anticipating pleasure to have among his army Todor Todorov, Mityu Ganev and Ivan Ignatov with their friends, whose fame of courage, audacity and talent haunted him.

The royal decree was delivered to Haskovo by a courier from Sofia on the same day, handed over to the 2 police agents, who immediately proceeded to the execution of the order. The agents immediately went in search of possible contacts to arrange a meeting with the cheta of the hajduks. And the hajduks, meanwhile, continued to perform their daring actions, after which they rested on the pinnacles of the hills among the fragrant herbs and flowers under the glowing July sun at the foot of the Rhodopes, drank crystal clear water from the streams, flowing from them and laved their beautiful young male bodies in them. They enjoyed the ongoing summer of 1924 and the thought that they had succeeded in taking vengeance on all their personal foes.

"The tsarist agents are seeking for a meeting with us," Todor told his friends the news, although, this was no longer news, but the well-known information, which the yataks respired to each other in all the villages. "I believe, it's high time to meet."

"Well, let them come to visit us here, on the pinnacle of Aida," Mityu Ganev smiled.

"They'll have to go far from Haskovo here. Maybe, we'll arrange a meeting somewhere to the north, closer?" Ivan Ignatov asked.

"They'll do it, let them walk," Todor said. "Our people will tell them where to go."

The information about the consent of the hajduks to meet with the tsar's envoys was conveyed from village to village along the chain of the yataks and in the final settlement near Haskovo, the owner of the tavern, the hajduks' yatak, informed the tsar's agents about this. Early in the morning at dawn, they set off by foot and without weapons, but with the tsar's decree. From one tavern to another they were told where to go, and they walked slowly along the goat paths, climbing the hills to the appointed place for meeting. From the top of the hill, overgrown with forest, the entire valley below was visible, and Ivan Ignatov vigilantly watched through binoculars 2 figures of the agents, moving alone in the distance below. It was evident that this was not a trap: the agents were alone, and no one followed them. Rusi Stoyanov, Mityu Panev and Kolyu Trendofilov were scanning the area from 4 other points, and Todor with Mityu Ganev prepared to receive the guests. 2 agents finally climbed the hill, where they were met by the young men, armed to their teeth, the fame of which thundered throughout Bulgaria. They greeted each other, and one of the agents took out from his field bag, hanging on a harness over his shoulder, a paper and handed it to Todor Todorov.

"His Majesty the tsar and the Minister-Chairman Mr. Alexander Tsankov authorized us to deliver you this decree, gentlemen the hajduks."

Todor unfolded the document, sealed and signed with royal signature, and began to read.

"Gentlemen, we have been authorized to inform you that His Majesty's government admired your fearlessness, courage, bravery and all your other talents and invites you to devote all your valor to serve the tsar and the fatherland. You are invited to become a personal guard of His Majesty's government to fight the mortal enemy of our state. You are even offered an officer rank, as well as 300 thousand leva in cash for each of you, a house where you want: in Plovdiv, Haskovo or in Sofia, and the most important: a complete amnesty for everything you have done before. If you accept this proposal, you'll be clean before the law, fully amnestied and become loyal fighters in the struggle against the enemies of our fatherland and help the government to exterminate the United Front Cheta of the Communists and Agrarians Hristo Botev."

The tsar's agent ended his speech and there was a tense silence.

"Todor, check, is it really all that's written there?" asked Mityu Ganev, who was not very literate.

Todor read the message of the tsar, which he was holding in his hands, and confirmed that everything was correct.

"Well, what do you say, Todor?" Mityu Ganev asked him again.

Todor, who was obsessed with idea, which he had uttered recently to his friends that he would give everything in the world to return to his house legally and live in peace, said:

"No, I do not accept the offer of the tsar and Tsankov and shall never serve the butchers and murderers of the Bulgarian people! What do you say, friends?"

"No!" Ivan Ignatov answered.

"No!" Rusi Stoyanov answered.

"No!" Kolyu Trendofilov answered.

"No!" Mityu Panev answered.

"And this is my response," Mityu Ganev said and took out of his pocket a 5-leva coin and handed it to Ivan Ignatov, "measure 50 paces and fix the coin on the tree."

The unarmed agents were intently watching the happening. Ivan Ignatov fulfilled the order of Mityu Ganev. He counted 50 paces toward a tree, growing in front of them, made a notch with a knife on the tree trunk and inserted the coin there, so that it stood close to the trunk perpendicular to the ground. Then he stepped aside. Mityu Ganev took aim and fired. There was a crash and ground of the wounded tree. Ivan Ignatov came to the tree, took the coin and returned it back; he handed the coin to Mityu Ganev, who handed it to the agents. The dumbfounded agents took the coin, pierced by a bullet exactly in the center.

"Take it to your tsar and Tsankov and give it to them: this is my answer! Todor, Ivan and all the others shoot exactly as accurately as I do. I tell them no! I'll not serve the fascists and the enemies of the Bulgarian people for any benefits, promised to me. As for freedom, we are already free: all the Rhodopes are ours, they are our home! Now get out!"

The agents didn't make them say it twice and hurried away down the hill.

"I'll keep it for memory," Todor said gloomily and hid the royal decree in his bag.

In the decree of the tsar they were offered the blessings of the world in exchange for their conscience. They refused these benefits, retaining their honor. They knew they had put their lives on the line, but they made their choice.

Chapter 43
Wedding in Bodrovo and Internment

On July Sunday the weather was fine, and in a house of Bay Kudyu Georgiev in the village of Bodrovo they celebrated the wedding. His son Hristo Kudev married a girl from the village. The house was full of guests, who were sitting at a long U-shaped table, bursting with food. Roasted lambs and piglets, stews and vegetables, appetizers and salads, pies were in abundance on the festive table in the large living room of Bay Kudyu Georgiev. Bottles of rakia and wine, to the delight of the guests, were standing densely on the table between the dishes with food. The newlyweds were sitting in the center of the table happy and content. The guests congratulated them, ate and drank to their health and had fun. The day was glowing; the door of the house was wide open into the courtyard, where the musicians were sitting and playing cheerful music. All of a sudden everyone was stunned and silent, staring at the front door. 3 young men, armed from head to toe were standing there, in whom everyone recognized Todor Todorov, Ivan Ignatov and Mityu Ganev. The musicians stopped playing, and it fell silent.

"Well. Why are you not playing? Play, musicians!" Ivan Ignatov turned to them and approached the newlyweds. "This is a gift from us to you!"

He handed the newlyweds a package tied with ribbon.

"Thank you, brother!" Hristo answered and invited them to the table. "Eat, drink and have fun, dear guests! Ivan Ignatov is my cousin! You know, he could not miss it to come and congratulate me."

The guests instantly came out of their stupor condition and pounced on food and rakia again. Todor, Mityu and Ivan joined them. The musicians merrily played with renewed vigor. Fun, an abundance of delicious food with rakia relaxed 3 friends, and they, having driven away all sad thought about their problems, indulged in general fun. Mityu Ganev filled one glass after another and soon could hardly sit at the table. Having had their fill and drunk, the guests went out into the yard, where the musicians were playing, and set off their favorite horo-round-dance. 3 friends followed them, supporting Mityu Ganev by the arms, as he, completely drunk, could barely dragging his feet. The young people joined the horo-dance. Mityu drew out his gun and began to shoot into the air, imitating the fireworks, and the frightened guests jumped aside, where they could.

"Hide the revolver! Have you gotten mad completely?" Todor commanded and together with Ivan dragged him back into the house.

"I salute to the health of the newlyweds!" barely dragging his tong, Mityu said, hardly understanding from the alcohol he drank, where he was.

"Well, it's high time to leave!" Todor said and together with Ivan Ignatov they dragged Mityu by the arms from the Kudyu Georgiev yard.

"We apologize, dear guests and hosts, for the trouble caused; our friend Mityu Ganev did not calculate his strength!" Todor apologized to everyone and in an instant dragged Mityu out of the yard with the help of Ivan.

Faithful yataks and 3 other companions were standing on guard from 4 sides of the hill, on which Bodrovo was located, and scanned all the roads, leading to it.

"Take some food with you," the good-natured Kudyu Georgiev said and quickly gathered a bag with food for the others.

"Thank you, Bay Kudyu!" they thanked and in a moment disappeared from the sight of all the present.

A week had passed. July 1924 came to an end. The Elijah's Day feast was approaching, and on the table of Ivan Todorov's house there were dishes prepared for the feast: cheese pies, meat stewed in a cauldron with vegetables, baked lamb and vegetables with fruits from their own garden. Policemen were scurrying around the house and urged the entire family to load quickly everything necessary into the cart for the journey to distant lands. Todor's father Ivan, a 47-year-old man, looked like a white-haired old man from the ordeals he had gone through. He loaded the wagon with the blankets, some cloths for change, bags with food and baklagas with water. Todor's mother Atanasa was already sitting in the cart together with her 3-year-old daughter. 18-year-old Maria was helping her father to collect the bags and put them in the cart. 15-year-old Gocho was driven from the field by the watchmen from the community.

Having abandoned their herd, horses, 2 dogs and the donkey, Gocho managed to get into the barn behind the house and hide his revolver in a lurking-place, and then he was forced to sit in the cart next to his family. A loaded cart harnessed by 2 oxen slowly moved along the central road of Bodrovo to exile. Their house was sealed, and accompanied by mounted police, a caravan of carts with the villagers, who had abandoned their houses, farms, fields, crops and livestock, moved in an unknown direction from Bodrovo. In the carts were the newlyweds, having celebrated their marriage a week ago, Hristo Kudev with his young wife and his brother, his little sisters Dalya and Vana together with a younger brother Blagoy, the entire family of Pancho Ignatov, the entire family of Tasho Kuzmov, the entire family of Kostadin Byalkov, the entire family of Dimitar Vylkov, the entire family of Georgy Zhekov and the entire family of Dimchev. The tsar Boris III and Tsankov took vengeance on all for the hajduks' refusal to take their side to exterminate the cheta of Hristo Botev.

From the church yard, where the kmet's building was situated, in which Ivan Todorov once worked as a kmet during the troubled times of the Great War, another police detachment rode out on horseback and reinforced the convoy. The caravan of carts, pulled by the oxen and accompanied by the convoy, descended from the hill, where Bodrovo was standing, drove to the highway and headed along the way to the village Varbitsa. The convoy warned everyone:

"If the Todorov-Ganev-Ignatov cheta appears to free you, I'll give the order to shoot all of you immediately!"

At that time the hajduks were watching the convoy from a hill overgrown with bushes. They had received the information about the upcoming internment in advance. Mityu Ganev took aim with the gun, Todor grabbed his hand:

"I forbid! Do not shoot! Suppose, we kill the entire convoy, then what? We shall not take our relatives to the mountains and yet with the small children, shall we? Well, they'll return home, and they will kill them all and burn our houses! No, in order to free them, it is necessary to change the entire system in the country and overthrow the fascist junta!"

Annoyed Mityu Ganev complied, realizing himself that Todor was right. Todor, Ivan and 4 companions were scanning from the hill, how the caravan of carts with their relatives moved in an unknown distance, going further and further away from their home and vanished from their sight.

Near the village Varbitsa on the Tsaregrad highway the convoy was divided into 2 parts. 2 carts with the families of Ignat Mitev and Ivan Todorov turned right toward Haskovo, and the rest turned left, and no one, including the convoy, knew where they were going. Near the village Gorsky Izvor the carts stopped to rest, eat some food, to water the oxen and continued their journey to the south-east along the Tsaregrad highway. The highway passed through the village of Klokotnitsa. The authorities drove all the villagers there in advance and lined them up along the road. When the cart with the Todor's family approached, the driven villagers began to boo the passers-by on the sign of kmet. Not all booed, some of the villagers looked with malice at their kmet, the policemen convoy and sympathetically at those sitting in the cart. Part of the scatter-brains, "not involved in politics," stared with curiosity with their open mouths at what was happening, part whistled and grimaced, laughed, exposing rotten teeth, and poked a finger at the persecuted, and part of the patriots, legal to the tsar and the fatherland, yelled with a throat distorted from anger:

"Why are you taking them anywhere? Kill them all: these Bolsheviks and Communists! Kill them! Kill them! Kill them!"

Mugs, snouts and muzzles, distorted by the malice of patriotism, stood before the eyes of Ivan Todorov for a long time, finishing off his already broken heart. Gocho's 47-year-old father, white from his ordeals, reminisced the past years. Before his eyes were the battles of 2 Balkan Wars, his fatal friendship with Guenov-Kamine, a fake "sworn-brother," who destroyed his whole life, work as kmet during the Great War, the suffering and glory of his elder son Todor, who became a legend among good people, and now the way to nowhere and the house abandoned in Bodrovo, the crops in the fields and cattle with horses, a donkey with dogs in a paddock near their koshara. He did not understand, why his life had turned out this way and why the villain-fate tormented him.

Meanwhile, the travelers reached Haskovo. They were sent to the first police station, where they were allowed to unharness the oxen, feed and water them and also eat themselves. 4 men: Ivan Todorov with Gocho and Ignat Mitev with the youngest son Zheko were taken to the investigation for interrogation.

"Did you feed your sons Todor and Ivan, did you supply their band with food?" the detective asked calmly.

"We could not do it, because we were under constant surveillance."

"Ok, let's write it down, you are free!" the detective let them go, thinking that if Todor, Mityu and Ivan change their mind and go over to the side of the authorities, then they'll become his bosses, and therefore it is better to treat their families neutrally, just in case.

In Haskovo they spent several hours resting, until a new convoy arrived to replace the old one, and 15 policemen went back, and 6 new escorts led the driven villagers from Bodrovo further on the way to the east. Night caught them in a small village, and they all fell asleep together right in their carts, and early in the morning they set off again. They passed hills covered with forests, fields with crops, groves with streams, and in the evening the tired oxen dragged them to Harmanly, where they spent the night, and in the morning 4 new guards separated them and sent to different directions: Ivan Ignatov's family in one direction, and Todor Todorov's family in another one.

They kept moving further and further south-east along the Maritsa River, passing orchards and vineyards and green hills nearby. They turned off the highway into the vicinity road and stopped for lunch near a cheshma with water. They spread the blanket on the grass, laid out food and invited 2 policemen-escorts. The latter sat down with pleasure, accepted a treat, talked in human way, joked, laughed, as if a cheerful company went to the countryside for a picnic. They enjoyed the company of 18-year-old Maria, Ivan's daughter. The glowing sun was in the sky, illuminating the unprecedented beauty of nature around. There was not a cloud in the sky, the soft breeze carried the heady aroma of flowering herbs and flowers.

Suddenly, in the distance, a small cloud appeared in the sky, which approached closer and closer, blacking and blurring over the entire horizon. The sky vanished under a huge black veil. They quickly collected the rest of the food, put the blanket in the cart and set off. A sudden storm brought hail down on their heads, and after it streams of water erupted from heaven, blocking their path. The vicinity path turned into a swamp, in which the police horses fell through knee-deep, and the poor oxen strained with all their might to move the cart filled with water, but could not do it. In the cart, as in a cold bath, Todor's relatives were swimming. With an effort they managed to turn off the vicinity road to the highway, but it disappeared from the face of the earth, completely covered with water; in front of the water a bridge over the stream stuck out, the water from which completely merged with a huge, giant puddle of deluge from rein.

The driven and the convoy stopped knee-deep in water, having no further path to move along. As soon as the water subsided and the outlines of the road appeared, they continued their way and reached the city of Lyubimets, where in some kind of hut they somehow dried themselves and spent the night, and in the morning they set off again and reached Svilengrad. The ancient city emerged before their eyes. Here the Thracians founded their city on the place of an ancient settlement, having left their artifacts and a chariot in the earth to the descendants. Here the Romans built their fortress on the way to the city Byzantine, which was later taken by storm by the Bulgarians, who had founded their kingdom with Asparuh.

Here the battles of all against all thundered on the direct route to Constantinople: the Byzantines against Bulgarians, the Bulgarians against crusaders, the Christians against the Muslims. Here the Ottoman Turks lingered for 500 years, erasing Bulgaria from the map of the earth. Here they were defeated in the First Balkan War, here Ivan Todorov fought for the capture of the city and then—in the neighborhood—for Adrianople. Now, he was going in a cart like a hostage of the regime, captured by the enemy, exposed to the crowd as a laughing stock.

The oxen cart rumbled over the ancient stones of the bridge over the Maritsa, built by the Turks in 1529. The ancient low arched bridge connected 2 banks of the river, on which the city was situated. They crossed the bridge and reached the police station, where 2 policemen left them, saying goodbye, and returned back to Harmanly. The hostages unharnessed the oxen, so that they could rest, and they themselves settled down on the ground near the wet cart. They waited in the police courtyard for 3 days, as it was not known where to send them further, and on the fourth day, having received a telegram, 2 new policemen took them further to the north-east through the villages Dimitrovche, Levka to the village of Mustraklii, handed them over to community and returned back. Kmet of Mustraklii took them to an abandoned, dilapidated, full of filth somebody's house, but the captives flatly refused to stay there, and then, ashamed, the kmet accommodated them in a large room in the school building. The exhausted travelers finally respired and lay down to rest, and Gocho, Todor's younger brother, fell down sick in semi-consciousness: he apparently caught cold under the rain. The strongest fever shook his body, it was burning, and he lay in semi-consciousness for many days, causing his relatives to suffer even more. Then gradually he began to recover, and the whole family merged into a daily life on a new place. As it turned out, they lived in a specious school room next to the library, and gradually, getting to his feet, he pounced at the books, absorbing them one after another. He began to go out into the field to graze his 2 oxen, and his relatives thought about what to do next. And then began to help to string tobacco leaves. They thought about their house, abandoned crops and the entire household and did not know, when they return home.

The inhabitants of the village of Mustraklii, dressed in bright costumes, sparkling with all the colors of rainbow and fresh flowers, decorated with embroideries, ribbons and belts, loved to sing and play musical instruments. They turned out to be good-natured and gentle; they received the new settlers in a friendly way, giving them all possible assistance.

Chapter 44
Cheta Hristo Botev

The last day of July 1924 came. Between the village of Bukovo and Voden on a high hill overgrown with dense forest there was a lawn-terrace, surrounded on all sides by thickets of bushes and trees. At the edge of the hill huge stones protruded from the ground, on which the hajduks were sitting. From this point a view down to the approach to the hill opened, to which a winding goat-path led. They were scanning the area.

"He is coming," Kolyu Trendofilov informed his companions, and everyone saw in a distance a lonely figure of a man, approaching from the side of the village of Bukovo the hill, on top of which they were.

"I've finally decided, I agree," Mityu Ganev answered.

"Why to drag this out? We must give them the answer. I agree," Ivan Ignatov said.

"I am like you," Kolyu Trendofilov supported his friends.

"Where shall I go without you? Of course, I am with you!" Rusi Stoyanov answered.

"Well, I decided long ago, I believe this is our destiny," Todor confirmed his word, "but you must understand that from the moment we answer them yes, we'll cease to exist."

"How is it?" Ivan Ignatov did not understand.

"It goes without saying, how can't you understand!" Mityu Ganev got angry.

"This means that from the moment we give them a positive answer, we'll cease to exist as the cheta of Todorov-Ganev-Ignatov. Our cheta stops the activities on this as a free, independent cheta of free rebellious hajduks, who challenged their foes. With responding them yes, we'll become a part of their organization and submit to their leadership. So, enjoy the freedom in the remaining minutes, until he climbs up the hill to us!"

"Actually, freedom is the main thing for me!" Mityu Ganev sighed.

"Well, the decision is yours," Todor answered.

"I am with you, friends! Where will Mityu Ganev go without you! And we really did have fun, there'll be something to remember, isn't that right!"

"One day we'll tell our children and grandchildren about it," Todor smiled.

"Yes, if we survive," Kolyu sighed.

The companions began to recall their brilliant actions and laughed merrily, interrupting each other with the question: "Do you remember?" Todor rejoiced especially having cruelly avenged his mortal foes. The foes wished for his death, he miraculously survived and punished them.

The man approached the hill, climbed up the goat's path and went out on the glade-terrace, where the hajduks were waiting for him. A middle-aged man appeared before them of pleasant appearance, clean shaven, in civilian clothes, on whose belt a hidden revolver was visible.

"Greetings, comrades! I am Dobri Zhelev," he told them.

"Welcome! We somehow met long ago," Mityu Ganev recalled.

"Yes. The world is small," Todor confirmed.

"Comrades, Dimitar Zahariev, the Haskovo District Communist Party Committee, instructed me to convoy to you again our common proposal to take our side in the fight against the fascists, to join us and join the Hristo Botev cheta. All of us are asking for this; the Hristo Botev cheta fighters, all our leadership, and the leadership of the BCP at the head of Georgy Dimitrov and Vasil Kolarov, as well as the leadership of the Agrarian Union. As for me, I myself am a member of the Agrarian Union of Alexander Stamboliysky, brutally tortured, as you know, by the fascists. And our cheta is a combat group of the United Front of the BCP and BANU; it also includes non-partisans. The United Front of Communists and Agrarians is preparing a new armed uprising against the fascist junta, that occupied our country, with the aim to overthrow the ruling regime of the monarchy and establish a republic with the workers' and peasants' government. All of us and our leadership of the BCP and BANU express to you our admiration of you courage, fearlessness, audacity and talent, with which you carried out your actions against your foes, and especially of your refusal the proposal of the tsar and Tsankov, from all the blessings they promised you in exchange for your honor. You refused the amnesty and big money and did not take the side of the butchers with their plans to destroy the cheta of Hristo Botev. All already are trumpeting this, the people is singing new songs about you. I'll not hide: we even envy your fame, but we envy in a good way, and we are all interested that such brave and fearless, experienced fighters with enemies, strong and courageous, join our cheta of Hristo Botev. But, remember, the tsar Boris III with Tsankov offered you amnesty, money and benefits in return for betrayal, but we not only don't offer you any benefits, but on contrary, we offer you hardships and adversity. Having joined our cheta, you'll be persecuted by the so-called authorities the same like us. You'll be driven and persecuted even more than before, and you'll be even more outlawed. You know that since April 4 of this year, the BCP has been outlawed. Although, the Agrarian Union has not been outlawed and it is the only legally existing opposition to the regime, it has been also crushed even more than the BCP, since all their leaders have been brutally tortured and killed, so having joined our ranks, you'll be even more outside the law than before. And only an armed uprising and overthrow of the fascist junta of the tsar Boris III and Tsankov can change the situation. I, our fighters from the cheta Hristo Botev, our leadership of the both parties, Communists and Agrarians, we ask you: 'Are you with us?' We know that Georgy Pilashev has been negotiating with you yet since winter, and he is counting on your agreement. Friends, are you with us?"

"Yes, I am with you, I decided it long ago," Todor answered.

"I've decided, yes, I am with you," Mityu Ganev said.

"I also agree," Kolyu Trendofilov said.

"Yes," Rusi Stoyanov uttered.

"Yes," Mityu Panev responded.

Excited, everyone shook hands with Dobri Zhelev, whose eyes became wet from emotions.

"Thanks, friends, I was not mistaken about you! Then we meet the day after tomorrow, on August 2. Let's no waste time! Come the day after tomorrow, on August 2, to Bukovsky Balkan."

"We'll come!"

"The United Front of the Agrarians and Communists has also organized other chetas in other regions and districts, we ask you, we suggest you to divide your cheta into 2 parts: Todor Todorov, Mityu Ganev and Ivan Ignatov will join the cheta Hristo Botev, which will act in the east, and Mityu Panev, Kolyu

Trendofilov and Rusi Stoyanov will join another cheta that will operate in the west. They'll be there to serve as an example of fearlessness and courage for others and share their experience of guerrilla warfare."

The companions looked at each other and nodded their heads.

"We agree," Todor answered, "yes, and also tell your leadership that we accept Georgy Pilashev's proposal and join the BCP."

"Wonderful!" Dobri Zhelev exclaimed. "Then, we'll organize along with your entry into the Hristo Botev cheta your entry into the BCP. See you on August 2!"

"See you!"

Dobri Zhelev hurried down the hill, where his horse was waiting for him, which carried his rider to the village of Tatarevo, near which the detachment of Hristo Botev was camped at that time. By relay the hajduks' decision was conveyed to the communist Dobri Delchev from the cheta, and he immediately went with it to Haskovo to the safe house of the District Committee of the BCP and conveyed the message to the secretary Dimitar Zahariev. The commander of the Hristo Botev cheta Radyu Delchev and his deputy Yanko Pavlitov also arrived there. A general decision was made to accept the hajduks into the Hristo Botev cheta according to all the rules of admitting to the cheta and at the same time to accept them into the BCP. The next day the communist Dobri Delchev led the cheta Hristo Botev from the village of Tatarevo, where they were camping, through the village of Bryastovo to the Bukovsky Balkan. They camped there on August 2, 1924 and began to wait for the hajduks.

On August 2, 6 young men emerged before them, whom the entire Bulgaria was buzzing about. It was Todor Todorov, perhaps the most handsome young man in Bulgaria: tall, slender, strong, with a beautiful oval of the face and chiseled sculpted features, burning black eyes and lush, shoulder-length parted hair. It was Ivan Ignatov, a tall hero with broad shoulders, ruby cheeks on the white handsome face and lush dark hair. It was Mityu Ganev, small in stature with a beautiful feminine type of face, with dark blond hair below his shoulders. It was Kolyu Trendofilov, a hero, a merry fellow, a handsome man, a bit like Ivan Ignatov. It was Rusi Stoyanov, of medium height, black-eyed, snub-nosed with full lips and lush dark hair. It was Mityu Panev, tall, thin, interesting young fellow with aquiline nose and piercing gaze. All were armed from head to toe.

The fighters of the cheta Hristo Botev, their leadership and numerous faithful yataks from different villages were looking at the legendary cheta with admiration and began to applaud loudly, greeting them. And the later, beautiful and proud, independent and free, courageous and fearless, who had challenged their foes and the entire system, were standing under the applause and admiring glances of the audience like idols before the fans and, embarrassed, were silent and smiled. With a special force they felt themselves needed by these people, who just as they fought against their common enemy. Not for a moment they regretted their decision to join them and were convinced of the rightness of their cause and the correctness of their choice finally.

A 27-year-old man of medium height, strong built, broad-shouldered with a pleasant face approached them and introduced himself, greeting the arrived guests.

"Hello, comrades! Welcome! I am the Voevoda of the Hristo Botev cheta, Radyu Delchev. I am very glad to welcome you here with us!"

He shook hands with each of them and introduced each to the audience, although they needed no introduction. He addressed everyone.

"Friends, in front of you are the legendary boys: Todor Todorov, Mityu Ganev, Ivan Ignatov and their friends, whom you have heard so much about and whom the people of Bulgaria sing songs about. These are 6 young men, the courage, fearlessness, talent to fight with the enemy and accuracy of shooting of which the people create legends about."

To the obvious delight of Todor and his friends the audience applauded again.

"Comrades," the Voevoda continued, "all of you know that the tsar Boris III and his henchman Tsankov offered them amnesty and a huge reward, if they go over to their side of evil, to the side of the butchers and murderers of the Bulgarian people and help the fascist authorities to destroy us, the cheta of the United Front Hristo Botev. But, as you know, they refused!"

An explosion of applause again interrupted the Voevoda, and after waiting them to subside, he continued:

"Well, friends, now you are seeing them in front of you, because they accepted our offer to join our ranks."

The Voevoda again waited until the audience applauded continued:

"Our leadership decided to accept Todor Todorov, Mityu Ganev and Ivan Ignatov in the Hristo Botev cheta and send 3 of their friends to another our detachment, operating in the western region; let them share their experience with our comrades. So, we've gathered here today to accept Todor Todorov, Mityu Ganev and Ivan Ignatov in our ranks."

Todor, Mityu and Ivan separated from their 3 friends and took a couple of steps forward, approached Ivan Velev, who was holding the banner of the cheta in his hands. The banner was of red color, on one side of it there was the inscription: "Haskovo District Cheta Hristo Botev" and on the other side there was a hammer and sickle, sparkled with the words: "Freedom or Death!"

"Let's take an oath, friends!" Voevoda Radyu Delchev addressed them: "Entering the United Front of Communists and Agrarians cheta Hristo Botev, I swear to be worthy disciple of Hristo Botev, revolutionary and fighter for freedom of the Bulgarian people, in order to fight to the end against the current bloody fascist government, which has seized power in Bulgaria on June 9, 1923 in a predatory way, for the liberation of the Bulgarian workers and peasants! I swear to be faithful to the Hristo Botev cheta, my comrades in struggle, to observe discipline and carry out the order of the Voevoda and higher leaders of the Agrarian Union and BCP! I swear to serve the people of Bulgaria and my fatherland for the benefits of the working people until the end of my revolutionary life!"

Voevoda Radyu Delchev pronounced the oath, and Todor, Mityu and Ivan repeated after him. After that they became the members of the cheta Hristo Botev. A joyful feeling swept through their entire being, and they became embarrassed, feeling their eyes wet. All the audience was sincerely touched and applauded again with joy that the legendary boys became a part of their cheta, and they themselves seemed to join the legend about them, and now they'll fight shoulder to shoulder with them against their common foe. Georgy Pilashev approached the new fighters of the cheta Hristo Botev and shook hands with them, then asked:

"Have you made a decision?"

"Yes, we have decided. Let's not postpone and proceed to 2 rites of acceptation, as the consent of the leadership has been received. Comrades, our legendary fighters have decided to join the BCP!" Georgy Pilashev addressed the audience.

He pronounced the oath, which Todor, Mityu and Ivan repeated after him and then one after another approached Ivan Velev, who was holding the banner, and raised the edge of the banner to their lips. A secretary, sitting on a large stone with a notebook and pencil in his hands, wrote down everything that was happening. Georgy Pilashev congratulated 3 friends on joining the BCP. Todor, Mityu and Ivan became the Communists.

"At ease!" Voevoda commanded, and all the chetniks flocked around 3 celebrities, hugging them and shaking their hands.

"This is Mityu Ganev, famous one that everyone knows about," Todor introduced his friend to all, who no less than others experienced a storm of joy and excitement feelings.

"Everyone knew Mityu Ganev even earlier than you and me, Todor," Ivan Ignatov said smiling, "he became famous rebel, when you and I were respectable citizens yet and peacefully grazed our flocks and worked in our fields, and his name already thundered all over Bulgaria!"

Everybody burst into laughing, shaking hands with Mityu Ganev and the later, happy from the attention to his personality, felt himself at the pinnacle of bliss. Small in stature, with a famine type of face, born in a large family with 3 brothers and a sister, having lost his father at the age of 11 and his mother at 13, from childhood he was forced to bend his back to the chorbadzhiis instead of studding, barely literate and not at all aware of a good attitude toward himself since childhood, beaten with sticks in the public station according to the vilifying slander of a chorbadzhii about allegedly stolen watermelon, Mityu Ganev was filled with anger and hatred to his offenders and a passionate desire for revenge on them and the others like them. Proud and conceited, ready to shoot for somebody's mocking of him, brave and daring, who did not know a feeling of fear, semiliterate, but smart with a heightened sense of his own dignity, Mityu Ganev was blissful, shaking hands with the soldiers of the Hristo Botev cheta and felt their respect to himself and their sincere admiration.

All shook hands with the other 3 friends: Mityu Panev, Rusi Stoyanov and Kolyu Trendofilov.

"Tomorrow we'll transfer you to the west to our other detachment, there too we need bold, fearless fighters with experience in guerrilla warfare," Voevoda told them.

"Well, we agree," 3 friends sighed sadly.

"Don't worry, we'll see you again, we'll fight together again!" Todor promised them.

"And now, boys, have lunch, it's a break!"

All together orderly, everyone knowing what to do, hurried to prepare a common meal, and soon on a glade surrounded by trees and bushes on the pinnacle of the Bukovsky Balkan mountain a lamb was roasted on a spit on a fire, emitting an unbearable desirable aroma for the hungry stomachs of the young men; several pieces of tarpaulin were laid out on the grass, around which, having prepared everything, everyone present sat down, except for one sentry, who according to the law of partisan struggle, was standing at the edge of the mountain, from which a view down on several km opened, and vigilantly scanned all the approaches to their secret place. Everything around was calm. Everyone received a piece of bread, cheese and baked lamb with vegetables, and a merry common meal began. Everyone had fun in his heart. Todor, Mityu and Ivan rejoiced at their choice to enter the BCP and Hristo Botev cheta, rejoiced, recalling their own daring actions that brought them fame throughout the country, they rejoiced at the perfect vengeance on their foes. Their 3 friends were glad that they were sent to another cheta to exchange experience, as they valued their experience, though they felt sad to part. And the warriors of the cheta rejoiced at the entry into their ranks of 3 boys, whose fame thundered throughout Bulgaria, who were unrivaled in audacity and accuracy of shooting.

They also rejoiced at the brilliant operations they themselves had just staged and shared their memories of them with the friends.

"You are great!" Mityu Ganev exclaimed. "You've campaigned right under the very nose of the Haskovo policemen! Ha-ha-ha!"

"Do you think, we've just come here empty-handed to accept you in our cheta? The day before yesterday, July 31, we just made this action to show you that we are not worse than you are!" Scheryu Atanasov declared cheerfully.

All laughed.

"But the most joyful thing is that the pursuers, when we had already disappeared, in confusion began to shoot at each other!"

"I wish it would always be like that!" Voevoda Delchev exclaimed, and everybody burst into laughing, cheerfully eating a baked lamb.

"Imagine: in 4 km from Haskovo, which is teaming with policemen, in broad daylight we detained 150 travelers on the highway between Haskovo and Konush. We escorted all of them to a glade in an oak forest near the highway. The banner of our cheta was placed there, on the glade we put them around our banner and kept there for 5 hours: from 9 am till 2 pm, waiting until more travelers approached, until 150 people were gathered. We allowed them to sit on the grass, but first, we rummaged them and took away the revolvers and knives only."

"You should've also taken the money!" Mityu Ganev exclaimed with annoyance, and all burst into laughing.

"Don't worry, Mityu, we've taken money from the tax collector and the butchers in the village of Momkovo 2 weeks ago. The most part of the money we gave to the party leadership to prepare a new uprising. And the day before yesterday, July 31, we had a different goal: information and agitation. All of our detainers, 150 people, first were shocked and trembled with fear, when they saw in front of them armed people in the new hajduk's clothes, similar to that one in which the rebels were dressed on Ilyin Day 20 years ago. By the way, these clothes were sewn for us by one tailor, our man, from the village of Lyubimets; our boss Dobri Terpeshev found him for us."

"It's a beautiful uniform!" Ivan Ignatov praised.

"We'll take your measurements, and he will sew an additional uniform for you, and we'll be all the same, all the fighters of the same cheta."

"Good!"

"So, the detained saw the chetniks, the young men in front of them with weapons, in beautiful uniform, shod in cervulis with belts on snow-white windings on their shins, girded with belts, to which daggers and grenades were attached with cartridges, and trembled with fear, expecting attack on themselves. And I told them: 'Do not be afraid, citizens, we are not the highwaymen as the tsar-Tsankov junta introduces us, we are the fighters of the Hristo Botev detachment, and I, the Voevoda of the cheta, am addressing you. We, Communists and Agrarians, as well as non-partisans, continue to fight against the gang of criminals, which illegally seized power in Bulgaria on June 9, last year, brutally tortured Prime Minister Alexander Stamboliysky and imposed hell on the land of Bulgaria. Since no rallies, meeting and demonstrations are possible, because of the fascist terror, we are forced to resort to this form of detaining you in order to convey our word to you. Know and tell the others that we, Communists and Agrarians, as well as non-partisans, are still acting as the United Front in the struggle against the fascist junta, we have not laid down our arms, but continue to struggle to overthrow that junta. Our cheta is political one and we are waging a political struggle, and victory will be ours! On behalf of the cheta, I apologize to you all for the detention! You are free!' Some were not even in a hurry to disperse, they wanted to listen more."

"Well done!" Todor exclaimed.

"You are also brave!" Mityu Ganev praised. "Under the nose of the Haskovo policemen you did it!"

"I think, we'll work well together," Ivan Ignatov said with a smile.

"But the funniest thing was later, when we let all the people go and disappeared ourselves, the policemen and gang of volunteers raided to this place from different sides, those who for a reward are looking for us under every bush, the same like for you. So, in confusion, they got everything mixed up and began randomly firing at each other."

Everyone laughed, and Todor remarked:

"For us, by the way, they promised more rewards."

"We do not mind," Voevoda Radyu Delchev agreed, "but now the reward for us will be increased, after we have united with you."

"It's only because of us!"

Young people, handsome, proud, noble, young warriors, the youngest of whom was 18 years old, who did not bend under the totalitarian power yoke and challenged it, brave, courageous, fearless, loyal to each other and to the idea, for which they fought, now, on August 2, 1924, arranged a small holiday for themselves and rested. They celebrated the entry of the legendary trio into their detachment, which marked a qualitatively new character of their cheta for the further struggle against the fascist butchers; they celebrated their small victories in recent daring actions that resonated throughout the country. They were sitting on the pinnacle, on which a delicious lamb was fried, ate it with bread and cheese, received from the yataks, and drank the water from their baklagas. They shared with each other the reminiscences of the past weekdays and sang old hajduks songs, glorifying the heroic struggle of the brave men against the enslavers.

"You haven't yet heard how Todor sings!" Ivan Ignatov exclaimed, and everyone immediately asked for confirmation of this.

"Todor, sing!"

Todor stood up and began to sing in full voice a hajduks song, and his voice of unprecedented beauty and strength, worth of a stage, echoed over the peaks of the mountains of the Bukovsky Balkan, reflecting from the peaks of Dragoina, Aida and Sakar Planina, awaking to life the heroic spirit of struggle and exploit of hajduks in the recent past and in the mists of time. And the same like in the past centuries, now Rhodopes have again opened their arms to handsome young men, with weapons in their hands risen to fight the fascist junta of usurpers. The Rhodopes, Dragoyna, Aida, Sakar Planina sheltered the folk heroes, provided them with their forests, caves for hiding place. Todor's voice penetrated to the depth of the young warriors' hearts, and they were listening and looked at him with admiration; their new comrade was standing in front of them, comrade-in-arms, perhaps, the most beautiful young man in Bulgaria, tall, slender, strong, with chiseled features, as if carved by a sculptor, with a piercing gaze of black eyes, like a symbol of struggle for freedom. Todor finished singing the hajduks song, and all applauded, happy with the historical event that took place today, August 2, 1924.

"You haven't yet heard how our Mityu reads the Hristo Botev's poems!" Ivan Ignatov, contented, said.

Everyone applauded in advance, inviting Mityu to speak. Not at all embarrassed, Mityu Ganev stood in front of the detachment and with a burning feeling read Hristo Botev's "Hadji Dimitar," which he learned orally by heart, when he heard the poem from Todor. Everyone applauded and almost shed a tear. Today was a joyful day for everyone: it was a day of rest for all. The Hristo Botev cheta had rest on the glade on the Bukovsky Balkan pinnacle under a clear sky and hot sun among the aroma of herbs and flowers, around like walls surrounding fortress, there was a green forest and reliably covered them from the enemies invasion, and the sentry vigilantly scanned from the top of the cliff the whole area below. Everything was calm. The villages of Voden and Bukovo lay below. When the sun began to roll to the west, moving further and further away from them, the cheta packed their things and set off. They walked along the goat-path, now going down, now going up through the thickets of bushes and dense forest and came to a small terrace on the pinnacle of the mountain, on which, hidden from prying eyes, was the entrance into the cave. In single file, one by one, they entered the cave, large enough to accommodate the entire squad, where the mattresses with straw had been placed in advance.

"This is one of our bases," Radyu Delchev explained to the new guests.

"We also have several like this," Todor replied.

"Make yourself at home for the night, tomorrow we are on the road!"

***

Having slept and rested the day before, the next morning the entire cheta was ready to set off. They descended from the mountain, where one of their cave-bases was, went to a glade on another hill, overgrown with forest, for training. Todor, Mityu and Ivan immediately hugged and parted with their 3 friends: Mityu Panev, Rusi Stoyanov and Kolyu Trendofilov, whom the courier escorted to another cheta to the west in the Plovdiv region.

"We'll meet again!"

"We'll win!"

"We do not farewell, see you soon!"

The Voevoda Radyu Delchev held the meeting and political information.

"Friends, warriors, let's bring our 3 new comrades up to date, although we've been negotiating with them since the winter, we told them a lot, they know much, but we'll clarify the details."

"First, there are 24 people in our cheta with the newly arrived fighters. To increase mobility, speed, ease and safety of passing, as well transitions from one place to another, as well as to facilitate the supply of food and quartering in the yataks' houses, especially with the onset of the cold weather, as well as to cover the territory of actions simultaneously in different areas in order to disorient the enemy, we divide our cheta into 2 parts for 12 people in each part. I, Radyu Mitev Delchev, your Voevoda, remain the Voevoda of the entire cheta and the Voevoda of the I detachment. You, Todor, will be my confident. So, Todor, by the father Ivanov, by the surname Todorov, by the linage name Karagochev, is my confident. Mityu Ganev-Armanov is appointed the commander of the II detachment. Mityu, by his father Ganev, by the surname Armanov, is the Voevoda of the II detachment."

"Second, each detachment is divided into 2 parts by 6 people in each. Our detachment is divided into 2 groups: there are 6 people in the I group. Our political commissar is Yanko Kuzmov Pavlitov, our standard-bearer is Ivan Velev. In the II group of our detachment the commander is Todor Todorov, political commissar is Scheryu Atanasov Tanev, and standard-bearer is Dimitar Ivanov Chirpanliata."

"The II detachment of the cheta is also divided into 2 groups by 6 people. In the I group of the II detachment Mityu Ganev-Armanov remains the commander, the political commissar is Georgy Slavov Neleza, and the standard-bearer is Ivan Ignatov Mitev."

"Mityu Ganev-Armanov remains the commander of the II group of the II detachment. The political commissar is Atanas Georgiev Zapryanov (Davkata), and the standard-bearer is Atanas Ivanov Meshkov."

"The remaining 12 people are distributed by 3 persons in each group. Yanko Kuzmov Pavlitov is our new chief of the BCP District Committee, and our main political leader of the BCP District Committee and military instructor is Georgy Pilashev (Daskala)."

All applauded, and the appointed commanders of the groups and under-Voevoda Mityu Ganev-Armanov was especially excited. For the first time in his life, Mityu Ganev felt unprecedented respect for himself and was ready to shed a tear, but with an effort, he restrained himself. Voevoda continued:

"Comrades, this division of our cheta Hristo Botev into the detachments and groups is conditional, and we'll regroup people or divide the Six in Triples, depending on the circumstances and tasks. And also the combat core of our cheta will always be headed by Todor Todorov, Mityu Ganev and Ivan Ignatov, but for now we'll stick to the division of the cheta in according with the way I told you."

"Further, as you know, our cheta did not appear by chance and does not act by itself. After June 1923, the BCP strongly condemned the betrayal of the certain members of its leaders about so-called 'neutrality' and the betrayal of the BANU and its leader Alexander Stamboliysky and founded the United Front with the Agrarian Union against the common enemy. And after the uprising in September, when the both our parties were defeated and suffered heavy losses, the United Front did not bow his head, did not surrender, did not lay down its arms, but headed for a new apprising."

"This is what the people of Bulgaria should know about, this is why our cheta Hristo Botev was created together with other cheats in all the district centers of the country. The activity purpose of our cheta is the political enlightenment of the people. Remember, it is not you, beautiful young warriors, brave and daring, skillful and fearless, who will liberate the people from the fascist tyranny of the criminal gang of murderers and thieves, who illegally seized power in our country on June 9, 1923! You are too few for that! The people himself will liberate himself! That's why you are here: to prepare and arm the people. That's why you will sneak into the villages of southern Bulgaria, rally the people and prepare him for the upcoming struggle; you'll hold secret meetings in the villages to inform the peasants about what's happening and that the uprising is coming."

"In the current conditions of lawlessness and terror of the fascist junta, when any word of truth is forbidden and total censorship reigns, when all the rights of citizens are violated and rallies and meetings are prohibited, you, the fighters of the cheta Hristo Botev, will be the connecting thread between the villagers and the United Front, you will carry them a living word and hope of the coming struggle, for which they must be ready. You will deliver to them illegal literature, so that they could distribute it among themselves."

"You will gather the villagers around the United Front and form the conditional groups by 6 people from them, let's call them militia-6, which will be ready to come out at the right time, having received a signal. To do this, you will collect the weapons and hide them in a secret place and train the peasants in the tactics of militant combat. You must act secretly, covertly and carefully, strictly observing conspiracy. Remember, our foes, the enemy of mankind, are traitors and rats, whom Bulgaria is teaming with! Beware of the scoundrels, do not make contact with strangers, but work only with the faithful yataks! Well, if you are hunted down and betrayed, and you are pursued, only then take the fight with the foe in order to retreat safely! Otherwise, avoid armed confrontation with the enemies, avoid skirmishes, leave quickly and quietly, engage in combat only as a last resort!"

"The actions need to be carefully designed to be successful and we'll plan each action with the help of our political and military leader Georgy Pilashev. All the appointed groups' commanders will develop action plans together with Pilashev."

"And also, our main task is agitation among the soldiers, penetration into the barracks for this purpose, political education of the soldiers, preparing them, so that they do not shoot at the people, but at the right time turn their bayonets against the criminals, who have illegally seized power in Bulgaria. Our task is to found the revolutionary military cores among the soldiers by means of agitation and to distribute among them the Bulletin of BCP and the 'Voinsky Glas'."

"In a word, summing up everything I've said: our main task is to help the United Front to prepare the masses for the armed uprising to overthrow the fascist junta of the tsar Boris-Tsankov and establish the workers' and peasants' government. Any questions?"

"There is a question: when will the uprising be?"

"When everything is ready for the uprising, and when everything is ready, you'll know about it. And when the day of the uprising comes, each of you will become a commander of a detachment of the revolution army. Your task is to prepare the army of resistance of the villagers for the beginning of the uprising and lead it as unit commanders. And now, let's proceed to our physical training. You, the militants of the Hristo Botev cheta, must be physically trained, you must be strong, dexterous, hardy and excellent shooters. Mityu Ganev will train you how to shoot accurately, and Todor will teach you hand-to-hand combat, they say you are the best."

"You never know what they say about you!"

"Come on, don't be modest, show us the master class!"

The militants of the cheta, having removed all the ammunition, began physical training on the pinnacle of the mountain, fenced with forest, preparing themselves for the upcoming battles. 3 friends, newly entered the cheta, were especially happy. They felt that a new stage had begun in their lives, a new and higher stage in their struggle with the hated enemy: now they'll fight the common foe for all the honest people of Bulgaria for freedom of the people, for the freedom of their country against the criminal gang of bandits, who illegally seized power in the country and exterminated all the best, what was in Bulgaria. All the other chetniks with their leadership were happy to join with the legendary triple.

Todor showed the comrades the hand-to-hand combat techniques, deftly dodging the blows in front of the astonished audience: it seemed, having overcome the force of gravity, he took off and instantly transferred over the overthrown adversary to take the right position to repel the blow.

Mityu Ganev demonstrated how to hit the target at a distance of 80 m, but no one could ever compare with him in terms of shooting accuracy.

The hero and strongman Ivan Ignatov deftly repulsed the attacks of several conditional opponents, scattering them at once on the soft grass in different directions.

3 friends felt in the depth of their hearts that a sincere friendship between them with all the Hristo Botev cheta members arose from the very first moment they joined the detachment and is growing stronger every moment for their forthcoming joint struggle shoulder to shoulder with a common enemy. The

political and military leader of the cheta Georgy Pilashev was sincerely happy with the results of his work, since he knew that it was his merit.

Chapter 45
Fight on the Pinnacle of Chala

Having rested and completed training on the peaks of the Bukovsky Balkan mountains, the Hristo Botev cheta with new members set off toward the southeast, fulfilling their mission of the United Front, and 4 groups with 6 people, bypassing Bryastovo and Miniralny Bani from the south, having appointed a meeting place at the peak of Chala near the villages of Dolno Botevo after completing the mission, dispersed in different directions toward the villages of Malak Izvor, Golyam Izvor, Tsareva Polyana and Bolyarsky Izvor to gather the villagers in the houses of the yataks, to form among them militia-6 for the upcoming struggle of all who wish to fight against the common enemy together with the United Front.

The group commander Todor Todorov led his 5 chetniks to the village of Bolyarsky Izvor. Bypassing settlements, and crowded roads, the chetniks made their way secretly, bypassing hills and ravines, securely hiding behind the green foliage of the bushes and trees. The detachment was led by the conductor Sava Kyzev, who knew this area from childhood, and therefore indicated to his friends the exact and safe hidden path.

Located in lower reaches at the foot of the Rhodopes Bolyarsky Izvor, after a long journey through the mountains and forests, finally appeared before them. The house of Bay Latyu Kuzev, the cheta's faithful yatak, opened its door to them.

"Dimitar, stay on guard!" Todor commanded and led his people into the house.

"Father! Rusi! How are you?" Sava Kuzev hugged his father and brother, who met the chetniks at the door.

"Son, are you all right, thank god!" Bay Latyu Kuzev hugged his son and cradled his head in his bosom, stroking his hair. "Where is Kuzi? Is he all right?"

"Do not worry, father, Kuzi is fine, he is in another detachment in the group of Mityu Ganev. The Voevoda and the leadership split our cheta into the Sixes to carry out the operational tasks. Brother, how are you?"

"I am fine, I am agitating the people," Rusi answered, pleased that he helped.

"Father, this is our Six, and this is our new Voevoda Todor Todorov, he and his 2 friends have joined our cheta, and his 3 friends are in another group."

Todor extended his hand, and Bay Latyu Kuzev with his son Rusi shook it hard.

"That one?" Bay Latyu asked, smiling. "Those same 3 friends?"

"Probably," Todor answered, "but now we are an integral part of the Hristo Botev cheta, and I am the commander of this group, and we are with you on the instructions of the United Front."

"Come in, friends, make yourself at home!" Bay Latyu said and led the group through the entry to a specious living room of his 2-story house and immediately seated them at a long table, set for dinner. 6 chetniks, who once left their houses and wandered through the caves, mountains and forests, now after a long journey, tired and hungry, were stunned with delight on seeing a laid table in a hospitable house, but for the sake of appearance Todor, embarrassed by the generosity of the host, still asked:

"Maybe, the business first?"

"We'll proceed to business after dinner," Bay Latyu answered, "respire after the passing first and have dinner."

The chetniks did not wait to be asked twice, but sat down at the table and preceded to dinner.

"Feel at home," Sava encouraged his friends, "this is my home."

The cozy, clean, spacious and hospitable house of the Kuzev family, the table set with everything that the fertile land of Bulgaria can bestow on harvesters in the month of August, filled the hearts of Todor's friends with warmth of the hearth and longing for the lost home. They firmly knew and believed that they could return their home only by overthrowing the hatred regime. And the thought that his own house is now empty and sealed in Bodrovo and his entire family is wandering in exile in remote lands stabbed with a dagger into his heart with pain and caused a new explosion of hatred and anger in him.

The chetniks devoured with appetite the treats gathered in the field by Bay Latyu, and the latter said:

"You eat and rest, and I'll go to bring our people."

"Are you sure about them?" Todor asked.

"Absolutely, as in myself!"

Bay Latyu hid behind the door, his son Rusi was standing on guard at the gate, and the chetniks enjoyed rare moment of relaxation and home comfort.

"How good is to be at home and to dine at the table!" Sava Kuzev signed.

"Soon we'll be at home, some more time, and we'll overthrow the fascist power and return home," Scheryu Atanasov exclaimed.

"It would be good," Todor said.

All of them believed that it would be so and were eager to bring this moment closer. After some time Bay Latyu returned home and brought 8 people with him, armed from head to toe. The chetniks were on the alert and vigilantly scanned what was happening. Everything was calm and went on as usual. Bay Latyu reported:

"My son Rusi is on duty at the gate, and 2 of our people are put on guard on the main road from different sides, there is a wide view there."

Todor nodded his head in approval, Latyu introduced his people. They took turns shaking hands with the chetniks and giving their names, adding BANU, or BCP, or non-partisan. Todor ordered.

"Sava, Yordan, you know your village and your people well, check the situation and replace 2 sentries at the post, they should be here."

"We'll do it," answered Sava Kuzev and Yordan Zhekov, who also was from Bolyarsky Izvor, and disappeared behind the door.

While waiting for 2 sentries, Latyu introduced in detail his fellow villagers to the chetniks. Everyone sat down on a long minder-sofa standing along the wall. Soon 2 men came in and introduced themselves. Todor attentively watched the visitors, all of them were the villagers from Bolyarsky Izvor, shepherds and farmers, men from 18 to 40 years old, all of them were united by hatred to the fascist regime. He addressed them:

"Comrades, as you can guess, we are the militants of the political cheta Hristo Botev, we are one group of the cheta, we are Six people. I, Todor Todorov, am a commander. We are fulfilling the task of the command of the

United Front of the Communists and Agrarians to prepare the conditions for the new uprising with the aim to overthrow the illegal rule of Tsankov, who usurped power on June 9, 1923. All of you know very well the essence of this regime: illegal and anti-people, what misfortunes and sufferings they subjected the people of Bulgaria. How beastly they tortured Prime Minister Alexander Stamboliysky and how unsuccessful 2 previous uprisings against them were. Therefore, our task is to prepare the ground for the new uprising, a mass uprising, nation-wide uprising in all the villages and cities of Bulgaria. We must prepare a rebel army among the villagers, armed and trained, which will know what to do at the right time, when the signal for the action is received. Our tactical task is to found groups of 6 villagers in each village, let's name the militia-6, headed by a chief, who'll become a fighting nuclear in the upcoming struggle. It must be close communication and interaction between the Sixes chiefs with all the faithful yataks and with the leadership of our detachment. Latyu, you'll be the head of the first Six. Divide your people into 2 groups!"

"Me, my son Rusi, plus 4 people will make up the first Six."

Rusi stood up and counted out 4 people, who were sitting on the sofa-minder.

"Nobody minds?"

"Agreed," the men replied.

"Then, now elect the chief of the second Six," Todor said.

"Let Hristo Georgiev be, he is an Agrarian."

"Who agrees?" Todor asked.

Everyone raised their hand, choosing Hristo Georgiev as the chief of the second Six.

"Congratulations!" Todor answered and shook hands with Latyu Kuzev and Hristo Georgiev. "Comrades, you've become militants of the United Front, fighters of the struggle for freedom, which is already going on today, combatants of the uprising against tyranny, which is rising by the decision of the leadership of the United Front, when everything is ready for it. Nobody changed his mind? If anybody has changed his mind, let him leave us right now!"

Nobody moved, and the glow of faith in the rightness of their cause burned in everyone's eyes.

"Fine, then, friends, let's take an oath according to the ancient tradition of our hajduks, who once fought for freedom in Bulgaria. Unfortunately, Bulgaria never gained freedom, and we, the young people of Bulgaria, are forced to rise again to fight for it." Repeat after me:

"I, a militant of the United Front, a member of the militia-6, voluntarily and of my own free will take path of fighting for freedom of the people of Bulgaria from illegal fascist power and swear to the end to be faithful to my comrades in the struggle, the Bulgarian people, and the struggle for his freedom, led by the United Front of Communists and Agrarians in alliance with all the progressive forces, joining this struggle!"

Todor was reading the oath, standing and holding a dagger in one hand and a revolver in another, crossing them in front of him. Each of the members of the newly founded Six repeated the oath after Todor and then approached Todor in turn and, according to the old hajduks tradition, kissed the crossed dagger and revolver.

"Congratulation, comrades, now you are the militants of the United Front! And now one more thing: in the atmosphere of total lie and fascist propaganda, when the opposition bulletins are destroyed and the venal journalists serve the fascist government and all the rallies and demonstrations are banned—it is important to convey the word of truth to the people. And so, we go through the forests and mountains, through the villages of Bulgaria to convey to people the information about what is really happening."

Todor took a pack file of newspapers "Rabotnichesky Vestnik" and "Zemledelchesky Vestnik" out from his bag and gave it to Latyu.

"Distribute among the villagers. And now our political commissar, Scheryu Atanasov, will say a few more words about the policy of the BCP."

Scheryu Atanasov made a speech, everyone listened attentively, inspired by the upcoming struggle. A kerosene lamp was burning on the table, and the night blackened outside the window.

"Thank you, friends!" Todor said. "And now carefully go back to your homes one by one, and tomorrow morning we'll meet on the pinnacle of the mountain south of the village, we'll do military exercises there."

The members of 2 newly formed militia-6 began to part with the chetniks and in some intervals left Latyu's house.

"We'll replace your sentries with our people, let the boys rest in the house!" Latyu said and receive the consent of Todor.

Latyu ordered 2 members of his Six, and after a while the chetniks Sava Kuzev and Yordan Zhekov entered the house. The Kuzev family prepared lodging for the night and accommodated everyone guest. Tired of the passing and full of emotions from the successfully completed task, 6 chetniks fell asleep soundly without parting with their weapons, and 3 members of the militia-6 guarded their sleep, standing on guard on both sides of the main road and at the gate of the house. A sound sleep strengthened the efforts of the young people, and in the morning at dawn they were ready to continue their journey, fulfilling the mission entrusted to them.

Latyu Kuzev fed and watered them and put food in a bag for them on the road. The chetniks thanked the hospitable hosts, 2 of whom: Sava and Kuzi were the chetniks themselves—Sava was in Todor's group, and Kuzi was in Mityu Ganev's group. Everyone left the house. The sentry from the militia-6, standing at the gate on guard, nodded to them that everything was calm. Bending down, shielded by lush green bushes, the chetniks safely slipped out of Bolyarsky Izvor and began to climb to the top of the mountain south of the village in the foothills of Rhodopes. Sava Kuzev, who had known this area from childhood, was going ahead of them and now pointed the chetniks which goat-path to turn and which pit or stone to bypass. Sheltering the cheta bushes and trees bloomed luxuriantly under the glowing sun in the crystal clear sky of Bulgaria in the last month of the summer of 1924.

Todor's group climbed to the top of the mountain, from which here opened a view on Bolyarsky Izvor and the road from it. On a glade of the mountain, covered with dense thickets of fragrant bushes with flowers, the chetniks camped and began to wait for 2 militia-6s from Bolyarsky Izvor. Soon the sentry at the post at the edge of the mountain gave a sign that the movement began, and from different parts of the village at some intervals their yesterday recruits were moving one by one to the mountain. Inspired by the example of the cheta, these handsome young men, fearless and noble, dressed in a beautiful hajduks uniform, who defended freedom with weapons in their hands, the villagers of Bolyarsky Izvor were eager to follow their example, became their support in the village and rise up at the right time to fight against the hatred regime of Boris III-Tsankov together with them. When all 12 people were at place, the training began. Todor turned to them:

"Comrades, as we have informed you, we are waiting for a signal from the United Front leadership to start the uprising, but for now, we'll prepare for it!

At the moment the uprising begins, you'll have to take the kmet's building, raise 2 fags over it: red and orange, capture and arrest the kmet, only if he is not our supporter, because there are many kmets, who are our yataks, helping us; you must know the political situation in your village and know who is who. If the kmet is a fascist, arrest him and put him under lock and key, and together with him—his henchmen, watchmen, police agents and counter-chetniks, if there are any in the village. Place guards over them and wait for the further orders."

"Having received the signal from our people to advance, you move out of the village with weapons in your hands and move toward Haskovo to join the rebel army to connect with other groups of Sixes from other villages in order to take Haskovo garrison, police and community. There are our supporters in the garrisons among the officers, they are working among the soldiers. We count on them. All of you must be brave, strong, physically trained, master the skill of hand-to-hand combat and professionally use the weapons. Who fought in the Great War?"

Half of the men raised their hands.

"It is clear that half did not fight due to their age. Who has a weapon?"

Half the men raised their hands.

"Clearly, our task is to provide you with weapons and teach you how to use them. Split into 2 groups. Who did not fight in the last war, come up to Scheryu Atanasov, although he himself did not fight because of his age, but he has a good command of the weapons, and he'll teach you how to assemble, disassemble and clean a revolver. With the others, we'll train in hand-to-hand combat."

2 militia-6s with the chiefs at the head were split into groups, and the training began. Soft green grass in the glade on the top on the mountain served them as a soft carpet, on which the chetniks showed the villagers the hand-to-hand combat technique, and next to them the bolts of the revolvers clicked, and the villagers learned to disassemble, clean and assemble military weapons. Both young boys and mature men were training, studying, restored their physical form and, inspired by the lofty idea, prepared to defend their lives with weapons in their hands from the hated gang of bandits that had seized Bulgaria. When the sun rose to its zenith and feeling of hunger made itself felt, all sat down on the grass, lay rugs, and the villagers took food out of their bags. The common meal even more united yesterday strangers; they all became a

part of a single whole, fighters of the United Front of the common struggle against the common foe. They were eating food, shared among everyone, talked in a friendly way and told each other about themselves, about their lives and problems and felt that they were becoming each other's faithful comrade-in-arms in the already ongoing struggle. They believed they would win. When they finished the meal, they put the leftovers in the bags, crammed to the top, and handed over to the chetniks to take with them on the road. Having refreshed themselves with lunch and rested, they returned to training, which lasted until evening. When the sun began to move faster and faster to the west, with its oblique rays barely illuminating the paths in the mountains, everyone got ready and began to part.

"And one more thing, it is very important," Todor said to them at parting, "if the fascist authorities begin to form a counter-cheta from the villagers of Bolyarsky Izvor, introduce your person into it to convey information and sabotage."

"We'll do it, don't worry," Bay Latyu and Hristo Georgiev, the heads of the Sixes, ensured, "we'll be in touch!"

12 villagers and 6 chetniks parted and dispersed in different directions. The villagers descended the mountain and went north to Bolyarsky Izvor, and the chetniks, carrying bags filled with food, went south-west toward mountain Chala. There was an appointment of the entire cheta there. They descended and ascended the hills, which became higher and higher to the south, and the sky above them became darker, and the sun rolled behind the horizon. Young and handsome, brave, strong and hardy, they overcame the way in the mountains and went to the goal. Finally, the mountain Chala, heavily overgrown with forest, rose before them. By zigzags along the path they climbed to its pinnacle, where the entire cheta of Hristo Botev was waiting for them. 4 commanders of the 4 Sixes reported to Voevoda Radyu Delchev about the completion of the task.

The cheta set up a camp under the trees, where they had dinner together and fell asleep soundly under the open sky, and 2 constant sentries from 2 sides on the top of the mountain guarded their sleep. The August days in Bulgaria were clear and hot, and they thanked nature for keeping them. They spent several days in the camp under the open sky, the hot sun warmed them, barely emerging from behind the horizon in the early morning, flowering shrubs filled the air with fragrance, the forest on the slopes of the mountain covered them from outsiders with e fortress wall. The friends continued their training in the open meadow, shared their experience and told how the formation of the militia-6 went in different villages. There were not enough weapons, and not everyone had a weapon, was the general result.

"This will be our first priority: to get weapons and provide with them the militia-6s," Voevoda said.

Down on the mountain side, on a small terrace, a stream was knocked out from under the mountain, flowed, murmuring, down into the lowland, and a wild pear tree grew nearby. The chetniks went down to the stream to drink and to fill their empty baklagas. A jet of crystal clear spring water fountained out of the rock, forming a stream. They washed their faces and hands with pleasure under a stream of cool water, as if under a shower, quenching their thirst and filled the baklagas-canteens. In the midst of their enjoyment of the water procedure, 2 girls suddenly appeared from behind the bushes, who came to collect wild pears. Everyone froze in surprise, when they saw each other.

"Hello, girls! Do you know who we are?" Delchev appealed to them without waiting for an answer, he himself told them: "We are the secret police agents from the secret department. We are here on a secret mission. You must not tell anyone that you saw us here! Do you understand?"

"Yes, of course," the girls answered in chorus, devouring with their eyes the young men.

"Promise us: you won't tell anyone that you saw us here!" the Voevoda addressed them sternly.

"We promise!" the girls answered in unison, backed away and vanished in the bushes.

The mood of the chetniks immediately fell, some kind of gloomy premonition seized Todor's heart, which rarely deceived him. They constantly took risks and walked along the razor's edge in their illegal activities, struggle, passings from one place to another, and a flock of enemies hunted after them. They were accustomed to taking risks, when they met strangers, but these girls with a stupid expression of their faces seemed to Todor a bad omen. The chetniks filled their flasks with water and climbed to the top of the mountain to their camp.

"What shall we do?" Todor asked Radyu.

"Let's wait and strengthen the security. In any case, here, on the pinnacle of Chala it is a convenient place for fight."

At that time 2 girls with a stupid expression on their faces, "not involved in politics," who promised not to tell anyone what they saw at Chala, were running, stumbling, racing with each other, to report what they had seen. They reached their village and told the gossipers that the Hristo Botev cheta was on the mountain Chala, not far from them. The gossipers conveyed to the other gossipers, and soon the most active gossipers dashed to the kmet's office to report. The kmet phoned another kmet, and the latter phoned the others, and the next day the news reached its main addresser: the head of the Haskovo district. The telephone was ringing from the district administration head office to all the kmets' offices of the district with the order to form the counter-chetas and move toward Chala Mountain, which is to be surrounded, until Haskovo police arrives; urgently the pro-fascist kmets from the vicinity villages dashed to fulfill the order. And on the top of the Chala Mountain the guard reported:

"A rider is coming here!"

Everyone had already collected his things, and weapons were always ready for any development of the events. The rider was driving the poor horse, galloped to the foot of the mountain, tethered the horse and hurried up on the mountain. The sentry recognized in him one of their yataks. Out of breath from quick walk, the yatak climbed to the pinnacle of the mountain and alerted the cheta, which was already waiting by the slope.

"Leave immediately!" the messenger hastily said, panting. "Police and military detachment are moving here from Haskovo together with the counter-chetas from all the villages. We took turns, riding from Haskovo, changing horses and messengers through the villages on the way here. I am the last messenger who has brought you the news here."

"Thank you, go away!" the chetniks thanked the messenger and hastily started to descend from the Chala Mountain together with him.

They got down, went to another mountain, which stood nearby close to the village Dolno Botevo. They climbed up. A wonderful view on the neighboring mountain Chala from all sides opened from the new mountain. The fighters took up positions, ready for battle, hidden behind the protruding stones and green bushes. From the southern side of the same mountain they could leave on the contiguous mountain. The whole night passed in tension.

Early in the dawn of the next day, when the rays of the rising sun illuminated the majestic nature around, the camouflaged and invisible chetniks saw that a counter-cheta, led by their yatak, was gradually approaching the mountain Chala. And at the considerable distance from them from different sides other counter-chetas were moving in the same direction, and on the horizon there was a detachment of police and military from the north from Haskovo. The chetniks froze and, clutching their weapons, were vigilantly scanning everything from the contiguous mountain. The first counter-cheta of the fascists-volunteers approached the Chala Mountain and began hastily to climb up.

"Let's hurry, we'll grab them first, and we'll first receive the reward! They promised big money for them, living or dead!" the leader urged on the counter-cheta and, hiding, hurried up to the top.

The pro-fascists climbed up, and the leader, having hidden behind a stone ledge of the mountain, shot down with the exclamation:

"They've already gone down! Fire! We'll shoot them from here!"

At that moment another counter-cheta ran up to the foot of the mountain, and its leader commanded:

"Fire! They are up there! There they are!" and hid behind a stone below. "Let's kill them and get the reward!"

Both groups fired at each other, and at that time the other counter-chetas from the nearby villages were running up to Chala from all sides and, just in case, in order to receive a reward for the Hristo Botev cheta, also started to shoot yet from a distance at those who were on the top of the mountain and below. The police with military detachment arrived to the place, having joined the general skirmish.

The long and bloody battle lasted for a couple of hours. Bullets whistled, flying down the mountain and up the mountain and also crossed in different directions, to where only someone was, raising clouds of dust, cutting off brunches of plants and scattering small pebbles in different directions, flying straight into the forehead of the battle participants. Under friendly fire all the participants in it for the dictatorship of the fascist power died a heroic death. The son of the village Stambolovo kmet fell in the heroic battle, thirsting for the reward no less than the others. In few hours the last shot fell silent, the mountain itself and the nearby land at its foot were littered with the corpses of all the participants in the historical battle on the Chala Mountain. Then, from behind all the ledges and stones the counter-chetas leaders, the faithful Hristo Botev cheta yataks, came out, gathered all weapons from the bodies of the dead in order to hide them safely in remote koliba and waved their hands to their friends, the chetniks, who were watching everything, what was happening on a contiguous mountain. Thus the historical battle on the mountain Chala ended, which the next day was trumpeted about all over the country by all the newspapers of Bulgaria.

Chapter 46
Popovo

In the last month of the outgoing summer of 1924, everyone who expected the uprising against the tsar Boris-Tsankov regime, was looking forward the onset of autumn, waiting for the uprising. The idea of the uprising against the hated regime of the butchers and murderers hung in the air and inspired the fighters to prepare for it. Inspired by the lofty idea of liberation their country from the fascist plague, the freedom fighters despised the fear before the "Law of Defense of the State," which forbade living and breathing free, believed in their victory over the forces of evil and steadfastly endured the blows of fate. Accused fate, as usual acting on the side of evil, did not fail to deal its vile blow on the forces of good. The lack of weapons was the main obstacle to a successful uprising. The main task of the United Front Military Organization was to provide the rebels with weapons and teach them how to use it.

Meanwhile, in August of 1924, he United Front lost a huge amount of weapons for the uprising. Under the cover of the August night the motor boats and sailboats from Sevastopol, loaded with weapons, docked one after another to a remote pier near Varna. Fearless freedom fighters unloaded the boxes with weapons from the boats ashore, risking their lives every second. The crates of weapons were carried away by trucks, and the crates were securely stored in a remote warehouse. 80 out of 120 boxes were unloaded ashore, taken away and hidden in a lurking-place. A fascist-patriot tracked them down and dashed to inform the police. The police seized the weapons and rent asunder the entire underground organization for delivery, unloading, transfer and shelter of the weapons for the uprising in Varna. The fascist-patriot rubbed his hands with pleasure, though he became embittered, not having received a reward.

In the atmosphere of failures and loss of weapons in Varna, when Yugoslavia, having supplied the United Front with 1000 rifles, then changed her mind and stopped deliveries, when Czechoslovakia failed to fulfill her promise to provide the Agrarian Union with 10 thousand rifles and 200 machine-guns, when every now and then between the leadership of the Agrarian Union and BCP again and again tensions flared up about who would lead the uprising, and the uprising itself, like a beautiful dream, moved further and further toward the horizon, as you approach it, the horizon recedes, and more and more signs emerged that the uprising from the autumn of 1924 seemed to be transferred to spring of 1925—the courageous Hristo Botev cheta fighters fought their successful battles on the local front allotted to them, and challenged the fascist authorities.

Passing like on a razor's edge, risking their lives every second, ready to enter combat with enemy any moment, the chetniks of Hristo Botev walked around the villages of southern Bulgaria, recruited supporters, relying on faithful yataks, formed the militia-6 with the chiefs at the head, taught them military affairs, and all prepared for to start of the uprising. Thus, August of 1924 and half of September of upcoming autumn ended.

The nature was still raging with lush greenery. Covering the hajduks-partisans with its green foliage, the sun was still shining hot, warming with its rays, but the air already smelled with the coming autumn and difficulties, associated with the onset of the cold weather, gleamed on the horizon. The idea of rebellion: only it warmed the soul and instilled hope.

On September 17 the weather was bad: it was overcast, the gloomy sky, covered with black clouds, did not let in a single ray of light. Heavy clouds, filled with water, periodically opened up, spewing out streams of downpour, after which it still did not get lighter, then closed again for a while, giving a respite to all living things that got wet on the ground. Of the 800 households of a large village of Popovo, there was not a single soul in the streets and yards. Dogs hid from the rain in their booths, and their owners locked themselves at home on latches from the weather. Not a single gossiper was sitting on a bench and peeped at what was happening. It was empty and calm. Only 13 Hristo Botev chetniks and their secret agent and faithful yatak from the vicinity village of Bukovo Ivan Petrov froze in waiting at the entrance to the village, on both sides of the road, hidden into the dense branches of bushes. They did not make a single sound, did not ask, did not answer, because they had worked out a plan of the operation in advance and only waited.

The day was coming to an end, but all the time it was gloomy as in evening. Disguised from outside, from under the brunches they were scanning the road from the village to the green fields. Finally a herd of cows appeared in the distance, returning from pastures. And next to them a shepherd was walking with a whip, lowered down. The cows were walking calmly, knowing the way themselves. The chetniks got ready for action, and when the shepherd with the cows came closer, they jumped out of the bushes and crammed among the cows, and the dumbfounded shepherd was grabbed by 2 chetniks, who covered his mouth and dragged him into the bushes. These 2 with the detained shepherd remained there to guard the road.

11 people together with Petrov, completely invisible from outside, slowly entered the village, hidden among the cows, who did not react in any way to the young men, who had joined their company, and peacefully were moving, kept walking along the familiar road, waving their tails like dogs. Peter Ivanov pointed to a rich 2-story house, and 2 people slipped out from under the cows and instantly found themselves at the gates of the house, hiding in the bushes. Not far away the second rich 2-story house was situated, which Petrov silently pointed to with his hand, and 2 people slipped out from under the cows and in a trice were hidden in the bushes at the gates. A kmet's building appeared on the horizon, the guide pointed on it with his hand and at the same moment slipped out from under the cows, hid in the bushes and hurried, unnoticed by anyone, back home to his village Bukovo.

In a trice 7 people were at the door of the kmet's building, and the cows went on their way for a walk. Kerosene lamps lit in the windows, and through the glass one could see who was where. There were several rooms along the corridor, there were people in 2 of them. In the first large room 30 people-fascist activists from the village were sitting on chairs with the revolvers on their belts, smoking cigarettes and loudly shouting, discussed how reliably they guarded the village from the chetniks and if they only come, they will immediately seize them alive and take them to Sofia directly to the tsar, because the tsar promised a big reward for them.

"But if they start shooting, we'll have to shoot them and deliver to the tsar dead, won't we?"

"What's the difference? The reward was promised for the living or dead the same!"

"And it seems to me that they'll give more money for the living, because ours will yet torture them to their own pleasure!"

"But while you'll catch them alive, they will shoot you! That's why we need to shoot at them right away, so that for sure, and get the reward even for the dead!"

"Well, I don't know."

Hum and rumble were in the room, and tobacco smoke clouded the eyes. The pro-fascist activists argued, interrupting each other, whether the tsar would give more money as a reward for alive of dead, they made noise and expelled smoke rings. Suddenly the door opened, and 2 military personal, dressed in military uniform, entered the room: Boris Hristov-Murletov and Kocho Vasilev.

"Newcomers? Are you joining our squad? Come in!"

Boris and Kocho moved forward from the door, clearing the way. Mityu Ganev, Todor Todorov and Ivan Ignatov burst into the room faster than lighting.

"Hands up! Be silent! Who makes a move, I shoot!"

The dumbfounded counter-chetniks, not realizing what was happening, raised their hands up. One, who was in close proximity to Boris Hristov, tried to draw the revolver, but did not have time to move, as he crashed to the floor, emitting a stream of blood from his stomach. In the blink of an eye Boris Hristov pierced him with a bayonet of his rifle. The fascists, numb with horror, were holding their hands up, not daring to breathe. Atanas Georgiev Davkata hurriedly walked around everyone with a large sack, took away the revolvers, pot them in the sack and carried it out into the street, where one chetnik was waiting, and gave it to him. Then he returned back.

A gramophone was playing in another room, clouds of smoke hung in a stuffy room, and at the table they were eating a stewed rabbit and drank rakia: a fascist kmet, a police bailiff from Borisovograd, a fascist, and 2 local policemen, the fascists. They were rumbling loudly about the same topic: would the tsar Boris give more money for alive or dead chetniks and savored the details of the torture of the captured rebels a year ago.

"And how shall we divide the money, if we all together capture them?" they pondered on the question, finding it difficult to answer.

"We have already caught!" 2 military said, who opened the door and pushed Mityu Ganev with his hands tied behind his back into the room. "We want to hand him over to you, this is their ringleader!"

"Can't be!" the kmet did not believe his eyes together with the policemen, who were all glowing with joy. "Mityu Ganev himself fell into our hands! What a miracle!"

The kmet jumped up from his chair, almost stumbling, leaped to Mityu Ganev and swung his hand to hit him on the face. In the blink of an eye, Mityu Ganev loosed his hands and with all his force hit the kmet in the teeth with his fist, so that the later fell to the floor with his tooth knocked out. Before the drunken policemen had time to figure out what was happening, they were disarmed and pushed in the neck along with the kmet into a large room with the others. Mityu Ganev, Todor Todorov, Ivan Ignatov, Boris Hristov, Kocho Vasilev and Atanas Zapryanov were holding 2 revolvers, aimed at them.

"Well, gentlemen fascists, how are you?" Todor asked them.

"Did you, gentlemen fascists, have a good time this evening?" Mityu Ganev turned to them.

"We could've finished you all off, as all of you are the fascist butchers, and the blood of innocent people is on your hands," Ivan Ignatov informed them.

"But we'll not kill you, as you are unarmed," Boris Hristov told them.

"We'll not kill you, as all of you would've killed us, because we are not you!" Kocho Vasilev explained.

"You are unarmed, but you did not give up your weapons yourself, it is us, 6 people, who disarmed all of you: 34 people!"

"And all of you at that time were splitting the tsarist money for our heads!" Todor reminded.

The entire audience of 34 people was gloomily smiled, horrified to see in front of them the muzzles of the revolvers. Todor Todorov continued.

"So, gentlemen fascists, we want to remind you: the Alexander Tsankov power in Bulgaria is illegal. This criminal gang of bandits on June 9, 1923, carried out a gangster coup in Bulgaria with help of such criminals like you, overthrew the legitimate government of the Agrarian Union, brutally tortured Prime Minister Alexander Stamboliysky, all the ministers of his government and staged unprecedented terror in the country. You, fascist scoundrels, do you understand that you are all criminals and accomplices in crimes against the people of Bulgaria? Answer!"

The arrested, trembling with fear, made a certain sound, akin to the cow's moo in agreement. Todor continued.

"So, if you understand that you are all criminals and abettors of the criminal power, why do you continue your criminal activity and persecute us, the militants of the cheta Hristo Botev, who are fighting against this criminal power for the freedom of Bulgaria? Or, do you, criminals and fascist abettors, understand that you are such, but do not repent at all and deliberately continue to commit crimes? Answer, do you repent of the crimes?"

The audience, already in the wet pants, looked at the muzzles of the revolvers and uttered inarticulate sounds in chorus.

"And do you remember that you robbed the poor in your village and took away the last from them?" Todor continued to speak, addressing the arrested, asking them questions to which there was no answer.

In the big room of the kmet's building 34 arrested men were sitting with their already ugly physiognomies, distorted with horror, in their shitted pants from fear and were shaking in nervous convulsions, and their antipodes were standing in front of them: handsome, proud, courageous and fearless young chetniks, cold-blooded and impudent to their madness; 6 young men, 4 of them dressed in the beautiful uniform of the historical hajduks and 2 in military uniform. And it was not clear whether the arrested were aware of their insignificance and criminal nature, looking at the beautiful young men, who were on the side of light and good, unlike themselves, because the arrested were sitting in their pants—sticky, wet and dirty from feces—shaking with fear and periodically making unarticulated sounds.

"So, gentlemen fascists, our Hristo Botev cheta is political," Todor continued, "this cheta is of the United Front of Communists and Agrarians, there are also non-party people there. But we have a political task: to overthrow the political regime of Alexander Tsankov and his fascist junta and establish the workers' and peasants' power in the country."

"This time we'll spare you, but if you continue to hunt us or deal with those who sympathize with us, there will be no mercy!" Mityu Ganev announced menacingly.

"I believe, we need to finish," Todor said, "it's already 6 hours, since we've captured Popovo and are busy with you, giving lectures. It's time to finish.

And finally: we announced to you that we, the political cheta of Hristo Botev, who have captured the village Popovo and have been holding it in our hands for 6 hours, impose a contribution in the amount of 300 thousand leva on you. We need this money for the maintenance of the cheta and for preparing the uprising against the illegal regime of Tsankov. You, kmet, come here!"

The kmet with a knocked out tooth and swollen physiognomy, neither alive nor dead from horror and fear, slowly approached Todor, and the later with 2 revolvers aimed at him pushed him outside the door. He, barely dragging his legs behind him, in shitted pants, obediently complied and went into the next room to his office, where Todor pushed him.

"Money and the keys to the rooms and the front door!" Todor demanded, and the kmet dutifully opened the safe, took out a bunch of keys and a suitcase with money and put everything on the table, where the remains of a half-eaten stewed rabbit and a half-drunk rakia were lying next to a telephone with a cut wire.

"Here it is, there are only 200 thousand leva here, there is no more," the kmet said sullenly, looking plaintively at Todor.

Todor took the bag and the keys, without putting away the revolver for a moment.

"You'll go with us! Call your assistant!"

In a second the kmet's assistant came out to the door, and Mityu Ganev pronounced at parting:

"We remind you, if you dare to make a move and pursue us, then you know yourself what will happen: we shall kill the kmet and all of you! It is me, Mityu Ganev who is telling you this, I'll shoot you from a distance of 80 meters!"

The arrested trembled with horror and put another portion of feces in their pants, and the chetniks backed up to the door, all the time holding the arrested at gunpoint, disappeared behind the door, and Todor locked the door with the key, received from the kmet, and everyone went out into the street, where one more person was waiting for them. Todor tied the hands in front of the kmet and his assistant, whom the chetniks pushed out. Todor locked the front door of the kmet's building, and all hurried to the exit from the village.

"Eh, it would be nice to raise 2 banners over the kmet's house: red and orange!" Boris Hristov sighed.

"Another time, let's go!" Todor said.

They approached the exit from the village, where 6 companions were waiting for them with 2 hostages—rich chorbadjis from rich houses, both were the fascist collaborators. Their hands were also tied, and 13 chetniks with 4 hostages hurriedly left the village and hid in the mountains, covered with forests. The rain stopped pouring like hell, but the black sky continued to splash in the face with fine drizzle, erasing all traces of the cheta on the ground. Unnoticed by anyone, the cheta retired to their camp at the top of the Bukovsky Balkan. They climbed the mountain, where they settled down for the night on a glade under the bushes. The bound hostages were nearby, and a sentry was sitting next to them, not taking his eyes off them for a second. Another sentry was standing at the edge of the mountain, which overlooked Popovo below. The chetniks, who brilliantly carried out their daring action, tired, but satisfied, fell asleep, clutching their weapons to their chest. The exhausted and devastated hostages also fell asleep with their hands tied up.

Next day morning the rising sun in a transparent sky instantly dried up all the traces of yesterday's downpour and began to shine merrily from the cloudless sky. Everyone was in a cheerful mood. They divided food among all, refreshed themselves and set off on their way, winding and confusing the tracks. They went to another glade and made a halt.

"You, gentlemen fascists, yourself have no idea where you are!" Mityu Ganev addressed them. "You are in the historical place, in the very place, where 3 of us, me, Mityu Ganev, and my friends Todor Todorov with Ivan Ignatov solemnly entered the Hristo Botev cheta exactly a month and a half ago!"

"On the same one!" Todor with Ivan confirmed, cheerfully smiling. "Next to your Popovo!"

"And this event changed our fate and joined us to the political struggle against people like you!"

"And before that your tsar Boris offered us all a house in the city and a lot of money, just so that we become like you, and a complete amnesty!" Ivan Ignatov reminded.

"But we refused!" Todor said. "Because we do not want to be like you, we are not like you, and we'll never be like you!"

The hostages were sullenly silent all the time, fearing that somebody from the cheta will change his mind and shoot them. But the chetniks acted in correct accordance to the plan. The chetniks began to talk among themselves, having waved their hands to the hostages.

"Shall we bring them to ours?" Todor asked Mityu.

"I don't think so," Mityu answered. "There are 40 our people there, plus us, 13 people, and some more 4—it's too many to move around easily. We'll release them as soon as we get 100 thousand leva, as we agreed."

Having heard about the number of chetniks in 40 people, who were somewhere nearby, the hostages put in their pants again. At noon the sentry, who was standing at the edge of the cliff behind a stone ledge, reported that a man had approached the appointed place, put down the bag and was moving away. There was no tail. One of the chetniks at the same moment hurried down from the top of the mountain, being watched by his friends from above, picked up a bag with money and returned up. There were 100 thousand leva in the bag. The required amount of 300 thousand leva was in their hands. The cheta held the hostages until evening, walked with them through the mountains, confusing their tracks, and released them in the evening. The baffled kmet of Popovo, his assistant and 2 chorbadjis dashed down to valley to their home, swearing to be damned, if they even think to act against this damn cheta of Hristo Botev.

The next day, on September 19, the tsarist troops cordoned all the crossroads, and the cheshmas, fountains and springs around the entire area of the village Popovo, Bukovo, Syrnitsa, Spahievo, Bryastovo and Susam, and it seemed that a mouse would not slip past the troops, and the cheta Hristo Botev was driven into a trap. But the cheta itself ambushed near one of the cheshmas at night on September 20, attacked the troops, who scattered after the first shoot of the chetniks, fled to where they came from, abandoning the dead and wounded on the battlefield.

13 chetniks, without losing anyone, went on to carry out their mission. Before the "Haskovskaya Poshta" newspaper informed a layman the next day that "The Hristo Botev cheta was ultimately exterminated by the valiant troops of His Majesty Tsar Boris III to the north-west of the Mineralny Bani in the town of Dushka," another messenger reported at the same time another news: "Today, September 20, the Hristo Botev cheta attacked the troops in the Malko Gradishche region." The superstitious layman crossed himself in fear and performed the other magic actions, which could protect him from evil spirits, as it was completely obvious that it could not have done without evil spirit!

How could the cheta, who was destroyed at the Mineralny Bani, resurrect and, as if on wings, be transported on the same day to the Ivaylovgrad region, 80 km to the east, and show up themselves?

The tsar Boris III, Tsankov and Rusev with all the rest evil spirit of Bulgaria flabbergasted and bit their lips with anger, and 13 chetniks, true friends, without losing a single person and having received 300 thousand leva for preparing the uprising and 34 revolvers, safely got out of the encirclement and went on their way, and the second part of the cheta at the head with Radyu Delchev were staging a distracting maneuver in the east in order to disorient the enemy and confuse him. They did not attack the troops, as the messenger reported, but carried on agitation among the travelers, whom they stopped at one of the turns of the undulated road southwest of Malko Gradishche and among the 100 detained travelers, in fact, there was a military captain with 7 soldiers, who listened to the speaker of the cheta with admiration. All the detainers spent time as if at picnic, sitting on the grass the whole day, until 100 people gathered, talking among themselves and with the chetniks, and then the speaker spoke to them. The chetniks did not take a single lev from them: they only collected the revolvers, which the faithful yataks from Malko Gradishche safely hid in a remote koliba until the signal to start the uprising.

The forest rustled around, touched by the yellowness of the coming autumn, a picturesque waterfall fell from the mountain, the grass on the glade was still pleasing the eye, but it was already drying and preparing to vanish until the next spring, to which the uprising was nevertheless postponed from the autumn of 1924.

Chapter 47
Returning Home

The village of Mustraklii on the eastern most outskirts of Bulgaria with carefree inhabitants, being in love with the colors of rainbow, with the colors of which they created their ornate costumes with embroideries, ribbons and fresh flowers, who lived in a world of dreams, legends and music, singing folk songs both at home and in the field, remained behind, and the cart, harnessed by 2 oxen, in which the entire family of Todor Todorov was riding, was moving further and further away from it in a western direction. Having received a letter from a postman, in which the authorities allowed the family to return home, Ivan Todorov immediately loaded the cart with their things, and the family, yearning for their home, set off, leaving the village Mustraklii, a place of exile, for the night, without waiting for the morning.

Todor's father Ivan was driving the oxen and led the cart, again passing the same places, where he fought during the Balkan War, he recalled the past years and lamented at the hardships, which disastrous fate had laid on his shoulders. And next to him there was his faithful wife Atanasa, hugging a 4-year-old Mitra, her 19-year-old daughter Maria and 15-year-old son Gocho, thin as a skeleton, emaciated by a serious illness, having swallowed during the exile a mountain of books from the library in Mustraklii, in one of the rooms of which the entire family lived all that time. With each new book he read, the horizon of acquired knowledge opened up before him more and more and retired from him more and more, as he approached it, as he realized how much more he would have to read and learn. His inquisitive mind greedily absorbed all the new knowledge, and his tenacious memory captured pictures of what he personally experienced with a passionate desire to write about it one day, if he survives.

The cart was shaking over bumps and impassable roads, as they were riding at random at night, and the faithful Bulgarian oxen, who had carried out on their shoulders the Balkan and Great wars, carrying shells to the battlefields, were now dragging the cart with their family back home to Bodrovo. They were riding all night, having gone astray in the darkness, only in the morning unfamiliar places flashed before their eyes and stopped only at noon at an unknown stream to quench their thirst, water the oxen and wash themselves. They drove on further and did not think about anything else, but their home. Finally, the road along which they were driven into exile appeared, and now they were approaching their native places. The last stretch of the road, the last turn of the way, and now they are driving up the hill after the turn and drive along the main road of the native village. Their house is on the main road on the left behind the kmet's building. The oxen themselves stopped, having recognized their home. The dogs, all that time fed by the Ivan's brother Dimitar, who lived nearby, whined plaintively, waved their tails and in a fit of joy rushed to rub against the legs of the hosts, who entered the house. A strange feeling seized them, as if they had not left anywhere, because with all their thoughts there were with their home during all these few months, being in a foreign land.

The next day all the other families, expelled from their homes, returned back to Bodrovo. The whole herd, abandoned to the mercy of fate, was intact, as there was somebody to take care of it, and the next day Gocho, taking with him another book in a sack, led the herd to graze on the already cool and yellow October meadows. October nights were cold, and he no longer spent night in the field, like in summer, but in the evening he drove the animals into the koshara and came home for night. From a distance, he saw a crowd of soldiers near the gates of his house, and the boy's heart sank from a bad promotion. When will they be left alone? He squeezed through the soldiers and entered the house. Inside 3 police agents bossed like at home: Angel Kazaka, Lieutenant Hadji Stoyanov from Asenovograd and Nikolov from Sofia.

"With your help or without you, we'll find the cheta and receive 20 million leva a reward that the tsar Boris promised," the civil agent Angel Kazaka announced, unceremoniously walking around the house and peering into all corners.

"Tell me, Gocho, where did you bring food to your brother Todor, where you met?" the military Hadji Stoyanov asked.

"If my brother counted only on my food, he would've died of hunger: I could not bring him food, because I have not been here for several months!" Gocho replied sullenly, cursing all of them, the persecutors of his family taken together.

The agents and the military spoke among themselves and agreed, apparently they had some plan.

"Today we'll stay overnight with you, and tomorrow we'll see," the agent Angel Kazaka announced and together with the lieutenant Hadji Stoyanov accommodated in one of the rooms, like at home.

The Sofia agent Nikolov came out of the house and with a crowd of the military men, flocked at the gates, went to the kmet's building, where they were quartered in safe houses for that night. And the night in Todor's house passed in anxious anticipation of the unknown.

Next morning, the agents, accompanied by the soldiers, proceeded to carry out their plan in order to receive 20 million leva reward, promised by the tsar. The civilian agent Angel Kazaka with one blow of his fist threw 15-year-old Gocho to one side of the floor, and with another blow he knocked his mother Atanasa to the floor, who fell, having hit her head under the cry of little Mitra. At that time the soldiers with lieutenant Hadji Stoyanov pushed Todor's father Ivan out of the house into the street, and the entire procession moved along the road from the village, joining Ivan Ignatov's brother Zheko, who had been taken hostage in the same way. On the Bansko Highway a group of military men joined to them the third hostage: Atanas Ganev-Armanov, the brother of Mityu Ganev, who was captured in the village of Aidanlar.

"Now the chetniks will not dare to attack us, if we run into them, and then we'll capture them dead or alive!" the Sofia agent Nikolov was rubbing his hands with pleasure.

A truck with the military was driving slowly along the road, car with 3 agents was driving in front of them, and a cart, pulled by 2 oxen, was driving in front of them, in which 3 hostages from Bodrovo and Aidanlar were sitting under the custody of the military. They were driving very slowly, entering every village on the way to rummage, they were driven from one koliba to another koshara on their way stopped and rummaged. They were driving from morning to night, and at night they settled down for night, kindly provided to them by the loyal kmets of the cities and villages, also by the loyal counter-chetniks, who secretly informed them of everything. They were driving slowly along the road and tuned into the vicinity roads, making raids deep into the forests on foot, and not finding anyone, drove on further.

The withered grass under their boot yellowed and died up completely. And yet recently, the green foliage of bushes and trees turned yellow and purple on their eyes and fell off, blown away by the cold wind, exposing the brunches, through which they still could see anything and could not capture the chetniks, though they had been hunting for them for a whole month. Cold November of 1924 came, bringing closer winter.

Having traveled and zigzagged all the settlements of southern Bulgaria, a pack of hounds, dragging along the hostages behind them, reached Asenovograd and not finding the cheta Hristo Botev there, headed to Bukovo. The mirage of 20 million leva, promised by the tsar, drove the pursuers forward, and now they arrived to the Bukovo kmet's house. It was evening. A flock of military with the hostages remained at the kmet's office, and the agent Angel Kazaka, accompanied by 2 soldiers, went to the local tavern-korchma. He left the soldiers to guard the door in the street and came inside, and sat down at the table in the corner, ordered a glass of wine for show and began to peer through the clouds of smoke at what was happening. On the stand of the korchma-keeper, as usual, a gramophone was playing, in the twilight of the kerosene lamps the circles of smoke were flying before the eyes from the cigarettes, which the villagers smoked one after another; the korchma was crammed with them. In the opposite corner at the table there was a young man sitting of fine appearance, with refined features of a handsome face, black, short hair with a thin line of black mustache above his lip, slender, fit, with a bearing of an officer, dressed in civilian clothes. The villagers who, were sitting at the same table with him and at the next to him tables, were discussing something vividly. The agent Kazaka began to listen to the conversation, but at a distance through the whole korchma and under the sound of gramophone he could not make out anything.

"Who is it?" he asked a peasant, sitting at the next table.

"This is our Georgy Pilashev," the man answered indifferently, drinking rakia.

Kazaka got up and walked closer, straining his ears.

"We are poor!"

"We are being robbed!"

"We are driven!"

"We are tormented!"

"They kill our children!" he heard from the villagers and from Georgy Pilashev.

"The Tsankov government, the tsar Boris, and the entire ugly society of Bulgaria are to blame for this!"

"Who is to be blamed and for what?" Kazaka asked menacingly, approaching Georgy Pilashev. "How dare you to slander the head of the Bulgarian government and personally His Majesty Tsar Boris?"

"The Tarnovo Constitution guarantees freedom of speech to the citizens of Bulgaria." Georgy Pilashev replied calmly, looking contemptuously at the tsarist agent.

"I'll show you Tarnovo Constitution! I'll show you freedom of speech! The State Protection Law abolishes all the laws and freedoms in Bulgaria!" Kazaka yelled and immediately called 2 soldiers standing at the door outside. "You are under arrest!"

The frozen with horror and frightened by the repressions the villagers did not dare to repel Pilashev, whom 2 soldiers and the tsar's agent led out of the korchma. Georgy Pilashev did not lose his composure and was pondering on the further actions. They approached the kmet's office, next to which a flock of soldiers were standing, and came in. In one of the rooms there were 3 hostages and Georgy Pilashev's father-in-law Radyu Hristov, who was arrested on a tip from one of the village's activists.

"Are you staying overnight in Bukovo?" kmet asked the agent.

"No, with such a prey we'll go immediately to Mineralny Bani!" agent Nikolov answered.

They loaded 2 arrested and 3 hostages into a cart, guarded by the soldiers, and the truck with the car moved east from Bukovo to Mineralny Bani. There was a commandant's office of the 10th Rhodope Infantry Squad, into which the 10th Rhodope Regiment was reorganized after the Treaty of Neuilly. The hostages were locked up separately from 2 arrested, and in the morning of the next day the commandant and also he himself, the chairman of the so-called military court, trumpet up the next day, Captain Ivan Jordanov Hubenov from the village of Karadjalovo hastily sentenced a verdict: "Georgy Pilashev and Radyu Hristov, as the enemies of the state, are sentenced to death by firing squad!"

2 arrested men, sentenced to death, were locked in one of the rooms and dispassionately were thinking over further actions; they had the rest of the day and the evening until midnight.

At that time another interrogation was going on in the next room. Sitting on a bench was an old man, who had been captured from his villa on the hill south of Bodrovo, organized by the agent from Sofia Nikola Nikolov and hurriedly brought by cart to Miniralny Bani. A 90-year-old white-haired old man, Ivan Duban, was sitting on a bench and looking contemptuously away from the tsarist agent, who was interrogating him. Nearby there were 4 officers from the commandant's office of Mineralny Bani.

"Answer, old man, do you know Mityu Ganev, Todor Todorov and Ivan Ignatov? Did they come to your house? Did you accept them?"

"Yes, I do, I do know them," Ivan Duban answered in a calm senile voice, "they came to my house, and I received them with pleasure."

"But how does it happen that these 3 robbers rob the chorbadjis, but made friends with you? After all, you are a chorbadji, aren't you?"

"First, they are not robbers, but hajduks, and now they are the members of the political cheta Hristo Botev, and they are fighting not with the chorbadjis, but with the murderers of the people, executioners and butchers in power!"

"How dare you insult the authorities?"

"I am not afraid of you," the old man answered calmly, "I have lived 90 years, 44 of them were under the Turks. I've seen a lot, but I know for sure: there were no such butchers of the Bulgarian people as the current government under any Turks! You, Bulgarians, are worse than the Turks!"

The enraged agent hit Ivan Duban on the head with all his might, and the old man could not stay in the chair and fell on the floor. The agent nodded his head to those standing near him, and they began to kick him with their legs.

"Speak, old robber, where is this gang of bandits? Where is Todor Todorov, Mityu Ganev and Ivan Ignatov and the entire gang? Answer! Answer! Answer!"

Each question of the royal agent and "answer!" was accompanied by a kick of the boot on the body of Ivan Duban. The old man no longer made a sound, and 4 officers of the former 10th Rhodope Regiment kicked him with their legs on his head, face, sides, arms and legs, turning his body into a bloody mess. The 90-year-old man, who survived 44 years of the Ottoman yoke, did not survive the blows of boots on his body by the 10th Rhodope Regiment officers, or rather what was left from this regiment. He was lying on the floor, bleeding, and the pictures of his life flashed before his eyes. He saw the face of his beloved wife, her rounded belly, in which the life of their third child began, and death of both of them, death of the first 2 children, loneliness, a large house with a garden on the top of the hill near Bodrovo, which he turned into a fortress, visit of 3 hajduks-friends, who brightened up his loneliness. They were waving to him and, moving away, parted. Gradually, the outlines of the pictures in his eyes blurred, became indistinct, he heard the voice of his loved ones, calling him from the pictures, disappearing before his eyes, and suddenly everything vanished, and all the voices subsided. He no longer saw, heard or felt anything. He died. And the officers of the 10th Rhodope Regiment continued to beat with their boots his lifeless body, lying on the floor.

"It'll be enough, he is already dead!" one of them noticed, but they could not stop and continued to knead the body of Ivan Duban with their feet.

Another retired Bulgarian officer Georgy Pilashev was sitting, locked up with his father-in-law Radyu Hristov in the next room, waiting for the execution, which was only a few hours away. They looked out of the window, overlooking the courtyard of the commandant's office, and assessed the situation. The tense moments flew by at breakneck speed. It was dark outside. Having dealt with the enemy Ivan Duban, a faithful yatak of the chetniks, the officers of the 10th Rhodopes Regiment flocked into korchma nearby to celebrate the valiant victory. Pilashev and Hristov saw that there was nobody under the window. Suddenly the door opened, and the soldier, standing on guard in the corridor, handed them a chisel and a revolver and said:

"Run through the window, as there is no one in the yard!"

Pilashev with Hristov grabbed the chisel and revolver, quickly shook hands with the soldier, who immediately vanished behind the door and stood at his post. With a chisel the arrested men tampered the window, on which there was no lattice, the window opened, they jumped out of it and, dinging to the wall, reached the end of the building, ran to the fence and jumped over the low fence. In a trice they vanished into the mountains, which were contiguous to Mineralny Bani. And the officers of the 10th Rhodope Regiment were drinking in the korchma-tavern, celebrating the victory over the 90-year-old Ivan Duban and Georgy Pilashev with Radyu Hristov death sentence.

***

At the end of November 1924, in the village of Bodrovo in the house of Dimitar Todorov Karagochev, wedding was celebrated. His son Georgy married his beloved girl from the village. They laid the table, invited guests: life went on. Best man, 15-year-old Gocho Todorov was sitting next to his friend-cousin. Ivan Todorov came in and sat down between them.

"Georgy, do you know at all whom you married?" he asked almost in a whisper. "Do you know who her parents are? Do you know that they are the fascists, close to the power?"

"Uncle, it's not her fault," Georgy answered quietly, and their whisper was muffled by the playing music.

"Nephew, I wish you only the best," Ivan said, "this is my advice to you: leave after the wedding for another city or village so that no one finds you and no one knows where you are! Leave, listen to me, Georgy!"

No one heard these words, except for Gocho, sitting next.

The police agents not only did not kill 3 hostages, believing that they would be more useful alive and would still be need in search of the chetniks, but they even delivered them directly to the wedding in Bodrovo. And they themselves sat up an ambush, expecting that the chetniks would come to the wedding, despising the danger. But vainly the policemen and the military were waiting for a long time, having sat in already bare bushes. Todor, Mityu and Ivan along with their fellow-companions from the cheta Hristo Botev were in a completely different place, fulfilling their mission.

Chapter 48
Second Internment

On November 21, in Plovdiv there was a fierce skirmish near one of the secret apartments of the Military Regional Organization of the BCP. The apartment of the widow Shishkova at the very beginning of the Tsaregrad Street opposite the Catholic church was surrounded on all sides and fired upon by numerous Plovdiv policemen. They were brought there by the agent-provocateur Kuzinchev, introduced by the "public security" into the very heart of the BCP. From inside the apartment, Hristo Gyulemetov and Boyan Bolgaranov, the leaders of the Regional Military Organization of the BCP in Plovdiv, were firing back, waging an unequal battle. The military organization headquarters in Plovdiv actually led the Military Organizations of the District headquarters in Burgas, Sliven, Haskovo, Stara Zagora and Plovdiv itself, operating throughout Bulgaria between Stara Planina in the north, the Black Sea in the east and the village of Belovo in the west. The brilliant officers of the BCP and BANU party leaders, who did not bow their heads before the fascist junta, presided over the underground activities of the United Front, having at their disposal illegal apartments, secret addresses, couriers who organized communications, weapons deportment, preparing the uprising, the plan of which was developed in June.

 The Hristo Botev cheta and their associates in the other arrears successfully formed militia-6s in the villages and taught them military affairs, and the activists from the both parties penetrated the barracks, enlightening the soldiers. The 6th Infantry Regiment, the 3rd Cavalry Regiment, the 3rd Artillery Division, the 7th Gendarme Infantry Squad and many others took the side of the revolution for freedom.

 In defiance of them, the fascist junta released the agents-provocateurs from their rat-traps. One rat-agent-provocateur, successfully introduced under the guise of their own into the underground organization, was able to destroy it with his poison. Such a provocateur Nikola Kuzinchev, having disguised as an anti-fascist, managed to get close to some of the leaders of the United Front and now led the army of policemen to the Shishkova's apartment. Separate well-aimed shots from the window put down the policemen at the entrance, in response continuous fire broke into the apartment. The leaders of the Regional Party Military Organization Hristo Gyulemetov and Boyan Bolgaranov fired back at the army of policemen and at the same time were destroying the party documents.

"Let's run out the window!" Bolgaranov called and jumped out straight to the flying bullets.

He rushed to run through the garden, trying to escape. At that time his companion and comrade-in-arms Gyulemetov was tattering the remaining secret documents and swallowed them, while shooting back at the policemen. If one more moment, he would've jumped out of the window, but a police bullet knocked him to the floor, and flock of the policemen burst into the room.

"Look, he was swallowing the documents!" one of the policemen exclaimed, picking up a piece of paper that had fallen to the floor.

"What do you think, we'll not get...?" the senior policemen growled and commanded: "Hold him!"

Gyulemetov, dying from his wounds, was lying on the floor and gazed into nowhere. The policemen grabbed him, pressing to the floor, opened his clothes, cut the still breathing body of Gyulemetov, and the later breathed his last. The policemen cut open his esophagus and stomach and hastily began poking around in his intestines, pulling out pieces of the swallowed documents. For a long time the policemen had to make a mosaic from them, and finally they saw a text about secret places, addresses, passwords, couriers, as well as a map of the future uprising with the deployment of the military-political forces of South Bulgaria with the lists of the battle groups, militia-6s, chetas and squads: everything that Gyulemetov did not have time to destroy.

The secret address of the Hristo Botev cheta in Haskovo in the sewing workshop of Penyu and Kiro and the secret place in the house of Dobri Delchev in Bukovo, where there was one of the bases of the cheta, were disclosed. Autumn of 1924 ended without uprising, bringing winter and the hardships of life outside home for all the fighters of the cheta Hristo Botev. They continued to carry out their mission. They prepared the masses for the uprising, which was postponed to spring, while the fighters themselves were ready to act at any moment. And now it was necessary to survive at winter time.

On December 6, the Nikul Day, knee-deep snow covered the empty streets and gardens of Bodrovo, whose inhabitants locked themselves in their homes from the bitter frost and had fun at the sitting-gatherings in one house or another, where the guests, close or sometimes hostile in interests, gathered. In the house of Dimitar Todorov Karagochev, which was located next to 2 houses of his brother Ivan, young people from both families were sitting at the gathering in beauty, warmth and comfort: happy, recently married Georgy and Ivanka, Ivan's eldest daughter Mariyka and her fiancé Penyu Dimitrov, daughter of Dimitar Mika and Gocho. Young girls traditionally did needlework, singing a folk song. Gocho asked Georgy, who was sitting next to him:

"Do you remember the words of my father, said to you on your wedding day?"

"I do remember, but how to follow his advice? It's scary to imagine just how to run away from your own home to no one knows where! Yes, even with the young wife."

"What will be next for all of us?" Gocho sighed. "I miss my brother...how is there our Todor? We are still better than him and his friends. At least, we are sitting at home in our house, and he wanders somewhere. How I would like to see him!"

Georgy smiled mysteriously and replied:

"You'll see him soon."

It was late evening, and Gocho, who was always tired in company, as he always pondered on his own things, said goodbye to the young people and went home. He went through the garden, entered the contiguous yard. The whole ground, bushes and trees were covered with like a snow-white blanket with snow, which silently fell on the head with soft flakes. Mute silence reigned in the yard. Gocho opened the door at the back of the house, which led to the veranda and from there to the huge kitchen. Suddenly, somebody grabbed him, covered his mouth with his hand, pressed to himself and began to cover his head with kisses. The dumbfounded Gocho froze in place, tears rolling down from his eyes. His brother was standing in front of him, who was hard to recognize. It seemed to Gocho that Todor had become twice as big:

tall, broad-shouldered, with strong arms; Todor's lush black hair fell to his shoulders, and still a beautiful face, along which the tears were also rolling.

"Brother!" Gocho whispered, who had been missing Todor all this time.

"Let's go, be quiet," Todor pressed his finger to his lips, "don't be scared."

They opened the door from the veranda to the huge kitchen in his new house, and Gocho, amazed, entered the room. The entire detachment of Hristo Botev was there. Men from 18 to 30 years old, large, brave, but exhausted, were resting, filling the entire huge kitchen space in his house. Some were slipping on a long minder-sofa, which stood almost along the whole wall, some were sleeping on the floor on the spread matrasses, covered with rugs and woolen blankets, some were sitting on them and quietly whispered. Half of them had beards and mustaches, half had clean-shaved faces, but all had shoulder-length hair tousled.

The warriors were sleeping with full ammunition, never parting with it, and pressed the rifle that lay next to them: the bandoliers, filled with the bullets, crossed their chests, and daggers with a pair of grenades hung from their wide belts. Gocho was gazing, as if spelled, at the picture, opened before him, as if an illustration of a historical novel. By the opposite wall from the sofa his father Ivan and uncle Dimitar were cooking a sheep on a large stove, and his mother was busy near the table in the large contiguous living room. All the windows were tightly closed with curtains and shutters, and in the semi-darkness the kerosene lamps lit the living room, and many thin candles, stuck in the round bowl with grain in the kitchen lit the space. It was very warm in the house, and the happy faces of the warriors, enjoining the warmth and comfort, glowed in the twilight from the reflections of fire from a large stove, on which the caldron with a sheep emitted a sweet aroma.

"It's ready," Ivan informed, "Todor, son, wake up everyone."

"This is not an easy task," Todor smiled, "especially to wake up Mityu."

Quietly he approached all the sleeping people and began to shake them by the shoulders. One by one they woke up and breathed in the smell of cooked meat, looking forward to the meal. Every one woke up, except Mityu Ganev.

"Who will wake up Mityu Ganev?" Todor asked in a cheerful tone.

"Not me," all the chetniks chuckled in respond.

"Georgy, come on, wake up Mityu Ganev, you are the chief here," Todor joked, turning to Pilashev.

"Why me? Go ahead, wake him up, because you are friends since childhood, aren't you?"

"We were not exactly friends since childhood," Todor replied, smiling, "Ivan Ignatov is a witness."

"Then let Ivan wake him up."

"No way," Ivan protested and all laughed softly.

"Come on, Todor, as the host of the house."

"Damn you," Todor greened and went up to wake up Mityu Ganev, who was sleeping like dead on the sofa by the wall.

"Mityu, wake up, we'll have dinner!"

Everyone giggled. Todor extended his hand and gently pushed Mityu by the shoulder:

"Get up!"

Ganev, immersed in deep sleep, was only snoring, smiling happily in his dream. Todor shook him more by the shoulder and immediately jerked his hand back. Ganev jumped up, drew his revolver and shouted half-asleep:

"Hands up!"

Everyone laughed, covering with their hands their mouths.

"Get up, dinner is ready," Todor called, and Mityu Ganev, inhaling the aroma of the cooked meat, woke up completely and attacked everyone:

"Why did not you wake me up earlier?"

Everyone laughed merrily, pressing their palms to their lips as hard as they could.

Ivan, Dimitar and Atanasa put food on the plates for the guests, who thanked fate for the bliss to rest in the spacious, warm, hospitable house of their friend Todor and ate an amazing dinner. Todor addressed to the chetniks, who had had dinner and ordered them to change 2 sentries in the street, the latter entered the house from the frost and plunged into the bliss that reigned inside.

"Fill the bags with food now, don't put it off for later," Ivan ordered, and the chetniks began to put bread and cheese in their bags.

Mityu Ganev handed Ivan a suitcase, filled with bundles of banknotes.

"Here it is, take it, Bay Ivan! And thank you for everything you've done for us!"

"I won't take any money, keep it for yourself," Ivan Todorov replied.

"Take it, please, we all ask you," Mityu Ganev insisted, and all the chetniks nodded their heads.

"I categorically refuse," Todor's father answered.

"Bay Ivan, no offense, take it! You and your family suffered because of us! You and your family were interned to the end of the earth! You suffered losses because of this, you abandoned your farm."

"We suffered a lot, it's true, we suffered some loss by this exile. But they did not ruin us, we are chorbadjis ourselves; we have 2 houses, fields, herds, we have some funds. And keep this money for yourself, use it for your cause, for the uprising, demolish the power of the butchers, and this will be the greatest reward for all of us! I am not helping because of money, Mityu, use it for the needs of the cheta and our common cause. I am not helping because of money; Todor is my son, you are my children."

Mityu Ganev, being overwhelmed, hugged Ivan Todorov and shook his hand warmly, and all the chetniks pressed their palms together and shook them in the air as a sign of support.

"Listen to me, boys, I have to tell you the following," Ivan turned to them and told in detail how he, Ivan Ignatov's brother Zheko and Mityu Ganev's brother were taken hostages and were carried all over southern Bulgaria for a month in search of the cheta, how they beat to death the old Ivan Duban in the commandant's office of the Mineralny Bani.

"They dragged us all together from Bukovo to Mineralny Bani, and they locked us in different rooms, and we did not see anything," Georgy Pilashev and Radyu Hristov confirmed. "Then we fled."

Everyone frowned and commemorated old man Ivan Duban with a kind word.

"Blessed memory of him!" Mityu said.

"He loved us, hosted us at his villa and helped us," Todor said. "I am going to change sentry."

"In no case!" the father objected. "Dimitar and I'll go, Georgy is already there at the post; 3 of us and 2 of yours, 5 of us will guard you, and you all and you, Todor, go to bed and rest."

Atanasa laid out a few more mattresses with blankets on the floor in 2 rooms: in a large living room and in the kitchen, and everyone went to bed and, like cats, stretching out their legs and arms with pleasure, instantly fell into a deep sleep. All the cheta always slept in clothes and ammunition, clutching their rifles. Gocho and Todor fell asleep on the mattress on the floor, and in the street their father Ivan with his brother Dimitar and his son Georgy and 2 chetniks guarded their sleep, standing outside in the snow. Flakes of white snow fell silently, frost drew lacy patterns on the glass of the windows, the fire cracked hot in the stove, warming the whole house, young soldiers slept soundly on soft beds, having eaten hearty meal, the sentry on guard vigilantly guarded their sleep. The moments of bliss continued slowly for all. Silently silver stars and the moon shone in the sky, illuminating the snow-white cover. 2 chetniks replaced 2 sentries, and the latter hurried up to lie down in the warmth in bed.

When the hand of the clock approached 4 in the morning, suddenly the snow-white silence of the night was blasted by the chorus of the barking dogs. They stuck their muzzles out of their booths and burst into hysterical barking. Ivan, Dimitar and Georgy shuddered and told 2 chetniks:

"This is how our dogs always bark, when the military and police troops surround the village."

"What shall we do?"

"Cursed bastards, be damned! They don't let people sleep peacefully!" Ivan exclaimed.

"Let's inform the cheta," one sentry said and hurried into the house.

The awakened warriors were extremely unwilling to get up and leave the Todor's house and began to confer what to do.

"We have to leave," Radyu Delchev said, "boys, get up, the dogs are barking all over the village, they say that they always bark like that, when the troops approach."

In a few minutes the entire cheta, fully equipped, was ready to leave. They took things, sacks filled with food, left the house through the back door through the veranda, barn and disappeared into the night. Gocho continued to sleep and see happy dreams. When he woke up in the morning, there was no trace of the cheta, and he thought that he had seen all this in his dream…

In a few days 10 soldiers with an officer raided Ivan's house; they rummaged and searched everywhere, turning everything upside down, but found nothing. And Ivan was called to the kmet's office. With a heavy heart Ivan came into the office, where 11 years ago he himself worked as the kmet, heading the village, pulling on his shoulders the entire burden of the Great War hardships, protecting the villagers form the German requisitions, and now he was called here by the hostile people.

"Ivan, I am warning you: in a couple of days you will be interned, it's better to pack your things in advance so that not to turn out like the last time, when you had to pack in a hurry," Peter Kostov warned him.

Having returned home darker that a storm cloud, Ivan called his son:

"Gocho, go and call Georgy."

Gocho brought his cousin from his house next door in a moment.

"George, we are interned again by the tsarist butchers. I don't know, when we shall return home. This is what I want to convey to you: get in touch with Todor or any of his people and tell them that Zagon Ganev Zabanarov is a traitor!"

"It can't be!" George was amazed. "He does know everything, allegedly he is the yatak, and therefore, they trust him; once he even handed over the weapons to them. He knows the secret places and liaisons. Uncle, how do you know that Zagon is a traitor?"

"Listen to what I say, nephew, and do not argue! I've never been wrong. I have been suspecting him for a long time, and today I've seen him in the kmet's office. He was talking with a police agent in the next room, the door was ajar, they did not expect me to come, I saw them: he was giving the information to the policeman."

"That's a hit!" Georgy was dumbfounded. "He knows all the yataks from the village and knows that I am the very first one."

"This scum sold himself to the authorities," frowning, Ivan sighed, "several years ago he incited this fool Ivan Ignatov to steal the other people sheep and thus to become the hajduks. Ivan Ignatov, the fool, succumbed to a provocation and dragged out Todor into this affair. Although Todor did not steal these damned sheep, but Ivan forced Todor, as a friend, to be present at the sale-deal of the sheep. It was a trap, they were set up, they were captured, tortured, tormented, damn my former 'sworn-brother', fake friend, and damn myself for letting this scum into our house! In general, then, as you remember, they were all thrown to jail, and since then Todor was deprived of his home and still can't legally return here. Urgently tell them that Zagon Ganev Zabanarov is a traitor and a police agent, he works for the fascists! And also, Ilya Zapryanov Chakalov, the false yatak, is a traitor. They take money from the cheta, allegedly for help and hand over all the information to the police, from whom they also take money."

Georgy was listening, dumbfounded and convulsively pondered on how he could find Todor. The Todor's family involuntarily began to gather things, and in a couple of days a detachment of military kicked them out of their house, sealed the front door, and at parting, the police agent said sarcastically to them:

"Now you'll not see your home soon, if you ever see it at all!"

The cart, harnessed by 2 oxen, with everyone, except daughter Maria, who married Penyu Dimitrov and moved into his house, rolled with difficulty along a snowy road. Faithful oxen, driven out of a warm barn in the cold, pulled a cart with the entire family through the snow. On the main road they were joined by the cart with the family of Ivan Ignatov, and both families were taken to the nearest station Skobelevo, where they loaded the oxen, the cart with people into a fright car and sent them to Svilengrad. From there they were unloaded and sent further on their own to Alada on the eastern edge of Bulgaria. It was snowing, it was frost.

"Look for a roof over your head yourself," they were told.

"They sealed only the front door," Ivan said to his family, "and the other doors from the back entrance were not sealed, because they did not know about them. I hope, Todor with his companions will find the entrance to the house."

The Hristo Botev cheta did just that. Todor knew perfectly how to get into the house from the back door, and his friends found shelter and food in the house, unnoticed by anyone behind the sealed front door from the main entrance. As soon as they entered the house, Georgy Dimitrov was already there and told them the main information.

"Todor, beware: Blagon Ganev Zabanarov is a traitor!"

"I knew it! This was to be expected!" Todor answered with annoyance, turning white with anger; pictures of 3 years ago emerged before his eyes. "Ivan, do you hear? Mityu, do you hear?"

Both approached Todor, next to whom Radyu Delchev was standing, and entered the conversation.

"What's happening?"

"Zabanarov is a traitor, that's what it is!"

"I don't believe it," Ivan Ignatov answered complacently.

"Can't be!" stubborn Mityu Ganev objected.

"George, repeat!" Todor addressed his cousin.

"I warn you. I tell you: beware, Blagon Zabanarov is a traitor! Uncle Ivan told me to warn you before they were interned. The kmet invited him to warn that they would be interned so that they would be ready. He came to the kmet's building and saw Blagon there in the other room, he was whispering with a police agent, the door was ajar, and he saw them. And also, uncle Ivan said that he had known it before long ago that he was a traitor-provocateur and ordered to warn you."

"This can't be!" both Ignatov and Ganev objected.

"Have you forgotten, how 3 years ago he pushed you to steal those ill-fated sheep in order to become the 'hajduks', and you forced me to be present at the sale-deal of these sheep! And we all ended up in the jail and have not been able to return home legally since then! And now the father says that he saw how he whispered with a policeman, says that he is a traitor, and you don't believe it? This bastard should be killed!"

"We'll figure it out," Georgy Pilashev answered, "we'll get evidences and figure it out!"

"It can be too late for that!" Todor flared up.

Chapter 49
Manastir

On Saturday, December 14, 1924, in 2 km north-east of Haskovo in the area Karayamach, closer to the north, all travelers, heading to Rakovsky railway station, or from it, stopped for political information. The Hristo Botev chetniks, who were in ambush, at the agreed moment, went out on the highway and one by one began to detain everyone, who was moving in both directions on the road in carts, cars, chaises or by foot.

"Gentlemen, we ask all for a political meeting!" the chetniks politely addressed, escorting them out of their vehicles and gathering them on the side of the road. "Don't worry, we don't have bad intentions toward you, we'll only inform you about what's happening in our common country."

"Except this one!" they explained, pointing to Vasil Borachev, whom Todor and Ivan Ignatov took by arms, pulling out of the car, having the information, received in advance.

"What is your name?" Voevoda asked, addressing a stout middle-aged citizen, shaking with fear, dressed in expensive fur coat and a fur hat.

"Vasil Borachev," the latter answered in a whisper, lowering his eyes to the ground.

"Citizen Vasil Borachev, tell us all, which party to belong to and what you did on June 9 last year."

"To the National-Liberal," the citizen answered and fell silent.

"Why are you silent? Wouldn't you like to tell us about what you were doing on June 9, 1923?"

The assembled audience, overwhelmed by contradictory feelings—horror and fear of being detained by the armed warriors of Hristo Botev, dressed in a beautiful uniform, to curiosity and interest in what was happening—nervously shifted from foot to foot. The Voevoda continued the interrogation.

"Or, maybe you'll tell us why you party is called 'National-Liberal', if it opposed the Bulgarian nation and liberal freedom?"

"And it supported the upheaval in the country, carried out by the so-called 'Democratic Collusion', which is in fact not democratic at all, but it is anti-democratic, anti-people and fascist by its essence!" Todor said.

"You, all the foes of the Bulgarian people, not only carried out the fascist coup in the country, but also perverted and turned inside out the very concepts and definitions of 'national', 'liberal', and 'democratic'."

"Exactly so," Radyu Delchev confirmed and continued the interrogation, "So, do you, the so-called 'national-liberal', remember, how you actively participated in the fascist coup d'état in Haskovo on June 9, 1923 and how you helped the gang of bandits of tsar Boris III-Tsankov to seize power and overthrow the legal government of Alexander Stamboliysky? Why are you silent? You don't remember? But we remember! We remember and on behalf of the district military organization of the United Front of the Communists and Agrarians, we sentence you to death!"

Frightened exclamations waved over the crowd, and Borachev pleaded, turning to the chetniks: "Have mercy! Save me! I want to live!"

"And Alexander Stamboliysky, didn't he want to live, in your opinion?" Todor asked him. "Or maybe Raiko Daskalov didn't want to live?"

"And all the government ministers and members of the Agrarian Union, whom you, the butchers, tortured to death, didn't they want to live?" Atanas Georgiev Zapryanov, the BANU representative, asked him.

"I did not kill! I did not torture! I did not want! I was forced! I was wrong! Have mercy! I'll be useful to you! I'll help you!" Borachev pleaded, addressing the chetniks.

Radyu Delchev, Todor Todorov, Ivan Ignatov and Mityu Ganev stopped aside and after conferring returned back, and Mityu Ganev announced:

"We, the commanders of the detachments of the cheta Hristo Botev, consulted and decided to cancel the death sentence to Vasil Borachev in view of his sincere repentance and pardoned him."

2 chetniks, holding Vasil Borachev by the arms, let him go, and he remained standing free, closing his eyes and praying in a frenzy to all the gods of the world taken together of all times and all the peoples. Joyful exclamation of amazement and approval swept through the crowd, to which Radyu Delchev addressed:

"Gentlemen, friends, we, the warriors of the cheta Hristo Botev, were forced to stop you here on the road, because there is no other way to convey to people information about what is happening. All rallies and demonstrations, all the public events are prohibited, except those which glorify a gang of bandits in power. And the entire Bulgarian press sold out itself in bulk to this gang and serves the anti-people regime. This fascist regime and the venal press call our cheta Hristo Botev a band of robbers, while the gang of robbers is they: tsar Boris III, who organized the bandits upheaval on June 9, 1923, and his henchmen: Tsankov, Vylkov, Rusev and all the leaders of the 'Black Bloc', who participated in the coup. This gang of the bandits, as you know, on June 9 last year committed a villainous crime against our country and the Bulgarian people. They overthrew the legitimate government of the Agrarian Union of Alexander Stamboliysky, brutally tortured almost all the government ministers and cut to pieces the Prime Minister Stamboliysky for several days! He died a martyr and heroic death. They tortured tens of thousands of people in Bulgaria, who did not humble themselves and did not bow before the criminal bandit regime, and all who sympathize them. Therefore, it's not us who is a gang of robbers, as the fascists impudently lie, but they themselves are the gang of criminals and butchers of the Bulgarian people. And we are the political cheta of the United Front of the Communists and Agrarians; our goal is political: to prepare the masses for the anti-fascists uprising in Bulgaria with the aim of removing the fascist junta, bringing them to justice and establishing the workers-peasants government of the United Front. Let all people know about it, tell your friends about it, and let them, in turn, tell the others. And now you are free! We apologize for we delayed you!"

The crowd was standing and did not disperse, began to applaud, as if wanted to listen to more words that gave them strength of mind and instilled hope. But the Hristo Botev cheta warriors turned round, in an instant left them and vanished from sight. They walked without looking on the road, to the south, passed Haskovo and entered the village of Malevo, hiding and running from one shelter to another, approached and knocked at the house, where they expected to find shelter. The latch clanged, the door opened, and the secretary of the party organization, their comrade-in-arms and friend Milyu Georgiev Djezveliev appeared on the threshold.

"Come in, quickly!" he told them, looking around.

The entire detachment hurried inside, and Milyu closed the door.

"Comrades, I am not inviting you, sorry, in your own safety," he addressed them, standing right at the door, "it's very dangerous here; my younger brother Latun fired at the fascist kmet, but the gun misfired, and my brother fled to the vicinity village and hides somewhere there, and our house is under surveillance, like the whole village. It is very dangerous here, you must immediately go to another place. Go to Manastir to the house of Georgy Yorse, the password is following…the answer is…"

"We understand," Radyu Delchev answered, "boys, let's go!"

Milyu unlocked the door, looked out and, not noticing anything suspicious, nodded his head to them, and they hurriedly left the house. Evening twilight was thickening over the villages, a dank wind cut through to the bones; they left Malevo, vigilantly looking around, and went toward west, where the village Manastir was located. The detachment was led by Delcho, the Voevoda's brother. During the cheta's transitions from one place to another, they always appointed a guide, who was from that area and knew it very well from childhood. The Voevoda's brother Delcho Delchev Mitev, like his brother Radyu himself, was born and raised in the village of Voevodovo, located in the vicinity on the western side, became its kmet, but when he found out that he was suspected of helping the cheta Hristo Botev and his arrest was being prepared, he abandoned the village, the kmet's office, his native house and went into illegality, entered the cheta. Now he was leading his cheta through the vicinal territory to the village Manastir. It got quite dark. They entered the village and began to make their way to its northern part, walking along its eastern side.

"Right here," Delchev said, pointing to a lonely house, standing on the north-east of the village.

Radyu Delchev knocked at the gate. In a few minutes an unfamiliar voice asked:

"Who is there?"

Radyu said the password. There was no answer.

"What's your name?" Radyu asked.

"Georgy Dobrev, and who are you?"

The Voevoda with the cheta was stupefied by surprise, anxiously looking around. It was quiet around.

"Sorry, we've made a mistake," Radyu apologized.

The physiognomy of the host peeked out from behind the gate with curiosity and began to scan, where the armed men moved.

"Unforgivable negligence!" Voevoda gritted through his teeth to his brother, who already cursing himself.

They went to the north-western outskirts of the village and finally found the house of George Yorse. Georgy Yorse, the faithful yatak of the cheta, and his son opened the door and let the entire squad in. After the action on the road, the crossing and nervous tension, the chetniks sat down with pleasure in the large living room and proceeded to dinner, which Georgy Yorse and his treated the warriors. They told how they had made a mistake with the house, Yorse frowned and said:

"We must be alert!"

In a short time there was a knock at the door. All froze and fell silent Yorse asked through the door:

"Who is it?"

"It's me, Petko Georgiev. So, I've come to ask you if you would build a cheshma in front of my house."

"Why did you come so late?"

"Well, so, I don't know, so, I decided to ask," the newcomer mumbled.

"Go home, I am going to bed already, we'll talk another time."

Petko Georgiev swirled around the door and peered into all the windows, tightly closed with curtains, and suddenly he found a corner of the window, where the curtain moved a little aside, and stuck his physiognomy to the glass, looking inside. The room was dim, and only one kerosene lamp lit, but he could make out some shadows of people. He immediately skipped running to the house of kmet, who was already resting after work.

"Yes, yes, they are there!" out of breath Petko Georgiev reported with a sense of accomplishment. "Georgy Dobrev said correctly: they went to Georgy Yorse house!"

"I am telling you that Georgy Dobrev told me himself that the armed men came to his house by mistake and then went to the house of Georgy Yorse!" Georgy Dobrev's friend Todor Kolev confirmed gladly. "But you don't believe me!"

"Delche, immediately run and report to the military post, let them urgently move here!" the Manastir's kmet ordered his activist Delcho Stamov, who together with Todor Kolev and Petko Georgiev also were whirling around kmet, and each of them excitedly anticipated his part from the promised royal reward for the cheta Hristo Botev.

"Wow, it's 2 km to run!"

"Come on, run!"

And Delcho Stamov dashed into the darkness for reward. At that moment, there was another knock at the Yorse door.

"Run, save yourself!" out of breath, a yatak from the village reported. "Kmet sent Delcho Stamov for the military, their post is in 2 km from Manastir!"

"Make sure that the kmet does not organize a counter-cheta in the village!" Yorse ordered, and the yatak disappeared behind the door.

"What shall we do?" Radyu Delchev asked.

"I think that we have no way to leave the village," Todor answered, "there is an open area around, the village is in full view."

"We'll take the fight!" Mityu Ganev decided.

"The battle!" Ivan Ignatov exclaimed.

"Who is for taking the fight?" Voevoda asked his friends, and everybody raised their hands.

"It's decided: fight!" Radyu Delchev said and turned to Yorse and his son: "Go outside and watch the highway to Haskovo and the situation in the village so that a counter-cheta does not appear."

Yorse and his son hurried out of the house, which stood on the north-western side of Manastir not far from the highway, leading from Haskovo and crossing the village from north-west to south-east. The whole highway was visible from long distance. Parallel to the highway, from both sides of it, 2 streams flowed nearby, flowing into the river to the south, which flowed from west to east, flowing down from the mountains near Asenovograd, and flowed into the Maritsa beyond Harmanly; it made a half-loop, went around Manastir in 1 km to the south of the village.

"We divide the cheta into 2 squads: I command the first one, and Mityu Ganev commands the second one," Radyu Delchev said and on the run developed an action plan, putting everyone in a certain place and indicating what to do, "are there additions?"

"We retreat to Oludere to the south after the battle," Todor suggested.

"Yes, and 3 cover the retreat."

The chetniks got ready. Radyu Delchev and Gueno Radev took a position at the window, overlooking the highway, and began to watch, all the others prepared for the battle, everyone knew his action. In 2 hours Yorse with his son ran into the house and said:

"They are coming, they are few: 7 people!"

"Wonderful, let's proceed!" Radyu Delchev commanded.

He and several fighters slopped out of the house and hid in a shed, which stood from the side of the house. The others hid at the exit. 7 soldiers slowly approached the house. 4 of them separated from the rest and began to move behind the back of the house, believing that there was a back exit, and 3 went straight to the front door, all were holding the revolvers cocked. All of a sudden, Radev and Atanasov jumped out of the shed with a lightning speed and killed 2 soldiers with 2 shots. One fell dead, another was seriously wounded, and the third one turned round and fled. Scheryu Atanasov rushed to catch up with him. At that moment all the rest jumped out of the house with lightning speed, a couple of people remained in front of the house, and the others divided into 2 parts, rushed to the back of the house and surrounded the military, having killed 2, the other 2 raised their hands and surrounded. The chetniks took away from them all the weapons and binoculars. Radyu Delchev wrote a note on a piece of paper:

"To the commander of the regiment. Do not send your soldiers to kill us, but better fight the criminal gang of bandits, who illegally seized power in Bulgaria! It is them who are guilty of all the troubles of the Bulgarian people! Not we are! We are the political cheta named after Hristo Botev!"

"Take and give this message to your boss!" Radyu Delchev said and gave the letter to the soldiers standing with the hands up. One of them took the note, and they started walking from the Yorse's house to the Haskovo highway, gradually quickening the pace, and then dashed to run.

"Let's go!" Radyu Delchev commanded.

"It's late, we stay," Todor said, pointing to the highway from Haskovo.

A large number of military men were approaching the village, stretching out in a chain for encirclement. They were in 700 m distance. 2 commanders were riding with great pomp ahead.

"Let's attack!" the Voevoda commanded, and all the chetniks took a convenient position in front of the house and first opened fire, when the enemy came closer. Lieutenant Asen Stoyanov fell dead from his horse to the feet of his subordinates, and immediately after him the agent of the Public Safety Draganov fell dead. The soldiers, who did not expect fire from the chetniks and were left without a commander, stopped in confusion, not knowing what to do. Panic gapped them. Some began to shoot on random into the void, not seeing in the darkness where they were shooting. The others dashed to opposite directions to run away. And the chetniks, taking advantage of commotion, prepared to retreat.

"Come with us, quickly!" they addressed the hosts: Georgy Yorse and his son.

The latter were standing silently and did not move from place.

"Faster!" they were called.

"I'll not go," Yorse answered, "and you, son?"

"I'll stay with you, father."

"Where shall we go?" Yorse sighed. "This is our house, all our household, we've been living all our life here."

He felt impossible to abandon his house, where he spent his life, to leave warmth, comfort, food, household and go to nowhere, cold and void.

"I'll stay with you, father," his son confirmed.

"Let's go!" Radyu Delchev commanded, and all hurried to retire south to the Oludere River.

The soldiers rushed in all directions in panic, some continued to shoot at random, imitating a battle. A stray bullet wounded the standard-bearer Ivan Velev in the left shoulder, he fell and continued to shoot at the soldiers. The chetniks quickly moved from Manastir. Under the cover of the night they safely made their way further and further south, where the hills rose at the foot of the Rhodopes, and then east to the village of Belitsa, where their comrades-in-arms were waiting for them. Single shots remained far away behind them, becoming more and more muffled, then subsided.

With an incredible effort of will, overcoming pain and losing of blood, the standard-bearer of the cheta Ivan Velev, left alone in the ring of the enemies, managed to crawl, make his way, get to his feet and run, he escaped from the encirclement and saved his life. At black night, hiding and bending down, he moved further and further from Manastir in the south-eastern direction and, finally, reached the village of Dolno Botevo. His last strength was only enough for him to crawl to the house of the party secretary Yordan Boynuzov and to knock at the door. Boynuzov dragged his comrade to the house of Mariyka

Miteva, where it was safer. Velev told them both about their action and the battle in Manastir, when they bandaged his wound, which fortunately turned out not fatal.

"It's risky to stay here during the day," Mariyka said worriedly.

"Before it dawns, let's take him to the koliba in the mountains," Yordan suggested.

"Can you go?" they asked him.

"I'll try."

They grabbed him under the arms and headed south from the village, where the mountains rose—a heaven and salvation for all the hajduks of all times. They climbed a hill along a familiar path and reached the koliba, hidden from prying eyes. In a small hut the matrasses were laid out, blankets and warm clothes lay. He spent a day there, and at night they came for him and lowered him to the village, and so on for a couple of days. Then Yordan Boynuzov with the yatak Gocho Valev transported him to another village of Tynkovo at night, where they left him in a house of the Marev brothers until full recovery. He did not stay there long: a few days later, getting stronger enough, he headed east to the village of Belitsa, where he met with his friends. The cheta Hristo Botev did not lose a single person.

And the embittered fascist junta, enraged with daring courage of the freedom fighters, raised to the feet all the policemen, military and fascist activists around Manastir, who vainly searched for them in all the kosharas and kolibas in the area and, finding nobody, brought down revenge on the yataks. They grabbed Georgy Yorse with his son and enjoyed themselves for long time, torturing them to half-death. They cut off pieces from their bodies: finger after finger on their hands and feet, beat them, hung them by their feet, poured quicklime down their throats and, when they were almost dead, shot them, "when trying to escape." Thus the hero of the BANU of Alexander Stamboliysky Georgy Yorse and his son, who provided shelter to the cheta Hristo Botev in the village Manastir died a martyr's death. Exactly the same fate befell the secretary of the party organization in the village of Malevo Milyu Georgiev and the activist of Voevodovo Manol Chalakov.

"Find and eliminate!" the tsar Boris III raged, sending orders down to the subordinates.

Chapter 50
Belitsa

Right now they could raise a red and orange banner over the village of Belitsa, as the whole village was theirs. There was not a single family in the village, not a single house with the fascist activists for a counter-cheta and traitors—all people were their faithful yataks-helpers. But they could not raise the banners right now, as they kept secrecy and expected the uprising, postponed to the spring of 1925, which they themselves carefully prepared. The village, the same as Kirilovo on the other side of the Maritsa River, on its left bank, was their main base and headquarters for the both parties of the United Front. Here they held their conference at the end of December 1924.

The military leaders of the Regional and District Organizations for preparing the uprising gathered in the house of Angel Minchev. In the spacious 2-story house of Minchev, sitting next to each other were Nedelcho Dimitrov Manev (George) from the Regional Military Administration in Plovdiv; Todor Kostov, the head of the District Military Organization in Haskovo; Dobri Terpeshev, the secretary of the Lyubimets' District Party Committee; Zhelyazko Dobrev (Consula) from Kirilovo, serving illegal channels across the border to Turkey and further to the USSR, and the other the United Front helpers from the village of Belitsa.

The island of freedom Belitsa, in an atmosphere of total terror and repression, located on the eastern outskirts of the Haskovo district, became a heaven for freedom fighters. Young beautiful, fearless, proud, dressed in beautiful uniform, the chetniks with weapons that they never parted with, girded crosswise with bandoliers, at any moment ready to enter in battle with enemy, were sitting in front of the audience as the main heroes of the event, real warriors of the revolution in full combat readiness, confident in the rightness of their cause and victory. The faithful yataks from Belitsa were on the post from both sides on the outskirts of the village and guarded the road. The conference in the Minchev's house proceeded without any interference. Voevoda Radyu Delchev said:

"Comrades, I am glad to inform you that the task set before us by the leadership of both parties of the United Front has been successfully completed. The Hristo Botev cheta, founded 10 months ago, is successfully operating and fulfilling its mission, its wonderful fighters are sitting in front of you."

All applauded. The chetniks felt like heroes. Radyu Delchev continued, "The Hristo Botev chetniks are cohesive squad of fighters, and there are real friendly relations between them, and they are ready to cover the other in an hour of battle with a foe and shoulder to shoulder to fight together against the foe. The Hristo Botev chetniks are the Agrarians, Communists and non-party people, and all of them are united by political coherence, a common foe and common goal. These wonderful fellows are real heroes, they have a combat training, discipline, excellent command of the tactics of guerilla warfare, and each of them has a desire to participate in actions and fulfill the tasks assigned to them. Their courage and readiness to sacrifice themselves are well-known. During all this time we have not lost a single warrior."

Radyu Delchev was speaking for a long time, talking about the successful actions of the cheta. The floor was taken by Yanko Kuzmov Pavlitov, the 22-year-old political leader of the District Committee of the BCP from Haskovo.

"Friends, the activities of the Hristo Botev cheta wouldn't have been possible without help of our faithful yataks. We have them in almost all the villages and cities of the region, except the village of Popovo."

All laughed.

"Perhaps, the yataks or sympathizers appeared in Popovo after September 17," one of the guests remarked.

"In any case, when we pass by Popovo, they don't shoot at us, neither chase, though they see us," Todor reminded.

All applauded.

"Friends," Pavlitov continued, "we must pay tribute to all of our yataks, to their courageousness, fearlessness and valor! All these simple villagers, mostly poor, gave us shelter in their homes, often shared the last piece of bread with us, risking their lives, the lives of their relatives and their home, as the butchers fascist regime and the so-called 'Law of the Protection of the State' threatens them with the death penalty and the burning of the houses. They, these simple villagers, are real heroes!"

All applauded.

"It should be noted," Pavlitov continued, "that our liaisons with the yataks-helpers in all the villages are becoming more and more difficult, it is becoming more and more difficult to supply us with food due to the wide spread terror from the bandit authorities and repressions."

He recounted in detail the horrendous inhuman martyrizing that the butchers' power subjected the poor yataks, if they discover them, and the executions without any trial and investigation for these unfortunate ones, who did not die under torture and survive. All are killed under the pretext of "trying to escape." Pavlitov listed the names of the victims and the villages, where the unfortunate peasants, who gave shelter to the cheta, were subjected to unimaginable suffering and were killed at the denunciations of the traitors. He told how the executioners broke the legs of the unfortunate and cut off their toes, and then finished them off "when trying to escape." The names of the heroes, these ordinary people-yataks, whose life was taken by the tsar Boris III with the butcher Tsankov for the roof over the head for the Hristo Botev cheta and a piece of bread for them, sounded like a bell tocsin from Yanko Pavlitov and arose the anger of the present and their passionate desire for vengeance. They were silent, frowning their faces. They honored in silence the memory of the yataks-helpers, martyrized by the junta. Dobri Terpeshev, the secretary of the party organization in Lyubimets, addressed the chetniks:

"Comrades, we know that the Central Committee offered you to go abroad for winter and spend the winter time there at our secret places, but you refused and remained in Bulgaria. It is already a month the winter time, it's hard time for you, it's hard to hide. The Central Committee defined your tasks as follows: you divide your cheta into small groups with 3–5 people and continue your mission—go around the villages, continue to organize the militia-6s, led by chiefs, teach them to use weapons, check their combat capability and support the spirit of the masses. You continue your everyday hard, painstaking work to prepare the villagers for the upcoming uprising. This is the task for today. At the same time you refrain from any actions so that not to endanger yourself and our party organizations. No action! It's not time for it now."

"Settle down for night for 2–3 days at the houses of our yataks in the villages that you know about and carry out the underground work hidden from other eyes. But if our leadership needs you to take some action, we'll inform you, and for this work we are creating a combat core with Voevoda Radyu Delchev, Todor Todorov, Mityu Ganev and Ivan Ignatov, some other chetniks can join them, if it is needed."

All the leaders from both parties spoke, and the chetniks vividly discussed each item on the agenda with them. It was already past midnight, when all the issues had been discussed, and the conference ended. Some of the guests stayed to spend a night in the house of the host Angel Minchev, and the rest were taken to their homes by the yataks-friends from Belitsa.

The village of Belitsa was located on the right bank of the Maritsa, one of its tributaries ran from west to east. It flowed from the mountains that rose to the west of the village and together with the other streams ran down into the valley and flowed into the Maritsa. The picturesque mountains, covered with forests, low, akin to the hills, they were called Gradischeto, preserved on themselves the traces of the ancient Thracians. On the very top of their middle hill, named Kaleto, the Thracian fortress towered, where the first Europeans-Thracians had lived and created works of art thousands years ago, laying down the foundation of the European civilization. They fought with enemy besieging the walls of the fortress; and battles and time left for eternal memory of posterity only thoroughly laid stones of the remnants of the walls with oval encircling the entire plateau on the top of Kaleto from south to north, along which a moat stretched. Ruined by enemies and time, the Thracian fortress, as a living witness of history, gazed down at Belitsa from the top of the hill, narrating about the eternal struggle.

The Hristo Botev cheta spent a couple of days in the village of Belitsa thanks to the hospitality and loyalty of the villagers, then split onto 2 parts and left Belitsa. One detachment left west, closer to Bolyarsky Izvor, where there were many yataks in the nearby villages and militia-6s already had been founded. The chetniks checked their fighting capability, supported moral spirit and staged meetings. After spending 2–3 days in one of the houses, not to endanger the hosts, they moved on to another house, being in constant motion.

A detachment of 10 people, led by the commander Todor Todorov left Belitsa and went east across Maritsa to the village of Kirilovo. Located on the left bank of the Maritsa not far from the river, the village stood on ancient land, where human being found shelter for himself yet in pre-historic times, on the land of the Thracian civilization, absorbed by the Greeks, where the Romans paved the way on the lands, seized from the Greeks at the turn of the 2 eras. The village, situated on the slopes of the hills, was called Bunakli under the Turks and in 1903, Kirilovo, in honor of the second son of the Tsar Ferdinand Kirill, a pretender to the Bulgarian thrown, although he was absent from the country, as he fled with the father Ferdinand after the abdication to the city Cobourg.

In the village of Kirilovo a comrade-in-arms in the fight against fascism Zhelyazko Dobrev (Consula) gave shelter to the cheta in his house for a couple of days, and then they split into 2 groups and set off again. A group of 5 people with commander Todor Todorov, consisting of Scheryu Atanasov, Georgy Naydenov, Dimitar Ivanov and Hristo Pavlitov went south to Svilengrad. They walked 16 km by foot along the left bank of Maritsa by the hills and dales, hiding from prying eyes, overcoming distances, cold and wind, and finally reached the very south of Bulgaria before the border with Greece, in 2 km from it. And in 14 km to the south-east Turkey began, which owned Svilengrad before the Balkan War.

In the depth of the millennia Homo sapiens mastered these lands, and the Adrysian Kingdom of the Thracians raised culture to unprecedented height so that the Greeks, out of envy, wanted to merge it, passing it off as their own. And then Rome, which had merged them, built here his fortress Burdeniss on his road to ancient Byzantium. Here, at the crossroads of all paths, all fought with all from century to century. This land of Byzantium was devastated by the Bulgarians. Here nearby they fought with Baldwin's crusaders. The Turks reigned here for half thousand years. They founded the village of Kipekli and built a bridge across the Maritsa in 1529, which became a masterpiece of architecture, and next to the bridge a village of Mustafa Pasha arose, which grew into the city. The battles were fought for it with the Turks in the Balkan Wars; it passed from the hands of the Turks to the hands of Bulgarians and back, when the Turks burned it in their rage of the Second Balkan and again ceded it to the Bulgarians in 1913. The city became Svilengrad and was rebuilt after the fire on both banks of the Maritsa River.

Todor's detachment entered Svilengrad in its left-bank part, where near the half-dried river Kanaklia, running parallel to the left and flowing into it to the south—there was a quarter of the same name there. The house of Ivan Samandjiev, an associate and companion of the chetniks, was there in that quarter. The Todor's detachment, tired from the road, found a hospitable welcome in his house. 5 people of Todor were seated at the table and, first of all, fed.

"Welcome, friends!" the host and 2 comrades-in-arms, who were waiting in Ivan's house: Todor Kirkov and Georgy Yankov, the head of the military organization, addressed them.

"We greet you!" the chetniks answered, sitting down at the table.

"Eat first, rest from the road, then we'll talk."

A warm, hospitable house with food after long transition through murk and cold was a delight for the exhausted travelers. Having eaten and rested from the road, they proceeded to the work.

"How are things in Svilengrad? How are our militia-6s?" Todor asked Georgy Yankov.

"Things are going well with the 6s, the 6s are formed, everyone is armed and looking forward the uprising." Georgy Yankov answered.

It was a reserve officer with a large experience, a noble man with convictions, who took the side of resistance to the fascist authorities in Bulgaria, young, handsome, slender and very pleasant to talk with.

"We'll meet with everyone, we'll speak, we'll support the moral spirit."

"Certainly."

All of a sudden Scheryu Atanasov ordered him in a commanding voice:

"Immediately report to me the details of the armament of the 6s!"

His voice was not only commanding, but unceremonious and rude. Todor was stupefied.

"You, Scheryu Atanasov, do not order me, and even with a raised tone!" Georgy Yankov calmly replied. "You are not my commander, and I am not your subordinate. I am the officer and much older than you. We are comrades-in-arms in the fight against a common foe, and I, as the head of the military organization, together with the chiefs of the 6s, have made a lot of efforts to provide all the members of the 6s with the weapons."

"Friends, calm down!" Todor addressed both of them. "Georgy, forgive Scheryu, we are all very tired and everyone's nerves are on edge. We move from one settlement to another and are in a constant danger. We hide in the other people houses, form the 6s, we are responsible for their readiness for battle."

"It's all right, Todor," Georgy Yankov answered calmly and reported in detail about the armament of people.

Scheryu Atanasov, annoyed to have been curbed, bit his lips with vexation: he wanted very much to command. In the house of Ivan Samandjiev the Todor's group spent a week, enjoying the hospitality of the host, doing their painstaking work every day. They met with all the 6s, checked their weapons and made sure that everyone was armed. All were waiting for the signal to revolt, having taken an oath of allegiance to their common struggle.

And at the last evening of their stay in the Ivan Samandjiev's house all gathered at the table, and Hristo Pavlitov, the chetnik from Haskovo, said:

"Friends, today, January 5th of the New Year of 1925, our commander Todor has a birthday! He turned 24 years old! Let's congratulate our wonderful commander with his birthday and wish him well-being, long life and success in our common struggle, the same as we all can be wished it!"

"Thank you!" Todor answered. "It is rightly said: we wish this to all of us!"

"Congratulations!" each of the present said with a smile, and the host immediately gave the guests a sip of rakia to the health of commander.

The modest celebration of Todor's birthday completed the work in Svilengrad. Having parted with the host, the owner of the house Ivan Samandjiev, the secretary of the party organization Todor Kirov, the officer Georgy Yankov, the head of the military organization, Todor's group set off on their way back north to the village of Kirilovo. 16 km walk by foot through the mountains and forests, and dank January cold.

Kirilovo after Belitsa was their second main base, where comrades-in-arms and faithful yataks were waiting. And from Kirilovo to Lyubimets. The vast village of Lyubimets lay on the right bank of the Maritsa River, and a highway passed through it, in which all the other roads merged from west to east and from north to south, linking all the cities of Bulgaria toward Tsaregrad. Renamed Lyubimets from Turkish Hebibche in 1906, when Bulgaria was getting rid of the Turkish heritage, the village appeared in 1573 on the ancient Thracian land, having gone through change of eras and civilizations. In 1925, there was one of the centers of resistance, headed by Dobri Terpeshev.

It seemed that evil fate, always and everywhere, turned everything upside down in a sane world and played a cruel joke with him. She deprived him of everything when he was only 8 years old, having taken away his parents, childhood and a tolerable life, and pushed him out in the street as an orphan to work for a piece of bread. That force that is stronger than us ruined people's plans for human life, taking away from the worthy and throwing blessings under the feet of the scoundrels. The struggle for survival from childhood as a farmhand for the other people—that's what filthy fate slipped Georgy, and he threw back in her filthy mug his unbending spirit and desire for knowledge, and resistance to her intrigues in response.

In the continuous struggle that his life had become since his childhood, he merged all the books, one after another, without stopping self-education. In Izvorovo, where he was born, he founded the first socialist organization in 1903, which he headed and, like the chetniks now, 12 years ago, in cold, heat and rain, he walked around the villages in the region, staging meetings and creating the party cores. He fought against delusional ideas of Ferdinand about "Great Bulgaria" in the Balkans wars and miraculously survived in front of a company of soldiers, placed under shooting, because the soldiers refused to shoot at him. He fought of the creation of the socialist organization in Lyubimets, where he moved in 1913, he fought against the entry of Bulgaria into the Great War according to Ferdinand scenario, and here he showed solidarity with Alexander Stamboliysky. He fought against the regime during the Vladay revolution shoulder to shoulder with Stamboliysky.

Terpeshev headed the Regional Department of the Party and became a member of the District Committee, creating party structures from Simeonovgrad in the north to Svilengrad in the south. And in June 9, 1923, he fought against the butchers of Stamboliysky and shoulder to shoulder with the Agrarians raised the orange banner over Lyubimets, capturing the post office, bank and railway station. He continued to fight the fascists, ironclad in the Haskovo prison after June 1923 and pondered on plans of the revolt. In March 1924 he was released from prison, survived and returned to struggle. One of the founders of Hristo Botev cheta, he cherished her as his offspring, taking care of the chetniks, of their winter quarters, food and clothing. The faithful yataks in the towns and villages, despising the danger, let the cheta in their homes, and every time, when crossing, the chetniks knew in advance, where they would stop.

Todor led his people to Lyubimets, and Ivan Karageorgiev opened the door of his house for Todor's detachment.

"Come in, friends, feel at home, sit down at the table, have dinner, rest from the road!"

And after dinner…again meetings, inspections, instructions. All the heads of the 6s in Lyubimets and the assistant of the head of the military organization Dimo Angelov came to the meeting; all shook hands of the chetniks.

"Comrades, we welcome the detachment of Todor Todorov in Lyubimets! Hello to all of you from my uncle Dobri Terpeshev. The goal of the United Front remains the same: the course for the revolt this spring," Zhelyazko Terpeshev said and reported on the domestic and international situation in Bulgaria and the degree of readiness for the uprising.

"How many weapons are there?"

"Are the weapons seriously covered?"

"Do all the members of the militia-6s have command of the weapons?"

Todor and his group tested the readiness of Lyubimets to fight. They spent several days in Lyubimets, thanked Ivan Karageorgiev for his hospitality, shook hands with the comrades-in-arms and set off. They went north-west from Lyubimets, the village of Belitsa was left behind below, and they entered the village of Biser. The further they moved west of Maritsa, the higher the hills rose; they surrounded Biser from all sides, rising more toward the sky from the south-western side, and the village, as if on waves, was situated right on the slopes of the hills, densely covered with forest. The Biserska River ran through Biser from the west, flowing down from the hills of the Eastern Rhodopes, and cut the village into 2 parts, and carried its waters further to the east, entering Maritsa from its right side. And the river, and the hills, and the forests were covered with snow and ice. And the Hristo Botev cheta, Todor's group was surmounting their path.

Faithful yatak Zhelyazko Darakgiev, secretary of the party organization and head of the 6, opened the house in front of them. Rest from transition, dinner under the roof in the warmth. Meetings, gatherings, checking. The militia-6s, ready for battle, demonstrated the combat readiness. Farewell to friends till meeting soon again on the road. They went north-west along Maritsa to the city of Harmanly. How old this land was for human habitation, the Neolithic megaliths that stuck out in the middle of the field to the south-west under Harmanly spoke for themselves. They remained to the left from the travelers. As if nothing had happened, they had been standing here for 9 thousand years as witnesses of history, having survived all the regimes and uprisings against them. It was as if they were challenging the chetniks and saying: "This is what ancient people could do! And what can you do?" It is not known now, by what miracle ancient people had built a stone house. It is not known how they placed 3 flat stones, which made up the walls, and covered the walls with the same stone as a roof. It appeared a stone house. Mystery kept a secret, creating the riddles, how they had moved these stones, gigantic heavy boulders, and where they dug them out. Here, apparently, there was an altar here, where the ancient people cried out to heaven, praying for salvation.

And Todor's warriors continued their way past them to call for the uprising. Harmanly lay between 2 rivers. Undulating and meandering, the Oludere flowed from the west and approached the city from the western side, rose to the north, turned east almost at a right angle and flowed into Maritsa from the right side. Harmanly lay in the interfluve, surrounded by rivers from 3 sides. Thracians, Romans and Bulgarian settlers left their traces here. The Turks built a caravanserai here in 1510, where the travelers from Istanbul stopped for a night and changed postal horses. The Turks erected across the Oludere River a stone bridge hunched over in an arc in 1585, a masterpiece of architecture. And a village arose nearby, where the villagers grew rye in the fields, and next to the water it was a large threshing floor, where rye was threshed. Threshing floor is "harmanly" in Bulgarian, and those who threshed the rye, were called "harmanly". This is how the city appeared, when in 1925 there were streets and houses, and churches, vocational schools, the library "Druzhba," museums, railway station, through which the Orient Express ran, and mosques remained after the Turks.

In January 1925 in Harmanly the Hristo Botev cheta had a strong military organization of Communists and Agrarians and 7 militia-6s ready to fight. The Todor's group was led by a guide from Biser, who went with them and brought them to the appointed place. They stopped in a guard booth in 1 km from Harmanly for security and secrecy. And next to the booth there was a cheshma "Belonogata" in a big park and the remains of brick wall from a medieval fortress. Next to the cheshma there is a white statue of the "Belonogata," White-legged Gergana, who according to a legend, allegedly, was met here by the Ottoman Vizier and invited to his palace, but the girl refused him. Here on the slab, the lines of the Petko Slaveykov's poem "The Spring of Belonogata" were written. The Bulgarians, who made the fascist coup d'état, loved the sentimental fables.

Observing secrecy, Todor's group stopped in a small booth outside the city near the "Belonogata" cheshma. They were met here and embraced by Atanas

Guenov, the head of the party and military organization, who had just returned from the Soviet Union via secret channel. Companions and comrades-in-arms from Harmanly brought them food, and in a small hut near the cheshma they held staged the necessary meetings, checks and instructions.

"We are ready for the uprising," all reported, "militia-6s are armed, and we are waiting for a signal from you."

"Soon, another month of winter and spring will come," Todor said.

They spent 5 days near Harmanly and went back to Kirilovo. And from Kirilovo, again to Belitsa, where the next conference was convened. Scheryu Atanasov was walking ahead of the Todor's group and showed the way. They crossed the Maritsa along the bridge, crossed Lyubimets, where Atanasov was from, and having gone outside the village, sat down on the stone to rest and smoke a cigarette. The bright moon in the winter sky illuminated their path.

"Let's go here, we'll turn here," Scheryu Atanasov said and led the Todor's group.

They went on, walking, turning and bypassing the ravines, and thus they were going for 2 hours.

"This way, we'll come soon," Atanasov said, walking ahead.

"Maybe we'll stop, sit down, have a smoke right here at this very place, where we were smoking 2 hours ago?" Todor asked him, showing everyone the cigarettes butts, which they had left on this place.

"Where have you taken us to?" the tired chetniks asked irritably.

"I've appointed you as a guide, because you are from these lands!" Todor exclaimed. "And you've been driving us in a circle already for 2 hours! You are not even fit to be a conductor, but you strike to command! In Manastir the guide had already made a mistake once and led the entire cheta to the wrong house and almost ruined us all! And you want to lead us into a trap?"

Scheryu Atanasov glared at Todor with hatred, whose appearance irritated him.

"We'll come soon," he muttered under his breath.

They reached Belitsa, when it started to get light, and all the chetniks recognized the road, which they had passed several times. The conference began the next evening, and all the associates from the region came to it. The head of the district military organization from Haskovo Todor Kostov had an important message.

"Comrades, we have received the information that General Nikola Zhekov, who, as you know, openly opposes the Tsankov regime, is preparing a military coup against it!"

Excited exclamations were heard among the present.

"Well done!"

"Right!"

"It's high time!"

Kostov continued.

"So, the BCP Central Committee, the leadership of the Agrarian Union and the Comintern declared their support for the United Front of General Zhekov and uniting of our common forces."

The encouraging news inspired the present even more and strengthened their complete confidence in victory in upcoming uprising. They vigorously discussed the news, talked about the readiness of their militia-6s in cities and villages to rise, and in high spirit Todor's group again set off on the road in the evening of the next day. From Belitsa to the village Lyubimets they already walked by memory without Scheryu Atanasov help, who demonstrated his inconsistency as a guide. They crossed the Maritsa over the bridge and reached safely Kirilovo on the left bank of it. The active members of the military organization from the village of Kirilovo Zhelyazko Dobrev (Consula) received them in his house, and in the evening of the next day the chetniks set off. They went north to the village Oryahovo, where the brothers Nikola and Ivan Borbatev received them in their house, in which they conducted inspection of militia-6 with the head of the military organization in Oryahovo Hristo Shishkov, Konstantin Karatyozov and Stanko Mitev.

"I have good news, friends," the Agrarian Stanko Mitev said, "the commander of the canister company in Harmanly told me that during the uprising we can count on his company."

The good news gave the strength to the Todor's chetniks, and after spending several days in Oryahovo, they headed north to Izvorovo in the evening. They walked at night along the southern slopes of the Sakar Planina from one village to another to prepare uprising. They spent several days at Yanko Mitev's house in Izvorovo, where checked the militia-6s. They had no time to kill 2 policemen, who had come to Izvorovo to kill Zhelyazko Terpeshev, the nephew of Dobri Terpeshev, because the policemen had fled before the chetniks arrived. They hid Zhelyazko Terpeshev and set off again.

"The 'Law on the Protection of the State' not only hasn't been canceled, but was strengthened," Dimo Kazaliev told them.

But, despising the danger, both the chetniks and the yataks continued to prepare the uprising. They climbed north along the slopes of Sakar Planina and came to the village Cherepovo, where the yataks Georgy and Dimitar Kadirev received them in their house. And the next day evening a group of Mityu Ganev came into this house, who also, moving from one settlement to another, did the same work.

"Mityu! Ivan!"

"Todor!"

3 friends hugged, when they met in the Kadirev's house.

"A little more is left, a couple of weeks, and the winter will end!"

"And the uprising is scheduled for spring!"

In high spirits, seeing a gleaming target on the horizon, the groups of Todor and Mityu dispersed in opposite directions from Cherepovo; Todor lead his people further north to Simeonovo, where the yatak Chertukov was waiting for them in his house. After checking the combat readiness of the 6 in Cherepovo, Todor and his warriors turned left, crossed the Maritsa and came to Zlati Dol, located from the south under the river, where Maritsa turns almost at a right angle and turns south from the west. The colleague Delcho Gurbanov received them in his house. He also told Todor:

"All ours are ready; we managed to contact a group of officers in the barracks of the 3rd Infantry Regiment. They are all on our side together with the soldiers."

"Good news, friends!" Todor answered, "It's not long to wait left!"

Then they went north; the Sazliyka River flowed south to their left; Navasen left aside by the river, and they came to Obruchische, the largest village in the district, where they met with Mityu Ganev's group again. The yatak Yurdan Ilchev received them in his house. Meetings, discussions, checking, instructions. With the secretary of the party organization Dimo Dichev and the militia-6s heads they excitedly discussed the uprising, which was almost around the corner. Having completed the task, the chetniks said goodbye, shook hands with each other and with the words "see you soon" left Obruchische and went to different directions.

They walked like the uprising pilgrims, sinking into the snow up to their knees, bypassing on foot the Bulgarian villages, in order to prepare revolt.

Their faces were weathered and ammunition was heavy, and they were all sure, it'll be soon revolution. Wanderers, driven and homeless, they marched relentlessly forward, and all were irreconcilable fighters, the Hristo Botev squad.

Chapter 51
Navasen

On March 30, 1925, the group of Hristo Botev chetniks of 5 people: Hristo Pavlitov, Atanas Davkata, Delcho Delchev, Radyu Hristov and the commander Ivan Velev, having left Obruchische after a successful checking of the militia-6s, headed south and stopped along the way in the village of Navasen. The small village lay on the left bank of Sazliyka River, which flowed further and flowed into the Maritsa from its left side. The guide from Obruchische suggested:

"Let us stop here. There is one uninhabited house, we can rest from the road there."

"Sure?" Ivan Velev asked.

"I know for sure, the house is abandoned, nobody is there."

"Well, lead," Velev answered.

They entered the village and safely passed through it to the southern outskirts, where the empty house stood alone on the side of the road. The chetniks came inside.

"Well, what did I say: the house is empty, there is nobody here, you can rest here."

"This village is unreliable, we don't have yataks here," Ivan Velev said cautiously.

"Why should we be afraid? How many times we have risked!" Radyu Hristov, Georgy Pilashev father-in-law, complacently answered.

"We'll stay!" all answered.

"Do you know anyone, whom we could speak with about founding of 6?" Velev asked the guide.

"I don't know anyone exactly well, though I am superficially familiar with some."

"Spring has already come. March is coming to an end, and people are not yet prepared for the uprising everywhere."

"And when is the uprising?"

"They postponed it for spring, but the exact date hasn't been set," Velev answered.

"But in our Obruchische all are ready long ago," the guide answered, "I'll be returning, and you'll find the way yourselves then. You'll walk along Sazliyka and go straight to Maritsa."

"Good, we'll not get lost."

The chetniks of Velev parted with the guide, and the latter left them, heading back to Obruchische. One chetnik sat down on guard by the window and began to scan the surrounding area, and 4 fell asleep in order to get enough sleep at last the rest of the night. Everything was calm outside the window. Having wakened up in the morning, 4 were on guard, and the night sentry fell asleep. The time was approaching noon. One villager approached the house, who was looking after the empty house for himself, pondering on how to get his hands on this house. It seemed to him that somebody had overtaken him and occupied the empty house. Seething with anger that somebody had overtaken him and occupied the empty house, he squatted down and quietly crept up to the window, clinging to the wall, brought his physiognomy to the glass and peered inside. He saw 5 armed people: 1 was sleeping, and 4 were sitting at the table and periodically looked through the window. The hunter for the stranger house immediately recalled back from the glass unnoticed and, pressing himself to the ground, hurriedly left.

"Now I'll buy a new house for myself, not just occupy the old empty one!" pounded in his brain. "His Majesty the tsar promised big money for them!"

Moving away from the house in a crouching position in the direction of the north side, he immediately straightened up and with all his might dashed to run to the kmet's house. At that time of a day the kmet was at home and ate healthy lunch. The runner began banging on the door with all his might and yelling:

"Open up!"

The indignant kmet told his wife to open the door. The runner burst into the house and, hardly breathing, reported:

"They are here! Chetniks are here! They are in the empty house! I've seen them myself!"

From the news the kmet choked on a piece of cheese, turned purple, coughed and ran out of the house, waving with his hand to the messenger to follow him. Both ran to the office of kmet, where there was a telephone. Continuing to cough, the kmet phoned to the city Galabovo, which was north up the stream of the Sazliyka River on its right side, calling the police.

"Fast! Fast! Fast!" the kmet repeated, coughing, raving about the reward.

"And you run along the houses and call our people! All!" he ordered the messenger, and the latter angrily went to fulfill the order, feverishly counting in his mind on how many people the reward will be divided. To be on the safe side, he did not call all. A group of the activists gathered near the kmet's office.

Meanwhile, the chetniks were sitting in the empty house, while one of them was sleeping, and discussed a plan of further action.

"We'll stay here until night, and, as it gets dark, we'll set off," Ivan Velev said.

2 hours had passed. Suddenly there was a knock at the door. Everyone froze and grabbed his weapon, which was always ready.

"Open, I am from this village, and I have to tell you something."

All 5 were at once on their feet, 3 took positions by the windows, 2 stood on both sides of the door and opened it. A miserable man was standing on the threshold and crumbling his hat in his hands. One of the chetniks grabbed him by the collar and dragged inside the house, and they closed the door.

"Who are you? What do you want?"

"I am a negotiator," the messenger replied, stuttering, showing a piece of white cloth, pulled out from his hat, "I've been sent to convey you to surrender, as you are surrounded, and you won't get out of here alive."

Ivan Velev assessed the situation in a trice and changed glances with the others. They understood each other.

"Tell the one who sent you, that is kmet, that we do not surrender. We are the Macedonian cheta on a secret mission from His Majesty Tsar Boris III. Let him immediately remove the encirclement and let us go, but if he does not remove his gang and the policemen, if decides to pursue us, we'll burn your filthy village and report to His Majesty that all of you are his enemies! Go!"

"If they don't leave, we'll take the battle," Ivan Velev said, "we'll run out of the house and open fire, we'll make our way south toward Maritsa, but it would be nice to wait until dark."

Another hour passed. Exactly this time the kmet with the policemen were scratching their skulls and wondering if they were really the Macedonians or not.

"And how do they look like?" the kmet inquired the negotiator. "Do they look like the Macedonians? Are there Mityu Ganev, Todor Todorov and Ivan Ignatov among them?"

"No, I did not see those among them: those are well-known by description! No, these are completely different!"

"Or maybe they are really the Macedonians of His Majesty? Only, what do they do in our village? Or maybe they just stopped for a night on the way to another place? Listen, go back to them and tell them that if they are really His Majesty's Macedonians, then let them come out, and we'll talk. Or if they are not them, but quite different, that is the Hristo Botev chetniks, then let them surrender, because they are surrounded."

The "parliamentarian," kept on counting in his mind how much he would receive the reward, if they are the chetniks, for handing them over and how much additionally for "being a parliamentarian." It turned out a good amount, and, inspired with the idea of buying a new house, he bravely knocked at the door. The door opened, and he was dragged inside.

"It was ordered to convey you that if you are the Macedonians, go out to talk, and if you are not the Macedonians, then surrender, as you are surrounded."

"You'll stay with us!" Ivan Velev ordered and pushed him into the rear of the house away from the door. "You'll stay with us, until we let you go! If you make a move, we'll shoot you!"

The "parliamentarian," trembling with fear, crawled under the table and convulsively continued to count in his mind how much he would receive the reward from His Majesty Tsar Boris III. The kmet with the policemen waited for some more time and, making sure that the "parliamentarian" was detained, they opened fire at the house. The chetniks were responding by returning fire from the broken windows. Their weapons were always ready for battle, and their bandoliers were always filled with hundreds of bullets. Carefully looking out of the windows, they figured out where they were shooting from and accurately shot back.

The roar of the broken things in the house and the whistle of bullets filled the entire space around. Trembling with fear, the "parliamentarian" closed his eyes and ears and, sitting under the table, continued to count the reward. Courageous Ivan Velev, Hristo Pavlitov, a 23-year-old communist from Haskovo, Atanas Zapryanov (Davlata), a 34-year-old Agrarian from Haskovo, Delcho Delchev Mitev, the Voevoda's brother and a former kmet of Voevodovo village, and Radyu Hristov Radev, a 56-year-old Agrarian from Bukovo, the father-in-law of Georgy Pilashev, were fighting in cold blood and accurately fired at the foe from the windows of the empty house. They played for time and waited for dusk. During 2 hours the policemen and armed fascist activists from the village of Navasen fired in vain at the house, and in response they received well-aimed shots from the chetniks from the windows and fell one after another. Ivan Velev commanded to abandon the house.

"Let's wade to Maritsa!"

They jumped out of the house, having pushed the "parliamentarian" out, and threw a couple of grenades at the attackers. In panic the remains of the activists rushed to their heels.

"Run, I'll cover!" Ivan Velev ordered and, crouching to the ground, continued to shoot at the fleeing foe. 4 with the "parliamentarian" ran across the yard and looked back in front of the fence. Ivan Velev was lying on the ground with a helpless hand, clutching the revolver.

"Back!" Hristo Pavlitov commanded and rushed to Velev.

The other followed him. They ran up to the standard-bearer, who was lying on the ground, picked up his revolver, grabbed him by the arms and dragged him back into the house. They rolled him on his back and put a pillow under his head. Velev's face was distorted from suffering, and dark blood flowed out from his left side.

"I am finished, friends..." he uttered with difficulty.

"It's nothing, we'll get out!" Radyu Hristov encouraged him, trying to bandage his wound.

At that moment, the whistling bullets flew again into the house from all the windows. The "parliamentarian" crawled back under the table, and the chetniks continued the battle. The battle lasted until nightfall, until the darkness fell. They had to do something to get out of the house. They bent over Ivan Velev; he was lying helplessly on the floor, bleeding, and the blood was flowing through the bandage. All saw that the wound was fatal.

"We'll carry you on the blanket," Atanas Zapryanov said, "all of us will take the ends of the blanket and we'll get you out."

"Kill…please…do not leave me to the enemy…" with difficulty moving his lips, dying Ivan Velev replied with his face, distorted from martyrdom.

It was midnight.

"We can't do it," each chetnik of the group said in turn.

"Give me a revolver…" the lips of the dying standard-bearer whispered imploringly.

The chetniks looked at each other; tears were in their eyes. Delcho Delchev put a revolver into Ivan's hand. The latter made the last effort in his life in the struggle against the fascist junta in Bulgaria: he raised his hand with a revolver and shot himself in the temple. His eyes were looking at his fellow-comrades-in-arms, with whom they had been fighting side by side during the last year against the common foe, which had taken away from them their homeland Bulgaria, for which they fought to liberate. He was looking at these noble men, who did not bow their heads before the boot of the butcher's power, kissing the banner of the Hristo Botev cheta, which he, Ivan Velev, the standard-bearer of the cheta, was holding in his hands, when they entered the cheta to fight for freedom. His eyes were looking through the faces of friends into eternity, frozen forever. The messenger-parliamentarian was peeping from under the table.

For the first time in a year of their activity, the cheta Hristo Botev lost its warrior. The standard-bearer of the cheta Hristo Botev, Ivan Velev Petkov, a 30-year-old communist from the village of Dobrich, died from the enemy's bullet in the village of Navasen. 4 chetniks, gray with horror of loss, closed his eyes with their palms, took the revolver from his hand, removed his ammunition and, having parted with the passed friend, jumped out of the house, taking the "parliamentarian" with them. They crossed the yard, jumped over the fence and hurried out of the village. The fascist activists, sitting in ambush, opened fire on them right on the road. The killed "parliamentarian" fell down, struck by a bullet of his own. The oncoming fire of the chetniks dispersed the counter-cheta. They got out of Navasen safely. Bypassing the rest of the villages on their way, they, moving south-east along the left side of the Maritsa River, finally reached Oryahovo, where they were met with the other chetniks. Their banner was left, lying in a bag next to the lifeless body of the standard-bearer Ivan Velev.

Cheta-squad «Hristo Botev»

Chapter 52
Photo, Plovdiv, Sofia

Yet the bare skeletons of bushes and trees were blackening after hibernation, ready to revive soon, but the April sun had dried the puddles of the melted snow and filled the air with the scent of spring. Grieving hard the loss of their friend Ivan Velev, the Hristo Botev cheta, almost in full force, set off on a journey from east to west, closer to the District Center of the United Front in Haskovo and the Regional leadership Center in Plovdiv. They were moving at night, and during the day they rested on the still cold, but already dry land under the open sky. From the south they approached the village of Knyaz Borisovo, named after the one, whom they fought with.

The village was situated on the slopes of the hills to the west from Bolyarsky Izvor, not far from it. The Biserska River flowed past both villages. To the south the hills rose, gaining height. On the glade of the hill near Knyaz Borisovo, the cheta set up a camp. Soon their faithful yatak, the Secretary of the Party and Military Organization in Knyaz Borisovo Mitko Trandev, who was also a photographer and had his own photo workshop, came from the village. He brought his camera with him up the hill, and all the chetniks gathered to memorize themselves for history. The deceased Ivan Velev was absent. Also Atanas Georgiev (Krasin) from Pleven was not with them: he was killed on March 28, when he went with the assignment to Haskovo.

"Boys, get ready!" Georgy Pilashev gave the command.

"But we have been ready long ago!" was heard from all sides. "We have shaved!"

"As for us, we don't even think to shave, because with a beard and mustache we have a more respectable look!"

"An older look, you are aging yourself!" Mityu Ganev remarked sarcastically.

"We don't need to disguise under a girl, like you always do!" the bearded men laughed.

"Disguised as a girl, I penetrated the camp of the foe many times, and nobody ever recognized me," Mityu Ganev answered cheerfully, "imagine, if you dress as a girl, would it be at least anyone who would not recognize you with your beards and mustaches?"

All laughed in unison and began to gather in a group for a picture. Pilashev helped to place the chetniks.

"Todor, you stand the first on the left, and you, Ivan, close the row and stand on the right. You stand between them in the top row. The others stand in 2 rows in front of them, and 3 of us: Mityu Ganev, Georgy Nelezov and I will sit in front of you."

The chetniks in ammunition, which they never parted with and always had with them, were put in the right places. Georgy Pilashev with Ganev and Nelezov sat in front, and the photographer Mitko Trandev pointed the "Laika" camera at them and snapped the picture.

"Wow, what a camera!" they were gazing with amazement at the small camera that Trandev was holding in his hands.

"It's expensive, probably, isn't it?"

"Very expensive," satisfied photographer answered, "our people brought it from Plovdiv. Well, we've gotten a group photo for history!"

"Perhaps, our children and grandchildren will study our history by it." Todor said thinking.

"Yes, if we live to have our children and grandchildren," Ivan Ignatov sighed.

"Well, what a sad mood!" Georgy Pilashev objected. "Of course, we'll live, we all shall live to see a bright day!"

"Let's take next photo," the photographer called, "come on, Todor, you are the most handsome of us, stand here, and I'll take a picture of you!"

Scheryu Atanasov grinned wickedly. Todor began to pose in front of the photographer. He was standing with his ammunition: belted around his chest with bandolier, holding a rifle in his hands. His lash black hair, parted in the middle, fell down on his shoulders, framing his handsome, but somewhat thin face. His gaze was serious and somewhat stern, he was pondering on who would look at his photo in future, and whether he himself would convey this photo to posterity. The photographer clocked the button of his small camera and imprinted a moment for ages...

"Come on, next!" Trandev invited, being pleased that he himself was fulfilling a historical mission and taking photos for future generations of the legendary boys from the legendary Hristo Botev cheta.

6 people of Mityu Ganev stood in front of him, and the commander himself lay down in front of them, leaning on his left elbow and holding the rifle obliquely. The photographer took a picture.

"When shall we see the photo?" Pilashev asked.

"I'll bring them tomorrow," the photographer answered, "I hope you'll be here."

"We'll not move until we get the photos," Pilashev replied.

Georgy Pilashev headed the cheta during the absence of the Voevoda Radyu Delchev, and Todor Todorov was his deputy. Photographer Mitko Trandev kept his promise and brought the photos in a day. The chetniks were delighted to receive the pictures and scanned them. In the common photo of the entire cheta each of them was imprinted for memory of the descendants of future generations. Todor liked his photo: a handsome legendary warrior looked from it. He carefully placed several photographs between the pages of his notebook and hid in his bag. Ivan Ignatov came up and said:

"It's such a pity that Voevoda is not with us on the photo."

"Radyu Delchev is in Plovdiv," Todor answered, "he is carrying out the task together with Velyu Hristozov."

**

At that time in Plovdiv Radyu Delchev, dressed in the civilian clothes, with the appearance of an indifferent to everything layman was walking slowly along the street and passed a 2-story house in the back of the courtyard, which was separated from the street by a lacing fence with a gate. A car drove up and stopped before reaching the gate. Likomanov, the head of the Plovdiv Public Security, got out of the car and let the driver go. The car left. Slowly Likomanov went to the gate, leading to the courtyard of his house, where he lived. He inhaled the fresh aroma of spring air with full breath, clearing his lungs after the stuffiness and screams of the torture chamber.

He loved to be present at the torture of the prisoners, enjoining the spectacle with particular pleasure, when his butchers were operating, and sometimes he even had a hand in this. But he did not like the stuffiness of the torture chamber. That's why he was slowly walking home after work now and breathed deeply. He also did not like, when the enemies of the state, shot at the back, fell uselessly in the streets of Bulgarian cities, as now it was impossible to torment their lifeless bodies for your pleasure. Likomanov, with a sense of pleasure and a sense of accomplishment of duty to the fatherland, according to the "Law of Defense of State," smiling and inhaling the aroma of the coming spring, approached the gate of his house.

Likomanov breathed in the fresh April spring air for the last time and fell from the bullet that pierced his heart. Radyu Delchev ran across to the other side of the street, where Velyu Hristozov was waiting for him, and both of them instantly vanished into the alley, into the passing courtyard, again in the alley and again split walked slowly at a distance from each other and safely reached the house of Sofia and Jordan Karapetkov in 37 Maria Louisa Street, where they were safely hidden by their loyal companions and associates.

"How was it?" the hosts asked.

"The task is completed," Radyu Delchev answered, taken breath.

"How many more such butchers are left!" Velyu Hristozov exclaimed excitedly.

"We'll try to get them."

"How is your cheta there? You haven't seen them for a month!" Jordan asked.

"The cheta is in good hands, everything should be all right with them. Some more tasks, and we'll meet."

Having left the cheta under the command of Georgy Pilashev, Mityu Ganev and Todor Todorov a month ago, the Voevoda Radyu Delchev with Velyu Hristozov by the order of the Military and the Party leadership were taken by car to Plovdiv to carry out special tasks. There were still tasks to be accomplished.

***

One and a half weeks have passed. Early in the morning, on April 14, east of Sofia, in the Arabakonak mountain pass through the Balkan Mountains on the way to the village Orhanie, on a hill behind the bushes at the edge of the cliff, 5 anarchists from the city Koprivshetsa were sitting in ambush: Vasil Popov, Nesho Tumangelov, Anton Ganchev and Nesho Mandulov at the head of a commander Vasil Ikonomov. From the top of the hill, where they were sitting, they had a good view of the highway below. Each member of the group had his revolver ready. At 10 am they saw a car approaching in the distance. Ikonomov was looking in the tsar's binoculars.

"Get ready!" Ikonomov commanded. "Look, don't shoot at the one, who is not to be shot!"

"Yes, we remember!" the subordinated replied.

The vehicle drove up closer, and Ikonomov gave the command to shoot. Shots rang out, the vehicle stopped, the killed driver leaned over the steering wheel, and one person was killed in the back seat: the scientist entomologist Delcho Ilchev. Next to him there was his bag, in which he carried new specimens of plants and insects to the Sofia Museum. A man sitting next to him was not hurt. He jumped out of the car and vanished into the bushes. It was the Bulgarian tsar Boris III. Vasil Ikonomov was looking in the tsarist binoculars.

"It's ok, let's go!" he commanded his people, and all 5 hid in the bushes and disappeared in the opposite directions.

In the evening of the same day in Sofia near the "Cathedral of 7 Saints" General Georgiev was shot, the leader of the Military Union in Sofia and one of the organizers of the coup d'état in Bulgaria on June 9, 1923, and a member of the National Assembly from the fascist junta "Democratic Collusion," as well as the member of the commission that carried out death sentences on the Communists and Agrarians. This one was shot by the military organization punitive group of Atanas Todovichen and Zhivko Dinov. The funeral service was scheduled for April 16.

The events piled up like a snowball from both sides of the barricades. Even more the best representatives of the Bulgarian people were burned alive in the furnace of the police stations, fell in the street shot in the back, and writhed in death throes from suffocation with a noose around their neck, which was tightened on both sides by the sadistic executioners to the malicious guffaw of the Tsankov's gang.

"Slaughter, strangle, eliminate them, first of all the intelligence!" squealed the frenzied Vylkov, voicing the will of his superiors and passing it down to the executors.

The regime of Boris-Tsankov completely exterminated Bulgaria from thought and free spirit. The butchers tortured in the torcher chambers for their own pleasure people free to think and free in spirit. The medieval torture of the Inquisition, revived by the Tsar Tsankov junta in Bulgaria, shocked the civilized world, and Winston Churchill exclaimed: "If I lived in Bulgaria, I would become a revolutionary!"

In the evening of April 15, in a secret apartment in Sofia, the revolutionaries Todor Pavlov and Pavel Iskrov, who had become the newly elected Executive Bureau of the Military Organization instead of the eliminated the old one, had a fierce argument between themselves.

"We should not do this, because the whole society will be against us!" Iskrov exclaimed, pacing nervously across the room in the Sofia clandestine apartment.

"Society? Which society? A society of fascists and their accomplices? Where is this society already for 2 years, when the Tsankov's gang has been exterminating all decent people in Bulgaria? The entire society is split into 2 camps, and the civil war is going on in the country! They are against us, and we are against them! And a la guerre comme a la guerre!" Pavlov retorted, striving for action.

"There will be many victims!" Iskrov predicted gloomily.

"Not more than ours!" Pavlov answered. "Not only not more, but much less! It is us who have had many victims since June 9, 1923: so many that it is impossible to count them all, beginning from Stamboliysky and the Central Committee of BCP and ending with a tortured peasant in a remote village together with his family and their burned house!"

"I am afraid, if we do this, the legal opposition to Tsankov will turn away from us and, on the contrary, will rally around the authorities," Iskrov insisted.

"Vice versa! The legal opposition will seize the opportunity that there are no more the fascist junta leaders and take power into their hands, and we'll unite with them," Pavlov objected.

The entire former composition of the Central Committee of the BCP was destroyed: some were tortured to death, some shot themselves under the threat of arrest, some perished in skirmish, some fled abroad, and Iskrov and Pavlov made up the newly elected Central Committee. They were arguing fiercely with each other, giving argument pros and cons, and thus the midnight approached. Excited from the argument, Pavlov went out of the apartment into the street in agitation, finally throwing to Iskrov:

"I'll go to talk to Kosta Yankov."

Iskrov remained at home, tormented by gruesome forebodings. The hands of the clock passed after midnight, and it was April 16, 1925. Pavlov came to the secret apartment, where Kosta Yankov and Ivan Minkov were staying.

"Is the 'Great Work' being postponed or will it be completed?" Pavlov asked.

"The 'Great Work' will be done today at the exactly appointed time," Yankov answered confidently.

Born in a military and revolutionary family, Kosta Yankov was married to the daughter of the founder of the Bulgarian Social Democracy Dimitar Blagoev and was himself imbued with the spirit of the revolution to the core. A brave officer, who went through 3 wars: 2 Balkan Wars and the Great War, a reserve major since 1919, declared resistance to the fascist junta on June 9, 1923, and defended the Stamboliysky's Agrarian Union. He was one of the organizers of the resistance in September 1923. A member of the Central Committee of the BCP since May 1924, a brilliant brave officer, he headed the headquarters of the military organization, and during already a year he had been preparing the uprising throughout the country, which the Central Committee continued to postpone for later.

"They've killed our liaison in the palace professor Delcho Ilchev yesterday in the passage Arabakonak."

"Somebody disclosed the professor, he was our invaluable agent in the palace," Ivan Minkov said, "probably the tsar himself organized and staged assassination attempt on himself."

Ivan Minkov was Kosta Yankov's deputy in the military organization and had much in common with him. Born in a military family, he became an officer and went through 3 wars. In the Great War he was a pilot, was wounded and fought bravely. A reserve major, a convinced revolutionary, he was preparing the uprising together with Kosta Yankov.

"Iskrov is against it," Pavlov said.

"Cowards, not capable for anything!" Minkov exclaimed.

"He says there will be many casualties."

"Only supporters of the fascist junta will be there: its opponents will simply not go there!"

"The Central Committee is against it," Pavlov informed.

"I'll take care of everything!" Kosta Yankov exclaimed. "They have been dragging their feet for 2 years: soon none of us will be left! They are exterminating all of us and yet the survived Agrarians. They took away from us our country—we must take it back! We'll exterminate them all together, all at once, all the gang ringleaders and their accomplices! These are not officers; they dishonored the officer's honor! They committed the fascist upheaval in the country and began to torture and destroy the Bulgarian people. We'll not retreat, it's time to finish them off!"

"I am with you," Pavlov said, "just informed that the others are against."

"Who is against—let him step aside!" Minkov said confidently. "We have everything ready."

Todor Pavlov left the military organization headquarters leaders and went to his place in anticipation of the event that would decide their fate. It was not too long to wait. On April 16, 1925, at 2.30 pm in the church of "St. Resurrection" they brought a coffin with the body with Kosta Georgiev. Due to his high status, the entire top of the ruling junta gathered for the funeral. General Zhekov and the tsar Boris III were absent. The coffin with the body was put in the central place under the dome of the cathedral in front of the altar. Around the coffin there were Tsankov, Rusev, Vylkov and all the members of the self-proclaimed government, ministers and officials standing. The military accomplices were standing behind the ministers, and behind them there was a crowd of their close people. The church servant, as it was expected, distributed candles among the standing in front and suddenly moved the coffin with the body closer to the altar, with a jester of his hand inviting everyone to move forward and stand directly under the dome. The funeral service began at 3 pm. All the ringleaders of the fascist gang took fatal for Bulgaria a couple of steps forward, and all saved their skin. Exactly in 20

minutes after the beginning of the funeral service, the ignited wick reached the dynamite placed above the top of the central column at the altar and brought down the dome on everyone along the perimeter, except for the main ones, who were directly under the dome. Tsankov, Rusev, Vylkov and the ministers only scratched their ears.

Tsar Boris III, having returned from the funeral service of the professor Delcho Ilchev, murdered agent of the revolutionaries, went to the church "St. Resurrection" for the funeral service of the butcher Konstantin Georgiev. He stopped the car at a safe distance from the church and began to watch from outside, glancing at his watch.

"Boo!" he slapped his lips exactly at 3, 20.

On the same evening, April 16, the tsar-Tsankov junta hit Bulgaria on the head with the "martial law", drafted yet in January 1925. All the survived by the evil irony of fate, escaping only with their scratched ears during the explosion in the church, the fascist junta continued its work begun in June 9, 1923 with renewed vigor. The army, which betrayed its people and loyal to Tsankov, was sent to the home front. They scoured addresses according the pre-complied lists, turned everything upside down, grabbed people and dragged them to the barracks, tortured, cut to pieces, strangled and shot. The wounded and half-dead were buried in pits that rose above the surface from the ground from the last breath of tormented flesh. They turned the whole Bulgaria upside down, reaching the villages of her remote regions. The jets of black smoke from the chimneys in the police stations, where the freedom fighters were burned alive in furnaces, rose even thicker to the sky.

On April 21, the police tracked down the address in Sofia in Malgar Street, where Kosta Yankov was hiding in the house of the officer Hristo Kodjeykov. The veteran of 3 wars, awarded for bravery with the order of "St. Alexander," Colonel Kodjeykov was standing next to Kosta Yankov near the wall by the window and looked through the glass. The house was surrounded from all sides by the police and military, there was nowhere to run.

"Kodjeykov, give us Yankov, and you'll stay alive!" a senior policeman shouted from the street.

2 officers were looking at each other in the eyes, realizing that they were parting. Before the eyes of both scenes of the battles of the Balkan Wars and the senseless Great War were flashed, where both fought bravely, fulfilling their military duty. Both fulfilled their duty to the end, challenging the bandits who seized the country on June 9, 1923, and both, as part of the military organization of the United Front, have been preparing an uprising for 2 years. They wanted to eliminate this gang of thugs by placing explosive under the dome of the church, but the evil force that was stronger than them destroyed their plan. The evil chance or evil fate saved the main thugs, having killed the

rest. And the main thugs, having survived, hit with a black hammer on the remnants of life in Bulgaria.

"Kodjeykov, do you hear? We guarantee your life, just give us Yankov! We know: he is with you!" was heard from the street from the policemen. "Open the door for us and give him up!"

Without waiting the response, the besiegers opened fire. Glass of the windows shattered, through which the whirlwind of bullets flew into the room. Kodjeykov and Yankov shook hands and embraced for farewell. Everyone took place at the window, and the battle began. With well-aimed shots they hit the fascists, and they sent a hail of bullets through the windows, which crashed everything in the house that made life of Hristo Kodjeykov. The battle went on for a long time, the fascist evil spirit fell in the street and then set on fire the house. The besieged were running out of bullets, and they shot themselves with almost the last ones. The 37-year-old reserve Major Kosta Yankov, the Head of the Military Organization of the BCP and the remaining faithful to him Colonel Hristo Kodjeykov, a member of the military organization of the BCP, who was 51 years old, passed away.

※ ※ ※

At that time in Plovdiv, it was impossible to walk along the street calmly and imperceptibly, because the military patrols and policemen checked the documents of all the passers-by. The Voevoda of the Hristo Botev chcta Radyu Delchev was walking along the street, keeping cool, with air of a common man, with false documents in his pocket and 2 loaded revolvers. Velyu Hristozov was walking at some distance from him on the other side of the street. He was somewhat nervous from the constant intense struggle and began to betray himself with a confused look. Ahead of both on different sides of the street their associates Sofia Karapetkova, Matyu Toshev Iliev and Sasho Daskalov were walking at a distance from each other. They were showing them the way how to get out of the city from its eastern part in the direction to the Tsaregrad highway. A patrol of 2 policemen checked the documents of each of them in turn and, not finding anything suspicious, let them go further. They approached Velyu and began to examine his documents for a long time and looked at him.

"You seem to be nervous, don't you?" one policeman asked.

"Why to be nervous? I am a simple citizen, I haven't done anything wrong," Velyu answered as calm as possible.

"I don't like you!" one policeman said. "Let's search him! Raise your hands!"

Velyu raised his hands, and the policeman began rummage in his pockets of his jacket.

"And what is this?" the policeman yelled, pulling a loaded revolver out of the Velyu's pocket.

"This is only for my self-defense," Velyu babbled, pretending to be a fool, "in case of some Communists or Agrarians attacks. And I really don't know how to shoot, my brother taught me to shoot."

"I don't like your papers," the policeman did not get off, holding the revolver aimed at Velyu.

"Oh, I've confused, it's my brother's document, I took it by mistake, mixed it up, and my document remained at home."

"Where is your home?"

"Over there."

Velyu pointed forward along the street.

"Go ahead, show the way!"

The policemen pushed Velyu in the back to go in front of them, while they themselves followed him, holding his document and a revolver in their hands. They approached the Catholic church and commanded: "Stop!" as they saw their acquaintances. They stopped and began to chat and to share impressions of the day. At that moment they fell on the ground, pierced by Radyu Delchev's bullets, and Velyu drew his second revolver and in a trice put a bullet in the forehead of a policeman, who was following Radyu. There was a commotion, passers-by screamed and rushed to run in different directions, and Velyu managed to grab his revolver from the hands of the dead policeman, lying on the ground, and together with Radyu they hurriedly left the Catholic church. They were walking along a small street, turning into alleys, and soon found themselves far from the place of skirmish and again walked along the street like indifferent townsfolk. They passed by a korchma; one policeman suddenly jumped out of it. Without hesitation, he drew a revolver and fired at Velyu just in case, but missed. At the sound of a shot another policeman jumped out of the korchma with a revolver in his hand, not knowing whom to shoot at. Velyu laid them down both in a trice. And in another instant both vanished in the alleys of the outskirts of the city, from where they got out to the Tsaregrad highway and headed along it toward to the villages Sadovo and Cheshnegirovo to the east.

Chapter 53
Georgy Pilashev

The Hristo Botev cheta, led by Georgy Pilashev and his deputy Todor Todorov, descended from the mountain near Slavyanovo and slowly made their way at night into the forests of Aidanlar to the north-west. Forests covered the hilly area and isolated mountains, and the entire valley, framing the village of Aidanlar. Buds swelled on the trees one after another, exploded, giving rise to green life. The leaves were born before the eyes, and the forest turned green. The April sun awakened nature from hibernation. The greenery hid the fighters of Hristo Botev.

The armed chetniks continued their way. They had been walking all the winter by passing all the villages Bulgaria, preparing the uprising, and now they were waiting for the outcome.

"It's my native village, I was born here and raised here," Mityu Ganev sighed, "only we never had a normal house: it was such a dilapidated tiny hut so that all of us will never fit in it."

"Wait here, I'll scout the situation," Todor said.

He carefully beat his way to the neighboring 2-story houses, where his Uncle Gocho with his sons Vidyu and Todor lived once. Memories of the past years stabbed a dagger in his heart. Kolyu and Tanyu Kiryakov-Buchevs, who bought their houses and lands on the cheap, turned out, fortunately, to be their yataks. Their houses stood on the edge of the village, surrounded by forest, and behind them their fields stretched, separated by clearing with kolibas, paddocks and kosharas. Todor approached the massive gate of the high fence, enclosing the yard and the house, and knocked. The gates opened, and Kolyu Buchev shook his hand.

"How is the situation?" Todor asked.

"Everything is very bad," Kolyu answered, "very dangerous and stressful."

"The entire cheta is here," Todor respired.

"Come in everyone, but so that no one sees."

"Thank you."

Todor vanished into the darkness, and after a while one by one the chetniks of the Hristo Botev cheta silently entered the house of Kolyu Buchev, and the gate behind them was locked on latch. Hungry and tired chetniks found shelter and food with Kolyu, who risked his life, like everyone else, who let them into their homes. He told them the gruesome news.

"2 days ago the Military Organization in Sofia blew up the dome of the church 'St. Resurrection' to eliminate the entire ruling elite, but all the fascist ringleaders were not injured, but it was secondary ones and the others who died. And now the fascists declared martial law and even more intensified repressions. They capture, torture and kill all."

The chetniks became dumfounded and speechless, foreboding a catastrophe. And finally after silence Radyu Hristov exclaimed:

"No other way than the devil himself saved them so that they continue to torment the people!"

"Bay Radyu, there is no devil, and there is no god either, correspondingly!" Todor retorted.

"Then, what is it? Neither tsar, nor Tsankov, neither Vylkov nor Rusev died under such an explosion, but completely others died?"

"If anyone knew!"

"They went for broke, having decided that with one blow they would exterminate all the ringleaders, and thus the fascist junta would be overthrown, and then it would be possible to form a coalition government together with the bourgeois parties, which are not satisfied with the Tsankov's regime, together with the General Zhekov forces," Georgy Pilashev reflected. "I hope, General Zhekov was not in the church?"

"Of course not, he was not there. There was no tsar either." Kolyu answered.

"The tsar is a cunning fox, like his father Ferdinand, he plays for his own game and wants to rule alone without any tsankovs, vylkovs and rusevs," Georgy Pilashev replied. "I'll go to Bukovo and try to find a connection with the region leadership."

"I'll come back soon, I'll go to talk with Todor Trendofilov," Todor said and slipped out the door.

The nocturnal chetniks were accustomed to move around at night, and Todor, unnoticed by anyone, merging with the darkness, went to the other side of the village and knocked with a conditional sign on the gate of Todor Trendofilov, their yatak. He had recently married and enjoyed his honeymoon with his beloved sweet wife, who was his faithful companion and a helper. Both Todors met in the middle of the night and embraced.

"I hasten to tell you the most important, I was afraid that I would not be in time, I already warned my wife, if they kill me, let her warn you! How good it is that I see you and can tell you myself that Kityu Panev is a traitor!"

"It's bad," Todor answered gloomily, "he knows a lot."

"He got job as a forester. Now he is a warden of our forest for the authorities."

"Do you know that for sure?" Todor asked.

"Absolutely. He betrayed himself: he spied after me and fished out the information that did not concern him."

"But he gave us a couple of rifles, pretending to be the yatak."

"He took these rifles from the Haskovo police to ingratiate himself. And also, Blagon Ganev Zabanarov is also a traitor, he serves for the policemen."

"I know about him, my father passed it on through Georgy, my cousin, yet in winter. Where does this venal scum only come from? They pretended to be the yataks, even sold us a couple of rifles, we paid him money."

"But the policemen gave these rifles for him too to ingratiate himself to you."

"Ivan Ignatov and I once ended up in prison because of him. Ok, Todor, I'll go, I must hurry."

"Be careful!"

"You too, and take care of your wife too!"

Todor disappeared in the darkness and soon returned to his comrades-in-arms. On April 19, during the day time the chetniks had rest from night crossings in the house of Kolyu Buchev, and he with his brother Tanyu guarded them to be sure that everything was calm. Todor could not forget and all the time remembered how they were hiding in the same house with Vidyu...

In the evening, on April 19, the commander Georgy Pilashev ordered:

"You, Todor, try to get into your Bodrovo, check the connection with the District leadership: if there are any messages and get some food. Take 5 people. I'll go with Bay Radyu, Kocho Vasilev and Hristo Pavlitov to my village of Bukovo and try to find connection with the region leadership. We must receive the instructions on our further actions. And we'll get food too. You, Mityu, stay here to wait for us."

2 small groups: 6 and 4 people shook hands and, when it got dark completely, went in different directions. Georgy Pilashev with 3 men went to south-west to Bukovo, and Todor with 5 people headed for Bodrovo to the north-west. Todor and his group crossed the forest, hills and fields, approached Bodrovo from the east and bypassed it from the north, safely entered the sealed house through the courtyard from the back door. The sealed front door from the main entrance showed everyone that there was nobody in the house. 6 chetniks accommodated inside without turning the light. The walls of his native home stirred up the reminiscences, and his heart sank at thought of how was his family, driven out to a foreign land.

They wished, it would rather be better if everything is resolved! It would rather be the uprising, which they had been preparing for so long time, and the victory over the junta, would rather everyone return home!

They spent the rest of the night, resting after the crossing, and in the evening they froze motionless with the revolvers in their hands: someone opened the back door. The door opened, and Georgy appeared on the threshold. They embraced with Todor, barely holding back tears. Cousins, they grew up together and were friends since childhood, lived as neighbors, and for a long time Georgy had been Todor's faithful supporter, since Todor went into illegality. Faithful friend and yatak, Georgy knew the places of liaison and always helped. Georgy greeted the chetniks.

"Today is Easter," he said, "we are all preparing a festive dinner."

"We don't believe in priestly fairy tales," Todor said, "but we won't refuse from food."

"I'll bring it now."

Georgy hurried home and soon returned, carrying food in a bag. The chetniks immediately lifted their spirits.

"Georgy, you know where to go. Go and check if there is a message for us, we have been out of touch with the leadership for some time," Todor said.

"I'll do it, wait."

Georgy left, and the chetniks were sitting silently in the Todor's sealed house behind tightly closed shuttered windows, and life was in full swing outside the windows and inside the walls of other houses in Bodrovo. The villagers baked paska and kalachi-cakes, decorated them on the dishes with in all colors painted eggs, baked lambs, slaughtered for the feast and set the tables with all kinds of dishes. Life went on in spite of everything, and the villagers, who believed in god Christ, believed or wanted to believe that just as the object of their faith Christ, allegedly, resurrected on the third day after death, they will also be resurrected for eternal life, where there will be no more suffering and grief. They decorated their houses for Easter and prepared a festive dinner.

At the end of the day Georgy brought the news to the chetniks that there were no messages for them from any couriers. The loss of contact with the leadership and the complete uncertainty of what would happen next confused the chetniks.

"Go and take a break from business," Georgy told Todor, "go to Maria and Penyu. They are preparing a festive dinner."

"This is my sister Maria, she recently got married," Todor explained to his friends, "but all of us can't go, it's not safe either for them or for us. Maximum 3 people can go."

"I'll go!" Ivan Ignatov was the first to say.

"Will you take me?" Gueno Radev asked uncertainly.

All the others were modestly silent, though each of them wanted to go to visit for a festive dinner.

"Ok, 3 of us will go: Ivan, Gueno and I, and the rest will have dinner here at my place. Uncle Dimitar promised to cook dinner for us."

"Everything is ready," Georgy confirmed, "father slaughtered and baked 2 lambs, we've cooked delicious food."

3 chetniks were in good mood. Georgy and his father brought lambs, wine, bread, Easter cakes with colored eggs.

"It's for everyone."

"Thank you, uncle!" Todor clung to Dimitar, who pressed his head to his shoulder and stroked his hair.

"How mature you are, Todor! You became a grown up man!"

Tears shone in Dimitar's eyes.

Twilight was falling over Bodrovo. Covering themselves with it, Todor, Ivan Ignatov and Geno Radev slipped out of the yard through the northern exit, turned left toward the river and went around the village along the Kayaliyka River from the western side. The house of Penyu Dimitrov Dimov, whom Todor's sister Maria married, was situated on the south-western corner of Bodrovo and presented by itself almost a fortress with a stone fence and narrow loopholes in the walls, surrounding a vast courtyard. The 2-story house stood on the basement for food storage and towered on a hill, under which the Kayaliyka River flowed from south to north. From the windows of the house there was a magnificent view on all the directions of the world. Chorbadji Doygovets built his house yet back in the Kardzhali time, and his inhabitants did not know the need. Todor's sister Maria successfully married, both loved each other and were reliable support to each other in trouble. Maria's new family did not think that they all were risking their lives by letting the chetniks into their house: they let them in, because they were on their side. Armed from head to toe, with rifles on their shoulders, Todor, Ivan and Geno hid behind the gates of the Dimov's house and were cordially received in the house. Todor hugged his sister Maria.

"Come in, feel at home, sit down at the table!"

The eyes of the chetniks, accustomed to the camp food, which the yataks supplied them, diverged at the sight of a long table, covered with luxurious dishes. The smell of roasted lambs overwhelmed them. The paska-cakes in the form of the turrets, from which raisins stuck out, surrounded by the eggs, painted in all colors, decorated the table. The sweet aroma emanated from the baked Easter cakes and resurrected in them the reminiscences of their own home, which they abandoned long ago. Todor with 2 friends and all the hosts sat down at the table and raised a glass of wine for the quickest onset of a peaceful life.

"Actually, we are forbidden to drink alcohol," Todor said, and all his friends looked pleadingly at the commander, "but for the sake of the feast, we can drink 1 wineglass, or rather, not for the sake of the feast, as we are not believers, but for the sake of our meeting and the hospitality of the hosts."

"To our victory!" they raised a common toast and took a sip of wine.

"It would rather be the uprising and victory in it!" each of them was thinking, enjoying the dinner.

They feasted long after midnight, and then the hospitable hosts put them to bed.

In the morning of April 21, the inhabitants of Bodrovo in a cheerful mood greeted and congratulated each other on the fact that Christ, allegedly, had risen. Todor and his friends woke up, had a luxurious breakfast and began to ponder on how to return home safely. It was about 11 o'clock. The April sun was shining brightly, illuminating the spectacular picture of awakening nature. The chetniks stood by the windows and from the height of the hill, on which the Dimov's house stood, watched what was happening. All of a sudden the alarming tocsin sounded from the south-west, where Ezerovo lay: all the bells were ringing there. It was echoed by the bell on the Bodrovo tower. The bells chimed, as if they were competing to see which one was louder, announcing the alarm. Thus the chetniks planned to call the people to uprising. But it was not the uprising, otherwise they would've known about it. Icy fear pierced the inhabitants of the house, and the fearless chetniks took up positions at the window.

"Forgive us, sister! Forgive us, everybody! We should not have come!" Todor said contritely. "We've been betrayed."

"We must leave," Geno said.

Todor raised his hand, indicating not to move, and was looking through his binoculars out of the window. A detachment of mounted police was approaching the house. The policemen drove up to the house and drove further to the south. Todor saw through binoculars that from the direction of Bodrovo and Ezerovo detachments of infantry men and trucks with soldiers and canister-guns were moving south, as if they were preparing to onslaught a fortified fortress. All were moving south toward Bukovo.

After some time, explosions of shells, gunfire and the roar of a canister shook the air and flew from Bukovo to Bodrovo, and Todor with his friends could only imagine what was happening. Gloomy and furious, they were ready to enter the battle, but realized that they could not do it. All they had to do was to wait until it gets dark. The roar of the battle continued until night. The dark night opened the way for them. The hosts collected bags with food for them and for the rest of the chetniks and parted with them. The chetniks said goodbye, thanking the hosts for everything, they were both glad and not glad that they had come, endangering the Dimovs, but both the hosts and the guests hated the ruling power and only were waiting for it to collapse. Todor led 2 friends to his house, where the other 3 ones were waiting. They collected the food that Georgy and his father brought, and without delay under the cover of night quietly left the empty house of Todor. They got out through the northern exit from his yard, went around the village from the north and went to Aidanlar. Leaving his house, Todor felt his heart stab and shrink from a bitter foreboding that he would never see it again.

***

The group of 4 people under the command of Georgy Pilashev left Aidanlar together with the Todor's group, parted with it until meeting and headed in the opposite direction to Bukovo in the south-west. The way to Bukovo from Aidanlar was 2 times longer than from Aidanlar to Bodrovo, and they were walking half the night, passing the hills and ravines. The moon and the stars in the sky lit their path. They passed Woden, which lay in their path, and went further and further to the south-west, where the hills rose higher and higher. They went round the hill and went into the valley, where Bukovo flaunted, surrounded from all sides by the mountains, covered with forest. The heart of Radyu Hristov was beating with joy at the sight of his native village. The night covered them and guarded to be unnoticed by anyone. All came into the house of Radyu Hristov. Radyu's wife hugged her husband and son-in-law, whom she had not seen since autumn.

"Tomorrow is Easter. I've cooked food, how good it is that you've come!" she greeted the guests.

"We are very tired from the road, we need to sleep," Radyu answered for all 4 ones.

"We are leaving tomorrow night," Georgy Pilashev said. "Are there any letters for me?"

Yes, there are, in your room in the drawer, the mother-in-law answered, "they are delivered, Dobri Delchev brought it."

In the village of Bukovo Dobri Delchev carried out direct liaisons between the cheta and the Regional Military-Party Command in Plovdiv. Georgy Pilashev went to his study in the house of his father-in-law, and 3 travelers went to sleep after the journey. Georgy opened the dresser drawer, took out a sealed envelope, opened it and pulled out a blank sheet of paper. He sat down at the table, where a kerosene lamp lit dimly. He brought a blank sheet of paper to the hot glass of the lamp, and the text began to appear faintly on the paper.

"The Foreign Representation of the Central Committee of the BCP has withdrawn the course for the armed uprising. Activities of the cheta Hristo Botev for preparing the uprising are to roll up. You are to work to create a broad coalition with opposition bourgeois parties. You are to reorient the cheta activities to protect the peaceful demonstrations and meetings. The internal and international situation does not allow us to hope for the success of the armed uprising."

After reading the letter, Georgy Pilashev experienced an explosion of emotions: his blood throbbed and beat in his temples, and thoughts ran one after another. He was thinking: "What meetings, rallies and demonstrations! Dimitrov with Kolarov in Moscow do not understand what is happening, though they should've known! They shoot us in the back and don't let us walk on the ground at day time, what meetings, what rallies, what demonstrations! We can't hold a meeting, we can't live in our own houses, in our own country! They capture people and subject them to monstrous torture and burn their homes! BCP is outlawed and membership in it is punished by death! According to their bandit 'Law', a person, who gave us a piece of bread, is to be eliminated! They have already destroyed all the Agrarians and now set to work on us, the Communists, and they are there in Moscow giving us the directive of peaceful protest! There is only one method of struggle with the bandits: armed struggle! All of us, both we and they made a strategic mistake: the uprising should've been raised last autumn! A lot of was ready then! The boys have done a gigantic job, walked around the entire south-central Bulgaria and prepared the people. And now the Tsankov's junta is simply destroying the people. It would be better to die in the battle than to die from torture in their torture chambers. They offer us to capitulate, to surrender, to the butchers so that they beastly torture us to death!" Before his eyes the faces of the young men from the cheta passed: young, beautiful, fearless, noble and dedicated. They did not bow their heads to the scum, which had captured the country, and did not become traitors like the others. Risking their lives, they chose the path of struggle for freedom. He recalled how in winter of the last year here in the house of his father-in-law he invited Todor Todorov, Ivan Ignatov with Mityu Ganev to join him and join the cheta Hristo Botev, and 2 became the commanders, though at first, they hesitated a lot. How many km they traveled on foot, how many dangers they overcame, what a gigantic work they have done to prepare the uprising! "Parliamentary methods of struggle are possible only in a democratic country, and they are impossible in a fascist one!"

The night was coming to an end, and in order to restore his strength, Georgy Pilashev fell into a deep sleep. All woke up in the afternoon, and sat down at the table. Bay Radyu's wife laid the festive table, having prepared all kinds of dishes for Easter. Baked Easter cakes with raisons intoxicated you with their smell alone. Bay Radyu, Georgy Pilashev, Hristo Pavlitov and Kocho Vasilev, hungry yet from the previous days, sat down at the table.

"Drink some wine!" the hostess offered.

"We are forbidden to drink alcohol," her son-in-law objected, "although today you can drink, but very little."

The friends rejoiced.

"A couple of sips only, no more!" Pilashev reminded.

Hungry chetniks, including the host of the house, energetically began to devour the food on the table.

"Friends, I've received the order from the Central Committee to roll up our activities," Georgy Pilashev informed them.

All 3 froze with their mouths open.

"And now what?" Radyu asked.

"In Moscow, the Central Committee reversed the course toward the armed uprising. They gave us instructions for the peaceful struggle and the protection of rallies, demonstrations and meetings."

"After all, we were preparing the uprising for this in order to overthrow the fascist junta and return Bulgaria to a democratic path, where these same rallies, meetings and demonstrations are possible!" Radyu exclaimed.

"It turns out that everything we did was in vain!" Kocho Vasilev exclaimed. "And finally, we were preparing the uprising to return home! We can't go home now! And now we'll not be able to return! What will happen to us now?"

"Georgy Pilashev was gloomy silent, he had no answers to the questions of his friends; he asked himself these questions. The void and hopelessness tormented him, and gloomy pictures rose before his eyes."

"Such is reality, friends, such is the directive from Moscow from Dimitrov and Kolarov. Dimitrov and Kolarov are in Moscow, and we are here," Radyu Hristov said gloomily. "Help yourself, friends, at least we'll enjoy a festive dinner for Easter!"

"Eat, but don't drink, rest, and we'll hit the road at night. I'll go to work with the documents," Georgy Pilashev said.

He left his friends and went to his study and sat down at the table to write. He kept detailed records of the course of events, the activities of the cheta Hristo Botev, the chetniks, and the work they did.

"Someday people will know about us, read my notes and learn about our work," Georgy Pilashev thought, writing down the events of the last days.

Then he lay down for a little rest before the next crossing and, waking up, collected all the papers in the bag and went into next room, where his friends were resting. Hristo Pavlitov looked at him with a guilty gaze, pointing at 2 friends and shrugged his shoulders. Radyu Hristov, the owner of the house, and Kocho Vasilev were deadly drunk and therefore unable to go anywhere: they were lying on the sofa and slept soundly.

"We have nothing to lose already, let's wait until they wake up," Georgy Pilashev said.

He went to his room and sat down at the desk again, then lay down to rest himself. The night was coming to an end and was on the verge of dawn.

"Get up, it's time, let's hurry!" he raised his friends.

Radyu Hristov and Kocho Vasilev looked guilty and immediately quickly gathered for leaving. The hostess packed food for the rest of the chetniks in the bags, and they hurriedly slipped out of the house. Dawn gleamed on the horizon.

"Dawn is coming soon, we can't move during the daytime," Georgy Pilashev said, "we'll climb the mountains to wait for the evening there and return to Aidanlar in the dark."

"We could've waited another day at home and come out in the evening."

"Probably, though it is dangerous to stay in the house for a long time too."

They scurried south of Bukovo, where a coppice began, and behind it the mountains rose, completely covered with dense forest. They safely left the village and were approaching the rescue forest.

"Look, Georgy!" Radyu showed his son-in-law to the side, where a young shepherd was grazing sheep early in the morning. "What are we going to do now?"

"Let's detain him!" Hristo Pavlitov exclaimed.

"This is Paun Delchev from our village," Georgy Pilashev said, "he is a known bastard, yet young, but has already rotted inside ultimately!"

"Shall we get him?"

"I suppose, he did not notice us, he is looking in another direction, let's better scurry to the forest and mountains!"

They quickened their pace, and Paun Delchev from Bukovo abandoned his sheep and rushed with all his might to the kmet in the village. He was running faster than wind, sticking out his tongue like a dog and panting. In a few moments he banged on the door of the kmet, who was still sleeping, with a message about the chetniks and a mirage of the reward. The kmet of Bukovo Hristo Grozdanov jumped up as scalded and rushed to his office for the reward and in a trice the phone rang to all the police stations in the nearby villages. Troops were raised from there, while the troops were gathering, the kmet raised the entire village of Bukovo and put together a detachment of the fascists-volunteers. They ran in the direction, where the shepherd Paun Delchev was pointing, he was running ahead and yelled: "It's me who found them! It's me! It's me! The reward is mine!"

"Shut up or I'll shoot you!" the villagers answered him one by one.

Not at all discouraged, Paul Delchev continued his business.

"There they are!" Delchev yelled, pointing in the direction, where he saw the Georgy Pilashev group.

The fascist activists from Bukovo opened random fire there, where the shepherd's hand directed them. Not sparing the cartridges, given them by the police, they fired at random, not seeing a target in front of them, and each one hoped for a reward, believing that it would be his bullet to kill the fighters of the cheta Hristo Botev.

Pilashev, Hristov, Pavlitov and Vasilev had long ago moved away from the place, where the bastard shepherd had seen them, and heard gunfire far behind them. They did not respond to the shooting so that not to disclose their place. Suddenly a stray bullet, fired at random by a chase, pierced Georgy Pilashev left shoulder and flew out. An exit wound was not dangerous, and overcoming the pain, Georgy Pilashev with his friends scurried up the stream of the Klokotnitsa River, which flowed from the mountains south of Bukovo. The young forest at the foot of the hills was replaced by an old dense forest, completely covering the hills and mountains, which were the higher the further south. The fascist dogs that galloped in their tracks were soon left far behind and simply fired at random in different directions.

The Georgy Pilashev's group quickly receded, rising up in the direction of the south along the Klokotnitsa. Ahead a mill appeared, standing on the bank of the river, flowing down from the mountains: it was called the Karabadzhakov's mill. The chetniks hurried to go around the side of the mill, but suddenly another gang of fascists with dogs jumped out from behind the mill.

"Bite!" they unleashed their dogs, having noticed the Pilashev's group, and opened fire.

Petko Kristov from Bodrovo fired at Georgy Pilashev, and the latter fell on the ground, hit by the bullet and pain: Petko Kristov's bullet pierced Pilashev's thigh, tore an artery and broke his femur. Hristo Pavlitov destroyed Petko Kristov with one shot. After him another fascist from Bukovo Vakril Korokia fell, and after these ones all the rest fell. Their dogs, having lost the command "Bite!" barked, howled, wagged their tails and, receding away from the chetniks, fled into the bushes. Friends leaned over Georgy. He was lying helplessly on the ground, blood was gushing from his lifeless leg, his face was contorted in excruciating pain. Radyu Hristov took of the medical bag from his belt, which each of the group of the cheta carried with them, going on a mission, took off the baklaga from the belt, opened the lid and brought it to Georgy's lips. Pilashev drank a couple of sips of rakia.

"But the alcohol is prohibited," Georgy said with difficulty, trying to smile and joke.

"Forgive me, Gyonyu," Radyu said, "I couldn't resist the temptation and took some rakia from home instead of water."

He wet the bandage with rakia and applied it to Georgy wound, and Hristo Pavlitov brought an oblong plank from the mill, to which they tied his leg after bandaging it and tightening it above the thigh.

"Can you move with one leg and hold on to us?" Radyu asked.

Georgy Pilashev could not move, lying on the ground.

"Abandon me, friends, do not waste time, save yourself, now the troops will come!"

"Shut up, Georgy!" Radyu Hristov commanded. "Boys, let's take Georgy!"

Radyu Hristov and Kocho Vasilev embraced their necks with his hands, crossed their arms under his back, Hristo Pavlitov lifted his healthy leg and held the wounded one. 3 of them picked him up from the ground and began to make their way south into the mountains. They moved as far as they could and reached the Black Rocks, found a place convenient for defense, they lowered Pilashev to the ground behind a huge protruding stone. Kocho Vasilev looked down from the height to the lowland and saw a lot enemy forces that were moving toward them from all sides.

"Leave me, go away!" Pilashev turned to his people again.

"Be quiet, commander, we'll accept the battle, command!" the chetniks answered.

At that moment the sounds of shots rang out, yet far away from them.

"Well, friends, we actually raised the uprising," Georgy Pilashev said in a low, suffering voice, "we are dying in battle…"

"We must hold out until evening, if we hold out, we can escape in the darkness."

The whistle of bullets flew in the distance, and Georgy Pilashev commanded:

"Take positions for battle! Save the bullets!"

"Yes, commander!" the chetniks answered.

They lifted him by the back and seated him so that he could rest his back against the trunk of a tree growing behind him, in front of him a big protruding stone protected him. Pllashev held a revolver in his hands. 3 of his friends took comfortable positions behind here and there huge stones, protruding on the mountains, which were called Black Rocks. Thick forest covered the hills and mountains, view down on the valley opened up before them. They saw in the distance mounted policemen approaching the mountain, trucks with military, infantry and numerous detachments of the fascists-volunteers, who were crawling from all directions. They had crawled out like cockroaches and lice on the body of Bulgaria from different villages of the area, and the fascist scum crawled in black clouds to get the 4 valiant. The first roar of the canister was heard and hit the trees and stones above the heads of the fighters, hitting no one yet.

"Fire!" Georgy Pilashev commanded, and first lay down the officer: he fell from the horse.

With well-aimed shots, the chetniks responded with oncoming fire. The battle thundered, the roar from which reached Aidanlar and Bodrovo. Without wasting a single bullet, the chetniks accurately hit the target, and the fascist scum fell one after another. They saw that the black hordes of the fascists activists with policemen were going around the mountain, on which they were fighting, from both sides and closing the ring not far from the place, where they were. Soon he chetniks were completely surrounded, and from all sides shells and bullets, and fragments of a canister flew past them. The roar of shells and whistling bullets, bouncing off steel of stones, shook the Rhodopes until evening, 4 brave fighters of Hristo Botev cheta fought off the attacks and fought at the Black Stones, and 1000 Bulgarian scum attacked 4 chetniks and could not submit them. Apparently, also saving shells, the fascist fire subsided with the onset of twilight, and the moment of decision came. 3 friends got out from behind the shelter and came closer to Georgy Pilashev. The latter was holding on as best as he could, but suffered terribly, losing strength and blood. Blood has seeped through the bandage long ago and flowed from the wound in an ominous omen.

"Get ready, Georgy, it's getting dark, we'll break through the encirclement," Radyu Hristov said, "we'll carry you."

"Friends, I would like to go with you, but it is impossible. I know, I feel to be doomed. If you take me, you'll perish yourself, but you must save your lives. You must escape from the encirclement, survive and continue fight."

"No…"

"I order! You'll breakthrough in this direction!" he pointed to the east. "You'll pass here! Hurry, while it's getting dark!"

"Georgy…"

"Commander…"

"Friends…Hristo, take my bag, there are the party documents there and my diary. Be sure to keep it and give it to Todor, and let Todor give it to Radyu Delchev, when he returns from Plovdiv. I hope, he returns. My diary: I wrote down all our history in it, one day it'll reach the reader, and they will know about us…"

Radyu Hristov took the Georgy Pilashev's bag and hung it over his shoulder, he did not hide his tears.

"Forgive me, Genyu, it's all because of me: I am an old fool, succumbed to weakness and drank too much, I got into my house, I haven't been at home so long, and here my wife laid such a festive table, I relaxed, got drunk and made Kocho drink!"

Kocho was sitting nearby and wiped away his tears with his hands.

"Forgive me, commander!"

"Come on, friends, we would've escaped if it were not the traitor Paun Delchev, damn him! Where do traitors and fascist accomplices only come from on our land!"

"We'll take revenge!" Hristo Pavlitov uttered, without hiding his tears.

"Hristo, take my cartridge belt, and you, Kocho, take my rifle, I'll keep only my revolver for myself. Don't worry, friends, I won't give them up alive…"

Hristo Pavlitov, a 23-year-old communist from Haskovo, removed the bandolier from the commander, and Kocho Vasilev, a 28-year-old communist from Haskovo, took his rifle, and Radyu Hristov, 56-year-old Agrarian from Bukovo, the oldest one in the Hristo Botev cheta, the father-in-law of Georgy Pilashev, his friend and comrade-in-arms, was holding the bag with the diary and the documents, and his binoculars. He leaned over Georgy and hugged him for farewell.

"Radyu, tell our relatives that I love them, but I failed to make them happy, let them forgive me. Friends, I am proud to have been your commander, and I am proud of all of you. All of you, the Hristo Botev cheta, are the most wonderful sons of Bulgaria! Tell everyone, let them survive, let them save their lives and live! Hurry…!"

Radyu Hristov, Kocho Vasilev and Hristo Pavlitov hugged Georgy Pilashev and parted with him forever.

"Go, I order!"

All 3 disappeared into the darkness, heading east. They were making their way silently forward, peering into the darkness. When they got to the enemy's position, they suddenly threw a few grenades and made a hole for themselves. The enemy rushed in all directions, and 3 brave men got out of the encirclement and hurried to Aidanlar under the cover of night. On hearing grenade explosions, the fascists resumed shooting in the darkness at the place, where the chetniks had just been. Georgy Pilashev responded them with single shots from the revolver, hitting the fascists. They decided that the chetniks were still there and intensified their shelling the mountain. Pilashev was counting the remaining bullets carefully, and when the last one remained, he brought the revolver to his temple and shot himself. His wonderful face froze forever, his eyes reflected the path of his life, the path of struggle for freedom.

42-year-old Georgy Pilashev, a communist from Bukovo, political leader of the District Bureau of BCP and a military instructor of the cheta Hristo

Botev, a retired officer, a teacher, who invited 3 friends: Todor Todorov, Ivan Ignatov and Mityu Ganev to the cheta, who did not bow his head in front of the fascist junta that seized Bulgaria, died so that the memory of him would never die. If there was only one Georgy Pilashev in the noble struggle for freedom, he alone would've saved the honor of the officers of Bulgaria.

Chapter 54
Parting

At the dark night on April 22, Todor's group of 6 people safely left Bodrovo, crossed the fields and hilly meadows, among which were the lands and fields of the Todorov family, they were looked after by the remaining relatives, and in the east they entered the Aidanlar forest. Soon they met with the cheta, who stayed in the house of Kolyu Kiryakov Buchev. Todor with his friends brought them 2 baked lambs, a lot of bread, Easter cakes and some wine in the baklagas.

"What, has our discipline been completely shaken lately?" Mityu Ganev asked, pointing to the wine.

"I allowed," Todor answered, "today is a special day. Share food, Mityu, you are our main food distributor manager."

They laid out the food on a large table in the Kolyu's kitchen, and Mityu Ganev by eye shared all the food between the boys exactly, as always, having left for himself less that for the others.

"Do not deprive yourself, Mityu," Todor said, "today all have feast, both believers and non-believers, a lot of food has been prepared at home, who knows, when and where we'll get food next time…"

All were tensely silent, not knowing what to talk about. All heard the roaring battle yesterday, April 21, in Bukovo region. Suddenly there was a knock at the gate. All shuddered and froze with tension. Kolyu, the owner of the house, went to the gate, there were their people: 3 friends of the group of Georgy Pilashev entered the house with gray faces. They put on the floor bags with food from the house of Radyu Hristov, Georgy Pilashev's rifle, his cartridge belt, and Radyu Hristov gave Todor his bag with the documents.

"Where is Georgy Pilashev?" Mityu Ganev asked, although everything was clear for everyone…

All were numb with horror, it was impossible to believe what had happened. All of them used to walk along the razor's edge, risking their lives every second, but the fact that Georgy Pilashev died killed them all. Mityu Ganev distributed a new portion of food among everyone, they poured several sips of wine, brought by Todor into the glasses, and together with the host Kolyu and his brother Tanyu honored the memory of Georgy Pilashev. Everyone had tears in his eyes. These men-heroes, brave fighters for freedom, could not hold back their tears, having pated with Georgy Pilashev.

"He was the best of us!" Todor said, not hiding his excitement.

The night was coming to an end. After waiting in Kolyu's house the whole next day, they set off again as soon as it got dark. They took 2 new boys with them: Vasil Angelov Metov and Atanas Delchev, who joined them after Todor Kostov, the District Military Organizer in Haskovo, whom they were hiding, was arrested, and they were also chased after. 2 fellows managed to escape and joined the cheta in the village of Aidanlar.

"Thanks, Kolyu!" Todor shook hands with his friend, and all the chetniks thanked him for the shelter.

"Thanks, Tanyu!" they also said goodbye to Kolyu's brother, who was always with him.

"We'll go around several villages to Novakovo and return to Aidanlar. We can stay in the forest."

"In the forest you'll be noticed faster," Kolyu answered, "we have common enemies, come to me, when you return."

Todor and Kolyu embraced, and they left Kolyu's house, the same house, where his cousin Vidyu lived once.

"See you!"

"See you!"

They slipped out of the village of Aidanlar into the darkness of the Aidanlar forest and, having divided into 2 detachments, set off. The first detachment was led by Mityu Ganev, and the second detachment by Todor Todorov. They were walking at the distance from each other, but in the same direction. They walked under the cover of the night, when the fascist traitors were sleeping, and hid during the day time, finding a hidden place. They were going north-west to the village of Karadjalovo, coming close to Borisovograd, tore their yatak out of the fascist teeth and turned south toward Bryagovo.

At that time, Blagon Zabanarov Ganev, who once inspired Ivan Ignatov to steal the other people sheep "to become the hajduks" with a note in his pocket was running as fast as he could to the kmet's building in the village of Bodrovo. He rightly considered himself the main police agent in the village and a false yatak, but still feared that some other competitor would overtake him.

"Here it is!" wheezing from running, Blagon gave the paper to the kmet in his office.

"Well, what else do you have?" the kmet asked irritably, constantly tormented by remorse and doubts.

"Read!" Blagon exclaimed triumphantly.

The kmet took the message in his hands and silently read:

The main yataks of the Hristo Botev cheta in Bodrovo:

I category:

1. *Angel Ivan Tonev, son.*
2. *Vylkov Nedev Buchev and his brother Peter.*
3. *Georgy Dimitrov Karagochev.*
4. *Ivan Tonev Angelov, father.*
5. *Peter Nedev Buchev.*

II category:

1. *Bozhan Vylkov Tenev.*
2. *Georgy Dimitrov.*
3. *Dimitar Markov Dimitrov.*
4. *Dimitar Todorov Karagochev.*
5. *Dimitar Gospodinov Tundjarov*
6. *Dimitar Dimov Delchev.*
7. *Ignat Byalkov Bodjanov.*

III category:

1. *Ivan Todorov Karagochev, Todor's father.*
2. *Gocho Ivanov Todorov Karagochev.*
3. *Ignat Mitev, Ivan Ignatov's father.*

4. *Zheko Ignatov Mitev, Ivan Ignatov's brother.*

"Here it is!" Blagon exclaimed, baring his teeth.

"Okay, we'll figure it out. Go, go away, I am busy!" the kmet uttered gloomily and threw the message into the drawer of the table.

Kityu Panev from Aidanlar, who recently got a job as a forester, was more cunning than Blagon Zabanarov from Bodrovo and did not show the list of the yataks to the Aidanlar's kmet, as he suspected him of not having particular zeal to serve the regime. Therefore, he mounted a donkey and drove him straight to Haskovo to the commandant.

"Why were you silent before?" the commandant Hubanov asked him sternly.

"I looked out, eavesdropped and tracked down!" Kityu Panev reported servilely and handed him a message.

The main yataks of the cheta Hristo Botev in the village of Aidanlar:

1. Todor Trendofilov.
2. Kolyu Kiryakov Buchev.
3. Tanyu Kiryakov Buchev.

"Look, do not pull with the following!"

"It will be done, mister officer!"

Kityu Panev hurried on a donkey back to Aidanlar to get the information, and subordinate officer to the commandant equipped 3 soldiers of the escorts on a campaign and gave a written order to the Aidanlar's kmet to extradite 3 persons by names on a list.

"On the way back to shoot them at the attempt to escape," these words accompanied the verbal order.

"Mister Captain, give me a written order to shoot them!" the senior in the convoy turned to the chief.

"Do you dare to rebel? Maybe you want to become the yatak yourself?"

"Yes, Mr. Captain!" the escort agreed, frightened.

3 guards went on foot to the village of Aidanlar and got to the kmet's building. They handed the order to the kmet. The kmet read the order and

thought excitedly: "When will this violence stop? All expected the uprising, and instead of the uprising there are endless executions!"

"Deliver the Buchev brothers to the kmet's office!" the kmet ordered, sending his assistants. "Only 2!"

He crossed out the name of Todor Trendofilov from the list of the order with his own hand, and it was the only thing he was brave to do.

"I'll not give you Todor Trendofilov, he is not the yatak. I know him, he is too young, he just got married, he has a honeymoon with his wife."

The guards were delighted themselves and did not object. After a short time, the brothers Kolyu and Tanyu Kiryakov Buchev were delivered to the kmet's office and, accompanied by 3 escorts, went to Haskovo.

"Well, Ivan, how are you?" Tanyu asked the senior of the convoy.

"Well, as you can see, I am serving," Ivan answered, "and how are you?"

"I am also serving."

They silently walked half way, when they saw 2 military horsemen approaching them. The riders approached them, and the foreman asked:

"And where is the third one?"

"There are only these 2, and the third is not involved," the escort Ivan answered.

The riders spurred their horses and rushed to Aidanlar. After a short time they were dragging Todor Trendofilov, who was tied by the hands to one of the horses with his legs shot through. After dragging him some distance, the riders cut off the rope and shot him. The murdered Todor Trendofilov, the faithful yatak of the cheta Hristo Botev and a friend of Todor Todorov, was lying on the ground, not far from the village of Aidanlar.

The riders again let their horses run after the convoy and, having overtaken it, asked:

"Why the hell, are you dragging them alive? Our place is crammed, you received the order to shoot them!"

The riders tried to draw the revolvers, but the escorts got ahead of them at the same instant and pointed their rifles at them.

"Get back, you bastards! We have a written order to deliver them to Haskovo! But we don't have a written order to shoot them!"

The riders retreated, not expecting such a rebuff from their own people and, threatening them with reprisals, they galloped to Haskovo.

"Maybe, you'll let us go?" Tanyu Buchev asked.

"We can't, we've gotten the order to deliver you…"

They walked in silence the rest of the way, and each of them was thinking about his own things.

"It would've been better if we have raised the uprising and fought against the fascists, even died, than to be tortured by the butchers," both brothers were thinking, moving further and further away from Aidanlar, where their 2 large houses, fields, meadows, kosharas and cattle left, once bought on the cheap from the Todor's cousin Vidyu Karagochev, distraught with grief after losing his brother.

"It would've been better if we have raised the uprising and fought against the fascists and maybe won or died in battle, than stupidly comply with the fascist order," 3 guards thought to themselves and servilely stepped on.

They delivered 2 Buchev brothers to the commandant's office to Hubenov, and he gloatingly remarked:

"Well, the worse for them! Take them away!"

The brothers Kolyu and Tanyu Kiryakov Buchev, who gave shelter to Todor's friends, vanished in the dangerous of the prison in the city of Haskovo.

***

And Todor with his friends continued their journey at night from Karadjalovo to Bryagovo, having taken with them the secretary of the party organization in Karadjalovo Todor Iliev Vanchev. The Hristo Botev cheta fighters realized that their task at that moment was to save those who helped them.

At night they approached the village of Bryagovo, which lay in the valley of the Kayaliyka River at the very foot of Dragoyna. Picturesque Bryagovo, surrounded by the forested mountains, was a place, where the cheta had many friends. Once founded by the Bulgarians, who fled from the north from Turkish slavery, Bryagovo breathed with the spirit of freedom, and many villagers, defying the danger, helped the cheta, shared their houses with them. Both detachments approached the village from the north-east and stopped in a large koliba in a dense forest at the foot of the mountain. The koliba belonged to yatak Dimitar Petkov Rumenov.

"Come with me, you'll cover!" Todor turned to the newcomer Vasil Angelov, who had just entered the cheta.

The newcomer was happy to join the cheta's activities immediately, and both stealthily crept in the darkness to the house of Dimitar Rumenov. There was a conventional knock on the door, and the door opened. Dimitar let them in the house. He looked unhappy. They embraced.

"How is the situation?" Todor asked.

"Everything is very bad!" Dimitar replied gloomily. "The policemen scout around the village, rummage everywhere, and look for yataks. Every minute they can break into the house and grab you."

"We are here with the entire cheta, we go around the villages and check the situation."

"So, there won't be the uprising?" Dimitar asked ruefully.

"Apparently not," Todor replied gloomily.

"But we have prepared! It's a pity! It would be better to fight than give up without fight!"

"Agree. The situation is very difficult. We don't know ourselves what will be next."

"Do not enter the village, it is dangerous."

"We are in your koliba; we'll wait until the next night and go south to Novakovo. There is where to hide in the mountains there."

"So, what, have we been abandoned, betrayed?"

"We missed time. It was necessary to raise the uprising last autumn, and now we are all hunted down and destroyed."

"The District Committee in Haskovo was crashed, Todor Kostov was arrested, and Vasil Angelov and his friend helped him and were forced to flee from home, now they are with us."

Vasil Angelov nodded his head.

"It's terror throughout the country."

"All right, I'll collect food from our friends Ilya Krystev and Vylko Gluhov, we'll give as much as we can and bring it to you to the koliba tomorrow, when it get dark. Don't leave without food. Wait for me with food," Dimitar said.

Todor and Vasil slipped out of Dimitar's house, got of the village and returned to the koliba. All were very tired and, posting a guard, lay down on the floor in the hut to rest. When it dawned, the danger always increased, and all the chetniks were sitting quietly in the koliba until it became dark again. The owner of the koliba Dimitar brought a bag with food on a donkey.

"I barely got through! Leave faster until it's dark."

Having thanked Dimitar for food and koliba-shelter, the pilgrims set off. As before, they were walking in 2 detachments with the commanders Todor Todorov and Mityu Ganev at a distance from each other, heading south. The further south, the higher the mountains were, and when they reached Novakovo, they felt safe. The mountains were contiguous to Novakovo and rose right after the village. Dense forests with small glades covered the mountains slopes to the very top. And in one of the mountains there was their base-cave. 2 detachments of the cheta Hristo Botev passed Popovo and from the north approached Novakovo, which lay in full view of the Rhodopes half a km above the sea level, climbed the mountain along their path and got into their cave, where they arranged their secret base yet in summer. The entire cheta settled down to rest. Oak and birch forests and tall firs completely covered the Rhodopes, and the mountains guarded the cheta like the towers on the fortress.

"Save food, friends!" Todor ordered. "It's not known, when we receive the products some more; it is quite possible that our supply with food will stop at all."

The chetniks broke off a small piece of bread and ate a small piece of lamb meat, received on Easter in Bodrovo and Bukovo.

"Let's go, Vasil!" Todor called his new friend, and both descended down to Novakovo until the night ended.

Little Tsaregrad was the name of the village before the fire, and once burned by fire, it was rebuilt and renamed New Novakovo. Neat houses were picturesquely scattered right on the slopes of the hills, entwined with vines, immersed in gardens. The coming May 1925 more and more awakened all living things after hibernation in winter. While the villagers were sleeping and the night was not over, Todor with Vasil made their way to the house of Ilya Spasov, a faithful friend of Hristo Botev cheta.

"Come on quickly!" Ilya looked around, everything was calm; he locked the door with a latch. "How did you get through? There are cordons everywhere, policemen snoop around, it is forbidden to take out any food outside the village. If they catch somebody with food, they immediately torture him and inquire: 'Where are you going?' and shoot."

"Is Kostadin Popov safe? How is he? Does he have any information for us from Plovdiv from the Regional Command?" Todor asked.

"He vanished, and no one knows where he is," Ilya answered contritely, "we are in hell, in captivity of the foe. It would be better, if we fought with weapons in hands."

"I am afraid, we missed the moment last autumn, and now it's too late…"

"Damn butchers, they are worse than the Turks!"

"We'll go, while it's dark. This is my new friend Vasil Angelov."

"Greetings, Vasil!"

"Ilya, if you can, get us some food. Leave it in the appointed place. We'll be near."

"I have everything in my shop, the problem is to get out of the village. I'll try to get through. Tomorrow night. Don't come here anymore, it's very dangerous."

As already experienced partisans, Todor with Vasil slipped out of the house of Ilya Spasov and quietly left the village in the darkness and returned to their friends. Reliably closed from prying eyes behind the thickets of the forest on the mountain side, the natural cave was the base of the cheta, where they could stay for a long time. The chetniks saved food, prolonging the pleasure, ate a small piece of bread and lamb meat, received from the Easter feast, and pondered on their further actions.

"What are we going to do, boys?" Yanko Pavlitov asked.

"It is you who should tell us what to do next: it is you who are our political leader."

"In fact, we have lost any connection with the district and region."

"Maybe we'll visit the Bochkov monastery?" Mityu Ganev suggested. "We'll borrow some food from them? It's right there, next to us."

"Priests will hand us over and slam us like in a mousetrap in their monastery," Todor answered, "if the troops appear there, we won't get out."

"After all, all of them are traitors: the entire church serves the fascist regime with the tsar at the head!" Ivan Ignatov exclaimed.

"There are few decent individuals, who are against fascism, but they are an exception," Vasil Angelov said.

"Such as our Novakovo pope Angel Cholakov," Todor reminded. "He was such like us and of our age. At the age of 20, he prepared the uprising against the Turks. Vasil Levsky was like our United Front now. He went around the villages and cities of Bulgaria and founded the revolutionary committees, just like we did: created the militia-6s. He came to Novakovo and created the revolutionary committee to prepare the April uprising, and it was the priest Angel Cholakov who headed it. And exactly like we staged our secret meetings in the homes of our yataks, Vasil Levsky gathered secret meetings with the villagers of Novakovo in the house of our priest Angel. His house was a secret base of the Novakovo revolutionaries, and they hid weapons with gunpowder in his house."

"The April uprising was crushed, but at least they tried! They fought! But what are we? We did not even try!" Ivan Ignatov exclaimed.

"Why are you like that? We are not on our own! It was not we who had to raise the uprising, but our leaders, the leadership of the Central Committee and the United Front, to which we are subordinated. As for us, we ultimately fulfilled our task: we prepared people for the revolt, and it is not our fault that the uprising was not raised."

"And now, it is evidently: it is too late. The regime was the first to strike and crush our structures."

"Of course, it's a shame!"

"Although the April uprising was defeated, all the same, exactly in a year after its defeat, the Russian-Turkish war began, and in a year Bulgaria was liberated from the Turks," Todor continued. "But after that Bulgaria was again divided into the North and South Rumelia, and our priest continued fight against the Turks. Actually our pope Angel became a hajduk, he led a cheta, fought and rode on a white horse as a winner to Plovdiv and himself consecrated the Act of Reunification!"

"But how did he end up, do all remember?" Geno Delchev asked. "The drunken Bulgarian traitors killed him!"

"Enemies put together a counter-cheta from eternally drunken villagers, and they beat him to death with sticks!" Todor reminded everyone.

"Time passes, but nothing changes: the eternal struggle, the eternal struggle for freedom and the eternal story of betrayal continues!"

"And I'll ask you an indecent question, boys: who were worse: the Turks or the Bulgarian junta after June 9, 1923?"

"In my opinion, the poet Strashimirov has already given the answer to this question; he stated publicly: the tsar and the tsarist junta killed the Bulgarians more than the Turks did!"

All were silent, thinking, and Yordan Zhekov said:

"Where did the Bulgarian butchers come from on Bulgarian soil?"

"Maybe it is slavery that generated them."

Hidden from the enemies in the cave, the chetniks rested and gained strength, pondering on their further actions. And as soon as it got dark, Todor with Vasil went to the appointed place nearby, where Ilya was supposed to bring them food. The helper-donkey brought on his back bags, in which they collected everything that they could get from the friends and in his shop that they gave them.

"Here it is, I've brought it," Ilya said, passing the bags with food.

"Thanks, Ilya! We, the chetniks of Hristo Botev cheta, have been existing all this time only thanks to the yataks, thanks to your help! You shared with us everything you could, sometimes you gave us the last! You let us in your homes, risking your lives! On behalf of our entire cheta, I thank you and all our friends!"

Todor hugged Ilya.

"We have a common foe!" Ilya answered. "But now I don't know what will happen to us."

"Unfortunately, neither I nor anybody of us knows what will happen to all of us. I hope, we'll meet."

"Farewell, I'll return home, as I already said, it is forbidden to leave the village at night. There are cordons of policemen everywhere, they are like mad dogs."

The chetniks brought the bags with food from where Ilya had unloaded them, to the cave, their safe haven from the enemies, and all of them saved food as much as they could. A cave in the depth of the mountain protected by oak and beech forests and a dense wall of tall evergreen firs, standing close to each other, was turned into the base for the cheta last summer, and straw-stuff mattresses and dishes were brought into it in advance. The chetniks spent several days in that cave, and went out, not being seen by anybody. Nearby a source of clean water was knocked out from the ground, and an amazing view opened from the top of the mountain. The foliage on the branches of the trees grew thicker and thicker, filling the air of spring with aroma. The uncertainty oppressed them.

Todor with Vasil came to the appointed place of meeting with the yataks at a distance from the cave for security purpose and checked if there was a courier with a message. In a few days, as it got dark, Ilya Spasov was at the place and the bags with food were hanging on the back of the faithful donkey.

"Here it is. I've managed to bring it, I got through the ambush of policemen."

"Thank you, you are a hero, Ilya! We eat very little: by a small piece of bread with some cheese, we save food."

"This is a message, Todor! The Regional leadership tells you to return back to Aidanlar, Radyu Delchev will be there soon."

Todor hugged Ilya.

"This is the most valuable news for the latter time!"

Ilya Spasov led his donkey-helper back to Novakovo, and the chetniks received food reinforcement and valuable news. They were ready to leave. Under the cover of night they left their base-cave, which became their home and refuge, descended from the mountain and began to make their way to the north-east back to Aidanlar in 2 detachments in a distance from each other. At night they advanced over the mountains, hills and valleys, they hid during the daytime in a dense forest and continued to move as soon as it got dark. Next night they passed through the Aidanlar forest and approached the village of Aidanlar. The cheta stopped to wait in a dense forest in the former koliba of Vidyu Karagochev, now owned by the brothers Kolyu and Tanyu Kiryakov Buchev, while Todor with Vasil Angelov hurried to the village. They, like shadows, merging with the darkness of the night, silently and deftly crept up to the house of Todor Trendofilov and knocked at the door with a conventional knock. After a while the door opened, and a young widow of Todor appeared on the threshold. Disheveled and untidy, with swollen red eyes, she quickly let the chetniks in, closed the door and threw herself on the neck of Todor Todorov. Her tears streamed down on his shoulder, and now he already knew what she would tell them.

"There is no more Todor!" bursting into tears, she said. "2 military broke into the house, grabbed him, shot in the legs, began to beat him, and then tied him to a horse and dragged him out of the village… They killed him because he helped you! He asked me to tell you, if anything happens to him, the forester Kityu Panev is a traitor. It is he who betrayed him…"

The girl sobbed, being mad with grief. After a moment of silence, Todor asked gloomily:

"And what is with the brothers Kolyu and Tanyu Buchev? We haven't visited them yet. Are they all right?"

"No, they are not! Kityu Panev betrayed them too! They were convoyed by the military, and there is no news from them… It was on the same day…"

She went to the kitchen and brought 2 large loaves of bread.

"Here it is, take it!"

With a heavy heart Todor and Vasil left the house and the village, bringing the ominous news to the chetniks.

"I can't believe it!" Mityu Ganev exclaimed angrily. "This must be checked! Maybe some another one betrayed them!"

"Check!" Todor rebuffed. "Another traitor: some more victims—our friends!"

The chetniks were waiting for their Voevoda, and during the daytime some of them were in the koshara, the sentries guarded the approaches to the area. Todor was at the top of the hill with his friends, watching through the binoculars. He was looking into the distance very carefully, suddenly he saw the forester Kityu Panev walking along the path through the forest in a cheerful mood and humming something under his nose, holding a rifle on his shoulder. Todor pointed to the figure below with his hand to his friends, and they hurried down the hill. While they were descending, Kerez Bonbashev, who was on duty, jumped out of the bush and in a trice took the rifle away from him.

"Hold on! Do not move! And now let's go!"

He pushed him in the back with the butt of the rifle and led to Mityu Ganev, who was not far with some chetniks at the foot of the hill. On seeing them, Kityu Panev got excited even more, and then stretched out in a wide smile, coming up to Mityu Ganev.

"Hello, friend! How are you doing and how are your friends?" the forester joyfully greeted the under-Voevoda.

"Hello, Kityu!" Mityu Ganev answered and nodded his head to Bonbashev. "Everything is all right."

"How are those 2 rifles that I gave you back in autumn? Do they shoot well?"

"Useful, Kityu, thank you! And you, as I see, you got a job as a forester?"

"Most recently, we need to have order in our forest, otherwise our Aidanlar forest is notorious," Kityu blurted out.

"What is notoriously?" Mityu asked.

"Well, they say that the hajduks-robbers use to dwell here all the time!" the forester nervously laughed and added: "It's a joke!"

"It's all right, Kerez!" Mityu Ganev turned to the sentry Bonbashev and then took the forester's rifle from him and returned it to the detainee. "Take it, Kityu, everything is all right! We've known each other all our life. Go where you were going."

At that moment Todor and his friends, having descended the hill, ran up and blocked the forester's path.

"Halt, bastard! Hands up!"

Todor grabbed the forester rifle so quickly that the latter had no time to come to his senses. Todor pointed his revolver at the forester and then turned it to the under-voevoda.

"What's the matter, Mityu? Has your flair betrayed you? Has your simple prudence betrayed you? Or maybe you are deaf? Did you hear what I've told you: he is a traitor?"

Enraged Mityu Ganev reached for his revolver. Todor's friends were ahead of him and pointed their revolvers at Mityu Ganev and the forester. The latter was standing like a chameleon changing in his face from joy to horror.

"Are you all crazy?" Ivan Ignatov interfered. "Yes, we all have nerves on edge from what is happening, but we cannot behave like this and lose our temper like this! Come to your senses!"

"I've told you clearly that Kityu Panev is a traitor! He betrayed Todor Trendofilov and the Buchev brothers! Todor himself told me about it, when I saw him for the last time, and now his widow has confirmed it!"

"But we can't act like the authorities and just crack down on suspects without any evidence!" Mityu Ganev explained, somewhat calmed down. "We need evidence!"

"Search him!" Todor commanded to Kerez.

Kerez rummaged in the forester's clothes and drew out a copy of the note, which the forester had written for himself so that not to forget and not to confuse anything. Todor read aloud.

"Copy: in the village of Aidanlar, the yataks of HB cheta have been already handed over to Captain Hubenov: Todor Trendofilov, Kolyu Kiryakov Buchev, Tanyu Kiryakov Buchev."

Todor turned purple from anger and poked the note in Mityu Ganev's face.

"Come on, read! Oh, I am sorry, I forgot that you are illiterate: you can neither read nor write!"

Mityu Ganev was dumbfounded by the explosion of all feelings taken together: from resentment at the friend's insult to horror from the confirmed betrayal of the forester, whom he knew from childhood and whom he trusted. While he was suffocating from the feelings that paralyzed him, Todor shot at the forester, and the latter fell dead.

"Drop dead, fascist scum!" he gritted through his teeth with all the force of hatred for the death of all his friends taken together. Then he turned to the under-commander.

"Listen to me, Mityu Ganev! I warned you before and now I'm warning you: Blagon is also a traitor! Remember, if you fall for his tricks and do not kill him, but trust him again, you'll ruin the cheta! The death of our comrades will be on your hands!"

"Take him away!" Todor commanded, and the chetniks dragged aside the corpse of the traitor, lying under their feet.

"What's going on here?" Radyu Delchev asked, coming up to the cheta.

"The Voevoda is back!"

Friends threw themselves on his neck. Velyu Hristozov and another young man were standing nearby.

"Meet Matyu Toshev Iliev: he helped us in Plovdiv, has gone into illegality, like us, and now he will be with us."

The chetniks shook hands with him.

"Come on, Voevoda, tell us, how is it, what is it there?"

"Let's come in the koliba, put up a guard!" Radyu Delchev commanded.

2 people took the positions to guard the approaches to the place of cheta, and all the others came inside a spacious koliba, which accommodated them all. Radyu Delchev and Velyu Hristozov, although were glad to have a successful meeting with the cheta, still could not hide their depressed mood.

"Friends, I think all of you are aware and know that the Military Organization in Sofia, headed by Kosta Yankov, blew up the dome of the church 'St. Resurrection' on April 16 with the aim to eliminate all the fascist ringleaders taken together at one fell swoop and demolish the hated regime. Actually, for the same purpose we have been preparing the uprising for the past year. And they wanted to ensure the victory of the uprising by destroying the entire criminal elite. The Central Committee inside the country and abroad were at first for it, but then—against. Part of the Military Organization in Sofia was also against. But nevertheless, Kosta Yankov and another part of the headquarters went for it and took all responsibility for themselves, because the junta began to launch a pre-emptive strike long before the explosion. Almost all the members of the headquarters and the military organization, as well as the Central Committee, were captured and tortured to death. They formed a new composition of the headquarters, and they carried out what they planned. By a monstrous coincidence, as you know, all the ringleaders of the bloody gang were not injured and remained alive, but completely different ones died. The junta imposed martial law in the country on the same evening and further intensified the terror, which actually did not stop since June 9, 1923. A day before the explosion, on April 15, the Foreign Representation of the Central Committee, that is Dimitrov and Kolarov in Moscow, reversed the course of the armed uprising. That is: there will be no uprising. Terror is rampant throughout the country. Our friends, all those who helped us—they seize them and subject to horrendous torture and burn their houses. Our task today is to survive, to save our lives and save as many comrades as possible and take them with us."

"And where shall we go?" Mityu Ganev asked.

"We'll split into 2 detachments. One detachment, smaller in number, with the commander Mityu Ganev, will go around the villages of the Borisovograd and Asenovograd regions, maybe they will find our liaisons with the leadership and take with them the yataks, those who can be saved yet. And the most part of the cheta, the second detachment, of which I remain the commander and my deputy, as before, Todor Todorov—we'll go to the east, we'll go around the villages, we'll look for the liaisons and take the yataks with us. We all meet in the Belitsa area. In any case, it is closer to the border. In fact, we are on our own now. The District Committee in Haskovo is destroyed, the Regional Committee in Plovdiv is also destroyed, and the Military Organization in Sofia no longer exists. Its head Kosta Yankov is killed."

Everybody was listening silently in a depressed mood.

"It would be better if we raised the uprising last autumn, we had everything ready!" Georgy Nekezov, a political instructor from Borisovograd, exclaimed in despair. "It would be better to fight than just give up and die!"

"I agree," Radyu Delchev answered, "I also consider that we had everything ready last autumn, but the Central Committee leadership in Moscow thought differently, in fact, Moscow let us down, or rather betrayed us! And now it's too late: almost the entire leadership of the BCP and the

Agrarian Union had been destroyed, including our yataks in the villages and cities. Our task now is simply to survive."

There was a painful silence. On top of the gloomy news, Todor came up to Radyu Delchev and handed him the Georgy Pilashev's bag.

"Our Georgy died in the battle at the Black Rocks on April 21, and before his death he handed me his bag with the party documents and his diary so that I would give it to you, Voevoda…"

"Comrades, we are moving out tonight!"

The chetniks lay down on the floor in the koliba-cabin to rest in order to set off at night. The day was coming to an end, the evening was coming, and all prepared for the campaign. They split the cheta into 2 unequal parts. Mityu Ganev came up to Todor and sat down near him.

"I was wrong, Todor, that I wanted to let Kityu Panev go, I admit my fault, just I did not want to believe that he was a traitor. I grew up in Aidanlar, I knew him from childhood, and I trusted him: he was considered to be our yatak. Why did not he betray us before?"

"He was waiting for the right moment to break the bank: it's for sure, he was going to do it today after he saw all of us together."

"It's good, Todor, that you interfered and killed him!"

"Mityu, forgive me for calling you illiterate, I know what kind of childhood you had."

"I am not illiterate anyway," Mityu smiled, "the boys taught me to read and write!"

Ivan Ignatov approached them.

"Well, I see you've reconciled, haven't you? I wonder how you did not shoot each other today!"

"We all have our nerves on edge," Todor answered. "How are there are parents, Ivan?"

"I am afraid even to think about it," Ivan Ignatov answered, "all the same, we can't help them in any way."

"And how are there our friends: Mityu Panev, Kolyu Trendofilov and Rusi Stoyanov? Nothing is known about them. They joined another cheta closer to Plovdiv, and since then nothing has been known about them. Do you remember?"

The 3 friends smiled, remembering the time, when they had not yet joined the cheta.

"Yes, I'll tell you right away, I'll remind you once again that Blagon Zabanarov, because of whom we once ended up in a jail, is a traitor! Remember this, Ivan! Remember this, Mityu!"

"How do all the friends become traitors at all, it's not clear?" Ivan Ignatov asked with a sad sigh, recalling how together with Blagon, they "slipped cabbage soup" in Haskovo prison and then fled together.

"Nonsense, real friends never become traitors!" Todor answered. "It means that only fake 'friends' become traitors, because they were enemies from the very beginning."

"Boys, get up, we are moving!" Radyu Delchev commanded, and 2 detachments lined up near the koliba.

As always, they were in full combat readiness, ready to engage the battle against foe at any moment: bandoliers were filled with the bullets, bolts of the revolvers and rifles were full of cartridges, bombs were on their belts with daggers and a rifle was on the shoulders. The remains of food and baklagas with water were in the bags across the shoulders.

"Farewell, friends!"

The brothers Kuzi and Sava Kuzev from Bolyarsky Izvor were parting. Sava remained in the Radyu's detachment, and Kuzi stayed with Mityu Ganev. Mityu Ganev, Todor Todorov and Ivan Ignatov hugged for parting, not hiding their excitement.

"Goodbye, see you in the east of the country near Belitsa!"

"Maybe in a couple of weeks," Mityu Ganev said and hugged Todor again for parting.

Both squads shook hands, waved goodbye and disappeared in different directions. Mityu Ganev led the smaller detachment to the west, and the larger detachment Radyu Delchev and Todor Todorov led to the east.

Chapter 55
Mezek

The detachment of Radyu Delchev moved south and approached the village of Tatarevo, where there were faithful yataks, and stopped in front near the hill outside the village. Todor Todorov and Vasil Angelov went to the village. Moving from bush to bush, bending in the darkness, they managed to enter the village and come up to the house of the yatak Dobri Kolev. A conditional knock on the door, it opened, and they disappeared behind the door inside. Frightened, Dobri Kolev asked with surprise:

"How did you get through? In the village the policemen and the military are constantly snooping around, blocking the village, at night no one can go out or enter."

"Probably, the policemen and the military also want to sleep at night," Todor joked, "but I agree: things are very bad. Don't you want to leave with us?"

"Maybe not, where will you go from the native home? I hope that the danger will pass over me: Bay Angel Rusev did not betray me…"

"What is with him?" Todor asked.

"Recently he was seized, they suspected him to be your yatak. They tormented, tortured him, mocked him like barbarians, broke his legs, tried to find out who else was helping you in the village. He withstood inhuman torment and did not betray anyone. So, I am safe thanks to him."

"Hold on, we all have to survive this plague that has fallen on our heads. Is there any news for us?"

"No, there is not: nothing is known. So, there won't be any uprising?"

"Now we can definitely say no; we missed the moment last autumn. We'll go, Dobri, thank you for everything!"

"Take the bread."

He handed Todor a loaf of bread and a piece of cheese. Todor and Vasil slipped out into the darkness and reached the detachment, which halted to the north, not reaching the village. A loaf of bread and a piece of cheese were cut into thin slices for everyone, and the detachment set off. They approached the Banska River, which, undulating with waves, flowed from the peaks of the south-west, skirted the Tatarevo from the north and turned north-east in the direction of Maritsa. At the very edge of the village a military detachment was sitting in ambush. They spotted the chetniks and opened fire.

"Spread out, we make our way along the river to the rocks!" Voevoda gave the order. "Open fire!"

The chetniks scattered across the territory in a trice, took over behind the trees and began to shoot at the military. The first dead fell, the rest retreated north away from the river. The military fired at the chetniks and retreated further and further, and the latter sent bullets after them and made their way along the riverbed. Without losing a single man, the Delchev's detachment hid behind the rocks, through which the Banska River cut a gorge in the mountains of Boaz.

They climbed to the top of the forest-covered mountain and took up a convenient position for defense. Below the river rustled in the gorge, flying quickly through the stones. It could be waded over the large stones in a narrow place, then the river fell down in a small waterfall, then widened and deepened to fly down with waterfall again and break on the stones. High cliffs stood along the coast, and on them the chetniks met the dawn. They could move only at night, hiding somewhere during daytime. The sun rose in the east, and the rays illuminated the beautiful landscape. Nature seemed to tease them, saying: "Admire my beauty, but it is not for you, because you are chased behind!"

In a distance from Tatarevo the military appeared again and the fascists activists nearby. The authorities armed all the volunteers from the villages and gave them 50 leva each. There were volunteers in every village. Assistants to the military and policemen, they huddled together in their flocks and followed on the hills of the combatants of the cheta Hristo Botev. Having approached a shooting range, they scattered, losing those, who were going ahead. The marksmen from the top of the cliff laid down one scum after another. The military opened fire at the top of the cliff, but kept missing, as the bullets bounced off the huge stones.

"Hold out until evening!" Todor ordered.

The bullets were whistling over the Boaz Gorge. The military fell dead, but the living continued to shoot. So the May day passed, and the shooting stopped as soon as it began to get dark to be resumed in the morning.

"Are you ok, boys?" Voevoda asked.

The chetniks came out from under the shelters of the stones and gathered all together.

"Roll call!" Delchev said and called everyone by name.

All the boys were intact, but very emaciated. They shook hands. After conferring with Todor, Radyu said:

"Unfortunately, there is no time to rest, until night we'll make our way along the river in the direction of Garvanovo. When we go out of the gorge, we turn south to cover our tracks."

"We wish we could eat!" said the chetniks, who had eaten the last piece of bread.

"Be patient, boys, we'll get some food somewhere," Todor said.

Tired and hungry, the chetniks followed the planned route. They descended from the mountain in the easterly direction, where the Banska River flowed, and went along the gorge, following the river, which, undulating, made its way through the rocks. On the top of the troubles, it started to rain. It poured on the chetniks' heads, flowered down the collar, making it difficult for them to step. Their clothes got wet, their onuchis unwounded, and their cervulis fell off. The hungry stomachs of the young healthy men made themselves felt. After walking 5 km along the stones of the gorge, they turned to the south and began to move away from the Boaz Gorge, where the battle had recently been going on. They trudged through the swamp, into which the rain had turned their path, splashing with their cervulis, through the puddles, and retired further and further during the night. Dawn was approaching. They passed from the eastern side Trakietsa and hid in refuge in the dense forest on the top of the mountain from the rays of the rising sun. The stone remains of a Thracian fortress adorned the top of the mountain. As soon as the sunbeams illuminated the valleys and mountains, far behind them in the rocks of the Boaz Gorge of the Banska River, rifles shots and explosions of a canister were heard: the fascist blockhead warriors resumed the attack on the empty rock, where the chetniks had been fighting with them yesterday afternoon. The fascist shots thundered in the Boaz Gorge, kicking up dust and breaking the brunches.

Todor with Radyu were looking through the binoculars from the top of the mountain near Trakietsa: soldiers and policemen were scurrying around the village. They blocked the entrances and exits from the village and scurried around the surrounding area. Hungry chetniks in wet clothes lay down to rest on the top of the mountain. There were no more food supplies. A wild pear tree grew on the mountain, the unripe fruits somewhat satisfied hunger of the young men. The chetniks did not lose heart and determined to get food somewhere.

"I have a plan!" Todor told Radyu, and they shared it with the detachment.

As soon as it got dark, the chetniks set off. Covered by darkness and trees, they descended the mountain near Trakietsa so that the military did not notice them in the distance and continued to make their way to the south-east. They splashed across the wet ground with their cervulis, shapeless from wear, and their clothes was still damp from the night rain. They trudged in the darkness, not afraid of anything. They came up with a daring plan. While the policemen with the military and the fascist activists blocked the villages in the district, the chetniks set up an ambush in a distance from the villages on the road between Voevodovo and Mandra, leading to the fair in Haskovo. The fair was on that day, on Saturday, and the movement on the road was supposed to start early in the morning. The chetniks came up close to the road at night and hid behind the bushes at the very edge of the road. Traders on carts appeared on the road to the fair, and the chetniks blocked their path.

"Halt! Hands up!"

Not expecting the appearance of the chetniks, as the newspapers had already reported their ultimate abolition, the merchants stopped the carts and raised their hands.

"Citizens of Bulgaria!" Todor appealed to them. "This time it's a robbery! That is expropriation! Please, remain calm and understand us correctly! The army, which was called upon to protect our country from the external enemy, was thrown by the illegal authorities to the internal front to fight with us, the soldiers of the people. The fascists: Boris III, Tsankov, Rusev and Vylkov set their army on us to destroy us, but we are fighting it and are still alive to fight! Unable to destroy us, the army of the butchers destroys the defenseless villagers, who help us. The criminal butchers in military uniform break into the villages, seize good peasants, and subject them to barbaric torture, torment them, maul, break their arms and legs, pour quicklime down their throats, kill them together with their families and burn their houses for helping us! At the moment, our liaisons with our yataks are difficult! Therefore, we are in dire need of food, money, clothes, shoes, and we are earnestly ask you, merchants, who are going with goods to the fair in Haskovo, to share it with us! We, the cheta Hristo Botev, are fighting for our and your freedom against our common foe, who has enslaved our country! I hope, you don't mind to share something with us!"

The traders on carts filled with all sorts of good things listened to the speaker and were imbued with sympathy. They were gazing at the young people, dressed in hajduks uniform, once new, spectacular and beautiful, but worn out during the year of struggle, wet from the night rain, and saw their beautiful, proud faces, devoid of fear, with mockery in their eyes over the misfortune. They were gazing at them with sympathy, pity, admiration and pride for that not everyone in the country complied with a difficult fate. Each of the merchants handed out to the chetniks what he had: money, food, clothes and cervulis. Having taken everything they gave, the chetniks thanked the merchants and hastily retired from the Mandra-Voevodovo Road. They walked a few km, moving east, and halted in the forest, not reaching Knizhovnik. They stopped there to respire, to put on new shoes and continue the way. A hail of bullets whistled over their heads: from the direction of the village, across the field, policemen were approaching, accompanied by a platoon of the fascists activists: one of them tracked them down.

"Take up defensive position!" Radyu Delchev commanded. "Save cartridges!"

The chetniks disappeared behind the trees and returned fire. The battle continued until night, while the remains of the policemen and activists retreated. Without losing a single person, the cheta Hristo Botev set off. They were going in the same direction, their goal was Belitsa. They walked at night, and during the daytime they had to engage in battle with foe, who scoured the villages, fields and forests in search of the chetniks. In a day after the battle in Knizhovnik they approached Bolyarsky Izvor at night and took refuge in the forest on the top of the mountain, where they used to train the militia-6s and take photos. Emaciated and tired, the chetniks made a halt under the trees, and Voevoda turned to Todor:

"Try to get into the village, maybe you'll make it."

"Let's go, Vasil," Todor called his friend, and both went down from the mountain, got into Bolyarsky Izvor and crept up to the house of Latyu Kuzev, the head of the militia-6. On hearing a conventional knock on the door at night, Latyu Kuzev shuddered with excitement, no longer believing that this was possible. He hurriedly opened the door and let Todor with Vasil in.

"How are you, Latyu, how is your son?" Todor asked.

"I believe, you know yourself, Todor, our affairs are very bad," Latyu answered, "they can break into the house at any moment and seize you."

"Get ready and come on with us with your son," Todor called him, "even though our things are worse than ever, but at least, we are fighting with weapons in our hands."

"I have been ready long ago to leave together with you," Latyu answered, "it's better to fight than to be tormented to death. Now I'll raise my son."

Latyu went to another room and soon returned with his third son.

"Get ready, son, come on to cheta, it's dangerous here, they can grab you at any minute."

"Where shall I go, father?" Rusi answered. "2 brothers have left, you'll leave, what will happen to our house? At least someone should stay at home and take care of the household!"

"Son, Rusi, you don't understand, if you stay here, there will be no one to take care of our house, but if we leave with the cheta, maybe we survive and return back one day to our home!"

"Hurry up, Latyu, and you, Rusi! The father tells the truth: if you are suspected that you are the yatak, they will destroy you together with the house! If you have decided to leave together with us, hurry up, we must go!"

"Come on, son!" Latyu pleadingly looked at Rusi.

"Father, I am staying, I won't go, I've decided so," Rusi answered, "you go, if you decided to leave, then go!"

Latyu quickly gathered his bag with things, put the food that was in the house into another bag and hugged his third son for parting. Tears were shimmering in the father's eyes.

"Farewell son!"

"Farewell father, farewell friends, be careful, come back!"

Todor with Vasil shook hands with Rusi Latev Kuzev, and all 3 slipped out of the house into the darkness. Todor put his finger to his lips, showing: not a sound, and they quietly got out of the village, reached the mountain and climbed up.

"Hello son!" Bay Latyu hugged his second son Sava. "Where is Kuzi?"

"Hello father, Kuzi left with Mityu Ganev. Where is Rusi? Why didn't he come?"

"Rusi did not want to go," the father sighed sadly, "he preferred to stay at home and to look after the household. We used to train our 6s here." Bay Latyu reminded. "I wonder how is there our photographer."

"Boys, we must go!" Radyu Delchev addressed the cheta. "We must make our way further to Belitsa, while it's night and dark."

After a short rest during the halt, the chetniks got up and set off on their way. They trudged through nights, mountains and forests, and during the daytime they fought until it got dark. They walked at random without any guides from the local villages, without communications with the leadership and yataks, without any information about the troops. The policemen, military and activists tracked them down, when it was light, and without losing a single fighter, they fought until night and fled. Finally, Belitsa emerged on the horizon. The hearts of the chetniks beat with excitement. They had passed, fighting, through half of the country and without losing a single person, overcoming all the troubles that fell on them, and reached their goal. They were standing on a hill, and below them a dale stretched, where Belitsa lay in full view. In this village almost all people were their yataks, and Belitsa was the base of the cheta. Joy and excitement overwhelmed them, as there was uncertainty.

"Hands up!" came from behind them, and shuddered with surprise, they drew their revolvers and turned around.

Laughter and joy, hugs and shaking hands in a trice replaced fear. A detachment of their comrades-in-arms was standing behind them. The companions laughed and hugged.

"We have been waiting for you," Nikola Tryndev from Belitsa said.

"Friends, here we are!" Voevoda Radyu Delchev exclaimed joyfully.

"But the fact that you are here, but not at home does not bode anything good," Todor remarked.

"How is there Belitsa?" Voevoda asked.

"Your base in Belitsa no longer exists," Nikola Tryndev answered with a frown, "Dobri Terpeshev was seized, the Party Secretary Angel Minchev was seized. You can imagine what is happening with them now. All of us who are here managed to leave, left their homes, and we have been sitting in the mountains and waiting for you. Here we are, all who are here—my brother

Georgy Tryndev, Gavril Georgiev, Hristoz Andreev—we are from our Belitsa. And these are our friends from Nova Mahala: Party Secretary Georgy Boytsev, Secretary of the Komsomol Organization Toncho Georgiev, as well as Zafir Georgiev, Belcho Boydev, Kiro Stoikov, Kosta Lambov. So, we have our own cheta."

"Folks, in the evening we all set off on a journey to Malko Gradishte," Voevoda said. "Mityu Ganev platoon should come there in early June, and we'll wait for them there."

"There is still time, there are still 2 weeks," Todor answered.

After waiting on the mountain near Belitsa all day, they got ready to go as soon as it began to get dark. For the last time they looked down into the valley, where Belitsa, to east of them, lay as if in a cradle, giving them home and shelter. Their hearts ached with pain, when they remembered the past winter and autumn. In each house in Belitsa there were their yataks, they gave the fighters home and comfort. When a winter blizzard howled outside and a knee-deep snow covered all the paths, Belitsa opened its doors to the fighters, and in the warm houses by the fireplaces they discussed the uprising. This was their struggle, the struggle of free people against slavery. They remembered the faces of friends, faithful, brave and kind; they shared their home and bread, sometimes giving the last. Rebellion was their hope, and they were all ready for it. They dreamed to free their land from the fascist invaders.

A dark haze was advancing from west, when the sun had rolled behind the mountains; this darkness covered the village, and Belitsa hid under it. The soldiers of Hristo Botev cheta did not see it any more. They set off on their way to Malko Gradishte. For the first time lately their moving was not difficult. A detachment from Nova Mahala and Belitsa, which had joined the cheta, confidently led them forward. The guides from Belitsa knew the ways and paths, walked ahead and led all the others. By midnight they had reached their destination.

Malko Gradishte lay south of Belitsa, and the same distance remained to the border of Bulgaria. Rising on 200 meters above the sea level, the village was contiguous to the mountains, surrounding it. On one of the mountains, covered with trees, there was a cave—another base of the cheta Hristo Botev. Here already every chetnik knew the way to it. Climbing along a familiar path through the densely standing trees, they finally came to their destination. Hidden from view, the entrance to the cave in the rock opened its doors, and the cheta finally found peace in it. Everything was untouched and had been in place, since they had left everything: the weapons in the cache, cookware and the mattresses with straw. The chetniks, falling from their feet with fatigue, fell right on them.

After lying half an hour, Todor with Vasil got up and set off on their way, while it was dark. They could not move during the daytime. Having mastered the tactics of penetrating a village under the cover of night, Todor and Vasil safely reached the house, which stood on the hill, covered with greenery. The secretary of the party organization, Dimo Georgiev Kostov lived there. He opened the door on the conditional knock, and 2 chetniks slipped inside. The companions hugged and shook hands.

"Tell me, how are things? Is everyone safe?" Dimo asked.

"Fortunately, everyone is safe, here, at the end of the world, fortunately, the executioners have not reached yet, but this does not mean that they can't get here at any moment," Todor answered gloomily. "Is there any message for us?"

"The Central Committee has ordered you to leave Bulgaria and go abroad. The rebellion is out of the question. All our organizations throughout the country have been destroyed, people have been tortured and killed. They've ordered you to leave, to save yourselves, to save your life. You are the most valuable thing that we have."

"Yes, the uprisings must be raised in time," Todor said, "it would be better if we acted last autumn, when everything was ready. Moscow betrayed us, they did not support us and thwarted the uprising!"

"By all indications, it was so," Dimo Kostov answered, "now it's useless to remember the past: you have to build your new future in a foreign land. We, all our people from Malko Gradishte, will leave together with you, will not wait until the executioners appear here. A lot of people have already left through our illegal channels."

"We all are in our place, you know where it is. We need food supplies, the boys have been starving already for half a month."

"We'll provide you," Dimo answered, "there is no problem with this. We'll bring it tomorrow evening, but for now, take what I have."

Dimo prepared 2 bags with food from his house and 2 large loaves of bread, the smell of which made Todor and Vasil dizzy. But they did not break off a single piece, thanked Dimo, said goodbye to him and hurried to their friends.

The chetniks were impatiently waiting for Todor with Vasil, waiting for the news they bring. And when they entered the cave at the end of the night, everyone sat down on the mattresses and was all ears.

"Boys, here it is food!" Todor and Vasil happily announced and laid out the contents of 2 bags on the blanket spread on the floor of the cave.

They carefully cut 2 huge loaves of bread, 2 kg each, for everyone: each got a tiny piece of cheese to sniff. They ate slowly, stretching the pleasure.

"Well, tell!" Radyu Delchev addressed Todor.

"The Party Organization in Malko Gradishte is safe: the policemen with military have not reached there yet. There are no local fascist activists either," Todor said to his friends, smiling, "so, all the people are safe, but all the same they are going to abandon their homes to join us to go abroad together with us!"

There was silence.

"Abroad?" Radyu Delchev asked again.

"Yes, abroad! The Central Committee ordered us to leave Bulgaria and go abroad! Many of our people from the other cities and villages have already left Bulgaria! But why are you so surprised, as if you yourself did not guess where we were going all this time! After all, it was the border to the east, where we were advancing."

"Anyway, it's unexpectedly," thought and said each of the chetniks, who were aware of this necessity to themselves, but did not want to admit it.

"The best people have left Bulgaria—who will remain in it!" Radyu Delchev exclaimed.

"Ok, boys, the morning is wiser than the evening; we all need rest before starting a new path!" Todor turned to his friends.

"But it is already almost morning!" Vasil Angelov noticed.

All the chetniks fell into a dead sleep for the first time lately, and 2 sentries, as always, guarded their sleep outside the cave. They woke up after noon, went out of the cave to bask in the sun. Bright rays illuminated the magic view on Malko Gradishte. For the first time in a while they had nowhere else to hurry. They admired the view from the top of the mountain. The grandiose rocks with an impregnable barrier, like the walls of the fortress, guarded them from the foe, and far to the south-west, sheer cliffs rose to the sky even higher, the "Deaf Stones" of the ancient Thracians, who by some miracle cut the niches like trapezoids through the walls. The Thracian niches blackened on the rocks like eye sockets, making the contemporaries shudder, and it seemed that through them the owners of this land were watching them. The impossibility of carving such niches in the rocks appeared to be possible for the ancient Thracians and inspired awe, horror and fear for those, who gazed at them in the ages.

In the distance, to the south-east, Mezek blackened as a dot—the last wharf before the border. And around, the foliage raged with greenery, which in mid-May grew even more from heavy rains. Malko Gradishte could be seen from the top of the mountain as the last memory of their home in Bulgaria, lying quietly on the slope of the hills, immersed in greenery and in white lace of flowering fruit trees. For the first time in a long time the chetniks rested openly on the top of the mountain and discussed their entire path traveled. And the unknown was ahead. When it began to get dark, Dimo Georgiev Kostov and his brother Angel Kostov lifted bags with food up the mountain, loaded on the back of a faithful donkey, helping a man in the dales and mountains. The food problem had been resolved.

"Comrades, we'll leave together with you," Dimo told the chetniks and once again conveyed to them the order of the Central Committee, "you are ordered to go abroad."

"We've already got used to this idea," Radyu Delchev answered, "we are waiting here for the Mityu Ganev detachment, and we are leaving!"

"We'll join you in a few days," Dimo said.

Accustomed to making transition at night and hiding during the day or, as lately, fighting daily, the warriors of Hristo Botev in the cave under Malko Gradishte returned to normality. Now they slept enough at night with mandatory sentries, and during the day time they rested on the top of the mountain. The feeling of hunger no longer tormented them, as the comrades from Malko Gradishte regularly supplied them with food, and they could only wait, enjoying nature. Below on the terrace, 3 waterfalls replaced each other. The water, flowing down from the mountains, fell from a stone ledge, forming a pool like in a stone bath, and flowed out further along the mountain side in a stream. The chirping of birds that arrived in spring broke the silence on the top of the mountain, and the greenery of the bushes and trees grew brighter every day. It was their rest before a long journey, and they would have rested in body and soul, if not their thoughts about the future and past. They had been waiting for the platoon of Mityu Ganev for 2 weeks, the platoon did not come. The comrades-in-arms from Malko Gradishte, who joined them, insisted on crossing the border.

"We can't wait here anymore! Do you want us to be tracked down here and ruined?"

"It's ought to be conveyed to our friends in Malko Gradishte, who decided to stay, so that they inform Mityu Ganev, when his detachment comes here, that we left for Greece through our channel, he knows it," Radyu Delchev said, "let them, if they can, pass on to all the other villages through our liaisons, who is still alive, that we have gone abroad."

"I'll pass on everything," Dimov said, "I am returning to the village for the last time, I'll take something else with me, and I'll be with you this evening."

"We are moving out tonight!" Radyu and Todor decided, and they were supported by all the other chetniks, who faced a choice either to be destroyed or go abroad.

The Hristo Botev fighters gathered their belongings, cleaned their clothes, put on new cervulis, combed their curls and shaved off the beards those who had them, and by the evening they were ready to set off. Their hearts were beating faster than when they fought in battle. Dimo Georgiev Kostov returned together with his friends: Angel Kostov, Kerez Binbashiev, Stoycho Djurov and Hristo Kabanvanov. All people started on their journey. For the last time they looked down at Malko Gradishte, which gradually disappeared before their eyes in the darkness. They descended the mountain and walked in the dark on the dales and hills. They moved further and further south-east, approaching the border. At dawn they reached Mezek. Like Malko Gradishte, Mezek was contiguous to the mountains with forests, and on them to the way south they camped for the day. A cave on the mountain was at their service. Having walked on all night through the mountains, they lay down to sleep in the vast cave and, having slept just a little, began to prepare again for the journey.

"We leave all the extra weapons here!" Radyu and Todor commanded. "Boys, get to work, we leave with us only one revolver and a rifle."

Each of them wiped dry the second revolver, wrapped it in a piece of cloth, which he had, everything was neatly folded in the depth of the cave: bombs, bandoleers, cartridges.

Everything was covered with stones.

"We'll use it one day, if we return."

At the top of the mountain, along the slopes covered with forests, all the chetniks took up positions for observation. A panorama unfolded before them that stirred their hearts. In the east, the Maritsa undulated, absorbing tributaries from both sides. On the both sides of the river they could see the villages, where their comrades had received them last winter. Free, brave, kind, who did not want to endure humiliating oppression; they together with them created detachments, militia-6s, to follow the cheta at the moment of the uprising. They all expected the uprising and wanted to overthrow the hated junta. And now they were left alone. The majority had been already tortured to death by the butches. The hearts of the chetniks ached with pain, but they had nothing to reproach themselves with. They were fulfilling their duty on the instructions of the United Front. It was not their fault that the uprising was not destined to be realized. The entire valley of Maritsa lay before their eyes on 3 cardinal points: north, west and east—except for the south. Ahead of them to the south there was the frontier post. They scanned the movement at the frontier, discussed the actions together and were ready to set off in the evening.

For farewell they gazed from the top of the mountain at the whole Bulgarian land: behind them, on mount Kaleto, the Mezek fortress towered, or rather what was left from it, but a little remained. Thousand-year-old walls of stone and brick towered on 10 m at the top of Kaleto; they stood on the western side close to Mezek with towers in the corners and along the walls. The fortress Neutzikon was preserved best of all and reminded the descendants of Byzantium that had gone into oblivion. Her stones, as living witnesses of a 1,000-year history stood before the eyes of Hristo Botev cheta and parted with them. And next to Mezek, the treasures of the ancient Thracians were buried under the ground.

It was getting dark, and the Hristo Botev cheta was ready to set off. They looked for the last time around.

"One day we'll return," Voevoda said, "maybe, not now, maybe in 10 years, maybe in 20 years, but we'll definitely return and take revenge on the butchers, all the traitors, fascist activists, we'll avenge each of our tortured friend, we'll take vengeance for everyone!"

"We'll be back, if we survive," Todor said.

The chetniks looked around for the last time and moved south from Mezek. The border was close, and they could see it ahead. They approached it and crossed over the border. Farewell native land! Farewell Bulgaria, the country of the folk heroes and the traitors, who betrayed them all! Farewell the motherland of cheta Hristo Botev: young and fearless men, crazy brave and proud, born free and free in spirit. They challenged the fascist scum and fought them bravely in battle. They did not comply with the bandit power and never recognized the bastards, who usurped power in Bulgaria and rent asunder Alexander Stamboliysky. Farewell Bulgaria, which betrayed Stamboliysky and Raiko Daskalov, a country of traitors, slaves and serfs, servile servants, who kissed the tsarist boot, with which he beat their stinking teeth to the chimes of the churches bells and the stench of the chrism!

Chapter 56
Mezek 2

Having left Aidanlar, the detachment of Mityu Ganev set off in the west-north direction. After consulting with each other, they started a daring action that no one expected from them. They went directly to Bodrovo.

"I haven't been in my native village for a long time!" Ivan Ignatov said sadly.

"Here we go!" Mityu Ganev delighted him.

Midnight was approaching. The chetniks crossed the hills and meadows between Aidanlar and Bodrovo and came close to the village. They froze, hiding behind the bushes on both sides of the road and scanned the situation around them for a while. There was nothing suspicious; stealthily they sneaked into the village. Soon there was a knock at the door of the Bodrovo kmet. The kmet was frightened by the night knock, but came to the door and asked:

"Who is it?"

"Open, Bay Peter, it's me, Ivan," the kmet heard the voice of Ivan Ignatov and was scared even more.

"What do you want, Ivan?"

"Open, let me in!"

The kmet pushed the latch with a trembling hand, the door swung open, and the cheta Hristo Botev entered the house, pushing him into the rear. The kmet was trembling with fear and hated himself for that; in the depth of his soul he dreamed to be as brave as the chetniks.

"Don't be afraid, Bay Peter, we need food only, we have a problem with the supply of food lately. So, will you treat us?"

"Well, come on," he called the uninvited guests, having decided, come what may now.

12 chetniks came in a specious dining room.

"With your permission, we'll sit down at the table, do you mind?" Ivan Ignatov asked.

"Sit down, make yourself at home," frightened kmet squeezed out of himself.

"Sit down, boys, Bodrovo kmet invites us for dinner," Ivan invited his friends, and the chetniks hurried to sit down at a long table.

"Bay Peter, feed the hungry wonderers from the road."

"Of course, just a minute."

In a minute on the table in front of the chetniks there were the remains of a baked lamb, bread, cheese, vegetables, milk and boiled eggs.

"Only, Bay Peter, we won't be able to pay you off: at the moment we don't have enough money and food, and liaisons with our yataks are difficult. I think, you know it yourself," Mityu Ganev turned to him.

"Don't worry, Bay Mityu, no payment is required," the frightened kmet responded.

"We'll pay you off some other day," Mityu Ganev promised.

"And where is Todor?" kmet interested.

"Todor is on a responsible mission now," Ivan answered, eating the food, offered by kmet.

"I understand."

"How good is with you, Bay Peter," Mityu said, "it is so cozy, clean, a lot of food. We are so tired and hungry, don't you mind, if we rest here at your place until morning?"

"Have rest, since you've come. What is it now?" kmet sighed. "Ivan, I regret that your relatives and the relatives of Todor were interned! It's not my fault, you know. Now we are not the masters in our village, in our native home! Now military are in charge everywhere."

"That's why we exist: to fight them!" answered Mityu Ganev, whom unexpectedly kmet stopped to be afraid of. "That's why we, the cheta Hristo Botev, are fighting against these military fascists in order to be masters again in our house, in our village and in our country, which they have deprived of us."

Kmet sighed and pondered on, not believing what was happening: not only Mityu Ganev, not only Ivan Ignatov, but the entire cheta Hristo Botev, or a part of it, is sitting at the table in his house as a guest. "If the military saw!" he was thinking with horror.

That night the chetniks enjoyed coziness and dinner as uninvited guests in the house of the kmet of Bodrovo Peter Kostov until dawn. At dawn they took with them the bags with food, which the kmet gave them for journey, and parted with him.

"We hope, you Bay Peter, that it goes without saying, you will not tell anyone about our night visit!" Mityu Ganev addressed him.

"Of course, I won't tell!" the kmet replied.

The Mityu Ganev detachment sneaked out of the kmet's house and vanished outside Bodrovo. In the morning the kmet Peter Kostov came to his office to work, sat down at the table and pondered on. He recalled the past years; before his eyes the pictures of 3 wars passed, in which he fought: 2 Balkan Wars and the Great War. He recalled how during the last was Todor's father Ivan Todorov Karagochev, was sitting in this same office, he was the kmet at that time, and saved the whole village from Ferdinand's and German robbery. His wife told how Ivan did not allow the deprivation of the last from the villagers, as it used to happen everywhere. He recalled what happened then, how their country was rolling into the abyss and fell on the very bottom. If the Second Balkan War was the first catastrophe, and the Great War was the second catastrophe, then the tsarist-Tsankov upheaval on June 9, 1923, with all the consequences was nothing but the third national catastrophe, and now they are prisoners of the military, who took the side of the putsch. And these brave men are real heroes and are fighting for the liberation of their country from the fascist oppression. Kmet was tormented by thoughts that he just tried to do his job and did not think about whose side he was on. Of course, he was not a scoundrel, he did not want to be on the side of the butchers' power, but he neither wanted to be on the side of resistance solely out of fear, because he knew how the butchers dealt with the rebels. He just wanted to live peacefully and not to risk with anything. He realized that he was just a coward, incapable of any act, and he despised himself for this cowardice. And here he got a chance, and he did the act: he fed the chetniks and did not tell anyone about it. No, this is not enough, and he will make another bold act, and come what may! He opened the drawer of his desk, in which Blagon's denunciation lay, pulled out the list of the yataks of the cheta Hristo Botev, and resolutely burned it. For the first time in 2 years of the fascists' coup, he felt satisfaction and peace in his soul.

Meanwhile, the detachment of Mityu Ganev, unnoticed by anyone, sneaked out of Bodrovo and managed to get to the neighboring Varbitsa, which was in 3 km north from Bodrovo at a crossroads. The highway from Plovdiv to Istanbul passed through the village, which was crossed by the road from Bodrovo to Skobelevo to the north to Maritsa. The chetniks hid in the dense greenery of the bushes next to the trees near the highway, and in the east the orange arc of the rising sun slowly emerged from behind the mountains, piecing the passing night with its rays.

The sentry Peter Filippov climbed a tree, whom which the highway was clearly visible in both directions, and the chetniks froze, lying in the bushes. The sun rose higher and higher, giving birth to one more day in the life of Bulgaria. On the highway in both directions trucks passed by them, and the warriors, sitting in them, went to war with the yataks in the cities and villages of Bulgaria. Being unable to leave the shelter during the day time, the chetniks of Mityu Ganev were sitting in it until the nightfall, and as soon as it began to get dark, they got out of the bushes and set off. They got their yatak from Varbitsa and all together went in the direction of the west. The darkness of the night was even darker, the stars in the sky were not visible, they were covered by heavy clouds, which soon broke through, having brought down streams of water to the ground. Soaked to the skin, the chetniks trudged the puddles across the fields and hills; the Tsaregrad highway ran to their right, and the northern outskirts of Bodrovo were visible to the left. Ivan Ignatov wondered, if he ever sees his native village. They trudges along the northern outskirts of the village of Pravoslaven and began to move south from the Tsaregrad highway. Small in size, but dense copies with a glade in the center on the hill side seemed to them a suitable place for rest after a night travel.

"Boys, halt!" Mityu Ganev said.

"We'll rest until the evening!" Jordan Zhekov rejoiced.

They carefully looked around, studied the area, divided into groups by 3 people and lay down to sleep under the trees at a distance from each other at the 4 different sides, outlining retreat routs in case of attack. Heavy wet clothes stuck to the body, wet shapeless from wear cervulis slipped from wet onuchis, but the chetniks, accustomed to the hardships, fell asleep, clutching their rifles. The rain stopped, the darkness dissipated, and the rising sun heralded a new day. Ivan Ignatov took the position of the sentry. An oak tree grew a little to the side, and mighty branches descended close to the ground. Ivan climbed up the branches of the tree and began to guard the rest of his friends. A view opened into the distance from the height of the branches of the oak tree. Ivan really wanted to sleep himself, but the duty of his service kept him awake. He was gazing from a height into the distance at the miracle of nature, admiring its beauty. From 3 sides, like the corners of a triangle, he could see Tatarevo, Konush and Dalbok Izvor, and between them the bends of the hills and meadows undulated. The sun dried everything that the rain had soaked at night, and the heady aroma of a fresh morning invigorated the young bodies of men. Ivan Ignatov recalled his past life, how he was sitting as a sentry, when it was Todor turn to sleep, when 2 of them had already almost become the hajduks. Ivan fell asleep, and the Macedonian, passing by, stole the dagger from Todor. After that Todor was furious, and they quarreled. How many events have passed since then, and how turbulent their young life was! He was thinking about his poor relatives, who were expelled from their native home along with the Karagochev family and sent to no one knows where. How are they there, far away on the eastern end of the fascist Bulgaria? Their house, their fields, their herds, their sheep in the village were abandoned, and they were rather wealthy. Probably, the father's brother and other relatives, his nephew look after the household and the cattle. How will their epic end? No one knows.

Suddenly Ivan Ignatov saw a dark mass approaching in the distance, it was moving straight toward them. The detachment of one of the counter-chetas, as the junta called them, fascist activists, whom the junta handed weapons and sent them on a handful of freedom fighters. There were such counter-chetas in every village, and now this pack was moving straight toward them from the Konush village from the west. Ivan jumped down from the tree, and having let the activists closer, shot at them. One of the bastards, walking in front, fell dead on the wet ground, and the rest opened fire, shooting in different directions.

"Boys, get up!" he woke up his friends, who themselves already woke up from the sounds of shooting.

He pointed to them with his hand in the direction of Konush, from where the gang of fascists was moving, and in a trice they took up positions for battle.

"Give up, you are caught, you are surrounded!" the fascists yelled, believing that there was only one Ivan Ignatov alone, but they immediately shut up, having received bullets from different sides.

Having lost part of their composition, the gang threw down their weapons and took to their heels.

"What shall we do?" Ivan Ignatov asked.

"As soon as the gang reaches Konush, there will be army here soon," Mityu Ganev said.

"The Rhodopes are far to the south, we won't have time to hide there before they catch up with us," Kuzi Kuzev rightly remarked.

"There is an open area nearby, mostly fields and meadows," Dimo Kafedzhiev said.

"We need horses! What if we take horses in Dalbok Izvor? It is to the south, all the same we must go south to the mountains," Latun Grozev advised.

"It is unlikely," Yordan Zhekov objected, "what if there are fewer horses than us, what will the others do?"

"We need transport in which all of us can fit! Peter Filipov exclaimed."

"A truck, for example!" Velyu Delchev promoted.

"Only, where can we get it?" Geno Radev asked.

"Wait, there is a brick factory nearby here in Poroyna," Mityu Ganev remembered.

"And where the factory is, there should be transport: that is a truck! They must transport their bricks on something!" Ivan Ignatov concluded.

"Boys, on the horses! We are moving toward Poroyna, let's hurry!" Mityu Ganev ordered.

The chetniks left the forest at a brisk pace and before the eyes of the astonished villagers, who were already working in the fields, moved southwest to the village of Poroyna in broad daylight. Poroyna lay as a peninsula between the Chinardere River and its tributary Mechka, which at an angle went around the village from the east and flowed into Chinardere from the north side. A low bridge across Chinardere led to Poroyna from the western side, it almost touched the river, which was rather shallow, but wide, overflowed after rain. The chetniks crossed the bridge, entered Poroyna, and after a short time, the village was theirs.

The brick factory was right across the bridge by the river at the edge of the village. They cut the connection and entered the factory, where the owner Yanko Gatev produced bricks by hand of hired workers.

"Stay where you are and don't move!" Mityu Ganev commanded, and those present at the factory saw alive Mityu Ganev himself and his squad of the cheta Hristo Botev. "Citizens, workers and heads of the brick factory, we ask you not to be nervous and remain calm! We need your truck only for the shortest possible time. We've planned one journey, but there is no transport, so we decided to borrow your truck. Who is in charge here?"

"Here he is!" the workers pointed a finger at a man standing next to him. "Here he is, the boss's brother."

"Wonderful!" Ivan Ignatov addressed him. "Prepare the truck for the trip!"

"There is no gasoline," the master replied gloomily.

"Really?" Mityu Ganev asked again menacingly, moving close to him.

"Oh, I forgot, there is gasoline!"

"Fill up a full tank!"

"Mityu, tell the master to tell the owner to pay us more: we work for cheap!" the factory workers began to complain, turning to Mityu Ganev.

"Do you hear what the workers are asking?" Mityu Ganev asked. "Where is your brother?"

"He went to Plovdiv," the master answered.

"Tell Yanko Gatev to pay the workers a normal salary, otherwise we shall visit here again! Tell your boss that it is Mityu Ganev who said it!"

The workers smiled and applauded.

"All the best, citizens, do not lose heart! The Tsankov regime will collapse soon, and all the butchers and blood suckers of the people will answer for their atrocities before the court!"

The workers applauded even louder.

"Boys, get in the truck! These 2 will go with us: the owner's brother and another head. Take them to the back of the truck, and I'll sit next to the driver!"

The truck filled with gasoline pulled out of the factory. The entire detachment and 2 hostages were sitting in the back of the truck, and Mityu Ganev was sitting next to the driver with a revolver in his hands.

"Come on, go as it should be, where I say, otherwise you won't collect your brains!"

The workers were standing yet for a long time and waved after the departing truck. It crossed the bridge over the Chinardere and turned south toward Rhodopes. The truck quickly moved away from the meeting point with the fascist detachment and from the brick factory in Poroyna, it drove along the vicinity road to the south, approached the village Dalbok Izvor and passed it along the eastern outskirts.

"This is our village!" Dobri Yankov Kovachev and Slavi Velichkov Temarev exclaimed, pointing in the direction of Dalbok Izvor.

Everywhere people were already working in the fields, and the chetniks' hearts ached with anguish, as they had their homes and fields abandoned. Mityu Ganev looked back: there was no pursuit of them.

"Slow down at this well!" he ordered the driver, and the truck stopped.

There was a cheshma at the edge of the road, and the villagers worked in the fields nearby.

"Get out of the truck!" he ordered the driver, and the latter obediently left the cabin.

"Boys, smoke! Let's drink some water!"

On seeing a truck with people, curious villagers began to approach it closely. Part of the chetniks got out of the body. Suddenly one girl stood out from the group of people, approaching the truck, and rushed to run forward. She ran up to Slavi Velichkov Temarev and threw herself on his neck, screaming:

"Brother, why did they grab you? My poor brother!"

Overjoyed and embarrassed, Slavi from Dalbok Izvor embraced her with the words:

"Calm down, sister, they did not capture me: this is my detachment Hristo Botev! These are my friends, and this is Mityu Ganev himself, you heard songs about him and his friends, and you sang them yourself, didn't you!"

The stupid village woman, who did not understand what was happening, however calmed down and began to stare around, scanning the chetniks, and the villagers, who approached at that moment, applauded. Mityu Ganev climbed into the back of the truck and addressed the villagers.

"Citizens, villagers, we are the detachment of the cheta Hristo Botev, we are the peoples fighters for freedom! The fascist government is persecuting us, it organized whole detachments of the fascists activists almost in every village from ordinary villagers like you, but unlike you, good people, they are traitors and murderers, fascist accomplices. The bandit authorities gave them weapons and 50 leva each so that they would kill us! They scour everywhere like packs of wolves! No, sorry, wolves have nothing to do with them! Wolves are driven: unfortunate animals! It's rather us are like the wolves that are being hunted. No, these gangs of scumbags for 50 leva are scouring the fields and forests in search of us, the peoples' defenders, to kill us! And the fascist authorities have thrown the entire army against us, they are torturing and killing our yataks in all the villages! Fascist terror rages all over Bulgaria! But do not lose heart, villagers, do not give up, hold on! Sooner or later the illegal fascist power in Bulgaria will collapse and all the butchers will answer for their atrocities before the people's court!"

The villagers applauded. Dobri addressed them:

"Friends, all of you know me: I am Dobri Yankov Kovachev from Dalbok Izvor! You all know that we are the cheta Hristo Botev, the freedom fighters against the fascist force that enslaved our country! The day will come, when people of Bulgaria condemn all the butchers: Boris III, Tsankov, Vylkov, Rusev and their henchmen, all the executioners who torture and kill the people of Bulgaria and burn their houses! They can't get out of court!"

The villagers applauded, tears flowed down their cheeks, the chetnik's sister was completely calmed down that her brother was safe, and now she was crying with happiness.

"It's time, boys!" Mityu Ganev gave a signal to go.

Everyone sat down in the truck again in their places, having filled their baklagas with fresh water from the cheshma, and the truck drove further south toward mountains. The truck was driving along the vicinity roads, approaching the Rhodopes. The further south the higher the hills rose, and the path between them became meandering. Mountains emerged in the distance, and a dense forest began at the foothills and rose to the very peaks. It was impossible to drive further.

"Stop," Mityu Ganev ordered the driver, "boys, get out! And you 3, you can go home, it was a pleasant company with you and especially with your truck, you are free! But don't dare to tell anyone where we've driven! If we are chased by your denunciation, we'll not be here all the same, but we'll find you!"

2 hostages and the driver hurried to leave, having experienced an exciting day in their lives, and the detachment of Mityu Ganev hurried toward the forest at the foot of the Rhodopes. In the distance they saw a large detachment of the counter-chetas from the vicinity villages blocking their path to Rhodopes.

"We'll have to take the fight!" Mityu Ganev said. "4 people—Ivan, Geno, Latun and Kuzi—make up a strike group, you'll move forward, throw grenades at them. We'll cover, punch a hole, get behind their lines and open fire at their flanks for the rest to break through!"

"Let's go, boys!" Ivan Ignatov called.

All the rest, having found a shelter, opened frequent fire on the fascists from behind the cover, the latter rushed in different directions, firing back; a passage was formed in the center. 4 striking fighters threw the grenades at them and broke through to their rear, opening fire on the phalanges. The main group fired from the front. The fascists fired back and fell dead. The rest took to their heels, dropping the weapons. The chetniks picked up all the weapons from the ground and hid in the forested Rhodopes, without losing a single person. They climbed to the top of the mountain, from which an amazing view opened, and without going down, moved east away from the battle field. In the distance at the foot of the mountains Lenovo floated past them. And when they reached Popovo, it was already getting dark. They found a convenient place for a halt, and there they stopped for a short time. Down in the valley Popovo lay, which they had so spectacularly captured on September 17 last year. The hearts of the chetniks ached at the recalling of the autumn, when the uprising, which they so carefully prepared, did not take place. After resting for a couple of hours, they set off again, walking along the Rhodopes in the darkness. At dawn they looked for a heaven to rest in order to sleep, and at night they went on their journey.

They reached the top of Aida, below on the left they could see Bukovo and Bryagovo on the right, and below at the foot of the mountains, Black Rocks stuck out, where Georgy Pilashev heroically died on April 21, on Christian Easter. Tired from crossings, they lay down to rest on the top of Aida. An overactive fascist activist tracked the chetniks down and denounced them. Jordan Zhekov, guarding the chetniks' sleep, raised the alarm and woke them up. Troops were approaching the mount Aida.

"Get up boys, we'll have to take a fight!" Mityu Ganev turned to his friends.

They all leaned down from Aida and looked down at the valley: the military, policemen and fascist activists platoons were approaching the foot of the mountain in a chain.

"We must hold out here until evening," Mityu Ganev said.

"Well, we have a convenient position for a fight!" Ivan Ignatov noticed.

"Take positions for battle!" Mityu Ganev ordered.

All the chetniks took comfortable positions behind the ledges of rocks on the top of Aida, they like the battle towers on the walls of the fortress stuck out along the edge on the top of the mountain, forming loopholes in between. The chetniks appreciated the exceptionally convenient position for the battle on the top of Aida.

"There they are! There! I've seen them!" the activist squealed below, pointing to the top of the mountain. "I was watching! I tracked them down! The reward is mine!"

"Fire!" The officer commanded, and the soldiers opened fire at the top of the mountain.

Bullets whistled over the heads of the cheta, but most often somewhere at the level of the middle of the mountain, not reaching its top. They crashed into the steel shells of the rocks and bounced back, raising dust and bringing down an avalanche of small stones, mutilating plants and disturbing birds.

"Fire!" Mityu Ganev commanded, and the chetniks returned fire.

They fired accurately from loopholes in the gap behind the rocky teeth, reliably protecting themselves behind the stones. One by one the attackers from the hostile force fell.

"Boys, are you safe?" Mityu Ganev periodically asked his friends, and everyone answered that they were alive.

The bullets of Mityu Ganev hit the target at any distance, but all the other Hristo Botev fighters were not inferior to him. The battle continued without interruption until the evening and stopped, when it began to get dark. The attackers retreated, and the chetniks, having carried out a roll call, safely set off on their way in the dark. Emaciated by battle, hungry and tired, they went forward in the direction to the east. As usually, they walked at night and rested during day time, finding a convenient place on the top of the mountain. The last supply of food had run out long ago, and the famine began. They tried to satisfy their hunger with unripe fruits of the wild fruit trees and washed down with spring water. Having passed 40 km along undulated bends of the mountains and hills, the Mityu Ganev cheta approached the village of Knizhovnik and descended into the valley.

"Boys, this is not for the first time for us to do such actions, shall we risk once again? We have no way out: either we die of hunger, or we'll set up an ambush," Mityu Ganev asked his boys.

"It's better to die in battle, than from starvation!" Ivan Ignatov exclaimed.

"No more delay! We must get some food!" Kuzi Kuzev exclaimed.

"This is the plan," Mityu Ganev informed them, having conferring with all.

And early in the morning of June 3 they lay in ambush by the road between Haskovo and Malevo. The sun rose and illuminated all the beauty around with bright light. The first travelers appeared.

"You are detained, citizens, for short time!" the chetniks announced to them, blocking the road.

"Extreme circumstances force us to detain you and urgently ask you to share with us the funds that you have."

The travelers on carts handed them loaves of bread, pieces of cheese and small sums of money, which the chetniks gratefully put into their bags. A car drove up and stopped behind the carts, and the chetniks immediately surrounded it. An engineer from Haskovo was sitting at the back seat, holding a bag with money.

"How much is there?" Mityu Ganev asked, taking away the bag, which he obediently held out into his hands.

"22 thousand leva," the engineer answered.

"Dobri, write a receipt!" Mityu Ganev said. "I'll sign it."

Dobri Yankov Kovachev took a piece of paper of his bag and wrote:

"Receipt. Communist Mityu Ganev confiscated from the engineer the sum of 22 thousand leva in favor of the revolution. General Rusev with all his thugs and accomplices in all villages is outlaw. June 3, 1925, field. Mityu Ganev."

Mityu Ganev put his initials on the receipt and handed it to the engineer under the applause of all the present.

"Thank you for your attention!"

Mityu Ganev bowed to the entire audience and commanded to the cheta:

"Let's go, boys!"

They vanished from the sight of the travelers in the direction of the mountains. On June 4 at dawn they approached Knyaz Borisovo and set up a camp on the top of the mountain at the very place, where they were photographed 2 months ago. The reminiscences pierced the hearts of the young men, then they still hoped for the uprising and victory.

"Boys, do you remember how we took pictures here?" they asked each other, clutching their photos like a treasure to their chests.

"We rest until the evening, and in the evening we'll go down and visit our photographer."

Having posted a sentry for protection, the chetniks fell into a sound sleep under the trees, pressing their rifles to themselves. A sound sleep in nature in complete peace invigorated them, and in the evening they were ready for action.

"Let's visit the photographer!"

They decided to go all together. As soon as it got dark, the chetniks descended from the mountain covered with forest, waded across the shallow Biser River and approached Knyaz Borisovo. Everything was calm. Silently and noiselessly, hiding behind the bushes already lush with greenery, they entered the village and knocked with a conventional knock on the door of the house that stood on the edge of the village, in which Mitko Hristov Kolev Tryndev, secretary of the party organization and their photographer, lived. There were no signs of life in the house, and nobody answered. Cautiously they repeated the agreed knock and retreated from the house, when did not receive the answer. Without saying a word, but only with gestures, which everyone understood, without any words, they went to another house that stood next door and knocked at the gates.

"Welcome, we have been waiting for you, we want to leave with you!" the owner of the house Ivan Laikov and Dimo Todorov, who was visiting him from the village of Elena, greeted them.

The chetniks came inside the house and took a seat which found.

"Eat first!" Ivan Laikov offered and brought from the kitchen everything he had.

"Having swallowed a piece of bread with cheese and drank milk, the chetniks got down to business."

"We knocked at the Mitko's door, but nobody opened."

"Somebody saw a photo of the cheta in his workshop and denounced. Soldiers astride broke in the village yesterday and seized him," Ivan Laikov said, frowning.

"They tortured him, beat him all day, then tied him to a horse and drove him back and forth through the village and shouted: 'It'll be like this with every yatak'!"

The chetniks were listening with bated breath, and their hearts were beating with anger. Dimo Todorov continued.

"They dragged him, being tied to the horse, to our village Elena and threw him into a prison, and he is there now."

Hatred, anger and desire for revenge invigorated the chetniks, depriving them of any fear, which they never had from the beginning. After consulting for a couple of minutes, they announced: "Let's move, boys! Ivan, are you with us?"

"I was going to leave with you since long time ago, I have been waiting for you; at any moment they can seize me. I am ready to go."

"I'm waiting for you too!" Dimo Todorov informed. "And the most importantly: the detachment of Radyu Delchev and Todor Todorov has left for Greece through Mezek. They instructed to tell you to follow them: that was the order of the Central Committee. Everything is lost in Bulgaria, and you just need to save your lives."

The news struck the Mityu Ganev platoon, although everyone understood long ago that this is the thing everything was going to.

"On your horses!" Mityu Ganev ordered, and the chetniks together with the owner of the house Ivan Laikov and the guest from the village of Elena Dimo Todorov left the house and keeping secrecy, hiding behind the bushes and checking the road, moved north to the village of Elena in 6 km from Knyaz Borisovo.

They entered the village from the south side, quickly reached the kmet's building on the main road.

"I'll go for Staiko Kolev Petkov and take my donkey," Dimo Todorov whispered.

"If you are not in time to get here, we'll meet at the exit from the village from the south, where we entered here," Mityu answered.

Dimo Todorov vanished in the darkness and rushed home. And the chetniks crept up to the kmet's building, near which 10 military horses were tethered. Mityu Ganev tampered the lock with a chisel, the door opened, and the chetniks sneaked inside, having left Ivan Laikov on guard in the street, and silently began to move around the place. They opened the door to a large room, turned into the temporary barracks: 10 military were sleeping on the mattresses there on the floor after the torture of Mitko Tryndev. They remained there to sleep forever that night, each having received a bullet in his forehead. The chetniks shot the butchers and quickly began to open the doors of the other rooms. In one of them, the torture chamber, Mitko Tryndev was lying on the floor unconscious, turned into a mess. His internal organs were beaten off, and his face was unrecognizable: it was like a swollen crimson ball.

"Boys, quickly make a stretcher!"

Somewhere they found 2 boards, removed the curtains from the window in the office of kmet and, tying them tightly to the boards, they carefully lifted Mitko from the floor and laid him on the stretcher. Everyone hurried out of the kmet's building.

"Maybe we'll take the horses?" Ivan Ignatov asked.

"There are still fewer than us, it will not work."

4 chetniks took the stretcher with Mitko from 4 sides and all got out of the village. 2 yataks were waiting for them there: Dimo Todorov and Staiko Kolev Petkov with a faithful donkey.

"Maybe we'll sit him on a donkey?" Dimo asked.

"He can't sit, later, let's hurry!" the chetniks answered. "Bring the donkey here!"

They headed south-east, carrying the unconscious Mitko Tryndev on a stretcher, taking turns carrying their friend. The night came to an end. The top of the hill, covered with forest, served them as a shelter for day time. Mitko showed no signs of life, and only a faint heart beat indicated that he was still alive. They moistened his parched lips with water and hoped. The faithful donkey was nearby and carried bags with food. They were no longer hungry.

"How scary it is to abandon your house," Dimo Todorov sighed, "and go to no one knows where! To abandon everything what you've lived and worked for!"

"But it's even scarier not to abandon and remain at home so that the butchers grab you and torture to death and burn your house and all property!" Staiko Kolev Petkov answered.

The day in the shelter passed quickly, and in the evening they set off. On June 7, they approached Malko Gradishte and took refuge in their cave on the top of the mountain. Mitko Tryndev opened his eyes for the first time: he saw the beautiful faces of his friends and smiled with the swollen face.

"Mitko, how are you?" all the chetniks pounced on him, but he still could not speak.

The most important was that he was alive!

"Eat, Mitko!" Ivan Laikov put a piece of bread and cheese into his mouth and gave him some water to drink. To everybody's delight, he swallowed it all. The chetniks left him alone to rest and began to get ready for a journey. A couple of remaining yataks from Malko Gradishte climbed up to their cave.

"Tonight we move to Mezek," the yataks said, "we'll lead you to Mezek."

"Everything is so unexpected!" Ivan Ignatov suddenly exclaimed. "What awaits us there?"

"But what is waiting for us here?" Peter Filipov asked.

"But we so much hoped to liberate Bulgaria from the fascists and live in our homes!" Yordan Zhekov sighed.

"We must leave, otherwise we'll all die here," Slavi Velichkov Trandev said.

"Mityu, what about you, what do you think" all looked at the Voevoda.

"I think that if to go abroad, we should go to Yugoslavia. If we go to Greece, they can return us back. And Turkey can betray us too."

All were puzzled and began to discuss possible escape routes.

"But we simply shall not reach Yugoslavia! We've just come from there, we've walked half the country, miraculously remained alive! We won't go back, we won't be able to go through! Come to your senses! There is the border: you can see it from here!"

"Of course, we'll go here to Greece through Mezek!" Mityu Ganev said. "There is no other way out!"

They rested before the road, decided their fate, argued and argued all day on June 8, and in the evening they got ready to go. Mitko Tryndev came to his senses, they sat him on the donkey, he leaned forward, put his arms around the donkey's neck; 2 chetniks held him from both sides. They abandoned their cave on the mountain near Malko Gradishte and slowly set off on their way. 2 yataks from Malko Gradishte showed them the way. At night they reached Mezek. All day long they were watching the border from the height of the mountain, and in the evening on June 9 they set off.

"Today is exactly 2 years since the fascist coup in Bulgaria!" they all remembered.

The faithful donkey was carrying Mitko Tryndev, and together with the chetniks they crossed the border.

"Farewell Bulgaria!" they all whispered to themselves.

The chetniks crossed the border and went along the Greek territory.

"Farewell friends!" suddenly unexpectedly Mityu Ganev said and stopped. "I've been thinking all this time and finally decided: I can't go with you! I can't! If the Greek or Turkish authorities detain me, they'll extradite me back to Bulgaria. I have old affairs with them, old scores. And I can't be captured by the Bulgarian butchers! As for me, I'll come back, go through Rhodopes and go to Yugoslavia. We'll meet somewhere there one day. I am proud to have been your commander! Farewell!"

Tears rolled down Mityu Ganev's face, and at that moment no one, looking at his pretty feminine face, long hair and short stature, could believe that this was the same legendary Mityu Ganev, whose name alone, like as well as the names of his friends: Todor Todorov and Ivan Ignatov, terrified all the evil spirits in Bulgaria. Mityu Ganev was weeping helplessly, parting with his friends. The latter stopped and became dumbfounded from the surprise. All of a sudden, the mighty giant Ivan Ignatov separated from the chetniks, came up to Mityu Ganev and stood next to him, he also had tears in his eyes.

"Mityu, I am with you! Where shall I go without you? I won't leave you alone!"

"So do I, perhaps," Geno Radev Delchev joined them.

One after another 6 more people separated from the group: Dimo Todorov Kafedjiev, Peter Zhelyazkov Filipov, Yordan Zhelev Zhekov, Kuzi Latev Kuzev, Velyu Hristozov Delchev and Latun Georgiev Grozev.

"We'll not abandon our Voevoda," they said, "we'll stay and cross Rhodopes to Serbia."

There was a dramatic moment of silence: no one knew what to say. Finally Mityu Ganev said to the others:

"Hurry up, friends, we'll meet somewhere in a safe area. Take care of Mitko Tryndev! He is our photographer! He took historical pictures of the cheta for us!"

"For us and for history!" Geno Radev Delchev added.

A group of the chetniks together with a donkey, on whom the photographer Mitko was sitting, hurried forward to Greece, and 8 people with Mityu Ganev turned back and again crossed the border of Bulgaria.

Chapter 57
Political Emigration

From Svilengrad far to the north-east in a remount mountain village in kmet's building, like in many Bulgarian villages turned into a torture chamber, Ivan Todorov, father of Todor Todorov, his 16-year-old son Gocho, Ignat Mitev, father of Ivan Ignatov and his youngest son, were lying on the floor—they had been beaten by the Bulgarian officers. They were beating their tortured bodies for no reason and without asking anything. The executioners had nothing to ask, since the latter did not know anything, having been interned from Bodrovo 6 months ago. They did not know where their boys Todor and Ivan, who not only refused to serve Boris III, Tsankov, Rusev and Vylkov for a large reward, but also united with the Hristo Botev cheta to fight together against them.

The platoon of Radyu Delchev and Todor Todorov, having crossed the Bulgarian border near Mezek, was moving further and further away from it and walked all night through the territory of Greece. The terrain was reminiscent of Bulgaria: the same fields and hills, and very close to them on the right hand there was the frontier of Bulgaria, along which they were walking from the north side to the south. A strange feeling overwhelmed them: escape from danger, the joy of salvation and the complete uncertainty of what lay ahead of them. They passed a Greek village on 5 hills, which they saw in the morning rays of the rising sun, and continued their way south-west until Arda blocked their path.

Flowing from the mountains of Bulgaria, far away in the south-west and crossing all the Rhodopes in a raging stream to the north-east, undulating with wavy ribbon between the mountains, Arda crossed the Greek border and now slowly continued its way again, escaping from chase, until it merged with Maritsa into a single whole. Arda emerged before the travelers as a wide, slow and calm current, smoothly flowing around sandy islands from one to another of which one could wade knee-deep. The travelers stopped on the left bank and scanned the unfamiliar area. Suddenly they saw a man nearby, who having seen them, was frightened and was about to run away.

"Good man, do not be afraid of us!" Radyu Delchev addressed him, before he became the Voevoda of the cheta Hristo Botev, fought in the National Revolutionary Thracian Organization and had extensive experience to deal with the Greeks. "Do not be afraid of us, we'll not harm you, we are the members of the Stamboliysky Agrarian Union, who seek asylum in Greece."

The man first with fear, then with curiosity looked at the platoon of armed people. Radyu Delchev speech reassured him and, making sure that they had no hostile intentions, he approached them closer. He saw the beautiful faces of the young people, tired of crossing and looking for shelter.

"How can I be useful to travelers?" he asked them.

Radyu Delchev continued.

"We need to cross to the right bank of the Arda and find an outpost to talk to the chief. Couldn't you help us to find a boat to cross the river and take us to the outpost?"

"I'll help," the villager answered, "there is a boat nearby, and then I'll guide you."

The chetniks smiled and followed him. Soon a boat, tied to a tree on the bank of the river, was at their disposal, and they transported the first half of the people across Arda and then all the rest. The peasant, who felt that he was doing a useful thing for the strangers who needed help, escorted them to the outpost and remained on the sidelines to watch. The sentry at the outpost in the light of the glowing day saw a large group of armed people and froze in place in horror with his mouth open in amazement. Without moving or making a sound, he waited until they came up close to him.

"Stop, I'll shoot," he whispered with his eyes open wide with fear and without moving.

"Belay shooting!" Radyu Delchev ordered him. "We are the members of the Bulgarian Agrarian National Union of Stamboliysky, we want to talk with the head of the outpost!"

The sentry saluted the chetniks and disappeared into the outpost cabin, where the military had a lunch break. In a minute he returned back with the boss. The Greek major was dumbfounded, when he saw the armed detachment of Hristo Botev, but sensibly considered that there was no reason for them to attack the outpost, and having pulled himself together, risked to approach the chetniks.

"Who are you?" he asked them.

Radyu Delchev, who fluently spoke Greek, addressed him:

"Mr. Major, we are the members of the Alexander Stamboliysky Bulgarian Agrarian Union Party, whose power was overthrown by the fascist coup of Boris III, Tsanko, Rusev and Vylkov 2 years ago, on June 9, 1923. We resisted the upheaval and fought against it all this time, were persecuted and now were forced to leave the homeland, because it is no longer possible to stay in Bulgaria. We intend to surrender to the authorities of Greece and seek for political asylum. We ask you to take us to Dimotika, where we intend to apply to the representative of the Greek authorities. We'll give up our weapons; let they put them in a cart that will follow us, accompanied by 2 officers, for example."

After thinking for a minute, the major agreed, and the preparation to move began. A cart pulled by horses drove up, and each of the fighters of Hristo Botev for the first time since joining the Hristo Botev cheta, parted with the weapons. One after another they approached the cart, took off their military ammunition and put on the bottom of the cart their guns, rifles, cartridge belts, bombs, daggers, with which they had been slept all that time, pressing to themselves. Appeared to be disarmed, everyone experienced a feeling of anxiety that they had never experienced during a battle with foe. Only at that moment each of them felt that the Hristo Botev cheta was no more; their glorious past had ended, and now they are in a foreign land, and each of them is on his own. Only the memory of the past binds them forever. The last rifle, the bandolier with the revolver and bombs neatly fell on the loaded cart, and it set off after the truck, on which the chetniks were riding. The truck moved slowly from north-west to south-east across the hilly territory of Greece, which jutted north, like a wedge, separating Turkey from Bulgaria. Dimotika emerged by evening.

Ancient Dimotika lay in the plain as if at the bottom of a huge dish, fringed on the edges by hills with forests, merging into the mountains in the west. On the site of the ancient human settlement, the Thracians founded the city here, later merged by the Geeks, who lost it for the Romans. Here, at the confluence of the Luda River with Maritsa, the Roman Trajan built a fortress on the top of the hill and named it Plotina in honor of his wife Pompeia Plotina, and later

Septimus Severus left his bust of pure gold for the descendants for memory. Here Justinian built new fortification on a high hill, and in 30 years after his death, the whole castle was called "Double Fortification," which means Dimotika. This city was captured by the Bulgarian king Krum, exterminating the population of Greeks, the Byzantine general Bardas Skleros was in exile here, and then the crusaders captured it, and it was a part of the Latin Empire. Then the Bulgarian tsar Kaloyan again seized these lands, which were again taken from him by the Latins. Then the Bulgarian Asen ruled here again, until the Byzantines knocked him out. The Turks won the battle of Dimotika and made the city their first capital in Europe, where they enjoyed relaxing after the bloody campaigns. Here they hid Charles XII after the Peter's victory near Poltava. The Bulgarians captured it again during the First Balkan War and during the Second Balkan War they gave it back. It was taken again by the tsar Ferdinand, who entered the Great War on the wrong side, and according the agreement in Neuilly near Paris lost it forever together with the Bulgarian throne. The entire coast of the Aegean Sea and the Thracian Dimotika was controlled by the Entente forces after the victory, and in the end, was given to Greece.

The chetniks were riding along those lands, where the battles had raged in the past, and now they were seeking refuge from the Greek government.

"But if Bulgaria had not lost in the Second Balkan War and in the Great War, if these lands were Bulgarian, we would've died. Don't you think about it?" Todor asked his friends, and the latter replied that they were thinking about it.

The truck drove into the city, behind it the horses harnessed to the cart carried their weapons, to which they said goodbye forever, thinking: "Farewell to arms!" They drove along the narrow streets of the city, old houses with red roofs floated past them. In the west on the bank of the Luda River, the remains of the ancient fortress towered majestically. A half-ruined arch, the entrance to the fortress, high towers and stone walls stuck out on the top of the hill, towering from the past. They entered the military unit and stopped in the yard. The military removed their weapons to the warehouse, and the colonel on duty approached the travelers.

"Who are you?" the same question was asked.

Radyu Delchev answered again.

"We are the Agrarians, the members of the Agrarian Union of Bulgaria. Our government was illegally overthrown on June 9, 1923. We resisted, defending the legitimate authority, but now we are forced to leave Bulgaria and seek for asylum in Greece as the political emigrants."

At the words "Illegally overthrown" the colonel grimaced with displeasure, as in Greece one government replaced another one only as the result of the illegal upheavals and, scanning them suspiciously from head to toe, replied:

"While temporarily stay in jail until the circumstances are clarified."

He addressed his subordinates:

"Escort them!"

The prison was located near the military unit in an old Turkish building. They were all sent to one cell and locked up. Moss-covered broken stone walls conveyed the smell of centuries-old, the pitted earthen floor was covered with sewage, and there was not enough air for everyone. The entire cheta Hristo Botev was taken under custody in a medieval building. Those who were hungry and wanted to eat immediately lost their appetite, having inhaled the aroma from the time immemorial.

"Boys, we won the battles, and we'll survive the Greek prison in Dimotika!" Todor said.

"There is nothing else left for us," the friends answered.

Several days passed, no one remembered how many days, because they lost count of days and nights. And suddenly the door opened, and a visitor came in: Peter Georgiev, a member of the BCP Central Committee and the editor of the "Our Days" bulletin, emerged before them.

"Here we are all in Greece!" he greeted the prisoners sadly.

"Is there anything you can do for us?" the chetniks asked.

"Boys, don't lose hearts, wait, we'll think of something," Georgiev answered, "you are the legend, and everyone knows about you, but here in Greece keep quiet about it. The situation is complicated here: their own upheavals, their own junta etc., keep your mouth shut!"

"We do just that," Todor answered, "we did not say that there are Communists among us, we all named ourselves Agrarians."

"You did the right thing," Georgiev answered, "but I'll connect you with the Greek Communists, they'll help. They have their bulletin 'Resonance', if you are oppressed, we'll make it public. In Greece, unlike Bulgaria, there is still a free press, and a lot depends on public opinion."

The visit of Peter Georgiev brightened up their stay in prison, the term of which no one knew, and they began to look forward to his visits. The days went one after another; they lost count of them.

"How long will they keep us here some more?" Radyu Delchev asked the warden. "We were told that they would put us here temporarily, until the circumstances are clarified."

"We'll keep you here as long as we need!" the jailer answered rudely. "If you rebel, we'll send you back to Bulgaria!"

Peter Georgiev visited them constantly, and they enjoyed his visits. Once he brought 2 more Bulgarian emigrants: Peter Stanev and Dimo Ivanov. Friends brought newspaper in French, and Peter Georgiev read the news aloud to them. They felt friendly support, and this invigorated them. They informed friends that the wardens threatened to send them back to Bulgaria, if they are unhappy with that prison.

"Here's what we'll do," Peter Georgiev said, "We'll inform the Greek Communists about it, and they'll make it public: they'll publish in the newspaper that the General Pangalos, who has just carried out another upheaval and seized power, is going to extradite the political emigrants to the Bulgarian fascists. I think that Pangalos will be afraid of the condemnation of public opinion."

"Free press is the most important guarantee of security!" Todor exclaimed.

"Fortunately, in Greece it is still there!"

In a day, the news that the General Pangalos was going to extradite the political emigrants to the Bulgarian fascists spread throughout Greece, and in a couple of days later the wardens opened the cell door and took them out into the fresh air, which made the chetniks dizzy.

"You misunderstood," the warden explained, "no one is going to send you back to Bulgaria! Was it worth to raise the noise on the whole country! On the contrary, you are being transited deep into Greece. Now you are going to the railway station and you'll go to Alexandroupolis."

Moving at least anywhere in Greece was better than sitting in a cell, and the former chetniks went to the railway station with hope. They were loaded into a horse carriage, and Dimotika was left behind. The train was moving south down to the Aegean Sea along the Maritsa River, along which was the Turkish border, along the tracks of the Oriental Express, laid in 1897. Then the mouth of the river remained to the east, and the train smoothly turned to the west and arrived at the military station of Alexandroupolis. The chetniks were taken out of the car and sent to a new prison. They walked along straight, wide, parallel streets of the young city and breathed with fresh sea air before they were locked up in a new prison. They walked past neat houses along the streets of the city, for which their fathers fought during the past 3 wars and which passed from hand to hand to the conquering side and was eventually given to Greece, in which they now sought refuge. The city was young, built within the last 50 years, although it stood on the land of the ancient Thracians and the ruins of their city of Sale. By the beginning of the Russian-Turkish war of Alexander II, which liberated Bulgaria from the Turkish possession, the village Dedeagach appeared here on the shore of the Aegean Sea, meaning "old man's tree," in the shade of which the Turkish dervish Dede gave instructions to his students about what is good and what is bad. The troops of Alexander II occupied the village, recaptured from the Turks, and turned it into the city of large scale constructions until the Berlin Congress annulated the Treaty of San-Stefano and returned it to the Turks again. During the I Balkan War the allies took the city from the Turks, and mortal enemies to each other during the II Balkan War, they fought for the city, killing each other. The victorious Greeks occupied the city, but by the Peace of Bucharest they returned it back to the Bulgarians. And the latter lost it now forever, following the tsar Ferdinand during the Great War. The Turkish Dedeagach was named after Alexander, who was the king of Greece for a short time and died from a bite of a macaque, yielding the throne again to his father Konstantin, the author of the Nazi manual on the destruction of the Bulgarians during the II Balkan War.

The chetniks walked along the new streets of the city and came to the old building. They were locked up again either in a cell or in a closet, or in a storeroom close to each other and put a warden.

"Boys, move close to the walls so that everyone fits," "Radyu Delchev turned to his friends."

"There is no air here, nothing to breathe with!" they answered.

"Break the window!" Todor said.

Broken glass flew out, and machine-gun fire rang out from outside. Then everything calmed down, and everybody survived again.

Fortunately, they did not have to sit close to each other in the cell for a long time, and next day they walked again along the streets of Alexandroupolis as tourists to the same railway station, where they were again loaded into a horse carriage and sent further along the territory of the former Bulgarian Belomorska Thrace. They were brought to Komotini. 2 thousand years BC, the ancient Thracians founded a city here, where long before them an ancient man found a comfortable place to live here. The Greeks invaded here later, and later they were captured by the Romans. And the last of them Theodosius I built a fortress here at the crossroads. 2 Roman paths here, crossing, led from south to north and from east to west: Komotini-Philippopolis through the Rhodopes and Constantinople—the Adriatic Sea. The Bulgarian tsar Kaloyan destroyed the settlement here and killed the locals until the Ottoman Turks captured them all. Like Dedeagach, the city was captured by the Bulgarians during the I Balkan War and lost again during the II one, returned by the Bucharest Peace and left forever after the Great War. Here in the museum of archaeology on a pedestal the golden bust of Septimus Severus, which was dug out in Dimotika, flaunted to the envy of the descendants.

The chetniks got off at the Komotini railway station and walked to a prison. Behind the city the Rhodopes immediately rose, behind which on the other side Bulgaria groaned from the fascist yoke. Again they were locked in a cell, this time larger than in Alexandroupolis, and their mood improved.

"How are you, boys?" Radyu Delchev asked.

"We hold on, hope, this will be over soon," the chetniks answered.

The next day some visitors came to them: the Komotini Communists.

"Greetings to the cheta Hristo Botev!" they exclaimed and shook hands with everyone. "We've heard about you!"

The Greek Communists brought fresh bread and fried fish with them, for which the chetniks were sincerely grateful. Delicious food made their stay in detention easier. This time it was not long, and they were again taken to the streets of the city to be escorted to the station. The chetniks saw the Thracian-Greek-Roman-Bulgarian-Turkish city and the native Rhodopes just behind it. They said goodbye to Komotini and continued on to Thessalonica. The train traveled for a long time from Komotini along the coast of the Aegean Sea through the land, where the war raged 13 years ago, where the names of the city became symbols of carnage and mutual destruction, where their fathers fought to make these cities Bulgarian. They were riding along the bloody path of the Balkan Wars: Xanti floated past them, on the coast was Kavala, to the right closer to the mountains there were Doksato, Drama, Prosotsani, Serres, Sidirokastro, Kilkis. Here the former allies against Turkey slaughtered each other in a brutal battle for these lands, and in the end they were given to Greece, in which the chetniks now sought rescue.

"We live, because this is the territory of Greece," Todor said.

"Yes, it is, such is the paradox and irony of fate!" the chetniks agreed.

The train approached Thessaloniki and stopped at the station not far from the sea. They got out of the car, and the city of history emerged before their eyes. Founded in 315 BC by the Macedonian tsar Cassander and named after his wife Thessalonike, the sister of Alexander the Great, the port city belonged to all the nations in turn. It was owned by the Greeks and Romans, Paul wrote his letters here, Bulgarians and Goths, Slavs and Saracens flashed for a while here, Byzantium and the Latin Empire firmly established here, until Turkey defeated them all, making these lands their own. Bulgarians and Geeks came here simultaneously during the I Balkan War, and the latter were ahead of the Bulgarians on one hour and captured the city forever.

The chetniks gazed at the city of discord like the tourists in a museum. Majestically he rose like an amphitheater on the slopes of the hill, and in front of him the sea surface-stage was. Burned down on a third 8 years ago, the city shook the ashes of the fire and emerged to the astonished gaze of those who saw it for the first time. It was a mixture of styles of all times and peoples, new buildings after the fire and buildings of antiquity, interspersed between them: Turkish baths, the Basilica of St. Dimitar of the 4th century, Triumphal Arch and the palace of the emperor Galerius, who was from Serdika-Sofia, the late Roman church of St. George, the church of St. Sofia of the 7th century, the 5th century St. David's church and the majestic Byzantine walls on the top of the hill, behind which the prison was.

Convoyed by the guards, the chetniks were led through the city to the north-east. A fresh sea breeze invigorated them, and over the heads in the distance on the top of the hills the Byzantine walls towered. They stood like a gigantic bulk on the top of the hill and seemed to be even taller. The half-thousand-year-old walls of the Byzantine Empire emerged before the travelers with frightening force. The brave fighters, who did not flinch during the battles, felt a chill of superstitious fear. Having approached the masonry walls of antiquity, they seemed to be taking a step into the past. They took that step and stepped beyond the walls. The 10-tower fortress of Yedi Kule was situated inside the walls; it glowed in front of them with its terrible beauty, hugeness and might like a living ghost of the Byzantine past. They walked through the territory of the fortress, and it seemed to them immense. They were led into a room down a narrow staircase, pushed into a cell, and a massive door was latched. A tiny window high overhead barely let in any light. The walls of the cell were all completely covered with the names and messages of the prisoners, who were jailed here. There were whole lists of the Bulgarian names from the time of the II Balkan War. They reported that they were being transported to the island. Frost of horror passed along the skin of the fearless fighters, now prisoners.

"It would've been better if we have died in battle at home than to be buried alive here!" Vasil Angelov exclaimed.

"Wait to die, we'll live some more!" Todor answered him.

The chetniks sat down on the floor of the underground and were afraid to think about what waited them next. But it turned out to be not so bad. Soon they were fed and taken out for a walk in the yard. To their joy, they met many prisoners here. There was a whole group of Bulgarian political emigrants here; they said they were waiting to be transferred to the island. Here in the yard they also met the editor of the communist bulletin.

"I've made too bold articles about the government," he explained why he had been imprisoned.

"Why, isn't there freedom of speech in Greece?" Todor asked.

"It is more than in Bulgaria, but not as much as in the other democratic countries," the editor answered. "I am not here for long, and you need to get out of here. I'll put you in touch with the IROR: International Relief Organization for Revolutionaries, and they will help you."

The chetniks immediately perked up and were ashamed of their superstitious fear of the prison at first. The jail is like a jail, only is situated in the ancient Byzantine walls of the 4th century! It is even interesting: exotic! The editor of the newspaper kept his promise and through his visitor contacted the IROR, who soon asked them where they wanted to go from here.

"To Serbia!" Todor replied.

"In Serbia there are 2 camps for the Bulgarian emigrants: one is in Gorni Milanovats, and another one is in Pozharevats."

"To Pozharevats!" Radyu Hristov exclaimed. "There are Agrarians there!"

"We'll arrange it, don't worry, you'll be there soon."

The fighters of Hristo Botev spent 2 weeks in the historical prison of the Byzantine fortress. They wrote their names on the wall and informed that they were going to Serbia. On that day they were guided like on a tour along Thessaloniki to the railway station, put on a train and sent to Serbia. IROR kept its promise and facilitated their move. The train carried them north to the border with Serbia, and at the station of the frontier Gevgelija the Greek warden handed them over to the Serbs.

"Gentlemen, you are free! You can go wherever you want! And you can travel wherever you want!" they were told in Gevgelija.

"To the market! To the market!" the chetniks rejoiced.

"But we have no Serbian money!"

"Maybe we'll find somewhere to change!"

For the first time since crossing the Greek border, the chetniks found themselves free and in a joyful mood went for a walk around the city, and went to the market. A small town of Gevgelija was located near the border with Greece in a southern Yugoslavia along the Vardar River. A highway from Belgrade to Athens ran along it. He healed the wounds of 3 wars that raged here 13 years ago, when Serbia, Bulgaria and Greece wrested him from the Turkish Empire and then bit into each other's throats to capture him first. And during the Great War the freshly-minted allies Bulgaria-Turkey fought together with Germany against the Entente. Having healed his wounds from the wars, the border-lined Gevgelija on the territory of Serbia covered his lands with gardens and orchards. The chetniks went along his streets like free birds, for the first time nobody chased them with weapons, and licked their lips, looking at the food stalls, having no Serbian money.

Breathing with air of freedom, they returned to the railway station, and the next morning the train carried them further north. They drove through the territory of Serbia, passing cities and villages, where the Bulgarians and Serbs fought for the Undisputed and Disputed zones, destroying each other, and arrived in the Serbian city of Pozharevats.

Fringed by the Danube, the Great Morava and Mlava, the city lay at the foot of the Chachalitsa hill on the ancient land of the same Thracians and kept the memory of struggle an inseparable part of human history. Here the emperors of Rome beat each other in the civil war: Diocletian against the troops of Carinus, here the Hun Attila commanded, making peace with Byzantium, and even rested somewhere nearby, according to a legend. Here there were the lands of the Byzantine Empire and briefly Bulgarian, as well as Hungarian, until the Serbian tsar Stefan Dragutin made the city his own. And under Stefan Dusan, he became a part of the Serbian Empire. The Turks invaded here as well as all the Balkans, and Pozharevats became their sanjak, until the Austrians drove them out, securing the seizure of the territory by the treaty in Pozharevats in 1718. But the agreement did not help, and the Turks won again and bossed here for other 100 years before the Serbs uprising. Here the Serbian prince Milan Obrenovich led 2 revolutions and put the Turks army to flight, achieved autonomy for the country and made Pozharevats the capital. And after the Balkan and Great wars the Turks parted with the Balkans forever. Now this country is the Kingdom of Serbs, Croats and Slovenes.

The train stopped at the Pozharevats station, and the chetniks entered the city. They arrived to the camp of the Bulgarian political emigrants in Pozharevats, where the leaders of the Agrarian Union were staying.

Here they learned what had happened with the rest of their friends.

Chapter 58
Georgy Dimitrov Karagochev. Susam

Todor's cousin Georgy, the son of uncle Dimitar, recently got married and enjoyed family life with his beloved wife, in whom he found a true friend and supporter. Both of them were happy, as a man could be in a time of terror.

"Georgy, do you remember what uncle Ivan said before leaving for exile?" his young wife asked him from time to time, being anxious. "He ordered you to leave Bodrovo!"

"I remember, but how can I leave! And what about you?" he answered, hugging his wife.

"I'll go with you! After all, Uncle Ivan said: *Take your wife and leave from here somewhere!*" Ivanka exclaimed.

"Where shall we go together, what shall we do there! After all, we have a house here, fields, livestock, multiplied by 2: after all we must cultivate and the fields of uncle Ivan and graze his animals, until they return from exile! After all, we can't leave their household and ours for our father alone, he alone will not cope! We have 2 households, and we must take care of them. And besides, 6 months have already passed since he spoke about it before his leaving. After all, we are still safe, maybe the trouble will not happen."

He pressed his beloved wife to his chest and was happy that he had a true friend. The wife took care of the household, maintained the garden and orchard of the neighbor uncle Ivan, and they all worked together in both fields and grazed both herds of animals. Hot June pleased with the sun and promised a harvest. Everything around was fragrant and glowed with all the colors of rainbow. Cherries ripened, ears of wheat rose, the hills were covered with green and yellow velvet.

Blagon Zabanarov Ganev watched with irritation how Georgy Dimitrov went with his father to the fields, worked, led herds to graze in the meadows and could not understand what was happening. Then suddenly a suspicion against the Bodrovo kmet crept into his insides: what if the kmet is a traitor himself and did not report the thing he had to do? Anger twisted the physiognomy of Blagon Zabanarov Ganev; he sat on a donkey and drove the poor animal, whipping on his sides, through the fields, hills and meadows straight to the Haskovo Mineral Baths to the commandant's office and personally handed the captain of the 10th Rhodope Regiment Hubenov a copy of the list of the yataks from the village of Bodrovo, handed initially to Bodrovo kmet, the devil knows when.

"Well done, Blagon! Continue to serve the fatherland the same honestly and faithfully!" Hubenov praised him, reading the list.

Blagon wanted to hint about the kmet, but he did not dare and thought: "I'll get him later, when the yataks are captured!" He servilely bowed to Hubenov and went home satisfied, Suspicions against the kmet tormented his insides, but he did not dare to take any active measures against him as he did not have accurate evidence. But yet he did not resist not annoying him. Having arrived to Bodrovo, Blagon set off the donkey directly to the kmet's building. The kmet was in his office, and next to him his secretary Naiden Nikolov was doing his job.

"I want to inform you, Bay Peter, that you don't go anywhere from your office tomorrow, but be present here at a historical event: tomorrow the Hristo Botev yataks will be convoyed here!" Blagon announced gloatingly and began to sing a cheerful song.

"Get out of here!" the kmet shouted irritably and was frightened of himself, added:

"Don't bother me, I have a lot of work to do! Who allowed you to break into my office without permission?"

The clerk-secretary Naiden Nikolov did not react to what was happening and continued indifferently to dig in his papers. The embittered Blagon even more suspected him of betraying the fatherland and, clenching his fists, left the office.

"And we'll deal with you!" Blagon gritted through his teeth, but nevertheless he went home joyfully.

The working day came to an end, and the kmet with his secretary locked the room with the key and went home. Having come home, kmet lay down on his bed without undressing and without supper, stared at one point on the ceiling and lay like that all night. That was the end of his protest.

In the evening in the house of Dimitar Karagochev, as usual, the entire family was sitting at the table, had dinner and discussed plans for tomorrow. The feeling of anxiety had not left Georgy lately, but he did not want to overshadow the peaceful dinner of the family. Having had dinner, he left the table and came out into the garden.

"Georgy!"

He winced and turned around. Naiden Nikolov, the kmet's secretary, was standing in front of him. Georgy put his finger to his lips and dragged him into the shed behind the house. He looked around, there was no one, and he followed him into the shed.

"Something happened?" he asked Nikolov quietly.

"Escape immediately! Run right now!" the secretary pronounced excitedly. "They will seize you tomorrow! Blagon went himself to Miniralny Baths and denounced the yataks, after our kmet did not betray you. He showed up at the kmet's office and announced that all the yataks would be seized tomorrow."

"Where shall I run? I have no liaison with the cheta. I have not seen them for a long time, I don't even know where they are. Otherwise I would go together with them. I have the wife, we got married recently."

"Run somewhere, then you'll contact your wife! Now you must save your life! Now is the worst time in the history of Bulgaria! We all walk on a razor's edge! That's all, I've warned you! Run right now! Tomorrow will be too late!"

Secretary Nikolov left Georgy's shed and vanished behind the bushes. Georgy left his yard and went to the house of Angel Tonev. It was already dark, and ominous silence spread in the air, which was periodically broken by the crackling of cicadas: they seemed to warn of danger. The Tonev's house was in the south in Bodrovo, and soon Georgy was there. Father Ivan Tonev Angelov and his son Angel Ivanov Tonev were devoted yataks of the cheta. Excitedly Georgy told about the kmet's secretary report.

"Why didn't the chetniks kill Blagon?" Ivan Tonev was indignant.

"I asked myself this question," Georgy answered. "I told Todor yet in winter, but then they left, apparently all this time they were far from these lands. Uncle Ivan, Todor's father, warned me that Blagon is a traitor."

"Well, what is it now! Now we have to save ourselves!" said Ivan Tonev. "Run, son!"

"And you, father?" Angel Tonev asked at a loss.

"I shall somehow turn away, I am not strong enough to run somewhere."

"I shall go to the Buchevs, then I'll come back, we'll run away together," Georgy said and disappeared behind the door.

Georgy was walking in the dark through his native village, not knowing what to do. Where to run? How to live? How to abandon the wife? If to run, what will be with her? The questions pulsed one after another, scattering his attention. He could not concentrate and was looking for a way out. Georgy came up to the Buchevs house and knocked on the door. Peter and Valko Buchev lived in one 2-story house, divided into 2 parts. Both cheerfully met Georgy.

"Why are you so gloomy, Georgy," they asked cheerfully.

"Run, tomorrow they'll seize all the yataks, who helped the Hristo Botev cheta."

"But we have not seen them for a long time, and we do not even know where they are now, maybe they they've been staying abroad long ago!" the brothers answered, good-naturedly interrupting each other. "How do you know this? Why do you think so?"

"A trusted person told me that they'll arrest everybody tomorrow. Blagon went to Miniralny Baths and denounced all the yataks."

"Can't be! The Buchev brothers exclaimed, without believing."

"That's all! I can't argue with you anymore! I've warned you that Blagon is a traitor and handed over all the yataks to the military!" Georgy exclaimed irritably. "Are you escaping with us: me and Angel Tonev?"

"Are you crazy?" the brothers exclaimed. "Look, what a house we have, what a household! How is it to abandon everything and run nobody knows where!"

Georgy dumbly turned around and left their house. He did not know where to go. His feet led him home to his family, to his wife, he was very tired from work all day in the field and really wanted to sleep, and tomorrow early in the morning he had to go back to the field. He made an effort on himself and went in the opposite direction from home again to Angel Tonev.

"Angel did not wait for you and left himself," his father Ivan answered.

"And you?" Georgy asked.

"I am not strong enough to run, I am not in that age to run," father answered, "run toward Aidanlar, Angel is there, you'll meet there!"

Georgy went outside; it was late, dark and damn lonely. He looked toward Aidanlar forest, which lay further south-east of Bodrovo, and his legs against his will led him home. He came home and went to bed, thinking that morning is wiser than evening. That night before dawn, the dogs outstripped the roosters: before the roosters had time to crow, foreboding the dawn, the dogs barked furiously in all the yards of the village, warning of danger. These faithful friends of human seemed to sense the approach of the fascist dark force and barked angrily, getting loose from a chain to protect their house.

2 trucks with military drove into Bodrovo like in their own home in order to carry out the massacre. One truck stopped at the entrance to the village, and the military poured out of the truck to block the entrances and exits. The second truck was met by a local guide from the village of Bodrovo Hristo Kolev, who specially got up early in the morning for the upcoming event. Lieutenant Peychev had in his hands the list of the yataks, compiled by Blagon Zabanarov Ganev. Part of the soldiers unloaded at the kmet's building and took up the positions, and the Bodrovo guide got into the truck next to the driver to show him the way. Lieutenant Peychev showed him the list of the places where to go, but the latter brushed it aside and assured him that he himself knew where and for whom to go.

They went around the houses of the Bodrovites, burst inside and pulled out the "II category yataks" according to the list of Blagon and crammed them into the truck. When all 10 yataks were captured, the truck took them together with the part of the soldiers back to Miniralny Baths to Hubenov, the captain of the 10th Rhodopes Infantry Squad, into which the 10th Rhodopes Regiment was reorganized by decision of the agreement in Neuilly. And the guide Hristo Kolev with lieutenant Peychev on the second truck made the second detour of the village and seized "the main enemies of the fatherland": "yataks of the I category." When they arrived to the kmet's building, the door was already open, and the kmet was sitting in his office. There were several rooms in the building, and the military pushed several people into them: Georgy Dimitrov

Karagochev, Todor Todorov's cousin, Peter and Valko Buchev, the Ivan Ignatov cousins, and Ivan Tonev Angelov. Soon father Ivan was joined by his 17-year-old son Angel Ivanov Tonev, who was dragged from Aidanlar forest by 2 fascist activists: Dimo Rusev Vermezov and Todor Georgiev Kontilev. And soon the 6th yatak Kolyu Konstandinov from Ezerovo joined the arrested.

The kmet of Bodrovo Peter Kostov was sitting in his office and silently gloomily stared at one point. His secretary Naiden Nikolov was standing by the window with his back to him without uttering a word. Suddenly a heart-breaking cry deafened the kmet, he heard the cries of men, escaping from their throats against their will; the cries filled all the space around, and the kmet could not stand it. He ran out of the office, ran along the road that led to the north from the village. There at the entrance to the village, there was an old cheshma with spring water. He washed his face and hands with this water, went down to the bank of the Kayaliyka River, sat down on the ground and stared at one point, at the quietly murmuring water of the river. The cries of men from the kmet's building burst out and spread throughout the village, and they were echoed by the plaintive howl of dogs, rending a soul.

"Who are you? What is your name?" Lieutenant Peychev began the interrogation.

"Georgy Dimitrov Karagochev."

"So, you are the cousin of Todor Todorov Karagochev, aren't you?"

"Yes, I am."

Peychev waved his hand to the soldiers, who surrounded Georgy, and they began "to carry out the task of defending the fatherland." One of them hit Georgy on the face with a backhand, and blood came out of his nose and mouth.

"Where is your brother?" Peychev continued the interrogation.

"I don't know, I have not seen him for a long time," Georgy said, and these were his last words.

He did not utter a sound any more. He concentrated in himself all the strength of hatred and content for these butchers, for the traitor-rat Blagon, who denounced the yataks, for the entire fascist junta, which seized their homeland, for the criminal loathsome Saxe-Coburg-Gotha bitch on the Bulgarian throne, who organized the upheaval in the country, for his fascist henchmen: Tsankov, Rusev, Vylkov and other lackeys, for the Bulgarian servile people, who allowed everything to happen. He hated all of them, and the power of hatred killed fear in him. He no longer heard any questions that made no sense and even more so did not answer them. His ears were buzzing, and everything floated before his eyes; he recalled his childhood, his cousin Todor, whom he was proud of. In the depth of his soul, he admired him and wanted to be like him.

At that time the enraged butchers, who got excited, tormented his young body. They hammered nails under his nails, crushed his toes with a hammer, each in turn. They broke his right arm and continued to twist it, when it hung on nothing but veins. They put a bag of quicklime on his head, and all his lungs burned. They beat him with clubs, broke his ribs, and kneaded his half-dead body, and when they got tired, they, spewing curses, went out into the street to rest and smoke, and the others began torturing.

Kolyu Konstandinov, the cheta's yatak from Ezerovo, did not give the butchers pleasure to torture him for a long time, as he died from torture. And the rest—the Buchev brothers Peter and Valko, father Ivan Tonev Angelov and his 17-year-old son Angel—the butchers-warriors continued to torture them in the same way as Georgy. The dogs wailed plaintively in response to the soul-rending cries of the fascist terror victims. Thus, 2 days passed: June 15 and 16, 1925. The butchers, tired of torturing, were replaced by the others, and having tormented them without interruption for 2 days, the Bulgarian warriors threw their barely alive bodies into a truck and left Bodrovo.

This was the last journey of the yataks along their native land. Lieutenant Peychev with his henchman sub-officer Petko Kolev from the village of Karadzhalovo drove the truck from Bodrovo south past the hills and fields and stopped not far at the foot of the hill, where the villa was of Ivan Duban, 92-year-old man, beaten to death by the officers of the 10th Rhodopes Regiment. There, where the vicinity path led to the highway to Miniralny Baths, in a place called Sasipaka, they threw half-corpses on the ground and open fire.

Lieutenant Peychev with the lieutenant officer Petko Kolev from the village of Karadzhalovo with the rest warriors began to shoot them first in the legs, then rose higher, piercing their bodies with bullets, and enjoyed the spectacle of their blood gushing from the wounds. Finally, after riddling their bodies with bullets, they shot them in the heart and head. The yataks-friends of the cheta Hristo Botev passed away, dying the death of martyrs in the morning of June 17, 1925, in Fascist Bulgaria.

***

5 days had passed. The platoon of Mityu Ganev, consisting of 9 people, including him himself, having crossed the Bulgarian border from Greece, safely passed a third of the way from Mezek to Aidanlar, not noticed by anyone, heading toward Serbia. They stopped on the outskirts of the Aidanlar forest at the entrance to the village on June 22, 1925.

"Boys, let's take some extra cartridges and canned food from our cache in the Vidyu's old shed. Tomorrow evening we set off," Mityu Ganev said.

"Our path would be rather shorter and faster, if we went straight to Serbia along the Rhodopes and did not enter here, where it is dangerous!" Velyu Hristozov remarked.

"Really, Mityu, why have we made such a big detour and came to Aidanlar, where a hunt has been declared on us?" Ivan Ignatov did not understand.

"After all, we've just been at my place in Malevo, we rested there and replenished some supplies! Why have we come this way?" Latun Georgiev asked.

"But we have already come here, what it is now!" Mityu Ganev answered. "And since we've come, we'll take the opportunity and pick up from our hiding place everything that we need for a long journey and tomorrow evening we'll hit the road. And since we are already here, we must spend a day in hiding. I suggest to go to my house. Actually it is not a house, but an old wreck, a tiny hut, where I grew up, but we'll fit there, as we are only 9 in number. I am sure, it'll not occur to anyone to look for us there."

Dawn was already breaking and without wasting any more time on useless arguments about why they had come here, since they had already been here, the chetniks hurried out of the forest to the village of Aidanlar, where Mityu Ganev empty abandoned tiny hut stood on the outskirts. They took refuge in the hut, having left a sentry by the door.

"This is my house, I grew up here and remained an orphan since childhood," Mityu Ganev said. "We rest, boys, and in the evening, as it gets dark, we'll move out."

Meanwhile, Blagon Zabanarov Ganev, who once dreamed vainly to become a "hajduk" and incited the fool Ivan Ignatov to steal other people's sheep for this purpose, though the hajduks were always a symbol of the struggle for freedom, but not sheep thieves. Ivan Ignatov was from a wealthy family and did not need other people's sheep, as he had many of his own; he never realized his dream and never became a "hajduk". He only helped

Guenov-Kamine to throw himself together with Ivan Ignatov and Todor Todorov, whom they both set up, behind bars. Blagon Ganev, who once dreamed to become a "hajduk" and be like the hajduks the same brave, fearless and elusive folk hero, whom songs are sung about, and famous, with a fierce malice hated his fellow villagers and former cellmates Ivan Ignatov and Todor Todorov, because he had never become like them. He hated all the fighters of the cheta Hristo Botev, because he never became like them. He hated his nothingness and hated the entire cheta even more. He betrayed all the yataks in his native Bodrovo and could not calm down. He knew that the chetniks killed another traitor from Aidanlar, the forester Kityu Panev, his competitor, and it meant that no competition could thwart him anymore.

That's why Blagon Ganev went to Aidanlar, perhaps to catch at least someone else. He knew that Aidanlar was a homeland of Mityu Ganev and Aidanlar forest was a nest of insurgent rebels. He spied, eavesdropped, trying to fish at last anything. Blagon Ganev scoured the village of Aidanlar first in one direction, then in another one and came across the abandoned hut of Mityu Ganev. He hid in the bushes aside from the hut and began to scan. He peered tensely into the dark windows, the neglected courtyard, overgrown with bushes, and suddenly he noticed that one of the bushes moved. He turned into sight and hearing and fixed his eyes on that bush.

"Maybe it seemed to me," he thought, "maybe a dog ran through."

He stared at that bush for a long time, but there was nothing. He was sitting in ambush for a long time, then could not stand it anymore, crawled out from behind a bush and hurried back home to Bodrovo.

Meanwhile, the Mityu Ganev's platoon was sleeping at least during the day after the night transition and before the upcoming campaign in the evening toward the Serbian border. The sentry, sitting in the bushes, was replaced by another sentry, and the first one went to sleep. Silently and imperceptibly they were sitting in Mityu Ganev's hut and in the evening began to gather for a journey. The sun was receding to the west, and they were preparing to the saving land of Serbia.

"Stay where you are! Who are you?" the sentry grabbed in the yard a young man by the hand, when he opened the gate of the fence with a straight move and headed toward the house of Mityu Ganev.

"I am looking for Todor Todorov, Ivan Ignatov and Mityu Ganev," the visitor said.

The sentry grabbed him by the hand and dragged the visitor behind the house, sending a prearranged signal through the window. Mityu Ganev came out of the hut and approached the sentry and the visitor.

"What do you want, Ignat?" he asked the visitor, being alert. "What are you doing here?"

"They have been captured! They all have been captured!" Ignat exclaimed, twitching nervously.

"Who was captured? Speak clearly!" Mityu Ganev threatened him.

"All your yataks were seized: Georgy, Peter, Valko, Ivan, Angel and all the others! They are being kept in the kmet's building and tomorrow they will be taken along the main highway to Miniralny Baths!"

"At what time?"

"From 8 to 9 am!"

"How do you know about that? Mityu Ganev asked suspiciously."

"I've seen it myself: they are in the kmet's building. There were talks among the military that in the morning they would be taken to the Miniralny Baths."

"How did you know we were here? Why have you come here?"

"Blagon sent me," Ignat blurted, stuttering.

"What? What?"

"Blagon sent me. He told me: *Go there and check if there is the cheta there, only they alone can save the yataks. And if the chetniks appear to be there, tell them to save the yataks.*"

Mityu Ganev was listening in confusion, not realizing what was happening.

"Yes, is Todor also there with Ivan?" Ignat enquired.

"None of your business, go!" Mityu commanded, and Ignat rushed to run away.

Chetnik on guard and Mityu looked at each other and shrugged, showing their confusion. Mityu returned to the hut. It was time to move out.

"What's wrong with you, Mityu?" friends asked.

"Ivan, Ignat Byalkov, your nephew, has come and said that our yataks from Bodrovo were all arrested, they are being kept in custody in the kmet's building, and tomorrow morning thy will be taken along the Bansko Highway to Miniralny Baths."

Deathly silence reigned for a minute, and then Ivan Ignatov answered:

"My nephew is a fool."

"That's not the point, the question is whether he is telling the truth," Latun Grozev said.

"How did he even know at all that we were here? Why has he come here?" Kuzi Latev Kuzev asked incredulously.

"He says that it is Blagon who sent him here; go, they say, check if there are chetniks there, as only they, that is us, can save the yataks."

"What? Blagon? After all, Todor did tell you that Blagon is a traitor!" Yordan Zhalev Zhekov flared out.

"But what if he is telling the truth?" Mityu Ganev asked himself. "There is one of two things: either this is trap, or he is telling the truth. And if it is true, we must save our friends!"

"All this seems suspicious to me!" Peter Zhelyazkov Filipov exclaimed. "We've just come here, and they immediately find us and inform about the arrested! And this is reported by one, about whom Todor clearly said that he is a traitor!"

"Ivan, who is your nephew? Can he be trusted?" Dimo Todorov Kafedzhiev asked.

"I would say he is a prankster," Ivan Ignatov answered irritably, "the son of my older sister. Well, a relative of some kind, he even helped us somehow in something before. But I don't know. I don't know for sure now if we can trust him."

"What shall we do, boys?" Geno Delchev Radev asked.

"I think that all this is very suspicious and looks like a trap! We must leave, while it gets dark, we must move toward Serbia!"

Everyone looked at Mityu Ganev.

"Boys, we need to stay," Mityu Ganev uttered finally. "What if it is true and if they are now being tortured in the Bodrovo kmet's building and tomorrow they'll be taken along the Bansko Highway to Miniralny Baths, where they will be continued to be tortured and killed? And we, as cowards and traitors, could save them, but did not take risks and calmly handed them over to the executioners to be tormented and hid ourselves in Serbia! I stay!"

"Everyone was silent. The time passed. It was getting dark. Night has come."

Finally, Ivan Ignatov pronounced:

"What can you do alone? I am staying with you, Mityu!"

Mityu Ganev turned to his friends:

"Boys, I am not keeping anyone. I am not forcing anyone to stay. I am just saying that I'm staying. Let those who want to leave, leave, and hurry up, while it's night! And let those who want to stay and save our friends—stay!"

There was an ominous silence. Nobody moved. They were sitting in the Mityu Ganev's hut all night without any light, and in their mind each of them imagined how far he could've been from here, if he had set off last evening. But none of them spoke their thoughts aloud any more. Before dawn they finally set off. They abandoned the miserable hut of Mityu Ganev, and Mityu Ganev himself parted with his native home, where he was born and raised, knowing that he would not return here again, and slipped out of the village of Aidanlar. On the way in the old koshara that once belonged to Vidyu, they picked up additional cartridges and canned food.

"We'll free the yataks and go with them to Serbia," they thought with hope.

9 chetniks headed south to the Bansko Highway and stopped near the village of Susam in the area called Shiroko Dere. Each of them knew what to do, when the convoy appears on the highway. They looked around. To the south of them the village of Susam lay, named after the sesame plant, which was grown by the villagers in the vicinity fields for food and medicine. The Bansko Highway was crossed by the Banska River in the very center of the village, and further down the highway to the south, Miniralny Baths could be seen in 2 km away. Behind them mountains covered with forests rose, which had to be reached. And next to the highway there was an open space, and here and there the oases of green forest were scattered in the distance.

"As if a palm of a hand, this is like a mouse trap!" each of them thought, but remained dump.

The hours of waiting dragged on like eternity. In the east the orange hoop of the rising sun emerged over the mountains, which soon flooded everything with its light. An ominous silence reigned in the air, and nervous tension fettered the soul of the brave fighters. The hands of the clock crept slowly, as if leaving them time for life. Here and there the villagers began to appear in the fields, starting work on their land. The shepherds took their cattle for a walk. 8, 9, 10, 11 am passed. The chetniks were waiting for the convoy to free Georgy and the rest of the yataks, whose bodies had been rotten in the sun for a week in the Sasipaka area.

"Let's go, it's a trap!" Velyu Hristozov Delchev exclaimed.

"Check the road!" Mityu Ganev said.

Delchev got out from behind the shelter and climbed a small hill that towered nearby and looked around.

"Let's go, it's a trap!" he shouted to his friends, but at that moment the first bullets whistled over their heads.

"Spread out, take up places for defense!" Mityu Ganev exclaimed.

He himself climbed the hill and looked around.

"It's too late," he whispered to himself and began to curse himself: "It's all your fault, Mityu Ganev! It's you who have led your friends into a trap! They and you together with them would've already been on the Greek territory, but you provoked them to return to Bulgaria, because you were afraid that the Greek authority would extradite you! Todor warned you, Mityu Ganev, that Blagon is a traitor and should be killed, but you did not listened and fell for his primitive trick and brought all the boys here to death! The fair of prudence and instinct of a commander have betrayed you, Mityu Ganev! But it's you, Mityu Ganev, who was chosen as the commander of the detachment of the cheta Hristo Botev! After all, Todor warned you that the blood of all the boys would be on your hands, if you don't give heed to his warning! But everyone could've been in Greece long ago, or on the way to Serbia, if not you, semiliterate idiot, Mityu Ganev! Damn you forever!"

These thoughts-curses of himself were pondering in the head of Mityu Ganev, who saw that this was the end. They won't escape from here. He himself led them all into the trap. He saw through binoculars in the distance, how black ring was shrinking and approaching them from all the villages along the perimeter: from Tatarevo, Bryastovo, Susam, Bukovo, Voden, Ezerovo, Bodrovo, Bryagovo, Dragoynovo, Varbitsa, Gorni Izvor, Klokotnitsa and Garvanovo. The priests beat the bells of the Christian churches, calling the fascist filth, and all the evil spirits crawled out of the villages, armed with whatever they could. With pitchforks and knives, with weapons received from power and with a thirst of reward, everyone was moving toward Shiroko Dere in exactly indicated direction. Captains Hubenov and Pondichev solemnly moved at the head of the 10th Infantry Rhodope Squad, 6th Cavalry Regiment, 8th Infantry Regiment from Haskovo, Harmanly and Kardzhali garrisons, policemen astride on the horses from Borisovograd and Haskovo—all were approaching the 9 chetniks. Countless hordes of fascist scum were advancing on 9 boys from the cheta Hristo Botev on a tip from Blagon Ganev from the village of Bodrovo and Ivan Ignatov's nephew Ignat Byalkov.

Bullets whistled over the heads of the chetniks, and the famous unequal heroic battle began. The warriors were carrying cannons, canisters, artillery on carts and sent them in action.

"Forgive me, friends! I've led you into a trap!" Mityu Ganev addressed the cheta.

"We'll have a good fight today!" Ivan Ignatov exclaimed.

"We won't give up alive!"

"Let's take with us to the grave as much of fascist filth as possible!"

"We must hold on until dark!"

"Maybe we'll break through!"

"Let's try to hide in the woods over there!"

"Let's run!"

They tried to get to a small forest to the south-west of them, but the grapeshot blocked their way. Bullets, shells, fragments of shells rained down on them from all sides, cutting off any path to retreat. Fascist activists hurried to their reward from all sides, squeezing the ring. The chetniks fired back, accurately hitting the target. Nearby rye undulated in the field, and from there a canister fired. Mityu fired several shots in that direction, and the shotgun fell silent. He rushed there to grab the canister, but did not run a few paces, fell next to it, pierced through with bullets in the abdomen by the fire shots from the other side.

The battle went on for several hours. The bullets of the chetniks hit the target accurately, but began to run out. Velyu Hristozov and Latun Georgiev crawled along the ground in a south-western direction to break through the encirclement toward the forest. They ran out of grenades, with which they laid down a mass of enemies, and ran out of bullets that hit the target. The grapeshot hit them, and they were left lying on the ground. Kuzi Latev Kuzev and Peter Zhelyazkov Filipov fought to the last bullet and fell to the ground dead, looking at the Bulgarian sky.

Thunder rumbled from grenade explosions, bullets flew, almost crashing into each other. Shootings moved down the crops in the fields. Shooting back, hitting the target, Dimo Todorov Kafedzhiev and Geno Delchev Radev were saving the precious bullets and, having used the last bullets, fell dead.

Yordan Zhelev Zhekov and Ivan Ignatov continued to hit the enemy, and the enemy had already come close.

"Yordan!" Ivan Ignatov called his friend, but the latter did not answer.

Ivan saw him lying on the ground with his eyes closed. Ivan Ignatov remained alone, and there were still a few cartridges in reserve. He filled the last clip with them and inserted them into the revolver.

"Give up!" they yelled from the foe side.

"Now I'll surrender to you!" Ivan replied.

He took out a white handkerchief and covered with it his revolver with the last cartridges, which he was holding firmly in his hand. He was holding in his hand the revolver and the edge of the handkerchief. The handkerchief unfolded and closed the revolver. Ivan Ignatov slowly came out from behind the tree, where he was fighting, and began slowly to approach the enemy. Lieutenant Borisov with a group of soldiers hastened toward him for their glory and reward. Having let them closer, Ivan Ignatov in a blink of an eye with a revolver, which he was holding under a white handkerchief, fired at them, having unloaded the entire clip, and fell, wounded in the stomach. Lieutenant Borisov, killed by a bullet from Ivan, fell: it was he, who as a second lieutenant plunged a bayonet into a stomach of a wounded Turk during the I Balkan War. Next to him the soldiers were lying, on whom Ivan Ignatov's bullets were enough.

The whole area around was littered with the corpses of the military and fascists activists, and on a small patch of Shiroko Dere 8 bodies of the Hristo Botev cheta fighters were lying. Critically wounded, Ivan Ignatov was still alive. The entire foe force rushed to him, and the fascist activists grabbed the corpses of 8 chetniks, tearing them out from each other, and dragged them to Ivan Ignatov. They piled the bodies next to Ivan, pushing each other away, and began to poke their knives into them, hoping for rewards. They inflicted 17 knife blows on the body of Mityu Ganev.

"Cut off their heads!" captain Hubenov commanded. "And you look!"

He grabbed Ivan Ignatov by the hair and put his head back so that he would watch. 8 heads were cut off and put on the bayonets of the rifles.

"Now cut of his head!" Hubenov pointed to still living Ivan Ignatov.

And the butchers began slowly to cut off his head. Finally, the head of Ivan Ignatov was cut off and put on the bayonet of a rifle, and a victorious procession began. A brass military band appeared from somewhere, which slowly followed the military, and began to play "patriotic music." To the sound of the victorious march, all the dark countless multitudes started after the warriors, who solemnly carried in front 9 heads of the fighters of the cheta

Hristo Botev, put on the rifles bayonets. The solemn procession moved south to Susam and to the music walked through the village along the main road, along which the villagers gathered and saw off their idols on their last journey. The procession went another 2 km to the Miniralny Baths, triumphantly marching along the main streets to the curiosity, disgust, ridicule and tears of various segments of the Bulgarian population, and then the warriors, carrying the heads of the chetniks on the bayonets, got into a truck with them and hurried east through Bolyarovo to Haskovo, where, no longer hurrying, they went by a solemn march through the streets of the city.

The orchestra of the musicians walked in front, and "non-political" musicians, always and everywhere serving any cannibal regime, enthusiastically played "spiritual music." There were 3 dames standing in a crowd of the idles and carried on a conversation.

"Oh, I don't see that handsome man among them! What a pity!" the first dame exclaimed, peering into the heads. "I don't know what his name is, but everyone told me that he is very handsome! It's too bad: I wanted to look at him!"

"How stupid you are! For example, I would like to look at all of their heads; there are few of them here; only 9!" the second dame exclaimed.

"What are you about politics and about politics all the time!" the third dame exclaimed. "For example, I don't care what heads to look at and how many of them are there! I don't care about politics!"

And the procession of the winners solemnly walked further and further through the city to the sounds of the "spiritual music." The barbarians of Bulgaria carried the heads of 9 chetniks, as the Turks once carried the heads of the defeated enemies in the lands they captured.

On the same day, the third son of Bay Latyu Kuzev—Rusi Latev Kuzev, who refused to leave with his farther to cheta and stayed at home to take care of the household in the village of Bolyarsky Izvor—got rid of mortal agony, having died after inhuman torture that lasted for several days.

Thus, the day of June 23, 1925, ended in fascist Bulgaria.

Chapter 59
Epilogue

In Serbia, Radyu Delchev's detachment was met at the Pozharevats railway station by a trusted person of BANU, and everyone was led to the Headquarters of the Foreign Representation of the Agrarian Union, which was situated in a small 2-story house, surrounded by a garden. The surviving elite of the Agrarian Union of the Stamboliysky government, as well as now the cheta of Hristo Botev, found shelter and political asylum in Serbia. The chetniks were accompanied into the house. They came into a specious room of the headquarters, where they were met by 3 leaders of the Agrarian Union: Nikola Zahariev, Alexander Obbov and Kosta Todorov.

37-year-old Kosta Todorov, a former plenipotentiary ambassador of Stamboliysky government in Yugoslavia, was a revolutionary and rebel from birth. Not tall in stature, somewhat similar to Mityu Ganev, almost from childhood Kosta Todorov did not tolerate even a hint of any humility to any despotism, and from his youth he participated in the revolutionary struggle that he only met on his way. Born free, he fought for freedom in that era of struggle for freedom, in which all of them were destined to live. His life rushed like a comet across the sky of struggle.

He was 17 years old when the Turks sentenced him to death and announced a reward on his head for the liquidation of the Turkish ruler in Thessalonica Ibrahim Agha. He participated in a conspiracy against Sultan Abdul Hamid II in Istanbul. He was sentenced to death in Russia in Odessa for attempt to assassinate the chairman of the Odessa military court and was imprisoned in Odessa. Already as a journalist for the "Balkan Tribune Bulletin", he was in Sofia prison for ridiculing Ferdinand and Radoslavov. Awarded with orders, he bravely fought on the fronts of the Great War in the ranks of the French Foreign Legion and again was thrown by Ferdinand behind bars in the Sofia prison, where he fortunately became close to Alexander Stamboliysky and Raiko Daskalov.

He was present in Neuilly at the signing of the treaty as the agent in favor of the Bulgarian prisoners of war. He became a diplomat for Alexander Stamboliysky and was appointed as the Bulgarian ambassador to Belgrade. Together with Obbov, he became a leader of the Agrarian Union after the fascist upheaval in Bulgaria on June 9, 1923 and the assassination of Raiko Daskalov, and all this time he had been negotiating with the BCP for the creation of the United Front for general uprising against the junta.

Now, Kosta Todorov shook hands with the chetniks and greeted them in Yugoslavian Pozharevats. Alexander Obbov greeted them next to him.

Together with Kosta Todorov, Obbov headed the Stamboliysky's Agrarian Union, of which he was a member from age 17, and at 18 he already entered the leadership. The associate of Alexander Stamboliysky, Minister of Agriculture in his government, deputy of the National Assembly, he managed to escape to Romania after the fascist coup in Bulgaria, and he had been negotiating with the BCP about the United Front and general uprising against the junta.

The chetniks were greeted by 27-year-old Nikola Zahariev, who was the leader of the Bulgarian Agrarian Union. 3 leaders of the Agrarian Union shook hands with the chetniks and welcomed them on the land of Yugoslavia.

"Congratulations on the safe crossing the Bulgarian border and arrival to Serbia!" Nikola Zahariev said. "We are all political emigrants now. You boys, have honestly fulfilled your duty, conscientiously prepared our common uprising against the fascists, who seized our country! But the fascist executioners turned out to be stronger than us, and the uprising was never destined to take place."

"But let's not lose hope, life goes on, and the day will come, and Bulgaria will be free!" Alexander Obbov said.

"The main thing is that you are all alive and managed to get out of that hell!" Kosta Todorov said. "Unfortunately, unlike the other part of the cheta, Hristo Botev, which was with Mityu Ganev."

The chetniks froze at these words and a cold chill ran down their backs.

"What's with them?" they asked anxiously.

"They are all killed. Apparently, they were heading to Serbia, but for some reason they appeared to be in the Aidanlar forest and fell into a trap near the village of Susam. The details are not known; it is not clear why they were there, but it was there, near Susam, near the Bansko Highway where they were surrounded by the military and fascist activists they were all killed in an unequal battle. They all died heroically, like many of our friends, like our Prime Minister Alexander Stamboliysky…"

Tears welled up in the chetniks' eyes, and the poor father Latun Kuzev sobbed from terrible grief.

"Sun, Kuzi! Come back!" Bay Latyu sobbed, clutching his son Sava, and the latter sobbed himself, trying to calm the father. Both did not know that the third son of Latyu-Rusi died of torture on the same day that Mityu Ganev's platoon perished. Todor's heart sank with pain and a terrible suspicion crept into his soul.

"I think I know why they ended up at Susam," he said with pain, "they were lured into a trap, and it is only Blagon Zabanarov who could do it. After all, I did warn everyone that Blagon is a traitor and he must be killed!"

"Let's honor the memory of our friends with a minute of silence," Radyu Delchev said, and everyone fell silent, mourning their comrades-in-arms.

"We'll try to help you here in Serbia, you must get settled for the first time," Kosta Todorov broke the silence.

"I want to go away from here!" Scheryu Atanasov declared irritably, no longer hiding his dislike for the Agrarians. "I want to go to Gorni Milanovats: the emigrants from BCP are there!"

"We need to talk to the city authorities," Kosta Todorov answered, "but for now accommodate yourself in the emigrant camp of the Agrarians!"

The chetniks were accompanied to the Agrarians' camp for a night.

"We need to talk, boys," Radyu Delchev addressed everyone, "you have understood for a long time that the cheta Hristo Botev of the United Front has fulfilled its historical mission, for which it was created: to prepare the uprising against the fascist bandits, who seized power in Bulgaria—and ceased to exist. We did prepare the uprising, our leaders failed to raise it for the combined set of reasons taken together, and this is not our fault. We have fulfilled our duty. There is no more cheta Hristo Botev, she has been gone since the moment we crossed the border."

"It exists only in the history of Bulgaria, in our memory, in the memory of the people and in our photographs, which Mitko Trindev from Knyaz Borisovo made for us. I am no longer your commander, and Todor Todorov is no longer my deputy and confidant; we are civilians now, and everyone is now on his own."

"We've known this since we crossed the border," Todor said, "though it's hard to get used to."

"Get used to it," Radyu Delchev answered.

"We are used to fighting together, waging a guerrilla war against a common foe, but now what? What shall we do here?" Kocho Vasilev asked.

"We have to get used to a new life in a foreign land," Todor answered.

Bay Latyu Kuzev continued to mourn his son Kuzi, who perished with the platoon of Mityu Ganev.

"I want to go to Gorni Milanovats! There are Communists there!"

"Calm down! Don't whine!" Todor interrupted Scheryu Atanasov.

The leaders of the Agrarian Union kept their promise and with the help of the city authorities, transported the former chetniks to Gorni Milanovats in a short time. Again, they rode to the south-west along the foreign land and saw a landscape reminiscent of Bulgaria. The new city, founded 60 years ago, lay like at the bottom of a ditch, surrounded by the high mountains, covered with forests. The city was built in the wild field on the idea of Prince Milosh Obrenovich, the leader of 2 Serbian revolutions against the Ottomans, and named after deceased half-brother Milan Obrenovich.

Mount Rudnick towered above the new city, where the ancient ruins of a Roman temple from time immemorial reported that this land, like the land of all the Balkans, was inhabited almost at the dawn of mankind. Dacians, Thracians, Celts, Goths, Greeks and Romans left their traces on it one after another. Artificially created new city on the ancient land with planned streets, parks and gardens became a refuge-camp for the political emigrants-Communists from Bulgaria. They died here of boredom, as there was nothing to do. Here, even the land was given free of charge to those who decided to settle down here.

The chetniks arrived and stayed in Gorni Milanovats for several days and set off again. They arrived by train to the village Indjia, a large village in Voevodino. The village of Indjia lay north-west of Belgrade near the Danube and had more than half a millennium years of history, when it passed from hand to hand to different owners: from the Serbian despot Yovan Brankovich to the Habsburgs and the Ottoman Empire. A large village, almost a town, had the development of many crafts, factories and agriculture. The chetniks were accommodated in an emigrant camp in rural cottages and assigned to work in the gardens and orchards, and fields outside the village.

Having finished the partisan struggle against a common enemy in Bulgaria, the former chetniks remained alive and safe in a foreign land, each alone with himself, with his own problems, his own inner world, memories of the past and complete fog about the future.

Todor worked in agriculture, having experience in this work since childhood, and often remembered his home, his childhood and relatives.

Thus, summer of 1925 passed. One day in early September, a man got in touch with him, who received instructions from Moscow. He found Todor in the village and took him aside for a conversation.

"The Foreign Representation of the Central Committee of the BCP requests your arrival to Moscow," the messenger informed him.

The news struck Todor like thunder from the blue sky and his thoughts were connected only with the past and the calm, dreary, unadventurous present. And here—Moscow: new horizons, receding into the distance endlessly! Unusual excitement seized Todor, and he was afraid that this messenger was only joking. But the stranger handed him an envelope and said: "There is money and documents here, as well as train tickets. You are leaving in a couple of days. You are of interest to them."

"Am I going alone?" Todor asked excitedly.

"2 more are going: Scheryu Atanasov and Doncho Kalaydjiev. Freshen up, buy new clothes, and bon voyage!"

The man hurried away, without drawing attention to himself. Todor opened the envelope and saw in it everything that the messenger had listed. Stunned, Todor pressed the envelope to his chest, hid it securely and began to prepare for his departure.

The day of departure had come. Clean, in new clothes, with money and documents in his pocket and with the train tickets, Todor together with 2 former chetniks boarded the train and went to Vienna. Serbia remained behind with the emigrant camp in Indjia; lands, foreign villages and cities floated outside the window. They crossed Hungary, entered Austria and arrived in Vienna. The capital of the former Habsburg Empire, now only the Austrian capital, Vienna met them with splendor and glory of the past. There they stayed for a week like tourists, admiring the magnificent monuments, then transferred to another train and went to Moscow.

Todor, from the ancient lineage of Karagochev, where his great-grandfathers were the hajduks, from whom he inherited the will to freedom, free-spirited, a fighter by nature, smart, handsome and proud, forever abandoned his past life for an unknown future.

Next to him Scheryu Atanasov was traveling, a communist to the marrow of his bones, who belonged to that part of the party in whose face Alexander Stamboliysky rightly threw accusations, trying in vain to find allies among them to fight the common foe: doctrinaires and sectarians! Atanasov secretly and viciously hated all Agrarians and tolerated them due the circumstances of the struggle of the United Front in one cheta Hristo Botev. He believed that only his party of Communists was the correct one. He was going to Moscow to make a career and was already pondering on how he would later lie that it was he, Scheryu Atanasov, who was the main Voevoda and political commissar in the cheta Hristo Botev, but not Radyu Delchev and Todor Todorov, Yanko Pavlitov and Georgy Pilashev. Only, it would be nice if by that time, there were no living witnesses left.

Doncho Dimitrov Kalaydjiev was traveling together with them: a member of BCP from Haskovo, smart, handsome, noble and courageous, a friend, who could be relied upon in trouble.

3 people, different in character, who were united by one heroic past in the cheta Hristo Botev, were going into the unknown, dream and reality. They were going to Moscow. They had heard so much about it, but knew nothing for sure. They knew that 8 years ago, a communistic revolution had taken place there and the power of Communists was established, that no Agrarians and no other parties were in the government, that there was a bloody civil war and the country was dying of hunger.

Alexander Stamboliysky, being the minister-chairman, collected products from all the villages of Bulgaria, which were loaded into the carts, and oxen dragged them to the port of Varna, where everything was loaded onto the ships and sent to Russia. They knew that Lenin, the leader of the revolution, had died a year ago, but they did not know what was happening there now. They were going to their future life in a distant foreign unfamiliar land.

The train carried them away from Vienna, and outside the windows of the train, foreign lands of Europe flashed. They were going to Soviet Russia.

What awaited them in a foreign land?

Todor Todorov Karagochev was traveling to a foreign country into the unknown, and next to him lay a newspaper, where it was reported that he, the commander of the detachment of the political cheta Hristo Botev, was sentenced to death by hanging in Bulgaria by the regime of Boris III-Tsankov.